Advanced Programming Using Visual Basic

Version 6.0

Julia Case Bradley
Mt. San Antonio College

Anita C. Millspaugh
Mt. San Antonio College

D1501759

Boston   Burr Ridge, IL   Dubuque, IA   Madison, WI   New York   San Francisco   St. Louis
Bangkok   Bogotá   Caracas   Lisbon   London   Madrid
Mexico City   Milan   New Delhi   Seoul   Singapore   Sydney   Taipei   Toronto

McGraw-Hill Higher Education

*A Division of The **McGraw-Hill** Companies*

ADVANCED PROGRAMMING USING VISUAL BASIC 6.0

Published by Irwin/McGraw-Hill, an imprint of the McGraw-Hill Companies, Inc. 1221 Avenue of the Americas, New York, NY 10020. Copyright © 2001 by The McGraw-Hill Companies, Inc. All rights reserved. No part of this publication may be reproduced or distributed in any form or by any means, or stored in a database or retrieval system, without the prior written consent of The McGraw-Hill Companies, Inc., including, but not limited to, in any network or other electronic storage or transmission, or broadcast for distance learning.

This book is printed on acid-free paper.

3 4 5 6 7 8 9 0 VNH/VNH 0 9 8 7 6 5 4 3 2 1

ISBN 0-07-239815-9

Publisher: *David Kendric Brake*
Senior sponsoring manager: *Jodi McPherson*
Associate editor: *Beth Cigler*
Marketing manager: *Jeff Parr*
Senior project manager: *Jean Lou Hess*
Production supervisor: *Debra R. Sylvester*
Freelance design coordinator: *Craig E. Jordan*
Senior supplement coordinator: *Marc Mattson*
New media: *Steve Schuetz*
Compositor: *GAC Indianapolis*
Typeface: *11/13 Bodoni Book*
Printer: *Von Hoffmann Press, Inc.*

Library of Congress Cataloging-in-Publication Data

Bradley, Julia Case.
    Advanced programming using Visual Basic 6.0 / Julia Chase Bradley, Anita C. Millspaugh.
        p. cm.
    ISBN 0-07-239815-9
    1. Microsoft Visual BASIC. 2. Computer programming. I. Millspaugh, A. C. (Anita
C.) II. Title.

QA76.73.B3 B695 2000
005.26'8--dc21   00-020914

http://www.mhhe.com

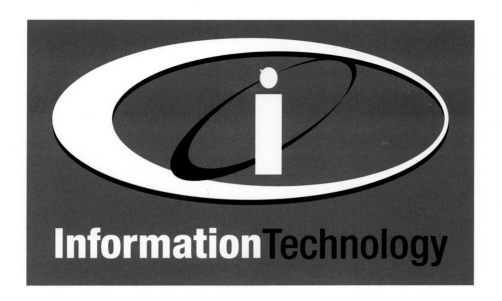

InformationTechnology

At McGraw-Hill Higher Education, we publish instructional materials targeted at the higher education market. In an effort to expand the tools of higher learning, we publish texts, lab manuals, study guides, testing materials, software, and multimedia products.

At **Irwin/McGraw-Hill** (a division of McGraw-Hill Higher Education), we realize that technology has created and will continue to create new mediums for professors and students to use in managing resources and communicating information with one another. We strive to provide the most flexible and complete teaching and learning tools available as well as offer solutions to the changing world of teaching and learning.

Irwin/McGraw-Hill is dedicated to providing the tools for today's instructors and students to successfully navigate the world of Information Technology.

- **Seminar series**—Irwin/McGraw-Hill's Technology Connection seminar series offered across the country every year demonstrates the latest technology products and encourages collaboration among teaching professionals.

- **Osborne/McGraw-Hill**—This division of The McGraw-Hill Companies is known for its best-selling Internet titles *Harley Hahn's Internet & Web Yellow Pages* and the *Internet Complete Reference*. Osborne offers an additional resource for certification and has strategic publishing relationships with corporations such as Corel Corporation and America Online. For more information visit Osborne at **www.osborne.com.**

- **Digital solutions**—Irwin/McGraw-Hill is committed to publishing digital solutions. Taking your course online doesn't have to be a solitary venture, nor does it have to be a difficult one. We offer several solutions that will allow you to enjoy all the benefits of having course material online. For more information visit **www.mhhe.com/solutions/index.mhtml.**

- **Packaging options**—For more about our discount options, contact your local Irwin/McGraw-Hill Sales representative at 1-800-338-3987 or visit our Web site at **www.mhhe.com/it.**

Preface

Introduction

This textbook is intended for use in an advanced programming course, which assumes completion of an introductory course. The topics include those required for the MCSD Exam 70-176, Visual Basic 6 Desktop Applications.

About the Authors

Both of the authors have taught courses in beginning and advanced Visual Basic for several years at Mt. San Antonio College. They have also taught Visual Basic at the National Computer Educator's Institute at the University of Central Oklahoma.

Julia Bradley developed the Faculty Computing Center at Mt. San Antonio College and acted as director during the first year of operation. Anita Millspaugh has served as the department chair of Computer Information Systems for several years.

About This Text

This text incorporates the basic concepts of programming, problem solving, programming logic, as well as the design techniques of an event-driven language.

Chapter topics are presented in a sequence that allows the programmer to learn how to deal with a visual interface while acquiring important programming skills such as creating projects with loops, decisions, and data management.

The chapters may be used in various sequences to accommodate the needs of the course, as well as a shorter quarter system or a semester-long course.

Chapter Organization

Each chapter begins with identifiable objectives and a brief overview. Numerous coding examples as well as hands-on projects with guidance for the coding appear throughout. Thought-provoking feedback questions give students time to reflect on the current topic and to evaluate their understanding of the details. The end-of-chapter items include a chapter review, questions, programming exercises, and two case studies. The case studies provide a continuing-theme exercise that may be used throughout the course.

Acknowledgments

We would like to express our appreciation to the many people who have contributed to the successful completion of this text. Most especially, we thank the students at Mt. San Antonio College and Theresa Berry who helped class-test the material and who greatly influenced the manuscript.

Many people have worked very hard to design and produce this text, including Jodi McPherson, Jean Lou Hess, and June Waldman. Thanks to Alfonso Hermida for the technical edit.

We greatly appreciate Theresa Berry, and for their thorough technical reviews, constructive criticism, and many valuable suggestions. Thank you to Eric Millspaugh, Tim Blek, and Jim Neptune for their "on-the-job" suggestions. And most importantly, we are grateful to Dennis and Andy for their support and understanding through the long days and busy phone lines.

We want to thank our reviewers, who have made many helpful suggestions:

Kurt Kominek, Northeast State Technical Community College
Anita Phillipp, Oklahoma City Community College
Scott Lord, Bainbridge College
Janet Dunford, Central Virginia Community College

We have had fun teaching and writing about Visual Basic. We hope that this feeling is evident as you read this book and that you will enjoy learning or teaching this outstanding programming language.

Julia Case Bradley
Anita C. Millspaugh

To The Student

Welcome to the exciting new features of Visual Basic. You have probably already learned that the best way to learn how to program is to actually sit at a computer and code, change things, and test it again. Stepping through existing code is also a great tool in learning new techniques. With that in mind, we have included all of the code from the examples within the chapters on your student CD. Please feel free to load the programs, change things, and test it again.

But, if you really want to learn how it works, it is critical that you create a blank project and try the techniques yourself. If you run into a problem, take a look at the sample and compare properties and code.

There are several tools in this text to help you on your way.

- Each chapter begins with a list of topics and ends with a summary. Combine these for a thumbnail review of the chapter. Understanding the terminology is an important part of learning any new language that's also true with programming languages.

- A list of key terms is at the end of each chapter. Each of those terms is in boldface within the chapter. There is also a glossary at the end of the text where you can look up the definition of the terms.

- Test yourself with the feedback questions as you work through each section of a chapter. The review questions at the end of the chapter can test your understanding of the topics.

- Tips are included to give suggestions in situations where you may run into problems caused by the version of software installed/not installed or with settings.

- Each chapter also includes hints and topics for the MCSD exam. If you plan to take the exam, it is a good idea to also obtain a CD or book that contains sample exams.

J.C.B.
A.C.M.

Contents

Advanced Programming Using Visual Basic

Version 6.0

1

Installing and Configuring Visual Basic

At the completion of this chapter, you will be able to . . .

1. Select the correct edition of Visual Basic (VB) based on software features and hardware requirements.

2. Install VB, selecting the features you will need.

3. Set up the VB environment options.

4. Use the debugging tools and windows.

5. Understand the purpose and functions of Visual SourceSafe.

Because you are beginning an advanced programming text, we assume that

- You have completed an introductory text or a course, or have some experience programming in Microsoft VB. If this assumption is not true, you will need to do some catching up, either by spending some time with an introductory text or by studying Appendix C.

- You want to be a good programmer. That is, you want to write good programs. The projects in this book demonstrate good programming practices as well as good user-interface design.

- You want to master the advanced features of VB. You can see from the table of contents that you will cover many advanced topics.

- You *may* want to take Microsoft's certification exam for VB. This text prepares you for exam 70-176, Designing and Implementing Desktop Applications with Microsoft Visual Basic 6.0. Some of the information included in this text appears strictly to prepare you for test questions.

This first chapter covers installing VB on your computer, setting up the environment, using the VB debugging tools, and working with Visual SourceSafe.

Visual Basic

Visual Basic is big. In recent years it has become the most popular language for development. If you count Visual Basic for Applications (VBA), VBScript, the Control Creation edition (CCE), and the full version of VB, more developers are using this language than any other.

Each new release of VB includes additional and more powerful features. Using the VB environment and tools, you will find that rapid application development is relatively easy to perform.

Editions of Visual Basic

According to Microsoft's documentation, three versions of VB are available: the **Learning edition,** the **Professional edition,** and the **Enterprise edition.** However, you may have used another version, the **Working Model,** which is licensed for distribution with VB textbooks and cannot be purchased independently. The Working Model is designed for learning the language. It includes more controls than the Learning edition, but does not include the Help files (Microsoft Developer Network documentation CDs). The Working Model does not allow programs to be compiled and does not include the Data Environment or Data Report Designer. The Working Model is clearly not appropriate for advanced programming.

You can create applications for most small to medium-size companies by using the Professional edition. The Enterprise edition is designed for large-scale enterprisewide applications, usually with teams of programmers.

Most of the exercises in this text can be done with the Professional edition. But the MCSD (Microsoft Certified System Developer) exam includes some questions about features found only in the Enterprise edition, so those topics are included. Unless you have the Enterprise edition, you won't be able to complete the exercises, but you *will* be able to learn the concept to prepare for the test questions. For example, the section on Visual SourceSafe later in this chapter applies only to the Enterprise edition.

Features of Each Visual Basic Edition

You will want to select the VB edition that best suits your needs.

- The Learning edition includes
  - Intrinsic controls.
  - Grid, Tab, and data-bound controls.

- The Professional edition includes
  - All features included in the Learning edition.
  - Additional ActiveX controls.
  - Internet Information Server (IIS) Application Designer.
  - Integrated data tools and the Data Environment.
  - ActiveX Data Objects (ADO).
  - Dynamic HTML (DHTML) Page Designer.
  - A native code compiler.

- The Enterprise edition includes
  - All features included in the Professional edition.
  - SQL Server.
  - Microsoft Transaction Server.
  - Internet Information Server.
  - Visual SourceSafe.
  - Visual Database tools (Query Designer and Database Designer).
  - SNA Server.
  - Application Performance Explorer.
  - Visual Modeler.
  - Stored Procedure Editor.
  - Visual Component Manager.
  - Remote Data Control.
  - Other BackOffice tools.

For the Microsoft certification exam, you must be familiar with the various editions of VB, the features, and the minimum hardware requirements for installation.

VB 6 requires Windows 95, Windows 98, or Windows NT 4.0 running on a 486DX/66 megahertz or higher processor (Windows NT should have a Pentium processor). The system must include a CD-ROM and a mouse. Table 1.1 shows the hardware requirements, and Table 1.2 shows the disk space needed for VB.

Table 1.1

Hardware Requirements for Running VB

Hardware Requirements	Operating System	
	Windows 95/98	Windows NT
Memory (RAM)	16MB	32MB
Processor (minimum)	486DX/66 megahertz	Pentium

T a b l e   1 . 2

Disk Space Needed to Install VB

	Disk Space Needed for	
Edition of Visual Basic	**Typical Installation**	**Full Installation**
Learning/Professional	48MB	80MB
Enterprise	128MB	147MB

Many questions on the MCSD exam refer to systems that do not meet the minimum hardware requirements.

Installing Visual Basic

You can install Visual Basic 6.0 as a stand-alone product or as part of the Visual Studio package. The setup details depend on the version and edition you are using and whether you previously installed another version of VB or Visual Studio on your system.

One of the first screens in the setup program holds the End User License Agreement. You cannot continue with the installation if you do not accept the terms of the agreement.

The next screen gives you the opportunity to retain or delete any previous versions of the software, for example, a stand-alone product such as VB 5 or a full version of Visual Studio. If you opt not to uninstall your previous version(s), it will not conflict with the new product that you are installing.

The screen that prompts for information about you requires the CD key; the name and company information is read from the Windows Registry. If the information is incorrect, you may change it on the installation screen.

A product ID appears on the next screen. This information is available in two places: during installation and as the serial number under the *About* option on the *Help* menu after installation.

Visual Studio Professional Edition

When you run the Visual Studio setup program, choose the *Custom* option (Figure 1.1); this choice enables you to select the options that you need. In the

F i g u r e   1 . 1

When installing Visual Studio Professional edition, click on the Custom button to select your choices.

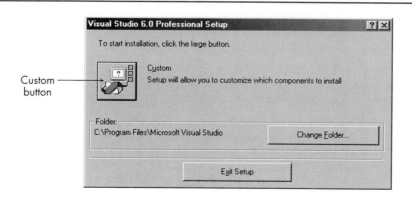

Custom button

Custom dialog box (Figure 1.2), you can elect to install VB along with several other languages and tools.

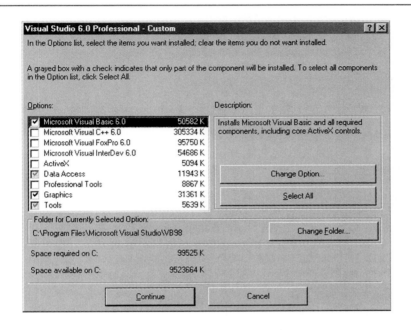

In the Custom dialog box, select your options. To install only Visual Basic 6.0, the only required options are Microsoft Visual Basic 6.0 and Data Access.

If you want to install *only* VB, deselect all options except *Microsoft Visual Basic 6.0* and *Data Access.* You will likely want to also choose *Graphics* to install the graphic files used in this text. Other useful components are *ActiveX, Professional Tools,* and *Tools.* Fortunately, you can rerun the setup program and install or remove components at a later time.

Visual Studio Enterprise Edition

The setup procedure for the Enterprise edition gives you a few more options than the Professional edition does. You will want to select *Microsoft Visual SourceSafe 6.0* and *Enterprise Tools.*

Installing Microsoft Developers Network

After you install the VB software, the setup program prompts you to install the **Microsoft Developers Network (MSDN)** CDs. The MSDN library holds the VB Help files, code samples, technical articles, and extra utilities. It also holds the documentation for all of Visual Studio, including Visual C++, Visual J++, Visual Interdev, and Visual FoxPro. Even if you have only the Professional edition of VB, you will have the documentation for the Enterprise edition, including Visual SourceSafe.

You have three installation choices (Figure 1.3), which determine the amount of disk storage required and whether or not you need to keep the CD in the drive when you use VB.

Figure   1.3

Choose the MSDN option that works best for your system.

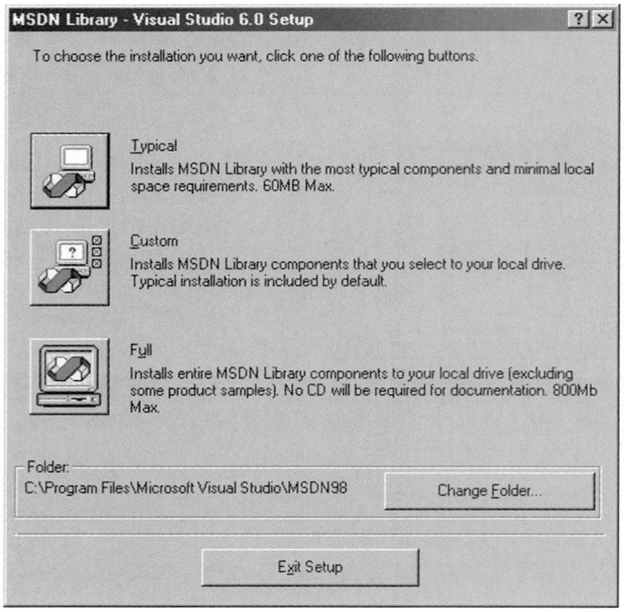

- Choose *Typical* to install a preselected set of components. This option uses the least amount of hard drive space, and in the future you will be prompted to insert the CD when you ask for components that are not on the hard drive.

- The *Custom* option gives you the most control. You can select the components that you want to store on your hard drive. All components from the typical installation are included, plus the ones you select.

- Choose *Full* if you are installing all of Visual Studio and you have lots of hard drive space available. With this option you will never have to insert the MSDN CD while you are running VB.

If you choose *Custom* (the recommended choice), you will see the *Custom* dialog box (Figure 1.4). Choose the options for VB.

The MSDN library comes on two CDs, which will have the current set of files. Microsoft updates MSDN often; to see the current components, visit the MSDN Web site: http://msdn.microsoft.com/.

Feedback 1.1

1. Can you install and run VB 6 on a 386 computer running Windows 95?
2. Can you install and run VB 6 on a 486 DX2 running Windows 95? Windows 98? Windows NT?
3. How is installation handled for a computer that doesn't have a CD drive?
4. Which useful features in the Professional edition are missing from the Learning edition?
5. Name three useful features in the Enterprise edition that are missing from the Professional edition.

Figure 1.4

Select the MSDN components for VB.

Configuring Your Visual Basic Environment

The VB environment, also called the **Integrated Development Environment (IDE),** consists of the windows, menus, tools, and designers that you use to develop your applications (Figure 1.5). You can customize the IDE to fit your own preferences, which makes programming and debugging easier.

Figure 1.5

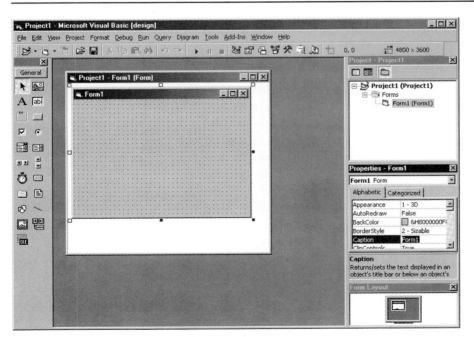

The VB environment.

Note: Be careful about customizing the environment when you are using a shared computer in a campus computer lab or an office.

Setting Environment Options

To customize your VB environment, make sure that you have a project open and select *Tools/Options.* (The *Options* command is grayed if no project is open.) In the *Options* dialog box (Figure 1.6), you can specify that all variables must be declared, control when errors halt execution, change the editor's font size and color, and select many other useful features. Notice that the dialog box has tabs for Editor, Editor Format, General, Docking, Environment, and Advanced.

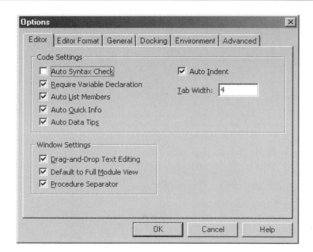

Choose Tools/Options to display the Options dialog box.

The Editor Tab

On the Editor tab (refer to Figure 1.6) make sure that *Require Variable Declaration* is checked. This option places the `Option Explicit` statement in the top of every new module that you create, requiring all variables to be declared. The other choices on the Editor tab allow you to set the number of spaces for indent and to turn off some features of the "smart" editor. *Auto List Members* displays a box that can complete an expression, *Auto Data Tips* displays a variable's value when the cursor is over the field, and *Auto Quick Info* shows the format of functions. You may wish to remove the check mark from *Auto Syntax Check.* If you are comfortable with the language, sometimes move to another line prior to completing a statement, and don't like to have an error dialog box appear, this option is for you. The syntax checker still colors the offending line red but does not display the dialog box.

Full Module View allows you to see multiple procedures on the screen at one time.

CHAPTER 1

The Editor Format Tab

The Editor Format tab (Figure 1.7) controls the font and size of the source code as well as the colors used for elements such as comments. If you are having difficulty seeing your code or displaying it on an overhead projector, you might try increasing the font size.

Figure 1.7

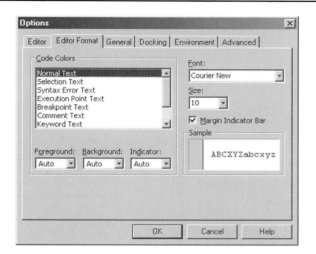

On the Editor Format tab of the Options dialog box, you can change the font, size, and color of various text elements.

The General Tab

On the General tab (Figure 1.8) you can specify whether you want the grid dots on your form at design time and the spacing of those dots. The unit of measure is twips, which you may recall is a screen-independent measurement. There are 1440 twips per inch, or 567 twips per centimeter.

Figure 1.8

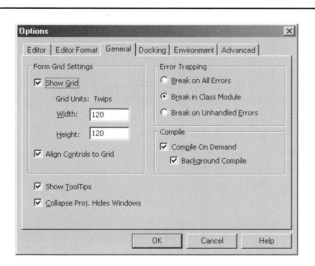

The General tab of the Options dialog box.

The Error Trapping options on the General tab allow you to choose how errors are handled when your code runs. If you choose *Break on All Errors* (instead of the default *Break in Class Module*), VB will enter break mode when any error occurs, even if you have written an error handler. The option to *Break on Unhandled Errors* causes VB to halt when you trap an error but don't have a handler for that particular error.

You will probably want to leave the default settings for the compile options. *Compile on Demand* means that the project can begin running before the compile is complete, and the *Background Compile* option specifies that idle time can be used to compile.

The Docking Tab

The Docking tab (Figure 1.9) controls the ability to "dock" the various windows that make up the IDE. This tab should not be confused with "docking" hardware available with some laptop systems.

F i g u r e   1 . 9

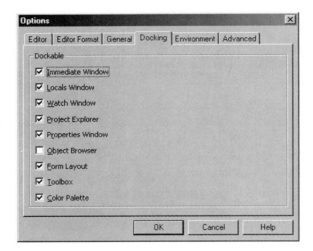

Choose the windows that can be docked on the Docking tab.

Any windows that are deselected will "float" rather than dock when you move them around.

The Environment Tab

On the Environment tab (Figure 1.10) you can also choose whether you want to automatically create a new default project when VB starts or to prompt for the project to open. If you choose *Prompt for project,* you can either open an existing project or create a new project based on templates.

Have you ever made a lot of changes to a project and then had the system lock up before the changes are saved? You can keep that from happening again by selecting either *Save Changes* or *Prompt to Save Changes* on the Environment tab.

The Environment tab controls the location of the project templates and allows you to select which ones appear in the dialog box when you add a component.

Figure 1.10

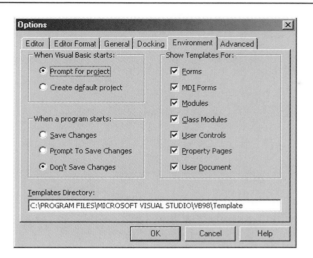

The Environment tab of the Options dialog box.

The Advanced Tab

The one option on the Advanced tab (Figure 1.11) that you may want to try changing is *SDI Development Environment*. SDI stands for single-document interface, and with this option selected the Windows desktop is visible while you use the VB IDE.

Figure 1.11

The Advanced tab of the Options dialog box.

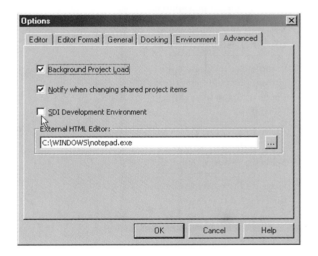

Feedback 1.2

1. What step forces all variables to be declared?
2. Explain how to force a project to be saved automatically before it is executed.

continued

3. What option controls the display of error dialog boxes while you are editing code?
4. What would cause *Tools/Options* to be grayed out?
5. Where is an `Option Explicit` statement placed in code?
6. What feature (when turned off) displays only one procedure at a time in the Code window?
7. Explain the purpose of *Compile on Demand*.

Debugging

To be a good programmer, you will want to master the VB debugging tools. Use these powerful tools to help you find and eliminate run-time and logic errors. You can also use the debugging tools to follow the logic of an existing project to better understand how the program works. Table 1.3 shows the debugging tools.

T a b l e   1 . 3

The Debugging Tools and Their Shortcuts

Debugging Tool	Shortcut	Button	Purpose
Toggle breakpoint	F9		Sets code statement where execution should break. Toggles on and off.
Step Into	F8		Executes next line of code; steps into called procedures.
Step Over	Shift + F8		Executes next line of code; steps over called procedures.
Step Out	Ctrl + Shift + F8		Completes execution of the current procedure and breaks at the next line in the calling procedure.
Run to Cursor	Ctrl + F8		Continues execution and breaks again at the statement that holds the insertion point.
Quick Watch	Shift + F9		Displays the current value of the selected expression in Break mode.

The debugging tools allow you to set breakpoints, step through code, and display the current contents of variables and properties. Special debugging windows are the Immediate, Watch, Locals, and Call Stack.

Save yourself time by displaying and using the Debug toolbar (Figure 1.12) while debugging a project. You can use the toolbar buttons to start and stop execution, as well as to set breakpoints, step through execution, or display the debugging windows. You can either float the toolbar or dock it—try docking it along the right edge of the screen (Figure 1.13).

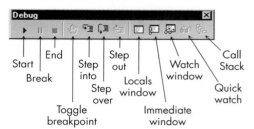

The Debug toolbar.

You may want to dock the Debug toolbar along the right edge of the screen.

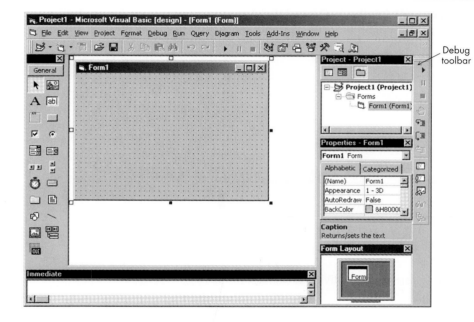
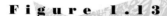

Break Mode

To debug a project, you must be in **Break mode** (also called ***break time***). Of course, if the program generates a run-time error, VB goes into Break mode automatically. Otherwise, you can manually enter Break mode. VB provides several ways to enter Break mode, including clicking the Break toolbar button, pressing Ctrl + Break, choosing *Break* from the *Run* menu, setting a breakpoint in code, or placing a `Stop` statement in code.

Setting Breakpoints

During the debugging process, you often want to stop at a particular location in code and watch what happens (which branch of an `If . . . Then . . . Else`; which procedures were executed; the value of a variable just before or just after a calculation). You can force the project to break by inserting a **breakpoint** in the code.

To set a breakpoint, place the cursor in the gray margin indicator bar at the left edge of the Code window and click; the line is highlighted in red, and a large red dot displays in the margin indicator bar (Figure 1.14). You can also set a breakpoint by placing the cursor on the line before which you want to break and clicking on the Set Breakpoint button, by choosing *Toggle Breakpoint* from the *Debug* menu, or by pressing F9, the keyboard shortcut. The breakpoint line changes to red (unless colors have been altered on your system).

F i g u r e   1 . 1 4

Toggle breakpoints on and off by clicking in the gray margin indicator bar.

Breakpoint

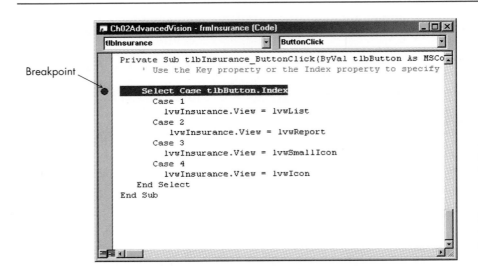

After setting a breakpoint, start (or restart) program execution. The project will halt, display the line, and go into Break mode upon reaching the breakpoint.

You can use *Toggle Breakpoint* again to turn off an individual breakpoint or clear all breakpoints from the *Debug* menu.

Manually Pausing Execution

You can click on the Break toolbar button to pause execution. This step places the project into break time at the current line. The disadvantage of this method is that you don't have much control over where execution stops; usually you want to break in the middle of a procedure. To choose the location of the break, use a breakpoint.

Debugging Techniques

The techniques that you will use most often are stepping through your code and displaying the contents of variables by using Data Tips, Watch expressions, or the Immediate window.

Stepping through Code

The best way to debug a project is to thoroughly understand what the project is doing every step of the way. You can use the VB stepping tools to trace program execution line by line and see the progression of the program as it executes your code.

VB has three methods of stepping, which execute the next line of code and again pause the program in break time. **Step Into** (F8) executes one line at a time, including the lines in called sub procedures and functions. **Step Over** (Shift + F8) shows the line-by-line execution of the current procedure but does not show the code in any called procedures. **Step Out** is used only when you are single-stepping in a called procedure and decide to quickly finish execution of the current procedure; execution breaks again after the call in the calling procedure.

Starting the Step Process To step through code, you must be in break time. You can enter break time by using one of the methods mentioned in the preceding section. Another method of entering break time and stepping through code is to choose one of the step commands, such as Step Into, from design time. The program begins running and immediately transfers to break time.

Executing a Line at a Time The current statement appears highlighted in the Code window (Figure 1.15). That is, the highlighted line is the next statement to execute. When you choose either Step Into or Step Over (F8 or Shift + F8), the highlighted statement executes. You can repeatedly step execution and watch as each code line executes. You can tell which branch of an If statement is taken, follow the execution of loops, and check the value of variables and properties as you go.

Tip

Save yourself time by learning the keyboard shortcuts for the most-used debugging commands. Press F8 repeatedly to step through program statements; press F5 to continue execution; press Shift + F5 to restart execution from the beginning.

Figure 1.15

The current line is highlighted in the Code window. Press F8 to execute the highlighted line.

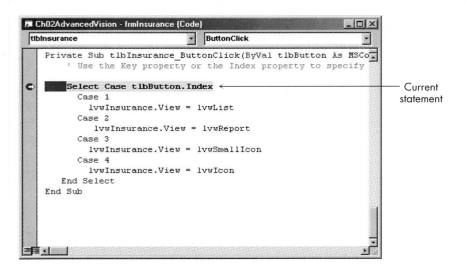

Current statement

When the current procedure finishes, you may need to click on the program's taskbar button to again display the running form. At that point you can click one of the command buttons on the form; the button's Click event occurs, and you transfer to the Code window in break time, ready to continue single-stepping.

Stopping and Starting If you want to continue rapid execution without stepping, choose the *Continue* command (from the *Run* menu, the toolbar button, or the F5 shortcut).

Sometimes you find yourself stepping though a lengthy process, such as a loop with many iterations. You can click in the statement following the loop and choose *Run to Cursor* (Ctrl + F8) from the *Debug* menu. VB will rapidly execute the code and break again at the line holding the insertion point.

One more debugging command that you may find useful occasionally is *Set Next Statement* (Ctrl + F9). When you want to skip some lines of code and execute a statement out of order, click in the line you want and choose this command. Be careful though—none of the intervening lines will execute, and data values might not be what you expect.

Data Tips

Data Tips are great. They look like ToolTips but display the current contents of a variable or property in the Code window. The project must be in break time, and the variable must be in scope. That is, to display the contents of a local variable, execution must currently be halted in the procedure where the variable is declared. You can display the contents of a global variable from anywhere in the project, and a module-level variable from anywhere in the module.

To display a Data Tip, pause the mouse pointer over the variable name or property you want. Figure 1.16 shows a Data Tip in the Code window.

Figure 1.16

Pause the mouse pointer over a variable or property to see the current contents.

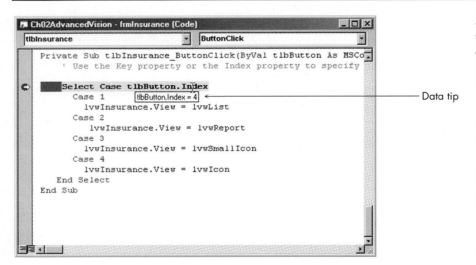

Watch Expressions

You can set up a variable, property, or expression that you want to monitor as you single-step program execution. For example, you can choose to watch the value of a variable called intCount; an expression such as `curTotal / intCount`, which displays the result of the calculation; or `intCount = 0`, which displays True or False (Figure 1.17).

Display the **Watch window** by using the *View* menu or the toolbar button. Then you can drag and drop a variable name from the Code window to the Watch window to automatically set a **Watch Expression.** Or you can choose *Add Watch* from the *Debug* menu or the shortcut menu; right-click in the Watch window to see the shortcut menu (Figure 1.18).

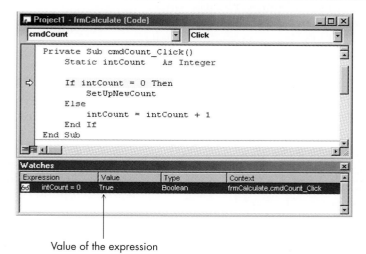

Figure 1.17

The Watch window displays the current value of an expression only when the variables are in scope.

Value of the expression

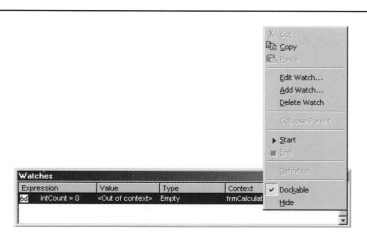

Figure 1.18

You can edit, add, or delete a Watch Expression on the shortcut menu.

The Watch window displays the current contents of all Watch Expressions as long as the variables are in scope. If the variables are out of scope, the Value column shows the message <Out of context> (Figure 1.19).

Figure 1.19

Out-of-scope expressions display <Out of context>.

Quick Watch

You can quickly check the current value of an expression, such as a variable, a condition, or an arithmetic expression, by using **Quick Watch.** During break time display the Code window, select the expression that you want to view, and choose *Quick Watch* (*Debug* menu, toolbar button, or Shift + F9). The *Quick Watch* dialog box pops up with the current content of the expression (Figure 1.20). You can click the Add button to add the expression to the Watch window. (Quick Watches were much more useful before Data Tips were added to VB in version 6.0.)

A Quick Watch immediately shows the value of an expression. You can optionally choose to add the expression to the Watch window.

The Debugging Windows

You can choose to display any of the extra windows used for debugging. Table 1.4 shows the purpose of the Call Stack, the Immediate window, the Locals window, and the Watch window.

The Debugging Windows

Debugging Window	Shortcut	Purpose
Call Stack	Ctrl + L	Shows procedures that have been called but not yet completed.
Immediate window	Ctrl + G	Directly executes statements or displays values in Break mode.
Locals window		Shows current value of local variables.
Watch window		Shows values of selected variables or expressions.

The Call Stack

The **Call Stack** can help you debug a series of nested procedures. The Call Stack is a dialog box that displays the *active procedures*—the procedures that have been called but have not yet completed. The most recently called procedure appears at the top of the list (Figure 1.21). You can display the Call Stack during Break mode by using the toolbar button, by selecting the *View/Call Stack* menu command, or by pressing Ctrl + L.

The Immediate Window

The **Immediate window** (Figure 1.22) is available at design time, run time, and break time. You can display the values of data or messages in the Immediate window while the project is executing. In break time you can use

The Call Stack displays the names of procedures that have been called but not completed. It can be useful for debugging nested procedures.

Immediately execute single lines of code in the Immediate window.

the Immediate window to view or change the contents of variables or to execute lines of code. At design time you can view the window to see values from the previous run, but you cannot execute any code.

You can display the window by selecting it from the *View* menu, using the shortcut Ctrl + G, or clicking the toolbar button. You may want to move and resize the window to make it more visible.

In earlier versions of VB, the Immediate window was called the Debug window. You will still find references to the Debug window in the documentation. For example, the statement `Debug.Print` displays its output in the Immediate window. And the keyboard shortcut, Ctrl + G, is based on the term *Debug window.*

You can execute any single line of code in the Immediate window. Type the line and press Enter; the code executes. You can even reexecute any line in the Immediate window by placing the cursor anywhere in the line and pressing Enter.

To display the contents of a variable, property, or expression in the Immediate window, use the window's Print method. Note that you can omit the object name (Debug) and even use a shortcut for the keyword `Print`.

```
Debug.Print intCount
Print intCount
? intCount (The question mark is a shortcut for the Print keyword.)
```

The Locals Window

At break time you can display or change the values of local variables in the **Locals window** (Figure 1.23). Display the window by using *View/Locals Window* or the toolbar button.

The Locals window can save you lots of time. You can view all local variables at once, rather than displaying each variable individually. Another great feature is that you can view the current properties of the active form and any objects that are in scope. Click on the boxed plus sign to view the properties of

Figure 1.23

The Locals window shows the contents of local variables as well as objects that are in scope, including the current form.

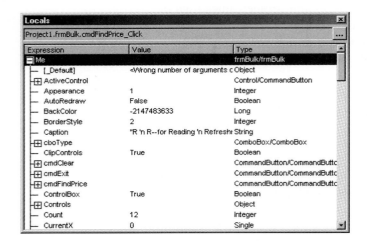

```
            intGame1 = Val(txtScore1.Text)
            intGame2 = Val(txtScore2.Text)
            intGame3 = Val(txtScore3.Text)

            'Perform all calculations
            curAverage = curFindAverage(intGame1, intGame2, intGame3)
            intSeries = intFindSeries(intGame1, intGame2, intGame3)
            strHighGame = strFindHighGame(intGame1, intGame2, intGame3)
            curHandicap = curFindHandicap(curAverage)

            lblAverage.Caption = FormatNumber(curAverage, 1)
```

Locals

Project1.frmBowling.mnuFileCalc_Click

Expression	Value	Type
⊞ Me		frmBowling/frmBowling
curAverage	158.3333	Currency
curHandicap	0	Currency
intSeries	475	Integer
strHighGame	""	String
intGame1	140	Integer
intGame2	160	Integer
intGame3	175	Integer

Figure 1.24

Click on the boxed plus sign to display the properties of an object.

Locals

Project1.frmBulk.cmdFindPrice_Click

Expression	Value	Type
⊟ Me		frmBulk/frmBulk
— [_Default]	<Wrong number of arguments c	Object
⊞ ActiveControl		Control/CommandButton
— Appearance	1	Integer
— AutoRedraw	False	Boolean
— BackColor	-2147483633	Long
— BorderStyle	2	Integer
— Caption	"R 'n R--for Reading 'n Refresh	String
⊞ cboType		ComboBox/ComboBox
— ClipControls	True	Boolean
⊞ cmdClear		CommandButton/CommandButtc
⊞ cmdExit		CommandButton/CommandButtc
⊞ cmdFindPrice		CommandButton/CommandButtc
— ControlBox	True	Boolean
⊞ Controls		Object
— Count	12	Integer
— CurrentX	0	Single

an object (Figure 1.24). (Recall that Me is a shortcut that refers to the current form.) And you can display all elements of an array or a typed variable—just click on the boxed plus sign to drill down to see the elements (Figure 1.25).

The Watch Window

In the Watch window you can view or alter the values of any variables or expressions that you want to watch. The Watch window is also a useful tool for watching property values at run time. Setting and viewing Watch Expressions were covered in the earlier sections "Watch Expressions" and "Quick Watch."

Another important feature of the Watch window is that you can watch the values of array elements and the elements of typed variables. Add a Watch Expression by dragging the name of an array or typed variable to the Watch window; the array name or typed variable name is preceded by a boxed plus sign (Figure 1.26). Click on the plus sign to view the elements of the structure and click on the minus sign to again hide the elements.

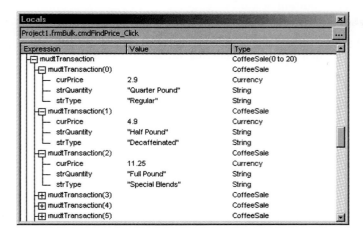

Display each element of an array or a typed variable by clicking on the boxed plus sign for its name. Hide the elements again by clicking on the boxed minus sign.

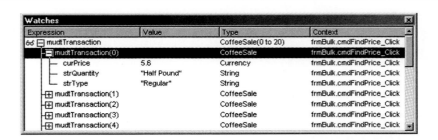

The Watch window can also be used to display elements of arrays and typed variables.

Feedback 1.3

1. Assume that you are getting strange results from a calculation. How can you examine each value and watch the calculation happen?
2. Describe how to display the contents of a variable by using Data Tips, the Immediate window, the Watch window, and the Locals window.
3. You are in design time and want to run a project, single-stepping every line. Explain how to do this.
4. Explain two methods of displaying the contents of all elements of the strName array.
5. How can you view the properties of the current form during break time?

Visual SourceSafe

If you have ever worked on a really large project, you know the importance of keeping track of the version of each component. You need to know which is the most current version and, in some cases, revert to an earlier version. **Visual SourceSafe (VSS)** creates a database of users (developers) and versions of source code. The program is designed to accommodate a team environment in which numerous developers may be making changes to a project. As you might expect, VSS is included only with the Enterprise edition of VB.

Each developer (user) in the team must have an account with VSS. Although you do not need to be familiar with VSS for the Microsoft desktop developer exam, you must at least know that a user cannot log on to VSS without a valid username and password. These are established by the VSS administrator.

If you have the Enterprise edition and have installed VSS, take a peek at the VSS options. Select *Tools/SourceSafe/Options* from the menu. If you click on the Advanced button, you can see your username and password. The database name also appears. For most situations you will use the default database called *Common* (Figure 1.27).

F i g u r e   1 . 2 7

The advanced options of Visual SourceSafe.

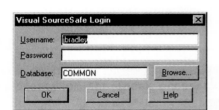

MCSD Exam Notes

Exam Objectives Covered in This Chapter

Establishing the Development Environment

● Establish the environment for source code version control.

● Install and configure VB for developing desktop applications.

Testing the Solution

Set Watch Expressions during program execution.

Monitor the values of expressions and variables by using the Immediate window.

● Use the Immediate window to check or change values.

● Use the Locals window to check or change values.

Given a scenario, define the scope of a watch variable.

Questions/Tricks to Watch for

● Be familiar with the tabs and settings on the dialog box for *Tools/Options*.

● Know the purpose of the debugging windows.

● For each edition of VB, know the hardware requirements.

- A project must be open for *Tools/Options* to be enabled.

- Visual SourceSafe branching creates a new project B as a copy of project A; changes to project A are not reflected in project B.

S u m m a r y

1. Visual Basic (VB) 6.0 is sold in three editions: Learning, Professional, and Enterprise. In addition, the Working Model is packaged with some Visual Basic textbooks. To select the correct edition, a person should be aware of the hardware requirements as well as the software features.
2. VB may be installed as a stand-alone product or as part of Visual Studio.
3. After installing VB, you must also install MCSD, which holds the Help files and all documentation.
4. The VB IDE can be customized from the *Options* dialog box. Options include requiring variable declaration, automatic syntax checking, full-module view, editor font size and color, error trapping, and project-saving options.
5. Debugging tools are used to locate program errors. Tools include the ability to set breakpoints, step through code as it executes, and examine the contents of variables and properties.
6. Code stepping commands include Step Into, Step Over, Step Out, Run to Cursor, and Set Next Statement.
7. You can examine the contents of variables, properties, and/or expressions by using Data Tips, Watch Expressions, Quick Watches, the Immediate window, and the Locals window.
8. The Call Stack shows procedures that have been entered but not yet completed.
9. The Locals window and the Watch window can display the properties of objects, the elements of an array, and the elements of a variable declared as a user-defined type.

K e y   T e r m s

Break mode   *13*
break time   *13*
breakpoint   *13*
Call Stack   *18*
Data Tip   *16*
Enterprise edition   *2*
Immediate window   *18*
Integrated Development Environment (IDE)   *7*
Learning edition   *2*
Locals window   *19*

Microsoft Developers Network (MSDN)   *5*
Professional edition   *2*
Quick Watch   *17*
Step Into   *15*
Step Out   *15*
Step Over   *15*
Visual SourceSafe (VSS)   *21*
Watch Expression   *16*
Watch window   *16*
Working Model   *2*

Review Questions

1. What are the hardware and operating system requirements for each edition of VB?
2. Explain how and when to use the various step tools for debugging code.
3. List and explain the purpose of the various debugging windows.

Computer Exercises

1.1   Create a project to test the debugging tools and windows.
Form: Place a text box, a label, and a command button called ADD on the form. Use appropriate naming conventions for your objects.
Processing: Include a module-level integer variable called mintCount. The Click event of the ADD command button adds the contents of the text box to mintCount and displays the result in the label on the form.
Testing: Place a breakpoint on the calculation line in the command button's Click event. View the Watch window. Click on the boxed plus sign to view object properties.

1.2   Modify the program to use a Static local variable and view the Locals window.

2

Interfacing with the User

At the completion of this chapter, you will be able to . . .

1. Understand the sequence and purpose of form events.

2. Visualize and use the Forms collection and Controls collection.

3. Create an MDI project with a parent and child forms.

4. Add and remove controls at run time.

5. Modify menu commands during program execution.

6. Create pop-up (context) menus.

7. Use a group of ActiveX controls: ImageList, Toolbar, StatusBar, TreeView, and ListView.

8. Create a Tabbed Dialog control.

9. Perform error handling.

10. Declare and call Public procedures.

Interfacing with the User

One goal of good programming is to create programs that are easy to use. The user interface is the part of a program through which you interact with your user. The interface consists of the visual components as well as the behavior of the program. In designing the interface you need to consider the screens as well as what will happen if an error occurs.

Your user interface should be clear and consistent. One school of thought says that if users misuse a program, it's the fault of the programmer, not the users. Because most of your users will already know how to operate Windows programs, you should strive to make your programs look and behave like other Windows programs. One way to do so is to use Windows controls such as the Toolbar and the StatusBar. The TreeView and ListView provide an interface similar to Windows Explorer.

On the behavior side your program should incorporate error-handling routines in case of problems during execution. Help is another part of interfacing with the user and is addressed in Chapter 13.

Designing the User Interface

The design of the screen should be easy to understand and "comfortable" for the user. The best way to accomplish these goals is to follow industry standards in relation to color, size, and placement of controls. Once users become accustomed to a screen design, they will expect (and feel more comfortable with) applications that follow the same design criteria. Design your applications to match other Windows applications. Take some time to examine the screens and dialog boxes in Microsoft Office as well as those in VB.

Microsoft has done extensive program testing with users of different ages, genders, nationalities, and disabilities. Programmers should take advantage of this research and follow Microsoft's guidelines.

One recommendation about interface design concerns color. You have probably noticed that Windows applications are predominantly gray. One reason is that many people are color blind. Also, gray is easiest and best for most users. Although you may personally prefer brighter colors, if you want your applications to look professional, stick with gray.

Colors can indicate to the user what is expected. Use a white background for text boxes to indicate that the user is to input information. Use a gray background for labels, which the user cannot change. Labels that display a message or result of a calculation should have a border around them; labels that provide a caption on the screen should have no border (the default).

Group your controls on the form to aid the user. A good practice is to create frames to hold related items, especially those controls that require user input.

This visual aid helps the user understand the information that is being presented or requested.

Use a sans serif font on your forms, such as the default MS Sans Serif, and do not use boldface. Limit large font sizes to a few items, such as the company name.

Objects

The form is the basic *object* of a user interface. Recall that an object is a "thing" that has properties (characteristics) and methods (actions). A project may contain many forms, and each form may contain other objects called *controls*. The controls you should be familiar with include labels, command buttons, text boxes, and list boxes.

Collections

A special object that refers to a group of objects is called a **collection.** A collection has properties and methods just like any other object. VB has some default collections, for example, the **Forms collection** and the **Controls collection.** The loaded forms in a project make up the Forms collection; the controls on a form make up the form's Controls collection.

You will be using collections extensively as you program in VB. Fortunately, you can identify collection names, as they are always the plural of the individual object's name. For example, you can refer to an individual Form or to the collection of Forms. Collections always have a Count property and usually have Add and Remove methods. For now you will use the built-in collections in VB; in Chapter 6 you will learn to create your own collections.

Form Events

We need to do a quick review of forms, since the sequence of events that occur with forms is important. Remember that you can use the Load statement or the Show method to load a form; the Show method does an automatic Load if the form is not yet loaded. Also, VB automatically loads a form that is set as the startup object when the project begins execution.

When a form loads, the first event to occur is the Initialize, followed by the Load. When the form load is complete and the form displays or becomes the active window, the Activate event occurs. If all the form's controls are disabled, the GotFocus event is triggered instead of the Activate event.

The sequence for unloading is QueryUnload, followed by Unload, and then Terminate. Table 2.1 shows the form events in sequence.

Using the Form Events

In designing programs you will usually use the startup form's Load event procedure to initialize variables, properties, and any other startup code. Likewise, the "cleanup" code such as unloading other forms and releasing object variables belongs in the Unload event procedure. Use the QueryUnload to prompt the user to save changes and to provide a Cancel to avoid the Unload.

Unload Rather Than End a Project Although you may have learned to end an application with the End statement, you must now break that habit and end your applications properly by unloading forms. When all forms are unloaded, the project ends.

Event	Caused By
Initialize	Created in memory before loading. Occurs when an instance of a form is created.
Load	Form is loaded into memory. Use this procedure for initialization code.
GotFocus	Form becomes active, and all visible controls are disabled. Often is the case for splash screens.
Activate	Form becomes the active window or becomes visible with the Show method or Visible property.
LostFocus	Another form becomes the active window, and all visible controls are disabled.
Deactivate	Another form becomes the active window.
QueryUnload	Occurs before form is unloaded; use to check for saving changes or canceling Unload.
Unload	Form is unloaded from memory.
Terminate	All variables have been set to nothing.

The End statement ends an application immediately—no code after the End statement is executed, and no further events occur. In particular, VB does not execute the QueryUnload, Unload, or Terminate event procedures for any forms. Object references are freed, but if you have defined your own classes, VB does not execute the Terminate events of objects created from your classes.

To properly end a project, set all object variables to nothing and unload all forms. See "Ending an Application" later in this chapter.

Screen Resolution

Have you ever created a form on a computer with a large screen and/or very high resolution and then tried to run that form on a computer with a small screen or low resolution? The result is frustrating: You cannot even see the controls that are off the edge of the form.

If you work on a computer with high resolution or a large screen and know that your programs might be run on a screen that is smaller or has a lower resolution, you need to be aware of the problem. You can totally avoid it by always creating forms for the lowest resolution: 640 × 480. Or if you know the resolution of the computer(s) on which your program will run, set your resolution to match (using the Windows Control Panel).

You can see how your form will appear on a 640 × 480 display by using the Form Layout window. Right-click on the form display and select *Resolution Guides* to display guidelines on the window's display (Figure 2.1).

Display the resolution guides in the Form Layout window to make sure your form will display in 640 × 480 resolution.

If you find yourself stuck on a small-screen computer, trying to work on a program with out-of-sight controls, here's a workaround. In the Properties window, drop down the Object list and select the name of a control that you cannot see. Then change both the Left and the Top properties to zero. This step moves the control to the upper-left corner of the form from which you can move the control to a new location.

MDI and SDI Projects

Your VB projects can use a **multiple-document interface (MDI)** or a **single-document interface (SDI).** An MDI project resembles applications such as Word and Excel, which have a parent window (the main window) and child windows (the document windows that appear inside the parent window). With SDI each form acts independently of the others. In an MDI project one form is the **parent form** (main window) that controls the other forms, referred to as **child forms.** When you unload the main form, all child forms are also unloaded. An advantage of using MDI is that the child forms display within the boundaries of the parent, giving more control over resizing forms to the user.

Creating an MDI Project

In any one VB project you can have only one MDI form, which is the parent. You can make any other forms into child forms by setting the MDIChild property to True. Note that in an MDI project you *should* make all nonparent forms into child forms, with the exception of the splash screen. Any forms not set as child forms operate independently and are not confined to the parent window.

To add an MDI (parent) form to a project, choose *Project/Add MDI Form.* Notice in the Project Explorer window that the symbols for the MDI parent form and child forms differ from the symbols for SDI forms (Figure 2.2).

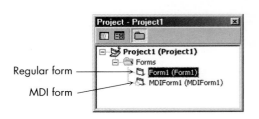

Regular form

MDI form

The Project Explorer window displays different symbols for MDI forms and regular forms.

Adding Menus to an MDI Project

If you add menus to an MDI project, you need to consider carefully where to specify the menus. If an MDI (parent) form has a menu, its menu displays only if no child form with a menu is displaying. If any child form that has a menu is displaying, its menu replaces the parent's menu. You can see this concept in action by opening Word or Excel and watching the menus. If no document (child) is open, you see one menu; if a document is open, you see a different menu on the main window.

Creating a Windows Menu

You can make your MDI project behave like other Windows applications by adding a *Window* menu. The *Window* menu typically has options to cascade and tile the child windows. Also, a list of open child windows displays with the active window checked. The user can switch to another window by selecting it from the menu (Figure 2.3).

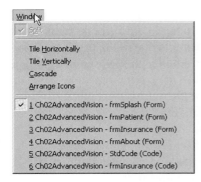

F i g u r e   2 . 3

The Window menu displays a list of open windows with the active window checked.

Displaying the WindowList

It's easy to make your *Window* menu display a list of open child windows. In the menu editor set the WindowList property to True for the *Window* menu (Figure 2.4).

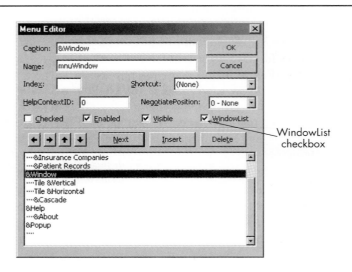
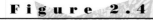

F i g u r e   2 . 4

Select the WindowList property to make the list of open windows appear on the Window menu.

Arranging the Child Windows

Give your user the option of arranging the open child windows within the parent window by using the **Arrange method.**

The Arrange Method—General Form

```
FormName.Arrange vbConstant
```

The constant can be vbCascade, vbTileHorizontal, or vbTileVertical.

The Arrange Method—Examples

```
frmMain.Arrange vbCascade
frmMain.Arrange vbTileHorizontal
```

```
Private Sub mnuWindowCascade_Click()
    'Cascade Open Forms

    frmMain.Arrange vbCascade
End Sub

Private Sub mnuWindowTileHorizontally_Click()
    'Tile Open forms horizontally

    frmMain.Arrange vbTileHorizontal
End Sub

Private Sub mnuWindowTileVertically_Click()
    'Tile open forms vertically

    frmMain.Arrange vbTileVertical
End Sub
```

Using the Forms Collection

The Forms collection consists of all of the forms in a project that are loaded into memory. The collection may contain MDI forms; MDI child forms; and regular, non-MDI forms. You can refer to each form by using an index, which begins with zero. For example, if your project has three forms, you can refer to them as Forms(0), Forms(1), and Forms(2). The Forms collection has a Count property, so the highest index is Forms.Count−1.

Ending an Application

An event-driven application stops running when all forms are unloaded and no code is executing. If a hidden form still remains loaded when the last visible form is closed, your application appears to have ended (because no forms are visible) but in fact continues to run until all the hidden forms are unloaded. This situation can arise because any reference to an unloaded form's properties or controls implicitly loads that form without displaying it.

The best way to avoid this problem when closing your application is to make sure that all of your forms are unloaded. If you have more than one form, you can use the Forms collection and the **Unload statement.** For example, on your main form you might have a command button named cmdExit that lets a user exit the program. If your application has only one form, the Exit event procedure could be as simple as this:

```
Private Sub cmdExit_Click ()
    Unload Me
End Sub
```

If your application uses multiple forms, unload all the forms in the Unload event procedure of your main form. You can use a `For/Each` loop and the Forms collection to make sure that you find and close every form. Each loaded Form object is an individual member of the Forms collection.

```
Private Sub Form_Unload (Cancel As Integer)
    'Loop through the forms collection and unload each form.
    Dim OneForm as Form 'Declare variable for a single form

    For Each OneForm In Forms
        Unload OneForm
    Next
End Sub
```

Notice in this example that OneForm is created as a Form object, whereas the loop refers to Forms, the collection. These Microsoft names follow their standard naming convention of collections being the plural of the single object name.

Dynamically Adding and Removing Controls at Run Time

If you're reading this book, you already know how to add controls at design time. In fact, you can create controls that are invisible and make them visible at run time in response to some action or condition. But you may also want to create new controls at run time, based on an action of the user. You can dynamically add and remove many classes of controls, such as option buttons, command buttons, text boxes, and labels. You can also add and remove ActiveX (nonintrinsic) controls, but the process is a bit more difficult.

VB provides two ways to add controls at run time: by using control arrays and by using the Controls collection. Programmers have been using control arrays for a long time; the Controls collection method is new to VB 6.

Adding Controls by Using Control Arrays

To add a new control by using the control array method, at design time you must create a control array with at least one control of the class you want to add. The first control typically has an Index property of zero, may be set to invisible, and serves as a template for the added controls. For example, add an option button called optChoice to a form. Set the button's Index property to zero (which makes it a control array). In code these statements add another option button and make it visible (newly loaded controls are invisible by default).

```
Load optChoice(1)
optChoice(1).Visible = True
```

Where will this new option button appear? Right on top of the first one unless you change its properties.

After you create a new control, you are likely to want to change several of its properties. The following event procedure allows the user to create multiple option buttons and sets the properties of each button. (Note that this procedure uses a module-level variable called mintButtonIndex. This variable is included to allow for removing the controls in another procedure.)

```
Private Sub cmdAddOption_Click()
    'Add an option button

    mintButtonIndex = mintButtonIndex + 1    'Get the next higher index
    Load optChoice(mintButtonIndex)          'Create a new button

    With optChoice(mintButtonIndex)                'Set properties for new button
        .Caption = "Button " & mintButtonIndex
        .Top = optChoice(mintButtonIndex − 1).Top + 300
        .Visible = True
    End With
End Sub
```

Removing Controls Added with Control Arrays

You can dynamically remove any controls that you added during run time by using the Unload statement. For example, this statement removes the optChoice button created earlier:

```
Unload optChoice(1)
```

You can only unload controls that you have added during program execution. If you try to unload a control that was added at design time, you receive a run-time error.

This code allows the user to remove the option buttons added in the previous event procedure:

```
Private Sub cmdRemoveOption_Click()
    'Remove an option button

    If mintButtonIndex > 0 Then
        Unload optChoice(mintButtonIndex)     'Remove the button
        mintButtonIndex = mintButtonIndex − 1
    Else
        MsgBox "Cannot remove original button", , "Dynamic Controls"
    End If
End Sub
```

Responding to Events for the Added Controls

You can respond to events for the added controls in the same way that you respond to any control array. A control array has only one Click event procedure with an Index argument that indicates the selected control.

```
Private Sub optChoice_Click(Index As Integer)
    'Respond to option button event
    'Note: Normally the only action you take in an option button
    '       Click event is to save the index for processing in
    '       another event procedure.

    mintSelectedOption = Index 'Save the index for processing elsewhere
    MsgBox "You selected Button " & mintSelectedOption, , "Dynamic Controls"
End Sub
```

If you have dynamically added command buttons, you can use the Index argument to determine the action to take.

```
Private Sub cmdNew_Click(Index As Integer)
    'Respond to the Click event of an added command button

    Select Case Index 'Take a different action for each button
        Case 0
            MsgBox "Taking action for Button 0", , "Dynamic Controls"
        Case 1
            MsgBox "Taking action for Button 1", , "Dynamic Controls"
        Case 2
            MsgBox "Taking action for Button 2", , "Dynamic Controls"
        Case Else   'Add as many more Cases as you wish
            MsgBox "Taking action for Button " & Index, , "Dynamic Controls"
    End Select
End Sub
```

You can find the complete program for adding and removing option buttons and command buttons in the folder Ch02DynamicControlArray.

Adding Controls by Using the Controls Collection

In VB 6 you can dynamically add and remove controls by using a form's Controls collection. The Controls collection, like other VB collection objects, has methods for Add and Remove, as well as Count and Index properties.

The Controls Collection You can quickly iterate through all controls on a form by using the Controls collection. For example, this bit of code enables all controls on a form:

```
Dim OneControl As Control
For Each OneControl In Me.Controls
    OneControl.Enabled = True
Next
```

You can also check the type of control and enable only certain ones:

```
Dim OneControl As Control
For Each OneControl In Me.Controls
    If TypeOf OneControl Is TextBox Then
        OneControl.Enabled = True
    End If
Next
```

Adding New Controls to the Collection Adding a new control to the Controls collection is a two-step process: First declare an object variable to refer to the new control and then use the collection's **Add method** to add the control.

Tip

Remember that the singular (Control) refers to a single control; the plural (Controls) refers to the collection.

The object variable for your new control should most likely be declared at the module level, since you will want to refer to the control in multiple procedures. (Remember that object variables have scope, just like all other variables.) If you want your new control to be able to respond to events (and who doesn't?), you need a **WithEvents clause.** You use the As clause to declare the class of the control, which may be TextBox, Label, CommandButton, or any of the intrinsic controls.

Note: You can also add ActiveX (nonintrinsic) controls, but the task is a little more complicated. And if the ActiveX control is not registered on your system, you must also add to the Licenses collection. Read about adding ActiveX controls in MSDN under "Add Method (Controls Collection)" and "Add Method (Licenses Collection)."

Declaring a New Control Variable—General Form

```
Private|Public [WithEvents] Identifier As ObjectType
```

Declaring a New Control Variable—Examples

```
Private WithEvents mcmdNew    As CommandButton
Private WithEvents mtxtNew    As TextBox
Public mtxtNewData            As TextBox
Public mobjAdded              As Object
```

As mentioned earlier, you generally place these declarations at the module level (hence the *m* prefix).

In the last example above, the variable is declared as type Object. Although this declaration is legal and will work, you'll generate inefficient code that causes late binding, which means that the compiler cannot assign the type during the compile process; the type cannot be determined until the program runs.

To actually add the control, you set the object variable by using the Add method of the Controls collection.

The Controls object is a member of the Form and can be accessed as frmMain.Controls. The Add method contains two arguments: the type of control called and the name that will be assigned to the control.

The Controls.Add Method—General Form

```
Set ObjectVariable = Controls.Add(strProgID, strControlName, [Container])
```

The object variable is the name of the variable that you previously declared. The **ProgID (programmatic ID)** is a string that represents the class name of the control from the library. For the compiler to locate the correct module, you must prefix the intrinsic control name with "VB" (example: VB.CommandButton). The strControlName argument is the name by which you will call the new control and should be the same as the object variable. Use the optional Container argument if you want the new control to belong to another control, such as a frame or a picture box.

The Controls.Add Method—Examples

```
Set mtxtName = Me.Controls.Add("VB.TextBox", "mtxtName")
Set moptNewColor = Controls.Add("VB.OptionButton", "moptNewColor", fraColors)
```

Note that the ProgID and the control identifier are placed in quotation marks.

After you add a new control, you need to set its properties. By default, new controls are invisible and located in the upper-right corner of the container. The following code adds an option button and a text box and sets their properties. Assume that optBlack already exists.

```
Option Explicit
```

```
Private moptNewColor        As OptionButton
Private WithEvents mtxtName As TextBox

Private Sub cmdAddOption_Click()
    'Add an Option Button

    Set moptNewColor = Controls.Add("VB.OptionButton", "moptNewColor", _
          fraColors)
    With moptNewColor
      .Caption = "New Color"
      .Left = optBlack.Left
      .Top = optBlack.Top + 300
      .Width = optBlack.Width
      .Visible = True
    End With
End Sub
```

```
Private Sub cmdAddTextBox_Click()
    'Add a textbox to the form

    Set mtxtName = Controls.Add("VB.TextBox", "mtxtName")
    With mtxtName
      .Left = 1800
      .Top = 240
      .Height = 375
      .Width = 2400
      .Visible = True
    End With
End Sub
```

Removing a Control

You can use the **Remove method** of the Controls collection to remove a control that was dynamically added. Note that you cannot use this method to remove any controls that were created at design time.

Example
```
Me.Controls.Remove mtxtName
```

Control Errors You need to include error handling in a project that adds and removes controls. If you attempt to add a control that is already loaded or to remove a control that wasn't loaded at run time, you get a run-time error. See the section "Handling Errors during Execution" later in this chapter.

Complete Program Listing

```
'Project:      Chapter 2 Dynamic Controls 2
'Date:         2/2000
'Programmer:   Bradley/Millspaugh
'Description:  Dynamically add and remove controls at run time
'              using the Controls collection
'Folder:       Ch02DynamicControlsCollection

Option Explicit
```

```
Private moptNewColor        As OptionButton
Private WithEvents mtxtName As TextBox

Private Sub cmdAddOption_Click()
   'Add an Option Button

   Set moptNewColor = Controls.Add("VB.OptionButton", "moptNewColor", _
      fraColors)
   With moptNewColor
      .Caption = "New Color"
      .Left = optBlack.Left
      .Top = optBlack.Top + 300
      .Width = optBlack.Width
      .Visible = True
   End With
   cmdAddOption.Enabled = False   'Do not allow another add
   cmdRemoveOption.Enabled = True
End Sub
```

```
Private Sub cmdAddTextBox_Click()
   'Add a textbox to the form

   Set mtxtName = Controls.Add("VB.TextBox", "mtxtName")
   With mtxtName
      .Left = 1800
      .Top = 240
      .Height = 375
      .Width = 2400
      .Visible = True
   End With
   cmdAddTextBox.Enabled = False 'Do not allow another add
   cmdRemoveTextbox.Enabled = True
End Sub
```

```
Private Sub cmdExit_Click()
   'End the project

   Set moptNewColor = Nothing
   Set mtxtName = Nothing
   Unload Me
End Sub
```

```
Private Sub cmdRemoveOption_Click()
    'Remove an option button
    'Must add error handling later

    Me.Controls.Remove moptNewColor
    cmdRemoveOption.Enabled = False  'Do not allow another remove
    cmdAddOption.Enabled = True
End Sub
```

```
Private Sub cmdRemoveTextbox_Click()
    'Remove a text box
    'Must add error handling later

    Me.Controls.Remove mtxtName
    cmdRemoveTextbox.Enabled = False  'Do not allow another remove
    cmdAddTextBox.Enabled = True
End Sub
```

Adding and Modifying Menu Commands at Run Time

When you create a menu at design time, you can set many properties. You can also change most of the same properties for menu commands at run time. You can enable and disable menu commands, place or remove a check mark on a menu command, make menu commands invisible, and add new menu commands.

Disabling a Menu Control

When a menu command is disabled, it is still visible but dimmed (Figure 2.5). The user cannot select a disabled menu item. You can set a menu control's Enabled property to False or True in code.

F i g u r e   2 . 5

A disabled menu command is dimmed and cannot be selected.

Example
```
mnuEditCustomer.Enabled = False
```

Making a Menu Control Invisible

Instead of disabling a menu item, you can set its Visible property to False so that it does not appear. If you set a menu name to invisible, the menu does not appear and the rest of the menu names shift to the left. If you set a menu command to invisible, the rest of the menu items move up to replace the invisible menu control. Note: If you set a menu name to invisible, none of the items under that menu can be selected; this technique is used for pop-up menus, which are covered later in this chapter.

Example
```
mnuWindowCascade.Visible = False
```

Checking an Item on a Menu

Menu controls often use the Checked property to indicate whether a condition is on or off (Figure 2.6). You can set the Checked property at design time, using the menu editor. You can also change the property at run time.

A check mark next to a menu item indicates that the option is currently selected.

```
Select
    By Last Name
    By First Name
  ✓ All Patients
```

Example
```
mnuEditBold.Checked = True
```

Adding Menu Controls at Run Time

At times you may need to add an item to a menu in code. Use the control array method of loading controls to add a menu or menu item. You can define a menu control array by using the same name for a series of menu items. The menu controls that are members of the array must be contiguous in the menu list and must be at the same indentation level. You then refer to the elements in the control array by using the Index property to indicate the relative position of the array element.

One common menu that requires adding controls at run time is the *Most Recently Used File List* frequently found on a *File* menu. Another common application for adding menu items is for pop-up menus. In the hands-on example at the end of this chapter, you will see an application that loads the menu items for pop-up menus on the fly; that is, the shortcut menu for each control is built as it is needed.

Defining a Menu Item Control Array To create a menu item control array, define a menu item with an Index of zero (Figure 2.7). You can create additional menu items with the same name and Index values of 1, 2, 3, and so on.

Set the Index property of a menu item to zero to create a control array.

Set Index property

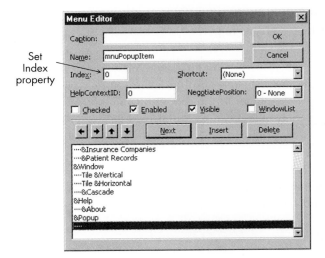

Responding to a Menu Item Control Array You will recall that a control array has only one Click event. When the user selects any of the menu commands in the array, the Click event executes. In the event procedure, you can use the Index argument to determine which command the user selected.

```
Private Sub mnuFileItem_Click(Index As Integer)
    'Respond to menu click events

    Select Case Index
        Case 0
            'Execute commands for first menu command
        Case 1
            'Execute commands for second menu command
        Case 2
            'Execute commands for third menu command
    End Select
End Sub
```

Another approach is to check the Caption property of the selected menu command, rather than use the Index property. We use the Caption property method in the chapter hands-on example, since the menu items depend on the control the user clicks on.

```
Private Sub mnuFileItem_Click(Index As Integer)
    'Respond to menu click events
    '  Check the Caption of the selected menu command

    Select Case mnuFileItem(Index).Caption
        Case "&Save"
            'Execute commands for the Save menu command
        Case "&Print"
            'Execute commands for the Print menu command
        Case "E&xit"
            'Execute commands for Exit menu command
    End Select
End Sub
```

Loading Additional Menu Items If you plan to add menu items at run time, you must define a menu control with at least one element at design time. You can make the one element invisible if you wish.

Use the Load method that you learned earlier in this chapter to add menu items. You must change properties of the new item after loading it.

```
Load mnuFileItem(1)
mnuFileItem(1).Caption = "&Save"
```

Feedback 2.1

1. Why are most windows gray instead of brightly colored?
2. Place these form events in the correct sequence: Activate, QueryUnload, Unload, Load, Terminate, Initialize. In which event are program initialization tasks usually performed? In which event would you ask the user, "Are you sure you want to quit?"
3. Write the VB statement(s) to disable cmdPrint.

4. Explain the difference between using the `End` statement and the `Unload` statement to end an application. How can you unload all forms by using the Forms collection?
5. Code the statement to create a new menu command at run time and make it visible. Then code the statement to remove that same menu command.
6. Code the statement to add a command button called cmdCancel to frmSummary.

Pop-up Menus

When running Windows applications, do you use **shortcut menus?** Shortcut menus pop up when you right-click an item and are also called **pop-up menus, context menus,** and **right-mouse menus.** You can add shortcut menus to your projects by using the Menu Editor and a new event. And you can display different shortcut menus, depending on the location of the mouse pointer.

Defining a Pop-up Menu

You can choose to display one of your existing menus when the user right-clicks, or you can create a separate menu specifically as a shortcut menu. To create a menu as a shortcut menu, make the top-level menu name invisible (Visible property unchecked; Figure 2.8). Create the menu items following the standard naming conventions. Your menu must have at least one command beneath the menu name.

Menu	Control Name
&Form	mnuForm
....C&olor	mnuFormColor
....&Close	mnuFormClose

Figure 2.8

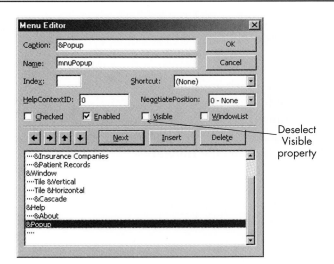

To create a pop-up menu, deselect the Visible property for the menu name.

Deselect Visible property

Coding the Pop-up Menu

You can make a shortcut menu pop up for a form or any control on the form. Write code in the MouseUp or MouseDown event for the selected form or control. (Microsoft recommends using the MouseUp event.) For example, the code for a form's MouseUp event appears as follows:

```
Private Sub Form_MouseUp(Button As Integer, Shift As Integer, _
        X As Single, Y As Single)
```

   The Button argument holds an integer that indicates which button was pressed; 1 = left button; 2 = right button. You can use the numeric constant in your code or use the intrinsic constant vbRightButton for the right button.

   The statement that causes the menu to appear is the PopupMenu statement. Follow the command with the name of the menu (the top-level menu name).

```
Private Sub Form_MouseUp(Button As Integer, Shift As Integer, X As Single, _
        Y As Single)
    'Display a menu when the right mouse button is pressed

    If Button = vbRightButton Then           'Right mouse button pressed
        PopupMenu mnuForm
    End If
End Sub
```

Windows Common Controls

You can improve the usability of a user interface by adding many of the common items found in Windows programs. Familiar tools for the user include the status bar at the bottom of the form and the toolbar for quicker access to menu commands. Toolbar and StatusBar controls are included with the common Windows controls. Other controls in this group are the ImageList, TreeView, and ListView, which allow a more graphical display of information. The ImageList is considered a "helper control"; its purpose is to store the images used in other controls, such as the Toolbar and ListView.

Adding a Toolbar and a Status Bar to the Interface

Most Windows programs have a **toolbar** with buttons, which are shortcuts to using menu commands. Toolbars, also called control bars or ribbon bars, can make your application more intuitive and easier to run.

   Although you can create toolbars manually, using a PictureBox control as a container, it's much easier to use the **Toolbar control** and the **ImageList control.** You store the graphics for the buttons in the ImageList control and then reference the images in the Toolbar control. For the graphics you can use many different file formats, such as bitmaps and icons. The ImageList control is invisible during program execution—its function is to provide the pictures for the Toolbar control.

Before you can create the Toolbar and ImageList controls, you must add the controls to your toolbox. Select *Projects/Components* (or right-click on the toolbox) to display the *Components* dialog box. Select *Microsoft Windows Common Controls 6.0*; the two controls you want, plus several more, are added to the toolbox (Figure 2.9).

Figure 2.9

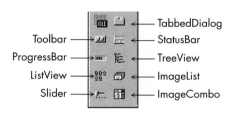

Add Microsoft Windows Common Controls 6.0 to the toolbox.

The ImageList Control

You should create an ImageList control and add the graphics you want before creating the Toolbar control. Adding the images and connecting the ImageList to a Toolbar are easy, but changing the images after the connection is made is relatively difficult.

Add an ImageList control to your form and change the control's Name property, using *ils* as the prefix. Then display the Property Pages by right-clicking on the control and selecting *Properties*, or by selecting *Custom* from the Properties window and then clicking on the build button (…).

On the Property Pages, select the Images tab and click the Insert Picture button to add a graphic (Figure 2.10). You can refer to each picture in an ImageList by its Index or by an optional Key property. The Key property is a unique string that you make up to identify the picture. Assigning and using keys is usually better than using indexes. When you insert and delete pictures, the indexes change but the keys do not.

Tip

Once you open a Property Pages dialog box, you can move from control to control and view or modify the properties of each control.

Figure 2.10

Add a graphic to the ImageList control by clicking on the Insert Picture button.

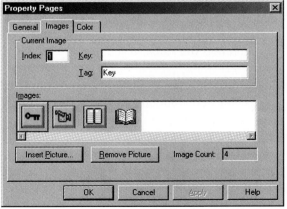

Insert each picture that you want and assign each a Key property. You can select a picture and remove it by clicking the Remove Picture button. When you insert a new picture, it appears after the selected picture.

You can use any graphical image for the pictures. The ones in the following examples are taken from *Program Files/Microsoft Visual Studio/Common/Graphics*. Some were selected from *Icons* and others are from *Bitmaps/Assorted*.

The Toolbar Control

Double-click on the Toolbar icon to place an empty Toolbar control on your form (Figure 2.11). Name the Toolbar control using *tlb* for the prefix.

F i g u r e   2 . 1 1

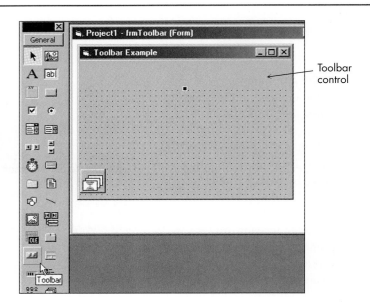

Add a new Toolbar control to a form.

Toolbar control

As with the ImageList control, the best place to set the Toolbar properties is in the custom Property Pages dialog box. Right-click on the Toolbar control and select *Properties* or select *Custom* from the Properties window. The Property Page contains three tabs: General, Buttons, and Picture.

Use the General tab to set the ImageList for your pictures. You can also set the size of the buttons and the alignment of text (Figure 2.12).

Create the toolbar buttons by selecting *Insert Button* on the Buttons tab. The first button is assigned an Index value of one. You can connect the button to an Image in the ImageList in one of two ways: Set the button's Image property to either the image's Index number or its Key property. (Note that the Key property is case sensitive.) Also set the button's ToolTipText property if you want to display ToolTips. You can place as many buttons as you want on the toolbar.

You can use a button's Style property to modify the type of button. Insert a new button and set its Style property to tbrSeparator to create a separation between buttons. You can create a group of buttons that act like option buttons,

Tip

Older controls and programming tools usually start with an index of zero; the new 6.0 Windows tools conform to the newer trend of starting with one.

Figure 2.12

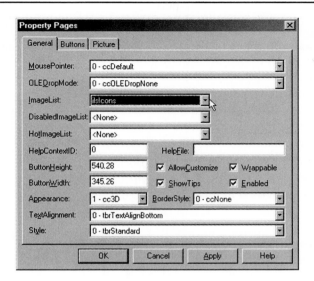

Connect the ImageList to the Toolbar using the ImageList property on the General tab.

where only one of the group may be selected at one time: set the Style property to each of the contiguous buttons to tbrButtonGroup.

Note: Once you connect an ImageList control to a Toolbar control, you can no longer make any additions or changes to the ImageList without disconnecting from the Toolbar. When you disconnect the ImageList, the Toolbar loses all Index and/or Key properties you have set. Save yourself time by making sure the ImageList is complete before beginning the Toolbar control.

Tip

Don't confuse the Microsoft recommended Toolbar prefix *tlb* with the constant prefix of *tbr*.

Coding the Toolbar's Events

The toolbar's ButtonClick event procedure receives a Button object as an argument. You can use the Button object's Key property or its Index property to determine which button was clicked.

```
Private Sub tlbDemo_ButtonClick(ByVal Button As MSComctlLib.Button)
    'Use the Key property or the Index property to determine the _
        button clicked

    Select Case Button.Key
        Case "Exit"
            mnuFileExit_Click
        Case "Save"
            mnuFileSave_Click
        Case "Print"
            mnuFilePrint_Click
    End Select
End Sub
```

Adding a Toolbar Button at Run Time

Although you usually create toolbar buttons during design time, you can also add and remove buttons at run time. If you plan to use images on the new buttons, make sure to store the extra button images in the ImageList control at design time.

Adding a Button at Run Time—General Form

```
ToolbarName.Buttons.Add [Index], [Key], [Caption], [Style], [Image]
```

All arguments for the Add method are optional and correspond to the properties that you set for a new button at design time. The Index property determines where the new button will appear. For example, set the new button's Index property to one to make the button appear at the left end of the toolbar; all other buttons will shift to the right. If you omit the Index entry, the new button will have the highest index and appear at the right end of the toolbar. If you plan to insert tools at the beginning of the toolbar, be sure to use the Key property rather than the Index property in your ButtonClick event procedure.

Adding a Button at Run Time—Examples

```
tlbDemo.Buttons.Add 4, "New", , , "Book"

tlbEdit.Buttons.Add 1, "Save", , , "Save"
tlbEdit.Buttons("Save").ToolTipText = "Save the file"
```

The StatusBar Control

You can easily create your own status bar by using the **StatusBar control.** A status bar is normally located at the bottom of a form and contains information about the status of the program and the keyboard, such as whether the Caps Lock and Num Lock keys are activated (Figure 2.13). Status bars often display the current date and time.

F i g u r e   2 . 1 3

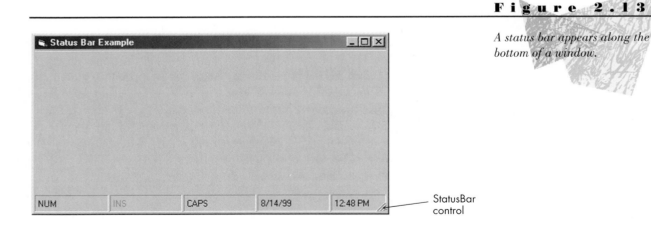

A status bar appears along the bottom of a window.

StatusBar control

Note: Toolbars and status bars can appear on both parent and child forms.

If the StatusBar control is not in your toolbox, open the *Components* dialog box and select *Microsoft Windows Common Controls 6.0.* Then add a StatusBar control to your form; the new control will have one **Panel,** but it's easy to add more Panels. Name your StatusBar with the prefix *sta.*

The StatusBar control is made up of Panel objects that divide the bar into sections. You can add panels either at design time or at run time, up to the maximum of 16 panels.

Each Panel object has properties and methods, so you can easily add many features to your status bar. For example, setting the Style property of a Panel to sbrTime makes the current system time automatically appear. If you also want the date to appear, add another Panel and set its Style to sbrDate. You can set up Panels to automatically display the status of many keyboard keys; you can also display text and/or graphics in a Panel. Table 2.2 shows the Style properties that you can use for the Panel objects. You usually set the Style property at design time. However, if you add a new Panel object at run time, you can also set the Style property in code.

Table 2.2

The Style Property Constants for StatusBar Panel Objects

Style Constant	Value	Purpose
sbrText	0	Text/Bitmaps.
sbrCaps	1	Caps Lock key.
sbrNum	2	Num Lock key.
sbrIns	3	Insert key.
sbrScrl	4	Scroll Lock key.
sbrTime	5	Current time.
sbrDate	6	Current date.

Setting up the Panels

After you add a StatusBar control to your form and change its Name property, right-click on the control and open its Property Pages dialog box. On the Panels tab (Figure 2.14), you can insert and remove Panels and set the properties for

Figure 2.14

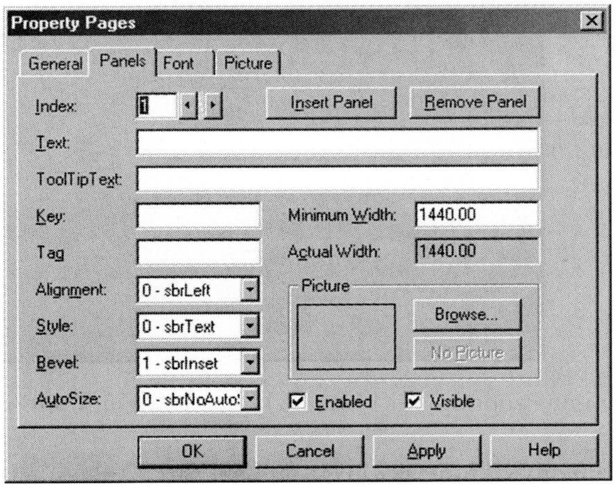

Add new Panel objects using the Panels tab of the StatusBar Property Pages dialog box.

each. The Text property holds any text that you want to appear in the Panel. The optional Key property gives the Panel a name that you can use to refer to it in code. Set the Style property if you want to select any of the automatic functions of the StatusBar control. Notice also that you can add a picture, as well as set Enabled and Visible properties.

Setting a Panel's Text in Code

You can set a Panel's Text property at design time or in code, in response to an action. To refer to a single Panel, you must use either its Index property or its Key property, as a member of the Panels collection. Notice that the Index is numeric (first example) and that the Key is string (second example).

```
staAdvVision.Panels(1).Text = "Patient Information"
staAdvVision.Panels("Info").Text = "Patient Information"
```

Adding and Removing Panels at Run Time

Panel objects belong to the Panels collection. You can use the Add and Remove methods of the Panels collection to add and remove Panels at run time.

Adding a Panel at Run Time—General Form

```
StatusBarName.Panels.Add [Index], [Key], [Text], [Style], [Picture]
```

All arguments for the Add method are optional. If you omit the Index, the new Panel appears at the right end of the status bar. If you want to insert the Panel, give it an Index that will cause it to be inserted. For example, if you want the new Panel to appear at the left end, give it an Index property of one; the other Panels will shift right, and their Index properties will change to reflect their new position.

The Key property assigns a name to the Panel that you can use to refer to the member of the Panels collection. Of course, the Text property assigns text that you want to appear in the Panel. Choose the Style constant from Table 2.2.

Adding a Panel at Run Time—Example

```
staDemo.Panels.Add 2, , "New Panel"     'Add a Panel 2, others will move to right
```

Note: You can find the completed project on your student disk in the sample program called *Ch02Toolbars*.

Feedback 2.2

1. Write the statement to display a pop-up menu. In what event procedure should the statement appear?
2. Assume that you have created an ImageList control and a Toolbar control and that you now want to add another image and toolbar button. Describe the steps necessary to do so.

3. Write the Add statement to place an additional Panel on a status bar called staOne.

4. What property determines what will display in a Panel?

The TreeView Control

Another handy Windows control is the **TreeView control,** which displays hierarchical information. The most familiar example of a tree view is the left panel of Windows Explorer (Figure 2.15). Each entry (a **node**) can have subentries (child nodes). You can expand the subentries by clicking on the plus sign, to show the level beneath, which may also have subentries. A tree view is an example of a style of display called a *drill-down interface.* And the process of moving down to progressively lower levels is often called *drilling down.*

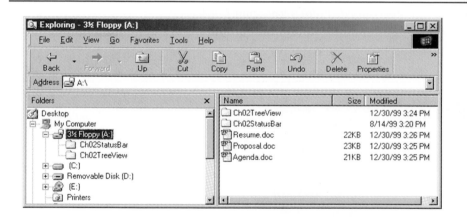

F i g u r e   2 . 1 5

Windows Explorer displays a tree view in the left pane and a list view in the right pane.

You are likely to find many uses for the TreeView control, such as for an address book with nodes for each letter of the alphabet, for an index, for folders and files, for an organization chart, for classifying relational data such as primary tables with related secondary tables, or for any data that are classified into groups.

When you create a TreeView control, you define **root nodes,** the top-level entries, and **child nodes** (all lower levels). The root nodes always display, but the child nodes display only when they are expanded, usually by using the plus sign that indicates that child nodes exist.

All nodes of a TreeView control belong to the control's **Nodes collection.** As with most other collections, the Nodes collection has a Count property and Add and Remove methods, so you can add and remove nodes at run time.

The TreeView control uses a family-tree metaphor. Each node (except root nodes) has a *parent.* Parent nodes have *child* nodes. All the child nodes of one parent are *siblings.* You even see references to *grandparent* and *grandchild* relationships. When you add a node, you specify a *relative* (the node related to) and then state the relationship (where to place the new node), such as before or after the relative, or a child of the relative.

Because the TreeView control is intended to give a visual representation of data, you will probably want to display pictures. The folder images of Windows Explorer are a good example of using pictures. You store the pictures you want to use in an ImageList control and attach the ImageList to the TreeView control at design time. Then you can assign the images to different nodes using the images' Key or Index properties. You can also specify a second image to a node so that you have a different image if the node is expanded, for example, an open folder and a closed folder.

Setting up a TreeView Control

The TreeView control, along with the ImageList control, belongs to the Windows common controls. If you don't have the controls in your toolbox, open the *Components* dialog box and select *Windows Common Controls 6.0.*

To create the name list in the following program example (Figure 2.16), add an ImageList control and a TreeView control to the form. Name your TreeView *treNames* and name the ImageList *ilsBook.* Add three icons to the ImageList (all found in *Graphics/Icons/Office*): Folder01.ico, Folder02.ico, and Crdfle08.ico. Set the Key properties to *FolderClosed, FolderOpen,* and *Card,* respectively.

F i g u r e   2 . 1 6

The project example holds a TreeView control and an ImageList control.

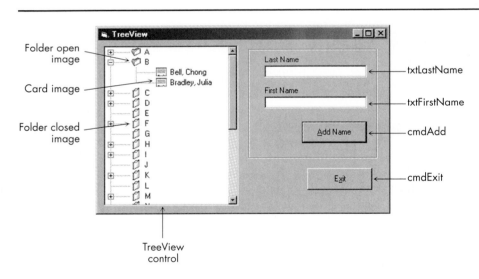

Open the *Property Pages* dialog box for the TreeView control and notice the properties on the General tab (Figure 2.17). The Style property has eight combinations to allow you to choose text, pictures, lines, and plus/minus signs (the default gives you everything). You can experiment with the LineStyle property—Figure 2.18 shows the tvwTreeLines style, and Figure 2.19 shows the tvwRootLines style. Set the Style property to tvwRootLines for this project. Set the ImageList property to ilsBook. That's all of the design-time properties to set; the rest you'll take care of in code.

Figure 2.17

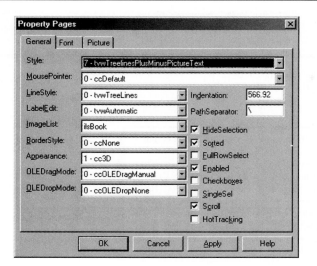

Set properties for the TreeView control on its Property Pages dialog box.

Figure 2.18

A TreeView control with its LineStyle set to tvwTreeLines.

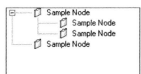

Figure 2.19

A TreeView control with its LineStyle set to tvwRootLines.

Note: The Sorted property refers to the root nodes only and sorts initial entries only. Any time you add new nodes, you need to set the Sorted property to True again to force the sort. Each node also has a Sorted property to sort its child nodes. We will set the Sorted properties in code.

If you're following along, now is the time to create the text boxes, labels, and command buttons you see on the form (refer to Figure 2.16).

Adding Nodes at Run Time

To add a node in code, use the Add method of the TreeView's Nodes collection. You must declare an object variable and set the variable to the result of the Add method.

The TreeView Nodes Collection Add Method—General Form

```
Set ObjectVariable = Object.Add([Relative], [Relationship], [Key], Text,
[Image], [SelectedImage])
```

All arguments except the text to display on the node are optional.
The arguments:

Relative	Key of a relative node. If you omit the argument, the node is placed at the top level (a root node).
Relationship	The relationship to the relative (if named). Use the constants in Table 2.3.
Key	A unique string to identify this node so that you can later refer to it in code. Needed if you plan to add child nodes to this node.
Text	The text string to display on the node.
Image	The Index or Key property of an image in the ImageList. The image displays for this node.
SelectedImage	The Index or Key property of a second image in the ImageList. This image displays when the node is selected.

T a b l e   2 . 3

Constants for the Relationship Property

Constant	Purpose
tvwFirst	Place node before all nodes at level of relative.
tvwLast	Place after all nodes at level of relative.
tvwNext	Place after the relative node (default).
tvwPrevious	Place before the relative node.
tvwChild	Place as a child of the relative node.

The TreeView Nodes Collection Add Method—Examples

```
Dim nodTemp As Node  ' Declare Node variable.
Set nodTemp = treNames.Nodes.Add(, , "A", "A", "FolderClosed", "FolderOpen")

Dim nodAdd As Node  ' Declare Node variable.
Set nodAdd = treNames.Nodes.Add("A", tvwChild, , strName, "Card")
```

The first example adds a new root node with a Key of "A", which also displays "A" for the node. The node displays the FolderClosed image (from the ImageList) unless the node is selected—then it displays the FolderOpen image.

The second example adds a child node to the root node with a Key of "A". This new node does not have a Key; it displays the text from a variable called strName and displays the Card image (from the ImageList).

Coding TreeView Events

You can respond in code to several TreeView events. The Expand event occurs each time a node is expanded; the procedure receives a Node argument to tell it which node was expanded. The Collapse event fires each time a node is collapsed; the procedure also receives a Node argument. In the program example that follows, the node's image is changed in the Expand and Collapse events.

Following is the (almost) complete program listing.

Program Listing

```
'Project:        TreeView and ImageList
'Date:           2/2000
'Programmer:     Bradley/Millspaugh
'Description:    Demonstrates the use of a TreeView with an ImageList.
'                Adds nodes at run time
'Folder:         Ch02TreeView

Option Explicit
```

```
Private Sub cmdAdd_Click()
    'Add a name to the name list
    Dim strLetter      As String
    Dim strName        As String
    Dim nodTemp        As Node

    If txtLastName.Text <> "" Then
        strLetter = UCase(Left$(txtLastName.Text, 1))
        strName = txtLastName.Text & ", " & txtFirstName.Text
        Set nodTemp = treNames.Nodes.Add(strLetter, tvwChild, , _
                    strName, "Card")
        treNames.Nodes(strLetter).Sorted = True 'Resort this node
        txtLastName.Text = ""
        txtFirstName.Text = ""
        txtLastName.SetFocus
    End If
End Sub
```

```
Private Sub cmdExit_Click()
    'Exit the application

    Unload Me
End Sub
```

```
Private Sub Form_Load()
    'Add the root nodes for the address book
    Dim nodTemp As Node

    Set nodTemp = treNames.Nodes.Add( , , "A", "A", _
            "FolderClosed", "FolderOpen")
    Set nodTemp = treNames.Nodes.Add( , , "B", "B", _
            "FolderClosed", "FolderOpen")
```

```
Set nodTemp = treNames.Nodes.Add(, , "C", "C", _
    "FolderClosed", "FolderOpen")
Set nodTemp = treNames.Nodes.Add(, , "D", "D", _
    "FolderClosed", "FolderOpen")
Set nodTemp = treNames.Nodes.Add(, , "E", "E", _
    "FolderClosed", "FolderOpen")
.
. 'The program file actually has all 26 letters
.
Set nodTemp = treNames.Nodes.Add(, , "X", "X", _
    "FolderClosed", "FolderOpen")
Set nodTemp = treNames.Nodes.Add(, , "Y", "Y", _
    "FolderClosed", "FolderOpen")
Set nodTemp = treNames.Nodes.Add(, , "Z", "Z", _
    "FolderClosed", "FolderOpen")
End Sub
```

```
Private Sub treNames_Collapse(ByVal Node As MSComctlLib.Node)
    'Change image for collapsed node

    Node.Image = "FolderClosed"
End Sub
```

```
Private Sub treNames_Expand(ByVal Node As MSComctlLib.Node)
    'Change image for expanded node

    Node.Image = "FolderOpen"
End Sub
```

Note: For a more elegant solution, use ASCII codes in a loop instead of defining each letter.

The ListView Control

If you have used Windows Explorer or My Computer, you have seen a ListView. Explorer uses a TreeView in the left panel and a ListView in the right. (Refer to Figure 2.15.)

You can add a **ListView control** to an application and choose the display style (Figure 2.20): large icons, small icons, list, or details (also called *Report*).

The ListView control has a lot in common with the TreeView control. Both are included in the Windows common controls, and both reference images stored in an ImageList control. To display both small icons and large icons, you need two ImageList controls—one for each icon size.

The ListView control is made up of a collection of ListItems. And the ListItems collection, like the other collections you have used, has a Count property and Add and Remove methods. Each ListItem object can also contain SubItems, which hold the extra information you see in the Details view.

The ListView also contains a ColumnHeader object, which you can use to set up the column headings for Details view. You can set the column headings at either design time or run time.

Setting up a ListView Control

To set up a project to use a ListView, make sure that the Windows common controls are in the toolbox. Add a ListView control to your form, give it a name with

Figure 2.20

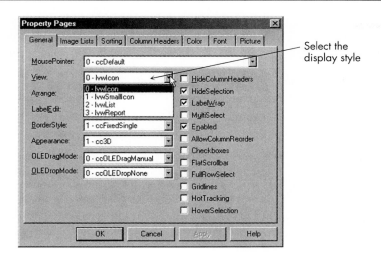

Select the
display style

*A ListView can display its contents
in four views: Large Icons, Small
Icons, List, and Report (details).*

a prefix of *lvw,* and add two ImageList controls. Call one ImageList
ilsSmallIcons and the other ilsLargeIcons. To set up the icons, open the
Property Pages dialog box for ilsSmallIcons and set the image size to 16 × 16
on the General tab (Figure 2.21). Add any images that you want to use, giving
each a Key property. Then set the image size for ilsLargeIcons to 32 × 32, add
the same images, and give them Keys. The Keys can be the same for both
ImageLists.

Figure 2.21

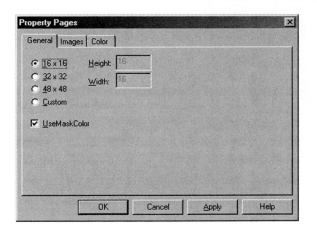

*Set the image size to 16 × 16 for
small icons and to 32 × 32 for
large icons.*

In the *Property Pages* dialog box for the ListView, on the General tab
(Figure 2.22) you can set many properties, such as the initial view and how you
want the icons to be arranged in the control. You can also set many appearance
properties, such as AllowColumnReorder, which allows the user to drag and
drop column headings to rearrange the columns in Details view.

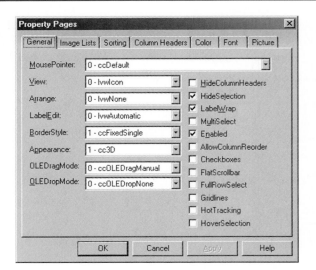

You set the two ImageLists on the Image Lists tab (Figure 2.23) and the column headers for Report (details) view on the Column Headers tab (Figure 2.24).

Note: Often you will fill a ListView control from data that you read from a database or file. You can set the column headers at run time from a file if you wish.

Adding ListItems to a ListView Control

You add the list items to the ListView control at run time. In fact, most likely you will fill the list with data that you read from a database. In the examples for this chapter, you will add constant data.

Figure 2.24

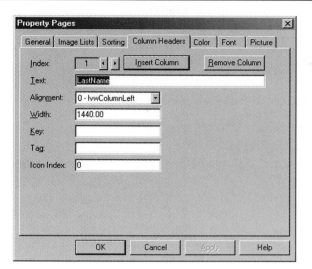

Create the column headers for the ListView on the Column Headers tab.

Use the Add method of the ListItems collection to add a new item. First declare an object variable of type ListItem and then set the variable to the result of the Add method.

The ListView ListItems Collection Add Method—General Form

```
Set ObjectVariable = Object.Add([Index], [Key], [Text], [Icon], [SmallIcon])
```

The Index property, if present, sets the Index of the new item. If missing, the new item is placed in the next position of the collection. You can give the new item a Key, which allows you to refer to the item by Key rather than Index. The Text property holds the text that you want to appear for the item, and the Icon and SmallIcon properties select the image to use with this item. You can set the two icon properties by using an Index property (numeric) or a Key property (string).

The ListView ListItems Collection Add Method—Examples

```
Dim itmNew      As ListItem
Set itmNew =   lvwBooks.ListItems.Add(1, , "My First Dictionary", _
               "Book", "Book")

Dim itmPerson As ListItem
Set itmPerson = lvwPerson.ListItems.Add(, , strPerson, 1, 1)
```

After you add a new item, you can add any extra information that you want to appear in Report view, using the ListSubItems collection of each ListItem.

Example:

```
lvwBooks.ListItems(1).ListSubItems.Add , , "Dr. Seuss"
```

The two missing arguments in this Add method are Index and Key, which you can assign for the list subitems if you wish.

Sorting the ListItems

You can make the ListItems appear sorted by setting the Sorted property of the ListView control to True.

Program Listing

```
'Project:       ListView
'Programmer:    Bradley/Millspaugh
'Date:          2/2000
'Description:   Demonstrate a ListView control
'Folder:        Ch02ListView
Option Explicit
```

```
Private Sub cmdAdd_Click()
    'Add a new item to the list
    Dim itmNew          As ListItem

    If txtLast.Text <> "" Then
        Set itmNew = lvwPersons.ListItems.Add(, , txtLast.Text, "Person", "Person")
        With itmNew.ListSubItems
            .Add , , txtFirst.Text
            .Add , , txtPhone.Text
        End With
        txtLast.Text = ""
        txtFirst.Text = ""
        txtPhone.Text = ""
        txtLast.SetFocus
    End If
End Sub
```

```
Private Sub Form_Load()
    'Add elements to the ListView
    Dim itmNew          As ListItem
    'Note: Usually You would read data from a database

        Set itmNew = lvwPersons.ListItems.Add(1, , "Beeson", "Person", "Person")
        With itmNew.ListSubItems
            .Add , , "Janice"
            .Add , , "(805) 555-1212"
        End With
        Set itmNew = lvwPersons.ListItems.Add(1, , "Mills", "Person", "Person")
        With itmNew.ListSubItems
            .Add , , "Pat"
            .Add , , "(818) 555-4444"
        End With
        lvwPersons.Sorted = True
End Sub
```

```
Private Sub mnuFileExit_Click()
    'Terminate the project

    Unload Me
End Sub
```

```
Private Sub mnuViewDetails_Click()
    'Set the View to Report

    lvwPersons.View = lvwReport
    lblView.Caption = "Report"
End Sub

Private Sub mnuViewLarge_Click()
    'Set the View to large icon

    lvwPersons.View = lvwIcon
    lblView.Caption = "Icon"
End Sub

Private Sub mnuViewList_Click()
    'Set the View to List

    lvwPersons.View = lvwList
    lblView.Caption = "List"
End Sub

Private Sub mnuViewSmall_Click()
    'Set the View to small icons

    lvwPersons.View = lvwSmallIcon
    lblView.Caption = "Small Icon"
End Sub
```

The Tabbed Dialog Control

You can create forms with tabbed pages, similar to the ones on a property sheet. You can use either the **Tabbed Dialog control** or the TabStrip control to create the tabs—both are ActiveX controls that come with VB but must be added to the toolbox. The following section uses the Tabbed Dialog control, which is a little easier to use than the TabStrip control.

To use a Tabbed Dialog control, select *Microsoft Tabbed Dialog Control 6.0* in the *Components* dialog box. Then use its toolbox tool to add a control to your form (Figure 2.25). Note: Both the tool and the class of the new control are named *SSTab*. Generally *sstab* is the prefix for the control's name.

Each tab page of the Tabbed Dialog control is a separate container. You can switch pages and place the controls you want on each page. But be careful—do not double-click to create your new control, or the control will "belong" to the form rather than to the tab page.

Setting Properties for the Tabbed Dialog Control

Use the General tab of the control's *Property Pages* dialog box (Figure 2.26) to modify the appearance of the Tabbed Dialog control. The tabs can appear on the top, bottom, left, or right. You can choose the number of tabs to display and the number of tabs per row. Using the Style property, you can make the control look like a Property Page, with flat tabs rather than 3-D. Set the Caption for each tab in the TabCaption property. You can switch the CurrentTab display and set the properties for each tab.

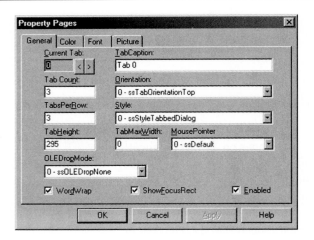

The hands-on programming example at the end of this chapter uses a Tabbed Dialog control.

Coding for the Tabbed Dialog Control

Very little coding is required for a Tabbed Dialog control. You may want to perform some action when the user switches tabs, such as set the focus to a particular control, and you may want to programmatically switch to a different tab. In both cases you need to remember that tab numbering begins with zero.

Use the tab control's Click event to determine whether the user switched tabs:

```
Private Sub sstabPatient_Click(PreviousTab As Integer)
    'User switched tabs?

    If sstabPatient.Tab <> PreviousTab Then 'Compare current tab to previous
        MsgBox "You switched "
    End If
End Sub
```

You can switch tabs in code by setting the control's Tab property:

```
Private Sub Form_Activate()
    'Display first tab

    sstabPatient.Tab = 0
End Sub
```

Feedback 2.3

1. Write the code to add a node to a TreeView. Explain the entries that you include for Relative and Relationship.
2. Write the code to change a ListView to display in Detail view.
3. What code is needed to make a ListView appear sorted?

Handling Errors during Execution

If it is possible for a user to do a "dumb thing" and make your program fail, be assured that someone will do it. A mark of a good programmer is that his or her programs are easy to use and don't generate run-time errors. Users should not have to deal with program termination or cryptic system error messages. You should anticipate possible errors and write your program to handle any situation.

When a run-time error occurs, VB generates an error number and checks it against a table of error codes. You can intercept the error number and take action without terminating the project. The statements used in this **error-trapping** process are the **On Error statement** and the Err object.

To trap errors, you must

1. Turn on the error-handling feature using the On Error statement.
2. Create error-handling code routines, which are set off from your other code with line labels.
3. Determine how and where the program is to continue after the error is taken care of.

The On Error Statement

You must place an On Error statement at the beginning of any procedure where errors might occur, such as loading a new object. If the object is already loaded, the program cancels with an *Object already exists* error. The following procedure generates a pop-up menu when the form is right-clicked. The procedure loads menu items at run time, which can cause an error if the object is already loaded. The individual statements and options are explained in the sections that follow.

```
Private Sub MDIForm_MouseUp(Button As Integer, Shift As Integer, _
        X As Single, Y As Single)
    'Pop up menu on right mouse click

    On Error GoTo HandleError
    If Button = vbRightButton Then
        mnuPopupItem(0).Caption = "Display &Patient Information"
        Load mnuPopupItem(1)
        mnuPopupItem(1).Caption = "Display &Insurance Information"
        Load mnuPopupItem(2)
        mnuPopupItem(2).Caption = "&Close Active Form"
        Load mnuPopupItem(3)
        mnuPopupItem(3).Caption = "E&xit Application"
        PopupMenu mnuPopup 'Display the menu
    End If
    Exit Sub                        'Exit this sub procedure


HandleError:
    If Err.Number = 360 Then     'Object already loaded

        Resume Next

    End If
End Sub
```

The On Error statement at the top of this sub turns on error trapping. If all goes well (no errors occur), execution proceeds through the If statement with no problems. Notice the Exit Sub statement, which transfers control out of the sub procedure. This practice keeps the logic from executing the statements in the HandleError subroutine accidentally when no error has occurred. If any error occurs, execution jumps down to the HandleError line label and executes the code there.

You may not want to add error-handling statements until you have tested and debugged your project (assuming the possibility that your projects don't always run perfectly the first time you test them). You want your error-handling code to trap user errors, not programming errors. You may want to include the error-handling statements but remark them out while debugging. An alternative is to set the environment to disable error handlers while you complete your normal debugging. Choose *Options* on the *Tools* menu. On the General tab select *Break on All Errors* and then click OK.

Although the On Error statement has three forms, you will use form 1 and form 3 in most of your work. Form 1 turns on error trapping, and form 3 turns it off. Anytime error trapping is turned off, the project is subject to terminating with an *Error* dialog box.

The On Error Statement—General Form 1

```
On Error GoTo LineLabel
```

The On Error GoTo specifies the label of the line where your error-handling code begins. A **line label** is a name (following identifier naming conventions) on a line by itself and followed by a colon. The error-handling code must be in the same procedure as the On Error statement.

The On Error Statement—General Form 2

```
On Error Resume Next
```

Using the Resume Next option of error handling causes execution to skip the line that generated the error and to continue execution with the following line of code.

The On Error Statement—General Form 3

```
On Error GoTo 0
```

The GoTo 0 option of the On Error turns off error trapping. Any error that occurs after this statement executes causes a run-time error.

The Err Object

The **Err object** holds information about an error that has occurred. You can check the properties of the Err object to determine the error number and a description of the error. The name of the object or application that caused the error is stored in the Source property. The Number property contains the error number (ranging from 0 to 65,535) that is described in the Description property.

You don't need to define or include the Err object. It has global scope and is automatically a part of your project, similar to the Printer object.

If your program logic transfers execution to another procedure or executes a Resume statement, the properties of the Err object are cleared. If you need these values for further processing, make sure to assign them to variables before performing any action that causes them to clear.

The Err.Number Property

Table 2.4 includes a partial list of error codes. The complete list of errors may be found in the MSDN Visual Basic Documentation under the heading Trappable Errors.

Table 2.4

Partial List of VB Error Codes

Err.Number	Err.Description
7	Out of memory.
9	Subscript out of range.
11	Division by zero.
	continued

Err. Number	Err. Description
13	Type mismatch.
52	Bad file name or number.
53	File not found.
54	Bad file mode.
58	File already exists.
61	Disk full.
67	Too many files.
68	Device unavailable.
70	Permission denied.
71	Disk not ready.
75	Path/file access error.
76	Path not found.
360	Object already loaded.
482	Printer error.

Raising Error Conditions

You can use the Raise method to set the error code, effectively "turning on" an error, or making it occur. This step may be necessary when an error that occurs is not among those that you anticipated and coded for; you may want to turn on the error so that the system handles the error and displays a dialog box for the user.

```
Err.Raise Number:=71
Err.Raise Err
```

The full Raise method allows several arguments—only the error number is required.

The Raise Method—General Form

```
Object.Raise Number:=NumericValue
Err.Raise Err            'Raise the previous unhandled error
```

The numeric value that you assign may be a constant, a named constant, or a variable.

The Raise Method—Examples

```
Err.Raise Number:=76
Err.Raise Number:=intPathNotFound
```

Coding Error-Handling Routines

The code that you use to handle errors begins with a line label. Assuming that you have used the statement

```
On Error GoTo HandleErrors
```

your error-handling code begins with this line label:

```
HandleErrors:
```

A line label follows the rules for naming identifiers, is followed by a colon, must appear on a line by itself, and begins in column 1. If you attempt to insert spaces or a tab before the line label, the editor deletes them.

```
HandleErrors:
    'Check to make sure the user put a disk in the drive
    Dim strMsg              As String
    Dim intResponse         As Integer
    Const intErrorNoDisk    As Integer = 71
    strMsg = "Make sure there is a disk in the drive"

    If Err.Number = intErrorNoDisk Then         'Check for Err 71
        intResponse = MsgBox(strMsg, vbOKCancel)    'Returns button pressed
        If intResponse = vbOK Then                  'OK button pressed
            Resume                                  'Try again
        Else
            mnuFileExit_Click                       'Exit the project
        End If
    Else                                        'Any other error
        Err.Raise Err                           'Cancel with error message
    End If
```

The preceding example includes a routine that continues execution if the error is solved and also handles the situation for any unsolved errors.

Using Select Case to Check for Errors

You will probably find the `Select Case` statement very handy when you have a series of errors to check.

```
Select Case Err.Number
    Case 53                                     'File not found
        'Code to handle File not found error
    Case 71                                     'Disk not ready
        'Code to handle Disk not ready error
    Case 76                                     'Path not found
        'Code to handle Path not found error
    Case Else                                   'All other errors
        Err.Raise Err                           'Make the error reappear
End Select
Resume
```

The Resume Statement

When you have resolved the problem causing an error, your program should continue execution if possible. This step is accomplished with the **Resume**

> **Tip**
>
> **M**ake sure that you cannot reach a `Resume` statement without an error occurring. This condition causes an error that generates the message *Resume without an Error.*

statement. You can choose to continue with the statement that caused the error, with the statement following the one causing the error, or at a specified location in the code.

The Resume Statement—General Form 1

```
Resume
```

If you use the `Resume` statement in the procedure that originally generated the error, execution of the project continues with the line of code that caused the error to occur. If the error-handling routine calls a different procedure that contains a `Resume`, execution continues with the statement that called the second procedure.

The Resume Statement—General Form 2

```
Resume Next
```

Using the `Next` option of `Resume` continues execution with the statement immediately following the line that caused the error (assuming that the `Resume Next` appears in the same procedure as the line of code causing the error). Similar to form 1, if you call another procedure from the error-handling routine, `Resume Next` continues execution at the line following the call.

The Resume Statement—General Form 3

```
Resume LineLabel
```

Execution continues at the line label, which *must be in the same procedure* as the `Resume`.

Handling Errors

Your error-handling routine should do *something* to handle each error:

● If you identify the error type and the user can correct the problem (such as insert the correct disk in the drive), use `Resume`, which will reexecute the statement that caused the error. If another error occurs, execution returns to the error handler.

● If you identify the error type and execution can proceed without the error-causing statement, use `Resume Next`.

● If you prefer to check inline for a particular type of error (following the Open, for example), use `Resume Next`.

● If the error number is unexpected or unidentified, raise the error again so that VB will handle it. The system error message will display for the user.

- If you want to exit the current procedure and continue project execution, use `Resume` *LineLabel*. Make sure to code a line label before your `Exit Sub` statement. For an example, see the following section describing the `Exit Sub` statement.

- If you want to end your project execution without displaying the system error message, call your exit procedure code (e.g., mnuFileExit_Click or cmdExit_Click).

- If you want to turn off error trapping, use `On Error GoTo 0`. (Any further error will cause a run-time error and display the system error message to the user.)

The Exit Function and Exit Sub Statements

The statements in a VB procedure execute sequentially. To include an error-handling routine that will not execute accidentally (when no error occurs), you must exit the procedure before the line label. Precede the error-handling line label with an **Exit Sub** or **Exit Function statement** (depending on whether the code is in a sub procedure or a function procedure). The `Exit Sub` or `Exit Function` causes execution to exit the procedure immediately.

You can simplify your error-handling code if you adopt the following pattern for any procedure with error trapping:

1. Include an `On Error` statement at the top of any procedure that might require error handling.
2. Code a line label just before the `Exit Sub` statement. Name the line label the same as the procedure name, plus an underscore and Exit. Example: mnuFileSave_Click_Exit.
3. After the `Exit Sub` statement, code your error-handling routine.

```
'Template for procedure that includes error handling

    On Error GoTo HandleErrors              'Turn on error trapping
    'code

ProcedureName_Exit:
    Exit Sub

HandleErrors:                               'Error-handling routine
    'Code here to determine cause of error and display message

    Select Case Err.Number
        Case n
            'Code to handle error
        Case n
            'Code to handle error
        Case Else
            'Code to handle any other errors
    End Select
    Resume
End Sub
```

Feedback 2.4

What is the purpose of the following statements?

1. `On Error GoTo 0`
2. `On Error GoTo WhatToDo`
3. `Err.Raise Number:=53`
4. `Resume`
5. `Resume Next`

Coding Public and Private Procedures

When your project has multiple forms, at times you need to refer to objects, variables, and procedures in another form. In Chapter 6 you will learn about encapsulation, one of the concepts of object-oriented programming, in which each module attempts to hide its details and expose only certain variables and procedures. You will learn to declare all variables and procedures as Private, unless you specifically want to allow another module to modify a variable or execute a procedure.

If you *do* want the code in one module to be able to execute another module's procedure, the procedure must be declared as Public. And any variable declared as Public can be seen and modified by any other module (a global variable). Remember that good programming practices dictate that all global variables be declared in a standard code module, rather than in a form module.

In a project with an MDI form and child forms, you may need to execute a procedure in the main form from a child form. In this situation you can code the shared procedure in either the main form or the standard code module. Do not place a shared procedure in a child form—again, poor programming practice.

As an example, the hands-on programming example that follows needs a procedure to clear the pop-up menu. The menu is defined on the main form but displayed from the main form and two child forms.

In the main form declare the procedure as Public:

```
Public Sub ClearPopup()
    'Clear the entries on the popup menu
    Dim mnuEntry    As Object

    For Each mnuEntry In mnuPopupItem
        If mnuEntry.Index = 0 Then
            mnuEntry.Caption = ""
        Else
            Unload mnuEntry
        End If
    Next
End Sub
```

Then in a child form, call the procedure using FormName-dot-ProcedureName:

```
If Button = vbRightButton Then
        frmMain.ClearPopup              'Clear any previous popup menu
        . . .
```

You can also refer to the control on one form from the code in another form. For example, in the project that follows, you must load menu items on the main form from a child form:

```
Load frmMain.mnuPopupItem(1)
frmMain.mnuPopupItem(1).Caption = "C&lear Patient Information"
```

Your Hands-on Programming Example

For this example you will write a program for Advanced Vision and Beyond that uses many of the new controls and topics introduced in this chapter. You will need an MDI form, with a status bar and a toolbar, and child forms for Insurance and Patients, as well as an About form. The project also needs a splash screen, which is not a child form.

The toolbar on the main form should have three icons and a separator for a total of four buttons. Make sure to include ToolTips for the buttons. You can use the following information to set up the toolbar buttons.

Key	Icon	ToolTip
Close	Misc20.ico	Close Active Window
Patients	Misc28.ico	Patients
Insurance	Book02.ico	Insurance

The Insurance form must have a ListView control, and the Patients form must have a Tabbed Dialog control. Refer to the sketches for the layout.

Include a status bar with two panels. (You need to insert only one; remember that one exists by default.) Set panel 1 to no bevel with a size setting of sbrSpring. Place the time in panel 2, using the appropriate style, aligned right. Each time a different child form becomes active, display a message in panel 1 indicating *Patient Information* or *Insurance Information*.

Create pop-up menus during program execution. You will need them for the main form, for the Patients form and the Insurance form, and for the large controls on each form (the ListView and Tabbed Dialog controls).

The program must include error-handling routines.

Planning the Project

Plan the Interface

Sketch the forms (Figures 2.27–2.31), which your users sign off as meeting their needs. Note: Although this step may seem unnecessary, it is standard programming practice and documents that your users have been involved and approve the design.

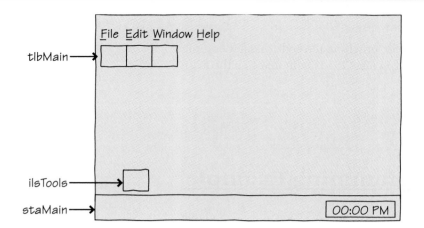

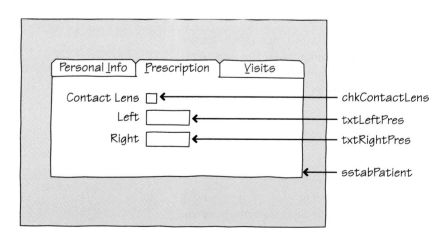

a.

b.

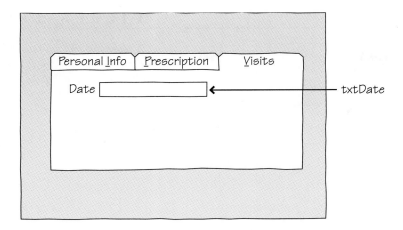

c.

Figure 2.29

A planning sketch of the Insurance form (frmInsurance) for the hands-on programming example.

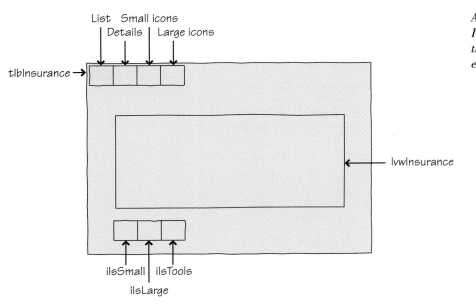

Figure 2.30

A planning sketch of the About form (frmAbout) for the hands-on programming example.

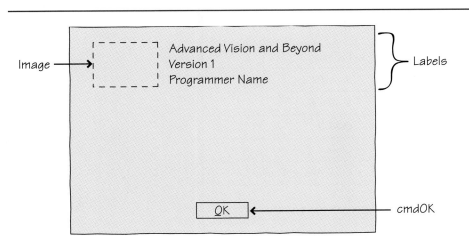

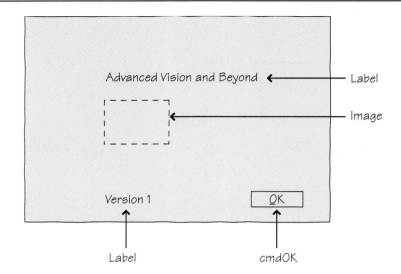

*A planning sketch of the splash
form (frmSplash) for the hands-on
programming example.*

Plan the Objects and Properties

Plan the property settings for the forms and for each control.

Main Form—MDI Form

Object	Property	Setting
frmMain	Caption	Advanced Vision and Beyond
	Icon	Eye.ico
staMain	NumPanels	2
Panel1	Bevel	0 - sbrNoBevel
	AutoSize	1 - sbrSpring
Panel2	Style	5 - sbrTime
	Alignment	2 - sbrRight
ilsTools	Name	ilsTools
Image1	Picture	Misc20.ico
	Key	Close
Image2	Picture	Misc28.ico
	Key	Patients
Image3	Picture	Books02.ico
	Key	Insurance
tlbMain	ImageList	ilsTools
Button1	Key	Close
	ToolTipText	Close Active Window
	ImageIndex	1

continued

Object	Property	Setting
Button2	Style	3 - tbrSeparator
Button3	Key	Insurance
	ToolTipText	Insurance
	ImageIndex	3
Button4	Key	Patients
	ToolTipText	Patients
	ImageIndex	2
mnuFile	Caption	&File
mnuFileExit	Caption	E&xit
mnuEdit	Caption	&Edit
mnuEditInsurance	Caption	&Insurance Companies
mnuEditPatient	Caption	&Patient Records
mnuWindow	Caption	&Window
	WindowList	True
mnuWindowTileVertically	Caption	Tile &Vertical
mnuWindowTileHorizontally	Caption	Tile &Horizontal
mnuWindowCascade	Caption	&Cascade
mnuHelp	Caption	&Help
mnuHelpAbout	Caption	&About
mnuPopup	Caption	&Popup
	Visible	False
mnuPopupItem	Caption	(blank)
	Index	0 (To create a control array)

Main Form (concluded)

Object	Property	Setting
frmPatient	Caption	Patient Records
	Icon	Eye.ico
	MDIChild	True
sstabPatient	TabCount	3
Tab(0)	Caption	Personal &Info
txtPatNum	Text	100
txtLastName	Text	Jones

continued

Patient Form

Patient Form (concluded)

Object	Property	Setting
txtFirstName	Text	Angela
txtPhone	Text	(909) 555-1111
Label1	Caption	Last Name
Label2	Caption	First Name
Label3	Caption	Phone
Label4	Caption	Patient Number
Tab(1)	Caption	&Prescription
chkContactLens	Name	chkContactLens
txtLeftPres	Text	3.75
	Alignment	1 - Right Justify
txtRightPres	Text	0.75
	Alignment	1 - Right Justify
Label5	Caption	Contact Lens:
Label6	Caption	Right:
Label7	Caption	Left:
Tab(2)	Caption	&Visits
txtDate	Text	2/20/2000
Label8	Caption	Date:

Insurance Form

Object	Property	Setting
frmInsurance	Caption	Insurance Information
	Icon	Eye.ico
	MDIChild	True
ilsSmall	General	16 × 16
Image1	Picture	Checkmrk.ico
	Key	Check
ilsLarge	General	32 × 32
Image1	Picture	Checkmrk.ico
	Key	Check
ilsTools	General	16 × 16
Image1	Picture	Graphics\Bitmaps\TlBr_W95\Vw-lrgic.bmp
	Key	Large

continued

Insurance Form (concluded)

Object	Property	Setting
Image2	Picture	Graphics\Bitmaps\TlBr_W95\Vw-smlic.bmp
	Key	Small
Image3	Picture	Graphics\Bitmaps\TlBr_W95\Vw-list.bmp
	Key	List
Image4	Picture	Graphics\Bitmaps\TlBr_W95\Vw-dtls.bmp
	Key	Details
tlbInsurance	ImageList	ilsTools
Button1	Key	List
	ImageKey	List
	ToolTipText	List
Button2	Key	Detail
	ImageKey	Details
	ToolTipText	Detail/Report
Button3	Key	Small
	ImageKey	Small
	ToolTipText	Small Icons
Button4	Key	Large
	ImageKey	Large
	ToolTipText	Large Icons
lvwInsurance	Arrange	1 - lvwAutoLeft
	Icons	ilsLarge
	SmallIcons	ilsSmall
ColumnHeader(1)	Text	Company
ColumnHeader(2)	Text	Rep
ColumnHeader(3)	Text	Phone

About Form

Object	Property	Setting
frmAbout	Caption	About Advanced Vision and Beyond
	Icon	Eye.ico
	MDIChild	True
picIcon	Picture	eye.ico

continued

About Form (concluded)

Object	Property	Setting
cmdOK	Caption	&OK
	Cancel	True
	Default	True
Line1	Name	Line1
lblTitle	Caption	Advanced Vision and Beyond
lblDescription	Caption	(Your name goes here)
lblVersion	Caption	Version 1

Splash Form

Object	Property	Setting
frmSplash	MDIChild	False
	BorderStyle	3 - Fixed Dialog
	Caption	(blank)
	ControlBox	False
	MaxButton	False
	MinButton	False
	WindowState	2 - Maximized
cmdOK	Caption	&OK
	Cancel	True
	Default	True
fraAbout	Caption	(blank)
imgLogo	Picture	Eye.ico
	Stretch	True
lblVersion	Caption	Version 1
lblCompany	Caption	Advanced Vision and Beyond

Plan the Code Procedures

Determine which events will need code and plan the code for each.

Standard Code Module

Procedure	Actions
Main	Show splash form.
	Load main form.

Object	Procedure	Actions
mnuEditInsurance	Click	Show frmInsurance.
		SetFocus.
mnuEditPatient	Click	Show frmPatient.
		SetFocus.
mnuFileExit	Click	Unload forms.
mnuHelpAbout	Click	Show frmAbout.
mnuWindowCascade	Click	Cascade windows.
mnuWindowTileHorizontally	Click	Tile windows horizontally.
mnuWindowTileVertically	Click	Tile windows vertically.

mnuPopupItem	Click	Select Case based on Caption of item selected.
		   Case Close form
		      Hide the form.
		   Case List
		      Change list view to List.
		   Case Report
		      Change list view to Report (details).
		   Case Small Icons
		      Change list view to Small Icons.
		   Case Large Icons
		      Change list view to Large Icons.
		   Case Display Patient Information
		      Execute mnuEditPatient_Click.
		   Case Display Insurance Information
		      Execute mnuEditInsurance_Click.
		   Case Close Active Form
		      Hide the active form.
		   Case Exit Application
		      Execute mnuFileExit_Click.
		End Select

Form	Unload	Unload all forms.

	MouseUp	If right button clicked
		   ClearPopup (clear any previous pop-up menu).
		   Load items for form's pop-up menu.
		   Display the pop-up menu.
		End If

(General)	ClearPopup	Clear all previous pop-up menu items.

tlbMain	ButtonClick	Select Case based on Key of button clicked.
		   Case Close
		      Hide the active form.
		   Case Insurance
		      Execute mnuEditInsurance_Click.
		   Case Patients
		      Execute mnuEditPatient_Click
		End Select

Patient Form

Object	Procedure	Actions
mnuFileReturn	Click	Me.Hide
Form	Activate	Display first tab.
		Set status bar text to show active form.

	MouseUp	If right button clicked
		   ClearPopup (clear any previous pop-up menu).
		   Load items for form's pop-up menu.
		   Display the pop-up menu.
		End If

sstabPatient	MouseUp	If right button clicked
		   ClearPopup (clear any previous pop-up menu).
		   Load items for form's popup menu.
		   Display the popup menu.
		End If

(General)	ClearPatientInfo	Clear all text boxes.
		Set the focus.

Insurance Form

Object	Procedure	Actions
mnuFileReturn	Click	Me.Hide
Form	Activate	Set status bar text to show active form.
	Load	Add each ListItem.
		Add extra information for each ListItem.

	MouseUp	If right button clicked
		   ClearPopup (clear any previous pop-up menu).
		   Load items for form's pop-up menu.
		   Display the pop-up menu.
		End If

lvwInsurance	MouseUp	If right button clicked
		   ClearPopup (clear any previous pop-up menu).
		   Load items for form's pop-up menu.
		   Display the pop-up menu.
		End If

tlbInsurance	ButtonClick	Select Case based on index of button clicked.
		   Case 1
		      Set view to List.
		   Case 2
		      Set view to Report.
		   Case 3
		      Set view to Small Icon.
		   Case 4
		      Set view to Large Icon.
		End Select

Object	Procedure	Actions
CmdOK	Click	Unload Me.

About Form

Object	Procedure	Actions
cmdOK	Click	Unload Me.
		Show main form.

Splash Form

Write the Project

Follow the sketches in Figures 2.27–2.31 to create the forms. Figures 2.32–2.36 show the completed forms.

Figure 2.32

The completed main form (frmMain) for the hands-on programming example.

Figure 2.33

The completed Patient form (frmPatient) for the hands-on programming example. (continued)

b.

c.

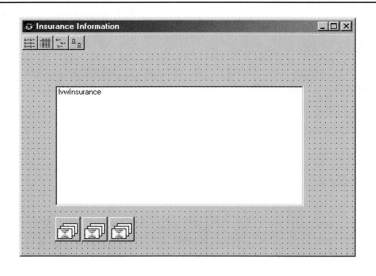

Figure 2.35

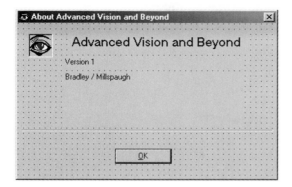

The completed About form (frmAbout) for the hands-on programming example.

Figure 2.36

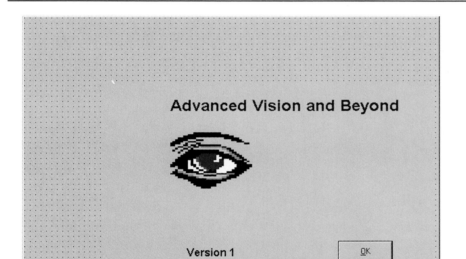

The completed splash form (frmSplash) for the hands-on programming example.

- Set the properties of each of the objects as you have planned.

- Working from the pseudocode, write each event procedure.

- When you complete the code, thoroughly test the project.

The Project Solution

The Standard Code Module

This module contains Sub Main, which is the startup for the project.

```
'Project:      Advanced Vision and Beyond
'Module:       Standard Code
'Programmer:   Bradley/Millspaugh
'Date:         2/2000
'Folder:       Ch02AdvancedVision
'Description:  Startup module—Holds Sub Main
```

```
Option Explicit

Private Sub Main()
    'Display splash screen while loading forms

    frmSplash.Show vbModeless
    Load frmMain
End Sub
```

frmMain

```
'Project:    Chapter 2 Advanced Vision
'Programmer: Bradley/Millspaugh
'Date:       2/2000
'Description:A demonstration using an MDI form with two child
'            forms, a ListView, and a Tabbed Dialog control
'Folder:     Ch02AdvancedVision

Option Explicit
```

```
Private Sub MDIForm_MouseUp(Button As Integer, Shift As Integer, _
            X As Single, Y As Single)
    'Pop up menu on right mouse click

    On Error GoTo HandleError
    If Button = vbRightButton Then
        ClearPopup 'Clear any previous popup menu
        mnuPopupItem(0).Caption = "Display &Patient Information"
        Load mnuPopupItem(1)
        mnuPopupItem(1).Caption = "Display &Insurance Information"
        Load mnuPopupItem(2)
        mnuPopupItem(2).Caption = "&Close Active Form"
        Load mnuPopupItem(3)
        mnuPopupItem(3).Caption = "E&xit Application"

        PopupMenu mnuPopup 'Display the menu
    End If
    Exit Sub

HandleError:
    If Err.Number = 360 Then    'Object already loaded
        Resume Next
    End If
End Sub
```

```
Private Sub MDIForm_Unload(Cancel As Integer)
    'Unload all forms
    Dim frmSingle    As Form

    For Each frmSingle In Forms
        Unload frmSingle
    Next
End Sub
```

```
Private Sub mnuHelpAbout_Click()
    'Display the About dialog

    frmAbout.Show
End Sub
```

```vb
Private Sub mnuPopupItem_Click(Index As Integer)
    'Handle popup menu for all project forms

    On Error GoTo HandleError
    Select Case mnuPopupItem(Index).Caption
        'Popup menu for frmPatient
        Case "&Close Patient Form"
            frmPatient.Hide
        Case "C&lear Patient Information"
            frmPatient.ClearPatientInfo

        'Popup menu for frmInsurance
        Case "&Close Insurance Form"
            frmInsurance.Hide
        Case "&List"
            frmInsurance.lvwInsurance.View = lvwList
        Case "&Report"
            frmInsurance.lvwInsurance.View = lvwReport
        Case "&Small Icon"
            frmInsurance.lvwInsurance.View = lvwSmallIcon
        Case "Large &Icon"
            frmInsurance.lvwInsurance.View = lvwIcon

        'Popup menu for frmMain
        Case "Display &Patient Information"
            mnuEditPatient_Click
        Case "Display &Insurance Information"
            mnuEditInsurance_Click
        Case "&Close Active Form"
            ActiveForm.Hide
        Case "E&xit Application"
            mnuFileExit_Click
    End Select

HandleError:
    Resume Next
End Sub
```

```vb
Private Sub mnuWindowCascade_Click()
    'Cascade Open Forms

    Me.Arrange vbCascade
End Sub
```

```vb
Private Sub mnuWindowTileHorizontally_Click()
    'Tile Open forms horizontally

    Me.Arrange vbTileHorizontal
End Sub
```

```vb
Private Sub mnuWindowTileVertically_Click()
    'Tile open forms vertically

    Me.Arrange vbTileVertical
End Sub
```

```vb
Private Sub mnuEditInsurance_Click()
    'Display insurance form

    frmInsurance.Show
    frmInsurance.SetFocus
End Sub
```

```
Private Sub mnuFileExit_Click()
    'End the application

    Unload Me
End Sub
```

```
Private Sub mnuEditPatient_Click()
    'Display patient Info

    frmPatient.Show
    frmPatient.SetFocus
End Sub
```

```
Private Sub tlbMain_ButtonClick(ByVal tlbButton As MSComctlLib.Button)
    'Use the Key property or the Index property to specify an action

    On Error GoTo HandleError
    Select Case tlbButton.Key
        Case "Close"
            ActiveForm.Hide    'Generates an error if no child form is active
        Case "Insurance"
            mnuEditInsurance_Click
        Case "Patients"
            mnuEditPatient_Click
    End Select
    Exit Sub

HandleError:
    If Err.Number = 91 Then    'No child form is active
        MsgBox "No form to close.", vbInformation, "Advanced Vision"
        Resume Next
    End If
End Sub
```

```
Public Sub ClearPopup()
    'Clear the entries on the pop-up menu
    Dim mnuEntry    As Object

    For Each mnuEntry In mnuPopupItem
        If mnuEntry.Index = 0 Then
            mnuEntry.Caption = ""
        Else
            Unload mnuEntry
        End If
    Next
End Sub
```

frmInsurance

```
'Project:   Advanced Vision and Beyond
'Form:      frmInsurance
'Folder:    Ch02AdvancedVision

Option Explicit
```

```
Private Sub mnuFileReturn_Click()
    'Hide Insurance form

    Me.Hide
End Sub
```

```
Private Sub Form_Activate()
    'Display status

    frmMain.staMain.Panels(1).Text = "Insurance Information"
End Sub
```

```
Private Sub Form_Load()
    'Add elements to the ListView
    Dim itmNew          As ListItem
    'Note: usually would read data from a database

        With lvwInsurance
            Set itmNew = .ListItems.Add(1, , "ABC Inc.", "Check", "Check")
            .ListItems(1).ListSubItems.Add , , "Mary Johann"
            .ListItems(1).ListSubItems.Add , , "(213) 555-4321"
            Set itmNew = .ListItems.Add(2, , "Optical C Specialists", _
                Check", "Check")
            .ListItems(2).ListSubItems.Add , , "Jerry Thaven"
            .ListItems(2).ListSubItems.Add , , "(520) 555-8888"
            Set itmNew = .ListItems.Add(3, , "Vision Services", "Check", _
                "Check")
            .ListItems(3).ListSubItems.Add , , "Juanita Lopez"
            .ListItems(3).ListSubItems.Add , , "(505) 555-6432"
            Set itmNew = .ListItems.Add(4, , "Diamond, Inc.", "Check", _
                "Check")
            .ListItems(4).ListSubItems.Add , , "Danny Freeman"
            .ListItems(4).ListSubItems.Add , , "(818) 555-2222"
    End With
End Sub
```

```
Private Sub Form_MouseUp(Button As Integer, Shift As Integer, _
        X As Single, Y As Single)
    'Pop up menu on right mouse click

    On Error GoTo HandleError
    If Button = vbRightButton Then
        With frmMain
        .ClearPopup    'Clear any previous pop-up menu
        .mnuPopupItem(0).Caption = "&Close Insurance Form"

        PopupMenu .mnuPopup 'Display the menu
        End With
    End If
    Exit Sub

HandleError:
    Resume Next
End Sub
```

```
Private Sub lvwInsurance_MouseUp(Button As Integer, Shift As Integer, _
        X As Single, Y As Single)
    'Pop up menu on right mouse click

    On Error GoTo HandleError
```

```
    If Button = vbRightButton Then
        With frmMain
            .ClearPopup              'Clear any previous popup menu
            .mnuPopupItem(0).Caption = "&Close Insurance Form"
            Load frmMain.mnuPopupItem(1)
            .mnuPopupItem(1).Caption = "&List"
            Load frmMain.mnuPopupItem(2)
            .mnuPopupItem(2).Caption = "&Report"
            Load frmMain.mnuPopupItem(3)
            .mnuPopupItem(3).Caption = "&Small Icon"
            Load frmMain.mnuPopupItem(4)
            .mnuPopupItem(4).Caption = "Large &Icon"

            PopupMenu .mnuPopup 'Display the menu
        End With
    End If
    Exit Sub

HandleError:
    Resume Next
End Sub
```

```
Private Sub tlbInsurance_ButtonClick(ByVal tlbButton As MSComctlLib.Button)
    'Use the Key property or the Index property to specify an action

    Select Case tlbButton.Index
        Case 1
            lvwInsurance.View = lvwList
        Case 2
            lvwInsurance.View = lvwReport
        Case 3
            lvwInsurance.View = lvwSmallIcon
        Case 4
            lvwInsurance.View = lvwIcon
    End Select
End Sub
```

frmPatient

```
'Project:   Advanced Vision and Beyond
'Form:      frmPatient
'Folder:    Ch02AdvancedVision
```

```
Option Explicit
```

```
Private Sub mnuFileReturn_Click()
    'Unload Patient form

    Unload Me
End Sub
```

```
Private Sub Form_Activate()
    'Display first tab

    sstabPatient.Tab = 0
    frmMain.staMain.Panels(1).Text = "Patient Information"
End Sub
```

```
Private Sub Form_MouseUp(Button As Integer, Shift As Integer, _
            X As Single, Y As Single)
    'Pop up menu on right mouse click

    On Error GoTo HandleError
    If Button = vbRightButton Then
        With frmMain
            .ClearPopup     'Clear any previous pop-up menu
            .mnuPopupItem(0).Caption = "&Close Patient Form"

            PopupMenu .mnuPopup 'Display the menu
        End With
    End If
    Exit Sub

HandleError:
    If Err.Number = 360 Then    'Object already loaded
        Resume Next
    End If
End Sub
```

```
Private Sub sstabPatient_MouseUp(Button As Integer, Shift As Integer, _
            X As Single, Y As Single)
    'Pop up menu on right mouse click

    On Error GoTo HandleError
    If Button = vbRightButton Then
        With frmMain
            .ClearPopup     'Clear any previous popup menu
            .mnuPopupItem(0).Caption = "&Close Patient Form"
            Load frmMain.mnuPopupItem(1)
            .mnuPopupItem(1).Caption = "C&lear Patient Information"

            PopupMenu .mnuPopup 'Display the menu
        End With
    End If
    Exit Sub

HandleError:
    If Err.Number = 360 Then    'Object already loaded
        Resume Next
    End If
End Sub

Public Sub ClearPatientInfo()
    'Clear out fields for patient

    txtPatNum.Text = ""
    txtLastName.Text = ""
    txtFirstName.Text = ""
    txtPhone.Text = ""
    txtLeftPres.Text = ""
    txtRightPres.Text = ""
    txtDate.Text = ""
    txtPatNum.SetFocus
End Sub
```

frmAbout

```
'Project:   Advanced Vision and Beyond
'Form:      About dialog
'Folder:    Ch02AdvancedVision

Option Explicit
```

```
Private Sub cmdOK_Click()
    'Unload About dialog

    Unload Me
End Sub
```

frmSplash

```
'Project:  Advanced Vision and Beyond
'Form:     Splash Screen
'Folder:   Ch02AdvancedVision

Option Explicit
```

```
Private Sub cmdOK_Click()
    'Unload splash screen

    Unload Me
    frmMain.Show
End Sub
```

MCSD Exam Notes

Exam Objectives Covered in This Chapter

Creating User Services

Implement navigational design.

- Dynamically modify the appearance of a menu.

- Add a pop-up menu to an application.

- Create an application that adds and deletes menus at run time.

- Add controls to forms.

- Set properties for controls.

- Assign code to a control to respond to an event.

Create data input forms and dialog boxes.

- Display and manipulate data by using custom controls. Controls include TreeView, ListView, ImageList, Toolbar, and StatusBar.

- Create an application that adds and deletes controls at run time.

- Use the Controls collection to manipulate controls at run time.

- Use the Forms collection to manipulate forms at run time.

Write code that processes data entered on a form.

- Given a scenario, add code to the appropriate form event. Events include Initialize, Terminate, Load, Unload, QueryUnload, Activate, and Deactivate.

Implement error handling for the user interface in desktop applications.

●   Identify and trap run-time errors.

●   Handle inline errors.

Questions/Tricks to Watch for

●   Menu items have only a Click event.

●   A control array must have at least one element at design time.

●   Know the sequence in which form events occur.

●   Learn the shortcut keys for bringing up IDE windows:
      F2—Object Browser
      F3—Properties window
      Ctrl + E—Menu Editor

S u m m a r y

1. The user interface should be clear and consistent and follow Windows standards.

2. Forms are the basic objects of a VB interface. The events for loading a form, in sequence, are Initialize, Load, and Activate or GotFocus. The events for unloading a form are QueryUnload, Unload, and Terminate.

3. All active forms in a project are members of the Forms collection. You can unload all members of this collection in the QueryUnload event procedure to assure that a program releases memory properly.

4. Forms may be SDI or MDI. An MDI form prevents child forms from appearing outside the parent form area and forces all child forms to close when the parent form is closed.

5. A project can have only one MDI (parent) form. Other forms in the project can be made into child forms by setting their MDIChild property to True.

6. An MDI form displays the menu for an open child form if one exists. Otherwise the menu defined on the MDI form displays.

7. A Windows menu can display a list of open windows and provide commands to arrange the open windows.

8. A project should be ended by unloading all forms, not by using the `End` statement.

9. The user interface can be modified at run time. It is possible to add and remove controls and to change the menu.

10. Two methods exist for adding controls at run time: using control arrays and using the Controls collection.

11. Use the `Load` statement to add a control as part of a control array. Any control added in this way can be removed by using the `Unload` statement.

12. Use the Add method to add new members of a Controls collection. Any controls added with the Add method can be removed by using the Remove method.

13. A menu can have controls added, disabled, checked, or made invisible. Menu items are added at run time by using a control array and the `Load` statement.

14. Pop-up menus, also called shortcut menus, context menus, and right-mouse menus, are displayed in the MouseUp event by using the PopupMenu statement.

15. Many extra controls are available in the Windows common controls, including the Toolbar, ImageList, StatusBar, TreeView, and ListView controls.

16. An ImageList is a collection of graphical images that are used with other Windows controls. The ImageList control is created first and then connected to a Toolbar, TreeView, or ListView control.

17. A StatusBar displays along the lower edge of a window and can be set up to automatically display the date, time, and status of several keyboard keys. You can display text and graphics in a StatusBar.

18. The TreeView is the familiar root-and-node setup from the left panel of Windows Explorer. The ListView represents the right side and can be set to view as large icons, small icons, a list, or a detailed report.

19. The Tabbed Dialog control maximizes the usage of a screen area by dividing information on different tabs. You can add controls to each tab page.

20. The `On Error` statement is used by the programmer to intercept or "trap" program errors. The errors are stored in an Err object to allow the programmer to handle the errors as needed. The `Resume` statement controls where execution of the program continues.

K e y   T e r m s

Review Questions

1. Name the events and their sequence that occur as a form is loaded and displayed.
2. Name two collections intrinsic to VB. How are they used?
3. What are some advantages of using an MDI rather than an SDI?
4. Describe the two methods for adding controls at run time. Which method would you use for adding menu commands?
5. What steps are necessary at design time and at run time to add a menu control during program execution?
6. What steps are necessary to add a control at run time by using the Controls collection?
7. Describe how to create and display a shortcut (right-mouse) menu.
8. Give an example of a situation in which each of these controls can be used: Toolbar, StatusBar, ImageList, TreeView, ListView, and Tabbed Dialog.
9. Why should error handling be considered during the design of a program?
10. Explain the purpose and properties of the Err object.
11. When is it necessary to declare a sub procedure as Public?

Programming Exercises

2.1 Create a project that contains a label. Add a menu, a pop-up menu on the label, and a toolbar that allow the user to change the color and font of the text in the label. You may use a common dialog box or hard code the changes to the color and the font.

2.2 Write a program that displays at least five names and phone numbers. Use a *View* menu to display the information as small icons, large icons, list, and detail. Use happy face icons, or if you have access to a scanner, scan in pictures of the individuals to use as icons.

2.3 Create an MDI application containing a main form and two child forms captioned and named as frmOne and frmTwo.
Place menu items under *File* to *Display Form 1*, *Display Form 2*, and *Exit*. A *Windows* menu will have options for *Tile Vertical*, *Tile Horizontal*, *Cascade*, and *Show WindowList*.
Each child form should have a Close command button to hide the form.
Try placing a menu on the child form that contains *File* with an option to close the form. Notice how the child's menu replaces the parent menu.
Now make sure that you can arrange the windows when a child form is visible.

2.4 Write a project that allows the user to add controls at run time. You can decide which controls to allow.

2.5 Create a project containing department names (accounting, HR, IT, sales, and shipping) in a TreeView. Allow the user to select a department from a control array of option buttons and then add a name in a text box. Add the name to the appropriate node on the TreeView.
Optional extra: Allow the user to add a new department (add to the TreeView and to the option buttons).

CASE STUDIES

Video Bonanza

Create an MDI project that contains a splash screen, a parent form, and child forms for Video Inventory and Customer Records.

Splash Screen

Include an appropriate company logo, the company name, and the version number. Use an OK, Cancel, or Close button to signal unloading the form. (With a small project like this, you need to hold the splash screen until the user responds. If you hide the splash screen after all forms are loaded, the screen disappears too quickly to view it.)

About Dialog

Your name should be included as programmer.

Main Form

The main form will include a toolbar and a status bar. Place the date and time on the status bar.

Video Inventory

Use a TreeView control to display categories for videos. The categories are Action, Comedy, Drama, Horror, and Sci-Fi. Place at least one node under each category.

Include a command button for Add that will place text boxes for Category and Title on the form, along with OK and Cancel buttons. The OK button will add the new title to the appropriate node of the tree.

Customer Records

Use a Tabbed Dialog control to display Customer information.
Personal Info
    Last Name
    First Name
    Phone Number
    Customer Number
Financial
    Credit Card Company
    Account Number

VB Auto Center

Create an MDI project that contains a splash screen, a parent form, and child forms for Auto Inventory and Salesperson Records.

Splash Screen

Include an appropriate company logo, the company name, and the version number. Use an OK, Cancel, or Close button to signal unloading the form. (With a small project like this, you need to hold the splash screen until the user responds. If you hide the splash screen after all forms are loaded, the screen disappears too quickly to view it.)

About Dialog

Your name should be included as programmer.

Main Form

The main form will include a toolbar and a status bar. Place the date and time on the status bar.

Auto Inventory

Use a ListView that defaults to a Report view. The column headers are Vehicle ID, Manufacturer, Model, Year, Color, and Price. Use an auto icon along with the Vehicle ID for the other views.

Salesperson Records

Display the information for one salesperson on the form by using a Tabbed Dialog. The first tab will contain the name (first and last), department name, and the Social Security number. The second tab will be labeled Address and will have fields for street, city, state, and ZIP code. On the third tab (labeled Reviews), place a field for Date of last review and Reviewed by. At this point, since we don't have a data file, just use constants for the information.

3

Writing Database Programs Using ADO

At the completion of this chapter, you will be able to . . .

1. Use database terminology correctly.

2. Create data-bound controls using an ActiveX data objects (ADO) data control.

3. Create a project with an ADO data control to view an existing database table.

4. Connect data from two data sources to display data in DataList and DataCombo controls.

5. Display data in a DataGrid control.

6. Use the VB Data Environment Designer to set up database access.

7. Navigate a database programmatically using an ADO data control and/or a Data Environment Command object.

8. Create relation hierarchies.

9. Display hierarchical relationships in an MSHFlexgrid control.

10. Create reports by using the Data Report Designer.

Visual Basic and Database Applications

Professional VB programmers spend most of their time on applications that involve databases. To be a good programmer, you will want to concentrate on the various methods of displaying and updating database information.

   With VB you can create very simple database applications that require virtually no coding, all the way up to very powerful client-server applications that access and modify data on multiple large-scale servers. You can create programs that display and/or update data on a single stand-alone computer as well as on multiuser networked databases. Although this text concentrates on Access databases, the techniques that you learn also extend to larger-scale databases, such as SQL Server, Oracle, Sybase, and DB2.

Universal Data Access

Microsoft's strategy for accessing data from multiple providers is called **Universal Data Access (UDA).** The goal of UDA is to be able to access any type of data from any application on any type of computer. The data could be from relational databases, text files, spreadsheets, email, or address books, stored on a desktop computer, a local network, a mainframe, an intranet, or the Internet.

OLE DB

UDA is a concept; **OLE DB** is Microsoft's technology designed to implement that concept. In theory, any type of data source can be an OLE DB provider as long as the proper library routines allow low-level access to the data, following OLE DB specifications. OLE DB is actually a standardized interface that allows the developer to use one set of programming tools to refer to data from any source, such as data stored in a database, a text file, or a spreadsheet.

   Using OLE DB, a programmer need not be concerned with the syntax and intricacies of a particular data format. However, the OLE DB interface is somewhat complicated, so VB adds another layer to simplify the programming.

ADO

ActiveX Data Objects (ADO) is Microsoft's latest database object model. The goal of ADO is to allow VB programmers to use a standard set of objects to refer to any OLE DB data source. Although you can still use the older technologies, such as the intrinsic data control, data access objects (DAO), and remote data objects (RDO), Microsoft urges you to use ADO for all new development. Therefore, this text concentrates on ADO.

   The ADO technology provides three methods for connecting to a data source. They are the ADO data control, the Data Environment Designer, and objects defined in code. This chapter and the next deal with the first two methods; Chapter 5 covers creating database objects in code.

A VB programmer can use OLE DB and ADO to use data from any source. However, this text focuses on using database files created in Access. The Access database, along with VB, uses the Microsoft Jet Engine, or Microsoft Jet OLE DB Provider.

Note: Jet is the name Microsoft uses to refer to the software that handles an Access database.

Database Terminology

To use database files, you must understand the standard terminology of relational databases. Although there are various definitions of standard database terms, we stick with those used by Access.

An Access **file** (with an .mdb extension) can hold multiple **tables.** Each table can be viewed as a spreadsheet—with **rows** and **columns.** Each row in a table represents the data for one item, person, or transaction and is called a *record.* Each column in a table is used to store a different element of data, such as an account number, a name, an address, or a numeric amount. The elements represented in columns are called *fields.* You can think of the table in Figure 3.1 as consisting of rows and columns or of records and fields.

Figure 3.1

A database table consists of rows (records) and columns (fields).

Patient	Last Name	First Name	Street	City	State	Zip Code
100	Jones	Angela	1245 Club Dr.	Pomona	CA	91763
110	Jones	Brian	1245 Club Dr.	Pomona	CA	91763
120	Berry	Christine	1100 Nieces	Rancho	CA	91772
121	Berry	Heather	1100 Nieces	Rancho	CA	91772
122	Berry	Lisa	1100 Nieces	Rancho	CA	91772
130	Riebli	Erin	897 Couise	Rancho	CA	91772
131	Riebli	Raymond	897 Couise Ave	Rancho	CA	91772
140	Lemaster	J. Michael	9154 College	Diamond Bar	CA	91765

Record → 121 ... Field

Most tables use a **key field** (or combination of fields) to uniquely identify each record. The key field is often a number, such as employee number, account number, identification number, or Social Security number; or it may be a text field, such as last name, or a combination, such as last name and first name.

Creating Database Files for Use by Visual Basic

The files used in this textbook were created using Access. If you want to create a new database file, you can use Access or the Visual Data Manager add-in application that comes with VB.

You can run the VB Visual Data Manager by selecting *Visual Data Manager* from the *Add-Ins* menu. In the VisData application window (Figure 3.2), you can create a new file or open and modify an existing database file. The application is quite straightforward; you can use Help if you need instructions. Other handy features included in the Visual Data Manager are a QueryBuilder utility and a DataForm Designer. And if you like to see how things are done, you will be pleased to know that the Visual Data Manager is written in VB and that you can examine its source code. Look in the MSDN VB sample projects for the VisData project.

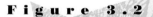

F i g u r e   3 . 2

Create a new database or modify an existing one by using the Visual Data Manager (VisData) window.

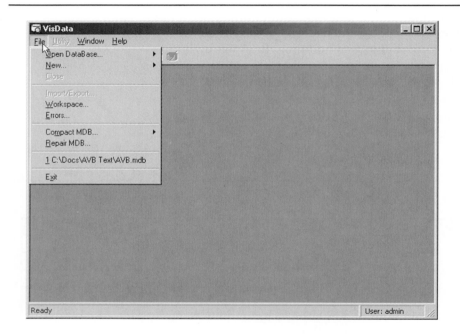

Using the ADO Data Control

Programming with the VB ADO data control is quite easy and powerful. And if you have previously used the older intrinsic data control, you will be glad to know that very few programming changes are required.

Adding the ADO Data Control to the Toolbox

Before you can use an ADO data control, you must add a reference to the control so that it appears in your toolbox. Select *Project/Components*, or right-click on the toolbox and choose *Components*, to display the *Components* dialog box. Then select *Microsoft ADO Data Control 6.0 (OLEDB)* and close the dialog box. The tool for the ADO data control will appear in your toolbox.

Figure 3.3 shows the toolbox tool for creating an ADO data control, and Figure 3.4 shows a data control on a form.

Figure 3.3

Figure 3.4

Note: You'll have a chance to do this for yourself in the section "Viewing a Database Table—Step by Step."

The Data Control and Data-Bound Controls

Using a data control is a two-step process. First you place a data control on a form and set the properties to link the control to a file and to a command. Each control can reference one table, stored procedure, or query. Then you create controls, such as labels and text boxes, to display the actual data. Each control is bound to a particular field in the table. In this example the label is called a **data-bound** control and automatically displays the contents of the bound field when the project runs. Figure 3.5 shows a form with a data control and four data-bound labels.

Figure 3.5

Microsoft also uses the term *data aware* for controls that can be bound to a database field. You might say that labels are data aware; therefore, you can use a label to create a data-bound control. The data-aware intrinsic controls include labels, text boxes, check boxes, list boxes, combo boxes, images, and picture boxes. VB also includes some ActiveX (nonintrinsic) data-aware controls, including the DataList, DataCombo, DataGrid, MSHFlexGrid, DataRepeater, and Chart. Use labels for any fields you don't want the user to be able to change; use text boxes if you want the user to update the field content.

Use check boxes for fields with a True/False or Yes/No value; the check box will display a check mark for True or Yes and remain blank for False or No.

A data control generally links one form with one table or query. If you want to have data-bound controls on a second form, you must place a data control on that form. You may place more than one data control on a single form when you want to reference more than one data source.

Properties of the Data Control

After you place a data control on a form, you must set the control's properties in the Properties window. By default, the Name and Caption are set to Adodc1. You should change the Name property, using *ado* as its three-character prefix.

You can set the other properties using the *Property Pages* dialog box (Figure 3.6), displayed either by right-clicking on the control and selecting *ADODC Properties* or by clicking on Custom and then on the Build button. You will need to change settings on the General tab and the RecordSource tab.

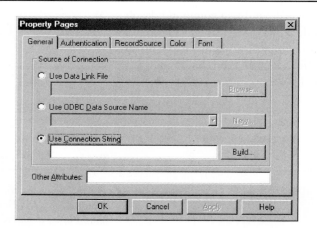

F i g u r e 3 . 6

Set the properties for the ADO data control by using its Property Pages dialog box.

Required Properties To access data, the minimum you must do is

- Specify a **ConnectionString,** which declares the database path, filename, and an optional UserID and password.

- Specify the RecordSource, which selects the data you want from within the database file. The RecordSource may be a table name, a stored procedure name, or an SQL statement. The CommandType property specifies which type of RecordSource you are using.

The ConnectionString Property Use the General tab (refer to Figure 3.6) to define the source of the connection (Table 3.1). Unless you have previously created a Data Link File or DSN (data source name), select *Use Connection String* and click the Build button. In the *Data Link Properties* dialog

Tip

You can look up all properties, events, and methods for the data control in the Object Browser. Select *Object Browser* from the *View* menu, drop down the *Project/Library* list, choose *VB*, and then select *Data*.

box that opens (Figure 3.7), enter the values to generate the ConnectionString property.

Table 3.1

Sources of Connection

Option	Purpose
Data Link File	The connection parameters are stored in a file with the extension .udl.
ODBC Data Source Name	Parameters are stored in a DSN, which must be created at the operating system level.
Connection String	Parameters are included in a string that can be built with the help of the *Data Link Properties* dialog box.

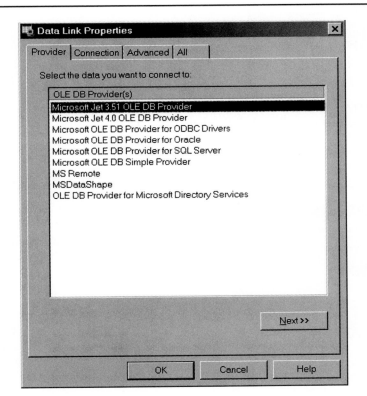

Figure 3.7

Build a connection string using the Data Link Properties dialog box. Set the database type on the Provider tab.

First set the *OLE DB Provider* on the Provider tab. For Access 97 files select *Microsoft Jet 3.51 OLE DB Provider;* for Access 2000, select *Microsoft Jet 4.0 OLE DB Provider.* Click the Next button, which displays the Connection tab (Figure 3.8). You can enter or browse for your filename and then click on the Test Connection button, which checks the access to the file.

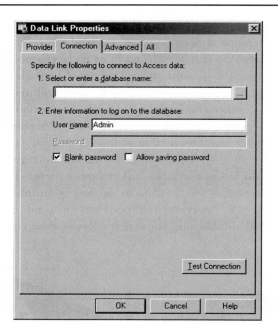

The Connection tab. Browse for the path and filename and then click the Test Connection *button.*

The CommandType and RecordSource Properties Display the Record-Source tab (Figure 3.9) to set the properties that actually select the data.

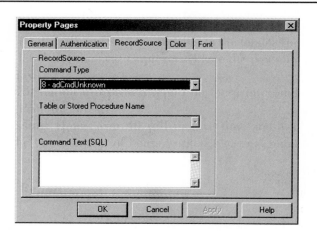

Specify the data to select on the RecordSource tab. For a table, set the Command Type and the table name.

The CommandType indicates how you will specify the data to select (see Table 3.2). The default setting is adCmdUnknown, but you will change that to adCmdTable to select a specific table from the database.

Table 3.2

The CommandType Settings

Setting	Purpose
adCmdUnknown	The default setting. The CommandType is unknown.
adCmdText	An SQL statement will select the data.
adCmdTable	Use a table.
adCmdStoredProc	Use a stored procedure.

When you select adCmdTable, the drop-down list labeled Table or Stored Procedure Name is filled. Drop down the list to select the table name (Figure 3.10). The table name that you select becomes the data control's **RecordSource property.** This property contains the name of the table, the stored procedure, or the SQL statement, depending upon the CommandType property.

Figure 3.10

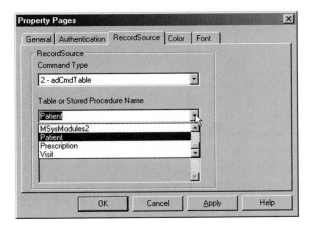

Select the table name from the list.

Access Permissions Be sure to take a look at the Advanced tab of the *Data Link Properties* dialog box (Figure 3.11). The *Access permissions* settings determine how much access your user has to the data. The choices are Read, ReadWrite, ShareDenyNone, ShareDenyRead, ShareDenyWrite, ShareExclusive, and Write. The default, ShareDenyNone, means that your user can read and write the data and that other users can have the data open at the same time. In this chapter we change this setting to Read so that the user cannot accidentally make changes to the data. In the next chapter you will learn to update the data and will need to set the access to ReadWrite.

Set the Access permissions on the Advanced tab of the Data Link Properties dialog box.

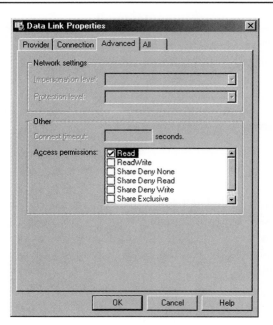

After setting the properties for the data control, you are ready to set the properties for the data-bound controls.

Properties of Data-Bound Controls

After setting the Name and Text or Caption properties of your bound controls, you must set the DataSource and DataField properties that bind the control to a particular field in a table.

First set the **DataSource property** of the bound control to point to the data control. Click on the down arrow in the Settings box to drop down the list of data controls on the form (Figure 3.12). Once you have selected the data control, VB knows the name of the file and table. Next you specify the particular field to bind to the control.

Select the name of the data control for the data-bound control's DataSource property.

Set the **DataField property** by clicking on the down arrow in the Settings box. The list of fields in the selected table will appear (Figure 3.13). After choosing the field name for one of your data-bound controls, set the DataSource and DataField properties for the rest of your controls.

Set the DataField property to the name of the field to bind to the control.

Later in this chapter you will learn about two other handy properties of bound controls: the DataMember property for use with the Data Environment Designer and the DataFormat to specify the display formatting style for a field.

That's all there is to it. Once you have bound the table and fields to the controls on your form, you are ready to run the application. With no code at all, the fields fill with data when your project begins. You can use the navigation buttons on the data control to move from one record to the next.

Viewing a Database Table—Step by Step

In this step-by-step tutorial you create a simple project to display the data from the Patients table for Advanced Vision and Beyond. The only code required is for the Exit procedure.

Design and Create the Form

Figure 3.14 shows the initial user interface for this project.

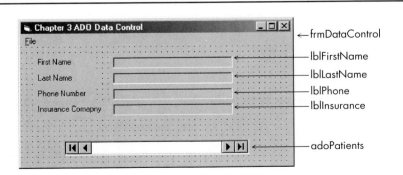

The user interface for the database step-by-step tutorial.

The Project

STEP 1: Create a new folder for this project and copy the AVB.mdb database into the folder. (The database is included on the CD that accompanies this text.)

STEP 2: Create a new standard project and maximize the Form Designer window. Resize the form, if necessary, to allow room for the controls.

STEP 3: Set the form's Name, Caption, and StartUpPosition properties to the settings of your choice.

STEP 4: Save the form and project into the new folder that you created in step 1.

The Controls

STEP 1: Right-click on the toolbox, select *Components*, and select *Microsoft ADO Data Control 6.0 (OLE DB)* from the *Components* dialog box. This step adds the control to the toolbox.

STEP 2: Add an ADO data control along the bottom of the form.

STEP 3: Create the labels to identify the data: "First Name", "Last Name", "Phone", and "Insurance Company".

   Hint: Recall that you can Ctrl-click on the toolbox tool to draw multiple controls of the same type.

STEP 4: Create the labels for the four data-bound controls.

The Menu

STEP 1: Open the Menu Editor and create a *File* menu with an *Exit* command. Name the menu *mnuFile* and the command *mnuFileExit*.

Set the Properties for the ADO Data Control

STEP 1: Select the data control and use the Properties window to change the Name to adoPatients and delete the Caption.

STEP 2: Right-click on adoPatients and select *ADODC Properties*.

STEP 3: Select *Use Connection String* and then click on *Build*. On the Provider tab, click *Microsoft Jet 3.51 OLE DB Provider* for Access 97 files or *Microsoft Jet 4.0 OLE DB Provider* for Access 2000 files and click *Next*.

STEP 4: On the Connection tab, select the AVB.mdb datafile that you added to the project's folder.

STEP 5: Click on the Test Connection button. You should get some good news next—your connection to the database should be confirmed.

STEP 6: Switch to the Advanced tab. Deselect *ShareDenyNone*, select *Read*, and click OK. This step protects your database from accidental updates.

STEP 7: On the *Property Pages* dialog box, switch to the RecordSource tab and change *CommandType* to *2 - adCmdTable*.

STEP 8: Drop down the list of tables and select the Patient table. Click on OK.

Set the Properties for the Data-Bound Controls

STEP 1: Select the label for First Name. In the Properties window set the Name to lblFirstName and delete the Caption.

STEP 2: Click on the Settings down arrow for the DataSource property and select adoPatients (the name of the ADO data control).

STEP 3: Click on the Settings down arrow for the DataField property; the list of fields in the Patient table appears. Click on FirstName.

STEP 4: Set the properties for the rest of the data-bound controls.

Object	Property	Setting
lblLastName	Name	lblLastName
	Caption	(blank)
	DataSource	adoPatients
	DataField	Last Name
lblPhone	Name	lblPhone
	Caption	(blank)
	DataSource	adoPatients
	DataField	Phone
lblInsurance	Name	lblInsurance
	Caption	(blank)
	DataSource	adoPatients
	DataField	Insurance Company Code

STEP 5: Select all four data-bound controls and change the BorderStyle property to *1 - Fixed Single.*

STEP 6: Optional, but a good idea: Check and set the TabIndex properties of all controls so that they are in the correct sequence.

Write the Code

The coding for this project may surprise you. All you need are a few remarks and an Exit procedure.

STEP 1: Select the *Exit* command from the *File* menu to open the mnuFileExit_Click procedure.

STEP 2: Type the following code:

```
'Exit the project
Unload Me
```

STEP 3: Switch to the General Declarations section and type the remarks:

```
'Program:       Display Patient Table
'Programmer:    Your Name
'Date:          Today's date
'Description:   Display the Patient information in the
'               AVB database.
'Folder:        Your folder name
```

Run the Project

STEP 1: Save the project and then start it running. You should see data in the form's labels.

STEP 2: Try the navigation buttons on the data control: Click on the arrows for Move Next, Move Previous, Move First, and Move Last (Figure 3.15).

Figure 3.15

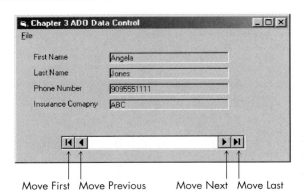

Move First   Move Previous   Move Next   Move Last

STEP 3: Select the *File/Exit* command to stop program execution.

Format the Phone Number Field

STEP 1: Select lblPhone, click in the DataFormat property in the Properties window, and click on the ellipses button. Select *Custom* and create this format string:
(###) ###-####

STEP 2: Run again.

STEP 3: Save again.

Feedback 3.1

1. Use this information to fill in the answers to the following questions.

Database Name:	Classes.mdb
Table name:	Teachers
Field name:	Name
Data control name:	adoClasses
Text box name:	txtTeacher

   You want to display the name field in txtTeacher. How should these properties be set?
   (a) txtTeacher.DataSource
   (b) txtTeacher.DataField
   (c) txtTeacher.Text
2. What properties must be set for the ADO data control to connect to a database table?
3. What is the purpose of the CommandType property? To what values can the property be set?

Using Bound DataList and DataCombo Controls

Looking back at the preceding example, wouldn't it be better to display the name of the insurance company instead of the company code? You can use several methods to do that, but the easiest and best way is to use one of the data-bound list box controls, which can display a list of all possible values for the field taken from another table. In the insurance company example, the Patient table holds a code for the insurance company and a second table, called InsuranceCompany, holds the complete name, address, and phone number for each company. You can place a second data control on the form and a **DataList control** or a **DataCombo control** to display the insurance company name.

The two data-bound list controls actually link the data from the first table to their corresponding values in the second table. Besides the usual DataSource and DataField properties, the DataList and DataCombo controls have properties called RowSource, ListField, and BoundColumn. The **RowSource property** indicates the data control used to retrieve the data for the list. You specify the field to display in the list by using the **ListField property,** and the field used in the lookup is the value of the **BoundColumn property.**

For the insurance company example, assume that you have a DataCombo control with these properties set to display the correct insurance company code for each person:

Property	Setting	Purpose
Name	dbcInsurance	
DataSource	adoPatient	Control that refers to the Patient table, which contains the insurance company code for the patient.
DataField	Insurance Company Code	Field in the Patient table containing the code for the insurance company.

These properties bind the control to the Insurance Company Code field in the Patient table.

Now, to fill the list with the names of all of the insurance companies, create a second ADO data control called adoInsurance, which connects to the InsuranceCompany table of the database. Set these additional properties of the DataCombo control:

Property	Setting	Purpose
RowSource	adoInsurance	Control that refers to the Insurance table, which contains the insurance company name that matches the code.
ListField	Name	The Insurance table field that displays in the List property of the DataList control; the full name of the insurance company.
BoundColumn	Code	The Insurance table field that contains the value to be matched with the DataField in the Patient table.

Creating a DataList or DataCombo Contol

The two controls, DataList and DataCombo, are new to VB 6; they are designed for use with OLE DB and ADO. Although the older DBList and DBCombo controls can be used, you should stick with the newer ones.

To use one of the data-bound list controls, you must add the tools to your toolbox by using the *Components* dialog box. Select *Microsoft DataList Controls 6.0 (OLE DB)* to add both the DataList and DataCombo tools (Figure 3.16).

Your choice of DataList or DataCombo depends on how you want the UI (user interface) to look and behave. Just as with the intrinsic ComboBox control, the DataCombo has a Style property, which provides for a dropdown list and an optional text box for user data entry. For the examples in this chapter, use Style *2 - dbcDropDownList*. In the next chapter the user can add data, so we will use other styles.

When naming the data-bound list controls, use the prefix *dbl* for a DataList and *dbc* for a DataCombo.

Adding a Dropdown List—Step by Step

In this continuing step-by-step tutorial, you will add a dropdown list that displays insurance company names to the chapter project.

Open the Project

STEP 1: Open the project that you created in the earlier step-by-step example.

Add the Second Data Control

STEP 1: Add a second ADO data control.
STEP 2: Set the Name to adoInsurance.
STEP 3: Set the ConnectionString to the same database file (AVB.mdb) and set the RecordSource to the InsuranceCompany table.
STEP 4: Set the Visible property to False.

Add the DataCombo Control

STEP 1: Open the *Components* dialog box and select *Microsoft DataList Controls 6.0 (OLE DB)*.
STEP 2: Delete lblInsurance and add a DataCombo control in its place (Figure 3.17).

STEP 3: Name the control dbcInsurance and delete the Text property.
STEP 4: Set the Style property to *2 – dbcDropDownList.*
STEP 5: Set the following properties:

DataSource	adoPatients
DataField	Insurance Company Code
RowSource	adoInsurance
ListField	Name
BoundColumn	Code

STEP 6: Set the Locked property to True so that the user cannot select or enter a new insurance company name.

Run the Project

STEP 1: Save and run the program.
STEP 2: Navigate from record to record; you should see insurance company names rather than the codes. Then drop down the list of insurance companies.

Feedback 3.2

Assume that you have a relational database with tables for Customer and Sales. The Customer number is the primary key of the Customer table and is also included in the Sales table. Your form, designed to display sales information, should display a list of customers in the dbcCustomer DataList control. The form has two ADO data controls: adoSales and adoCustomers.

Sales Table Fields	Customer Table Fields
InvoiceNumber	CustomerNumber
Date	Name
CustomerNumber	Phone

Fill in the properties of these controls:

Control	Property	Setting
lblInvoiceNumber	DataSource	
	DataField	
lblDate	DataSource	
	DataField	
dbcCustomer	DataSource	
	DataField	
	RowSource	
	ListField	
	BoundColumn	

Navigating the Database in Code

You can use the navigation buttons on the data control to move from record to record, or you can make the data control invisible and provide the navigation in code. You use the **Recordset object** to manipulate the database.

The Recordset Object

When you set the RecordSource property of a data control to the name of a table or a query, you are defining a new object called a *Recordset*. The Recordset object has its own set of properties and methods, which you can use to move from record to record, check for the beginning or end of the file, and search for records to match a condition.

When you refer to the Recordset object, you must first name the data control:

```
DataControl.Recordset.Property
DataControl.Recordset.Method
```

Using the MoveNext, MovePrevious, MoveFirst, and MoveLast Methods

The MoveNext, MovePrevious, MoveFirst, and MoveLast methods provide the same functions as the data control navigation buttons. Each method is applied to the Recordset object created by the data control.

```
adoPatient.Recordset.MoveNext      'Move to the next record
adoPatient.Recordset.MoveLast      'Move to the last record
adoPatient.Recordset.MovePrevious  'Move to the previous record
adoPatient.Recordset.MoveFirst     'Move to the first record
```

Checking for BOF and EOF

Two handy properties of the Recordset object are **BOF** (beginning of file) and **EOF** (end of file). The BOF property is automatically set to True when the record pointer is before the first record in the Recordset. This condition happens when the first record is current and the user chooses MovePrevious. The BOF property is also True if the Recordset is empty (contains no records).

The EOF property is similar to BOF; it is True when the record pointer moves beyond the last record in the Recordset and when the Recordset is empty.

When you navigate using the data control's navigation buttons, you can ignore the BOF and EOF conditions. When the user tries to move previous to the first or after the last record, the action depends on the settings of two properties of the data control: **BOFAction** and **EOFAction.** The choices for the BOFAction property are adDoMoveFirst and adStayBOF (default adDoMoveFirst). The EOFAction property choices are adDoMoveLast, adStayEOF, and adDoAddNew (default adDoMoveLast).

When you are doing your own navigation in code, you need to check for BOF and EOF so that run-time errors do not occur. If the user clicks MoveNext when on the last record, what do you want to do? Have the program cancel with a run-time error? display a message? add a new record? wrap around to the first record? keep the record pointer on the last record? (The last approach matches the action of the navigation buttons on the data control.)

In the example that follows, we use the wrap-around method. If the user clicks on the MoveNext button when on the last record, the first record becomes the active record.

Adding Record Navigation—Step by Step

In this continuation of the chapter step-by-step tutorial, you will add record navigation in code.

Open the Project
STEP 1: Open the project that you created in the earlier step-by-step example.

Add the Navigation Buttons
STEP 1: Add the four command buttons for navigation (Figure 3.18).

F i g u r e   3 . 1 8

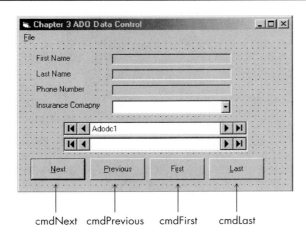

Add the four command buttons to use for navigation.

cmdNext   cmdPrevious   cmdFirst   cmdLast

STEP 2: Set the Name and Caption properties for the four buttons.
STEP 3: Set the Default property of cmdNext to True.

Set up the ADO Data Control
STEP 1: Set the Visible property of adoPatients to False.

Write the Code
STEP 1: Change the remarks in the General Declarations section to reflect the changes.

STEP 2: Add coding for each command button. See the following listing for help.

```
'Program:        Display Patient Table
'Programmer:     Bradley/Millspaugh
'Date:           2/2000
'Description:    Display the Patient information in the
'                AVB database using buttons for navigation.
'Folder:         Ch03SBS3

Option Explicit

Private Sub cmdFirst_Click()
    'Move to the first record

    adoPatients.Recordset.MoveFirst
End Sub

Private Sub cmdLast_Click()
    'Move to the last record

    adoPatients.Recordset.MoveLast
End Sub

Private Sub cmdNext_Click()
    'Move to the next record

    With adoPatients.Recordset
        .MoveNext
        If .EOF Then
            .MoveFirst
        End If
    End With
End Sub

Private Sub cmdPrevious_Click()
    'Move to the previous record

    With adoPatients.Recordset
        .MovePrevious
        If .BOF Then
            .MoveLast
        End If
    End With
End Sub

Private Sub mnuFileExit_Click()
    'Exit the project

    Unload Me
End Sub
```

Feedback 3.3

1. What is the purpose of the BOFAction property? Where is it set? When can it be used?
2. Write the code for the cmdNext command button, assuming that you want to remain on the last record if the user tries to go beyond the last record.

Moving a Project

Do you ever move a project folder from one location to another? from your hard drive to a diskette? from one computer to another? If so, you will have problems with the ADO data control, since its ConnectionString property includes the path as well as the filename.

To see the ConnectionString generated by the *Data Link Properties* dialog box, select a data control and view the property in the Properties window. The ConnectionString property for the preceding step-by-step exercise on the author's machine is (all on one line):

```
Provider=Microsoft.Jet.OLEDB.3.51;Persist Security Info=False;Data
Source=C:\Docs\AVBProjects\Chapter03\Ch03SBS3\AVB.mdb;Mode=Read
```

The solution to the path problem is to store the database file in the same folder as your project and assign the ConnectionString property, as well as the CommandType and RecordSource properties, at run time. You can then specify that the database file resides in the current directory, rather than hard code the complete path at design time.

The App Object

The predefined VB object called *App* holds properties for your application. You can use App.Path to refer to the path from which the current application is running. To assign a ConnectionString, include App.Path in place of the system-generated path.

```
adoPatients.ConnectionString = "Provider=Microsoft.Jet.OLEDB.3.51;" & _
          "Persist Security Info=False;Data Source=" & _
          App.Path & "\AVB.mdb;Mode=Read" 'Set the ConnectionString
```

Note: For this method to work, your project *must* be in a folder. A project running from the root level generates a run-time error using App.Path. Also notice the backslash included in front of the filename.

Opening the Recordset

The ADO data control wants to automatically open its Recordset before your form is loaded. If you want to take charge and open it yourself, you must omit the ConnectionString, CommandType, and RecordSource properties at design time and assign them yourself in the Form_Load procedure. (To create your data-bound controls, first set the data control's properties, create the bound controls, and then delete the data control's properties.)

Use the ADO data control's Refresh method to open the Recordset.

The Refresh Method—General Form

```
adoControlName.Refresh
```

The Refresh Method—Example

```
adoPatients.Refresh
```

The Refresh method opens or reopens the database.

Making the Project Example Portable

To make the project example in this chapter portable, delete the ADO data control's ConnectionString, and on the RecordSource tab, set the CommandType to adCmdUnknown, delete the table name, and add this code:

```
Private Sub Form_Load()
    'Set up Connections for the two ADO data controls

    With adoPatients
        .ConnectionString = "Provider=Microsoft.Jet.OLEDB.3.51;" & _
            "Persist Security Info=False;Data Source=" & App.Path & _
            "\AVB.mdb;Mode=Read"                    'Set the ConnectionString
        .CommandType = adCmdTable                    'Set the CommandType
        .RecordSource = "Patient"                    'Set the table name
        .Refresh                                     'Open the Recordset
    End With

    With adoInsurance
        .ConnectionString = "Provider=Microsoft.Jet.OLEDB.3.51;" & _
            "Persist Security Info=False;Data Source=" & App.Path & _
            "\AVB.mdb;Mode=Read"                    'Set the ConnectionString
        .CommandType = adCmdTable                    'Set the CommandType
        .RecordSource = "InsuranceCompany"           'Set the table name
        .Refresh                                     'Open the Recordset
    End With
End Sub
```

Displaying Data in Grids

Another good way to display data is in **grids,** which present tables in rows and columns similar to a spreadsheet. VB comes with several grid controls. In addition, many companies sell powerful grid controls that you can include in your project. In the following example, you will create a simple application that uses the Microsoft DataGrid 6.0 control. You will add the control by using the *Components* dialog box and use *dgd* for the naming prefix.

A DataGrid Control—Step by Step

This step-by-step tutorial shows you how to create an application that displays the Patient table for AVB. You also learn how to display the record number and record count. Figure 3.19 shows the completed form.

Figure 3.19

The completed form using the DataGrid control. The record count appears in the data control's Caption.

This project only displays the data. It does not allow for updating.

Create the Form and Controls

STEP 1: Create a new folder for the project and add the AVB.mdb database to the folder.

STEP 2: Begin a new project and widen the form. You may want to close the Project Explorer and Form Layout windows and float the Properties window to allow room to work on the wide form.

STEP 3: Save the project into your new folder.

STEP 4: Open the *Components* dialog box and select *Microsoft ADO Data Control 6.0 (OLEDB)* and *Microsoft DataGrid Control 6.0 (OLEDB)*.

STEP 5: Create an ADO data control along the bottom of the form. Set the control's Name property to *adoPatients* and build the ConnectionString for AVB.mdb, setting *Access permissions* to *Read*. Set the RecordSource to the *Patient table*.

STEP 6: Click on the DataGrid tool and draw a large grid on the form. Then, using the Properties window, change the control's Name property to *dgdPatients* and the DataSource property to *adoPatients*.

STEP 7: Create the menu bar. It should have a *File* menu with only an *Exit* command.

STEP 8: Set the form's Name property to *frmPatient* and the Caption property to *Advanced Vision and Beyond*.

Code the Exit Procedure

STEP 1: Code the mnuFileExit procedure with an `Unload Me`.

Set the Properties of the Grid

STEP 1: Point to the DataGrid control and right-click to display the shortcut menu. Select *Retrieve Fields* and *Yes*. Watch as the grid changes to display the fields from the Patient table. One column is set up for each field, with the field name at the top of the column as a Caption.

STEP 2: Start the project running. You should see the grid fill with data. Scroll to the right and view all the fields. You can also scroll down to see more records. After viewing the data, test your *File/Exit* procedure.

STEP 3: Right-click the DataGrid control and choose *Edit*. In Edit mode you can delete and resize columns.

STEP 4: Point to the first column heading for Patient Number; the mouse pointer should change to a down-pointing arrow (Figure 3.20). Right-click and select *Delete*.

F i g u r e   3 . 2 0

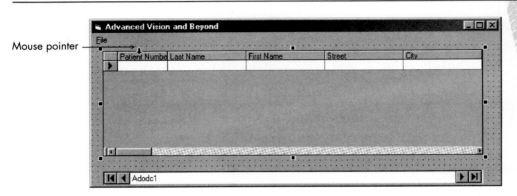

Mouse pointer →

Select the first column in the DataGrid. Notice the shape of the pointer.

STEP 5: Delete the columns for Street, City, State, and Zip Code.

STEP 6: Point to the divider between two columns and drag to resize a column (Figure 3.21).

F i g u r e   3 . 2 1

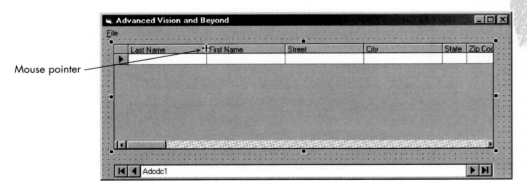

Mouse pointer ——

Resize a column by dragging the column divider. Notice the shape of the pointer.

STEP 7: Open the *Property Pages* dialog box. On the General tab, deselect *AllowUpdate*. Make sure that *AllowAddNew* and *AllowDelete* are also deselected.

STEP 8: Switch to the Columns tab and change the Caption for the Insurance Company Code column to *Insurance*.

STEP 9: On the Format tab, select the Phone column and create a custom format "(###) ###-####" (without the quotes).

STEP 10: On the Splits tab, set the Locked property to True for Split 0. A *split* is a group of contiguous columns; you are setting the property for all the columns in the grid.

STEP 11: Investigate the other properties on the Splits tab and those on the Layout tab, where you can set properties for individual columns.

STEP 12: Run the project again. Then use either Edit mode or the *Property Pages* dialog box to make any more changes that you think will improve the display.

STEP 13: Save but don't close the project.

Displaying the Record Number and Record Count

Often it is useful to display the record number and record count when viewing database records. You can use the **RecordCount** and **AbsolutePosition properties** of the Recordset to display both, for example, *Record 10 of 45*. You can make the count display in a label or in the Caption of an ADO data control.

The RecordCount and AbsolutePosition Properties

The RecordCount property holds the number of records in a Recordset; the AbsolutePosition holds the position of the current record in the Recordset. For an ADO Recordset the AbsolutePosition is one based (the first record is AbsolutePosition 1), as opposed to the older data controls that are zero based.

Examples

```
intCurrentRecord = adoPatient.Recordset.AbsolutePosition
intCurrentRecord = deAdvancedVision.Recordset.AbsolutePosition
```

If the Recordset is at BOF or EOF, the AbsolutePosition property has a value of zero.

Note: You cannot use the AbsolutePosition property as a record number because the position number changes as records are added and deleted.

To display the record number and count in the Caption of the ADO data control, create a sub procedure and use this code:

```
Private Sub SetRecordNumber()
    'Display the record number
    Dim intRecordCount      As Integer
    Dim intCurrentRecord    As Integer

    With adoPatients.Recordset
        intRecordCount = .RecordCount
        intCurrentRecord = .AbsolutePosition
        If .EOF Then
            adoPatients.Caption = "EOF"
        Else
            adoPatients.Caption = "Record " & intCurrentRecord & _
                " of " & intRecordCount
        End If
    End With
End Sub
```

You can display the current record information in a status bar panel by assigning the text to the correct panel:

```
staDemo.Panels(1).Text = "Record " & intCurrentRecord & _
    " of " & intRecordCount
```

The MoveComplete Event

To display the record number as the user moves from record to record, use the ADO data control's **MoveComplete event.** The MoveComplete event occurs each time a new record becomes current and at BOF and EOF.

```
Private Sub adoPatients_MoveComplete(ByVal adReason As ADODB.EventReasonEnum, _
    ByVal pError As ADODB.Error, adStatus As ADODB.EventStatusEnum, _
    ByVal pRecordset As ADODB.Recordset)
    'Set the record number

    SetRecordNumber
End Sub
```

Finish the Grid

STEP 1: Add the code for the adoPatients_MoveComplete event procedure and the SetRecordNumber procedure to the DataGrid example.

STEP 2: Run the project. Navigate through the records and view the record count.

Make the DataGrid Project Portable

If you want to be able to move the DataGrid project to a different computer, disk, or path, follow these additional steps.

STEP 1: Display the *Property Pages* dialog box for the ADO data control and cut the ConnectionString property to the Clipboard.

STEP 2: Close the dialog box, switch to the Code window, place the insertion point into the Form_Load procedure, and paste. The entire ConnectionString should appear. We'll come back and fix it up in a minute.

STEP 3: Reopen the ADO data control's *Property Pages* dialog box. Make sure that the ConnectionString property is empty, switch to the RecordSource tab, delete the Table name, and then change the CommandType to *adCmdUnknown.*

STEP 4: Switch back to the Form_Load procedure in the Code window.

STEP 5: Write the code to set the properties and open the ADO data control's Recordset. Edit the ConnectionString that you pasted by deleting the path and inserting App.Path.

```
Private Sub Form_Load()
    'Open the Recordset

    With adoPatients
        .ConnectionString = "Provider=Microsoft.Jet.OLEDB.3.51;" & _
            "Persist Security Info=False;Data Source=" & _
            App.Path & "\AVB.mdb;Mode=Read"
        .CommandType = adCmdTable
        .RecordSource = "Patient"
        .Refresh
    End With
End Sub
```

Feedback 3.4

1. Write the code that will place the record number and record count ("Record n of nn") in a panel of a StatusBar control.
2. Tell where in code your statements should appear so that the record number is always up-to-date.

The Data Environment Designer

New to VB 6 is a tool designed to expedite your work with databases. The **Data Environment Designer** is a visual interface that allows you to set up all the database connections and Recordsets for a project in one location. Then all forms and modules can refer to those Recordsets. Using the Data Environment Designer (Figure 3.22), you can specify a hierarchy among the data in the project. You can also drag-and-drop fields to your forms, which automatically creates bound controls.

Figure 3.22

A Data Environment Designer can manage all connections and commands in a project.

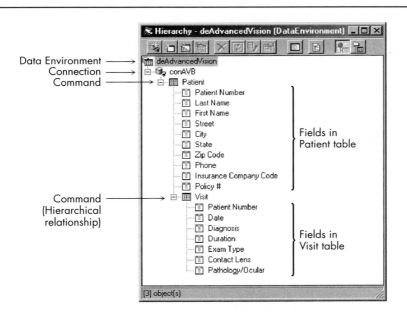

If you choose to use a Data Environment instead of an ADO data control, you no longer have the visible navigation buttons available. You will have to code the navigation, as you did in the preceding example.

Using the Data Environment Designer, you set up and refer to a series of objects. A **DataEnvironment** is an object that consists of **Connections.** Each Connection can hold one or more **Command** objects.

Connection and Command Objects

Connection: Specifies the physical database file, how it will be accessed, and with what permissions. Also called a **DEConnection.**

Command: Source of the data within the file. May be a table name, a stored procedure name, or an SQL statement. A Command corresponds to the RecordSource property of an ADO data control. The Command can also specify actions to perform on the data, such as grouping and updating. Also called a **DECommand.**

Adding a Data Environment Designer

You can add a Data Environment Designer to a VB project by selecting *Project/Add Data Environment* (or *Project/Add ActiveX Designers/Data Environment* in some configurations). If *Add Data Environment* doesn't appear on the *Project* menu, select *Project/Components,* switch to the Designers tab, select *Data Environment*, and close the *Components* dialog box. Then you can select *Project/Add Data Environment.* (Your menu may have *Add Data Environment* under a submenu *More ActiveX Designers.*)

When the Data Environment (DE) window appears (Figure 3.23), you will see an icon for the Data Environment and an icon for one Connection. (Each Data Environment must have at least one Connection.) In the Data Environment window, you can rename each object, add Connections and Commands, and set the properties for each object.

F i g u r e   3 . 2 3

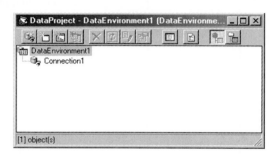

A new Data Environment window displays icons for the Data Environment and the first Connection.

It's a good idea to rename the Data Environment before adding any Connections or Commands. Click on the Data Environment icon and change the name in the Properties window; the recommended prefix for a Data Environment is *de*; for example, *deAdvancedVision* or *deCompanyDatabase.*

You can change the display of the objects in the Data Environment Designer. Using toolbar buttons, you can select *Arrange by Connections* (the default) or *Arrange by Objects.*

Adding Connections

To add a DEConnection to a Data Environment, right-click on the Data Environment icon and select *Add Connection* from the shortcut menu. You can rename the Connection in the Properties window or on the shortcut menu. Name each Connection with a prefix of *con*, for example, *conPatients* or *conPrescriptions.*

You can set many properties of the DEConnection object. Right-click on the icon and choose *Properties.* You will see the *Data Link Properties* dialog box; you also used this dialog box to set up a ConnectionString for the ADO data control. You can set the provider, database name, and access permissions, as well as test the connection.

Adding Commands

Although the term *command* can be somewhat confusing, for now just think of a Command as a table name or a query that returns a set of data, similar to the RecordSource property of an ADO data control. A Command creates a Recordset object with the data it returns. You will be able to use the Recordset in code, just as you used the ADO data control's Recordset.

To add a Command, right-click on the icon for a Connection and select *Add Command* from the shortcut menu. Change the name of the Command in the Properties window or the *Rename* command of the shortcut menu. Most programmers do not use a prefix for a Command, but rather choose a name that describes the data in the Recordset, such as Patients, Prescriptions, Employees, or Products.

After adding a Command, right-click the icon and display the *Properties* dialog box for the Patient Command object (Figure 3.24). The tabs are General, Parameters, Relation, Grouping, Aggregates, and Advanced. The Data Environment Designer works well to separate the database operations from your coding.

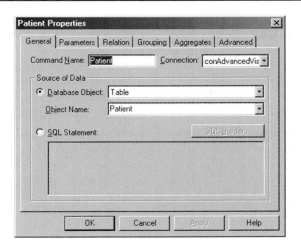

The Properties dialog box for the Patient Command object.

Creating a Data Environment—Step by Step

The following step-by-step tutorial creates a new application with bound controls using a Data Environment.

Begin a Project

STEP 1: Create a new folder and add the AVB.mdb data file to the folder.
STEP 2: Open a new standard project in VB.
STEP 3: Save the project into the new folder.

Add a Data Environment

STEP 1: Open the *Project* menu and select *Add Data Environment.* If you don't see it, look under *Project/More ActiveX Designers/Data Environment.* A Data Environment window will open.

Note: If *Add Data Environment* is not listed in the *Project* menu, open the *Components* dialog box, select the Designers tab, and click on *Data Environment.*

STEP 2: Click on the icon for DataEnvironment1 and change its Name property to *deAdvancedVision.*

Set up the Connection

STEP 1: Click on Connection1 and change its Name property to *conAdvancedVision.*
STEP 2: Right-click on conAdvancedVision and select *Properties*; the *Data Link Properties* dialog box appears.
STEP 3: On the Provider tab, select *Microsoft Jet 3.51 OLE DB Provider* and click *Next.*
STEP 4: On the Connection tab, for the database name, browse to find and select AVB.mdb. Click the *Test Connection* button to verify that your connection is set up correctly.
STEP 5: On the Advanced tab, select *Read* for *Access permissions* and deselect all other choices. Then click OK to close the dialog box.

Note: If you accidentally close the *Data Environment* window, reopen it by double-clicking on deAdvancedVision in the Project Explorer window.

Add a Command

STEP 1: In the deAdvancedVision Data Environment window, right-click on conAdvancedVision and select *Add Command* from the shortcut menu.
STEP 2: Right-click on Command1 and select *Properties* from the shortcut menu.
STEP 3: On the General tab, enter *Patient* for Command Name. The Connection should be set to *conAdvancedVision.*
STEP 4: For Source of Data, drop down the list for Database Object and select *Table.*
STEP 5: For Object Name, drop down the list and choose *Patient.* Click OK to close the dialog box. You have now set the data source to the Patient table of the AVB.mdb database.
STEP 6: Click on the plus sign for Patient to see a listing of the fields in the table (Figure 3.25).

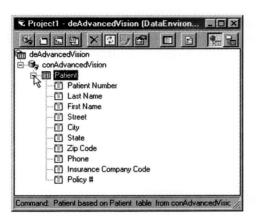

Expand the Command to view the field names for the Patient table.

Create Bound Controls

STEP 1: You may want to resize and move the Data Environment window so that you can view both the form and the fields in the window.

STEP 2: Drag and drop the LastName, FirstName, and Phone fields to the form. You now have labels and data-bound text boxes.

Run the Project

STEP 1: Run the project. You should see the fields filled with the first record in the Recordset.

Note that there are no navigation buttons. To navigate the Recordset, you will have to add the MoveNext, MovePrevious, MoveFirst, and MoveLast coding, as you did in the earlier example.

Modify the Project

STEP 1: Delete the labels and bound controls from the form.

STEP 2: Drag the Command object (Patient) to the top of the form. You have created labels and bound controls for all fields in the Patient table.

You can use the Properties window to view the properties set for a data-bound control. Notice that the DataSource is set to the Data Environment (deAdvancedVision) and the DataMember is set to the Command (Patient).

STEP 3: Run the project again.

STEP 4: Delete all labels and controls from the form.

STEP 5: Point to the Command object icon (Patient) and drag to the form with the *right* mouse button. When you release the mouse button, a menu allows you to choose the type of controls that you want: *Bound Controls* (like the ones from step 2), a *Data Grid*, or a *Hierarchical Flex Grid*. The hierarchical grid is covered later in this chapter. Choose *Bound Controls*.

Basing a Command on an Access Query

In the preceding exercise, we based the Command on a table in the Access database. You can also base a Command on an Access query, assuming that the query already exists in the database. When setting the properties for a Command, select *View* from the Database Object list. Then the Object Name list will show the names of any existing queries in the file. You may want to try this technique on the AVB.mdb database, which does have a query defined.

Record Navigation with the DataEnvironment Object

A Command object creates a Recordset object to which you can refer in code. The Recordset is automatically named with the name of the Command plus a prefix of *rs*. For example, in the previous step-by-step tutorial, you created a DataEnvironment object called deAdvancedVision with a Connection object conAdvancedVision, which contains a Command object called Patient. The Recordset is automatically created as *rsPatient*. You reference the Recordset in code as

```
DataEnvironmentName.RecordsetName.Property
```
or
```
DataEnvironmentName.RecordsetName.Method
```

Because the Data Environment does not provide an automatic navigation tool, you need to code command buttons to perform the navigation functions. You can use the same navigation methods as with the ADO data control's Recordset: MoveFirst, MoveLast, MoveNext, and MovePrevious.

The MoveNext method would appear as

```
deAdvancedVision.rsPatient.MoveNext
```

This method of navigation is referred to as *programmatically accessing objects*.

Making a Data Environment Portable

Making a Data Environment portable is easier than making an ADO data control portable (refer to "Moving a Project" earlier in this chapter). The Data Environment has its own code module where you can write code for its events. The Data Environment's Initialize event fires before any connections are made. Therefore, you can change just the Command object's ConnectionString property, and the connection will be made automatically.

To open the Data Environment's Code window, double-click on the Data Environment icon or on the View Code toolbar button.

```
Private Sub DataEnvironment_Initialize()
    'Make the project portable

    conAVB.ConnectionString = "Provider=Microsoft.Jet.OLEDB.3.51;" & _
        "Persist Security Info=False;Data Source=" & App.Path & "\AVB.mdb"
End Sub
```

Coding for Recordset Events

As the preceding code segment shows, you can write procedures in the Data Environment module. In fact, you need to write code there if you want to respond to events of the Data Environment, a Connection, or a Recordset object. (Command objects do not have events; only the resulting Recordset does.)

To display the current record number in the status bar of a form, the code must appear in the Data Environment's Code window.

```
Private Sub rsPatient_MoveComplete(ByVal adReason As ADODB.EventReasonEnum, _
    ByVal pError As ADODB.Error, adStatus As ADODB.EventStatusEnum, _
    ByVal pRecordset As ADODB.Recordset)
    'Display the record count

    With rsPatient
        frmAdvVision.staAdvVision.Panels(1).Text = "Record " & _
            .AbsolutePosition & " of " & .RecordCount
    End With
End Sub
```

Feedback 3.5

You have just added a Data Environment Designer to your project. Describe the steps necessary to set up access to a table and create bound controls on a form.

Data Hierarchies

You can set options in the Data Environment Designer to create hierarchies of data, joining data from more than one table. This procedure is especially useful for one-to-many relationships, which join a primary (parent) table with a secondary (child) table.

To see the advantage of a hierarchical Recordset over a "regular" relational table join, see the examples in Figures 3.26, 3.27, and 3.28. Figure 3.26 shows two related tables. The Patient Number field in the Patient table is the primary key; the Patient Number in the Visit table is called a *foreign key*; it is included to join, or relate, the two tables. Figure 3.27 shows a relational join. As you can see, the patient information is included for every visit, causing some patient data to be duplicated in this Recordset.

Patient Table

Patient Number	Last Name	First Name
100	Jones	Angela
110	Jones	Brian
120	Berry	Christine
121	Berry	Heather
122	Berry	Lisa
130	Riebli	Erin
131	Riebli	Raymond Jr.
140	Lemaster	J. Michael
141	Lemaster	Laurie

Visit Table

Patient Number	Date	Duration	Exam Type
100	11/4/98	15	Office
100	3/1/99	30	Office
110	1/15/99	30	Intermediate
120	11/12/98	30	Comprehensive
120	5/10/99	30	Office
121	11/4/98	30	Office
122	11/4/98	30	Intermediate
130	12/5/98	30	Intermediate
131	11/12/98	45	Comprehensive
140	11/2/98	15	Intermediate
140	11/15/99	45	Comprehensive
141	11/2/98	30	Comprehensive
141	1/15/99	15	Office
141	11/15/99	15	Office

Figure 3.27

A relational join of the Patient table and the Visit table. Notice that any patient with more than one visit has multiple records and that the patient information is repeated for each visit.

Patient Number	Last Name	First Name	Date	Duration	Exam Type
100	Jones	Angela	11/4/98	15	Office
100	Jones	Angela	3/1/99	30	Office
110	Jones	Brian	1/15/99	30	Intermediate
120	Berry	Christine	11/12/98	30	Comprehensive
120	Berry	Christine	5/10/99	30	Office
121	Berry	Heather	11/4/98	30	Office
122	Berry	Lisa	11/4/98	30	Intermediate
130	Riebli	Erin	12/5/98	30	Intermediate
131	Riebli	Raymond Jr.	11/12/98	45	Comprehensive
140	Lemaster	J. Michael	11/2/98	15	Intermediate
140	Lemaster	J. Michael	11/15/99	45	Comprehensive
141	Lemaster	Laurie	11/2/98	30	Comprehensive
141	Lemaster	Laurie	1/15/99	15	Office
141	Lemaster	Laurie	11/15/99	15	Office

Figure 3.28

A hierarchical Recordset created from the Patient table and the Visit table. The patient information (the parent) appears only once for each patient. The visit information (the child) appears as many times as necessary.

Patient Number	Last Name	First Name	Date	Duration	Exam Type
100	Jones	Angela	11/4/98	15	Office
			3/1/99	30	Office
110	Jones	Brian	1/15/99	30	Intermediate
120	Berry	Christine	11/12/98	30	Comprehensive
			5/10/99	30	Office
121	Berry	Heather	11/4/98	30	Office
122	Berry	Lisa	11/4/98	30	Intermediate
130	Riebli	Erin	12/5/98	30	Intermediate
131	Riebli	Raymond Jr.	11/12/98	45	Comprehensive
140	Lemaster	J. Michael	11/2/98	15	Intermediate
			11/15/99	45	Comprehensive
141	Lemaster	Laurie	11/2/98	30	Comprehensive
			1/15/99	15	Office
			11/15/99	15	Office

Figure 3.28 shows the same data in a hierarchical Recordset. As you can see, the parent data (for the patient) appears only once; the child data (the visits) can appear multiple times for one parent.

An ADO hierarchical Recordset includes one field for each element in the parent Recordset plus an extra field that holds the entire Recordset for the child data (Figure 3.29). This configuration enables you to treat multiple Recordsets as a single unit for navigation.

Patient Number	Last Name	First Name	Visit
100	Jones	Angela	\<Recordset\>
110	Jones	Brian	\<Recordset\>
120	Berry	Christine	\<Recordset\>
121	Berry	Heather	\<Recordset\>
122	Berry	Lisa	\<Recordset\>
130	Riebli	Erin	\<Recordset\>
131	Riebli	Raymond Jr.	\<Recordset\>
140	Lemaster	J. Michael	\<Recordset\>
141	Lemaster	Laurie	\<Recordset\>

The Patient_Visit Hierarchical Recordset. The Visit field for each patient actually holds an entire Recordset.

VB 6 includes a special control—called the Microsoft Hierarchical FlexGrid control (MSHFlexGrid)—for displaying the data in a relation hierarchy. In the following sections you will create a hierarchical Recordset and display it in a MSHFlexGrid control.

Relation Hierarchies

Creating a **relation hierarchy** is similar to joining two related tables of data. Using the Data Environment Designer, you create a parent Command object and a child Command object. The next example uses the Patient and Visit tables of the Advanced Vision database and relates the tables using the Patient number. The Patient table is the parent (primary) table, and Visit is the child (secondary) table.

You can use either of two methods for creating the parent/child relationship. In both methods you need a Command object for each table. In the first method you create both Commands at the same level and convert one into a child; in the second method you first create the parent and then add the child directly beneath the parent. The following step-by-step tutorial uses the first method but also describes the second.

Creating a Relation Hierarchy—Step by Step

Create the Project

STEP 1: Create a folder for the project and add the AVB.mdb database to the folder.

STEP 2: Open a new project, add a Data Environment named deAdvancedVision, and save the project into the new folder.

Build the Relation Hierarchy

STEP 1: Using the Data Environment Designer, build a Connection for the AVB database. Name the Connection conAVB and set its properties.

STEP 2: Add two Command objects, one called *Patient* with the Patient table as the record source and one called *Visit* with the Visit table as the record source (Figure 3.30).

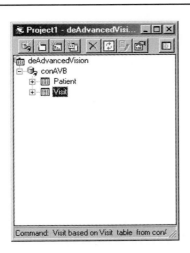

Figure 3.30

Create the Patient and Visit Command objects.

STEP 3: Right-click on the Visit Command object and select *Properties* from the shortcut menu.

STEP 4: On the Relation tab, check the box for *Relate to a Parent Command Object.*

STEP 5: Select *Patient* for the *Parent Command.* At this point VB tries to guess which fields form the relationship. When the fields have the same name, as in our database, VB usually makes a good guess.

STEP 6: For Relation Definition, make Patient Number appear for both the Parent Field and Child Field, if necessary.

STEP 7: Click *Add* and the relation will appear in the text box (Figure 3.31).

Figure 3.31

Click Add to make the relationship appear in the text box.

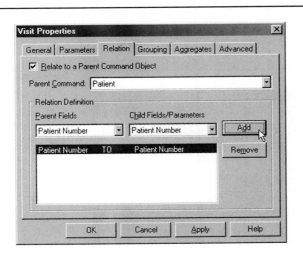

STEP 8: Click on OK. Note the indentation and relationship in the Data Environment (Figure 3.32).

The Visit Command object is a child of the Patient Command object.

STEP 9: Save your project.

Displaying Hierarchical Data in a MSHFlexGrid Control

What are you going to do with your data when they are in a hierarchy? How are you going to display them? One tool designed for this purpose is the Microsoft Hierarchical Grid Control (**MSHFlexGrid),** new to VB 6. This control is based on the VB 5 FlexGrid control but has more display options.

A MSHFlexGrid is also similar to the DataGrid control but is more secure because the user is not allowed to change the data. However, resourceful programmers can allow users to update the data in a MSHFlexGrid by adding a text box on top of the cell to edit.

To use the control, you need to select *Microsoft Hierarchical FlexGrid Control 6.0 (OLE DB)* from the *Components* dialog box; the suggested naming prefix is *msg.*

Displaying Data in a MSHFlexGrid—Step by Step

This step-by-step tutorial is a continuation of the preceding hierarchical data exercise. Figure 3.33 shows the finished grid.

The MSHFlexGrid filled with hierarchical data. Click a plus sign to expand the data for a patient.

Add the Grid

STEP 1: Add the Microsoft Hierarchical FlexGrid Control 6.0 to your toolbox and add a large grid control to the form of the preceding Relation Hierarchy project.

STEP 2: Using the Properties window, name the grid *flexPatientVisit*.

STEP 3: Set the DataSource property to *deAdvancedVision* and the DataMember to *Patient*. The DataMember property is used to hold a Command from a Data Environment.

STEP 4: Right-click the grid and select *Retrieve Structure* from the shortcut menu. Resize the form and the grid as needed.

STEP 5: Run the project and experiment with the plus and minus signs to view patient visits.

Modify the Grid

STEP 1: Stop the program and open the grid's *Property Pages* dialog box; click on the Bands tab.

STEP 2: Each data Command is considered a separate band, so this grid has two bands, one for Patient and one for Visit. Bands are numbered beginning with zero.

STEP 3: On Band 0 (Patient), uncheck all address fields and the two insurance fields.

STEP 4: Switch to Band 1(Visit) and delete all information except the date.

STEP 5: Run again.

STEP 6: Note which patients have more than one visit. You can return to Design mode and resize the grid and form if you wish. You can also experiment with many properties that control the appearance of the data. You may want to try some of the fonts and some of the choices on the General tab. Notice that you can allow the user to resize the columns.

The Data View Window

Another visual tool for working with databases is the **Data View window** (Figure 3.34). It looks very similar to the Data Environment Designer but has a different purpose. The Data View window interacts with the database structure, whereas the Data Environment Designer works with the application (interface and code).

Figure 3.34

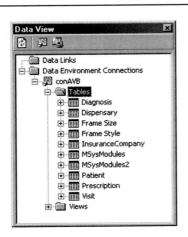

The Data View window. Drag data elements to the Data Environment Designer or to a form.

Use the Data View window to look at the way the tables are designed in the database. For some database formats, such as SQL Server and Oracle, you can even modify the structure of the database from the Data View window and create and view data diagrams. (You cannot use the Data View window for data diagrams or modifying the structure of Access databases.)

You can use the Data View window to view multiple Data Environments, showing the connections and field names. You can display the properties of any table or field by right-clicking and choosing *Properties* from the shortcut menu. You cannot create new Connections or Commands in the Data View window, but you can drag a table name or a field from the Data View window to the Data Environment Designer, which creates a new Command. However, you cannot drag items in the other direction (from the Data Environment Designer to the Data View window).

Display the Data View window by selecting *View/Data View Window* or by clicking its toolbar button (Figure 3.35).

Figure 3.35

The Data View window toolbar button.

The Data Report Designer

When you need to create a printed report based on a database, you can use the **Data Report Designer,** which is new to VB 6. You start by using the Data Environment Designer to set up a data source, and then you use the Data Report Designer to lay out the design of the report. Both the Data Environment and report become modules in your project. After you create the report, you can display it on the screen by using the report's Show method, or you can send the report to the printer with the PrintReport method.

When you design a report, you are creating a template for a report. Each time you display or print the report, VB uses current data values from the data source that you specify.

To create reports, you need *Add Data Report* to appear on the *Project* menu. If it doesn't, open the *Components* dialog box, click on the Designers tab, and select *Data Report.*

Tip

Previous versions of VB used Crystal Reports for data reports. Although it doesn't get installed when you set up VB 6, you can still find Crystal Reports on the Visual Basic or Visual Studio CD. Look on the last CD under *Common/ Tools/VB/Crysrept.*

Creating a Report—Step by Step

You can add a data source and report(s) to an existing project or create a new project for the report. In this step-by-step tutorial, we will create a new project that displays a report on the screen or sends the report to the printer. Figure 3.36 shows the completed report.

The completed report for the Report Designer step-by-step tutorial.

Advanced Vision and Beyond
Patient List as of 8/14/99   Page 1

Last Name	First Name	Phone
Jones	Angela	(909) 555-1111
Jones	Brian	(909) 555-1111
Berry	Christine	(619) 555-1112
Berry	Heather	(619) 555-1112
Berry	Lisa	(619) 555-1112
Riebli	Erin	(619) 555-1113
Riebli	Raymond Jr.	(619) 555-1113
Lemaster	J. Michael	(909) 555-1114
Lemaster	Laurie	(909) 555-1114
Patterson	Roman	(909) 555-4111
White	Tom	(909) 555-4321
White	Mary	(909) 555-4321
Raster	Ken	(619) 555-4322
Raster	Viola	(619) 555-4322
Mills	Tricia	(949) 511-4321
Mills	Eric	(714) 123-4567
Mills	Kenna	(714) 123-4567
Westley	Henry	(562) 145-6799
Westley	Irene	(562) 145-6799

Advanced Vision and Beyond
Patient List as of 8/14/99   Page 2

Last Name	First Name	Phone
Sedillo	Andy	(626) 555-7890
Navarro	Randy	(909) 777-7777
Pollard	Gary	(909) 222-2121
Picco	Joseph	(909) 552-3333
Johnson	Jay	(909) 552-3333

Number of Patients: 54

Begin the Project

STEP 1: Open a new standard project.

STEP 2: Save the project in a new folder called Ch03Report. Name the form file
Reports.frm and the project file Reports.vbp.

STEP 3: Move a copy of AVB.mdb into the new folder.

Set up the Data Source

Each report must be based on a data source, which can be any one of many
relational database formats, or even nonrelational data.

STEP 1: Add a Data Environment and change its Name property to *deAdvancedVision.*

STEP 2: Name the Connection *conAVB* and connect it to the AVB.mdb database file.

STEP 3: Add a Command called *Patient,* based on the Patient table. Click on the Command's plus sign to display the list of fields.

Design the Report

You will want to keep the Data Environment window open during most of the report design. At times you may close the window to get a better view of the report design. Open the window again by clicking on the deAdvancedVision icon in the Project Explorer window.

Begin the Report

STEP 1: Open the *Project* menu and select *Add Data Report.*

> *Note:* If *Add Data Report* is not on your *Project* menu, open the *Components* dialog box, click on the Designers tab, and select *Data Report.*

STEP 2: Resize the Data Report window to see more of the report. Notice the bands or sections on the report layout. You can add bound controls, labels, images, and other controls to each of the sections of the report.

STEP 3: When you are working on a report object, the toolbox changes to display the tools for a report (Figure 3.37). Take a minute to look over the available controls.

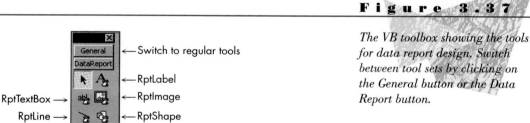

The VB toolbox showing the tools for data report design. Switch between tool sets by clicking on the General button or the Data Report button.

Set the Report's Properties

STEP 1: In the Properties window, change the Name property of the report to *rptPatient.*

STEP 2: Set the DataSource property to *deAdvancedVision* and the DataMember to *Patient.*

STEP 3: Set the Caption property to *AVB Patient Report.* The Caption appears in the window title bar when the report displays on the screen.

Close the Report Header Section

STEP 1: Point to the dividing line between the Report Header and Page Header sections. When your pointer changes to the two-headed arrow, drag upwards to close the Report Header section. Anything you place in the Report Header section appears at the top of the first page of a report.

Note: If the Data Report Designer does not show the Report Header and Report Footer sections, right-click on the report and choose *Show Report Header/Footer*. Then close the Report Header section (we use the Report Footer section later).

Place Titles in the Page Header Section

STEP 1: Drag the bottom edge of the Page Header section down to allow room for the title lines and column headings.

STEP 2: Select the RptLabel tool in the toolbox and draw a label in the Page Header section. Change the label's Caption property to *Advanced Vision and Beyond* (Figure 3.38).

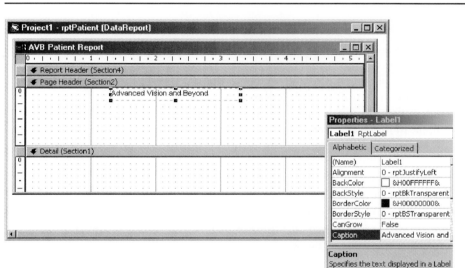

Figure 3.38

Change the Caption property of the report title label to Advanced Vision and Beyond.

STEP 3: Modify the label's properties to set the font to 12-point bold and the alignment to centered. While the label is still selected, you may want to resize the control and/or move it into a better position.

STEP 4: Add a second label; use the Caption property *Patient List as of.* Set the alignment of the label to right-justify.

Place Bound Controls in the Detail Section

STEP 1: Arrange your screen so that you can see the report layout and the Data Environment window. You may want to close the toolbox, the Project Explorer window, and the Properties window.

STEP 2: Click on Last Name in the Data Environment window and drag a control onto the Detail section of the report layout. Drop the icon at approximately the 1-inch mark at the top of the section (Figure 3.39).

STEP 3: The Designer creates a text box as a bound control and a label to indicate the field name. You can move the two controls independently, change their properties, or delete them to match your planning design.

STEP 4: Drag the First Name and Phone fields to the Detail section. You will move the fields and labels to match the report design next.

Move the Detail Fields and Column Headings into Position

STEP 1: Referring to Figure 3.40, move and resize the labels and text boxes. The labels should appear in the Page Header section, which appears once at the top of each page. The text boxes should appear in the Detail section because that section repeats once for every record in the data source.

F i g u r e   3 . 4 0

Move and resize the controls.

STEP 2: Click on the Phone field in the Detail section. Change its DataFormat property to a custom format "(###) ###-####".

STEP 3: Resize the Page Header section and the Detail section to remove any extra space. Any extra space in the Detail section is repeated for every row, giving the report wide spacing between lines.

STEP 4: Select the three column heading labels and change their font to bold.

STEP 5: Remove the colons from the Captions of the labels.

STEP 6: Close the Page Footer section by dragging its divider upward.

Add the Date and Page Number

STEP 1: Click in the Page Header section to select it, right-click, and select *Insert Control* from the shortcut menu. Then select *Current Date (Short Format)* from the pop-up submenu (Figure 3.41). A label appears with the code for the date (%d).

Figure 3.41

Insert a new control by using the shortcut menu.

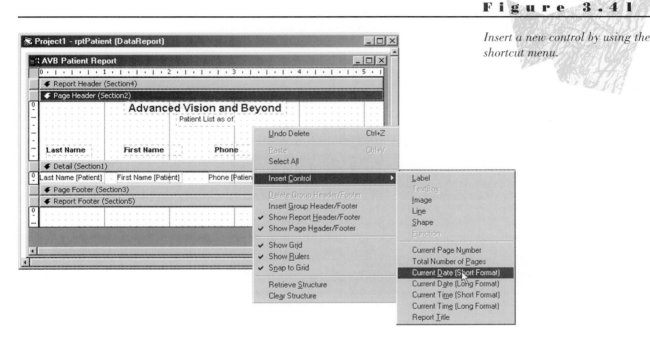

STEP 2: Move the new control to the right of the label for *Patient List as of*. Resize and align the two controls to make the date appear next to its label.

STEP 3: Right-click the Page Header section again, select *Insert Control*, and choose *Current Page Number*. The new control has the code for the page number (%p).

STEP 4: Move the page number control to the right and align it with the label holding the date.

STEP 5: Add another label control; use the Caption *Page* and position it next to the page number control. Make the alignment of the new label right-justified.

Add a Count in the Report Footer

The Report Footer section appears once, at the end of the last page of a report. Any summary information or report totals belong in this section.

STEP 1: Select the Report Footer section and right-click to open the shortcut menu.

STEP 2: Choose *Insert Control* and then choose *Function*.

STEP 3: Change these properties of the new control:

DataField	Patient Number
DataMember	Patient
FunctionType	rptFuncRCnt (row count)

STEP 4: Create a new label to the left of the counter control; use the Caption *Number of Patients.* Resize and align the controls as necessary.

Save the Report Design

STEP 1: Select *Save rptPatient As* from the *File* menu and save the report file. It will be named *rptPatient.dsr*. Your screen should resemble Figure 3.42.

Figure 3.42

The final layout of the report design.

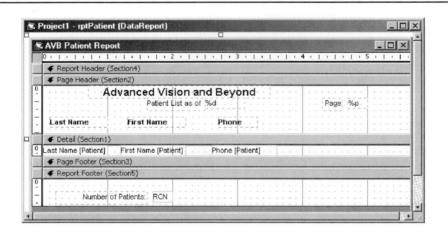

Printing the Report from a Form—Step by Step

You will now set up controls on the user interface so that the user can choose to display or print the report.

Set up the Form Properties

STEP 1: Set up your screen for working on a form: Click on the toolbox General tab to display form controls, display the form, and display the Properties window.

STEP 2: Change the form's Name property to *frmReport* and its Caption property to *Advanced Vision and Beyond Report.*

Tip

Switch among the various open windows in the VB IDE by using the F6 key.

STEP 3: Open the Menu Editor and create a menu with these commands:

Caption	Name
&File	mnuFile
&Report	mnuFileReport
&Display	mnuFileReportDisplay
&Print	mnuFileReportPrint
E&xit	mnuFileExit

Write the Code

STEP 1: In the mnuFileReportDisplay_Click procedure, code these lines:

```
Private Sub mnuFileReportDisplay_Click()
    'Display the report on the screen

    rptPatient.Show
End Sub
```

STEP 2: In the mnuFileReportPrint_Click procedure, code these lines:

```
Private Sub mnuFileReportPrint_Click()
    'Print the report on the printer

    rptPatient.PrintReport
End Sub
```

STEP 3: Code the mnuFileExit_Click procedure. Note that you must unload the report as well as the form.

```
Private Sub mnuFileExit_Click()
    'End the project

    Unload rptPatient
    Unload Me
End Sub
```

Test the Code and Report Layout

STEP 1: Save your project and run it.

STEP 2: Test the *File/Report/Display* command. Your report should display on the screen. You may need to return to the Data Report Designer to modify the layout of the report.

Formatting Numeric Fields

When you display numeric fields on a report, you need to set up the formatting. The report for VB Auto (Figure 3.43) shows a column for CostValue, which is totaled in the Report Footer section.

Figure 3.43

The VB Auto report has a formatted numeric field in the Detail section and a total in the Report Footer section.

VB Auto

Year	Manufacturer	ModelName	CostValue
1989	Chevrolet	Suburban	15,885
1987	Pontiac	Fiero	4,220
1993	Chevrolet	S-10	8,950
1991	Buick	Regal	8,525
1989	Chevrolet	Suburban	14,225
1991	Ford	Probe	12,295
1994	Pontiac	Firebird	19,145
1994	Dodge	Caravan	17,250
1994	Chevrolet	Astro	13,850
1993	Nissan	Sentra	6,845
1994	Hyundai	Excel	5,550
1994	Ford	Mustang	16,125
1995	Chevrolet	Suburban	23,175
1995	Toyota	Supra	25,400
1994	Ford	Probe	12,750
1990	Chrysler	LeBaron	5,800
1989	Buick	Regal	3,950
1992	Ford	Taurus	7,250
1994	Chevrolet	Lumina	10,950
1993	Mazda	RX-7	17,850
1985	Volkswagon	GTI	3,995
1995	Geo	Prism	9,999
1996	Pontiac	Grand Am	18,950
1989	Ford	Festiva	8,000
			290,934

To define the formatting for the CostValue field in the Detail section, set the following properties:

Property	Value
Alignment	rptJustifyRight
DataFormat	Number (or Currency) Set the number of decimal places and whether to use a comma separator.

Adding Totals to a Report

In the report for Advanced Vision, you added a record count to the report. You can just as easily add totals for numeric fields. Follow these steps to add the report total for CostValue in the VB Auto report:

● In the Report Footer section, right-click and choose *Insert Control/Function*. By default VB inserts the Sum function.

● Set the following properties:

Property	Value
DataField	Field name (CostValue)
DataMember	Connection name (Vehicle)
Alignment	rptJustifyRight
DataFormat	Number—zero decimal places and a comma separator
FunctionType	rptFuncSum

Note: For FunctionType, you can choose from sum, count, min, max, avg, and standard deviation.

Automatically Creating a Report

If you want to use all (or most) of the fields defined in a Connection, you can save a few steps when creating a report. Just drag the Connection from the Data Environment to the Detail section of the Data Report Designer. You will get two controls for each field: a label with the field name and a text box bound to the database field. You can then delete any unwanted controls and move the rest into the desired position.

Setting Report Margins

You can adjust the margins of your report, as well as determine the size of the Print Preview window displayed with a Show method. The following settings are in twips, a screen-independent measurement designed to give a consistent size regardless of the screen or printer resolution. There are 1440 twips to an inch or 567 twips to a centimeter.

The following properties determine the location and size of the Print Preview window:

Property	Default Value in Twips
Left	0
Top	0
Width	12,000
Height	9,000

To set the margins and printable area of the report, you can set these properties:

Property	Default Value in Twips	Size in Inches
LeftMargin	1,440	1
RightMargin	1,440	1
ReportWidth	7,500	5.2

Grouping a Report

Using the Data Report Designer, you can create groups in reports. To visualize grouping, think of subtotaling or breaking a report when the value of the chosen field changes. For example, you could group a report by department, division, state, region, company, or product. In the following example for Advanced Vision, the patient prescription information is grouped by last name. Notice (in Figure 3.44) that for each last name an extra line at the top identifies the group name and an extra line at the end provides summary information (in this case a count of the number of patients in that group). The extra information for the group is specified in a Group Header section and a Group Footer section (Figure 3.45).

You can even include grouping at multiple levels, such as a state within a region within an organization.

To create a report with grouping, first declare the grouping in the Command properties of the Data Environment. Then create the report from the Command.

Define the Grouping in the Data Environment

To set up grouping, display the *Property Pages* dialog box for the Command object. After you select the table or view, click on the Grouping tab, check *Group Command Object,* select the field for grouping, and send it to the *Fields Used for Grouping* box (Figure 3.46). The Data Environment Designer will rename your Command with an underscore and the word *Grouping* and add two subgroups—one for the summary (grouping) field(s) and one for the detail fields in the Command (Figure 3.47).

Note: The example for this section uses the view (Access query) Patient Prescription Query from the AVB.mdb data file.

Set up the Grouped Report

Once you have created a grouping Command object, you can define a report with the grouped data. Set the report's DataSource property to the Data Environment and the DataMember property to the Command (the one ending in *_Grouping*).

Display the Group Header and Group Footer sections by right-clicking on the report and choosing *Insert Group Header/Footer.* Then you can drag the summary field(s) to the Group Header and or Group Footer sections and drag the detail fields to the Detail section. Any functions that you add to the Group Footer section, such as `Sum` or `Count`, pertain to the group. Notice the `RCNT`

This report is grouped on last name. Notice the header and footer line for each group.

Patient Prescriptions Grouped by Last Name

Alfaro

3/1/99	Alfaro	David		Men's	Metal	PCB
3/15/99	Alfaro	Carmen	Contacts			

Count: 2

Berry

11/4/98	Berry	Lisa		Children's	Metal	PCB
11/15/99	Berry	Christine	Contacts			

Count: 2

Case

1/18/99	Case	Lennie		Men's	Plastic	PCB
1/18/99	Case	Dennie	Contacts			
2/1/99	Case	Jennie		Children's	Plastic	CR39 (Plastic)
2/1/99	Case	Bennie		Children's	Plastic	CR39 (Plastic)

Count: 4

Crow

1/18/99	Crow	Margaret		Women's	Plastic	CR39 (Plastic)
1/18/99	Crow	Paul	Contacts			

Count: 2

Hartley

2/1/99	Hartley	John		Men's	Metal	Glass
2/1/99	Hartley	James		Men's	Metal	PCB

Count: 2

The report layout for the grouped report. Notice the Group Header and Group Footer sections.

Figure 3.46

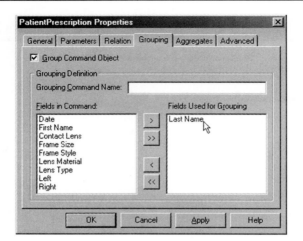

Select the field(s) on which to group on the Grouping tab of the Connection's Properties dialog box.

Figure 3.47

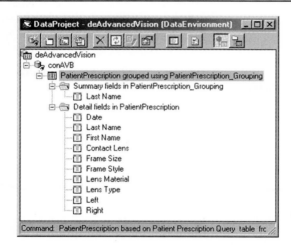

After selecting grouping, the Data Environment shows the grouped Connection object with subgroups for summary and detail fields.

(that is, row count) function in the Group Footer section in Figure 3.45 and the resulting output in Figure 3.44.

Feedback 3.6

1. Describe the function of each of these report sections:
   Report Header
   Page Header
   Group Header
   Detail

Group Footer
Page Footer
Report Footer
2. Explain how to add a record count to a report design. In which report section should the record count appear?
3. Explain how to add the page number to a report design. In which report section should the page number appear?
4. What is grouping? When is it useful?
5. Explain how to add a subtotal and a report total to a report.
6. How do you display a report in Print Preview mode?

Beginning a New Data Project

When you begin a new data project, you can save yourself a little time. Instead of selecting *Standard EXE* from the *New Project* dialog box, choose *Data Project*. Your new project will automatically have a form, a Data Environment Designer, and a Report Designer.

Tip

When using a DataCombo control with a Data Environment, set the DataSource and the Record-Source both to the DE name. Set the DataMember and RowMember properties to the Command that points to the specific table.

Your Hands-on Programming Example

This example for Advanced Vision and Beyond displays the Patient table and displays and prints a patient report.

In this project you will use a Data Environment with two Command objects—one for the bound controls and one to fill the list of a DataCombo control. You must add code in the Data Environment's code module to respond to the Recordset's MoveComplete event and display the record number.

Include a status bar with three panels. The first panel will display the record count ("Record n of nn"); the other two panels will display the date and time.

Set the *Access permissions* to *Read* and lock the bound controls so that the user cannot make any changes to the data. Although setting the *Access permissions* to *Read* might seem to be enough, the user can still make changes in the screen controls, which triggers an ugly run-time error.

Planning the Project

Plan the Interface

Sketch the form (Figure 3.48) and design the layout of the report (Figure 3.49), which your users sign off as meeting their needs.

Figure 3.48

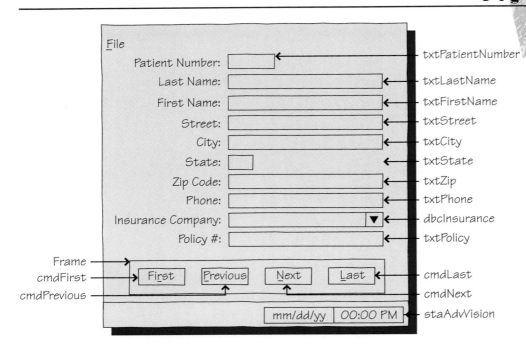

The planning sketch of the form for the hands-on programming example.

Figure 3.49

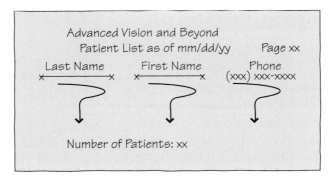

The planning layout for the report.

Plan the Objects and Properties

Plan the Data Environment.

Object	Property	Setting
Data Environment	Name	deAdvancedVision
Connection	Name	conAVB
	ConnectionString	Set up for AVB.mdb on your system
	Access Permissions	Read (only)

continued

Object	Property	Setting
Command	Name	Patient
	Source of Data	Patient table
Command	Name	Insurance
	Source of Data	InsuranceCompany table

Plan the property settings for the form and for each control.

Object	Property	Setting
frmAdvVision	Name	frmAdvVision
	Caption	Advanced Vision and Beyond
	Icon	Eye.ico
	StartupPosition	2 - CenterScreen
Data-bound text boxes	Name, DataSource, DataMember, DataField	Use default properties that occur when you drag a field or Command to the form from the Data Environment.
	Locked	True
txtZip	DataFormat	Custom - #####-####
txtPhone	DataFormat	Custom - (###) ###-####
Field labels	Name, Caption	Use default properties as set up by the Data Environment.
dbcInsurance	Name	dbcInsurance
	DataSource	deAdvancedVision
	DataMember	Patient
	DataField	Insurance Company Code
	RowSource	deAdvancedVision
	RowMember	Insurance
	ListField	Name
	BoundColumn	Code
fraNavigation	Name	fraNavigation
	Caption	(blank)
cmdFirst	Name	cmdFirst
	Caption	Fi&rst
cmdPrevious	Name	cmdPrevious
	Caption	&Previous

continued

Object	Property	Setting
cmdNext	Name	cmdNext
	Caption	&Next
	Default	True
cmdLast	Name	cmdLast
	Caption	&Last
staAdvVision	Name	staAdvVision
	Panels	3
Panel(1)	MinimumWidth	2880
	AutoSize	2 - Contents
Panel(2)	Style	6 - sbrDate
	AutoSize	2 - Contents
Panel(3)	Style	5 - sbrTime
	AutoSize	2 - Contents
mnuFile	Name	mnuFile
	Caption	&File
mnuFileReport	Name	mnuFileReport
	Caption	&Report
mnuFileReportDisplay	Name	mnuFileReportDisplay
	Caption	&Display
mnuFileReportPrint	Name	mnuFileReportPrint
	Caption	&Print
mnuFileExit	Name	mnuFileExit
	Caption	E&xit

Plan the Event Procedures

Determine which events will need code and plan the code for each.

frmAdvVision

Procedure	Actions
cmdFirst_Click	Move to first record.

cmdPrevious_Click	Move to previous record.
	If BOF Then
	    Move to first record.
	End If

continued

Procedure	Actions

cmdNext_Click	Move to next record.
	 If EOF Then
	    Move to last record.
	 End If

cmdLast_Click	Move to last record.
mnuFileReportDisplay_Click	Show the report.
mnuFileReportPrint_Click	Print the report.
mnuFileExit_Click	Unload report and form.

deAdvancedVision

Procedure	Actions
deAdvancedVision_Initialize	Set up ConnectionString to include App.Path.

rsPatient_MoveComplete	If not BOF or EOF Then
	    Set StatusBar text to record number.
	 End If

Write the Project

Follow the sketch in Figure 3.48 to create the user interface. Figure 3.50 shows the completed form, and Figure 3.51 shows the completed report.

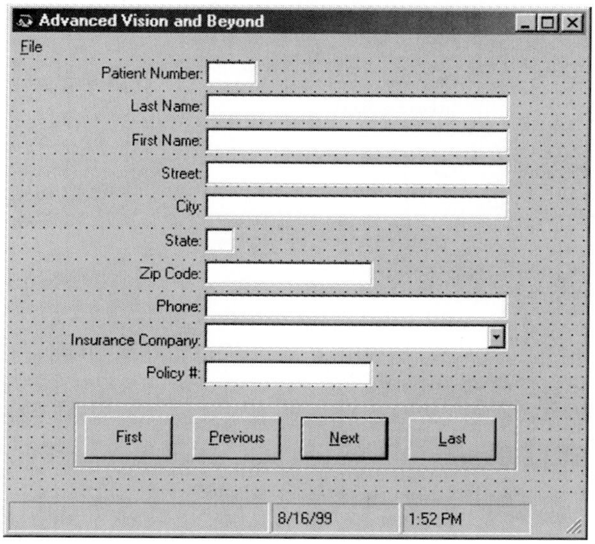

Figure 3.50

The form for the hands-on programming example.

The completed report for the hands-on programming example.

Advanced Vision and Beyond
Patient List as of 8/14/99   Page   1

Last Name	First Name	Phone
Jones	Angela	(909) 555-1111
Jones	Brian	(909) 555-1111
Berry	Christine	(619) 555-1112
Berry	Heather	(619) 555-1112
Berry	Lisa	(619) 555-1112
Riebli	Erin	(619) 555-1113
Riebli	Raymond Jr.	(619) 555-1113
Lemaster	J. Michael	(909) 555-1114
Lemaster	Laurie	(909) 555-1114
Patterson	Roman	(909) 555-4111
White	Tom	(909) 555-4321
White	Mary	(909) 555-4321
Raster	Ken	(619) 555-4322
Raster	Viola	(619) 555-4322
Mills	Tricia	(949) 511-4321
Mills	Eric	(714) 123-4567
Mills	Kenna	(714) 123-4567
Westley	Henry	(562) 145-6799
Westley	Irene	(562) 145-6799

Advanced Vision and Beyond
Patient List as of 8/14/99   Page   2

Last Name	First Name	Phone
Sedillo	Andy	(626) 555-7890
Navarro	Randy	(909) 777-7777
Pollard	Gary	(909) 222-2121
Picco	Joseph	(909) 552-3333
Johnson	Jay	(909) 552-3333

Number of Patients: 54

- Add the Data Environment Designer and set up the Connection to AVB.mdb. Add two Commands—one for the Patient table and one for the InsuranceCompany table.

- Add a Report Designer and create the report. If you already created the report in the step-by-step example in the chapter, add the report file to your project folder and select *Project/Add File* to add the report module to this project.

- Set the properties of the form and each of the controls, as you have planned.

- Working from the pseudocode, write each event procedure.

- When you complete the code, thoroughly test the project.

The Project Solution

The Form Module

```
'Project:        Chapter 03 Advanced Vision and Beyond
'                   Chapter Hands-On Example
'Module:         frmAdvVision
'Date:           2/2000
'Programmer:     Bradley/Millspaugh
'Description:    Display the Advanced Vision Patient table, using
'                   a Data Environment and bound controls.

Option Explicit

Private Sub mnuFileExit_Click()
    'End the project

    Unload rptPatient
    Unload Me
End Sub

Private Sub mnuFileReportDisplay_Click()
    'Display the report on the screen

    rptPatient.Show
End Sub

Private Sub mnuFileReportPrint_Click()
    'Print the report on the printer

    rptPatient.PrintReport
End Sub

Private Sub cmdFirst_Click()
    'Move to the first record

    deAdvancedVision.rsPatient.MoveFirst
End Sub

Private Sub cmdLast_Click()
    'Move to the last record

    deAdvancedVision.rsPatient.MoveLast
End Sub

Private Sub cmdNext_Click()
    'Move to the next record

    With deAdvancedVision.rsPatient
        .MoveNext
        If .EOF Then
            .MoveLast
        End If
    End With
End Sub
```

```
Private Sub cmdPrevious_Click()
    'Move to the previous record

    With deAdvancedVision.rsPatient
        .MovePrevious
        If .BOF Then
            .MoveFirst
        End If
    End With
End Sub
```

The Data Environment Code Module

```
'Project:        Chapter 03 Advanced Vision and Beyond
'                    Chapter Hands-On Example
'Module:         deAdvancedVision
'Date:           2/2000
'Programmer:     Bradley/Millspaugh
'Description:    Display the Advanced Vision Patient table, using
'                    a Data Environment and bound controls.

Option Explicit

Private Sub DataEnvironment_Initialize()
    'Make the data file moveable

    conAVB.ConnectionString = "Provider=Microsoft.Jet.OLEDB.3.51;" & _
        "Persist Security Info=False;Data Source=" & App.Path & _
        "\AVB.mdb"
End Sub
```

```
Private Sub rsPatient_MoveComplete(ByVal adReason As & _
    ADODB.EventReasonEnum, ByVal pError As ADODB.Error, & _
    adStatus As ADODB.EventStatusEnum, ByVal pRecordset As & _
    ADODB.Recordset)
        'Display the record count

    With rsPatient
        If Not .BOF And Not .EOF Then
            frmAdvVision.staAdvVision.Panels(1).Text = "Record " & _
            .AbsolutePosition & " of " & .RecordCount
        Else
            frmAdvVision.staAdvVision.Panels(1).Text = ""
        End If
    End With
End Sub
```

MCSD Exam Notes

Exam Objectives Covered in This Chapter

Creating Data Services

**Access and manipulate a data source by using ADO
and the ADO data control.**

Questions/Tricks to Watch For

- Make sure that you are familiar with the Data Environment, the Data View
  window, and the Data Report Designer.

- The properties List, BoundColumn, and RowSource apply to the DataCombo and DataList controls only.

- Know that a data control applies to one form only, but a Data Environment is for the entire project.

Summary

1. OLE DB is Microsoft's current database technology, using ADO as the programming interface.
2. Microsoft Access is VB's native format for database files.
3. In database terminology a *file* consists of *tables*, which consist of *rows* or *records*, which consist of *columns* or *fields*. Each record is identified by its *key* field. One record is always the *current* record.
4. A data control placed on a form links to a database file and a particular table within that file. Data-bound controls link to a data control for the table name and to a particular field within the table.
5. The data-aware intrinsic controls include labels, text boxes, check boxes, list boxes, combo boxes, images, and picture boxes. Others are the DataList, DataCombo, data-bound grid, MSHFlexGrid, DataRepeater, and Chart.
6. Set the ConnectionString, CommandType, and RecordSource properties of a data control to link it to a database table.
7. Set the DataSource and DataField properties of data-aware controls to bind them to a field in a database table.
8. The DataList control and DataCombo control can be used to look up and display data from two different tables. The control must be connected to both tables. Using an ADO data control, the DataSource and RowSource contain the appropriate data control names. With a Data Environment, the DataSource and RowSource both contain the name of the DE and the DataMember and RowMember are set to the Command object that specifies the correct table.
9. The Recordset object defined by the data control has its own properties and methods. Use the MoveNext, MovePrevious, MoveFirst, and MoveLast methods to navigate the database. The BOF and EOF properties indicate the beginning or end of file.
10. To make a data project portable, assign the ConnectionString property in the Form_Load procedure, using App.Path for the path of the database file. Open the Recordset by using the Refresh method.
11. You can display the Recordset of an ADO data control in a DataGrid control.
12. A Recordset's RecordCount and AbsolutePosition properties can display the number of records and the current record number. Use the RecordSet's MoveComplete event to display the record number.
13. The Data Environment Designer allows you to create a DataEnvironment object to contain all connections to all databases in a project. It can handle hierarchical relationships and can be accessed from all forms in the project.

14. A DEConnection object (Connection object) contains the connection information for a database. The DECommand object (Command object) specifies a table, stored procedure, or SQL text to be used to create the Recordset.

15. Relation hierarchies represent the relationships among Command objects similar to joining tables in an Access database. You can create Command objects with parent and child relationships.

16. The Data View window displays the structure of database files. You can drag table and field names from the Data View window to the Data Environment Designer to automatically create Connection and Command objects.

17. The Data Report Designer provides a tool to quickly create reports from database Recordsets. Reports are created in bands, with sections for Report Header, Page Header, Group Header, Detail, Group Footer, Page Footer, and Report Footer.

Key Terms

AbsolutePosition property *117*	EOF *110*
ActiveX data objects (ADO) *94*	EOFAction *110*
BOF *110*	field *95*
BOFAction *110*	file *95*
BoundColumn property *107*	grid *114*
column *95*	key field *95*
Command *119*	ListField property *107*
Connection *119*	MoveComplete event *118*
ConnectionString *98*	MSHFlexGrid *130*
data-bound control *97*	OLE DB *94*
Data Environment Designer *119*	record *95*
Data Report Designer *132*	RecordCount property *117*
Data View window *131*	Recordset object *110*
DataCombo control *107*	RecordSource property *101*
DataEnvironment object *119*	relation hierarchy *128*
DataField property *103*	row *95*
DataList control *107*	RowSource property *107*
DataSource property *102*	table *95*
DECommand *120*	Universal Data Access (UDA) *94*
DEConnection *119*	

Review Questions

1. Assume you have a database containing the names and phone numbers of your friends. Describe how the terms *file, table, row, column, record, field,* and *key* apply to your database.

2. Explain the difference between a data control and a data-bound control.

3. Which controls can be data bound?

4. Explain how the BOFAction and EOFAction properties are set and how they might be used in a project.

5. What is a connection string? Explain three sources of connection.

6. List and define the options for the CommandType property available for an ADO data control and for a DECommand object.

7. What is the default access permission for a database connected to an ADO data control?

8. How can you add code to a Data Environment? What procedures would you likely want to place in the Data Environment code module?

9. What is a hierarchical Recordset? When would it be useful to define one?

10. Explain the differences between the Data View window and the Data Environment Designer.

11. Explain the various sections of the Data Report Designer and how each section would be used.

Programming Exercises

3.1 Display the fields in the Prescription table of AVB.mdb using the ADO data control. Hide the data control and include command buttons for navigation. Make sure that the user cannot change the data.

3.2 Display the fields in the Prescription table of AVB.mdb using the Data Environment Designer. Include command buttons for navigation. Make sure that the user cannot change the data. Use menu choices rather than command buttons for the following program functions:

Menus

File	Record	Help
Exit	Next	About
	Previous	
	First	
	Last	

You may give each menu command a keyboard shortcut (in the Menu Editor) to make selecting a command quicker.

3.3 Write a project to display the Publishers table from the Biblio.mdb database that comes on the VB CD. (Biblio.mdb is not installed automatically on your computer but is on the CD.) Include command buttons for record navigation and hide the data control. Do not allow the user to change the data.

Hint: Copy the Biblio.mdb file to the directory where your project will be stored before setting the properties for the data control.

Note: The Biblio.mdb database included with VB 4 was 288 KB, small enough to easily fit on a diskette. The version included with VB 5 and VB 6 is 3.5 MB—too large for a diskette. The older version is included on the CD that accompanies this text. The two versions of the file have the same structure; the increased size reflects the large number of records added to the newer version.

3.4   Write a project to display the patient name and phone number along with the prescription information from AVB.mdb. Use a relation hierarchy and a MSHFlexGrid. Display a count of the number of patients in a label.

C A S E   S T U D I E S

Video Bonanza

Modify your project from Chapter 2 to display data from the VBVideo.mdb file for videos. Add a child form that contains text boxes and labels for the data fields.

The following fields must be displayed: Movie Number, Title, Length, Studio, and Category. Use a DataCombo control, dropdown list style, to display the studio name for the videos.

Use menu options or command buttons for navigation.

On the main menu include an option to print a report of the videos in stock.

VB Auto Center

Add a Customer menu to your parent form in the project from Chapter 2. Display data from the VBAuto.mdb file for customers on a child form. Use menu options or command buttons for navigation.

Include the following fields on the display: Customer Number, Customer Name, Manufacturer, Model, and Year. Use DataCombo controls to display the last three fields linked by the vehicle ID.

Place a command button on the form to display a report. The report should display the customer number, customer name, and vehicle ID.

4

Maintaining a Database File

At the completion of this chapter, you will be able to . . .

1. Set the CursorType, CursorLocation, and LockType according to application requirements.

2. Add, edit, and delete records in a database file.

3. Validate user input at the field level with the Validate event.

4. Recognize error types handled by ADO.

5. Use the WillChangeRecord event for form-level validation.

6. Find records that meet a specific criterion by using the Find method

7. Reorder records by using the Recordset's Sort property.

8. Select records with the Filter property of a Recordset.

9. Use Query Builder to create an SQL Command object.

In the preceding chapter, you learned to display database files using both a data control and a Data Environment. In this chapter you will write programs that allow the user to update the data. Updating or maintaining a file refers to the ability to add records, delete records, and make changes to existing records.

You need to be familiar with ADO cursors before programming database updates.

ADO Cursors

The term *cursor,* in database terminology, refers to the system resources needed to manage a set of data. The cursor enables you to move though the rows of a Recordset and keeps a pointer to the current record. ADO documentation sometimes uses the term *cursor* as another name for the Recordset; in addition, sometimes *cursor* refers to the library routines needed to create the Recordset, and in some locations *cursor* refers only to the current record pointer.

Cursors consume considerable resources, both memory and processing time. By setting properties of the cursor—the CursorLocation, CursorType, LockType, and Mode—you can greatly affect the system performance. You can choose to read a table or query as a single row, read only selected rows, make the table updatable or read only, and determine whether the access is forward only or scrollable (can move forward or backward). In a distributed application you must decide whether these resources should be used on the server side or the client side.

Setting Cursor Properties

You can set cursor properties for both the ADO data control and a DECommand object. For a data control set the CursorLocation, CursorType, LockType, and Mode properties in the Properties window. For DECommand properties set all but the Mode on the Advanced tab in the Recordset Management frame; the Mode is set for the DEConnection, as Access Permission.

The CursorLocation Property

The **CursorLocation property** determines where the data reside while they are being accessed and which machine manages the current-record pointer—the client machine or the server machine. For large client-server applications, CursorLocation is an important setting; it determines how much data pass over the network and which machine's resources manage the Recordset. Desktop applications always use the Client setting. Table 4.1 shows the available settings for CursorLocation.

T a b l e 4 . 1

ADO CursorLocation Property Values

CursorLocation	Constant
Client side	adUseClient
Server side	adUseServer

The CursorType Property

The **CursorType property** determines how you can move through the Recordset and the manner in which changes are made. The four types of cursors are forward only, static, keyset, and dynamic. Table 4.2 shows the types and the VB constants.

Cursor Type	Constant
Forward only	adOpenForwardOnly
Static	adOpenStatic
Keyset	adOpenKeyset
Dynamic	adOpenDynamic

With a forward-only cursor, you can only move forward through the Recordset. Any Move method, other than MoveNext, causes an error. Forward-only cursors use the least amount of system resources and perform the quickest. Although forward only does not allow you to return to the beginning of a Recordset, you can close the Recordset and reopen.

A static cursor uses more resources than a forward-only cursor but provides more flexibility. Using a static cursor, you can navigate in both directions. The drawback of a static cursor occurs only when more than one user is connected to a database. If user A makes any changes to data or adds or deletes a record, those changes won't show up in user B's static Recordset until the Recordset is closed and reopened. Note: When the cursor location is set to client side, forward-only and static are the only two choices. VB cannot actually implement a keyset or a dynamic cursor on a client-side cursor.

Compared to a static cursor, a keyset cursor uses more resources but also provides more information. When user A makes changes to data or deletes a record, those changes show up in user B's keyset Recordset. However, any new records added by user A do *not* show up in user B's Recordset.

A dynamic cursor uses the most resources and provides the most information. All changes made by user A, including adds and deletes, show up in user B's Recordset.

When you choose the type of cursor, be sure to select the type that uses the least amount of resources necessary for your application.

Note: The RecordCount property returns the correct number of records only for static and keyset cursors. For a forward-only cursor, the RecordCount is -1; for a dynamic cursor, the RecordCount returns either -1 or the actual count, depending on the data source.

The LockType Property

Locking is important when multiple users can open the same data, which is referred to as *concurrency*. What happens when user A has a record open and user B wants to look at the same data and/or make updates to the data? What happens if both users are making changes to the data at the same time?

If multiple users can update data, you must lock the data while an update is in progress. You can choose the extent of the locking with the **LockType property.** Table 4.3 shows the possible settings; the default for ADO is Optimistic, which does allow others to view and/or change the data.

Table 4.3

ADO LockType Property Values

Lock Type	Constant	Result
N/A	adLockUnspecified	
Read Only	adLockReadOnly	No edits can be made.
Optimistic	adLockOptimistic	Locked as each update submitted.
Batch Optimistic	adLockBatchOptimistic	Locked when all updates submitted.
Pessimistic	adLockPessimistic	Locked from Recordset creation.

If you will not be making any changes, it's best to set the LockType property to Read Only. Optimistic locking does not lock the file until updates are actually applied, while Pessimistic locking keeps the table locked the entire time that the Recordset is open. You should avoid using Pessimistic unless absolutely necessary. The Batch Optimistic setting allows all your changes to be submitted at one time.

Optimistic locking is usually the preferred setting, but here's a problem that can occur: User A is working on updating a record; user B opens the record and locks it (pessimistically); user A tries to save the updated record and is locked out. It's problems such as this that give database administrators gray hair.

The Mode Property

The **Mode property** determines the access rights of the user. In the last chapter we set the Mode to Read, since we didn't want the user to be able to make changes to the data. Table 4.4 shows the possible settings for Mode.

Table 4.4

ADO Mode Property Values

Constant	Result
adModeUnknown	Default. Access has not yet been determined or set.
adModeRead	Read-only permissions.
adModeWrite	Write-only permissions.
adModeReadWrite	Read-write permissions.

continued

Constant	Result
adModeShareDenyRead	Prevents others from opening connections with read permissions.
adModeShareDenyWrite	Prevents others from opening connections with write permissions.
adModeShareExclusive	Prevents others from opening connection.
adModeShareDenyNone	Prevents others from opening connection with any permissions.

Feedback 4.1

1. What cursor type should be used in the following situations:
   (a) Records will not be modified.
   (b) Changes must be made to a database on a single-user system.
2. What lock type should be used in the following situations:
   (a) Records will not be modified.
   (b) Changes must be made to a database on a single-user system.

Updating a Recordset

The term *update* refers to modifying the data in existing records, adding new records, and deleting records.

Modifying Records

When you are using bound controls, saving changes is practically automatic. If the Mode is set to give write permission, VB automatically saves any changed data any time the user clicks one of the navigation buttons or one of the Move methods executes.

You can also explicitly save changes by executing the Recordset's **Update method.**

Adding Records

When you want to add new records to a database, you have several choices. If you are using the data control's navigation buttons (rather than your own code for navigation), you can allow VB to do the adds automatically. Set the data control's EOFAction property to *2 - AddNew*. When the user moves to the end of the table and clicks the arrow for Next Record, an *Add* operation begins. The data in all bound controls are cleared so that new data can be entered. Then, when the user clicks one of the arrow buttons, the Update method is automatically executed and the new record is written in the file.

You need a different approach when you use code to accomplish record navigation. Assume that you have a command button or menu choice to add a new record. In the Click event for the command button, use the Recordset's **AddNew method:**

```
adoPatient.Recordset.AddNew          'ADO data control
deAdvancedVision.rsPatient.AddNew    'Data Environment
```

When an AddNew method executes, all bound controls are cleared so that the user can enter the data for the new record. After the data fields are entered, the new record must be saved in the file. You can explicitly save it with an Update method; or if the user moves to another record, the Update method is automatically executed.

```
adoPatient.Recordset.Update          'Save the new record
deAdvancedVision.rsPatient.Update    'Save the new record
```

You may want to use two buttons for adding a new record—a New Record button and a Save button. For the New Record button, use an AddNew method; for the Save button, use the Update method.

When adding new records, some conditions can cause errors to occur. For example, if the key field is blank on a new record, a run-time error halts program execution. See "Preventing Errors" later in this chapter for some solutions.

For a program that allows Adds, make sure that the user can enter a new key field. In the projects in Chapter 3, we displayed data in labels or locked text boxes. In this chapter you must use text boxes, which you may want to unlock when an Add is in progress and lock the rest of the time.

Using the DataCombo When Adding Records

In the preceding chapter you used a bound DataCombo control on a form. The dropdown list showed the names of insurance companies from the Insurance table, and the form displayed the Patient information from the Patient table. Now when adding new records, you will see the true value of using the DataCombo control: The user can select an insurance company name from the dropdown list, and the associated Insurance code is written to the Patient table.

In the examples for this chapter, you will find that the Style property for the DataCombo control is set to Dropdown Combo. That setting allows the user to enter a choice that is not on the list. You may notice that some of the records show Medicaid for Insurance, which does not appear in the list.

Using the MaskedEdit Control for Input and Display

The **MaskedEdit control** is a natural for displaying and inputting formatted data, such as a phone number or Social Security number. You can bind a MaskedEdit control to a data field, display formatted output using the DataFormat property, and supply input formatting by using the Mask property. You can choose whether to include the formatting characters in the Text property. If you don't set the DataFormat and Mask properties, a MaskedEdit control works exactly like a text box.

Note: To add a MaskedEdit control to your toolbox, select *Microsoft Masked Edit Control (6.0)* from the *Components* dialog box.

The Mask Property The **Mask property** is used only for data input. It supplies a template so the user can see the format of the data required. You can set the Mask property at design time or at run time.

Examples

Input Value	Mask Property	Prompt Showing in MaskedEdit Control
(202) 345-6789	(###) ###-####	(___) ___-____
555-44-3333	###-##-####	___-__-____
$25,215.75	$##,###.##	$__,___.__

Note: The pound symbol (#) represents a numeric character.

You can create masks for alphanumeric input, for date/time input, and to force uppercase or lowercase characters. See the MSDN topic *masks/formats in MaskedEdit control* for more information.

If you want to clear the contents of a MaskedEdit control, you must clear the mask and reset it:

```
With mskPhone
    .Mask = ""'Clear the mask
    .Text = ""'Clear the text
    .Mask = "(###) ###-####"      'Reset the mask
End With
```

The PromptInclude and ClipMode Properties The PromptInclude property determines whether the literals in the prompt (such as the parentheses in the phone number) are included in the Text property. Bound controls will not clear properly for an Add unless you set the PromptInclude property to False (the default is True).

The ClipMode property determines whether the prompt characters are included when you cut or copy the contents of the control to the Clipboard. The settings are *0 - mskIncludeLiterals* and *1 - mskExcludeLiterals*.

The DataFormat Property To set the output format of data, set the DataFormat property. For example, for the phone number field, select Custom Format and set the format to *"(###) ###-####"*.

Deleting Records

The **Delete method** deletes the current record. The user should display the record to delete and click a Delete command button or menu choice. When a record is deleted, the current record is no longer valid. Therefore, a Delete method must be followed by a MoveNext (or any other Move) method.

```
With deAdvancedVision.rsPatient
    .Delete
    .MoveNext
End With
```

But what if the record being deleted is the last record in the table? Remember that if a data control's navigation buttons are used to navigate, moving beyond EOF just resets the current record to the last record. No problem. However, if you are using event procedures for navigation, you must take care of this situation. If a MoveNext causes an EOF condition, then the program should do a MovePrevious. What will happen if the user deletes the *only* record in the Recordset? If the user deletes the last and only record in the Recordset, you must check for both EOF and BOF.

```
Private Sub cmdDelete_Click()
    'Delete the current record

    With deAdvancedVision.rsPatient
        .Delete          'Delete the current record
        .MoveNext        'Move to the following record
        If .EOF Then          'If last record deleted
            .MovePrevious
            If .BOF Then          'If BOF and EOF true, no records remain
                MsgBox "The Recordset is empty.", vbInformation, "No records"
                'Take any other desired action for empty Recordset
            End If
        End If
    End With
End Sub
```

Feedback 4.2

1. What will be the Recordset name of a Command object called Employee in a Data Environment with the name deAcmePayroll.
2. Write the statement(s) to add a record to the Recordset named in question 1.
3. Write the statement(s) to delete a record to the Recordset named in question 1.

Preventing Errors

When a computer program aborts and displays a cryptic system error message, who is to blame? the user? the programmer? the computer? Programmers sometimes tend to blame "stupid" users who just don't know what they are doing, but an amazing fact is that *really* good programmers seem to have "smarter" users who use programs correctly and make fewer errors. To become a good programmer, you must anticipate all possible actions of users. Any action that it is possible for your program to take will be tried by some user. If your form has a button or command that shouldn't be pressed in some situations, be assured that one of your users will press it.

You can do some fairly simple things to prevent user errors. It's a good idea to lock text boxes when data shouldn't be changed, disable buttons that shouldn't be pressed, and validate user input as much as possible. You can set the MaxLength property of text boxes so that the user cannot enter too many characters, and you can keep a user from causing many errors by disabling navigation buttons during an Add or a Delete operation.

Locking Text Boxes

You can lock text boxes that shouldn't be changed. In the Advanced Vision example, we don't want the user to change the Patient Number field, since that is the key field. However, we don't want to use a label for the Patient Number, since we need to be able to type in a Patient Number during an Add operation. Therefore, we will keep txtPatientNumber locked most of the time and unlock it when an Add is in progress.

In the procedure to begin an Add (cmdAdd_Click), include this statement:

```
txtPatientNumber.Locked = False
```

Because the only two actions that the user can take after beginning an Add are Save and Cancel, you should include the following statement in both the Save and Cancel routines:

```
txtPatientNumber.Locked = True
```

Limiting the Length of User Input

You can avoid many user input errors by setting the MaxLength property of a text box. Check the length of a field in the database and then set the MaxLength to the same size.

An easy way to check the field length in the database is to use the Data Environment or the Data View window. Right-click on a field name and select *Properties.* You will see the properties of the field, including the data type and size. Note, for numeric fields, the size is given in bytes of storage and does not represent the number of characters allowed.

Validating Data Using the Validate Event

When you want to make sure that a required field has an entry or that a field has valid data, the **Validate event** is a good location to check. If the field is not valid, you can display an error message and cancel the operation.

New to VB 6, most controls now have a new property and a new event that greatly aid in validating the entries in controls. The CausesValidation property can be set to True or False, which indicates whether validation will be performed on the control about to lose the focus. The Validate event occurs for the control just before it loses the focus.

For example, assume you have txtPatientNumber and txtLastName. The user is expected to enter a value in txtPatientNumber and tab to txtLastName. If you set the CausesValidation property of txtLastName to True, then the Validate event of txtPatientNumber occurs. Of course, the user may do something else, such as click in a different field or on a command button or exit the program. You must set the CausesValidation property to True for all controls that the user might select if you want validation to occur. Fortunately, the default setting for CausesValidation is True.

The Validate Event—General Form

```
Private Sub ControlName_Validate(Cancel As Boolean)
```

The Validate Event—Example

```
Private Sub txtPatientNumber_Validate(Cancel As Boolean)
```

In the Validate event procedure, you can perform any error checking and display a message for the user. If the data don't pass the error checking, set Cancel to True. When the sub procedure completes, the focus will remain in the control you are checking.

```
Private Sub txtPatientNumber_Validate(Cancel As Boolean)
    'Validate the PatientNumber for an Add
    '  Note: The control is locked unless an Add is in progress.
    Dim strMessage As String

    'All PatientNumbers must be numeric
    If Not IsNumeric(txtPatientNumber.Text) Then
        strMessage = "Invalid PatientNumber"
        MsgBox strMessage, vbExclamation, "Data Entry Error"
        With txtPatientNumber
            .SelStart = 0                    'Select the current entry
            .SelLength = Len(.Text)
        End With
        Cancel = True                        'Keep the focus
    End If
End Sub
```

Make sure to allow your user a way out. If *all* the controls on the form have CausesValidation set to True, *any* action puts the focus back in the text box. For example, if you have a Cancel button to cancel the operation, set its CausesValidation property to False.

Protecting an Add Operation

When the user clicks on the Add button, the cmdAdd_Click event occurs:

```
Private Sub cmdAdd_Click()
    'Add a new record

    deAdvancedVision.rsPatient.AddNew    'Clear out fields for new record
End Sub
```

Once the Add operation starts, you want the user to fill in the text boxes for the new record and click on *Save.* However, if the user clicks on one of the navigation buttons first, any data already entered in the text boxes are saved automatically. How can the user be forced to click on *Save*? How can he or she be allowed to cancel the operation?

Limiting User Actions

The best way to avoid errors is to avoid any extra options that can cause trouble. Once the Add begins, the user should have two choices only: *Save* or *Cancel*. The navigation buttons and the Delete button should be disabled or removed. (Recall from Chapter 2 that you can add controls at run time. Controls that are added at run time can also be removed during execution.) Figure 4.1 illustrates a data form used for updating; Figure 4.2 shows the same form during an Add operation with only two buttons available.

An update form as it appears before the user clicks on Add.

The update form as it appears during the Add operation. The Caption on the Add button changes to Cancel.

In the following example, when the user clicks on the Add button, several actions occur:

1. An AddNew method clears the bound controls to await entry of new data.
2. The focus is set in the first text box.
3. The navigation buttons and the Delete button are disabled.
4. The Save button is enabled.
5. The Caption of the Add button changes to *Cancel*, which gives the user only two choices: *Save* or *Cancel*.

Sharing the Functions of a Command Button

Another technique is to have one command button perform different actions depending on the situation. Notice in Figures 4.1 and 4.2 that the Add button becomes the Cancel button during an Add operation. Of course, this isn't the only solution: You could create a separate Cancel button and disable it.

To make a command button perform more than one action, you must change its Caption when appropriate. Then in the button's Click event, check the Caption before responding to the event.

```
Private Sub cmdAdd_Click()
    'Add a new record or cancel an add

    If cmdAdd.Caption = "&Add" Then
        'Code to handle Add
        cmdAdd.Caption = "&Cancel"   'Change the button's Caption
    Else        'A Cancel action is selected
        'Code to handle Cancel
        cmdAdd.Caption = "&Add" 'Reset the button's Caption
    End If
End Sub
```

Coding the Add Procedure

The cmdAdd_Click event performs two distinct operations: Add or Cancel. A new statement, the **CancelUpdate method,** also appears in the Cancel operation. CancelUpdate does what it sounds like—it cancels the Add and returns to the record that was active before the Add started.

```
Private Sub cmdAdd_Click()
    'Add a new record

    If cmdAdd.Caption = "&Add" Then
        deAdvancedVision.rsPatient.AddNew 'Clear out fields for new record
        txtLastName.SetFocus
        DisableButtons    'Disable navigation
        cmdSave.Enabled = True  'Enable the Save button
        cmdAdd.Caption = "&Cancel"   'Allow a Cancel option
    Else        'A Cancel action is selected
        deAdvancedVision.rsPatient.CancelUpdate   'Cancel the Add
        EnableButtons    'Enable navigation
        cmdSave.Enabled = False 'Disable the Save button
        cmdAdd.Caption = "&Add" 'Reset the Add button
    End If
End Sub
```

Procedures to Disable and Enable Buttons

These two general procedures simplify the disable/enable operations.

```
Private Sub DisableButtons()
     'Disable navigation buttons
     cmdNext.Enabled = False
     cmdPrevious.Enabled = False
     cmdFirst.Enabled = False
     cmdLast.Enabled = False
     cmdDelete.Enabled = False
End Sub

Private Sub EnableButtons()
     'Enable navigation buttons

     cmdNext.Enabled = True
     cmdPrevious.Enabled = True
     cmdFirst.Enabled = True
     cmdLast.Enabled = True
     cmdDelete.Enabled = True
End Sub
```

The Save Procedure

When the user clicks on Save, you must first save the new record by executing the Update method. Then reset the controls to their "normal" state.

```
Private Sub cmdSave_Click()
     'Save the current record

     deAdvancedVision.rsPatient.Update
     EnableButtons
     cmdSave.Enabled = False
     cmdAdd.Caption = "&Add"
End Sub
```

The WillChangeRecord Event

When the user takes any action that will change a record, add a record, or delete a record, the **WillChangeRecord** event fires just before the action is carried out. You can use the Recordset's WillChangeRecord event procedure to perform form-level validation. You can also determine the cause of the event, take appropriate action, and cancel the pending operation. Another related event, RecordChangeComplete, is fired after the database change has taken place.

When the WillChangeRecord event fires, VB passes the procedure an argument called *adReason*. This argument indicates which method is about to execute: Update, Delete, CancelUpdate, AddNew, UpdateBatch, or CancelBatch. Table 4.5 shows the constants for adReason. To cancel the pending action, set adStatus to *adStatusCancel*.

T a b l e   4 . 5

ADO Reason Constants

Constant	Associated Method Pending
adRsnAddNew	AddNew
adRsnUpdate	Update
adRsnDelete	Delete
adRsnUndoUpdate	CancelUpdate

continued

Constant	Associated Method Pending
adRsnUndoAddNew	CancelUpdate
adRsnUndoDelete	CancelUpdate

```
Private Sub rsPatient_WillChangeRecord( _
    ByVal adReason As ADODB.EventReasonEnum,  ByVal cRecords As Long, _
    adStatus As ADODB.EventStatusEnum, ByVal pRecordset As ADODB.Recordset)
    'Limit User Actions depending on Reason for change

    Select Case adReason
        Case adRsnAddNew
            With frmPatientData
                .txtPatientNumber.Locked = False
                .txtPatientNumber.SetFocus
                .cmdSave.Enabled = True      'Enable the Save button
                .cmdAdd.Caption = "&Cancel"  'Allow a Cancel option
            End With
    End Select
End Sub
```

Notice that this procedure checks the argument *adReason*. If an AddNew method caused this event to occur, the form is set up for an Add. You can include as many *Case* clauses to the *Select Case* as needed.

Trapping Database Errors

Several types of errors can occur while working with a database. The user may enter data that violate one of the rules of the database, such as attempting to add a duplicate key, a blank key, or a value that violates referential integrity.

Referential integrity, which is enforced by the database provider, is an important concept of relational databases. When a table includes a field, such as Patient Number, Part Number, or Employee Number, which refers to a key field in a second table, those values must match. For example, in the Advanced Vision database, the Patient Number is included in the Prescription table. If someone is allowed to delete a patient who has prescriptions in the Prescription table or enter a new prescription with an invalid Patient Number, that violates referential integrity in the database. If a user tries to do such a thing, ADO generates a provider error.

Some errors can occur from the VB statements; perhaps the requested operation cannot be performed. If an error occurs on a VB statement, you can trap the error using On Error GoTo and check the value of Err.Number. But an error that occurs because of a problem with the database is considered a provider error. Provider error codes are not listed in the VB documentation.

ADO provider errors are distinct from errors that are caused by VB. The error messages from ADO are even quite complete and acceptable to display to a user. For example, when the user tries to add a record with a duplicate key field, the system-generated message says, "The changes you requested to the table were not successful because they would create duplicate values in the index, primary key, or relationship." For most ADO error conditions, you can display the ADO error message, rather than check the cause and make up your own.

The ADO Errors Collection

Each ADO provider error is stored in an Error object. Because each action (such as a Move, Delete, or AddNew) can generate more than one error, ADO uses an **Errors collection,** which belongs to the Connection object. The Errors collection has a Count property and Clear and Item methods. The collection clears each time a new statement executes; the count of errors reflects those resulting from a single operation (Count = 0 means that no errors occurred).

If any provider errors occur for an operation, the Errors collection holds an object for each error. Then VB places the last provider error into the Err object. Therefore, you may be able to figure out the error from the Err object, but for the complete story you need to view each object in the Errors collection.

In your error handler you can check the values of the error numbers. But the only numbers that match the tables are the VB errors, not the provider errors. Table 4.6 shows some of the more common ADO VB errors.

Table 4.6

Selected VB ADO Errors

Error Number	Constant	Cause
3001	adErrInvalidArgument	Arguments are the wrong type, out of range, or in conflict.
3021	adErrNoCurrentRecord	Either BOF or EOF is True, or the current record was deleted.
3265	adErrItemNotFound	Could not find object.
3421	adErrDataConversion	Wrong data type for operation.
3709	adErrInvalidConnection	Closed or invalid Connection object.

You can use a `For/Each` loop to display the description of each Error object. Declare a variable of type ADODB.Error to represent each object in the collection and append the description of each error to a string.

```
Dim strMessage As String
Dim errDBError As ADODB.Error

For Each errDBError In deAdvancedVision.conAVB.Errors
    strMessage = strMessage & errDBError.Description & vbCrLf
Next
MsgBox strMessage, vbExclamation, "Database error"
```

Remember this rule: *Always place error handling in every procedure that accesses the database.* You must do so to avoid fatal program errors.

Feedback 4.3

1. When does the Validate event execute?
2. What problem would be encountered if all controls are set to CausesValidation = True?
3. For the following error conditions, which are caught by VB and which are ADO provider errors?
   (a) File not found.
   (b) Duplicate key field.
   (c) Empty key field.
4. Where does the Errors collection reside? What does it contain? How do you refer to a single Error object in the Errors collection?

Searching for a Specific Record

ADO provides several ways to search for a specific record. You can locate a particular name, account number, or phone number—any field stored in the database. You can search by using a **Find method,** or you can use a query or a stored procedure. In the following section you will learn to use the Find method.

Using the Find Method

The criteria specify the field name from the database and the contents for which you are searching. When we cover SQL statements later in this chapter, you will see that the criteria in a Find is like a *Where* clause in SQL, but without the word *Where.*

The Find Method—General Form

```
Recordset.Find SearchString [,[SkipRows], [search direction], [start]]
```

The search string contains the criteria or comparison for the record(s) you want to find. The SkipRows is an offset to the value of the start position and is set to zero by default. Your options for search direction are adSearchForward and adSearchBackward. You can optionally set a start point by using a Bookmark.

Note: The search string is not case sensitive.

The Find Method—Examples

```
adoPatient.Recordset.Find strSearch
deAdvancedVision.rsPatient.Find strSearch
adoPatient.Recordset.Find "[First Name] = 'Christine'"
deAdvancedVision.rsPatient.Find "[Last Name] = '" & txtSearch.Text & "'"
deAdvancedVision.rsDispensary.Find "Quantity < 20", , adSearchBackward
```

For a string search criterion, use a string variable or include the search string with the Find method. The comparison for a string field must be enclosed in single quotes. Notice that a database field that contains a space must be enclosed in square brackets as in [First Name] or [Last Name]. Because the Quantity field does not contain a space in the field identifier, no square brackets are required. In the fourth example the confusing mix of quotes produces the correct search string. Try concatenating the contents of txtSearch using a value of *Berry*. The search string becomes

```
"[Last Name] = 'Berry'"
```

When searching in a numeric field, do not enclose the numeric value in single quotes. The fifth example above includes a numeric constant. To specify a date constant, enclose the date in # signs, such as #1/1/2000#.

For the comparison operator, you may use =, >, <, or Like. To use the Like operator, use an asterisk as a wildcard character to match any character(s) in that position.

The Find method begins with the current record and moves forward. If you want to begin at the start of the Recordset, do a MoveFirst before the Find. To skip the current record and start with the next one, as for a Find Next, include the Offset argument:

```
adoPatient.Recordset.Find "[First Name] = 'Christine'", 1
```

Examples
```
"PayRate < 50000"
"LastName Like 'Ber*'"          'All last names beginning with "Ber"
"[End Date] > #2/2/2000#"       'Dates after 2/2/2000
```

No Record Found

If no record is found, the Recordset is at EOF (BOF for a forward search). Always test for end-of-file after a Find method.

```
If .EOF Then
    MsgBox "Record Not Found", vbExclamation, "Search"
End If
```

If a match is found, the record becomes current and is displayed in the data-bound controls. If no match is found, the current record number is unpredictable. A good way to take care of a no-match situation is to use a Bookmark.

Bookmarks

You can set a Bookmark on any record and use the Bookmark later to return to that record. Set a variable equal to the Recordset's **Bookmark property** to save it for future reference. Any time you set the Bookmark property to the variable name, the bookmarked record becomes the current record.

Note: Use the Variant data type for a variable to hold a Bookmark.

```
Private Sub cmdFind_Click()
    'Find a record by last name
    Dim strSearch   As String
    Dim vntBookMark As Variant

    If txtLastNameFind.Text = "" Then
        MsgBox "Type in Name to find before selecting command"
        txtLastNameFind.SetFocus
    Else
        strSearch = "[Last Name] = '" & txtLastNameFind & "'"
        With deAdvancedVision.rsPatient
            vntBookMark = .Bookmark      'Save pointer to current record
            .MoveFirst
            .Find strSearch
            If .EOF Then
                MsgBox "Record Not Found", vbExclamation, "Search"
                .Bookmark = vntBookMark 'Return to previous record
            End If
        End With
    End If
End Sub
```

Notice the `MoveFirst` before the `Find`. This Find will always find the first match in the Recordset. If you want to start the search from the current record, omit the MoveFirst method. Note: Not all searches will result in a match.

Feedback 4.4

1. Code the Find method to locate a Visit Date of 1/5/00.
2. Code the Find method to locate a date from the txtDate text box.
3. Write the statement(s) to check for a match after a Find.
4. What is the purpose of a Bookmark?

Working with Database Fields

In the sections that follow, we reference individual fields from a Recordset by name, read the contents of the fields, load field values into a list box, and select records using criteria.

Referring to Database Fields

At times you may want to refer to a single field in the current Recordset. You can use any of these formats to refer to a field:

```
DEObject.Recordset.Fields("FieldName")
```

or

```
DEObject.Recordset("FieldName")
```

or

```
DEObject.Recordset!FieldName
```

If the field name in the table is more than one word, you must enclose the name in quotes or square brackets:

```
deAdvancedVision.rsPatient!"Policy Number"
deAdvancedVision.rsPatient("First Name")
deAdvancedVision.rsPatient![Last Name]
```

Note: In the language of computer programmers, the exclamation mark is called the *bang.* To read the last of the three lines above, say "deAdvancedVision–dot–rsPatient–bang–Last Name."

Using Unbound Controls

All the database examples so far have used data-bound controls. The biggest advantage of using bound controls is that you can quickly create an application that automatically displays data and nearly performs automatic updates. However, for many programming tasks you cannot use bound controls. For example, if your controls need to appear empty at any time, you cannot use bound controls. Many applications allow the user to select one item of data and then fill in the rest of the controls based on the selection, such as these scenarios: choose a flight number, and the details for the flight appear; choose a customer number, a product number, or a patient name, and the details appear.

You can write a database project that has unbound controls. In fact, most complicated database programs written by professional programmers use unbound controls. For each control you must *not* specify a DataSource, DataMember, and DataField property. Instead, in code you must write the statements to assign field values to the controls. And if the user updates the data in the controls, you must assign the control's value to the database fields and perform an Update method. Although this approach seems like a lot of work, compared to using bound controls, it gives you much more control over what happens in the program.

To fill a screen control from the Recordset field:

```
txtLastName.Text = deAdvancedVision.rsPatient![Last Name]
```

Transfer from the control on the form to the database as needed:

```
deAdvancedVision.rsPatient![Last Name] = txtLastName.Text
```

If a database field may have a null value, you must take an additional step. If a null value is assigned to a text box, a run-time error occurs. Since an empty string (" ") is an acceptable value for a text box, append an empty string to each database field as you assign it to a text box:

```
txtLastName.Text = deAdvancedVision.rsPatient![Last Name] & ""
```

Chapter 5 contains an example of a complete program that uses unbound controls.

Loading Database Fields into a List Box

In the earlier examples for Find, the user entered the search value into a text box. Two better approaches might be to offer a list of possible values or to use a combo box that gives the user the opportunity to select or enter a new value. To fill a list with values from a Recordset, use a Do/Loop. You can place the loop in the Form_Activate procedure or in the Form_Load procedure.

When you decide whether to fill the list in the Form_Load or Form_Activate procedure, remember that Form_Load occurs once, the first time you show a form. Form_Activate occurs each time you show the form. If the data might have changed since the form was last displayed, use the Form_Activate procedure.

```
Private Sub Form_Load()
    'Fill the Patient list

    On Error GoTo HandleError
    With deAdvancedVision
        Do Until .rsPatient.EOF 'Fill the list
            If .rsPatient![Last Name] <> "" Then
                cboPatientName.AddItem .rsPatient![Last Name]
            End If
            .rsPatient.MoveNext
        Loop
        .rsPatient.MoveFirst
    End With

Form_Load_Exit:
    Exit Sub

HandleError:
    MsgBox "Unable to load patient list", vbInformation, "Advanced Vision"
    On Error GoTo 0
End Sub
```

Sorting and Filtering Data

You can sort a Recordset on any field by using the Sort property of the Recordset. You can also request a subset of a Recordset by setting a Filter property. ADO creates a temporary Recordset for display purposes; no changes are made to the underlying table.

The Sort Property

The **Sort property** allows you to reorder records in the Recordset by any field. Assign the property a field name, or multiple field names separated by commas.

The Sort Property—General Form

```
DEObject.Recordset.Sort = "FieldName[, MoreFields]"
```

The Sort Property—Examples

```
deAdvancedVision.rsVisit.Sort = "Date"
deAdvancedVision.rsPatient.Sort = "[Patient Number]"
```

To implement the sort for your users, you may want to create either menu options that give the fields for sorting or a list box with the field names.

```
Private Sub mnuSortDate_Click()
    'Sort by Date

    deAdvancedVision.rsVisit.Sort = "Date"
End Sub
```

```
Private Sub mnuSortDiagnosis_Click()
    'Sort by Diagnosis

    deAdvancedVision.rsVisit.Sort = "Diagnosis"
End Sub
```

```
Private Sub mnuSortDuration_Click()
    'Sort by Duration

    deAdvancedVision.rsVisit.Sort = "Duration"
End Sub
```

Note that you can also dynamically create an index for a field in a Recordset by setting the **Optimize property** of the field to True. Setting the Optimize property to False deletes the index. An index is a lookup table that the database engine uses to quickly locate records by a given field. An index provides much faster access for processing data in many circumstances.

The Optimize Property—General Form

```
Recordset.Fields(field).Properties("Optimize") = True|False
```

The Optimize Property—Examples

```
'Create an index
deAdvancedVision.rsPatient.Fields("Last Name").Properties("Optimize") = True
'Delete an index
deAdvancedVision.rsPatient.Fields("Last Name").Properties("Optimize") = False
```

The Filter Property

The **Filter property** allows you to create a new temporary Recordset by selecting records that match a specified criterion. For example, you might select all records with the same Last Name. Use the same criteria rules for the Filter as you used with the Find method.

The Filter Property—General Form

```
DEObject.Recordset.Filter = FilterString
```

The Filter Property—Examples

```
deAdvancedVision.rsVisit.Filter = "LastName = 'Berry'"
deAdvancedVision.rsVisit.Filter = "(Last Name) = 'Berry' AND (First Name) = 'Lisa'"
deAdvancedVision.rsVisit.Filter = strSearch
```

You can also use multiple criteria by combining the comparisons with AND or OR. Although you can combine multiple ANDs and ORs, there is no precedence for the AND/OR operators. You will want to use parentheses as needed.

For pointers to specific records, you can use the Filter property to return an array of Bookmarks to the records that match the criteria. See MSDN for more information.

If you want to display all records after you have set the Filter property, you must set the Filter property to empty quotes " " or use the Filter constant *adoFilterNone.*

Tables 4.7 and 4.8 summarize the properties and methods of ADO Recordsets.

T a b l e   4 . 7

Summary of Recordset Properties

Property	Purpose
BOF	Beginning-of-file marker.
EOF	End-of-file marker.
AbsolutePosition	Current record number—starts at 1.
RecordCount	Number of records in the Recordset.
Fields	Select specific field from collection.
Filter	Select records based on criteria.
Sort	Temporarily rearrange order of records.

T a b l e   4 . 8

Summary of Recordset Methods

Method	Purpose
Move	Move a specified number of records.
MoveFirst, MoveNext, MoveLast, MovePrevious	Move one record in direction specified.
AddNew	Clear bound controls and begin an Add.
Delete	Remove a record.
Update	Submit changes to the database.
CancelUpdate	Stop update processing.
Find	Locate a record by criteria.
Requery	Refresh the Recordset.

Feedback 4.5

1. Write the statement to find a record in deAdvancedVision.rsDispensary where the Quantity field is less than 20.
2. Code the command to sort the Employee command object of deAcmePayroll by
   (a) Rate
   (b) Employee Name
3. Write the statement to select records from the Employee command of deAcmePayroll. Create the set of records that contain a YTD salary of more than 45000.

Using SQL

VB uses Structured Query Language (SQL) to create files and/or indexes, to update database files, and to create new Recordsets. **SQL** (pronounced either "sequel" or "S, Q, L") is an industry-standard language for accessing relational databases.

You can base an ADO Command on an SQL statement, which creates a new Recordset. The Recordset may be a complete table, a subset of only certain fields of a table, or only the records that match a given criterion. A Recordset may also be the result of joining the data from multiple tables. As an example of a joined Recordset, consider an application to produce invoices in which a patient number must be joined with name and address information and must be joined with visit and prescription information.

This chapter provides a brief introduction to SQL, using the VB Query Builder. Chapter 5 contains a much more complete discussion, and you will learn to write your own SQL statements.

Basing a Command Object on SQL

When you use the Data Environment to create a Command object, you have several choices for Source of Data. In the past we used tables and views, but you can base the Recordset on an SQL statement. Just type the statement directly into the box (Figure 4.3) or use the Query Builder to help you. You can also assign an SQL statement at run time, which is covered in Chapter 5.

Note: If you are assigning a ConnectionString in code, you will want to also assign it in the Connection's Property Page. Otherwise you won't be able to set the properties of the Command at design time. After you have the project working, you can delete the design-time ConnectionString if you wish.

SQL Queries

Here are a few simple SQL queries. (For more advanced queries and additional explanation, see Chapter 5.)

Figure   4.3

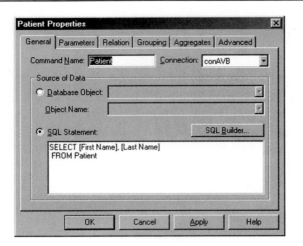

```
SELECT [Last Name], [First Name]
FROM Patient
```

The Recordset created from this SQL statement has only the Last Name and First Name fields from the Patient table.

```
SELECT *
FROM Patient;
```

This Recordset has all fields (* = all fields) from the Patient table.

```
SELECT Patient.[Last Name], Patient.[First Name],
    InsuranceCompany.Name
FROM Patient, InsuranceCompany
WHERE Patient.[Insurance Company Code] = InsuranceCompany.Code
```

This Recordset has three fields: Last Name and First Name from the Patient table and the Name field from the InsuranceCompany table. The SQL statement joins the two tables to retrieve the company name that matches the Insurance Company Code field from the Patient table.

Note: For field names that contain a space, you must enclose the name with either square brackets or the accent grave symbol (`).

```
SELECT `Last Name`, `First Name`
FROM Patient
```

Using Query Builder to Create SQL Statements

The Data Designer includes a Query Builder that can help you create an SQL statement. When you select the option button for SQL Statement on the *Properties* dialog box for a Command object, the SQL Builder button is enabled. Click on the button and the Query Design window opens, which is quite similar to the Query Design window in Access. The Data View window also appears, and you can set up your query by dragging tables from the Data View window to the top half of the Query Design window (Figure 4.4). Each field of the table has a check box so that you can select the fields that you want. Check the * (All Columns) entry at the top of the list if you want all fields in the table.

Figure 4.4

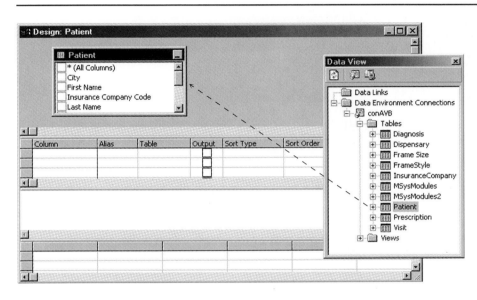

Drag table names from the Data View window to the top half of the Query Design window.

Creating SQL Queries—Step by Step

Begin the Project

STEP 1: Open a new standard project.

STEP 2: Save the project in a new folder called Ch04SQLQuery. Name the form file Patient.frm and the project file PatientQuery.vbp.

STEP 3: Move a copy of AVB.mdb into the new folder.

Set up the Data Source

STEP 1: Add a Data Environment and change its Name property to deAdvancedVision.

STEP 2: Name the Connection conAVB and connect it to the AVB.mdb database file.

Add a Command Object

STEP 1: Add a Command called Patient and open its Properties window.

STEP 2: Click the SQL Statement option button; then click on the SQL Builder button.

      The Query Design window and the Data View window open.

STEP 3: Resize and move the two windows as necessary to view both.

Build an SQL Query

STEP 1: Display the list of tables and drag the Patient table to the top half of the Query Design window.

STEP 2: Click in the check boxes for First Name and Last Name (Figure 4.5). Notice that the field names appear below in the grid and an SQL statement appears.

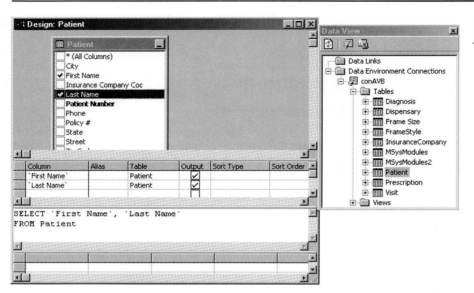

Place a check mark next to each field that you want to select.

STEP 3: Close the Query Design window, answering Yes to the "Save changes?" question. Also close the Data View window. You can reopen the Command's Properties window to see the SQL statement if you wish.
STEP 4: Expand the Patient Command in the Data Environment window (Figure 4.6). You should see the two field names below the Command.

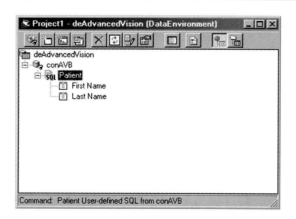

A Command object created with an SQL statement.

This Command creates a Recordset, which you can use to create bound controls on a form, just like any other Recordset. However, we are going to use it to fill a ComboBox with concatenated last and first names.

Fill a ComboBox with the Recordset

STEP 1: Place a Label and ComboBox on the form. Change the Label's Caption to *Select Patient Name.*

STEP 2: Change these properties of the combo box:

Name	cboName
Style	2 - Dropdown List
Sorted	True

STEP 3: Add a menu to the form with a *File/Exit* command.

STEP 4: Write code for the *File/Exit* command.

If a Recordset doesn't have any bound controls, it does not open automatically. In the Form_Load event procedure, we'll open the Recordset and step through the records, concatenating the names and adding them to the combo box.

STEP 5: Write this code in the Form_Load event procedure.

```
Private Sub Form_Load()
    'Fill the Patient list
    Dim strName As String
    Dim strSQL  As String

    With deAdvancedVision.rsPatient
        If .State = adStateClosed Then       'Recordset not opened
            .Open                            ' then open it.
        End If
        Do Until .EOF                'Fill the list
            If ![Last Name] <> "" Then
                strName = ![Last Name] & ", " & ![First Name]
                cboName.AddItem strName
            End If
            .MoveNext
        Loop
        .MoveFirst
    End With
End Sub
```

Test the Project

STEP 1: Run the project. Does the list fill with concatenated, alphabetized names? (If not, go back through the steps and check your work.)

STEP 2: Exit the project and save your work again.

In the next section, you will add unbound controls to the form and fill the controls during program execution. The user will select a name from the drop-down list. In the list's Click event procedure, you will first separate the first and last names and then open a Recordset based on an SQL query. The first name and last name will be supplied to the query as parameters, so the new Recordset will hold only the matching record(s).

Create a New Command for the SQL Parameterized Query

STEP 1: In the Data Environment window, create a new Command beneath conAVB. Name the Command FindName.

STEP 2: In the *FindName Properties* dialog box, select *SQL Statement* and click *SQL Builder.*

STEP 3: Drag the Patient table from the Data View window to the top of the Query Design window.

STEP 4: Place check marks next to First Name, Last Name, Patient Number, and Policy #. The query grid should show the four fields, and the SQL statement should appear in the lower pane of the window.

STEP 5: In the Criteria column for `First Name`, type "=?" (without the quotes). Notice the Filter icon that appears next to the field name in the upper pane.

STEP 6: In the Criteria column for `Last Name`, type "=?" (again, without quotes). Now both fields should display an icon next to their names (Figure 4.7).

F i g u r e   4 . 7

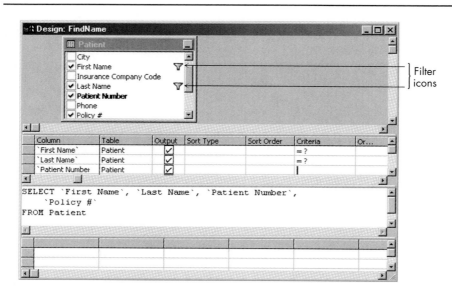

The Query Builder's Design window with the FindInfo parameterized query. Note the Filter icons next to the First Name and Last Name fields.

STEP 7: Click the Close button on the Query Design window, clicking Yes to the Save question.

STEP 8: Click OK on the message about setting parameters on the Parameter tab.

STEP 9: Open the FindName Properties window and look at the SQL statement.

```
SELECT `First Name`, `Last Name`, `Patient Number`, `Policy #`
FROM Patient
WHERE (`First Name` = ?) AND (`Last Name` = ?)
```

This query is asking for four fields from the Patient table that meet the criteria in the WHERE clause. Notice the two question marks. As you might guess, you probably won't know the value that the user wants to look for as you design the program. Obviously, a variable is the answer; this variable is called a **parameter.** A query that contains a parameter is referred to as a *parameterized query.*

The parameter value is replaced by a value at run time. This value usually comes from a text box or a variable. In the steps that follow, you will write code to run the query (create a new Recordset from the query) and assign the field values to unbound controls.

Set up the Parameters

STEP 1: Display the Parameters tab for Properties of the FindName Command object.

> The two names in the Parameters list are for First Name and Last Name.

STEP 2: Click on each of the two parameters and set the *DataType* to *adBSTR* and the *Host Data Type* to *String(VT_BSTR)*. You can also change the names of the parameters if you wish.

STEP 3: Click on OK to close the *Property Pages* dialog box.

Create the Unbound Controls

STEP 1: On the form, add Labels and Text boxes for First Name, Last Name, Patient Number, and Policy Number (Figure 4.8).

Figure 4.8

The form for the SQL query project. The combo box is filled in code from the Patient Recordset; the unbound text boxes are filled in code from the FindName Recordset.

You can create the controls by using the toolbox or by dragging fields from the Data Environment. However, the fields must be unbound, so if you drag from the Data Environment, you must delete the DataSource, DataMember, and DataField properties for each control. The text boxes should be named txtPatientNumber, txtFirstName, txtLastName, and txtPolicyNumber. (Beware! If you dragged the controls from the Data Environment, you must rename txtPolicyNumber.)

STEP 2: Run the program. The text boxes should all be empty. Go back to design time.

Code to Run the Parameterized SQL Query

To run the query and create the new rsFindName Recordset, you specify the query name followed by the values for the parameters:

```
deAdvancedVision.FindName strFirstName, strLastName
```

To run the query, the Recordset must be closed, so you will need this code:

```
With deAdvancedVision
    If .rsFindName.State = adStateOpen Then
        .rsFindName.Close
    End If
End With
```

After the query runs, you must assign the values of the fields to the controls on the form. First check the RecordCount property to determine whether you have a match. Then assign the values, appending an empty string to each field in case any has a null value.

```
With deAdvancedVision.rsFindName
    If .RecordCount > 0 Then
        txtPatientNumber.Text = ![Patient Number] & ""
        txtLastName.Text = ![Last Name] & ""
        txtFirstName.Text = ![First Name] & ""
        txtPolicyNumber.Text = ![Policy #] & ""
    Else
        MsgBox "Record not found", vbInformation, "Search for Name"
    End If
End With
```

The Project Code

This example concatenates the First Name and Last Name fields from the Patient table and loads them into the combo box during the Form_Load. After the user clicks on a name in the list, the function calls two procedures (GetFirstName and GetLastName), using string functions to separate the first and last names.

```
'Program Name: Advanced Vision and Beyond Database
'Programmer:   Bradley/Millspaugh
'Date:         2/2000
'Purpose:      Display patient information using SQL queries
'              and unbound controls.
'Folder:       Ch04SQLSearch

Option Explicit
```

```
Private Sub cboName_Click()
    'Display  Record from list as current record
    Dim strLastName    As String
    Dim strFirstName   As String

    strLastName = GetLastName 'Call function to read characters before ,
    strFirstName = GetFirstName
    With deAdvancedVision
        If .rsFindName.State = adStateOpen Then
            .rsFindName.Close
        End If
        .FindName strFirstName, strLastName
        ReadData
    End With
End Sub
```

```
Private Sub Form_Load()
    'Fill the Patient list
    Dim strName As String

    With deAdvancedVision.rsPatient
        If .State = adStateClosed Then     'Recordset not opened
            .Open                          ' then open it.
        End If
        Do Until .EOF                      'Fill the list
            If ![Last Name] <> "" Then
                strName = ![Last Name] & ", " & ![First Name]
                cboName.AddItem strName
            End If
            .MoveNext
        Loop
        .MoveFirst
    End With
End Sub
```

```
Private Sub mnuFileExit_Click()
    'Exit the project

    Unload Me
End Sub
```

```
Private Function GetLastName()
    'Get last name from cboName
    Dim intCommaPosition    As Integer

    'Find the comma
    intCommaPosition = InStr(1, cboName, ",")
    'Take left characters up to comma
    GetLastName = Left(cboName, intCommaPosition - 1)
End Function
```

```
Private Function GetFirstName()
    'Get first name from cboName
    Dim intLength           As Integer
    Dim intCommaPosition    As Integer

    'Find the comma
    intCommaPosition = InStr(1, cboName, ",")
    'Length of first name is length of full name - up to comma plus one for space
    intLength = Len(cboName) - (intCommaPosition + 1)
    'First name is to the right of the comma
    GetFirstName = Right(cboName, intLength)
End Function
```

```
Public Sub ReadData()
    'If a record is found display data

    With deAdvancedVision.rsFindName
        If .RecordCount > 0 Then
            txtPatientNumber.Text = ![Patient Number] & ""
            txtLastName.Text = ![Last Name] & ""
            txtFirstName.Text = ![First Name] & ""
            txtPolicyNumber.Text = ![Policy #] & ""
        Else
            MsgBox "Record not found", vbInformation, "Search for Name"
        End If
    End With
End Sub
```

Multiple Tables

Although this example used only one table for each query, you can drag multiple tables to the Query Builder. If fields from two tables have the same name, a hierarchical relationship is created automatically. If you drag the Patient and Visit tables, Query Builder relates the two tables on Patient Number (Figure 4.9).

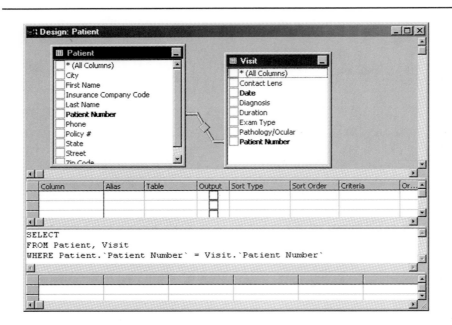

F i g u r e   4 . 9

The Query Builder automatically joins the two tables when the field names match.

You can also create a link between two tables yourself. Try dragging the Patient table and the InsuranceCompany table to the Query Builder Design window. No link appears because no two fields have the same name. Drag and drop the Insurance Company Code field from the Patient table to the Code field on the InsuranceCompany table. Now there is a relationship. Setting the relationship allows you to display the patient information along with the name of the Insurance Company from the Insurance table. If you check Last Name and First Name to print along with the Name field from the InsuranceCompany table, the Query Builder will create the following SQL statement:

```
SELECT Patient.`Last Name`, Patient.`First Name`,
   InsuranceCompany.Name
FROM Patient, InsuranceCompany
WHERE Patient.`Insurance Company Code` = InsuranceCompany.Code
```

Occasionally tables are automatically linked when they shouldn't be. They may have fields with the same name that are not really related. For example, you may have a Salesman table with a field called Name and a Vendor table with a field called Name. The two Name fields are not related to each other. To remove a relationship, select the line for the link and then press the Delete key.

Feedback 4.6

1. Use Query Builder and AVB.mdb to create an SQL statement containing the Patient Last Name, First Name, Patient Number, and Phone Number.
2. Use Query Builder to create an SQL statement to create a Recordset containing the Patient Last Name, First Name, Patient Number, Insurance Company, and Phone Number. Do not display the Insurance Code from the Patient table; use the Insurance Company Name from the Insurance table.

Your Hands-on Programming Example

This project for Advanced Vision and Beyond must update the Patient table as well as find, select, and sort the records.

For the updates allow the user to add new records, delete records, and modify existing records. Do not permit a change to a Patient Number (the key field) on an existing record. For an Add the user must be allowed only the options to Save or Cancel. Make sure to disable all other buttons and menu options that could change the current record.

Display the insurance company names in a dropdown combo box so that the user can select a company from the list or type in a new value.

Include these menu options:

File	Find	Select	Sort
Exit	Last Name	By Last Name	By Patient Number
	First Name	By First Name	By Patient Name
		All Patients	

For the Find option, use an InputBox and allow the user to enter a name (or partial name). Use a Find method with a wildcard to allow for the partial names.

For the Select option, also use an InputBox that allows the user to enter a (partial) name. Use a filter and make sure to include a check mark next to the currently selected menu option.

For the Sort option, use the Sort method. Make the currently selected option appear checked. When the program begins, make the current sort order by Patient Number.

Include a status bar at the bottom of the form. Show the record number ("Record n of nn") at the left end and the date and time at the right.

Make sure to include error handling in all procedures that access the database.

Note: This project is a continuation of the hands-on programming example in Chapter 3.

Planning the Project

Plan the Interface

Sketch the form (Figure 4.10), which your users sign off as meeting their needs.

A sketch of the form for the Advanced Vision and Beyond patient update project.

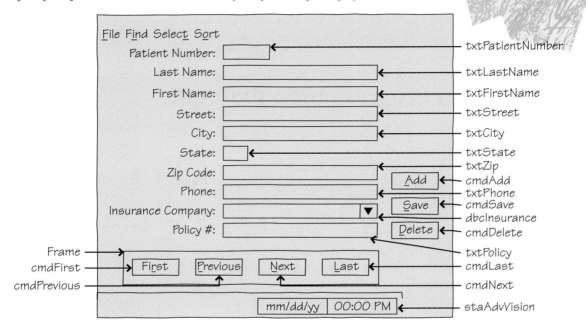

Plan the Objects and Properties

Plan the Data Environment.

Object	Property	Setting
Data Environment	Name	deAdvancedVision
Connection	Name	conAVB
	ConnectionString	Set up for AVB.mdb on your system
	Access Permissions	ShareDenyNone
Command	Name	Patient
	Source of Data	Patient table
Command	Name	Insurance
	Source of Data	InsuranceCompany table

Plan the property settings for the form and for each control.

Object	Property	Setting
frmAdvVision	Caption	Advanced Vision and Beyond Patient Information
	Icon	Eye.ico
	StartupPosition	2 - CenterScreen
Data-bound text boxes	Name, DataSource, DataMember, DataField	Use default properties that occur when you drag a field or Command to the form from the Data Environment.
	Locked	True
txtZip	DataFormat	Custom - #####-####
mskPhone	DataFormat	Custom - (###) ###-####
	Mask	(###) ###-####
	DataSource	deAdvancedVision
	DataMember	Patient
	DataField	Phone
	PromptInclude	False
	ClipMode	1 - mskExcludeLiterals
Field labels	Name, Caption	Use default properties as set up by the Data Environment.
dbcInsurance	DataSource	deAdvancedVision
	DataMember	Patient
	DataField	Insurance Company Code
	RowSource	deAdvancedVision
	RowMember	Insurance
	ListField	Name
	BoundColumn	Code
fraNavigation	Caption	(blank)
cmdFirst	Caption	Fi&rst
cmdPrevious	Caption	&Previous
cmdNext	Caption	&Next
	Default	True
cmdLast	Caption	&Last
staAdvVision	Panels	3
Panel(1)	MinimumWidth	2880
	AutoSize	2 - Contents

continued

Object	Property	Setting
Panel(2)	Style	6 - sbrDate
	AutoSize	2 - Contents
Panel(3)	Style	5 - sbrTime
	AutoSize	2 - Contents
mnuFile	Caption	&File
mnuFileExit	Caption	E&xit
mnuFind	Caption	F&ind
mnuFindLastName	Caption	&Last Name
mnuFileFirstName	Caption	&First Name
mnuSelect	Caption	Selec&t
mnuSelectLastName	Caption	By &Last Name
mnuSelectFirstName	Caption	By &First Name
mnuSelectAll	Caption	&All Records
	Checked	True
mnuSort	Caption	S&ort
mnuSortPatientNumber	Caption	By &Patient Number
mnuSortPatientName	Caption	By Patient &Name

Plan the Event Procedures

Determine which events will need code and plan the code for each.

frmAdvVision

Procedure	Actions
cmdFirst_Click	Move to first record.

cmdPrevious_Click	Move to previous record.
	If BOF Then
	   Move to first record.
	End If

cmdNext_Click	Move to next record.
	If EOF Then
	   Move to last record.
	End If

cmdLast_Click	Move to last record.
cmdAdd_Click	If button Caption is "Add" Then AddNew method. Disable all controls for movement. Change button Caption to "Cancel". Enable Save button.

continued

Procedure	Actions

	Unlock txtPatientNumber.
	Else (button is "Cancel")
	  CancelUpdate method.
	  Lock txtPatientNumber.
	  Enable all controls for movement.
	  Disable Save button.
	  Change button Caption to "Add".
	  Move to the last record.
	End If

cmdDelete_Click	Delete the current record.
	Move to the next record.
	If EOF Then
	  Move to the previous record.
	  If BOF Then (Recordset is empty)
	    Display message.
	    Disable all movement controls.
	  End If
	End If

cmdSave_Click	Update method. Lock txtPatientNumber. Enable all controls for movement. Disable the Save button. Change the Caption of Add button to "Add".
Form_Activate	Sort in Patient Number sequence. Check the menu option.
mnuFileExit_Click	Unload the form.

mnuFindFirstName_Click	Input requested first name.
	Save a bookmark.
	Find the record.
	If EOF Then (No match found)
	  Display message.
	  Return to bookmarked record.
	End If

mnuFindLastName_Click	Input requested last name.
	Save a bookmark.
	Find the record.
	If EOF Then (No match found)
	  Display message.
	  Return to bookmarked record.
	End If

mnuSelectFirstName	Input requested first name.
	Set the filter.
	If EOF Then (No records in the Recordset)
	  Remove the filter.
	Else
	  Check the menu option and uncheck others.
	End If

mnuSelectLastName	Input requested last name. Set the filter.

continued

4

Procedure	Actions

	If EOF Then (No records in the Recordset)
	    Remove the filter.
	Else
	    Check the menu option and uncheck others.
	End If

mnuSelectAll	Remove the filter. Check the menu option and uncheck others.
mnuSortPatientName	Sort by Last Name, First Name. Check the menu option and uncheck others.
mnuSortPatientNumber	Sort by Patient Number. Check the menu option and uncheck others.

txtPatientNumber_Validate	If not numeric Then
	    Display an error message.
	    Select the text.
	    Cancel the procedure.
	End If

DisableControls	Disable navigation buttons. Disable Find, Select, and Sort menus.
EnableControls	Enable navigation buttons. Enable Find, Select, and Sort menus.
SetUpAdd	Lock txtPatientNumber. Enable Save button. Change Caption of Add button to "Cancel".

deAdvancedVision

Procedure	Actions
deAdvancedVision_Initialize	Set up ConnectionString to include App.Path.

rsPatient_MoveComplete	If not BOF or EOF Then
	    Set StatusBar text to record number.
	End If

Write the Project

Follow the sketch in Figure 4.10 to create the user interface. Figure 4.11 shows the completed form.

- Add the Data Environment Designer and set up the Connection to AVB.mdb. Add two Commands—one for the Patient table and one for the InsuranceCompany table.

- Set the properties of the form and each of the controls, as you have planned.

- Working from the pseudocode, write each event procedure.

- When you complete the code, thoroughly test the project.

Figure 4.11

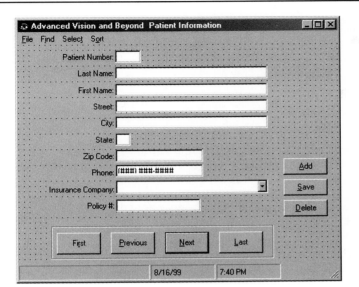

*The form for the Advanced Vision
and Beyond patient update
project.*

The Project Solution

The Form Module

```
'Project:       Chapter 04 Advanced Vision and Beyond
'                 Chapter Hands-On Example
'Module:        frmAdvVision
'Date:          2/2000
'Programmer:    Bradley/Millspaugh
'Description:   Display and update the Advanced Vision Patient table.
'                 Includes finding, sorting, and filtering.
'Folder:        Ch04AdvancedVision
```

```
Option Explicit
```

```
Private Sub cmdAdd_Click()
    'Add a new record

    On Error GoTo HandleError
    If cmdAdd.Caption = "&Add" Then
        deAdvancedVision.rsPatient.AddNew     'Clear out fields for new record
        DisableControls                       'Disable navigation
        SetUpAdd
    Else
        deAdvancedVision.rsPatient.CancelUpdate 'Cancel the Add
        txtPatientNumber.Locked = True
        EnableControls                        'Enable navigation
        cmdSave.Enabled = False               'Disable the Save button
        cmdAdd.Caption = "&Add"               'Reset the Add button
        deAdvancedVision.rsPatient.MoveLast
    End If

cmdAdd_Click_Exit:
    Exit Sub
```

```
HandleError:
    MsgBox "Unable to carry out requested action.", _
            vbInformation, "Advanced Vision"
    On Error GoTo 0
End Sub
```

```
Private Sub cmdDelete_Click()
    'Delete the current record

    On Error GoTo HandleError
    With deAdvancedVision.rsPatient
        .Delete                             'Delete the current record
        .MoveNext                           'Move to the following record
        If .EOF Then                        'If last record deleted
            .MovePrevious
            If .BOF Then            'If BOF and EOF true, no records remain
                MsgBox "The recordset is empty.", vbInformation, _
                        "No records"
                DisableControls
            End If
        End If
    End With

cmdDelete_Click_Exit:
    Exit Sub

HandleError:
    MsgBox "Unable to carry out requested action.", _
            vbInformation, "Advanced Vision"
    On Error GoTo 0
End Sub
```

```
Private Sub cmdSave_Click()
    'Save the current record

    On Error GoTo HandleErrors
    deAdvancedVision.rsPatient.Update
    txtPatientNumber.Locked = True          'Reset all
    EnableControls
    cmdSave.Enabled = False
    cmdAdd.Caption = "&Add"

cmdSave_Click_Exit:
    Exit Sub

HandleErrors:
    Dim strMessage As String
    Dim errDBError As ADODB.Error

    For Each errDBError In deAdvancedVision.conAVB.Errors
        strMessage = strMessage & errDBError.Description & vbCrLf
    Next
    MsgBox strMessage, vbExclamation, "Duplicate Add"
    On Error GoTo 0                         'Turn off error trapping
End Sub
```

```
Private Sub Form_Activate()
    'Establish sort order
```

```
    On Error GoTo HandleError
    deAdvancedVision.rsPatient.Sort = "[Patient Number]"
    mnuSortPatientNumber.Checked = True

cmdFind_Click_Exit:
    Exit Sub

HandleError:
    MsgBox "Unable to carry out requested action.", _
            vbInformation, "Advanced Vision"
    On Error GoTo 0
End Sub
```

```
Private Sub mnuFileExit_Click()
    'End the project

    Unload Me
End Sub
```

```
Private Sub cmdFirst_Click()
    'Move to the first record

    On Error Resume Next
    deAdvancedVision.rsPatient.MoveFirst
End Sub
```

```
Private Sub cmdLast_Click()
    'Move to the last record

    On Error Resume Next
    deAdvancedVision.rsPatient.MoveLast
End Sub
```

```
Private Sub cmdNext_Click()
    'Move to the next record

    On Error Resume Next
    With deAdvancedVision.rsPatient
        .MoveNext
        If .EOF Then
            .MoveLast
        End If
    End With
End Sub
```

```
Private Sub cmdPrevious_Click()
    'Move to the previous record

    On Error Resume Next
    With deAdvancedVision.rsPatient
        .MovePrevious
        If .BOF Then
            .MoveFirst
        End If
    End With
End Sub
```

```
Private Sub mnuFindFirst_Click()
    'Find by first name
    Dim strName      As String
    Dim vntBookmark As Variant

    On Error GoTo HandleError
    strName = InputBox("Enter the First Name that you want to find." _
            & vbCrLf & "Partial name OK", "Find by First Name")
    With deAdvancedVision.rsPatient
        vntBookmark = .Bookmark
        .Find "[First Name] Like '" & strName & "*'"
        If .EOF Then
            MsgBox "No records match '" & strName & "'", _
                    vbInformation, "Find by First Name"
            .Bookmark = vntBookmark
        End If
    End With

mnuFindFirst_Click_Exit:
    Exit Sub

HandleError:
    MsgBox "Unable to carry out requested operation.", _
            vbInformation, "Advanced Vision"
    On Error GoTo 0
End Sub

Private Sub mnuFindLastName_Click()
    'Find by last name
    Dim strName      As String
    Dim vntBookmark As Variant

    On Error GoTo HandleError
    strName = InputBox("Enter the Last Name that you want to find." _
            & vbCrLf & "Partial name OK", "Find by Last Name")
    With deAdvancedVision.rsPatient
        vntBookmark = .Bookmark
        .Find "[Last Name] Like '" & strName & "*'"
        If .EOF Then
            MsgBox "No records match '" & strName & "'", _
                    vbInformation, "Find by Last Name"
            .Bookmark = vntBookmark
        End If
    End With

mnuFindLast_Click_Exit:
    Exit Sub

HandleError:
    MsgBox "Unable to carry out requested operation.", _
            vbInformation, "Advanced Vision"
    On Error GoTo 0
End Sub

Private Sub mnuSelectAll_Click()
    'Select all records

    On Error Resume Next
    deAdvancedVision.rsPatient.Filter = ""
    mnuSelectFirstName.Checked = False
    mnuSelectLastName.Checked = False
    mnuSelectAll.Checked = True
End Sub
```

```
Private Sub mnuSelectFirstName_Click()
    'Select by first name
    Dim strName      As String

    On Error GoTo HandleError
    strName = InputBox("Enter the First Name that you want to select." _
            & vbCrLf & "Partial name OK", "Select by First Name")
    With deAdvancedVision.rsPatient
        .Filter = "[First Name] Like '" & strName & "*'"
        If .EOF Then
            MsgBox "No records match '" & strName & "'", _
                    vbInformation, "Select by First Name"
            .Filter = ""
        Else
            mnuSelectFirstName.Checked = True
            mnuSelectLastName.Checked = False
            mnuSelectAll.Checked = False
        End If
    End With

mnuSelectFirstName_Click_Exit:
    Exit Sub

HandleError:
    MsgBox "Unable to carry out requested operation.", _
            vbInformation, "Advanced Vision"
    On Error GoTo 0
End Sub
```

```
Private Sub mnuSelectLastName_Click()
    'Select by last name
    Dim strName      As String

    On Error GoTo HandleError
    strName = InputBox("Enter the Last Name that you want to select." _
            & vbCrLf & "Partial name OK", "Select by Last Name")
    With deAdvancedVision.rsPatient
        .Filter = "[Last Name] Like '" & strName & "*'"
        If .EOF Then
            MsgBox "No records match '" & strName & "'", _
                    vbInformation, "Select by Last Name"
            .Filter = ""
        Else
            mnuSelectFirstName.Checked = False
            mnuSelectLastName.Checked = True
            mnuSelectAll.Checked = False
        End If
    End With

mnuSelectLastName_Click_Exit:
    Exit Sub

HandleError:
    MsgBox "Unable to carry out requested operation.", _
            vbInformation, "Advanced Vision"
    On Error GoTo 0
End Sub
```

```
Private Sub mnuSortPatientName_Click()
    'Sort by Patient Name

    On Error GoTo HandleError
    deAdvancedVision.rsPatient.Sort = "[Last Name], [First Name]"
    mnuSortPatientName.Checked = True
    mnuSortPatientNumber.Checked = False

mnuSortPatientName_Click_Exit:
    Exit Sub

HandleError:
    MsgBox "Unable to carry out requested operation.", _
            vbInformation, "Advanced Vision"
    On Error GoTo 0
End Sub


Private Sub mnuSortPatientNumber_Click()
    'Sort by Patient Number

    On Error GoTo HandleError
    deAdvancedVision.rsPatient.Sort = "[Patient Number]"
    mnuSortPatientNumber.Checked = True
    mnuSortPatientName.Checked = False

mnuSortPatientNumber_Click_Exit:
    Exit Sub

HandleError:
    MsgBox "Unable to carry out requested operation.", _
            vbInformation, "Advanced Vision"
    On Error GoTo 0
End Sub


Private Sub txtPatientNumber_Validate(Cancel As Boolean)
    'Validate the PatientNumber for an Add
    '  Note: The control is locked unless an Add is in progress.
    Dim strMessage As String

    If Not IsNumeric(txtPatientNumber.Text) Then    'Must be numeric
            strMessage = "Invalid PatientNumber"
        MsgBox strMessage, vbExclamation, "Data Entry Error"
        With txtPatientNumber
            .Text = "000"                     'Eliminate any alpha characters
            .SelStart = 0                     'Select the current entry
            .SelLength = Len(.Text)
        End With
        Cancel = True                         'Keep the focus
    End If
End Sub


Private Sub DisableControls()
    'Disable navigation buttons

    cmdNext.Enabled = False
    cmdPrevious.Enabled = False
    cmdFirst.Enabled = False
    cmdLast.Enabled = False
    cmdDelete.Enabled = False
    mnuFind.Enabled = False
    mnuSelect.Enabled = False
    mnuSort.Enabled = False
End Sub
```

```
Private Sub EnableControls()
    'Enable navigation buttons

    cmdNext.Enabled = True
    cmdPrevious.Enabled = True
    cmdFirst.Enabled = True
    cmdLast.Enabled = True
    cmdDelete.Enabled = True
    mnuFind.Enabled = True
    mnuSelect.Enabled = True
    mnuSort.Enabled = True
End Sub
```

```
Private Sub SetUpAdd()
    'Set up controls for the Add

    With txtPatientNumber
        .Locked = False
        .SetFocus
    End With
    cmdSave.Enabled = True                      'Enable the Save button
    cmdAdd.Caption = "&Cancel"                  'Allow a Cancel option
End Sub
```

Data Environment Code

```
'Project:        Chapter 04 Advanced Vision and Beyond
'                   Chapter Hands-On Example
'Module:         deAdvancedVision
'Date:           2/2000
'Programmer:     Bradley/Millspaugh
'Description:    Display and update the Advanced Vision Patient table.
'                   Includes finding, sorting, and filtering.
'Folder:         Ch04AdvancedVision

Option Explicit
```

```
Private Sub DataEnvironment_Initialize()
    'Make the data file moveable

    conAVB.ConnectionString = "Provider=Microsoft.Jet.OLEDB.3.51;" & _
        "Persist Security Info=False;Data Source=" & App.Path & _
        "\AVB.mdb"
End Sub
```

```
Private Sub rsPatient_MoveComplete( _
    ByVal adReason As ADODB.EventReasonEnum, _
    ByVal pError As ADODB.Error, _
    adStatus As ADODB.EventStatusEnum, _
    ByVal pRecordset As ADODB.Recordset)
    'Display the record count

    On Error Resume Next
    With rsPatient
        frmAdvVision.staAdvVision.Panels(1).Text = "Record " & _
            .AbsolutePosition & " of " & .RecordCount
    End With
End Sub
```

MCSD Exam Notes

Exam Objectives Covered in This Chapter

Creating User Services

Write code that validates user input.

- Create an application that verifies data entered at the field level and the form level by a user.

- Create an application that enables or disables controls based on input in fields.

Creating Data Services

- Access and manipulate a data source by using ADO and the ADO data control.

Questions/Tricks to Watch for

- Know the various options for error trapping in the *Options* dialog box and know what each option does.

- Don't spend any time memorizing trappable error codes. For the exam you should know how to trap and handle errors and be familiar with the properties and methods of the Err object.

- The AddNew method has optional parameters to supply values for the new record.

Summary

1. A cursor refers to a Recordset, the resources needed to manage that Recordset, and a pointer to the current record. A cursor can be managed by the system containing the application (client) or the system containing the database (server). With a desktop application the client and server are the same machine.

2. The cursor type determines whether a Recordset is static, dynamic, or keyset driven. A forward-only cursor does not allow scrolling and provides the fastest access.

3. The locking provided by the cursor can be set to Read Only. For multiuser databases the locking strategy is important.

4. Updating a database includes adding records, deleting records, and making changes to existing records.

5. Bound controls provide automatic updating. You can use the Update method to explicitly save changes.

6. Add records by using the AddNew method, which clears the bound controls and allows the user to enter data. Then use the Update method to save the new record.

7. Use the Delete method to delete a record. You must move off the deleted record, since the current record is no longer valid.

8. A MaskedEdit control can provide a template for user input, supplying editing characters.

9. Adding and deleting records can cause a variety of errors. The programmer should take steps to avoid having the application abort for the user. This goal can be accomplished by limiting the actions that users can take, such as locking controls, limiting the length of user input, disabling commands, and trapping errors.

10. A good place to verify the reasonableness or accuracy of user input is the Validate event procedure.

11. The WillChangeRecord event of a Command object can be used for form-level validation.

12. The Find method is used to locate a specific record with a search string. This method works for both the data control and the Data Environment.

13. An EOF indicates that no records were found with the Find method search.

14. The Recordset's current record position can be saved by setting a variable to the Bookmark property. Setting the Recordset's Bookmark property to a saved bookmark makes that the current record.

15. Unbound controls give a programmer more flexibility but require the program to handle filling screen controls and explicitly saving changes in the database.

16. A Recordset contains a Sort property for temporarily reordering the records and a Filter property for selecting records using criteria. Filtering the Recordset creates a new temporary Recordset. An Optimize property set to True for a field actually creates the index on the client side.

17. Structured Query Language (SQL) can be used with VB to maintain or query a database. The Query Builder can help you build a query.

Key Terms

R e v i e w   Q u e s t i o n s

1. What cursor property should you set to make a Recordset forward only? scrollable?
2. What is meant by *cursor location*? What are the choices and the advantages of each choice?
3. List the steps needed to add a new record to a database.
4. List the steps needed to delete a record from a database.
5. How can you check for the user deleting the only record in a Recordset?
6. Why would it be desirable to use text boxes for an update form and then lock them?
7. Give an example for a Validate event for a Quantity field.
8. What statement(s) can you place in a text box Validate event procedure to prevent the user from exiting the control?
9. Write the statement(s) to instruct VB to ignore any error and just keep processing.
10. Write the statement(s) to check for an empty string in txtName (a data-bound control) in the txtName_Validate event procedure. If no data exist, display a message box.
11. Write an error-handling routine that executes a Resume Next for error numbers 3022, 3058, and 3109. For all other errors, display a message and exit the program.
12. What types of errors are not caused by VB statements and do not appear in the list of error codes?
13. Explain what will display for this statement:

```
MsgBox "Error " & Err.Number & ": " & Err.Description
```

14. What is a Bookmark? When would be an appropriate time to use a Bookmark?
15. Write the code necessary to assign the value of a field called *Employee Name* to txtEmployeeName. The field comes from a Recordset called rsEmployee, based on deEmployee.
16. When would it be preferable to use unbound controls rather than bound controls?
17. Write the code to sort the Recordset described in question 15. Use the Sort property and sort by the Employee Name field.
18. Give the search string to locate a record that contains less than 5 in a field called Count.
19. Explain the difference between the Find method and the Filter property. When is each appropriate?
20. How is SQL used in a Data Environment?

P r o g r a m m i n g   E x e r c i s e s

4.1   Create a project to update the InsuranceCompany table in AVB.mdb using a Data Environment. The project must contain buttons for Next,

Last, Previous, and First. The update features will include Add and Delete, as well as changing current records. Do not allow the user to change the Code field (the key field). During an Add, the only options available should be Save and Cancel.

Make sure to trap all possible program errors.

4.2   Modify project 4.1 to include validation. Make sure that the Code field is alphabetic and that the Name field is present.

4.3   Modify project 4.1 or 4.2 to include Find, Filter, and Sort.

4.4   Create a project that displays fields from the Patient table in a grid and allows the user to filter and sort the Recordset. Display only the Patient Number, Last Name, First Name, City, and Phone fields. Give the user the choice of filtering by Last Name (or partial name), filtering by City, or displaying all records. Allow the user the option of sorting by Last Name, by City, or by Phone. For both the Filter and Sort options, make the menu command of the currently selected option appear checked.

Make sure to trap all possible program errors.

4.5   Write a project that contains the Patient Number, Address, and Phone Number for patients in text boxes. Allow the user to select the specific patient, using Last Name and First Name.

Make sure to trap all possible program errors.

4.6   Write a project to update the Publishers table from the Biblio.mdb database that comes on the VB CD. (Biblio.mdb is not installed automatically on your computer but is on the VB CD.) Use a Data Environment and include command buttons for record navigation. The update features must include Add and Delete, as well as changing records. Do not allow the user to change the PubID field (the key field). During an Add, the only options available should be Save and Cancel.

Make sure to trap all possible program errors.

Note: The Biblio.mdb database included with VB 4 was 288 KB, small enough to easily fit on a diskette. The version included with VB 5 and VB 6 is 3.5 MB—too large for a diskette. The older version is included on the CD that accompanies this text. The two versions of the file have the same structure; the size difference is due to the large number of records added to the newer version.

4.7   Modify project 4.6 to include validation. Make sure that the PubID is numeric and that the Name field is present.

4.8   Modify project 4.6 or 4.7 to include Find, Filter, and Sort.

4.9   Write a project based on the Biblio.mdb database that allows a user to select a publisher's Company Name from a dropdown list and then fills in the rest of the information about the publisher in unbound controls. See the note about the Biblio.mdb database in project 4.6.

Make sure to trap all possible program errors.

4.10   Write a project based on the Biblio.mdb database that uses an SQL statement for the data source. Select only the PubID, Company Name, and Telephone fields for the Recordset.

Make sure to trap all possible program errors.

CASE STUDIES

Video Bonanza

Modify your project from Chapter 3 to use a Data Environment and allow updates. The user must be able to Add and Delete, as well as Modify, records. Validate to make sure that the Movie Number is numeric and that the Title is present. Do not allow the user to change the Movie Number field (the key field). During an Add, the only options should be Save and Cancel.

Allow the user to sort the movies by Title, by Studio, or by Category. Optionally, allow the user to filter by Studio, Category, or all records.

Make sure to handle all possible program errors.

VB Auto Center

Modify your VB Auto Center project from Chapter 3 to use a Data Environment and allow updates, including Add, Delete, and Modify records. Validate to make sure the Customer Number is numeric and that the Customer Name is present. Do not allow the user to change the key field. During an Add, the only options should be Save and Cancel.

Allow the user to find a specific customer by name (or partial name). Optionally, allow the user to sort by Customer Number, Customer Name, or Manufacturer.

Make sure to handle all possible program errors.

5

Using the ADO Programming Object Model

At the completion of this chapter, you will be able to . . .

1. Know the objects and collections in the ADO programming object model.

2. Create Connections, Commands, and Recordsets in code.

3. Recognize ADO events and their purposes.

4. Query the database asynchronously using ADO.

5. Understand the concept of a transaction.

6. Write SQL Select statements for querying a database.

7. Write and execute SQL statements that directly update a database.

8. Use the Data Form Wizard to create a form or program template.

9. Recognize the Shape command as a language for creating hierarchical Recordsets.

The ADO Hierarchy

In Chapters 3 and 4 you learned to display and update data using ActiveX Data Objects (ADO), using both a data control and a Data Environment. You can also use the ADO programming object model to create Connections and Recordsets directly in code. You will find that most professional VB database applications use ADO code except in "quick and simple" projects.

To program with the ADO object model, you must first add a reference to the library in your project. Choose *Project/References* and select *Microsoft ActiveX Data Objects 2.1 Library* (or the most current version). There are two ADO libraries: ADODB and ADOR. The one you want, **ADODB,** is called *Microsoft ActiveX Data Objects 2.1 Library* (MSADO15.DLL). The **ADOR** library is smaller and limited to Recordset objects; it is intended for browsers. To select ADOR, choose *Microsoft ActiveX Data Objects Recordset 2.0 Library* (MSADOR15.DLL). (If you plan to take the MCSD exam, you need to remember the DLL names.)

ADO Objects

The **programming object model** consists of objects and collections (Figure 5.1), which you can see by using the Object Browser (Figure 5.2). You are familiar with most of them: Connection object, Command object, Recordset object, Error object, Parameter object, Field object, and Property object. The Connection, Command, Recordset, and Field objects each has a Properties collection. Tables 5.1 and 5.2 show the ADO objects and collections.

The Connection Object

You are familiar with an ADO Connection from the Data Environment. The **Connection object** defines the provider and database name, as well as additional properties such as the allowable user access. You can create a Connection object in code.

Each Connection object has an **Errors collection,** which you learned about in Chapter 4. The collection holds all errors for a single operation.

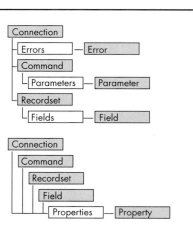

The ADO programming object model.

Figure 5.2

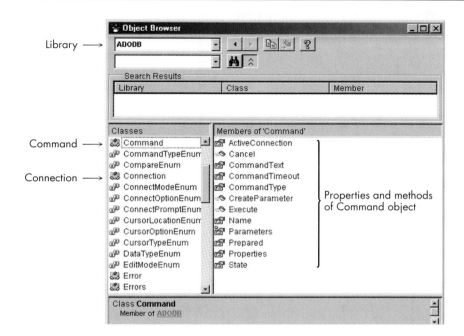

Table 5.1

Object	Purpose	Example
Connection	Connect to data provider	conAVB
Command	Contains an SQL statement	SELECT...
Recordset*	Current set of fields and records	rsPatient
Error	Individual error number and description	Err.Number
Parameter	Variable for SQL	[Last Name] = ?
Field*	Single column from a table	[Last Name]
Property*	Built-in or dynamic (from provider) properties.	Properties("Optimize")

ADODB Objects

*Objects available in ADOR.

The Error Object

An **Error object** is generated by each error returned from the provider. The error may relate to a connection problem, to a method being used on a closed connection, or to a problem with the Recordset such as a duplicate or missing key.

The Command Object

A **Command object** can be used to define a Recordset or perform actions on the database. A Command is based on an SQL statement, a table, or a stored procedure. With the correct SQL statement, a Command can also directly update a table. Using this technique, you write Commands that directly insert a new record, delete a record, or update a record in the database, rather than

Collection	Contains Objects of Type	Associated with
Errors	Error	A programming statement.
Parameters	Parameter	A Command object.
Fields	Field	A Recordset.
Properties	Property	A Connection, Command, Recordset, or Field.

use Recordset methods. You will see examples of this later in this chapter in the section on executing action queries.

Each Command object has a **Parameters collection** to hold Parameter objects.

The Parameter Object

A parameter supplies needed information to a Command. Recall the parameterized query in Chapter 4, where the user could enter the name desired, which was then supplied to the query as a variable. If you want to supply variable data to a Command, you will use a **Parameter object.**

The Recordset Object

The **Recordset object** is a temporary set of data that is kept in local storage. You can write code for a Recordset using the properties, events, and methods that you learned in Chapters 3 and 4.

Each Recordset must be based on a Connection. However, you don't need to create a Command to create a Recordset. Looking at the ADO object model in Figure 5.1, Recordset objects and Command objects are at the same level—both are subordinate to a Connection. You will see examples later in this chapter of creating Recordset objects with and without a Command object.

A Recordset has a Fields collection and a Properties collection.

The Field Object

Each row in a Recordset contains one or more columns of data. A column is referred to as a *Field object,* and the group of Field objects is called the *Fields collection.* Each Field has its own name, data type, and value.

The Property Object

The **Property object** represents the characteristics, descriptions, or behavior for each object in the ADO object model. There are two types of Property objects: built in and dynamic. You can access the built-in Properties of an ADO object at any time, using the *Object.Property* syntax. Dynamic properties are created through the connection to the provider and can be accessed only when the connection is open, using the Properties collection. Different types of databases have different dynamic properties.

The Properties Collection

Connection, Command, Recordset, and Field objects each has a **Properties collection.** The collection has methods for retrieving and returning the values of dynamic properties. For example, in Chapter 4 you accessed the Properties collection of the Recordset object with `rsPatient.Properties("Optimize")` = `True`.

ADO Events

Think of the events for the ADO objects in two groups—Connection events and Recordset events. The event handlers for each of these groups notify you before an action occurs and after it is complete. Examples are the Recordset's WillMove and MoveComplete event. Tables 5.3 and 5.4 show the ADO events.

Table 5.3

ADO Connection Events

ConnectionEvent	Group
WillConnect	
ConnectComplete	Connection
Disconnect	
WillExecute	
ExecuteComplete	Command Execution
InfoMessage	Information
BeginTransComplete	
CommitTransComplete	Transaction
RollbackTransComplete	

Table 5.4

ADO Recordset Events

RecordsetEvent	Group
FetchProgress	
FetchComplete	Retrieval Status
WillChangeField	
FieldChangeComplete	Field Change
WillMove	
MoveComplete	Navigation
EndOfRecordset	
WillChangeRecord	
RecordChangeComplete	RowChange
WillChangeRecordset	
RecordsetChangeComplete	Recordset Change

The advantage of being notified before an event occurs is that you can test the situation, perform validation, and cancel the operation if needed. You can have your program perform other tasks while database operations are occurring; this processing is referred to as ***asynchronous operations.*** To effectively use asynchronous processing you need to be notified when an action is complete.

An example of an asynchronous operation is a Recordset Open method. While the Recordset is being created, your application can perform other operations, such as initializing fields, displaying forms, or even creating additional Recordsets.

Creating ADO Objects

You create ADO objects by first declaring a variable and then assigning a value to the variable. Declare the object variable by using a `Dim` statement with the appropriate object type in the `As` clause. Precede the object type with the qualifier ADODB (the library name). You assign a value to an object variable by using the `Set` statement.

The Dim Statement for Objects—General Form

```
Dim [WithEvents] Identifier As [New] ObjectType
```

The Dim Statement for Objects—Examples

```
Dim conAVB        As ADODB.Connection
Dim FindName      As ADODB.Command
Dim FindZip       As New ADODB.Command
Dim ContactLens   As ADODB.Recordset
Dim WithEvents rsPatient As Recordset        'ADODB not required
```

The `Dim` statement declares the variable name and the object type but does not actually create an object. An object is created with the **New keyword.** You can use the `New` keyword directly in the `Dim` statement or on the **Set statement.**

Two possible ways to create objects:

```
Dim conAVB As ADODB.Connection         'Usually in the General Declarations
Set conAVB = New ADODB.Connection      'Usually in the Form_Load procedure
```

or

```
Dim conAVB As New ADODB.Connection        'Usually in the General Declarations
```

Of these two approaches, the first is preferred because it gives you control of when and where the object is created. If the `New` keyword is on the `Dim` statement, the object is created sometime in the initialization of the project, but you have no control over the timing.

Normally you will code the `Dims` for the Connection and Recordset or Command objects in the General Declarations section, making the variables module level. Then place the `Set` statements in the appropriate event procedures. The best place to create the Connection and Recordset is often in the Form_Load procedure; the best place to create a Command object might be in the procedure for a menu option or command button that performs some action on the database. You will see examples that open Recordsets in the sections that follow; examples using Command objects appear in the section on SQL later in this chapter.

If you want to be able to respond to events of the Connection or Recordset, you must use the **WithEvents keyword** on the `Dim` statement. This step places your Recordset under the list of objects on your Code window. You can now write code for all defined Recordset events.

Note: You cannot combine the `New` keyword and `WithEvents` on the same `Dim`. Write `WithEvents` on the `Dim` statement and code the `New` keyword on the `Set` statement.

```
Dim WithEvents rsPatient As Recordset      'In General Declarations
Set rsPatient = New Recordset              'In Form_Load procedure

Private Sub rsPatient_MoveComplete(ByVal adReason As ADODB.EventReasonEnum, _
    ByValpError As ADODB.Error, adStatus As ADODB.EventStatusEnum, _
    ByVal pRecordset As ADODB.Recordset)
    'Display the Record Number

    lblCount.Caption = rsPatient.AbsolutePosition
End Sub
```

Opening a Connection

After the objects are declared in the General Declarations section, they can be referred to in any module.

```
Option Explicit
'Create ADODB objects
Dim conAVB As ADODB.Connection
Dim rsPatient As ADODB.Recordset

Private Sub Form_Load()
    'Create the Connection and get the data
    Set conAVB = New ADODB.Connection
    Set rsPatient = New ADODB.Recordset

    conAVB.ConnectionString = "Provider=Microsoft.Jet.OLEDB.3.51;" & _
        "Persist Security Info=False;Data Source=" & App.Path & _
        "\AVB.mdb;Mode = readwrite"
    conAVB.Open                                 'Open the Connection
    With rsPatient
        .CursorLocation = adUseClient
        .CursorType = adOpenDynamic
        .LockType = adLockOptimistic
        .Open "Patient", conAVB, , , adCmdTable 'Open the Recordset
    End With
End Sub
```

Opening a Recordset

You have several choices of how to create a Recordset from a database. Later in this chapter you will see examples of performing an Execute method on a Connection or a Command object. However, the Recordsets created with the Execute method provide less flexibility than those opened with the Recordset's **Open method.**

The Recordset Open Method—General Form

```
Recordset.Open ([Source], [Connection], [CursorType], [LockType], [Options])
```

The Recordset Open Method—Example

```
rsPatient.Open "Patient", conAVB, adOpenDynamic, adLockOptimistic, adCmdTable
```

The source may be a Command object, an SQL statement, or the name of a table or stored procedure. The preceding example uses the name of a table enclosed in quotes. The Connection parameter is the name of an open Connection object or a ConnectionString enclosed in quotes. The Options parameter specifies how the data are to be retrieved from the data source and can be *adCmdTable*, *adCmdText*, or *adCmdUnknown* (the default).

These two techniques are equivalent:

```
rsPatient.Open "Patient", conAVB, adOpenDynamic, adLockOptimistic, adCmdTable
```

or

```
With rsPatient
    .Source = "Patient"
    .ActiveConnection = conAVB
    .CursorType = adOpenDynamic
    .LockType = adLockOptimistic
    .Open
End With
```

The first of the previous two techniques executes slightly faster.

You can also mix and match the two methods:

```
With rsPatient
    .CursorType = adOpenDynamic
    .LockType = adLockOptimistic
    .Open "Patient", conAVB, , , adCmdTable
End With
```

Important note: Although the Data Environment defaulted to CursorLocation = adUseClient, the ADO object model defaults to adUseServer. For Access databases to work correctly, you must also set the CursorLocation to *adUseClient*. Include this line before opening the Recordset:

```
    .CursorLocation = adUseClient
```

Working with Recordsets

After you open a Recordset, your coding can be nearly identical to the code you wrote in Chapter 4. You can use AddNew, Delete, Update, MoveNext, Find, and the rest of the Recordset methods, as well as the properties such as AbsolutePosition, BOF, EOF, Filter, and Sort. If you have specified WithEvents on the Recordset's Dim statement, you can code for events including WillChangeRecord and RecordChangeComplete.

Bound Controls

Using ADO code you can choose to have bound or unbound controls, just as with the Data Environment. To create bound controls, you must set the DataSource and DataField properties of each control. However, you cannot set the DataSource at design time when using a Recordset defined in code. You *can* set the DataField values, but you must bind the controls at run time by using a Set statement for the object property. Call this procedure after opening the Recordset in the Form_Load.

```
Private Sub BindData()
    'Bind the text boxes to the Recordset

    Set txtPatientNumber.DataSource = rsPatient
    Set txtLastName.DataSource = rsPatient
    Set txtFirstName.DataSource = rsPatient
    Set dbcInsurance.DataSource = rsPatient
    Set dbcInsurance.RowSource = rsInsurance
End Sub
```

Unbound Controls

If the controls on your form are not bound to a data source, you can transfer the field values from the Recordset to the text boxes.

```
Private Sub AssignData()
    'Transfer data from the Recordset to the form controls

    With rsPatient
        txtPatientNumber.Text = ![Patient Number]
        txtLastName.Text = ![Last Name]
        txtFirstName.Text = ![First Name]
        cboInsurance.Text = ![Name]
    End With
End Sub
```

Any time you move to a new record, call the AssignData procedure to place the field values on the form:

```
Private Sub cmdLast_Click()
    'Move to last record

    On Error Resume Next
    rsPatient.MoveLast
    AssignData
End Sub
```

Tip

Do not set a control's RowMember and DataMember properties at design time. Check to make sure that these values are deleted when converting from a project using Data Environments to one using the object model.

```
Private Sub cmdNext_Click()
    'Move to next record

    On Error Resume Next
    With rsPatient
        .MoveNext
        If .EOF Then
            .MoveFirst
        End If
        AssignData
    End With
End Sub
```

When you are using unbound controls, the AddNew method begins a new record but does *not* automatically clear the text boxes. You must clear the fields yourself.

```
Private Sub ClearTextFields()
    'Clear fields for add

    With txtPatientNumber
        .Text = ""
        .SetFocus
    End With
    txtLastName.Text = ""
    txtFirstName.Text = ""
    cboInsurance.Text = ""
End Sub
```

Tip

Use a regular combo box rather than a DBcombo box when using unbound controls.

Limiting User Actions

In the update project in Chapter 4, we placed some of the error-checking routines in the Data Environment code. If you include WithEvents on your Dim statement, you can place the error-checking code in the Recordset WillChangeRecord event procedure.

```
Private Sub rsPatient_WillChangeRecord(ByVal adReason _
    As ADODB.EventReasonEnum, ByVal cRecords As Long, adStatus _
    As ADODB.EventStatusEnum, ByVal pRecordset As ADODB.Recordset)
    'Limit user actions during updates

    Select Case adReason
        Case adRsnAddNew
            With txtPatientNumber
                .Locked = False
                .SetFocus
            End With
            cmdSave.Enabled = True
            cmdAdd.Caption = "&Cancel"
            DisableButtons                      'Disable navigation
    End Select
End Sub
```

The Find Method

The Recordset Find method, along with the Sort and Filter properties, is valid when using the object model.

```
strSearch = "[Last Name] = '" & txtLastNameFind & "'"
With rsPatient
    .MoveFirst  'Start at beginning of Recordset
    .Find strSearch
    If .EOF Then
        MsgBox "Record Not Found", vbExclamation, "Search"
        .MoveFirst
    End If
    AssignData
End With
```

Transactions

In server-side processing, you can use the transaction concept to submit a group of changes and not commit any of the changes until all have completed successfully. A **transaction** is a unit of work that succeeds or fails as a unit. It can be a single record update or a batch of updates. Imagine processing a payment that is deducted from your account, but the transaction fails before it credits the billing company. Not good; either both updates should be made or neither.

The **BeginTrans method** of the Connection object starts a transaction. The BeginTransComplete event then occurs. Once a transaction begins, no updates are actually made until you either commit the changes or roll back the transaction to cancel the changes. If no error occurs during the transaction, all updates can be submitted with the **CommitTrans method,** which saves all updates and ends the transaction. A **RollbackTrans method** cancels the changes.

```
conMyConnection.BeginTrans
    (transaction processing)

conMyConnection.CommitTrans
```

or

```
conMyConnection.RollbackTrans
```

Not all data providers allow transactions (Access does). You can determine whether transactions are allowed by checking the Transaction property in the Properties collection of the Connection object. You cannot use transactions with client-side cursors, which means that for a project using an Access file on a single computer, no transactions are allowed. Unfortunately, all the projects in this text use client-side cursors.

Feedback 5.1

1. Where in the ADO object model is the Errors collection?
2. Give an example of a Field object in the Patient table.
3. Your Code window does not show an object for your Recordset. What is wrong?

continued

4. Write the Open method to access the InsuranceCompany table assuming that a Connection object called conAVB is open.

5. Explain each parameter in the following line of code:

```
rsPatient.Open "Patient", conAVB, adOpenDynamic, adLockOptimistic, adCmdTable
```

SQL

Chapter 4 briefly introduced **SQL** and explained how to use the Query Builder to create an SQL statement. Using ADO and VB, you can write your own SQL statements and execute them in various ways. You can assign an SQL statement to the DataSource property of a data control or to the Source of Data in a Data Environment, or you can use an SQL statement in code to open a Command or Recordset. This chapter describes several ways to use an SQL statement in code to create a Recordset or to directly update a database.

Types of SQL Statements

SQL Select statements select data from a database and return that data to the program. You can specify which fields from which table or tables and select only certain records based on criteria.

You can also write SQL statements that perform actions on the database rather than just select data. The actions that you can perform include inserting records, deleting and updating records, and modifying the structure of a database, such as adding tables and fields.

This next section provides a brief tutorial on writing Select statements. Later in the chapter you will learn to write SQL statements that perform an action.

Writing SQL Select Statements

This section shows the syntax that you need to write your own SQL Select statements. But remember, you can always use VB's Query Builder. Even if you are not using a Data Environment, set one up temporarily, create the queries you need, and copy and paste them into your code. When the Query Builder is open, VB's *Query* menu becomes available, and you can write and test your own queries.

The SQL Select Statement—General Form

```
SELECT [Distinct] Field(s) FROM Table(s) [IN Database]
  [WHERE Criteria]
  [GROUP BY Field(s)]
  [HAVING GroupCriteria]
  [ORDER BY Field(s)]
```

For the field(s) you can list the field names or use an asterisk to indicate all fields from the named table(s). Multiple-word field names must be enclosed in square brackets or accent grave marks.

The optional *Distinct* drops out duplicates so that no two records are alike.

The SQL Select Statement—Examples

```
SELECT [Last Name], [First Name], Phone FROM Patient
   ORDER BY [Last Name], [First Name]
SELECT DISTINCT 'Last Name' FROM Patient
   ORDER BY 'Last Name'
SELECT * FROM Patient
   WHERE [Last Name] = "'" & txtSearch.Text & "'"
SELECT * FROM Patient, Insurance
   WHERE Patient.[Insurance Company Code] = InsuranceCompany.Code
```

Note that the preceding example joins the Patient and Insurance tables so that the actual name of the company, not just the code, is included in the results. This easy method for joining tables creates a Recordset that is nonup-dateable and does not include any patients without a matching entry in the InsuranceCompany table, including those with no insurance. To make a joined Recordset updateable and complete, you must use the Join clause of the SQL Select statement.

The Where Clause

You are already familiar with the syntax of a Where clause, since it's the same as the syntax for a Find method. You can use a Where clause to join tables:

```
"WHERE Patient.[Insurance Company Code] = InsuranceCompany.Code"
```

You can also use a Where clause to select only those records that meet specific criteria:

```
"WHERE Patient.[Insurance Company Code] = 'ABC'"
"WHERE Patient.[Insurance Company Code] = '" & strSelectedCompany & "'"
```

You can include multiple conditions in a Where clause:

```
"WHERE Patient.[Insurance Company Code] = InsuranceCompany.Code " & _
   "AND Patient.[Insurance Company Code] = '" & strSelectedCompany & "'"
```

Comparing Database Fields to Visual Basic Fields The syntax of the criteria in a Where clause depends on whether the field is in the Recordset or is a VB variable or property. And string fields must be compared only to string data; numeric fields must be compared only to numeric data. Otherwise, your user will get an ugly run-time error instead of a friendly informational message from you.

```
'Compare a string field to a string variable
"WHERE [Last Name] = '" & strName & "'"

'Compare a string field to a string constant
"WHERE [Last Name] = 'Jones'"
```

```
'Compare a string field to a string property
"WHERE [Last Name] Like '" & txtSearchName.Text & "*'"

'Compare a numeric field to a numeric variable
"WHERE [Duration] = " & intSearchMinutes

'Compare a numeric field to a property
"WHERE [Duration] = " & Val(txtSearchString.Text)

'Compare a numeric field to a numeric constant
"WHERE [Duration] = 15"
```

Tip

Some versions of SQL use a percent sign (%) rather than an asterisk (*) for the wildcard character.

The Order By Clause

Sorting your Recordset in SQL is incredibly easy—just use the Order By clause. You can order by one or more fields in ascending (ASC) or descending (DESC) sequence. If you don't specify the direction, ascending is assumed.

```
"ORDER BY [Last Name], [First Name]"
"ORDER BY InsuranceCompany.Name ASC"
"ORDER BY DateDue DESC"
```

Joins

A primary characteristic of relational databases is that data are stored in multiple tables that are related to each other by common fields. Data can be stored once and used in many places by using the relationships between tables. You will often want to select some fields from one table and other fields from another related table, maybe even fields from several related tables. You have already seen examples of this relationship by using a Where clause to join the Patient and InsuranceCompany tables. Joining the tables allows you to display the name of the company from the InsuranceCompany table rather than just the code stored in the Patient table.

Although you can use the Where clause to join tables, the resulting Recordset is not updateable. If you want the user to be able to update the data, you must use a **Join** clause in the SQL Select statement. Joins are of three types: **inner join, left join,** and **right join.** Table 5.5 shows the three types of joins. Note: The left join and right join are often called *left outer join* and *right outer join.*

T a b l e   5 . 5

SQL Joins

Join Type	Selects
INNER JOIN	Only records that have matching records in both tables.
LEFT JOIN	All records from the first table and only the matching records from the second table.
RIGHT JOIN	All records from the second table and only the matching records from the first table.

To best understand the three types of joins, refer to Figures 5.3, 5.4, 5.5, and 5.6. Figure 5.3 shows data in the Patient table and the InsuranceCompany table. Notice that two patients have no entry for Insurance Company Code and one has

Medicaid, which doesn't match any entry in the InsuranceCompany table. For an inner join (Figure 5.4), those three unmatched patients do not appear in the Recordset. Also notice the SQL statement that created the Recordset. Note: Using a Where clause to join the tables produces this same Recordset.

Figure 5.3

The Patient and InsuranceCompany tables from the Advanced Vision database. The two tables are joined by the insurance company code fields.

Patient Table (partial)

Patient Number	Last Name	First Name	Insurance Company Code	Policy #
150	Raster	Ken	ABC	234567
151	Raster	Viola	ABC	234567
160	Mills	Tricia		
162	Mills	Eric	VS	10034-0
163	Mills	Kenna	VS	10034-0
170	Westley	Henry	Medicaid	
171	Westley	Irene		
175	Crow	Paul	ABC	456789
176	Crow	Margaret	ABC	456789

Insurance Company Table (first two fields from the table only)

Code	Name
ABC	ABC Inc.
DIA	Diamond, Inc.
INT	International
OCS	Optical C
VS	Vision Services

Figure 5.4

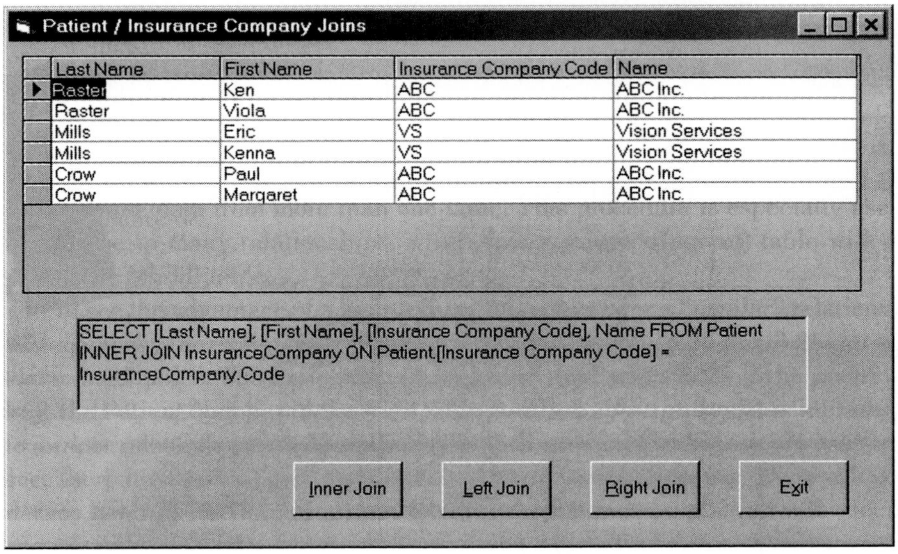

The Recordset that results from an inner join or a Where clause. Only the records that have a matching insurance company code from both tables are included.

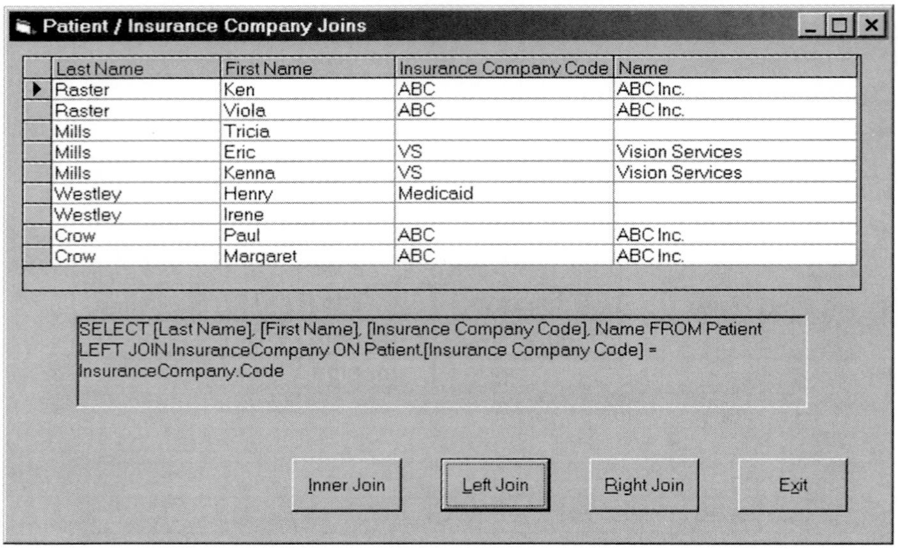
Patient / Insurance Company Joins
Last Name | First Name | Insurance Company Code | Name
Raster | Ken | ABC | ABC Inc.
Raster | Viola | ABC | ABC Inc.
Mills | Tricia
Mills | Eric | VS | Vision Services
Mills | Kenna | VS | Vision Services
Westley | Henry | Medicaid
Westley | Irene
Crow | Paul | ABC | ABC Inc.
Crow | Margaret | ABC | ABC Inc.
SELECT [Last Name], [First Name], [Insurance Company Code], Name FROM Patient LEFT JOIN InsuranceCompany ON Patient.[Insurance Company Code] = InsuranceCompany.Code
Inner Join
Left Join
Right Join
Exit

Figure 5.5

The Recordset that results from a left join. All patients are included and only those insurance companies where the insurance codes match.

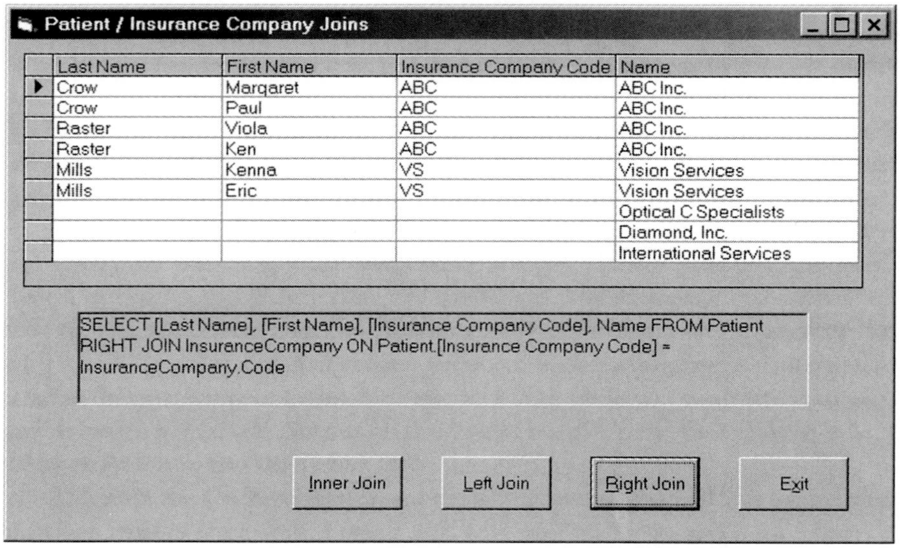
Patient / Insurance Company Joins
Last Name | First Name | Insurance Company Code | Name
Crow | Margaret | ABC | ABC Inc.
Crow | Paul | ABC | ABC Inc.
Raster | Viola | ABC | ABC Inc.
Raster | Ken | ABC | ABC Inc.
Mills | Kenna | VS | Vision Services
Mills | Eric | VS | Vision Services
Optical C Specialists
Diamond, Inc.
International Services
SELECT [Last Name], [First Name], [Insurance Company Code], Name FROM Patient RIGHT JOIN InsuranceCompany ON Patient.[Insurance Company Code] = InsuranceCompany.Code
Inner Join
Left Join
Right Join
Exit

Figure 5.6

The Recordset that results from a right join. All insurance companies are included and only those patients that have matching insurance codes.

In Figure 5.5 all patients appear. And if the patient has an entry for Insurance Company Code that matches an entry in the InsuranceCompany table, those data display. Notice the SQL statement used to create this left join.

Figure 5.6 shows a right join. All records from the InsuranceCompany table appear and only those patients that have matching records.

The Join Clause To code a Join clause, name only the first table in the FROM clause (this becomes the left table). Then specify the join type and the second table name; then write the relationship for the join using the ON.

```
SELECT [Last Name], [First Name], [Insurance Company Code], Name FROM Patient
    LEFT JOIN InsuranceCompany
        ON Patient.[Insurance Company Code] = InsuranceCompany.Code"
```

Joining Multiple Tables To join multiple tables, the joins must be nested within parentheses. The join inside the parentheses is performed first. The following Select statement selects all records from the Prescription table, only matching records from the FrameStyle table, and only matching records from the Patient table. For good measure, we included a Where and an Order By clause.

Big hint: Create complicated queries in Access. Display the query in SQL View; then copy and paste the query into your VB code.

```
SELECT Patient.[Last Name], Patient.[First Name],
       Prescription.[Frame Size], FrameStyle.[Frame Style] FROM Patient
    RIGHT JOIN (FrameStyle RIGHT JOIN Prescription
        ON FrameStyle.ID = Prescription.[Frame Style])
        ON Patient.[Patient Number] = Prescription.[Patient Number]
    WHERE (Prescription.Date>#1/1/99#)
    ORDER BY Prescription.Date
```

Opening a Recordset Based on SQL

You can base the Recordset's Open method on an SQL statement. In the `Open` statement the SQL statement is used in place of a table name, and adCmdText tells the method to interpret the command as SQL.

```
'Create the connection and get the data
    Dim strSQL      As String
    Set conAVB = New ADODB.Connection
    Set rsPatient = New ADODB.Recordset

    'Open the Connection
    conAVB.ConnectionString = "Provider=Microsoft.Jet.OLEDB.3.51;" & _
        "Persist Security Info=False;Data Source=" & App.Path & _
        "\AVB.mdb"
    conAVB.Open

    'Open the Recordset
    strSQL = "SELECT [Last Name], [First Name], " & _
                "[Insurance Company Code], Name FROM Patient " & _
              "INNER JOIN InsuranceCompany " & _
                "ON Patient.[Insurance Company Code] = InsuranceCompany.Code"
    With rsPatient
        .CursorLocation = adUseClient
        .Open strSQL, conAVB, adOpenDynamic, adLockOptimistic, adCmdText
    End With
```

Reopening a Recordset

You may want to change your query and open a different Recordset during program execution. If the Recordset is already open, you must close it and issue another Open method. This example, taken from *Ch05JoinsCode*, closes the current Recordset, opens a new one, and then refreshes the DataGrid control to display the new Recordset.

Note: Later in this chapter you will see an example using the Requery method, which is used only when the Recordset is based on a Command object.

```
Private Sub cmdRightOuter_Click()
    'Fill grid with data from right outer join
    Dim strSQL       As String

    strSQL = "SELECT [Last Name], [First Name], " & _
                "[Insurance Company Code], Name FROM Patient " & _
            "RIGHT JOIN InsuranceCompany " & _
                "ON Patient.[Insurance Company Code] = InsuranceCompany.Code"

    With rsPatient
        .Close              'Must close before reopen
        .Open strSQL, conAVB, adOpenStatic, adLockReadOnly, adCmdText
    End With

    Set dbgPatient.DataSource = rsPatient
    dbgPatient.Refresh  'Display new data
    DisplaySQL strSQL    'Display SQL string in label
End Sub
```

Opening a Recordset by Executing a Command

In all the chapter examples so far, we have opened a Connection object and a Recordset object without using any Command objects. You can also open a Recordset by using the Execute method of a Command object and a Connection object. The **Execute method** can execute an SQL Select statement, which opens a Recordset, or an SQL statement that performs an action, such as adding or deleting a record. This section illustrates Recordsets; later in the chapter you will see some action queries.

Recordsets that you open with the Execute method are considerably less flexible than those that you open with the Recordset's Open method. The Execute method does not allow you to specify the lock type or cursor type for the Recordset, so you must take the defaults: forward scrolling and read only. (It doesn't matter what you specify for the Mode in the ConnectionString.) So use the Execute method only when your application can be based on a static, forward-scrolling, read-only Recordset. The rest of the time, use the Recordset's Open method.

The Execute Method for Recordsets—General Form

```
Set RecordsetObject = ConnectionObject.Execute(CommandText, [NumRecords], _
                    [CmdTypeOption])
Set RecordsetObject = CommandObject.Execute([NumRecords], [Parameters], _
                    [CmdTypeOption])
```

The Set statement is used because this form of the Execute method returns a new Recordset. If you use the Execute method of a Connection, you don't need a Command object. The CommandText can be an SQL Select statement, a table name, or a stored procedure name. You can use a string variable that holds an SQL statement or write the statement directly in the Execute.

The Execute Method for Recordsets—Examples

Connections

```
Set rsPatient = conAVB.Execute("SELECT * from Patient", , cmdTypeText)
Set rsPrescription = conAVB.Execute(strSQL, , cmdTypeText)
Set rsVisit = conAVB.Execute("Visit", , cmdTypeTable)
```

Commands

```
Prescription.CommandText = "SELECT Date, [Patient Number] from Prescription"
Set rsPrescription = Prescription.Execute

Visit.CommandText = mstrSQL
Set rsVisit = Visit.Execute(, , cmdTypeText)
```

Remember that the database lock type and cursor type cannot be set when using the Execute method.

An Example Using a Connection, Command, and Recordset

The following example, which you can find on your CD as *Ch05SQLSearch*, opens a Connection and executes a Command, which returns a Recordset. The project also allows the user to select the records for the Recordset and sort by one of three fields.

Set up the module-level variables and object variables in the General Declarations section:

```
Option Explicit
Dim mstrSearchField As String
Dim mstrSQL As String
'Create ADODB objects
Dim conAVB     As ADODB.Connection
Dim Visit      As ADODB.Command
Dim rsVisit    As ADODB.Recordset
```

In the Form_Load procedure, create the new Connection and Command objects and open the Connection.

```
Private Sub Form_Load()
    'Create the Connection and get the data
    Set conAVB = New ADODB.Connection
    Set Visit = New ADODB.Command

    conAVB.ConnectionString = "Provider=Microsoft.Jet.OLEDB.3.51;" & _
        "Persist Security Info=False;Data Source=" & App.Path & _
        "\AVB.mdb;Mode = read"
    conAVB.Open
```

```
'Create the Command object
Set Visit = New ADODB.Command
Set Visit.ActiveConnection = conAVB

'Create the Recordset
Set rsVisit = New ADODB.Recordset
mstrSQL = "Select [Last Name], [First Name], Date, " & _
            "Diagnosis, Duration from Patient, Visit " & _
            "Where Patient.[Patient Number] = Visit.[Patient Number]"
Visit.CommandText = mstrSQL

Set rsVisit = Visit.Execute

'Bind the text boxes
Set txtLastName.DataSource = rsVisit
Set txtFirstName.DataSource = rsVisit
Set txtDate.DataSource = rsVisit
Set txtDuration.DataSource = rsVisit
Set txtDiagnosis.DataSource = rsVisit
End Sub
```

Requerying the Recordset

Creating a new Recordset is a two-step process. You set the Command's CommandText property to an SQL Select statement and then reopen the Recordset by using the Requery method.

After the user selects the field to use for selection (mstrSearchField) and enters the value to search for (txtSearch.Text), create a new SQL statement, set the Command's CommandText property, and use the Recordset's Requery method.

```
mstrSQL = "Select * from Visit, Patient " _
            & "Where " & mstrSearchField & "= " & Val(txtSearch.Text) _
            & " and Patient.[Patient Number] = Visit.[Patient Number]"
Visit.CommandText = mstrSQL
rsVisit.Requery
```

Checking for an Empty Recordset

When you open a Recordset, especially one in which the user is searching for particular values, it's quite possible for the Recordset to be empty—that is, no records match the criteria. If a Recordset is empty, both BOF and EOF are True after the Requery method.

```
strSQL = "Select * From Patient " & _
        "Where [Last Name] = '" & txtName.Text & "'"
Patient.CommandText = strSQL
With rsPatient
    .Requery
    If .BOF and .EOF Then
        MsgBox "No records match " & txtName.Text, vbExclamation, "No Match"
    End If
End With
```

Executing SQL Action Queries

So far, all of our database projects use Recordsets, and all SQL statements are Select statements. Now you will see a different way to program, using Command objects to directly update a database. You will write SQL action queries, such as **Insert, Delete,** and **Update,** and execute the queries by using the Execute method of the Connection or Command object (see Table 5.6).

Table 5.6

SQL Update Queries

Command	Purpose
INSERT INTO	Add a record.
DELETE FROM	Remove a record.
UPDATE	Change field values.

Action queries operate directly on the database, not on any open Recordset. To execute an SQL action query on a database, you must have an open Connection. But you don't need to have an open Recordset. You will nearly always use unbound controls in a project that uses action queries.

The Execute Method for Updating—General Form

```
ConnectionObject.Execute CommandText, [NumRecords], [CmdTypeOption]
CommandObject.Execute [NumRecords], [Parameters], [CmdTypeOption]
```

To use the Command object's Execute method, you must first set its CommandText property to an SQL statement.

The Execute Method for Updating—Examples

Connections

```
conAVB.Execute strSQL
conAVB.Execute strSQL, , cmdTypeText
conAVB.Execute "DELETE FROM Patient WHERE [Last Name] = 'Smith'"
```

Commands

```
Visit.CommandText = "UPDATE Visit SET Date = #2/15/2000# " & _
     "WHERE [Patient Number] = 100"
Visit.Execute

Visit.CommandText = strSQL
Visit.Execute , , cmdTypeText
```

You can use the SQL Insert, Delete, and Update commands to modify the contents of a database file. Make sure that a Connection is open and that the Mode is set to ReadWrite in the ConnectionString.

Some of the examples that follow are taken from project *Ch05SQLAction* on your CD.

The SQL Update Statement—General Form

```
Update TableName
    Set FieldName = FieldValue, FieldName = FieldValue, . . .
    Where Criteria
```

The SQL Update Statement—Examples

```
Update Patient
    Set [Last Name] = 'Bowser'
    Where [Patient Number] = 500

Update Visit
    Set Date = #1/1/2000#
    Where Date = #1/1/1900#

strSQL = "Update Patient " & _
            "Set [Last Name] = '" & txtLastName.Text & "', " & _
                "[First Name] = '" & txtFirstName.Text & "', " & _
                "[Policy #] = '" & txtPolicyNumber & "' " & _
            "Where [Patient Number] = " & txtPatientNumber.Text
```

The SQL Insert Statement—General Form

```
Insert Into TableName (Fieldlist) VALUES (ListOfValues)
```

The SQL Insert Statement—Examples

```
Insert Into Patient ([Patient Number], [Last Name], [First Name])
            Values (500, 'Berry', 'Terry')

strSQL = "Insert Into Patient " _
            & "([Patient Number], [Last Name], [First Name], [Policy #]) " _
            & "VALUES ('" & txtPatientNumber & "', '" & txtLastName & "', '" _
            & txtFirstName & "', '" & txtPolicyNumber & "')"
```

The SQL Delete Statement—General Form

```
Delete From TableName
    Where Criteria
```

The SQL Delete Statement—Examples

```
Delete From Patient
    Where [Patient Number] = 500

Delete From Patient
    Where [Last Name] = 'Berry'
```

```
strSQL = "Delete From Patient " _
            & "Where [Patient Number] = '" & txtPatientNumber.Text & "'"
```

To see a complete update program that executes SQL action queries, see project *Ch05SQLAction* on your CD.

Creating a Table or an Index

You can also use SQL to create new tables and indexes. The commands that modify the structure of a database are referred to as SQL Data Definition Language (**DDL**). The SQL DDL commands are Create Table, Drop Table, Drop Index, and Alter Table (see Table 5.7). You can use these commands to create or delete a table or to change the fields in a table at run time. You should know that these capabilities exist, but their implementation is beyond the level of this text.

Table 5.7

SQL DDL Commands

Command	Purpose
CREATE TABLE	Add a new table to the database.
CREATE INDEX	Create a new index.
DROP TABLE	Delete a table.
DROP INDEX	Delete an index.
ALTER TABLE	Change field list.

Feedback 5.2

Use these tables to write the requested SQL statements. For each statement, name the fields to select; do not use an asterisk to select all fields. (Both tables have more fields than those listed here.)

Patient
Patient Number
Last Name
First Name
Phone
Insurance Company Code

InsuranceCompany
Code
Name

1. Write the SQL statement to create a Recordset containing the patient's Last Name, First Name, Patient Number, and Phone Number fields.
2. Write the SQL statement to create a Recordset containing the patient's Last Name, First Name, Patient Number, Insurance Company, and Phone Number. Do not include the Insurance Company Code from the Patient table—instead include the insurance company name from the Insurance table. Use a Where clause, not a Join clause.
3. Use a Join clause to write the Select statement from question 2.

The Data Form Wizard

VB has an add-in that can generate much of the code needed for an application using the ADO object model. Check under the *Add-Ins* menu for *Data Form Wizard*. If you do not have this option, select the *Add-In Manager* option and then double-click on *VB 6 Data Form Wizard*. The *Load Behavior* will change to *Loaded*, and you can select OK to return to your project.

Try this—you'll like it. Begin a new project and store it in a folder along with your AVB database. Then begin the **Data Form Wizard** and let it do all the work.

Screen 1—Introduction

The first screen asks whether you want to use a profile. Because we have never created one, just click on *Next*.

Screen 2—Database Type

Select *Access* and click on *Next*.

Screen 3—Database

Use the Browse button to locate your AVB.mdb database. Click on *Next*.

Screen 4—Form

Complete the following items:

1. Type *frmInsurance* as the name for your form.
2. You can choose whether your form will contain a single record or display the data using a grid or chart control. Let's try *Single record*.
3. Select *ADO code*. Notice that another option is the ADO data control or a class module, which we cover in Chapter 6.

Click on *Next*.

Screen 5—Record Source

Complete the following items:

1. Select InsuranceCompany for the Record Source.
2. Add all fields to the Selected Fields list.
3. Set the sort column to *Name*.

Click on *Next*.

Screen 6—Control Selection

Leave all items selected but notice what your options are.
Click on *Next*.

Screen 7—Finished

This is the point where you could create a profile (for screen 1), but don't.
Click on *Finish*.
Your project now contains two forms; take a look at frmInsurance.

Running the Project

Before testing the project:

1. Remove Form1 from the project; don't save changes if asked.
2. Under *Project/Properties* set the Startup object to *frmInsurance*.
3. Start the project. Try the navigation buttons, which are actually command buttons and a label rather than a data control.
4. Exit and check out the code. Very interesting!

Hierarchical Recordsets

ADO 2.0 contains another language called the **Shape data manipulation language** designed for working with the parent/child relationship. The language is a part of the Client Cursor Engine of ADO. Microsoft refers to the use of the language as *data shaping.*

The **Shape command** is an efficient alternative to the SQL Join. Shape creates a hierarchical Recordset when joining tables, rather than returning multiple rows of the matching fields. To see an illustration of the difference, refer to Chapter 3, Figures 3.26, 3.27, and 3.28.

Although the Shape language is a little complicated, it's easy to have VB create Shape commands for you. You can then copy the commands into your code. Create a Data Environment and set up Parent/Child Command objects (or open *Ch03Hierarchy1* from your CD). Right-click on the parent Command (Patient) and select *Hierarchy info.* You will see the following Shape command that was generated by the Designer.

```
SHAPE {SELECT * FROM `Patient`} AS Patient APPEND ({SELECT * FROM `Visit`} AS Visit
RELATE `Patient Number` TO `Patient Number`) AS Visit
```

Your Hands-on Programming Example

This project for Advanced Vision and Beyond must update the Patient table as well as find, select, and sort the records. Use the ADO object model to open the Connection and Recordset in code. (Do not use a data control or Data Environment.)

For the updates allow the user to add new records, delete records, and modify existing records. Do not permit a change to a Patient Number (the key field) on an existing record. For an Add the user must be allowed only the options to Save or Cancel. Make sure to disable all other buttons and menu options that could change the current record.

Display the insurance company names in a dropdown combo box so that the user can select a company from the list or type in a new value.

Include these menu options:

File	Find	Select	Sort
Exit	Last Name	By Last Name	By Patient Number
	First Name	By First Name	By Patient Name
		All Patients	

For the Find option, use an InputBox and allow the user to enter a name (or partial name). Use a Find method with a wildcard to allow for the partial names.

For the Select option, also use an InputBox that allows the user to enter a (partial) name. Use a filter and make sure to include a check mark next to the currently selected menu option.

For the Sort option, use the Sort method. Make the currently selected option appear checked. When the program begins, make the current sort order by Patient Number.

Include a status bar at the bottom of the form. Show the record number ("Record n of nn") at the left end and the date and time at the right.

Make sure to include error handling in all procedures that access the database.

Note: This project is a continuation of the Chapter 4 hands-on programming example.

Planning the Project

Plan the Interface

Sketch the form (Figure 5.7), which your users sign off as meeting their needs.

F i g u r e   5 . 7

A sketch of the form for the Advanced Vision and Beyond patient update project.

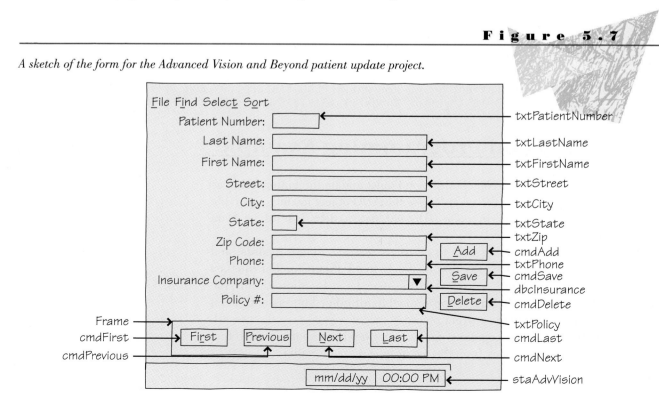

Plan the Objects and Properties

Plan the property settings for the form and for each control.

Note: If you are modifying your project from Chapter 4, you must delete the DataSource property from the bound controls.

Object	Property	Setting
frmAdvVision	Caption	Advanced Vision and Beyond Patient Information
	Icon	Eye.ico
	StartupPosition	2 - CenterScreen
txtPatientNumber	DataField	Patient Number
	Locked	True
txtLastName	DataField	Last Name
	Locked	True
txtFirstName	DataField	First Name
	Locked	True
txtStreet	DataField	Street
	Locked	True
txtCity	DataField	City
	Locked	True
txtState	DataField	State
	Locked	True
txtZip	DataFormat	Custom - #####-####
mskPhone	DataFormat	Custom - (###) ###-####
	Mask	(###) ###-####
	DataField	Phone
	PromptInclude	False
	ClipMode	1 - mskExcludeLiterals
Field labels	Name, Caption	Use default properties as set up by the DE.
dbcInsurance	DataField	Insurance Company Code

continued

Object	Property	Setting
	ListField	Name
	BoundColumn	Code
fraNavigation	Caption	(blank)
cmdFirst	Caption	Fi&rst
cmdPrevious	Caption	&Previous
cmdNext	Caption	&Next
	Default	True
cmdLast	Caption	&Last
cmdAdd	Caption	&Add
	CausesValidation	False
cmdSave	Caption	&Save
	Enabled	False
cmdDelete	Caption	&Delete
	CausesValidation	False
staAdvVision	Panels	3
Panel(1)	MinimumWidth	2880
	AutoSize	2 - Contents
Panel(2)	Style	6 - sbrDate
	AutoSize	2 - Contents
Panel(3)	Style	5 - sbrTime
	AutoSize	2 - Contents
mnuFile	Caption	&File
mnuFileExit	Caption	E&xit
mnuFind	Caption	F&ind
mnuFindLastName	Caption	&Last Name
mnuFileFirstName	Caption	&First Name
mnuSelect	Caption	Selec&t
mnuSelectLastName	Caption	By &Last Name
mnuSelectFirstName	Caption	By &First Name
mnuSelectAll	Caption	&All Records
	Checked	True
mnuSort	Caption	S&ort
mnuSortPatientNumber	Caption	By &Patient Number
mnuSortPatientName	Caption	By Patient &Name

Plan the Event Procedures

Determine which events will need code and plan the code for each.

frmAdvVision

Procedure	Actions
cmdFirst_Click	Move to first record.

cmdPrevious_Click	Move to previous record.
	If BOF Then
	   Move to first record.
	End If

cmdNext_Click	Move to next record.
	If EOF Then
	   Move to last record.
	End If

cmdLast_Click	Move to last record.

cmdAdd_Click	If button Caption is "Add" Then
	   AddNew method.
	   Disable all controls for movement.
	   Change button Caption to "Cancel".
	   Enable Save button.
	   Unlock txtPatientNumber.
	Else (button is "Cancel".)
	   CancelUpdate method.
	   Lock txtPatientNumber.
	   Enable all controls for movement.
	   Disable Save button.
	   Change button Caption to "Add".
	   Move to the last record.
	End If

cmdDelete_Click	Delete the current record.
	Move to the next record.
	If EOF Then
	   Move to the previous record.
	   If BOF Then (Recordset is empty)
	     Display message.
	     Disable all movement controls.
	   End If
	End If

cmdSave_Click	Update method. Lock txtPatientNumber. Enable all controls for movement. Disable the Save button. Change the Caption of Add button to "Add".
Form_Activate	Sort in Patient Number sequence. Check the menu option.
Form_Load	Create and open the connection. Create and open the Recordset. Bind the Recordset to the controls.
mnuFileExit_Click	Unload the form.

continued

Procedure	Actions

mnuFindFirstName_Click	Input requested first name.
	Save a bookmark.
	Find the record.
	If EOF Then (No match found)
	    Display message.
	    Return to bookmarked record.
	End If

mnuFindLastName_Click	Input requested last name.
	Save a bookmark.
	Find the record.
	If EOF Then (No match found)
	    Display message.
	    Return to bookmarked record.
	End If

mnuSelectFirstName	Input requested first name.
	Set the filter.
	If EOF Then (No records in the Recordset)
	    Remove the filter.
	Else
	    Check the menu option and uncheck others.
	End If

mnuSelectLastName	Input requested last name.
	Set the filter.
	If EOF Then (No records in the Recordset)
	    Remove the filter.
	Else
	    Check the menu option and uncheck others.
	End If

mnuSelectAll	Remove the filter. Check the menu option and uncheck others.
mnuSortPatientName	Sort by Last Name, First Name. Check the menu option and uncheck others.
mnuSortPatientNumber	Sort by Patient Number. Check the menu option and uncheck others.

txtPatientNumber_Validate	If not numeric Then
	    Display an error message.
	    Select the text.
	    Cancel the procedure.
	End If

DisableControls	Disable navigation buttons. Disable Find, Select, and Sort menus.
EnableControls	Enable navigation buttons. Enable Find, Select, and Sort menus.
SetUpAdd	Lock txtPatientNumber. Enable Save button. Change Caption of Add button to "Cancel".
DisplayRecordCount	Set status bar text to Recordset record count.
BindData	Set data source for controls on the form.

Write the Project

Follow the sketch in Figure 5.7 to create the user interface. Figure 5.8 shows the completed form.

Figure 5.8

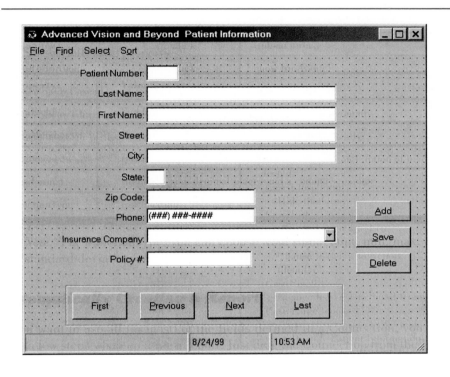

The form for the Advanced Vision and Beyond patient update project.

- Set the properties of the form and of each control, as you have planned.

- Add a reference to ADODB.

- Dimension the Recordset and Connection objects.

- Working from the pseudocode, write each event procedure.

- When you complete the code, thoroughly test the project.

The Project Solution

```
'Project:        Chapter 05 Advanced Vision and Beyond
'                  Chapter Hands-On Example
'Module:         frmAdvVision
'Date:           2/2000
'Programmer:     Bradley/Millspaugh
'Description:    Display and update the Advanced Vision Patient table
'                  using the ADO object model.
'                  Includes finding, sorting, and filtering.
'Folder:         Ch05AdvancedVision

Option Explicit
Dim conAVB       As ADODB.Connection
Dim rsPatient    As ADODB.Recordset
Dim rsInsurance  As ADODB.Recordset
```

```vb
Private Sub Form_Load()
    'Create the connection and get the data
    Set conAVB = New ADODB.Connection
    Set rsPatient = New ADODB.Recordset
    Set rsInsurance = New ADODB.Recordset

    conAVB.ConnectionString = "Provider=Microsoft.Jet.OLEDB.3.51;" & _
        "Persist Security Info=False;Data Source=" & App.Path & _
        "\AVB.mdb;Mode = readwrite"
    conAVB.Open
    With rsPatient
        .CursorLocation = adUseClient
        .CursorType = adOpenDynamic
        .LockType = adLockOptimistic
        .Open "Select * from Patient", conAVB, , , adCmdText
    End With
    With rsInsurance
        .CursorLocation = adUseClient
        .CursorType = adOpenStatic
        .LockType = adLockReadOnly
        .Open "Select * from InsuranceCompany", conAVB, , , adCmdText
    End With
    DisplayRecordCount
    BindData
End Sub
```

```vb
Private Sub BindData()
    'Bind the text boxes to the recordset

    Set txtPatientNumber.DataSource = rsPatient
    Set txtLastName.DataSource = rsPatient
    Set txtFirstName.DataSource = rsPatient
    Set txtPolicyNumber.DataSource = rsPatient
    Set txtStreet.DataSource = rsPatient
    Set txtCity.DataSource = rsPatient
    Set txtState.DataSource = rsPatient
    Set txtZipCode.DataSource = rsPatient
    Set dbcInsurance.DataSource = rsPatient
    Set mskPhone.DataSource = rsPatient
    Set dbcInsurance.RowSource = rsInsurance
End Sub
```

```vb
Private Sub cmdAdd_Click()
    'Add a new record

    On Error GoTo HandleError
    If cmdAdd.Caption = "&Add" Then          'Add button clicked
        rsPatient.AddNew                'Clear out fields for new record
        DisableControls                          'Disable navigation
        SetUpAdd
    Else                                      'Cancel button clicked
        rsPatient.CancelUpdate                'Cancel the Add
        txtPatientNumber.Locked = True
        EnableControls                          'Enable navigation
        cmdSave.Enabled = False               'Disable the Save button
        cmdAdd.Caption = "&Add"               'Reset the Add button
        rsPatient.MoveLast
    End If
```

```
cmdAdd_Click_Exit:
    Exit Sub

HandleError:
    MsgBox "Unable to carry out requested action.", vbInformation,_"Advanced Vision"
    On Error GoTo 0
End Sub
```

```
Private Sub cmdDelete_Click()
    'Delete the current record

    On Error GoTo HandleError
    With rsPatient
        .Delete                               'Delete the current record
        .MoveNext                             'Move to the following record
        If .EOF Then                          'If last record deleted
            .MovePrevious
            If .BOF Then            'If BOF and EOF true, no records remain
                MsgBox "The recordset is empty.", vbInformation, "No records"
                DisableControls
            End If
        End If
    End With

cmdDelete_Click_Exit:
    Exit Sub

HandleError:
    MsgBox "Unable to carry out requested action.", vbInformation, "Advanced Vision"
    On Error GoTo 0
End Sub
```

```
Private Sub cmdSave_Click()
    'Save the current record
    On Error GoTo HandleErrors

    rsPatient.Update
    txtPatientNumber.Locked = True            'Reset all
    EnableControls
    cmdSave.Enabled = False
    cmdAdd.Caption = "&Add"

cmdSave_Click_Exit:
    Exit Sub

HandleErrors:
    Dim strMessage As String
    Dim errDBError As ADODB.Error

    For Each errDBError In conAVB.Errors
        strMessage = strMessage & errDBError.Description & vbCrLf
    Next
    MsgBox strMessage, vbExclamation, "Duplicate Add"
    On Error GoTo 0                           'Turn off error trapping
End Sub
```

```
Private Sub Form_Activate()
    'Establish sort order
```

```
    On Error GoTo HandleError
    rsPatient.Sort = "[Patient Number]"
    mnuSortPatientNumber.Checked = True

cmdFind_Click_Exit:
    Exit Sub

HandleError:
    MsgBox "Unable to carry out requested action.", vbInformation, _
            "Advanced Vision"
    On Error GoTo 0
End Sub

Private Sub mnuFileExit_Click()
    'End the project

    Unload Me
End Sub

Private Sub cmdFirst_Click()
    'Move to the first record

    On Error Resume Next
    rsPatient.MoveFirst
    DisplayRecordCount
End Sub

Private Sub cmdLast_Click()
    'Move to the last record

    On Error Resume Next
    rsPatient.MoveLast
    DisplayRecordCount
End Sub

Private Sub cmdNext_Click()
    'Move to the next record

    On Error Resume Next
    With rsPatient
        .MoveNext
        If .EOF Then
            .MoveLast
        End If
        DisplayRecordCount
    End With
End Sub

Private Sub cmdPrevious_Click()
    'Move to the previous record

    On Error Resume Next
    With rsPatient
        .MovePrevious
        If .BOF Then
            .MoveFirst
        End If
```

```
        End With
        DisplayRecordCount
End Sub
```

```
Private Sub mnuFindFirst_Click()
    'Find by first name
    Dim strName      As String
    Dim vntBookmark As Variant

    On Error GoTo HandleError
    strName = InputBox("Enter the First Name that you want to find." & _
        vbCrLf & "Partial name OK", "Find by First Name")
    With rsPatient
        vntBookmark = .Bookmark
        .Find "[First Name] Like '" & strName & "*'"
        If .EOF Then
            MsgBox "No records match '" & strName & "'", _
                vbInformation, "Find by First Name"
            .Bookmark = vntBookmark
        End If
    End With

mnuFindFirst_Click_Exit:
    Exit Sub

HandleError:
    MsgBox "Unable to carry out requested operation.", _
        vbInformation, "Advanced Vision"
    On Error GoTo 0
End Sub
```

```
Private Sub mnuFindLastName_Click()
    'Find by last name
    Dim strName      As String
    Dim vntBookmark As Variant

    On Error GoTo HandleError
    strName = InputBox("Enter the Last Name that you want to find." & _
        vbCrLf & "Partial name OK", "Find by Last Name")
    With rsPatient
        vntBookmark = .Bookmark
        .Find "[Last Name] Like '" & strName & "*'"
        If .EOF Then
            MsgBox "No records match '" & strName & "'", vbInformation, _
                "Find by Last Name"
            .Bookmark = vntBookmark
        End If
    End With

mnuFindLast_Click_Exit:
    Exit Sub

HandleError:
    MsgBox "Unable to carry out requested operation.", _
        vbInformation, "Advanced Vision"
    On Error GoTo 0
End Sub
```

```vb
Private Sub mnuSelectAll_Click()
    'Select all records

    On Error Resume Next
    rsPatient.Filter = ""
    mnuSelectFirstName.Checked = False
    mnuSelectLastName.Checked = False
    mnuSelectAll.Checked = True
End Sub
```

```vb
Private Sub mnuSelectFirstName_Click()
    'Select by first name
    Dim strName     As String

    On Error GoTo HandleError
    strName = InputBox("Enter the First Name that you want to select." _
        & vbCrLf & "Partial name OK", "Select by First Name")
    With rsPatient
        .Filter = "[First Name] Like '" & strName & "*'"
        If .EOF Then
            MsgBox "No records match '" & strName & "'", _
                vbInformation, "Select by First Name"
            .Filter = ""
        Else
            mnuSelectFirstName.Checked = True
            mnuSelectLastName.Checked = False
            mnuSelectAll.Checked = False
        End If
    End With

mnuSelectFirstName_Click_Exit:
    Exit Sub

HandleError:
    MsgBox "Unable to carry out requested operation.", _
        vbInformation, "Advanced Vision"
    On Error GoTo 0
End Sub
```

```vb
Private Sub mnuSelectLastName_Click()
    'Select by last name
    Dim strName     As String

    On Error GoTo HandleError
    strName = InputBox("Enter the Last Name that you want to select." & _
        vbCrLf & "Partial name OK", "Select by Last Name")
    With rsPatient
        .Filter = "[Last Name] Like '" & strName & "*'"
        If .EOF Then
            MsgBox "No records match '" & strName & "'", _
                vbInformation, "Select by Last Name"
            .Filter = ""
        Else
            mnuSelectFirstName.Checked = False
            mnuSelectLastName.Checked = True
            mnuSelectAll.Checked = False
        End If
    End With
```

```
mnuSelectLastName_Click_Exit:
    Exit Sub

HandleError:
    MsgBox "Unable to carry out requested operation.", vbInformation, _
        "Advanced Vision"
    On Error GoTo 0
End Sub

Private Sub mnuSortPatientName_Click()
    'Sort by Patient Name

    On Error GoTo HandleError
    rsPatient.Sort = "[Last Name], [First Name]"
    mnuSortPatientName.Checked = True
    mnuSortPatientNumber.Checked = False

mnuSortPatientName_Click_Exit:
    Exit Sub

HandleError:
    MsgBox "Unable to carry out requested operation.", vbInformation, _
        "Advanced Vision"
    On Error GoTo 0
End Sub

Private Sub mnuSortPatientNumber_Click()
    'Sort by Patient Number

    On Error GoTo HandleError
    rsPatient.Sort = "[Patient Number]"
    mnuSortPatientNumber.Checked = True
    mnuSortPatientName.Checked = False

mnuSortPatientNumber_Click_Exit:
    Exit Sub

HandleError:
    MsgBox "Unable to carry out requested operation.", vbInformation, _
        "Advanced Vision"
    On Error GoTo 0
End Sub

Private Sub txtPatientNumber_Validate(Cancel As Boolean)
    'Validate the PatientNumber for an Add
    '  Note: The control is locked unless an Add is in progress.
    Dim strMessage As String

    If Not IsNumeric(txtPatientNumber.Text) Then    'Must be numeric
         strMessage = "Invalid PatientNumber"
        MsgBox strMessage, vbExclamation, "Data Entry Error"
        With txtPatientNumber
            .Text = "000"                    'Eliminate any alpha characters
            .SelStart = 0                    'Select the current entry
            .SelLength = Len(.Text)
        End With
        Cancel = True                        'Keep the focus
    End If
End Sub
```

```
Private Sub DisableControls()
    'Disable navigation buttons

    cmdNext.Enabled = False
    cmdPrevious.Enabled = False
    cmdFirst.Enabled = False
    cmdLast.Enabled = False
    cmdDelete.Enabled = False
    mnuFind.Enabled = False
    mnuSelect.Enabled = False
    mnuSort.Enabled = False
End Sub
```

```
Private Sub EnableControls()
    'Enable navigation buttons

    cmdNext.Enabled = True
    cmdPrevious.Enabled = True
    cmdFirst.Enabled = True
    cmdLast.Enabled = True
    cmdDelete.Enabled = True
    mnuFind.Enabled = True
    mnuSelect.Enabled = True
    mnuSort.Enabled = True
End Sub
```

```
Private Sub SetUpAdd()
    'Set up controls for the Add

    With txtPatientNumber
        .Locked = False
        .SetFocus
    End With
    cmdSave.Enabled = True              'Enable the Save button
    cmdAdd.Caption = "&Cancel"         'Allow a Cancel option
End Sub
```

```
Private Sub DisplayRecordCount()
    'Display the record count

    On Error Resume Next
    With rsPatient
        frmAdvVision.staAdvVision.Panels(1).Text = "Record " & _
            .AbsolutePosition & " of " & .RecordCount
    End With
End Sub
```

MCSD Exam Notes

Exam Objectives Covered in This Chapter

Creating Data Services

● Access and manipulate a data source by using ADO and the ADO data control.

Questions/Tricks to Watch for

● You have used events of Connections and of Recordsets. Note that we never discussed events of Commands because there aren't any. Beware of any questions that ask about programming for the events of Commands.

● Know the difference between the ADODB and ADOR libraries.

● Although you cannot use stored procedures with an Access (Jet) database, you should be aware of their existence and purpose. For client-server DBMSs (database management systems) such as SQL Server and Oracle, you can create and use stored procedures, which at their simplest level are just precompiled SQL statements. Stored procedures also allow parameters, conditions, looping, and branching and can be thought of as another programming language. These procedures are compiled and stored on the server, and they can run and return data much more efficiently than SQL statements issued by an application program.

● The ConnectionString for an ADO Connection can include the name of the server, a user ID, and a password, as well as many other possible arguments, depending on the provider.

● Closing a Connection while a transaction is in progress causes an error.

● *Blocking* is a term used to describe the wait in an asynchronous operation.

S u m m a r y

1. ADO has two libraries: ADODB, which contains the full ADO object model, and ADOR, for Recordset access only.
2. The object model contains objects for Connection, Command, Recordset, Error, Parameter, Field, and Property. The collections are Errors, Fields, Parameters, and Properties.
3. The Errors collection belongs to the Connection object, while the Parameters collection belongs to the Command object.
4. Each Recordset and Command must be based on an open Connection. It isn't necessary to code a Command to open a Recordset.
5. ADO events are usually paired; one fires prior to an action, and the other fires when the action completes.
6. Asynchronous operations allow your program to process other work while waiting for the database to complete an action and send an event.
7. Objects are created with the keyword `New`. `New` may be used in a `Dim` statement or later on a `Set` statement.
8. Use the `WithEvents` clause on a `Dim` statement to access the events for a Connection or a Recordset.
9. Use the Recordset's Open method to open a Recordset. Set the CursorType, LockType, and CursorLocation properties.
10. To use bound controls with a Recordset created in code, use the `Set` statement to set the controls' DataSource property to the Recordset.

11. To use unbound controls, you must write code to fill the controls and save any changed data.

12. Programming for a Recordset created in code is nearly identical to programming for the Recordset of a Data Environment or a Data control.

13. A transaction is one or more statements that execute or fail as a group.

14. The SQL Select statement is used to select records for a Recordset. A Select statement can select the fields, tables, relationships, and sorting.

15. The Select statement's Where clause can join tables, but the resulting Recordset is not updateable. To join tables and make the Recordset updateable, use a Join clause, which may specify an inner join, a left join, or a right join.

16. You must close an open Recordset before reopening it.

17. Use the Execute method of a Connection or a Command to open a Recordset based on an SQL Select statement. The Recordset will be forward scrolling and read only.

18. You can create a different Recordset by setting a Command's CommandText property and calling the Recordset's Requery method.

19. SQL Insert, Delete, and Update statements directly modify the database, rather than modify a Recordset. Use the Execute method of a Connection or a Command to execute an SQL action query.

20. SQL Data Definition Language (DDL) can modify the structure of a database.

21. The Data Form Wizard add-in can create a form that navigates and updates a database file using ADO code.

22. The Shape command can create a hierarchical Recordset.

K e y   T e r m s

R e v i e w   Q u e s t i o n s

1. List the objects contained in the ADO programming object model.
2. Differentiate between ADODB and ADOR. Where would you specify one or the other?
3. What is the purpose of a Parameter object?
4. Which objects have a Properties collection?
5. What is the purpose of the New and WithEvents keywords? Where are they specified?
6. Why would you want to use a Recordset.Open instead of a Command.Execute to return a Recordset?
7. Explain the purpose of these SQL statements: Select, Update, Insert, Delete.
8. Explain the differences between an inner join, a left join, and a right join.
9. What is SQL DDL, and what is its purpose?
10. What is the purpose of the Data Form Wizard? How could you create a template with the wizard?
11. What is data shaping?

P r o g r a m m i n g   E x e r c i s e s

5.1 Modify your project from Chapter 4 to remove the Data Environment and replace it with ADO objects created in code. Make sure to delete the DataSource property of all bound controls at design time.

5.2 Create a project that uses a Recordset's Filter property to display all patients or allows the user to select by last name or by city. Connect your project to the AVB.mdb file. Use a grid to display the information.

5.3 Modify project 5.2 to use SQL statements to create a new Recordset each time the user makes a new selection.

5.4 Use SQL to maintain the InsuranceCompany table in AVB.mdb. The update features will include Add, Delete, and Update. Do not maintain an open Recordset for the entire table; instead use a dropdown list to allow the user to select the record. Use unbound controls.

5.5 Create a project that uses SQL to display all patients or allows the user to select by last name or by city. Connect your project to the AVB.mdb file.

5.6 Use the Data Form Wizard to create a form containing the fields from the Visit table. Test the navigation and updating buttons.

CASE STUDIES

Video Bonanza

1. Remove the Data Environment from your Chapter 4 project. Make the code work using the ADO programming model.
2. Write a program that allows the user to select and display movies by movie number, title, studio, or category. Include dropdown lists for each of the fields for selection. When the user makes a selection from a list, use an SQL Select statement to create a Recordset of the selected records and display the first matching record in the form's (unbound) controls. Include navigation buttons and a record count of the current Recordset.
3. Modify the preceding exercise to include updating the data.

VB Auto

1. Remove the Data Environment from your Chapter 4 project. Make the code work using the ADO object model.
2. Write a project to display the fields from the Vehicle table in unbound controls. Allow the user to select the manufacturer from a dropdown list (each manufacturer name should appear only once on the sorted list). Use an SQL Select statement to create a new Recordset of the records that match the user's selection.
3. Write a project to update the Vehicle table using SQL action queries. Allow for adds, deletes, and updates.

6

Creating Class Modules

At the completion of this chapter, you will be able to . . .

1. Use object-oriented terminology correctly.

2. Differentiate between a class and an object.

3. Create your own objects and collections.

4. Create a class that has properties and methods.

5. Use property procedures to set and retrieve Private properties of a class.

6. Declare object variables and assign values to the variables by using the Set statement.

7. Instantiate an object in a project using your class.

8. Understand the purpose of the Class_Initialize and Class_Terminate events.

9. Create a collection of objects.

10. Use the Object Browser to get information about available objects, properties, methods, events, and constants.

11. Create a data-aware class module.

Visual Basic and Object-Oriented Programming

You have been using objects since Chapter 1. As you know quite well by now, **objects** have properties and methods and generate events that you can respond to (or ignore) if you choose. Until now the classes for all objects in your projects have been predefined; that is, you could choose to create a new object of the form class, a command button class, a text box class, or any other class of control in the VB toolbox. In this chapter you will learn to define your own new class and create objects based on the class.

Object-oriented programming (OOP) is currently the most acceptable style of programming. Some computer languages, such as Java and SmallTalk, were designed to be object oriented (OO) from their inception. Other languages, such as VB, have been modified over the last few years to accommodate OOP.

Each version of VB brings it closer to what many consider a true object-oriented language. Although not all of the concepts of object-oriented programming are completely supported by VB, most are. Certainly VB is close enough to an OO language for you to use it to write object-oriented programs.

Writing object-oriented programs is a mind set—a different way of looking at a problem. You must think in terms of using objects. As your projects become more complex, using objects becomes increasingly important.

Objects

Beyond the many built-in choices you have for objects to include in your projects, VB allows you to create your own new object types by creating a **class module.** Just like other object types, your **class** may have both properties and methods. Remember: Properties are characteristics, methods are actions that a class of object can perform, and events respond to actions by the user.

Think of a class as a new data type but much more powerful. Java refers to integer and string as "primitive" data types because they cannot include properties, methods, and events. Creating a class allows you to create a more complex data type.

An object is a *thing* such as a command button. You create a command button object from the command button tool in the toolbox. In other words, *command button* is a class, but *cmdExit* is an actual occurrence or **instance** of the class; the instance is the object. Just as you may have multiple command buttons in a project, you may have many objects of a new class type.

Defining your own class is like creating a new tool for the toolbox; this step creates a definition of what that type of object looks like and how it behaves but does not create the object. You may then create as many instances of the class as you need. Your class may be a student, an employee, a product, or any other type of object that would be useful in a project.

Many people use a cookie analogy to describe the relationship of a class and an object. The cookie cutter is the class. You can't eat a cookie cutter, but you can use it to make cookies; the cookie is the object. When you use a cookie cutter to make a cookie, you **instantiate** an object of the cookie class. Using the same cookie cutter, you can make cookies that differ from each other.

Although all cookies will have the same shape, some may be chocolate, some lemon, and some vanilla; some may have frosting or colored sprinkles on top. The characteristics such as flavor and topping are the properties of the object. You could refer to the properties of your cookie object as

```
Cookie1.Flavor = "Lemon"
Cookie1.Topping = "Cream Frosting"
```

What about methods? Recall that a method is an action or behavior—something the object can do or have done to it, such as Move, Clear, or Print. Possible methods for our cookie object might be Eat, Bake, or Crumble. Using object terminology, you can refer to Object.Method:

```
    Cookie1.Crumble
```

Sometimes the distinction between a method and an event is somewhat fuzzy. Generally, anything you tell the object to do is a method; if the object does an action and needs to inform you, that's an event. So if you tell the cookie to crumble, that is a method; if the cookie crumbles on its own and needs to inform you of the fact, that's an event.

Object-Oriented Terminology

The key features of an object-oriented language are **encapsulation, polymorphism, inheritance,** and **reusability.**

Encapsulation

Encapsulation refers to the combination of characteristics of an object along with its behaviors. You have one "package" that holds the definition of all properties, methods, and events. For example, when you create a command button, you can set or retrieve its properties, such as Caption or Width. You can execute its methods, such as SetFocus or Move, and you can write code for its events, such as Click or Double-click. But you cannot make up new properties or tell it do anything that it doesn't already know how to do. It is a complete package; you can think of all of the parts of the package as being in a "capsule."

Encapsulation is sometimes referred to as *data hiding.* Each object keeps its data (properties) and procedures (methods) hidden. Through use of the public and private keywords, an object can expose only those data elements and procedures that it wants the outside world to see.

Polymorphism

Polymorphism means "many shapes" and means that different classes of objects may have behaviors that are named the same but are implemented differently. Polymorphism allows you to request an action without knowing exactly what kind of object you are dealing with or how it will carry out its action. For example, you can specify Printer.Print, Form.Print, PictureBox.Print, and Debug.Print. Printer.Print sends its output to the printer object, Form.Print sends output to the form, PictureBox.Print sends output to a picture box control, and Debug.Print sends output to the VB Immediate window.

You can implement polymorphism in VB by using naming conventions. Always use standard names for your methods so that a programmer will recognize the action by its name. For example, don't use Clear for one class, BlankOut for another, and Empty for another. You can also implement polymorphism by implementing interfaces, which is discussed in Chapter 8.

Inheritance

Inheritance is the ability to create a new class from an existing class. From the OOP purist point of view, VB doesn't allow inheritance. For example, in theory you should be able to create a new class called MyCheckBox based on the check box class. MyCheckBox would have all the properties, methods, and events of check boxes, but you would specify that the shape of the check box is your company logo. If checked, it appears red; unchecked, it is black—everything else remains unchanged. This VB cannot do. Yet.

Reusability

The real purpose of inheritance is *reusability*. You need to be able to reuse or obtain the functionality from one class of object when you have another similar situation. VB *does* provide for reusability by implementing interfaces and a procedure known as *delegation*. Microsoft argues that reusability, not inheritance, is the important concept, but there are rumors of true inheritance for a future version of VB.

To share functionality by using delegation, you place the code you want to share in a base class, also called a *superclass*. Then you create other classes, called *subclasses,* that can call the shared functions. This concept is very helpful if you have features that are similar in two classes. Rather than writing two classes that are almost identical, you can create a base class that contains the similar procedures.

An example of reusability could be the option button and check box classes, which contain very similar functionality and could share a superclass. Each subclass would call the shared procedure from the base class and would contain any procedures that are unique to the subclass.

Reusable Objects

A big advantage of object-oriented programming over traditional programming is the ability to reuse objects. When you create a new class by writing a class module, you can then use that class in multiple projects. Each object that you create from the class has a set of properties, just like the built-in VB controls you have been using all along. For example, you can create two image objects: imgOne and imgTwo. Each has its own Visible property and Picture property, which will probably be set differently than for the other.

As you begin using classes in your projects, you will find many situations in which classes are useful. You might want to create your own class to provide database access. You could include methods for adding and deleting data members. If you work frequently with sales, you might create a product class. The product class would likely have properties such as description, quantity, and cost. The methods would probably include finding the current value of the product and issuing a message that the quantity is low and an order needs to be placed.

By convention, class names are prefixed with a *C*. For example, name the prescription class CPrescription and a patient class CPatient.

Classes

To design your own class, you need to analyze the characteristics and behaviors that your object needs. The characteristics or properties are defined as variables, and the behaviors (methods) are sub procedures or function procedures.

Properties of a Class

Inside your class module you define variables, which are the properties of the class. When deciding what properties belong to a class, think about the fields that are related to the object, along with field descriptions and data types. For a prescription in Advanced Vision, the properties could be:

```
Private mintPatientNumber      As Integer
Private mdtmDate               As Date
Private mintContactLens        As Integer
Private mintFrameSize          As Integer
Private mintFrameStyle         As Integer
Private mstrLensMaterial       As String
Private mstrLensType           As String
Private mintDuration           As Integer
Private mcurLeft               As Currency
Private mcurRight              As Currency
```

Notice that a property can be any data type depending on the characteristics of the field. When you use the word `Dim` to declare a variable, by default the variable is Public. Although you *can* define property variables as Public, you can gain some real advantages by making them Private.

Assigning Property Values

Theoretically you could declare all variables as Public so that all other project code could set and retrieve their values. However, this practice violates the rules of encapsulation that require that each object be in charge of its own data. Remember that encapsulation is also called data hiding. To accomplish encapsulation, you will declare all variables in a class module as Private. As a Private variable, the value is available only to the procedures within the class module, the same way that module-level variables are available only to procedures within the form module.

When your program creates objects from your class, you will need to assign values to the properties. Because the properties are Private variables, you will use special property procedures to pass the values *to* the class module and to return values *from* the class module.

The Property Procedures

Your class allows its properties to be set through a **Property Let** procedure. And to retrieve the value of a property from a class, you must use a **Property**

Get procedure. The Property Let and Property Get procedures serve as a gateway to assign and retrieve property values to the private members of the class module.

When you define the Property Let and Property Get procedures, the name you use becomes the name of the property to the outside world. Create "friendly" procedure names that describe the property without using a prefix, such as LastName or EmployeeNumber.

The Property Get Procedure—Format

The Property Get returns the current value of a property.

```
[Public] Property Get ProcedureName([OptionalArgumentList]) [As DataType]
    [statements in procedure]
    ProcedureName = PropertyName
End Property
```

Property procedures are Public by default, so you can omit the optional Public keyword. You can also define a property procedure to be Private, which means that the property is available only inside the class module. We won't be using any Private property procedures in this text.

Property Get procedures are similar to function procedures in at least one respect: Somewhere inside the procedure, before the exit, you must assign a return value to the procedure name.

The Property Get Procedure—Example

```
Public Property Get LastName() As String
    LastName = mstrLastName
End Property
```

The Property Let Procedure—Format

The Property Let assigns a value to a property. Inside the Property Let procedure, you can do validation to make sure the value is valid before assigning the incoming value to the property.

```
[Public] Property Let ProcedureName([OptionalArgumentList,] IncomingValue _
    [As DataType])
    [statements in procedure]
    PropertyName = IncomingValue
End Property
```

If you include any arguments in the argument list, the number of arguments, their data type, and order must exactly match the argument list in the Property Let procedure. If arguments are included, the incoming value must follow the list.

The data type of the incoming value must match the type of the return value of the corresponding Property Get procedure.

The Property Let Procedure—Example

```
Property Let LastName(strLastName As String)
    LastName = strLastName
End Property
```

Creating a New Class—Step by Step

In this step-by-step tutorial, you will create a new class to hold product information for an item in the dispensary (optometrist talk for "inventory"). Using the Advanced Vision term, we will call the class CDispensaryItem.

Define a New Class Module

A class module is part of a VB project, so the first step is to create a new project.

Begin the Class Project

STEP 1: Open a new project.

STEP 2: Select *Add Class Module* from the *Project* menu. The *Add Class Module* dialog box appears (Figure 6.1).

Figure 6.1

Add a new class to a project in the Add Class Module dialog box.

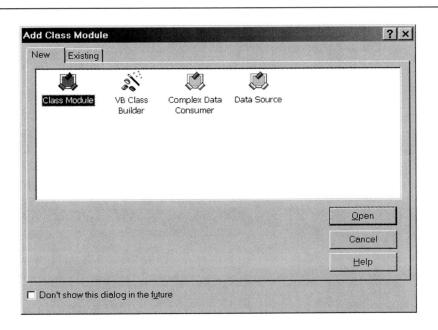

STEP 3: From the New tab choose *Class Module* and click on *Open*. You will see a Code window similar to the Code window for a standard code module.

STEP 4: Notice that the Code window is labeled *Class1*. Change the class name to *CDispensaryItem* by changing the Name property in the Properties window (Figure 6.2).

Change the class module's Name property.

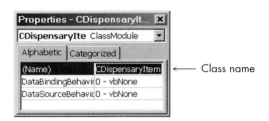

← Class name

Define the Class Properties

STEP 1: In the General Declarations section of the Code window, define the variables as Private. (If your Code window doesn't have an `Option Explicit` statement, add one.) These module-level variables become the properties of your new class.

```
Private mintQuantity    As Integer
Private mintFrameSize   As Integer
Private mintFrameStyle  As Integer
```

This class has three properties defined as Private module-level variables: mintQuantity, mintFrameSize, and mintFrameStyle. Because the properties and methods are declared as Private, they can be accessed only by procedures within the class module. To allow access from outside the class module, you must add property procedures.

Add Property Procedures

The Quantity Property

STEP 1: From the class module Code window, select *Add Procedure* from the *Tools* menu.

STEP 2: Type *Quantity* for the Name and select the options for *Property* and *Public* (Figure 6.3). Click OK.

Create property procedures for the Quantity property in the Add Procedure dialog box.

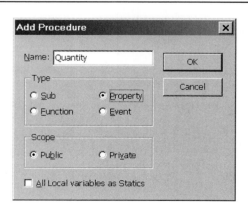

STEP 3: Look over the screen (Figure 6.4). Notice that you have both a Property Get Quantity and a Property Let Quantity( ) procedure. Note also that by default both procedures are declared as Variant return type.

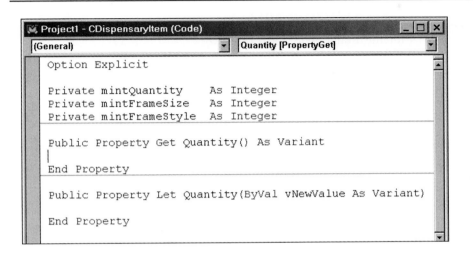

Figure 6.4

VB automatically creates the template for a Property Get and a Property Let procedure.

STEP 4: Change the return data type of the Property Get to Integer.
STEP 5: Write the code for the Property Get procedure (Figure 6.5).

```
Public Property Get Quantity() As Integer
        'Retrieve the current value

        Quantity = mintQuantity
End Property
```

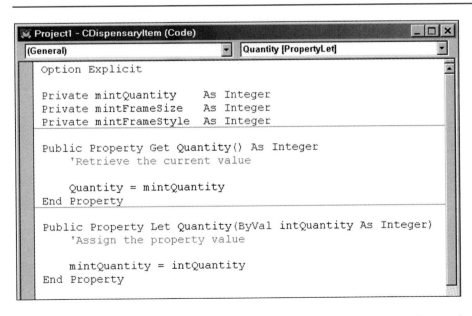

Figure 6.5

Code the Property Get and Property Let procedures

STEP 6: Code the Property Let procedure, changing the incoming value and data type.

```
Public Property Let Quantity(ByVal intQuantity As Integer)
    'Assign the property value

    mintQuantity = intQuantity
End Property
```

The FrameStyle and FrameSize Properties

STEP 1: Add Public property procedures for the FrameStyle and FrameSize properties.

STEP 2: Code the Property Get and Property Let procedures for both.

```
Public Property Get FrameStyle() As Integer
    'Retrieve the current value

    FrameStyle = mintFrameStyle
End Property


Public Property Let FrameStyle(ByVal intFrameStyle As Integer)
    'Assign the property value

    mintFrameStyle = intFrameStyle
End Property

Public Property Get FrameSize() As Integer
    'Retrieve the current value

    FrameStyle = mintFrameSize
End Property

Public Property Let FrameSize(ByVal intFrameSize As Integer)
    'Assign the property value

    mintFrameSize = intFrameSize
End Property
```

Code a Method

You can create methods by adding sub procedures and functions for the behaviors that the class needs. For this class you will add a function procedure to handle the receipt of a shipment.

STEP 1: From the class module Code window, select *Add Procedure* from the *Tools* menu.

STEP 2: Name the new procedure ReceiveItem and select the options for *Sub* and *Public.* Click OK.

STEP 3: Inside the parentheses add the argument *intNewAmount As Integer* to pass the quantity in the shipment.

STEP 4: Type the code.

```
Public Sub ReceiveItem(intNewAmount As Integer)
    'Increase the Quantity by shipment received

    mintQuantity = mintQuantity + intNewAmount
End Sub
```

STEP 5: Repeat the process for a method called ClearProperties.

```
Public Sub ClearProperties()
    'Set properties to zero

    mintQuantity = 0
    mintFrameStyle = 0
    mintFrameSize = 0
End Sub
```

Add General Remarks

STEP 1: Insert a new line before Option Explicit and add the general remarks.

```
'Module:        CDispensaryItem
'Programmer:    Your Name
'Date:          Today's Date
'Description:   Define methods and properties of the class.
'Folder:        Ch06SBSObject
```

Save the Class Module

STEP 1: Open the *File* menu and choose *Save CDispensaryItem As.* Note that VB assigns the file extension .cls to class modules.

STEP 2: Select the path, creating a new folder called *Ch06CreateObject* for this new project. Save CDispensaryItem.cls in your new project folder.

Feedback 6.1

1. Write the property declarations for a class module for a student that will contain the properties LastName, FirstName, StudentIDNumber, and GPA. Where will these statements appear?
2. Code the Property Let procedure to assign a value to the LastName property.
3. Code the Property Get procedure to retrieve the value of the GPA property.

Creating a New Object Based on a Class

Creating a class module defines a new class but does not create any objects. This process is similar to defining a new user-defined type; after you define the new data type, you must then dimension variables of the new type. To create an object based on your new class, you must create an instance of the class by using the New keyword and specify the class. This step is referred to as ***instantiating*** an object.

Dimensioning Objects Using the New Keyword General Form

```
Dim|Public|Private VariableName As New ClassName
```

The New Keyword—Examples

```
Dim Emp              As New CEmployee
Private mInventory   As New CInventory
Public NewForm       As New frmMain
```

Use the `New` **keyword** to create a new instance of an object class, just as you did to create ADO objects. The object class can be a class that you create or a standard VB object such as a form or a control.

Note: Using the `New` keyword sets up the memory location and references for the new object but doesn't actually create it. The first time your project refers to a property or method of the new object, the object is created.

Define and Use a New Object—Step by Step

To continue the step-by-step tutorial for the CDispensaryItem class, you must define a form in your project. The code in the form module creates an instance of the CDispensaryItem class. The user interface allows the user to enter the Quantity, Frame Style, and Frame Size of a DispensaryItem. Your project then assigns the input values to the properties of the CDispensaryItem class. Figure 6.6 shows the completed form.

F i g u r e   6 . 6

The completed form for the step-by-step tutorial.

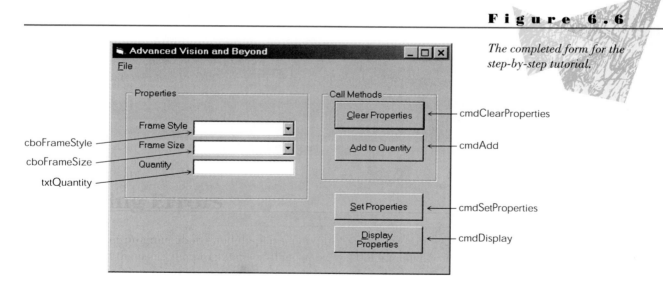

Create the Form

STEP 1: Open the form module and create your interface to match Figure 6.6.
STEP 2: Set the Name, Caption, and Text properties for the controls.
STEP 3: Set up the properties for the two combo boxes:

cboFrameStyle	Style	2 - Dropdown list
	List	1. Metal
		2. Plastic

cboFrameSize	Style	2 - Dropdown list
	List	1. Children's
		2. Men's
		3. Unisex
		4. Women's

STEP 4: Use the Menu Editor to add a *File/Exit* command.

Add Code

STEP 1: Type the comments and declare the new object.

```
'Project:       CreateObject
'Programmer:    Your Name
'Date:          Today's Date
'Description:   Create (instantiate) an object of CDispensary class.
'Folder:        Ch06SBSObject

Option Explicit
Private mDispensaryItem As New CDispensaryItem 'Instantiate the new object
```

STEP 2: Write the code for cmdSetProperties to assign the text box/combo box values to the corresponding properties.

```
Private Sub cmdSetProperties_Click()
    'Assign form control values to properties of object

    If cboFrameSize.ListIndex <> -1 And cboFrameStyle.ListIndex <> -1 Then
        With mDispensaryItem
            .FrameSize = cboFrameSize.ListIndex + 1 'Save size number
            .FrameStyle = cboFrameStyle.ListIndex + 1 'Save style number
            .Quantity = Val(txtQuantity.Text)
        End With
    Else
        MsgBox "Enter values for object properties.", vbInformation, _
                "Advanced Vision"
    End If
End Sub
```

STEP 3: Code the other command button event procedures.

```
Private Sub cmdAdd_Click()
    'Add the the object's quantity
    Dim intNewAmount As Integer

    intNewAmount = Val(InputBox("How many ?", "AVB Dispensary Item Shipment"))
    mDispensaryItem.ReceiveItem intNewAmount 'Call the object's method
    txtQuantity.Text = mDispensaryItem.Quantity 'Display the updated quantity
End Sub
```

```
Private Sub cmdClearProperties_Click()
    'Assign blanks to object property values

    mDispensaryItem.ClearProperties
End Sub
```

```
Private Sub cmdDisplay_Click()
    'Display object properties in a message box
    Dim strMessage As String

    With mDispensaryItem
        strMessage = "The object properties are: " & vbCrLf _
            & "Frame Style " & .FrameStyle & vbCrLf _
            & "Frame Size " & .FrameSize & vbCrLf _
            & "Quantity " & .Quantity
    End With
    MsgBox strMessage, vbOKOnly, "DispensaryItem object contents"
End Sub
```

STEP 4: Code the mnuFileExit_Click and Form_Unload event procedures.

```
Private Sub mnuFileExit_Click()
    'Exit the project

    Unload Me
End Sub
```

```
Private Sub Form_Unload(Cancel As Integer)
    'Release object references

    Set mDispensaryItem = Nothing
End Sub
```

Save the Form and the Project

STEP 1: Save the form as DispensaryItem.frm.

STEP 2: Save the project as DispensaryItem.vbp.

Run the Project

STEP 1: Run the project and fill in test values.

STEP 2: Click on *Set Properties.* Try *Display Properties,* then *Add to Amount,* and then *Display Properties* again.

STEP 3: When you finish experimenting, exit.

Step through the Project

Single-step through the project by pressing F8. Fill in the text boxes and click *SetProperties.* Then repeatedly press F8 and watch each step; you will see execution transfer to the code for CDispensaryItem for each Property Let. When cmdSetProperties_Click finishes, click on your project's Taskbar button to make the form reappear.

Click the other buttons, step through the code, and watch what happens.

Feedback 6.2

1. What is the difference between an object and a class?
2. Is mDispensaryItem an object or class? what about CDispensaryItem?
3. What actions are performed by the following statement?

```
mDispensaryItem.Quantity = Val(txtQuantity.Text)
```

Choosing When to Create New Objects

As you saw in Chapter 5, VB gives you more than one way to create a new object. The method you choose can affect the scope of your object and the performance of your program.

In the preceding step-by-step tutorial, you used one method of creating a new object—coding the New keyword on the Dim statement:

```
Private mDispensaryItem As New CDispensaryItem
```

This statement creates a new variable that can hold a reference to an object. The first time your code refers to mDispensaryItem, the object is actually created.

Although in this example the object variable, mDispensaryItem, is a module-level variable, object variables may also be defined to be local or global. For example, to create an object local to one procedure, you could use this statement:

```
Dim DispensaryItem As New CDispensaryItem
```

For an object defined as local, each time the Dim is encountered VB recreates the object variable. And the first time the procedure references the variable, the object is actually created. When the procedure terminates and the object variable goes out of scope, the object is "destroyed"; that is, the system resources used by the object are released.

Using the Set Statement

Another way to create an object is to dimension the object variable without the New keyword and use the Set statement in a procedure when you are ready to create the object. This method gives you more control over when the object is actually created. Because using this method can also improve program performance, it is the preferred choice.

```
'General Declarations section of your form
Private mDispensaryItem As CDispensaryItem

'Inside a procedure—generally Form_Load
Set mDispensaryItem = New CDispensaryItem
```

The Set Statement—General Form

```
Set ObjectVariableName = { [New] ClassName | Nothing }
```

A Set statement is an assignment statement for object variables. The variable name must already be declared (with a Dim, Public, Private, or Static statement).

Setting an object variable to Nothing terminates the object reference and releases the system resources.

The Set Statement—Examples

```
Set mDispensaryItem = New CDispensaryItem
Set MyDispensaryItem = mDispensaryItem
Set mDispensaryItem = Nothing
```

Using the New Keyword

When you create a new object, you have three choices for the statements. Note that all three methods use the New keyword in either the dimension or the Set statement.

Choice 1 (the preferred method)

```
Private mDispensaryItem As CDispensaryItem 'In the General Declarations section
Set mDispensaryItem = New CDispensaryItem  'In the procedure needing the object
```

The Set statement typically goes in the Form_Load procedure. The new object is created when the Set statement executes.

Choice 2 (the one used in the earlier step-by-step tutorial)

```
Private mDispensaryItem As New CDispensaryItem 'In the General Declarations section
```

This statement declares the new object; the object is actually created the first time mDispensaryItem is referenced in code. One disadvantage of this approach is that exactly when the object is created is unclear; small changes to the project can alter the sequence and cause unexpected results.

Choice 3 (the least efficient method)

```
Private mDispensaryItem As Object           'Using a generic Object type
Set mDispensaryItem = New CDispensaryItem 'In the procedure needing the object
```

Declaring the object variable as a generic Object is legal. On occasion you may need to use this format if the actual object type cannot be determined until run time. The disadvantage of this format is that VB cannot resolve the references to the object during compile, but must wait until execution. This coding method causes a condition called *late binding*.

Early Binding versus Late Binding

When you declare a new object, VB must locate the object definition to determine the available properties and methods. This process is called *resolving* the references. **Early binding** means that the compiler can resolve the object references during compile and is the most efficient binding method. Using either choice 1 or choice 2 in the preceding section causes early binding.

The third choice, with a variable declared as a generic object, is the least efficient approach and is an example of **late binding.** If you use late binding, your projects will run considerably slower than those with early binding.

The Initialize and Terminate Events

Each class module has two predefined events available for which you can write code if you wish. The **Class_Initialize event** is triggered when an object is created, and the **Class_Terminate event** occurs when an object goes out of scope or is terminated with a `Set ObjectName = Nothing`. These event procedures are useful for doing any setup work or for making sure that the memory allocated for an object is released.

```
Public Sub Class_Initialize
    'Create the collection object

    Set mDispensaryItems = New Collection
End Sub

Public Sub Class_Terminate()
    'Remove the collection from memory

    Set mDispensaryItems = Nothing
End Sub
```

Feedback 6.3

1. Write a declaration and a `Set` statement to instantiate an object of the CPerson class. Tell where each statement should appear.
2. What code should appear in the Class_Terminate event procedure?

Events

Most objects can generate events. The controls on the user interface raise events, such as Click, DoubleClick, MouseUp, and Move. The form (the container of the control) can respond to each event with code or ignore an event. Events are often caused by user action, such as a click or mouse move, but sometimes events are generated by the system, such as a timer firing or ADO events such as WillChangeRecord and RecordChangeComplete.

The objects that you create from your new classes can generate events, which the form can respond to (or ignore). For example, if a condition exists in an object and the user should be notified, your object *should not* display a message to the user; the user interface must display the message. Your object must either raise an event or raise an error, to which the form module can respond. This section covers raising and responding to events; raising errors is covered later in this chapter.

First we need a little terminology: An object that generates or raises an event is called the ***event source*** or the ***event provider.*** The object that responds to an event is called an ***event sink*** or an ***event consumer.*** For example, when the user clicks a command button and the form's cmdOK_Click event procedure executes, the command button is the event source and the form is the event sink.

Raising Events

Two things are needed for your class to generate events:

- Declare the event in the General Declaration section of the class module.

```
Public Event TaskComplete
```

- Raise the event in code. When a condition occurs that should generate the event, use the RaiseEvent statement.

```
If mblnJobFinished Then
    RaiseEvent TaskComplete
End If
```

The Event and RaiseEvent Statements—General Form

```
[Public] Event EventName([Arguments])
RaiseEvent EventName [(Arguments)]
```

An **Event statement** must appear at the module level and is Public by default. You may pass arguments with an event if you wish.

The Event and RaiseEvent Statements—Examples

```
Event QuantityBelowReorderPoint(intQuantity)
RaiseEvent QuantityBelowReorderPoint (mintQuantity)

Event TaskComplete()          'Declared at the module level
RaiseEvent TaskComplete       'In a code procedure
```

The **RaiseEvent statement** must appear in the same module as the Event declaration.

Responding to Events

Any module can be an event sink and respond to the events raised by your event source. (The exception is standard code modules, which cannot respond to events.) To respond to an event, you need to

- Declare the object using the **WithEvents keyword.**

```
Private WithEvents mMyTask As CMyTask
```

- Instantiate the object using the Set statement with the New keyword.

```
Set mMyTask = New CMyTask
```

Note: You cannot include both `WithEvents` and `New` in the same declaration. So you must first declare the object variable using `WithEvents`; then when the object is needed, use the `Set`.

- Write the code for the event procedure. You will find your object, mMyTask, in the Code window's Object list and all events that you have defined in the Procedure list.

```
Sub mMyTask_TaskComplete()
```

- When finished, release the object variable.

```
Set mMyTask = Nothing
```

Adding an Event to the Chapter Step-by-Step Tutorial

Next we will add an event to the chapter step-by-step example. In this example we will assume that management has declared that any quantity less than 10 is too low. So whenever an object is created or the quantity increased, if the quantity is less than 10, an event will be generated. The form will respond to the event by displaying a message to the user. Remember, the user interface should handle all interaction with the user—the class module should not display messages.

Add the Event to the Class Module

STEP 1: Open the CDispensaryItem class and declare the event in the General Declarations section.

```
Event LowQuantity()
```

STEP 2: Raise the event in the Quantity's Property Let procedure. Add the `If` statement to your existing procedure.

```
Public Property Let Quantity(ByVal intQuantity As Integer)
    'Assign the property value

    mintQuantity = intQuantity
    If mintQuantity < 10 Then
        RaiseEvent LowQuantity

    End If
End Property
```

STEP 3: Raise the event in the ReceiveItem method, after adding the current amount to the quantity.

```
    mintQuantity = mintQuantity + intNewAmount
    If mintQuantity < 10 Then
        RaiseEvent LowQuantity

    End If
```

Respond to the Event in the Form Module

STEP 1: Open the form module and modify the object declaration in the General Declarations. Remove `New` and add `WithEvents` to the declaration statement for CDispensaryItem.

```
Private WithEvents mDispensaryItem As CDispensaryItem
```

STEP 2: Instantiate the object in the Form_Load procedure.

```
Private Sub Form_Load()
    'Instantiate the object

    Set mDispensaryItem = New CDispensaryItem
End Sub
```

STEP 3: Write code to respond to the event. Drop down the Object list and select mDispensaryItem. Then write code for the LowQuantity event.

```
Private Sub mDispensaryItem_LowQuantity()
    'Display a message to the user
    Dim strMsg As String

    strMsg = "The quantity of this item is below the reorder point."
    MsgBox strMsg, vbInformation, "AVB Dispensary Items"
End Sub
```

Watch It Run

STEP 1: Run the project and enter new values for an object. Experiment with low quantities and add to the quantity. Use quantities < 10, = 10, and > 10.

STEP 2: Press Ctrl + Break to enter break time and single-step execution by using the F8. You will need to press your application's Taskbar button to bring the form to the top. Watch the event fire in the class module and your form's event procedure respond to the event.

Feedback 6.4

1. Write the statements necessary to raise an event called WillSoundAlarm in a class module. Where will each statement appear?
2. Write the statements necessary to respond to the WillSoundAlarm event in a form module. Where will each statement appear?

Collections

When you program with objects, you usually need more than one of each object type. One CDispensaryItem object is not very useful—you usually need to define multiple items. You can do so by creating a collection of objects.

A **collection class** holds references for a series of objects created from the same class or from different classes. Although in concept the collection *contains* the objects, actually the collection holds a reference to each of the objects, called *members* of the collection.

A collection can hold multiple objects, which is similar in concept to an array, which contains multiple variables. However, a collection can do more work for you. A Collection object has an Add method, a Remove method, an Item method, and a Count property. In fact, when you create a collection class, you are creating a collection just like the Forms collection or the Controls collection.

You can refer to the members of a collection in two different ways. Like an array, you can specify an Index number, which is the object's position in the collection. This method is convenient only if the members stay in the same order. Alternatively, you can give each object a string Key that uniquely identifies the object, and the collection object can store and retrieve the objects by their Key. Sometimes objects already have a field that is unique and can be used as a Key, such as a Social Security number, a customer number, or an account number. Or you can assign a sequential number to each object in order to have a unique Key. When objects are removed from a collection, the Indexes for the remaining objects change to reflect their new position, but the Key properties never change.

Microsoft has adopted a consistent naming standard for Collections: use the plural of an object for the name of the collection. Therefore, a collection of objects of the class CProduct is called CProducts, and the collection of CDispensaryItem objects is CDispensaryItems.

Creating a Collection

A collection is another type of object. You create a collection by writing a new class module and declaring an object variable. When you declare a class as Collection, you get all of VB's built-in functionality for a collection, which includes Add, Remove, and Item methods and a Count property.

We will continue the CDispensaryItem tutorial by adding a CDispensaryItems collection.

Creating a Unique Key in the CDispensaryItem Class

Before we create a collection of CDispensaryItem objects, we need to modify the class module to hold a unique Key. Note that the Key field for a collection must be string.

In this example you will assign the next sequential number to each object added to the collection. You will convert the sequential number to a string and assign the value to the new DispensaryItemCode property.

STEP 1: Open the CDispensaryItem class module Code window and add a module-level variable for the DispensaryItemCode property.

```
Private mstrDispensaryItemCode As String
```

STEP 2: Add property procedures to allow access to the new DispensaryItemCode property.

```
Public Property Get DispensaryItemCode() As String
    'Retrieve the current value

    DispensaryItemCode = mstrDispensaryItemCode
End Property

Public Property Let DispensaryItemCode(ByVal strDispensaryItemCode As String)
    'Assign the property value

    mstrDispensaryItemCode = strDispensaryItemCode
End Property
```

Creating the CDispensaryItems Class

STEP 1: Drop down the list of object types from the Add Form button on the toolbar (Figure 6.7). Select *Class Module*; then select *Class Module* from the New tab of the *Add Class Module* dialog box.

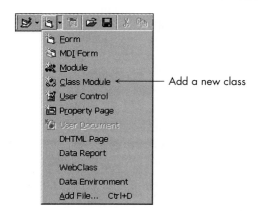

Add a new class module by using the Add Form toolbar button.

Add a new class

STEP 2: In the Properties window change the Name property to CDispensaryItems.

STEP 3: Write the general remarks at the top of the module.

```
'Class Name:     CDispensaryItems
'Programmer:     Your Name
'Date:           Today's Date
'Description:    Maintain the collection of CDispensaryItem objects.
```

STEP 4: Declare the new object variable, using the preferred method without the New keyword.

```
Option Explicit
Private mDispensaryItems As Collection
```

STEP 5: Code the Class_Initialize and Class_Terminate event procedures.

```
Private Sub Class_Initialize()
    'Create the collection object

    Set mDispensaryItems = New Collection
End Sub
```

```
Private Sub Class_Terminate()
    'Release the collection reference

    Set mDispensaryItems = Nothing
End Sub
```

STEP 6: Write the Private function that calculates the next product code. Use a static variable to keep the running count. Remember that a key field must be a string. You must use the `Trim` function to remove the extra space that VB includes when converting from numeric to string.

```
Private Function NextDispensaryItemCode() As String
    'Assign the next DispensaryItemCode
    Static intDispensaryItemCode    As Integer

    intDispensaryItemCode = intDispensaryItemCode + 1
    NextDispensaryItemCode = Trim(Str(intDispensaryItemCode)) 'Convert to string
End Function
```

Adding Objects to a Collection

A Collection object automatically has an Add method. If you declare the Collection's object variable as Public, code from any other module can use that Add method to add objects to the collection. However, to follow good OOP techniques, the collection should have control over each item that is added. Therefore, you should declare the object variable as Private (we did) and write your own Public Add method. This Public Add method is called a *wrapper* **method.**

The Add wrapper method creates a new object from the passed arguments and then executes the default (Private) Add method of the collection, adding the newly created object.

STEP 1: Write the Add wrapper procedure.

```
Public Sub Add(ByVal intFrameStyle As Integer, ByVal intFrameSize As Integer, _
        ByVal intQuantity As Integer)
    'Add a new member to the collection
    'Object variable to hold the new object
    Dim NewDispensaryItem As New CDispensaryItem

    With NewDispensaryItem    'Set up the properties for the new object
        'Call the function to assign the next key
        .DispensaryItemCode = NextDispensaryItemCode
        .FrameStyle = intFrameStyle
        .FrameSize = intFrameSize
        .Quantity = intQuantity

        mDispensaryItems.Add NewDispensaryItem, .DispensaryItemCode
    End With
End Sub
```

Removing a Member from a Collection

If you want to be able to remove objects from a collection, you must also write a Public Remove wrapper method. The new Remove method executes the Private Remove method.

Notice that the Key is passed as an argument to the procedure. The Key specifies which member object to remove. Recall that the Key must be string. If you are using numeric Indexes rather than Keys, then you should pass a Long (or Variant) data type.

Note: If the strKey field is not a valid Key value, this procedure will fail with a run-time error. We add error handling later in this chapter.

STEP 1: Write the Remove wrapper procedure.

```
Public Sub Remove(ByVal strKey As String)
    'Remove a member from the collection

    mDispensaryItems.Remove strKey
End Sub
```

Accessing a Member of a Collection

You also need to write a wrapper method to access an individual element of the collection. Again the string Key is passed as an argument. This function returns the object referenced by the Key as the Item method. Note that you must create a function not a sub procedure for Item.

Note: strKey must be a valid Key from the collection or a run-time error occurs. We add the error handling in the "Errors" section later in the chapter.

STEP 1: Write the Item wrapper function.

```
Public Function Item(ByVal strkey As String) As CDispensaryItem
    'Return one member from the collection

    Set Item = mDispensaryItems.Item(strkey)
End Function
```

Returning the Count Property

Each collection has a Count property that holds the number of members in the collection. Because we declare the collection as Private, we need a Property Get procedure to allow access to the count. Note: The Count property is read only, so you don't need a Property Let procedure.

STEP 1: Write the Property Get procedure to return the count.

```
Public Property Get Count() As Long
    'Return the number of members in the collection

    Count = mDispensaryItems.Count
End Property
```

Setting a Default Property

Each control you use on a form has a default property. Recall that you can refer to txtDescription.Text or txtDescription; the result is the same because Text is the default property of a text box control. You can also set a default property for your class. For a collection the Item property is normally used as the default, since it is used every time you access an object.

To set the default property, make sure you are displaying the code for your collection class and position the insertion point in the Item function. From the *Tools* menu, select *Procedure Attributes.* Click on the Advanced command button. Select *Item* from the *Name* dropdown list and then set the *Procedure ID* to Default (Figure 6.8).

Figure 6.8

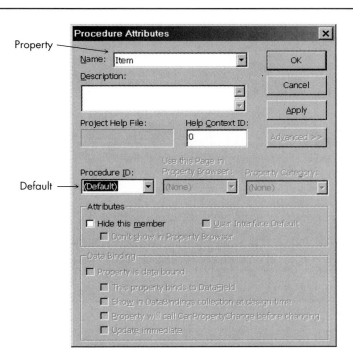

Make the Item property the default property of your class.

Using For Each . . . Next

When you want to access each object in a collection, you can use a `For/Next` statement. However, you must declare a loop index and use the Count property as the upper limit of the loop. For example:

```
'Display each product from the collection
Dim intIndex As Integer

For intIndex = 1 to mDispensaryItems.Count
    picDispensary.Print mDispensaryItems(intIndex).FrameStyle
Next intIndex
```

Note: We are using a picture box control in this example for a "quick-and-dirty" display. A picture box allows you to use the Print method to quickly view output. This code works only if the Item property of the collection is set as the default. If Item isn't the default, you must specify the property:

```
picDispensary.Print mDispensaryItems.Item(intIndex).FrameStyle
```

The For Each...Next statement is much handier for stepping through a collection. Although the statement is not available for user-defined collections, with a small workaround we can make it available.

You need several steps to be able to use For Each. A collection has an enumerator that VB stores as a hidden property. You can expose the enumerator by referencing this hidden property (_NewEnum) in a function in the collection's code.

The NewEnum Function

STEP 1: In the CDispensaryItems collection class module, write the NewEnum function procedure.

```
Public Function NewEnum()
    'Allow for the For Each…Next enumeration

    Set NewEnum = mDispensaryItems.[_NewEnum]
End Function
```

Note: The square brackets around _NewEnum are required because the underscore is not a legal character for a property. A leading underscore in a property name indicates a hidden property.

STEP 2: Now for the really strange step: With the insertion point in the Function NewEnum statement, open the *Procedure Attributes* dialog box from the *Tools* menu, choose *Advanced,* set the *Procedure ID* to −4 (negative four), and check the box for *Hide this member* (Figure 6.9).

To allow use of the For Each *statement, set the* Procedure ID *of the* NewEnum *function to* −4.

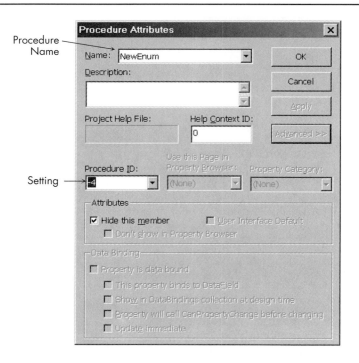

Once you have completed these two steps to expose the enumerator, you can step through the collection using For Each.

```
'Display each product from the collection
Dim DisplayItem As CDispensaryItem

For Each DisplayItem In mDispensaryItems
    picDispensary.Print DisplayItem.FrameStyle, DisplayItem.FrameSize, _
    DisplayItem.Quantity
Next
```

Note: As in the earlier `For Next` example, we are using a picture box control for a quick-and-dirty display of items.

Using a Collection in a Form—Step by Step

Now it's time to put this code together and make it all run. We will modify the form from the chapter step-by-step tutorial to use a collection. We'll add command buttons to add an object, display the collection, and clear the display. Note that the new objects created in the cmdAddObject_Click procedure are actually created by the collection.

Note: This exercise is a continuation of the earlier step-by-step tutorial.

Modify the User Interface

STEP 1: Open your form and remove the four command buttons and their associated code.

STEP 2: Add command buttons for Add Object, Display Collection, and Clear Display. Set the Name and Caption properties of the buttons.

STEP 3: Add a picture box control, named picDisplay. Figure 6.10 shows the completed form.

Figure 6.10

The form for the collection step-by-step tutorial.

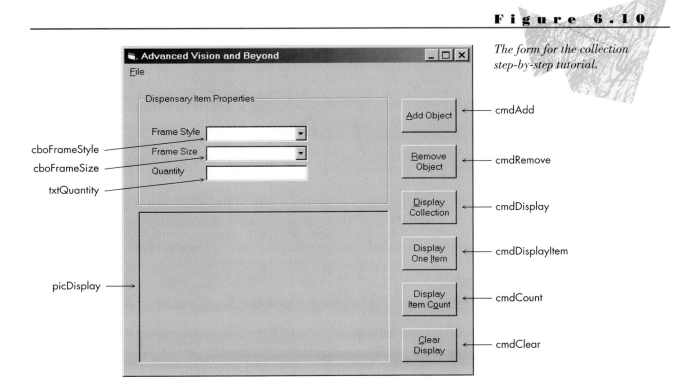

Assuming that you have completed all the numbered steps in the chapter, your CDispensaryItems collection class module has procedures for Add, Remove, Item, Count, and NewEnum and has exposed the enumerator so that you can use the For Each statement on the collection. Check your CDispensaryItems code to make sure all procedures are present.

Declare the Collection Object

You must declare a new object of the collection class in the form's General Declarations section.

STEP 1: In the form's Code window, add a declaration for the Collection object variable.

```
Private mDispensaryItems As New CDispensaryItems 'Instantiate the collection
```

STEP 2: Remove the declaration for mDispensaryItem. In this project all new CDispensaryItem objects are declared only in the collection class. You refer to a single object as a member of the collection.

STEP 3: Modify the Form_Unload procedure to release the Collection object (mDispensaryItems). (Add an *s* to the object name.)

STEP 4: Remove the mDispensaryItem_LowQuantity event procedure.

Tip

Make sure to always list the fields on the Add statement in exactly the same order as they are specified on the Add procedure in the collection class.

Code the Add Procedure

Your cmdAdd_Click procedure takes the contents of the combo boxes and text box on the form and uses the Add method of the mDispensaryItems collection. Recall that the Add method generates the next sequential DispensaryItemCode, creates a new object, and adds the object to the collection.

STEP 1: Code the cmdAdd_Click procedure in your form module.

```
Private Sub cmdAdd_Click()
    'Add an item to the collection

    If cboFrameSize.ListIndex <> −1 And cboFrameStyle.ListIndex <> −1 Then
        mDispensaryItems.Add cboFrameStyle.ListIndex + 1, _
        cboFrameSize.ListIndex + 1, _
        Val(txtQuantity.Text)
    Else
        MsgBox "Enter values for the item.", vbInformation, _
        "Dispensary Items"
        End If
        cmdClear_Click    'Clear out form controls
End Sub
```

Code the Display Procedure

The cmdDisplay_Click procedure uses a For Each statement to step through the collection. For an easy way to print quickly, we will use the Print method of a picture box control. The techniques you know for printing to the printer object work the same here—you can use commas and semicolons for spacing, as well as the Tab and Spc function. Notice the Cls (clear screen) method used to clear the contents of the picture box.

STEP 1: Code the cmdDisplay_Click procedure in your form module.

```
Private Sub cmdDisplay_Click()
    'Display the objects in the collection
    Dim DisplayItem As CDispensaryItem

    picDisplay.Cls              'Clear the display and print headings
    picDisplay.Print "Item Code", "Frame Style", "Frame Size", "Quantity"
    picDisplay.Print

    For Each DisplayItem In mDispensaryItems
        With DisplayItem
            picDisplay.Print .DispensaryItemCode, .FrameStyle, .FrameSize, _
                .Quantity
        End With
    Next
End Sub
```

Code the Count Procedure

STEP 1: Add the code for cmdCount_Click. You will display the Count property of the collection.

```
Private Sub cmdCount_Click()
    'Display the number of objects in the collection
    Dim strMsg As String

    strMsg = "The number of Dispensary Items is " & mDispensaryItems.Count
    MsgBox strMsg, vbInformation, "AVB Dispensary Items"
End Sub
```

Code the Clear Procedure

Clear all screen controls, including the picture box.

STEP 1: Code the cmdClear_Click procedure in the form module.

```
Private Sub cmdClear_Click()
    'Clear screen controls

    cboFrameSize.ListIndex = -1
    cboFrameStyle.ListIndex = -1
    txtQuantity.Text = ""
    picDisplay.Cls
End Sub
```

Run the Project

We will postpone coding the Remove and DisplayItem procedures until after the discussion of error handling. It's time to run the project. See what's happening in the project by single-stepping program execution by repeatedly pressing F8.

Tip

If you get the run-time error "438 - Object does not support this property or method," check the Procedure ID for the NewEnum procedure. It must be set to −4.

Feedback 6.5

1. Write the code to refer to a single item in a collection of the CPersons class using a Key. Then modify the code to use an Index instead of a Key.
2. Explain the differences between using an Index and using a Key for objects in a collection.

continued

3. Which property of a collection class should be made the default property?
4. Write the code to remove an object from the CPersons class.

Errors

If an error occurs in a class module, you need to handle it. However, you should not display error messages to the user in a class module; all user interaction should be handled by the user interface. As a general rule, you will raise an error in a class module and handle the error in the form module, using the `On Error GoTo`. Any errors that you generate can be handled by using standard VB error trapping. You can raise error conditions for validation errors as well as errors such as an invalid key for a collection or a file not found.

Setting the Environment Option for Error Handling

When you are working in the VB environment, as opposed to running compiled projects, you can choose whether a project cancels on error conditions. Select *Tools/Options* and display the General tab of the *Options* dialog box (Figure 6.11). In the Error Trapping section, select *Break on Unhandled Errors.* If you leave the default, *Break in Class Module,* your project will enter break time even when you correctly handle an error condition.

F i g u r e　6 . 1 1

Select Break on Unhandled Errors when you raise and handle errors from a class module.

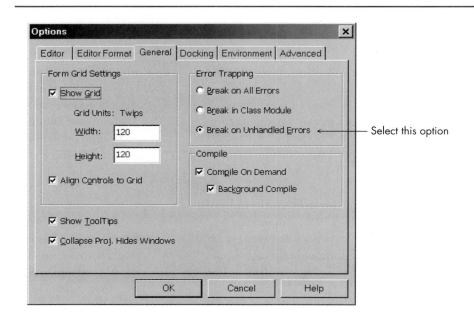

Setting up Error Numbers, Descriptions, and Constants

You can assign an error number to your error condition and then check for that error number in your error-handling code. The numbers that you choose should not conflict with any VB error codes. VB reserves 512 error numbers above a starting location called *vbErrorConstant.* So the first error number you should use in a program is

```
Const MyErrorCode1 = vbErrorConstant + 512 + 1     'Program error code 1
```

Using this constant declaration, you could code this statement:

```
Err.Raise MyErrorCode1, "My Class Module", "You have violated rule number 1"
```

This statement raises an error. It sets Err.Number to your error code, Err.Source to the name of the module generating the error (My Class Module), and Err.Description to "You have violated rule number 1".

In this example we declared a constant for the error code. However, there is a much better way to declare constants by using a VB `Enum`.

Using Enums for Constants

You are familiar with declaring constants by using the `Const` statement. But are you aware that `Const` declarations can only be Private? Therefore, if you declare constants in a class module, the constants are not available in any other module. However, you can declare numeric constants that are Public by using the Enum **statement.** In fact, any constants that you declare in a `Public Enum` statement become global to the entire project and appear in the Object Browser.

The Enum Statement—General Form

```
[Public|Private] Enum EnumName
    ConstantName [= ConstantValue]
    ConstantName [= ConstantValue]
    . . .
End Enum
```

You can code an `Enum` only at the module level. By default `Enums` are Public. The data type of the constants is Long, which holds a long integer. (You cannot declare string constants in an `Enum`.) The VB constants that you have been using such as vbOKOnly and adUseClient are actually `Enums` representing an integer value.

If you omit the constant value, the first constant is assigned a value of zero and each succeeding constant is assigned one number higher than the last. Good programming practice and documentation conventions dictate that you always explicitly declare the constant values.

The Enum Statement—Examples

```
Enum myConstants
    myPi = 3.14159
    myMaximumHours = 40
    myFirstError = 1
End Enum

Public Enum diError        'Dispensary Item Errors
    diItemCodeError = vbObjectError + 512 + 1
    diValidationError = vbObjectError + 512 + 2
End Enum
```

Make sure to give your Enum and constants a prefix. Doing so makes them appear in a group in the Object Browser and identifies the module that created them. Also, because constants declared with Enum are global to the entire project, you want to choose a unique prefix so that your names don't conflict with any VB constants.

Raising and Handling Errors—Step by Step

In this continuation of the collection step-by-step tutorial, we will add the code to remove an object and display a single object from the collection. Error handling is necessary in case the user enters a Key for an object that doesn't exist.

Write the Enum for the Error Code

STEP 1: In the Code window for the collection class module, add these statements to the General Declarations section.

```
Public Enum diError
    diItemCodeError = vbObjectError + 512 + 1
End Enum
```

Modify the Remove Method

In your Remove wrapper procedure, you must add error trapping to handle an strKey value for a nonexistent key. Turn on error trapping before the Remove. If the statement fails, raise your own error in the error-handling code.

STEP 1: Add the error handling to your Remove method.

```
Public Sub Remove(ByVal strKey As String)
    'Remove a member from the collection

    On Error GoTo HandleError
    mDispensaryItems.Remove strKey
Remove_Exit:
    Exit Sub

HandleError:
    Err.Raise diItemCodeError, "CDispensaryItems", "Invalid item key"
End Sub
```

Modify the Item Method

You must add similar code to your Item wrapper procedure because the user may enter an invalid key.

STEP 1: Add the error handling to your Item method.

```
Public Function Item(ByVal strKey As String) As CDispensaryItem
    'Return one member from the collection

    On Error GoTo HandleError
    Set Item = mDispensaryItems.Item(strKey)
Item_Exit:
    Exit Function

HandleError:
    Err.Raise diItemCodeError, "CDispensaryItems", _
        "Invalid dispensary item key"
End Function
```

Add Error Trapping to the Form Module

You must trap for errors in the cmdRemove_Click and cmdDisplayItem_Click procedures. If an error occurs, check the error code using your Enum constant and display an appropriate message.

STEP 1: Add error trapping and handling to cmdRemove_Click.

```
On Error GoTo HandleError
    '(Program statements here)
    Exit Sub

HandleError:
    If Err.Number = diItemCodeError Then
        MsgBox "Invalid Dispensary Item Code", vbInformation, _
            "Remove Dispensary Item"
    Else
        MsgBox "Unexpected Error", vbInformation, "Display Dispensary Item"
    End If
```

STEP 2: Add the same error trapping/handling code to cmdDisplayItem_Click.

Test Your Error Handling

STEP 1: Select *Tools/Options* and display the General tab. Make sure that *Break on Unhandled* Errors is selected and close the dialog box.

STEP 2: Run your project and add several objects to the collection.

STEP 3: Test the Remove button, first with a good Key and then with a non-existent Key.

STEP 4: Test the Display Item button, both with a good Key and with nonexistent Keys. Does your error trapping work properly?

STEP 5: Try single-stepping the code and watch the class module catch the error and raise your error. Then the form module should catch the error.

Feedback 6.6

1. Write an `Enum` statement to declare constants for validation errors. InvalidFrameSize should have a code of 1; InvalidFrameStyle should be code 2; InvalidQuantity should be code 3.
2. Write the code for a Property Let statement that checks the intFrameSize incoming argument. If the value is < 1 or > 4, raise the InvalidFrameSize error.
3. Write the code for a form module that traps and handles the InvalidFrameSize error.

Using the Object Browser

The **Object Browser** is an important tool for working with objects in VB. The Object Browser can show you the names of objects, properties, methods, events, and constants for VB objects, your own objects, and objects available from other applications.

Select *View / Object Browser,* click on the Object Browser toolbar button, or press F2 to display the Object Browser (Figure 6.12). In the *Project/Library* dropdown list, you can choose to display the objects in your own project or one of the VB libraries. You can type search text in the Search Text box to display matching text in the selected library or project.

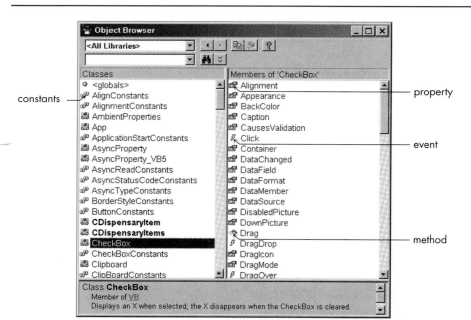

The Object Browser window. Notice the icons to indicate the member type.

The Object Browser uses several icons to represent items. Notice in Figure 6.12 the icons that represent properties, methods, events, and constants. At the bottom of the window you can see a description of any item you select.

Examining VB Objects

The Object Browser is the quickest and most reliable way to look up the available properties, methods, events, or constants of a VB object. You will find the lists to be more complete than those found in Help.

Try this: Select *VB* in the Project/Library list and click on *CheckBox* in the Classes list. Then examine the list that shows members of the CheckBox class; you will see the names of properties, methods, and events. Try clicking on a member name in the list; the description of that item shows up in the bottom pane of the window. And if you want more information on any member, click to select it and press F1 for its Help topic.

Examining Your Own Classes

You can see your own classes listed in the Object Browser. Make sure that the chapter step-by-step example project is open and then open the Object Browser. Select *Project1* from the Project/Library list and see the project's classes listed in the Classes list. Try clicking on each class name and viewing the list of properties and methods (Figure 6.13).

F i g u r e   6 . 1 3

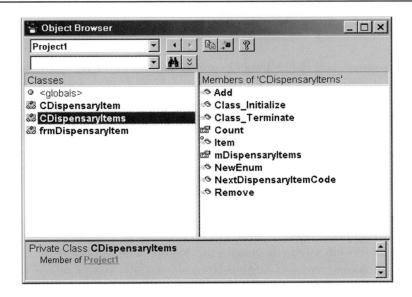

View the properties and methods for your own classes.

You can use the Object Browser to jump to the definition of any property or method by double-clicking on its name in the Members list. This is also a great way to jump to any of the procedures in your forms. Select your form name in the Classes list, then double-click on the name of the procedure you want to view.

Note: The MSDN Library has extensive information on using the Object Browser.

Your Hands-on Programming Example

The hands-on example in this chapter is the same as the chapter step-by-step tutorial for collections. If you have done each step of the tutorial, you have completed this exercise. You can use these specifications for reference.

This project creates and maintains a collection of DispensaryItem objects. The user should be given the options to add an object, remove an object, display the collection, display one item, display the item count, clear the display, and exit.

Display the collection and the single item in a picture box control.

Plan the Project

Sketch the form (Figure 6.14), which your user signs off.

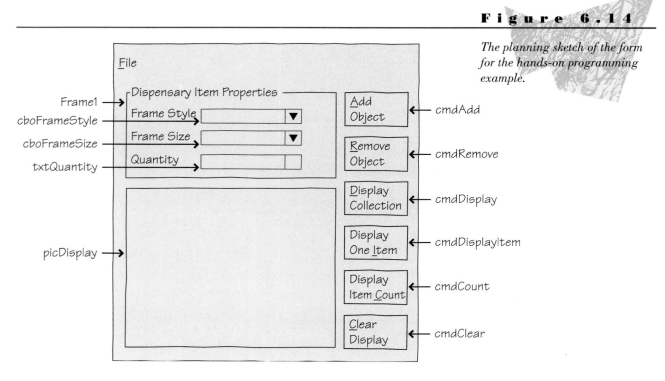

F i g u r e   6 . 1 4

The planning sketch of the form for the hands-on programming example.

Plan the Object and Collection Class

Identify the properties of the CDispensaryItem class and the CDispensaryItems collection class. The individual object class must declare a property variable for each property of the class.

CDispensaryItem Properties

Access Mode (Public or Private)	Variable Name	Data Type	Description
Private	mintQuantity	Integer	Quantity property

continued

Access Mode (Public or Private)	Variable Name	Data Type	Description
Private	mintFrameSize	Integer	FrameSize property
Private	mintFrameStyle	Integer	FrameStyle property
Private	mstrDispensaryItemCode	String	DispensaryItemCode property

CDispensaryItems Properties

No properties are needed for the collection class.

Plan the Form's Objects and Properties

Object	Property	Setting
frmDispensaryItem	Caption	Advanced Vision and Beyond
Frame1	Caption	Dispensary Item Properties
cboFrameStyle	Style	2 - Dropdown List
cboFrameSize	Style	2 - Dropdown List
txtQuantity	Text	(blank)
Label1	Caption	Frame Style
Label2	Caption	Frame Size
Label3	Caption	Quantity
cmdAdd	Caption	&Add Object
cmdRemove	Caption	&Remove Object
cmdDisplay	Caption	&Display Collection
cmdDisplayItem	Caption	Display One &Item
cmdCount	Caption	Display Item C&ount
cmdClear	Caption	&Clear Display
picDisplay	Picture	(blank)
mnuFile	Caption	&File
mnuFileExit	Caption	E&xit

Plan the Procedures

Plan the function and sub procedures for each class module and the form module.

CDispensaryItem Methods

Access Mode (Public or Private)	Return Type (for Function)	Procedure Name (Include Any Parameters)	Purpose
Public	Integer	Quantity	Property Let and Property Get.

continued

Access Mode (Public or Private)	Return Type (for Function)	Procedure Name (Include Any Paramenters)	Purpose
Public	Integer	FrameStyle	Property Let and Property Get.
Public	Integer	FrameSize	Property Let and Property Get.
Public	String	DispensaryItemCode	Property Let and Property Get.

CDispensaryItems Collection Methods

Access Mode (Public or Private)	Return Type (for Function)	Procedure Name (Include Any Paramenters)	Purpose
Public		Enum	Set up error constants.
Private		Class_Initialize	Instantiate the collection.
Private		Class_Terminate	Release the object variable.
Private	String	NextDispensaryItemCode	Assign the next key. Add 1 to count. Convert to string.
Public		Add(intFrameStyle, intFrameSize, intQuantity)	Instantiate a new object. Get the next key. Assign the properties of the new object. Add to the collection.
Public		Remove(strKey)	Remove the object from the collection. Raise an error if the Remove fails.
Public	CDispensaryItem	Item(strKey)	Return one item from the collection. Raise an error if the action fails.
Public	NewEnum	NewEnum	Set the NewEnum so the For Each works.
Public	Long	Count	Property Get (read only property).

Plan the Procedures for the Form

Procedure	Actions

cmdAdd_Click	If selection made from combo boxes then
	    Add to collection.
	Else
	    Display message.
	End If
	Clear the controls (call cmdClear_Click).

cmdRemove_Click	Input key of object to remove. Remove object from the collection. Display message if action fails.
cmdDisplay_Click	Clear the picture box. Display headings. For Each loop Display properties of one object. Next

continued

Procedure	Actions
cmdDisplayItem_Click	Input key of object to remove. Display item from the collection. Display message if action fails.
cmdCount_Click	Display collection count in a MsgBox.
cmdClear_Click	Set ListIndex of combo boxes to −1. Clear text box. Clear picture box.
mnuFileExit_Click	Unload form.
Form_Unload	Release object variables.

Write the Project

- Follow your plan to create the two class modules. Working from the pseudocode, write the procedures.

- Follow the sketch in Figure 6.14 to create the form. Figure 6.15 shows the completed form.

Figure 6.15

The completed form for the hands-on programming example.

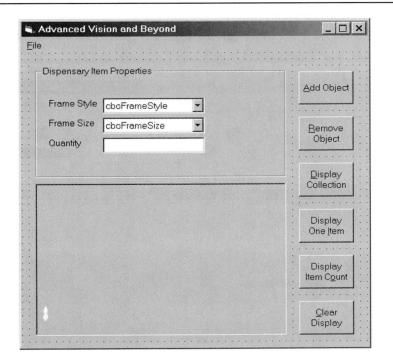

- Set the properties of the form and each of the controls, as you have planned.

- Working from the pseudocode, write each procedure.

- When you complete the code, thoroughly test the project.

The Project Coding Solution

CDispensaryItem Class

```
'Module:          CDispensaryItem
'Programmer:      Bradley/Millspaugh
'Date:            2/2000
'Description:     Define methods and properties of the class.
'Folder:          Ch06SBSObject

Option Explicit

Private mintQuantity       As Integer
Private mintFrameSize      As Integer
Private mintFrameStyle     As Integer
Private mstrDispensaryItemCode As String
```

```
Public Property Get Quantity() As Integer
    'Retrieve the current value

    Quantity = mintQuantity
End Property
```

```
Public Property Let Quantity(ByVal intQuantity As Integer)
    'Assign the property value

    mintQuantity = intQuantity
End Property
```

```
Public Property Get FrameStyle() As Integer
    'Retrieve the current value

    FrameStyle = mintFrameStyle
End Property
```

```
Public Property Let FrameStyle(ByVal intFrameStyle As Integer)
    'Assign the property value

    mintFrameStyle = intFrameStyle
End Property
```

```
Public Property Get FrameSize() As Integer
    'Retrieve the current value

    FrameSize = mintFrameSize
End Property
```

```
Public Property Let FrameSize(ByVal intFrameSize As Integer)
    'Assign the property value

    mintFrameSize = intFrameSize
End Property
```

```
Public Property Get DispensaryItemCode() As String
    'Retrieve the current value

    DispensaryItemCode = mstrDispensaryItemCode
End Property
```

```
Public Property Let DispensaryItemCode(ByVal strDispensaryItemCode As String)
    'Assign the property value

    mstrDispensaryItemCode = Trim(strDispensaryItemCode) 'Remove any extra spaces
End Property
```

CDispensaryItems Collection Class

```
'Class Name:    CDispensaryItems
'Programmer:    Bradley/Millspaugh
'Date:          2/2000
'Description:   Maintain the collection of CDispensaryItem objects.

Option Explicit
Private mDispensaryItems As Collection

Public Enum diError
    diItemCodeError = vbObjectError + 512 + 1
End Enum
```

```
Private Sub Class_Initialize()
    'Create the collection object

    Set mDispensaryItems = New Collection
End Sub
```

```
Private Sub Class_Terminate()
    'Release the collection reference

    Set mDispensaryItems = Nothing
End Sub
```

```
Private Function NextDispensaryItemCode() As String
    'Assign the next DispensaryItemCode
    Static intDispensaryItemCode    As Integer

    intDispensaryItemCode = intDispensaryItemCode + 1
    NextDispensaryItemCode = Trim(Str(intDispensaryItemCode))  'Convert to string
End Function
```

```
Public Sub Add(ByVal intFrameStyle As Integer, ByVal intFrameSize As Integer, _
        ByVal intQuantity As Integer)
    'Add a new member to the collection
    'Object variable to hold the new object
    Dim NewDispensaryItem As New CDispensaryItem

    With NewDispensaryItem    'Set up the properties for the new object
        'Call the function to assign the next key
        .DispensaryItemCode = NextDispensaryItemCode
        .FrameStyle = intFrameStyle
        .FrameSize = intFrameSize
        .Quantity = intQuantity

        mDispensaryItems.Add NewDispensaryItem, .DispensaryItemCode
    End With
End Sub
```

```
Public Sub Remove(ByVal strKey As String)
    'Remove a member from the collection

    On Error GoTo HandleError
    mDispensaryItems.Remove strKey
Remove_Exit:
    Exit Sub

HandleError:
    Err.Raise diItemCodeError, "CDispensaryItems", "Invalid dispensary item key"
End Sub
```

```
Public Function Item(ByVal strKey As String) As CDispensaryItem
    'Return one member from the collection

    On Error GoTo HandleError
    Set Item = mDispensaryItems.Item(strKey)
Item_Exit:
    Exit Function

HandleError:
    Err.Raise diItemCodeError, "CDispensaryItems", "Invalid dispensary item key"
End Function
```

```
Public Property Get Count() As Long
    'Return the number of members in the collection

    Count = mDispensaryItems.Count
End Property
```

```
Public Function NewEnum()
    'Allow for the For Each...Next enumeration

    Set NewEnum = mDispensaryItems.[_NewEnum]
End Function
```

Form

```
'Project:        Maintain Collection
'Programmer:     Bradley/Millspaugh
'Date:           2/2000
'Description:    Maintain a collection of DispensaryItems
'Folder:         Ch06SBSCollection

Option Explicit
Private mDispensaryItems As New CDispensaryItems 'Instantiate the collection
```

```
Private Sub cmdAdd_Click()
    'Add an item to the collection

    If cboFrameSize.ListIndex <> -1 And cboFrameStyle.ListIndex <> -1 Then
        mDispensaryItems.Add cboFrameStyle.ListIndex + 1, _
            cboFrameSize.ListIndex + 1, _
            Val(txtQuantity.Text)
    Else
        MsgBox "Enter values for the item.", vbInformation, "Dispensary Items"
    End If
    cmdClear_Click              'Clear out form controls
End Sub
```

```vb
Private Sub cmdClear_Click()
    'Clear screen controls

    cboFrameSize.ListIndex = -1
    cboFrameStyle.ListIndex = -1
    txtQuantity.Text = ""
    picDisplay.Cls
End Sub
```

```vb
Private Sub cmdCount_Click()
    'Display the number of objects in the collection
    Dim strMsg As String

    strMsg = "The number of Dispensary Items is " & mDispensaryItems.Count
    MsgBox strMsg, vbInformation, "AVB Dispensary Items"
End Sub
```

```vb
Private Sub cmdDisplay_Click()
    'Display the objects in the collection
    Dim DisplayItem As CDispensaryItem

    picDisplay.Cls              'Clear the display and print headings
    picDisplay.Print "Item Code", "Frame Style", "Frame Size", "Quantity"
    picDisplay.Print

    For Each DisplayItem In mDispensaryItems
      With DisplayItem
        picDisplay.Print .DispensaryItemCode, .FrameStyle, .FrameSize, _
            .Quantity
      End With
    Next
End Sub
```

```vb
Private Sub cmdDisplayItem_Click()
    'Display one item from collection
    Dim strKey      As String

    On Error GoTo HandleError
    strKey = InputBox("Enter item code to display.", "Display Dispensary Item")

    picDisplay.Cls              'Clear the display and print headings
    picDisplay.Print "Item Code", "Frame Style", "Frame Size", "Quantity"
    picDisplay.Print

    With mDispensaryItems(strKey)
        picDisplay.Print .DispensaryItemCode, .FrameSize, .FrameStyle, .Quantity
    End With

cmdDisplay_Click_Exit:
    Exit Sub

HandleError:
    If Err.Number = diItemCodeError Then
        MsgBox "Invalid Dispensary Item Code", vbInformation, _
        "Display Dispensary Item"
    Else
        MsgBox "Unexpected Error", vbInformation, "Display Dispensary Item"
    End If
End Sub
```

```
Private Sub cmdRemove_Click()
    'Remove an item
    Dim strKey        As String

    On Error GoTo HandleError
    strKey = InputBox("Enter item code to remove.", "Remove Dispensary Item")
    mDispensaryItems.Remove strKey

cmdRemove_Click_Exit:
    Exit Sub

HandleError:
    If Err.Number = diItemCodeError Then
        MsgBox "Invalid Dispensary Item Code", vbInformation, _
            "Remove Dispensary Item"
    Else
        MsgBox "Unexpected Error", vbInformation, "Display Dispensary Item"
    End If
End Sub
```

```
Private Sub Form_Unload(Cancel As Integer)
    'Release object variables

    Set mDispensaryItems = Nothing
End Sub
```

```
Private Sub mnuFileExit_Click()
    'Exit the project

    Unload Me
End Sub
```

MCSD Exam Notes

Questions/Tricks to Watch for

- Even though questions do not directly relate to naming conventions, recognizing the prefixes will help you to read questions more quickly.

S u m m a r y

1. Objects have properties and methods and can generate events.
2. You can create a new class module that can then be used to create new objects. The new object is called an instance of the class.
3. In object-oriented terminology, *encapsulation* refers to the combination of the characteristics and behaviors of an item into a single class definition. *Polymorphism* allows different classes of objects to have similar methods that behave differently for that particular object. *Inheritance* provides a means to derive a new object class based on an existing class. VB does not allow true inheritance but allows for reusability in another manner, using interfaces and delegation.

4. One advantage of object-oriented programming (OOP) is that objects you create for one project may be reused in another project.

5. Properties inside a class should be Private so that data values are accessible only by procedures within the class.

6. The way to make the properties of a class available to code outside the class is to use Property Get and Property Let procedures.

7. The methods of a class are Public sub procedures and functions.

8. To instantiate an object of a class, you must use the New keyword on either the declaration statement or the Set statement. The location of the New keyword determines when the object is created.

9. Declaring an object variable as a specific object type allows early binding; dimensioning a variable as a generic object type causes late binding, which is much less efficient than early binding.

10. The Class_Initialize event occurs when an object is created; the Class_Terminate event is triggered when an object is destroyed.

11. To raise an event from a class module, you must declare the event and use the RaiseEvent statement. The module that raises the event is called the *event source*. The module that responds to an event is the *event sink*.

12. To respond to the events in an event source, declare the object variable using the WithEvents keyword when the object is declared. WithEvents and New cannot appear in the same statement.

13. A collection holds a series of objects. You can create a new collection class and declare a new instance of the class. Members of a class can be referenced by a unique string Key or by a numeric Index.

14. Each collection class automatically has methods for Add, Remove, and Item and has a Count property. These methods should be made Private, and new Public wrapper methods should be written to give the class control over its methods.

15. You can set a default property of a class and enable the enumerator to allow using the For Each statement.

16. The Object Browser displays all properties, methods, and events for your new classes as well as all VB objects and objects from other available applications.

17. A class can raise an error that uses the VB Err object. Assign a unique error code and trap for the error in the form module.

18. Public constants can be created by using the Enum statement. Enums set up long integer values that are global to the project and appear in the Object Browser.

19. The Object Browser can display objects, properties, methods, events, and constants for VB objects as well as the classes that you create.

Key Terms

Review Questions

1. What is an object? a property? a method?
2. What is the purpose of a class module?
3. Why should properties of a class be declared as Private?
4. What are property procedures and what is their purpose?
5. Explain how to create a new object.
6. What steps are needed to assign property values to an object?
7. What actions trigger the Initialize event and the Terminate event of an object?
8. How can you write methods for a new class?
9. How can you write events for a new class?
10. What is a collection? Name one collection that is automatically built into VB.
11. What properties and methods are provided by the Collection object?
12. How can a program handle errors that occur in a class module?

Programming Exercises

6.1 Create a project that allows users to add to a collection of sandwich objects. Each sandwich member should have properties for name, bread, meat, cheese, and condiments.

   Use a picture box to display the object properties as they are added to the collection.

6.2 Modify project 6.1 to allow the user to remove sandwich objects and display a single object. Raise and handle an error if the user requests an invalid sandwich key.

6.3 Create a project that maintains a Collection of vendors. Each vendor should have properties for company name, phone, contact person, and email.

   Allow the user to add a vendor, display the list of vendors, display a single vendor, or remove a vendor. Display the vendor information in a picture box or a second form. Raise and handle an error if the user enters an invalid vendor key.

6.4   Modify project 6.3 to display the vendor names in a sorted dropdown list. Store the vendor name in the List property and the vendor's key in the ItemData property. (Remember that the ItemData property holds long integer values, so you will have to convert the string key to numeric to store it in ItemData.)

   As each vendor is added to the collection, add the name to the list; when a vendor is removed from the collection, remove the name from the list. Allow the user to select a vendor from the list and display the vendor's properties on the form or in a message box or on a second form.

C A S E   S T U D I E S

Video Bonanza

Create a project that maintains a collection of customers. Each Customer object should contain customer name, customer number (Key for Collection), and phone number. Allow options for adding and removing objects. Use a picture box to display the objects, giving the user the option to display the entire Collection or a selected customer. Raise and handle an error if the user enters an invalid Key.

VB Auto

Create a project that maintains a collection of advertisers. Each Advertiser object should contain company name, number (Key for Collection), and account representative's name. Allow options for adding and removing Advertiser objects. Use a picture box to display the objects, giving the user the option to display the entire Collection or a selected advertiser. Raise and handle an error if the user enters an invalid Key.

7

Designing a Multitier Database Application

At the completion of this chapter, you will be able to . . .

1. Define the stages of design: conceptual design, logical design, physical design, and deployment.

2. Understand how design decisions impact application performance, maintainability, extensibility, and availability.

3. Recognize Unifield Modeling Language (UML) class diagram symbols and relationships.

4. Create a data-aware class.

5. Understand the advantages of multitier data applications.

6. Implement a three-tier application using ADO.

This chapter introduces the design stages and UML as a design tool. In the previous chapter you learned to create a class module. In this chapter you learn to create a data-aware class and divide an application into several classes to create a **multitier database application.**

Designing a System

Sometimes you may have felt overwhelmed with developing a project. Can you imagine designing and implementing an entire system? Each example from Advanced Vision covers only one small portion of the system. The same is true of your case studies. In real life we would be working with all parts of the system or with a team with divided responsibilities for components of the system.

Ultimately everything (and everyone) must work together. Some thought must be given to the possibility of expanding, modifying, and maintaining the system. This level of integration is not going to happen without a plan.

The planning stages for a project are important. But even earlier, the planning for the entire system is critical. Programming professionals often say that the more time spent in planning, the less time needed for debugging. A logical design is needed to show how the components work together and what each component is responsible for.

Conceptual Design, Logical Design, Physical Design, and Deployment

The system design is sometimes referred to as the architecture of the system. Just as an architect goes through many stages of development before a project is built, an information system should go through several design steps. You can break the design phase into four stages: conceptual design, logical design, physical design, and deployment.

The **conceptual design** stage is for gathering information to determine the system or application requirements. This process involves input from many levels, from owner to manager to line personnel, depending on the size of the company. Unfortunately, one adage is very true: I'll know what I want when I see it. You must find out needs, how information flows, who does what, and what must be produced. In other words, what output is needed? What are the inputs? Where does each come from? And what must be calculated?

The **logical design** identifies the objects involved in the system. These objects may include customers or patients, vendors, orders, or prescriptions, any object that either supplies information (input) or receives information (output). Each object must then have a design for its interface (properties and methods) and its relationship to or dependency on other objects.

The logical design is compared to the conceptual design in a step referred to as **validation.** Just as you validate data and have errors, you may find that the conceptual and logical designs do not match, which indicates a need for further refinement.

The **physical design** applies the logical design to software components. Through reusability some of the components may already exist within the company; alternatively, some may be purchased from a third party, and some you may need to create.

Finally, the **deployment** stage determines how the components are distributed. Will the system be a desktop application or part of a network? Maybe the system will be distributed over the Web.

Performance, Maintainability, Extensibility, and Availability

You are probably already aware of many features that can improve the performance of an application. Let's review some guidelines for items to be considered during system design.

You can improve your application's **performance** not only in terms of speed of processing but also through optimizing features for the user. Do not use too many controls on the form at once. Think of applications that have an *Advanced* or *More* command button for additional features. You have also learned how to use a tabbed dialog box to "clean the screen." A program that is difficult to use will not be used.

Optimizing applications is discussed in Chapter 12, but you need to consider some items during design. Avoid late binding; use constants when appropriate; avoid the Variant data type. Improve the user's perception of the application's performance by loading frequently used forms while a splash screen displays.

If the program is designed to perform well and gets used for a long time (that's the idea), then maintenance will be needed at some point. For **maintainability,** insist that any applications within the system follow naming standards and conventions. All modules should be commented as needed. The design documentation also becomes a good source of information when modifications are needed.

Extensibility refers to the ability to add features to an application at a later date. If the application is well designed, adding features is relatively easy. An excellent example of extensibility is the *Add-In* menu in VB.

MSDN defines **availability** as "continuous operation regardless of failures." You can certainly understand a user's frustration when a bug occurs and a program suddenly shuts down. The design phase should consider how to avoid errors during execution.

Designing an Application in Tiers

The applications we have created so far have been small desktop applications designed to work on one computer only. If we consider the possibility of future expansion or enhancement, then we need to design in a different manner. Consider the possibility of your database application running on a server with multiple users, perhaps growing too large for Access Jet files and needing to migrate to a more powerful DBMS. Or maybe the application runs fine, but the user wants to change the user interface design or even run the application from a Web page.

One method for good system design is to break an application into independent components. The components should continue to do their job if the user interface (sometimes called the *front end*) changes or if the database (the *back end*) changes.

For some years the hot topic has been client-server (C/S) applications. In the first iteration of C/S, applications are broken into two tiers, or layers. The client operates on the user machine, and the server handles the database operations. Differences in design put more or less of the processing on the client machine. The term *thin client* means that little more than the user interface resides on the client machine.

Current thinking is that the ideal design separates an application into three or more tiers. The user interface should be only that; all validation, calculations, and business rules should be in separate components that may be stored on the client machine, the server, or on some other machine on the network. The database access should be handled by separate components that are tailored for the specific DBMS, such as SQL Server, Oracle, or Jet.

If you are designing a large application, it is very important to break the system into multiple tiers. But even for small projects that run on a single processor, the three-tier model has some advantages.

The Three-Tier Model

Think of an application as providing functionality for three "layers": User Services, Business Services or Business Objects, and Data Services (Figure 7.1). The **User Services** are seen directly by the user, in other words, they provide the user interface—forms, controls, and menus. The objects that we have created for applications, such as Product, Salesman, or Invoice, are the **Business Objects,** also called **Business Services.** The third tier is **Data Services,** for storage and retrieval of data. The three-tier model is often referred to as the *services model.*

Figure 7.1

The three-tier design model.

User Services	Business Services	Data Services
User Interface Forms, controls, menus	**Business Objects** Validation Calculations Business logic Business rules	**Data Retrieval** Data storage

Let's consider Advanced Vision as a multitier application. The User Services tier includes the update forms that we created in previous chapters. However, you will find that much of the coding must move from the form module to separate objects that are part of the Business Services tier. The entire system will require additional forms for updating the other tables, such as Patient, Visit, and Prescription.

The Business Services tier consists of the class modules for the various system objects. Each class will contain the appropriate properties and methods. Functions such as validation and navigation will appear in these modules.

For the Data Services tier, we need to create new data-aware classes, which interact with the DBMS to retrieve and save data. A data-aware class in VB can be a data source and can be bound to controls, similar to the functioning of a data control. A data-aware class can retrieve and save data in multiple sources, including multiple tables from more than one file or DBMS.

The major advantage of using multiple tiers is that you can make a change to a portion of the system without affecting all the code. Imagine that as the company grows, management wants to migrate from Access to SQL Server, Oracle, or Sybase, which should affect only the Data Services. On the other hand, the user may believe that a change to the interface could improve productivity. That change should have no effect on the Business Services or the Data Services objects.

Design Tools

Over the years computer professionals have used many methodologies for planning and documenting systems and projects. In recent years, with the emergence of object-oriented programming and multitier systems, the planning and design tools have become more and more similar. More recently the designers of the three most popular design methods (Booch, Jacobson, and Rumbaugh), along with many large corporations and the industrywide Object Management Group (OMG), agreed on the specifications for a single unified standard called **Unified Modeling Language (UML).**

UML

UML is a graphical language for visualizing, specifying, constructing, and documenting a software system. In this text we use only a small subset of UML to create class diagrams, which describe and illustrate the classes and their relationships. For a more complete description of UML, see *The UML User's Guide*[1] or the Rational Software Web site: www.rational.com/uml/index.shtml.

Creating Class Diagrams

You construct class diagrams by using symbols for the classes and lines to show relationships. Additional notation can give further information about the nature and constraints of the relationships. You can draw the symbols by hand or use a computer program. Visual Modeler, which comes with the Enterprise edition of VB, can automate the task for you.

The Symbols The symbol in UML for a class is a rectangle with two horizontal lines to represent properties and methods (Figure 7.2). Using Visual

Figure 7.2

The UML symbol for a class.

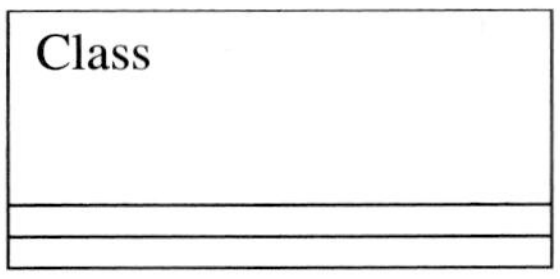

Class

---

[1]G. Booch, J. Rumbaugh, and I. Jacobson, *The UML User's Guide* (Menlo Park, California: Addison-Wesley Publishing Company, 1998).

Modeler, you enter the properties in the middle segment and the methods in the bottom segment; then you can choose whether to display or hide the properties and methods (Figure 7.3). When you create a class diagram by hand, do not list the properties and methods inside the symbol. Instead, document each class separately, using the class design form (Figure 7.4) or something similar.

a.

```
<<Class Module>>
    Customer
```

b.

```
<<Class Module>>
    Customer
pCustomerId : Variant
pName : Variant
pAddress : Variant

CreateNew()
Fetch()
Customer()
Clear()
<<Get>> CustomerId()
<<Get>> Name()
<<Let>> Name()
<<Get>> Address()
<<Let>> Address()
Class_Initialize()
Class_Terminate()
```

F i g u r e   7 . 3

The symbol for a class created in Visual Modeler. Note that the properties and methods can be (a) hidden or (b) displayed.

Another symbol used in UML is called a *utility module*. It represents a utility module or a user interface. Notice that the symbol looks similar to a class symbol but is wider and has a shadow (Figure 7.5).

The Relationships You indicate the relationships among the classes by using lines and arrowheads. You can also give each relationship a name, called the *role name*. Figure 7.6 shows the class diagram for a system called Ordersys, which comes from the Visual Modeler sample application in MSDN. Notice the lines between classes showing the relationships, and the role names next to each line. Also notice how the classes are arranged into the three tiers for User Services, Business Services, and Data Services.

Note: You can find the file that created this model (Ordersys.mdl), as well as the VB 6 application (Ordersys.vbp), in MSDN online[2] if it isn't on your MSDN CD. You will need Visual Modeler to open the .mdl file.

You can define relationships to be one of four types:

● An **association**—the most general type of relationship. You can initially define all relationships to be associations and add more precision later.

---

[2]The URL, as of this writing: http://msdn.microsoft.com/library/devprods/vs6/vstudio/vstool2/vesmpordersys demonstratesroundtripengineeringofvisualbasicapplication.htm.

Use this form to help design a new class.

Class Design

Class Name: _____

Class Properties

Access Mode (Public or Private)	Variable Name	Data Type	Description

Class Methods

Access Mode (Public or Private)	Return Type (for Functions)	Procedure Name (Include Any Parameters)	Purpose

F i g u r e   7 . 5

Use the UML utility symbol to
represent a utility module or a
user interface.

Utility Module

F i g u r e   7 . 6

This UML class diagram for the
Ordersys system was created with
Visual Modeler. The diagram is
included in MSDN as
Ordersys.mdl.

User Services	Business Services	Data Services

<<Class Module>>
Order

<<Module>>
Db

-Active_Order

-pPurchaser

<<Form>>
dlg_Order

-Active_Customer

<<Class Module>>
Customer

-pStorage

<<Class Module>>
Persistence

-pStorage

-My_Customers

<<Class Module>>
Customers

-pOrderrows

-pStorage

-pStorage

<<Form>>
dlg_OrderRow

-My_Articles

<<Class Module>>
Articles

-My_Orderrow

<<Class Module>>
OrderRow

-pArticle

<<Class Module>>
Article

Draw an association relationship using a solid line. You can also add symbols to indicate the number of objects required or allowed. For example, in
Figure 7.7 one patient may have zero-to-many related visits. The symbol 0
means *zero to many.*

F i g u r e   7 . 7

An association relationship can
indicate the number of each class
in the relationship. 1 = one;
0 = zero to many.

Patient

1

0

Visit

- A **dependency**—a relationship that indicates that the client class uses services from the supplier class. The provided services may be constants, variables, or methods of the supplier class. Draw a dependency relationship with a dotted line and an arrowhead. The arrow points to the supplier class (Figure 7.8).

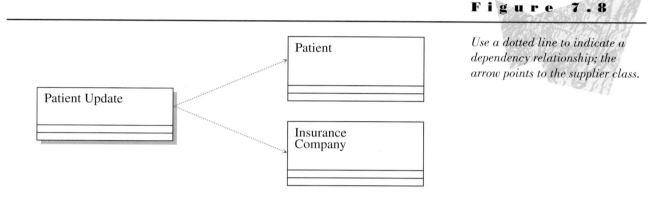

Use a dotted line to indicate a dependency relationship; the arrow points to the supplier class.

- An **aggregate**—a whole and part relationship. The whole end of the relationship (also called the aggregate class or the container) is the client. The supplier (the part) is the individual objects that make up the whole. Draw an aggregate relationship with a solid line and a diamond at the client class (Figure 7.9).

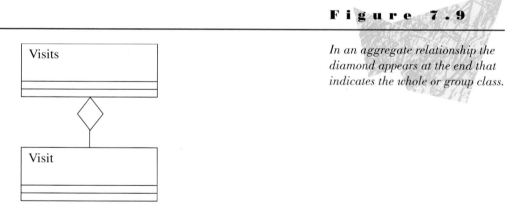

In an aggregate relationship the diamond appears at the end that indicates the whole or group class.

- A **generalization**—an inheritance relationship, which shows an "is a" relationship between classes. Create a generalization by using a solid line with an arrowhead pointing to the superclass (the general class). The other end of the relationship is the more specific, inherited class (Figure 7.10).

Designing the Advanced Vision Application in Tiers

When you design a multitier application, you need to separate the various services. For the Advanced Vision system (Figure 7.11), we'll first consider the

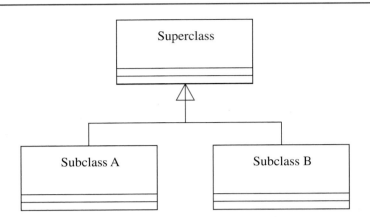

Business Services. These include Patient, Visit, Prescription, Insurance Company, and Dispensary. Each item requires a user interface to work with the object. For the Patient object we need forms for the update and navigation. However, the form we used in the earlier chapters also includes information from the Insurance Company object. In this situation the Patient update is dependent on the Patient object and on the Insurance Company object.

The relationship of objects is called an **object model.** In the next chapter we create objects based on Microsoft's standard Component Object Model (COM) that sets up methods for communicating among objects from different sources and possibly different development languages.

Feedback 6.1

1. During which stage of design do each of the following actions occur:
   (a) Distributing on a network.
   (b) Coding.
   (c) Interviewing users.
   (d) Designing an interface.
   (e) Determining objects and relationships.
2. What is the purpose(s) of drawing an object model?
3. List and define four types of relationships represented in UML.

Creating a Data-Aware Class

In Chapter 6 you learned to create a new class. This chapter introduces a different type of class—a **data-aware class.** New to VB 6, a class can connect to a database. The class module becomes the **data source;** the form or Business Object that uses the data is the **data consumer.**

The data-aware classes that you create can provide the Data Services in the services model. If the format or location of the data files changes, the data-aware class must change. But the objects that use the data shouldn't have to change at all—they will continue to use the same properties and methods, unaware of where the data actually come from.

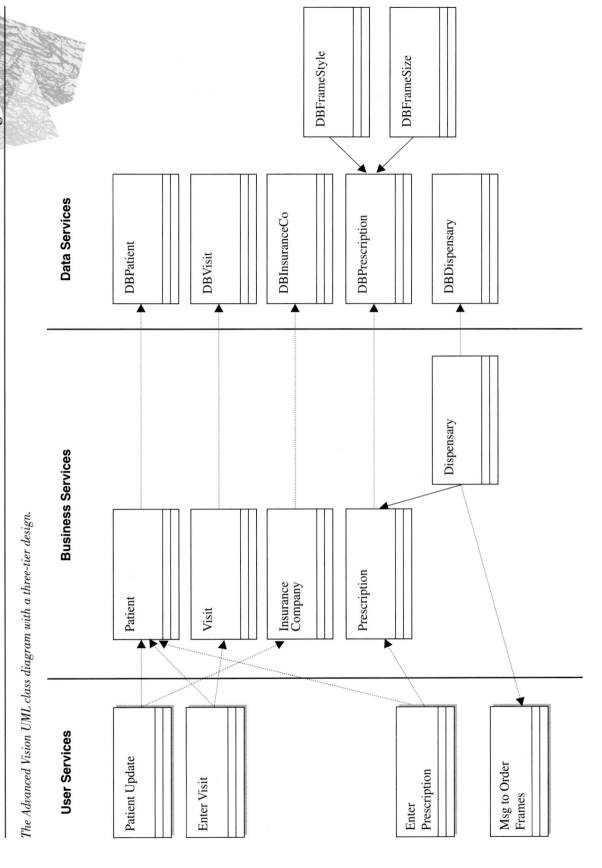

The Advanced Vision UML class diagram with a three-tier design.

Figure 7.11

The data-aware class example that follows uses a two-tier C/S model, illustrated by Figure 7.12. The form handles only the user interface and is the data consumer. The database navigation, validation, and business services are in the data-aware class module, which is the data provider.

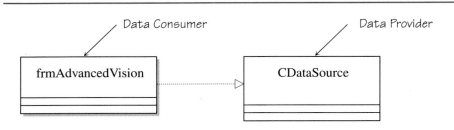

Data Consumer   Data Provider

frmAdvancedVision   CDataSource

The two-tier application using a data-aware class. The form handles only the user interface; all Business Services and Data Services are performed by the data-aware class.

Setting up the Class Module

You can make a class module data aware by setting its DataSourceBehavior property to vbDataSource. This step adds a new method called Class_GetDataMember to the class. The class can create Connection, Command, and Recordset objects and provide the resulting Recordsets to any data consumer object that has a reference to the class. Each Command and Recordset can be a DataMember of the class.

When you create an instance of a data-aware class and request a DataMember, VB calls the GetDataMember method to retrieve the Recordset. In the following code segment, either of two Recordsets can be returned.

Tip

To create a data-aware class, your project must have a reference to Microsoft ActiveX Data Objects.

```
Private Sub Class_GetDataMember(DataMember As String, Data As Object)
    'Determines the Recordset to return

    Select Case DataMember
        Case "Patient"
            Set Data = rsPatient
        Case "Insurance"
            Set Data = rsInsurance
    End Select
End Sub
```

To make this procedure work, you must explicitly add the names of the Recordsets to the DataMembers collection of the class. As a general rule, you will create the Recordsets and add their names to the DataMembers collection in the Class_Initialize procedure.

```
Private Sub Class_Initialize()
    'Create the Recordsets

    On Error GoTo HandleError
    Set conAVB = New ADODB.Connection
    Set rsPatient = New ADODB.Recordset
    Set rsInsurance = New ADODB.Recordset
```

```
'Open the connection
conAVB.ConnectionString = "Provider=Microsoft.Jet.OLEDB.3.51;" & _
    "Persist Security Info=False;Data Source=" & App.Path & _
    "\AVB.mdb;Mode = readwrite"
conAVB.Open

'Open the rsPatient Recordset
With rsPatient
    .CursorLocation = adUseClient
    .CursorType = adOpenDynamic
    .LockType = adLockOptimistic
    .Open "Select * from Patient", conAVB, , , adCmdText
End With

'Open the rsInsurance Recordset
With rsInsurance
    .CursorLocation = adUseClient
    .CursorType = adOpenDynamic
    .LockType = adLockOptimistic
    .Open "Select Code, Name from InsuranceCompany", _
        conAVB, , , adCmdText
End With

'Add Recordsets to the DataMembers collection

With DataMembers

    .Add "Patient"

    .Add "Insurance"

End With


Class_Initialize_Exit:
    Exit Sub

HandleError:
    Err.Raise dsOperationFailed, "CDataSource", "Recordset open failure"
End Sub
```

Dividing Functionality between the Form and the Class

When using a data-aware class for your data source, you should include all data handling in the class and remove it from the form. The class handles navigating, sorting, filtering, and any updating that you want to do. Create methods in the class to handle any functions that you need.

Remember, we want the form to perform the least amount of processing possible. The form is only the user interface. We want to have the option of creating a new user interface or switch to a Web page without rewriting any of the data-handling code.

Place all messages to the user in the form module. It's considered very poor form to display a MsgBox from a class module. The class module can raise an error or return a Boolean value to indicate that an error occurred, but the form must notify the user.

The form's command button event procedures call the methods of the class module as needed. The following code shows the MoveNext method from the class and the cmdNext procedure from the form.

Class CDataSource

```
Public Sub MoveNext()
   'Move to the next record

   On Error Resume Next
   With rsPatient
      .MoveNext
      If .EOF Then
         .MoveLast
      End If
   End With
End Sub
```

Form frmAdvancedVision

```
Private Sub cmdNext_Click()
   'Move to the next record

   mDataSource.MoveNext        'Call the MoveNext method of the class
   DisplayRecordCount
End Sub
```

Notice that all the work with the database, including the error checking, is done in the class module.

The next example shows the Find method with three arguments. It is the job of the form to input from the user the field and the search text. The form code then calls the Find method of the class to perform the Find operation. If the Find is successful, the Boolean argument blnMatchFound is set to True; otherwise, it's set to False. The coding in the form module should check the Boolean variable and display a message to the user if the Find is unsuccessful.

Class CDataSource

```
Public Sub Find(strFindString As String, strSearch As String, _
            blnMatchFound As Boolean)
   'Find a string in the specified field
   Dim vntBookmark As Variant

   On Error GoTo HandleError
   With rsPatient
      vntBookmark = .Bookmark
      .Find strFindString & " Like '" & strSearch & "*'"
      If .EOF Then
         blnMatchFound = False
         .Bookmark = vntBookmark
      Else
         blnMatchFound = True
      End If
   End With

Find_Exit:
   Exit Sub
```

```
HandleError:
    blnMatchFound = False
    Resume Find_Exit
End Sub
```

You can call the same Find method from the form to find both the LastName and the FirstName.

frmAdvancedVision

```
Private Sub mnuFindFirst_Click()
    'Find by first name
    Dim strName      As String
    Dim blnMatchFound As Boolean

    strName = InputBox("Enter the First Name that you want to find." & _
        vbCrLf & "Partial name OK", "Find by First Name")
    mDataSource.Find "[First Name]", strName, blnMatchFound
    If Not blnMatchFound Then
        MsgBox "No records match '" & strName & "'", vbInformation, _
            "Find by First Name"
    End If
End Sub
```

When you decide where to place a program function, think about its purpose. If the task affects the form, it belongs in the form module; but all database activities should be performed by the class. The cmdAdd_Click procedure demonstrates this division of tasks very well. The form's procedure calls an Add method in the class, which performs the AddNew and database error checking. The form handles the manipulation of controls.

frmAdvancedVision

```
Private Sub cmdAdd_Click()
    'Add a new record

    If cmdAdd.Caption = "&Add" Then
        DisableControls                     'Disable navigation
        SetUpAdd
        mDataSource.Add                     'Call the data source
    Else
        mDataSource.CancelUpdate            'Cancel the Add
        txtPatientNumber.Locked = True
        EnableControls                      'Enable navigation
        cmdSave.Enabled = False             'Disable the Save button
        cmdAdd.Caption = "&Add"             'Reset the Add button
    End If
End Sub
```

The form displays the record count in its StatusBar. Therefore, the class must provide a function or property that the form can use to retrieve the count. The following procedure returns the RecordCount from the data source class. You can also use a Property Get for the RecordCount if you declare a property first. Note that you will need another function (AbsolutePosition) to return the record number.

Class CDataSource

```
Public Function RecordCount() As Integer
    'Return the number of records in the Recordset

    On Error GoTo HandleError
    RecordCount = rsPatient.RecordCount

RecordCount_Exit:
    Exit Function

HandleError:
    RecordCount = 0
    Resume RecordCount_Exit
End Function
```

The form must access the data-aware class for the record count. The following procedure is called from all navigation command buttons and from the save and delete procedures.

frmAdvancedVision

```
Public Sub DisplayRecordCount()
    'Display the record count

    staAdvVision.Panels(1).Text = "Record " & _
        mDataSource.AbsolutePosition & " of " & mDataSource.RecordCount
End Sub
```

Binding a Form's Controls to the Data

A data-aware class creates a Recordset, just like the Recordsets you have used with data controls and ADO code. You can bind the data fields to controls on the form so that displaying and updating are practically automatic. In this section we bind the form's controls to the fields in the data source. Later in this chapter, in the three-tier project, you will learn to bind business services objects to a data source.

To bind a control, such as a text box, to a field in the data source, you must set three properties: DataSource, DataMember, and DataField. You can set the DataField properties of all controls during design time, but you must set the DataSource and DataMember properties in code after instantiating an object of the data source class. Note: You must set the DataMember before setting the DataSource.

> **Tip**
>
> **A**lways use the Set statement to assign a value to an object reference. The DataSource property refers to an object, so you must use Set.

```
Private Sub Form_Load()
    'This form is a data consumer, set data source to the class
    Set mDataSource = New CDataSource

    'Bind the controls to the data -- DataField set at design time
    With txtPatientNumber
        .DataMember = "Patient"
        Set .DataSource = mDataSource
End With
```

```
With txtLastName
    .DataMember = "Patient"
    Set .DataSource = mDataSource
End With
With txtFirstName
    .DataMember = "Patient"
    Set .DataSource = mDataSource
End With
```
(And so on . . .)

When you have more than two or three controls to bind, you can loop through the Controls collection and set the properties for all of the controls. Notice the use of the `TypeOf` keyword to check the type of each control. (You can find the correct name of each class of control in the Object Browser or the Properties window.)

```
Private Sub Form_Load()
    'This form is a data consumer, set data source to the class
    Set mDataSource = New CDataSource
    Dim ctlControl As Control

    'Bind the controls to their data fields
    For Each ctlControl In Me.Controls
        If TypeOf ctlControl Is TextBox _
            Or TypeOf ctlControl Is MaskEdBox _
            Or TypeOf ctlControl Is DataCombo Then
            ctlControl.DataMember = "Patient"

            Set ctlControl.DataSource = mDataSource
        End If
    Next
    With dbcInsurance
        .RowMember = "Insurance"
        Set .RowSource = mDataSource
    End With
    DisplayRecordCount
End Sub
```

Validating Data

You *can* check for valid data in the form module, but don't. Instead, always perform the validation in the data-aware class. Assume that the data-aware class will be used for more than one application; you don't want to have to rewrite the validation for every project. And if the company changes a policy to validate in a different manner, the change will have to be made in one place only.

This sample application validates only the Patient Number field. In the three-tier application later in this chapter, several more fields are validated. You will also see some different techniques for validation.

The best time to validate is at the field level so that the user receives instant feedback if the field just entered is invalid. The form's txtPatientNumber_Validate event procedure can call a Public validation function in the data-aware class.

frmAdvancedVision

```
Private Sub txtPatientNumber_Validate(Cancel As Boolean)
   'Validate the PatientNumber for an Add
   ' Note: The control is locked unless an Add is in progress.
   Dim strMessage As String

   If Not mDataSource.ValidKey(txtPatientNumber) Then 'Validate
      strMessage = "Invalid PatientNumber"
      MsgBox strMessage, vbExclamation, "Data Entry Error"
      With txtPatientNumber
         .SelStart = 0                        'Select the current entry
         .SelLength = Len(.Text)
      End With
      Cancel = True                           'Keep the focus
   End If
End Sub
```

Class *CDataSource*

```
Public Function ValidKey(strKeyField) As Boolean
   'Validate the key field (Patient Number)

   If IsNumeric(strKeyField) Then
      ValidKey = True
   Else
      ValidKey = False
   End If
End Function
```

The Entire Project

Load and run the project *Ch07DataAwareClass* from your CD. Examine the code in the form module and the code in the data-aware class. The form should handle only the user interface; all other processing should be in the class module.

> **Tip**
>
> As your projects get larger, the order of the procedures in each module becomes more important. By convention, place all property procedures (Gets and Lets) together, arranged alphabetically, ignoring the prefixes; then group all event procedures, arranged alphabetically; then place all general procedures, both functions and sub procedures, arranged alphabetically.

Feedback 7.2

1. Assume that you want to create a data-aware class for the Visit table. What steps would be necessary to connect to the Visit table?
2. Code the Add method for the class module to add *Visit* to the DataMembers collection of the data-aware class.
3. Write the statement to set the form's data source to *Visit*.
4. Write the code to bind the Visit Date field to a textbox called txtDate.

Coding for Multitier Applications

Now that you have seen how to create a data-aware class, we are going to divide the functionality into three tiers. We already have a form module (for the User Services tier) and a data-aware class module (CDataSource) for the Data

Services tier. We need to add a class module for Business Services and move some coding, such as the validation, to the correct tier. See Figure 7.13 for the class diagram.

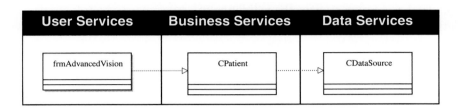

The class diagram for a three-tier application.

We will not complete the entire Advanced Vision system but rather just concentrate on the patient portion. Working on this component should give you a feel for how complex the application can become with all the components in place. In Chapter 8 we discuss converting some of the code components into ActiveX objects to improve the reusability of the components.

The Organization of a Multitier Application

When you break the tasks into three tiers, remember that your goal is to create components that can be reused and replaced. You shouldn't have to write a whole new application if the database changes, the user interface changes, or the validation rules change.

User Services	Business Services	Data Services
Handle the user interface.	Hold properties for each data field.	Create and expose Recordsets.
Display all messages to user.	Perform all validation, business rules, and calculation.	Provide all database access, including Add, Delete, Update, Sort, Filter, Find, RecordCount, and AbsolutePosition.
Maintain all user interface controls—Visible and Enabled properties.	Receive requests from User Services; call properties and methods of Data Services.	
Set and retrieve object properties in Business Services.	Properties can be bound to the fields in a Recordset by using a BindingCollection.	
Call methods from Business Services.		
Most controls cannot be bound to data fields in the Business Services class. Controls must be unbound.		

Data Services

With minor revisions, the data-aware class you created to handle the database activities can become the Data Services tier in a multitier project. Any validation, calculations, or business rules should be removed from the Data Services class and placed in the Business Services tier. In the continuing example for the patients in the Advanced Vision database, we must move the validation of the patient number to Business Services. We will also add some more validation and formatting to the properties in the Business Services class.

Business Services

The new layer in the Advanced Vision project is the Business Services tier. Although adding a layer seems to greatly complicate the project (it really *does*), the new layer provides encapsulation of the business rules, validation, and formatting of fields. The Business Object is a data consumer, since this object is bound to the Data Services module. But the Business Object is also a data source, providing the data to the User Services module.

A Business Services class module generally contains properties for each database field along with methods for each action that User Services will need. The Property Let procedures can perform any validation or formatting required for input data. Property Gets provide the property values to the form.

Binding the Data Fields to the Business Services Properties

You can bind the properties of the Business Object to the fields in a Recordset. You must set the class **DataBindingBehavior property** to vbSimpleBound and set up a **BindingCollection.** To create the BindingCollection, you need to declare an object variable in the General Declarations section; in the Class_Initialize procedure you will instantiate the collection and add a member for each field to bind. Note: Your project must include a reference to the *Microsoft Data Binding Collection* in the *References* dialog box.

```
'Project:        Chapter 07 Advanced Vision and Beyond
'                Chapter Hands-On Example
'Module:         CPatient
'Date:           2/2000
'Programmer:     Bradley/Millspaugh
'Description:    Business Services Tier.
'                Defines properties and methods for Patient objects
'Folder:         Ch07AdvancedVision
Option Explicit
```

```
'Create an instance of the Data Services class
Private mDataService     As CDataService

'Declare a BindingCollection to bind data source and data consumer
Private mbndPatient        As BindingCollection

'Declare properties for Patient (Note alphabetic order)
Private mstrCity                   As String
Private mstrFirstName              As String
Private mstrInsuranceCompanyCode   As String
Private mstrLastName               As String
Private mintPatientNumber          As Integer
Private mstrPhone                  As String
Private mstrPolicyNumber           As String
Private mstrState                  As String
Private mstrStreet                 As String
Private mstrZipCode                As String

'Enum for error codes
Public Enum paError
    paValidationError = vbObjectError + 512 + 100
End Enum
```

To set up the binding, you must set the BindingCollection's DataSource property to the data source object. Then you set up each field to bind by using the BindingCollection's **Add method** to add a member for each field.

Adding to the BindingCollection—General Form

```
BindingCollectionObject.Add DataConsumerObject, "Property", "DataField"
```

The DataConsumerObject should be the current module, which can be represented by the keyword Me. The property must be defined in the module, and the DataField must appear in the data source.

Adding to the BindingCollection—Example

```
mbndPatient.Add Me, "PatientNumber", "Patient Number"
```

Instantiating the Data Source and Binding Collection

In the Class_Initialize procedure for the Business Services object, instantiate the data source and binding collection. You must set the DataSource property of the binding collection object to the data source object and set the DataMember property to the correct data member (a Recordset, remember). Then you can add a member to the collection for each field.

```
Private Sub Class_Initialize()
    'Instantiate the data source and binding collection
    Set mDataService = New CDataService
    Set mbndPatient = New BindingCollection
```

```
'Set up the Binding Collection
Set mbndPatient.DataSource = mDataService
With mbndPatient
    .DataMember = "Patient"
    .Add Me, "PatientNumber", "Patient Number"
    .Add Me, "LastName", "Last Name"
    .Add Me, "FirstName", "First Name"
    .Add Me, "Street", "Street"
    .Add Me, "City", "City"
    .Add Me, "State", "State"
    .Add Me, "ZipCode", "Zip Code"
    .Add Me, "Phone", "Phone"
    .Add Me, "InsuranceCompanyCode", "Insurance Company Code"
    .Add Me, "PolicyNumber", "Policy #"
End With
End Sub
```

Binding a DataCombo or DataList Control

If you want to bind a DataCombo or DataList control to a data source, you must be able to refer to the original Recordsets. (You cannot set up the properties of a DataCombo or DataList control to work correctly by referring to individual properties of the Business Object.) For that reason the Business Services class will expose the data source as a property of the class. The form can refer to that property to set up the DataCombo.

CPatient Class

```
Public Property Get Insurance() As DataSource
    'Expose the data source to bind to the DataCombo box

    Set Insurance = mDataService
End Property
```

In the form module the Insurance property is actually a reference to the Data Services object. You can reference the two Recordsets: Insurance and Patient.

frmAdvancedVision

```
With dbcInsurance  'Bind DataCombo to data source
    .DataField = "Insurance Company Code"
    .DataMember = "Patient"
    Set .DataSource = mPatient.Insurance
    .RowMember = "Insurance"
    Set .RowSource = mPatient.Insurance
    .ListField = "Name"
End With
```

Validating and Formatting Input Data

In the past you have validated input data in the form module by using a control's Validate event. And in the preceding two-tier example, the validation was in the Data Source class. Now we're going to place it where it really belongs: in the Business Services tier.

When the user enters new data in a control, that data value should be validated. If it passes validation, the new value should be assigned to the correct property so that the update can occur. If the new data value requires any formatting, that also should occur. The validation and formatting rules should be part of the Business Services tier so that a new user interface could be written without having to rewrite all the rules.

Here are three sample Property Let procedures from the CPatient (Business Services) class. If the data pass validation, they are assigned to the correct property and the PropertyChanged method is called so that the data will be updated in the data source. If the data do not pass, the property procedure raises an error, which should be trapped in the form module.

The new function in the LastName procedure, StrConv, can change the format of a string. In this case StrConv sets the string to an uppercase first character and lowercase for the rest of the string.

CPatient Class

```
Public Property Let PatientNumber(ByVal varPatientNumber As Variant)
    'Assign property value

    If IsNumeric(varPatientNumber) Then
        mintPatientNumber = CInt(varPatientNumber)
        PropertyChanged "PatientNumber"
    Else
        Err.Raise paValidationError, "CPatient", "Invalid Patient Number"
    End If
End Property
```

```
Public Property Let State(ByVal strState As String)
    'Assign property value

    Select Case Len(strState)
        Case 2        'Right length
            mstrState = UCase(strState)
            PropertyChanged "State"
        Case 0
            'Empty field OK
        Case Else
            Err.Raise paValidationError, "CPatient", _
                "Invalid State Code. Must be two characters only."
    End Select
End Property
```

```
Public Property Let LastName(ByVal strLastName As String)
    'Assign property value

    mstrLastName = StrConv(strLastName, vbProperCase)
    PropertyChanged "LastName"
End Property
```

frmAdvancedVision

In the form module, use each control's Validate event to assign and check/format the new data. (Remember that the Validate event occurs only when the contents of a control change.)

```vb
Private Sub txtPatientNumber_Validate(Cancel As Boolean)
    'Validate a changed PatientNumber

    On Error Resume Next
    mPatient.PatientNumber = txtPatientNumber.Text

    If Err.Number <> 0 Then
        DisplayMessage txtPatientNumber
        Cancel = True                           'Keep the focus
    End If
End Sub
```

This procedure performs its error trapping with a technique called ***inline error handling.*** This method is quite common and has some advantages over using `On Error GoTo`. The `On Error Resume Next` tells VB to just keep processing if an error occurs. After any operation that could cause an error, you must check Err.Number. Any value other than zero means that an error occurred.

The DisplayMessage (local) procedure displays a message and highlights the text in the control.

```vb
Private Sub DisplayMessage(ctlCurrent As Control)
    'Display a message for field validation

    MsgBox Err.Description, vbExclamation, "Data Entry Error"
    With ctlCurrent
        .SelStart = 0                           'Select the current entry
        .SelLength = Len(.Text)
    End With
End Sub
```

Here are the Validate event procedures for the State and LastName fields, for which the Property Let procedures appeared above.

```vb
Private Sub txtState_Validate(Cancel As Boolean)
    'Validate a changed State

    On Error Resume Next
    mPatient.State = txtState.Text

    If Err.Number <> 0 Then
        DisplayMessage txtState
        Cancel = True                           'Keep the focus
    End If
End Sub
```

```vb
Private Sub txtLastName_Validate(Cancel As Boolean)
    'Validate a changed LastName

    On Error Resume Next
    mPatient.LastName = txtLastName.Text

    If Err.Number <> 0 Then
        DisplayMessage txtLastName
        Cancel = True                           'Keep the focus
    End If
End Sub
```

Notice that txtLastName_Validate traps for errors even though the Property Let procedure does not raise any errors. Once you have decided on raising errors for validation, every time you assign a property you must check for errors. That way, if next month the company policy changes and LastName must be validated, the only change necessary is to add or modify the validation rule in the Business Services class.

User Services

The form contains the visual components for the user. The form connects to the CPatient class and can reference the properties and methods of that class. This example uses unbound controls, so in code you must assign property values to the controls. New data values are assigned to the properties in each control's Validate event procedure, as described in the preceding section.

In the form's General Declarations section, declare an object variable for the CPatient class (the Business Services).

```
'Project:        Chapter 07 Advanced Vision and Beyond
'                   Chapter Hands-On Example
'Module:         frmAdvVision
'Date:           2/2000
'Programmer:     Bradley/Millspaugh
'Description:    User Services tier.
'                Handle user interface for Patient update.
'Folder:         Ch07AdvancedVision

Option Explicit
Private mPatient          As CPatient
```

In the Form_Load event procedure, instantiate a new CPatient object and set the binding properties for the DataCombo control.

```
Private Sub Form_Load()
    'Set up the form controls to handle data
    Set mPatient = New CPatient

    With dbcInsurance            'Bind DataCombo to data source
        .DataMember = "Patient"
        Set .DataSource = mPatient.Insurance
        .RowMember = "Insurance"
        Set .RowSource = mPatient.Insurance
        .ListField = "Name"
    End With
    AssignData                   'Display data in controls
    DisplayRecordCount
End Sub
```

Assigning Data Values to the Form Controls

Each time a new record is current, you must assign the properties from the CPatient class to the form's controls.

```
Private Sub AssignData()
    'Transfer the value from the Patient object to the interface

    With mPatient
        txtPatientNumber.Text = .PatientNumber
        txtLastName.Text = .LastName
        txtFirstName.Text = .FirstName
        txtStreet.Text = .Street
        txtCity.Text = .City
        txtState.Text = .State
        txtZipCode.Text = .ZipCode
        mskPhone.Text = .Phone
        txtPolicyNumber.Text = .PolicyNumber
    End With
End Sub
```

You will call the AssignData procedure each time a new record is current, including the Move procedures for navigation and the Add, Delete, and Save procedures for updates.

```
Private Sub cmdFirst_Click()
    'Move to the first record

    mPatient.MoveFirst
    DisplayRecordCount
    AssignData
End Sub
```

Assigning Values from the Form Controls to the Fields

Any time you have unbound controls, you are responsible for two-way transfer of data. You must not only place the data fields into the controls, you must also transfer updated data from the controls back to the database fields. We have already performed this task in the Validate event procedure for each control.

The Entire Multitier Project

Although you have seen parts of the code, you will understand this project better after going through the hands-on example at the end of this chapter. Try single-stepping through the code to see the transfer of data through the three layers.

Feedback 7.3

1. In which tier do the following belong? For the objects and Recordset, tell where they are first defined and where they will be referenced.
   (a) Patient object.
   (b) Visit Update form.
   (c) Visit object.
   (d) Patient Recordset.

2. What steps are necessary to set up a BindingCollection? Where is a BindingCollection used?

3. How are field values passed from the Business Services tier to the User Services tier?

4. How are new field values passed from the User Services tier to the Business Services tier?

Your Hands-on Programming Example

This project is a modification of the hands-on example from Chapter 5. The project uses three distinct tiers: one for User Services, one for Business Services, and one for Data Services. It also adds some new data validation and formatting in the Business Services tier. The rest of the program functions are unchanged.

The Advanced Vision and Beyond project must update the Patient table as well as find, select, and sort the records.

For the updates, allow the user to add new records, delete records, and modify existing records. Do not permit a change to a Patient Number field (the key field) on an existing record. For an Add, the user must be allowed only the options to save or cancel. Make sure to disable all other buttons and menu options that could change the current record.

Display the insurance company names in a dropdown combo box so that the user can select a company from the list or type in a new value.

Include these menu options:

File	Find	Select	Sort
Exit	Last Name	By Last Name	By Patient Number
	First Name	By First Name	By Patient Name
		All Patients	

For the Find options, use an InputBox and allow the user to enter a name (or partial name). Use a Find method with a wildcard to allow for the partial names.

For the Select option, also use an InputBox that allows the user to enter a (partial) name. Use a filter and make sure to include a check mark next to the currently selected menu option.

For the Sort option, use the Sort method. Make the currently selected option appear checked. When the program begins, make the current sort order by patient number.

Include a status bar at the bottom of the form. Show the record number ("Record n of nn") at the left end and the date and time at the right.

Make sure to include error handling in all procedures that could cause an error.

Planning the Project

The first step in planning is to lay out the three tiers and determine the functions for each class. In this case you will need a user interface for the User

Services, a CPatient class for the Business Services, and a CDataServices class
for the Data Services.

Plan the Data Services Class

CDataServices Properties

Note: Set the CDataServices DataSourceBehavior property to *vbDataSource.*

Access Mode (Public or Private)	Variable Name	Data Type	Description
Private	rsPatient	Recordset	Returns the rsPatient Recordset as the Patient DataMember.
Private	rsInsurance	Recordset	Returns the rsInsurance Recordset as the Insurance DataMember.

CDataServices Methods and Event Procedures

Access Mode (Public or Private)	Return Type (for Function)	Procedure Name (Include Any Parameters)	Purpose
Private		Class_Initialize	Open the Connection. Open the rsPatient and rsInsurance Recordsets. Add the Recordsets to the DataMembers collection.
Private		Class_Terminate	Release object variables.
Public	Integer	AbsolutePosition	Return the rsPatient.AbsolutePosition. If error occurred Set AbsolutePosition = 0. End If
Public		Add	rsPatient.AddNew. If error occurred Raise an error. End if
Public		CancelUpdate	rsPatient.CancelUpdate. rsPatient.MoveLast. If error occurred Raise an error. End If
Public		Delete	rsPatient.Delete. If EOF MovePrevious. If BOF Turn off error trapping. Raise an error.

continued

Access Mode (Public or Private)	Return Type (for Function)	Procedure Name (Include Any Parameters)	Purpose
			End If If an error occurred Raise an error. End If

Public		Filter(strFieldName, strSearchValue, ByRef blnMatchFound)	rsPatient.Filter using "Like".
			If EOF
			    Set blnMatchFound = False.
			    Set Filter = "".
			Else
			    Set blnMatchFound = True.
			End If
			If error occurred
			    Set blnMatchFound = False.
			End If

Public		Find(strFieldName, strSearchValue, ByRef blnMatchFound)	Set the Bookmark.
			rsPatient.Find using "Like".
			If EOF
			    Set blnMatchFound = False.
			    Reset Bookmark.
			Else
			    Set blnMatchFound = True.
			End If
			If error occurred
			    Set blnMatchFound = False.
			End If

Public		MoveFirst	rsPatient.MoveFirst.
Public		MoveLast	rsPatient.MoveLast.
Public		MoveNext	rsPatient.MoveNext.
Public		MovePrevious	rsPatient.MovePrevious.
Public	Integer	RecordCount	rsPatient.RecordCount.
Public		Save	rsPatient.Update. If error occurred Raise an error. End If
Public		ShowAllRecords	rsPatient.Filter = "".
Public		Sort(strSortString)	rsPatient.Sort. If error occurred Raise an error. End If

Plan the Business Services Class

CPatient Properties

Note: Set the CPatient DataBindingBehavior property to *vbSimpleBound*.

Access Mode (Public or Private)	Variable Name	Data Type	Description
Private	mstrCity	String	City property Set to proper case.
Private	mstrFirstName	String	FirstName property Set to proper case.
Public		DataSource	Insurance property to expose the data source object.
Private	mstrInsuranceCompanyCode	String	InsuranceCompanyCode property.
Private	mstrLastName	String	LastName property Set to proper case.
Private	mintPatientNumber	Integer	PatientNumber property Transfer as a Variant. Validate for numeric.
Private	mstrPhone	String	Phone property. Validate for numeric or blank.
Private	mstrPolicyNumber	String	PolicyNumber property.
Private	mstrState	String	State property Validate for two characters. Convert to uppercase.
Private	mstrStreet	String	Street property.
Private	mstrZipCode	String	ZipCode property Validate for len >= 5 or 0.

CPatient Methods and Event Procedures

Access Mode (Public or Private)	Return Type (for Function)	Procedure Name (Include Any Parameters)	Purpose
Private		Class_Initialize	Instantiate data source. Instantiate binding collection. Add each property to binding collection.
Private		Class_Terminate	Release object variables.
Public	Integer	AbsolutePosition	Call data source AbsolutePosition method to return the record number.
Public		Add	Call data source Add method to add a record. If error occurred Raise an error. End if

continued

Access Mode (Public or Private)	Return Type (for Function)	Procedure Name (Include Any Parameters)	Purpose
Public		CancelUpdate	Call data source CancelUpdate method to cancel an Add.
Public		Delete	Call data source Delete method to delete the current record. If error occurred Raise an error. End If
Public		Filter(strFieldName, strSearchValue, ByRef blnMatchFound)	Call data source Filter method to filter the Recordset.
Public		Find(strFieldName, strSearchValue, ByRef blnMatchFound)	Call data source Find method to find a record.
Public		MoveFirst	Call data source MoveFirst method.
Public		MoveLast	Call data source MoveLast method.
Public		MoveNext	Call data source MoveNext method.
Public		MovePrevious	Call data source MovePrevious method.
Public	Integer	RecordCount	Call data source RecordCount method.
Public		Save	Call data source Save method. If error occurred Raise an error. End If
Public		ShowAllRecords	Call data source ShowAllRecords method.
Public		Sort(strSortString)	Call data source Sort method. If error occurred Raise an error. End If

Plan the User Interface for User Services

Sketch the form (Figure 7.14, p. 328), which your users sign off as meeting their needs.

A sketch of the form for the Advanced Vision and Beyond patient update project.

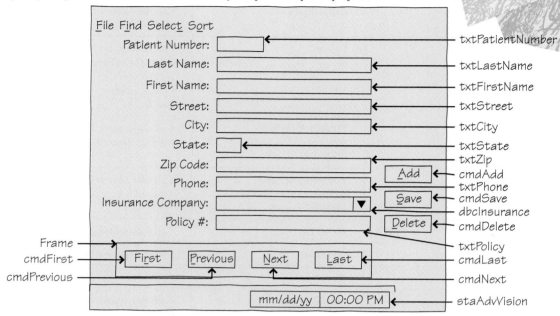

Plan the Form's Objects and Properties

Plan the property settings for the form and for each control.

Object	Property	Setting
frmAdvancedVision	Caption	Advanced Vision and Beyond Patient Information
	Icon	Eye.ico
	StartupPosition	2 - CenterScreen
txtPatientNumber	DataField	Patient Number
	Locked	True
txtLastName	DataField	Last Name
	Locked	True
txtFirstName	DataField	First Name
	Locked	True
txtStreet	DataField	Street
	Locked	True
txtCity	DataField	City
	Locked	True
txtState	DataField	State
	Locked	True

continued

Object	Property	Setting
txtZip	DataFormat	Custom - #####-####
mskPhone	DataFormat	Custom - (###) ###-####
	Mask	(###) ###-####
	DataField	Phone
	PromptInclude	False
	ClipMode	1 - mskExcludeLiterals
Field labels	Name, Caption	Default properties as set up by the DE
dbcInsurance	DataField	Insurance Company Code
	ListField	Name
	BoundColumn	Code
fraNavigation	Caption	(blank)
cmdFirst	Caption	Fi&rst
cmdPrevious	Caption	&Previous
cmdNext	Caption	&Next
	Default	True
cmdLast	Caption	&Last
cmdAdd	Caption	&Add
	CausesValidation	False
cmdSave	Caption	&Save
	Enabled	False
cmdDelete	Caption	&Delete
	CausesValidation	False
staAdvVision	Panels	3
Panel(1)	MinimumWidth	2880
	AutoSize	2 - Contents
Panel(2)	Style	6 - sbrDate
	AutoSize	2 - Contents
Panel(3)	Style	5 - sbrTime
	AutoSize	2 - Contents
mnuFile	Caption	&File

continued

Object	Property	Setting
mnuFileExit	Caption	E&xit
mnuFind	Caption	F&ind
mnuFindLastName	Caption	&Last Name
mnuFileFirstName	Caption	&First Name
mnuSelect	Caption	Selec&t
mnuSelectLastName	Caption	By &Last Name
mnuSelectFirstName	Caption	By &First Name
mnuSelectAll	Caption	&All Records
	Checked	True
mnuSort	Caption	S&ort
mnuSortPatientNumber	Caption	By &Patient Number
mnuSortPatientName	Caption	By Patient &Name

Plan the Form's Event Procedures

Determine which events will need code and plan the code for each.

frmAdvancedVision

Procedure	Actions
cmdFirst_Click	Call MoveFirst method of class module.
cmdPrevious_Click	Call MovePrevious method of class module.
cmdNext_Click	Call MoveNext method of class module.
cmdLast_Click	Call MoveLast method of class module.

cmdAdd_Click	If button Caption is Add Then
	    Call Add method of class.
	    Disable all controls for movement.
	    Change button Caption to Cancel.
	    Enable Save button.
	    Unlock txtPatientNumber.
	    Display text in StatusBar.
	Else (button is Cancel)
	    Call CancelUpdate method of class.
	    AssignData to controls.
	    Lock txtPatientNumber.
	    Enable all controls for movement.
	    Disable Save button.
	    Change button Caption to Add.
	    DisplayRecordCount.
	End If
	If error occurred
	    Display error message.
	    Update StatusBar text.

continued

Procedure	Actions
	Resume processing. End If

cmdDelete_Click	Call Delete method of class module.
	Check for errors.
	If no errors
	    AssignData to controls.
	    Update StatusBar text.
	Else
	    Display error message.
	End If

cmdSave_Click	Call Save method of class module.
	Select Case check for errors:
	    Case 0 (no errors)
	        Lock txtPatientNumber.
	        Enable all controls for movement.
	        Disable the Save button.
	        Change Caption of Add button to Add.
	        Update StatusBar text.
	    Case DuplicateAdd
	        Display error message.
	        Select PatientNumber text.
	        Update StatusBar text.
	    Case OtherError
	        Raise the error.
	End Select

Form_Load	Create object of CPatient class. Bind the DataCombo control. Call mnuSortPatientNumber_Click. DisplayRecordCount.
Form_Unload	Set object variables to Nothing.
mnuFileExit_Click	Unload form.

mnuFindFirstName_Click	Input requested first name.
	Call Find method of class module.
	If match found
	    AssignData to controls.
	Else
	    Display message.
	End If

mnuFindLastName_Click	Input requested last name.
	Call Find method of class module.
	If match found
	    AssignData to controls.
	Else
	    Display message.
	End If

mnuSelectFirstName	Input requested first name. Call Filter method of class module. If match found AssignData to controls.

continued

Procedure	Actions

	DisplayRecordCount.
	    Check correct option and uncheck others.
	Else
	    Display message.
	End If

mnuSelectLastName	Input requested last name.
	Call Filter method of class module.
	If match found
	    AssignData to controls.
	    DisplayRecordCount.
	    Check correct option and uncheck others.
	Else
	    Display message.
	End If

mnuSelectAll	Call ShowAllRecords from class module. AssignData to controls. DisplayRecordCount. Check the menu option and uncheck others.

mnuSortPatientName	Call Sort method of class module.
	If no error occurred
	    AssignData to controls.
	    Check the menu option and uncheck others.
	Else
	    Display error message.
	End If

mnuSortPatientNumber	Call Sort method of class module.
	If no error occurred
	    AssignData to controls.
	    Check the menu option and uncheck others.
	Else
	    Display error message.
	End If

txtCity_Validate	Assign value to City property.
	If validation error occurred
	    Display error message.
	    Cancel operation.
	End If

txtFirstName_Validate	Assign value to FirstName property.
	If validation error occurred
	    Display error message.
	    Cancel operation.
	End If

txtLastName_Validate	Assign value to LastName property.
	If validation error occurred
	    Display error message.
	    Cancel operation.
	End If

txtPatientNumber_Validate	Assign value to PatientNumber property. If validation error occurred Display error message.

continued

Procedure	Actions
	Cancel operation. End If

txtPolicyNumber_Validate	Assign value to PolicyNumber property.
	If validation error occurred
	   Display error message.
	   Cancel operation.
	End If

txtState_Validate	Assign value to State property.
	If validation error occurred
	   Display error message.
	   Cancel operation.
	End If

txtStreet_Validate	Assign value to Street property.
	If validation error occurred
	   Display error message.
	   Cancel operation.
	End If

txtZipCode_Validate	Assign value to ZipCode property.
	If validation error occurred
	   Display error message.
	   Cancel operation.
	End If

AssignData	Transfer all properties to controls.
DisableControls	Disable navigation buttons. Disable Find, Select, and Sort menus.
DisplayMessage	Display Err.Description. Select the text in the control.
DisplayRecordCount	Display record number and count in StatusBar.
EnableControls	Enable navigation buttons. Enable Find, Select, and Sort menus.
SetUpAdd	Lock txtPatientNumber. Enable Save button. Change Caption of Add button to Cancel.

Write the Project

- Add references to your project for the *Microsoft Data Binding Collection* and the *Microsoft ActiveX Data Objects 6.0 Library.*

- Create the Data Services class module. (If you created the data-aware class earlier in this chapter, very little is needed to turn it into the Data Services class. You must move the validation from this module to the Business Services class.)

- Create the Business Services class module. Set up all properties, property procedures, and methods.

- Follow the sketch in Figure 7.14 to create the user interface. Figure 7.15 shows the completed form.

*The form for the Advanced Vision
and Beyond patient update
project.*

- Set the properties of the form and each of the controls, as you have planned.
- Working from the pseudocode, write each event procedure.
- When you complete the code, thoroughly test the project. Single-step the execution to see the interaction of the three tiers.

The Project Solution

frmAdvancedVision

```
'Project:        Chapter 07 Advanced Vision and Beyond
'                Chapter Hands-On Example
'Module:         frmAdvVision
'Date:           2/2000
'Programmer:     Bradley/Millspaugh
'Description:    User Services tier.
'                Handle user interface for Patient update.
'Folder:         Ch07AdvancedVision

Option Explicit
Private mPatient        As CPatient

'****Event Procedures****

Private Sub cmdAdd_Click()
    'Add a new record
```

```
      On Error GoTo HandleError
      If cmdAdd.Caption = "&Add" Then         'Begin an Add
         mPatient.Add
         SetUpAdd
         DisableControls                                'Disable navigation
         staAdvVision.Panels(1).Text = "Add--Enter data for new patient"
      Else
         mPatient.CancelUpdate
         AssignData                                     'Refill controls
         txtPatientNumber.Locked = True
         EnableControls                                 'Enable navigation
         cmdSave.Enabled = False                        'Disable the Save button
         cmdAdd.Caption = "&Add"                        'Reset the Add button
         DisplayRecordCount                             'Reset the StatusBar
      End If

cmdAdd_Exit:
   Exit Sub

HandleError:
   MsgBox "Operation Failed", vbInformation, "Advanced Vision Add Operation"
   staAdvVision.Panels(1).Text = "Add Failed"
   Resume cmdAdd_Exit
End Sub
```

```
Private Sub cmdDelete_Click()
   'Delete the current record

   On Error Resume Next
   mPatient.Delete

   Select Case Err.Number        'Inline error check
      Case 0                      'No error occurred
         AssignData
         staAdvVision.Panels(1).Text = "Record Deleted"
      Case dsEmptyRecordset   'All records deleted
         MsgBox Err.Description, vbInformation, _
            "Advanced Vision Delete Patient"
         cmdAdd_Click
      Case dsOperationFailed  'Error occurred
         MsgBox "Delete Failed", vbInformation, _
            "Advanced Vision Delete Patient Record"
         staAdvVision.Panels(1).Text = "Delete Failed"
      Case Else
         Err.Raise Err.Number
   End Select
End Sub
```

```
Private Sub cmdFirst_Click()
   'Move to the first record

   mPatient.MoveFirst
   DisplayRecordCount
   AssignData
End Sub
```

```
Private Sub cmdLast_Click()
   'Move to the last record
```

```
    mPatient.MoveLast
    DisplayRecordCount
    AssignData
End Sub

Private Sub cmdNext_Click()
    'Move to the next record

    mPatient.MoveNext
    DisplayRecordCount
    AssignData
End Sub

Private Sub cmdPrevious_Click()
    'Move to the previous record

    mPatient.MovePrevious
    DisplayRecordCount
    AssignData
End Sub

Private Sub cmdSave_Click()
    'Save the current record

    On Error Resume Next
    mPatient.Save

    Select Case Err.Number      'Inline error check
        Case 0                   'No error occurred
            txtPatientNumber.Locked = True
            EnableControls
            cmdSave.Enabled = False
            cmdAdd.Caption = "&Add"
            staAdvVision.Panels(1).Text = "Record Saved"
        Case dsDuplicateAdd      'Duplicate add
            Dim strMsg As String
            strMsg = "Duplicate or missing Patient Number"
            MsgBox strMsg, vbInformation, "Advanced Vision Add Patient"
            With txtPatientNumber
                .SetFocus
                .SelStart = 0
                .SelLength = Len(.Text)
                staAdvVision.Panels(1).Text = "Duplicate Add"
            End With
        Case Else                'Unidentified error
            Err.Raise Err.Number
    End Select
End Sub

Private Sub Form_Load()
    'Set up the form controls to handle data
    Set mPatient = New CPatient

    With dbcInsurance          'Bind DataCombo to data source
        .DataMember = "Patient"
        Set .DataSource = mPatient.Insurance
        .RowMember = "Insurance"
        Set .RowSource = mPatient.Insurance
        .ListField = "Name"
    End With
```

```
      mnuSortPatientNumber_Click   'Set initial sort order & display data
      DisplayRecordCount
End Sub
```

```
Private Sub Form_Unload(Cancel As Integer)
    'Release object references

    Set mPatient = Nothing
End Sub
```

```
Private Sub mnuFileExit_Click()
    'End the project

    Unload Me
End Sub
```

```
Private Sub mnuFindFirst_Click()
    'Find by first name
    Dim strName       As String
    Dim blnMatchFound As Boolean

    strName = InputBox("Enter the First Name that you want to find." _
            & vbCrLf & "Partial name OK", "Find by First Name")
    mPatient.Find "[First Name]", strName, blnMatchFound
    If blnMatchFound Then
        AssignData
    Else
        MsgBox "No records match '" & strName & "'", vbInformation, _
            "Find by First Name"
    End If
End Sub
```

```
Private Sub mnuFindLastName_Click()
    'Find by last name
    Dim strName       As String
    Dim blnMatchFound As Boolean

    strName = InputBox("Enter the Last Name that you want to find." & _
            vbCrLf & "Partial name OK", "Find by Last Name")
    mPatient.Find "[Last Name]", strName, blnMatchFound
    If blnMatchFound Then
        AssignData
    Else
        MsgBox "No records match '" & strName & "'", vbInformation, _
            "Find by Last Name"
    End If
End Sub
```

```
Private Sub mnuSelectAll_Click()
    'Select all records

    mPatient.ShowAllRecords
    AssignData
    DisplayRecordCount
    mnuSelectFirstName.Checked = False
    mnuSelectLastName.Checked = False
    mnuSelectAll.Checked = True
End Sub
```

```
Private Sub mnuSelectFirstName_Click()
    'Select by first name
    Dim strName       As String
    Dim blnMatchFound As Boolean

    strName = InputBox("Enter the First Name that you want to select." _
            & vbCrLf & "Partial name OK", "Select by First Name")
    mPatient.Filter "[First Name]", strName, blnMatchFound
    If blnMatchFound Then
        AssignData
        DisplayRecordCount
        mnuSelectFirstName.Checked = True
        mnuSelectLastName.Checked = False
        mnuSelectAll.Checked = False
    Else
        MsgBox "No records match '" & strName & "'", vbInformation, _
            "Select by First Name"
    End If
End Sub
```

```
Private Sub mnuSelectLastName_Click()
    'Select by last name
    Dim strName       As String
    Dim blnMatchFound As Boolean

    strName = InputBox("Enter the Last Name that you want to select." & _
            vbCrLf & "Partial name OK", "Select by Last Name")
    mPatient.Filter "[Last Name] ", strName, blnMatchFound
    If blnMatchFound Then
        AssignData
        DisplayRecordCount
        mnuSelectFirstName.Checked = False
        mnuSelectLastName.Checked = True
        mnuSelectAll.Checked = False
    Else
        MsgBox "No records match '" & strName & "'", vbInformation, _
            "Select by Last Name"
    End If
End Sub
```

```
Private Sub mnuSortPatientName_Click()
    'Sort by Patient Name

    On Error Resume Next
    mPatient.Sort "[Last Name], [First Name]"
    If Err.Number = 0 Then          'Sort operation successful
        AssignData
        mnuSortPatientName.Checked = True
        mnuSortPatientNumber.Checked = False
    Else                            'Sort operation failed
        MsgBox "Unable to sort", vbInformation, _
            "Sort by Patient Name"
    End If
End Sub
```

```
Private Sub mnuSortPatientNumber_Click()
    'Sort by Patient Number

    On Error Resume Next
    mPatient.Sort "[Patient Number]"
    If Err.Number = 0 Then          'Sort operation successful
        AssignData
        mnuSortPatientNumber.Checked = True
        mnuSortPatientName.Checked = False
    Else                            'Sort operation failed
        MsgBox "Unable to sort", vbInformation, _
            "Sort by Patient Number"
    End If
End Sub
```

```
'****Validate Events****

Private Sub txtCity_Validate(Cancel As Boolean)
    'Validate the City

    On Error Resume Next
    mPatient.City = txtCity.Text

    If Err.Number <> 0 Then
        DisplayMessage txtCity
        Cancel = True
    End If
End Sub
```

```
Private Sub txtFirstName_Validate(Cancel As Boolean)
    'Validate a changed First Name

    On Error Resume Next
    mPatient.FirstName = txtFirstName.Text

    If Err.Number <> 0 Then
        DisplayMessage txtFirstName
        Cancel = True                           'Keep the focus
    End If
End Sub
```

```
Private Sub txtLastName_Validate(Cancel As Boolean)
    'Validate a changed LastName

    On Error Resume Next
    mPatient.LastName = txtLastName.Text

    If Err.Number <> 0 Then
        DisplayMessage txtLastName
        Cancel = True                           'Keep the focus
    End If
End Sub
```

```
Private Sub txtPatientNumber_Validate(Cancel As Boolean)
    'Validate a changed PatientNumber

    On Error Resume Next
    mPatient.PatientNumber = txtPatientNumber.Text
```

```vb
    If Err.Number <> 0 Then
        DisplayMessage txtPatientNumber
        Cancel = True                          'Keep the focus
    End If
End Sub

Private Sub mskPhone_Validate(Cancel As Boolean)
    'Validate the Phone

    On Error Resume Next
    mPatient.Phone = mskPhone.Text

    If Err.Number <> 0 Then
        DisplayMessage mskPhone
        Cancel = True
    End If
End Sub

Private Sub txtPolicyNumber_Validate(Cancel As Boolean)
    'Validate a changed PolicyNumber

    On Error Resume Next
    mPatient.PolicyNumber = txtPolicyNumber.Text

    If Err.Number <> 0 Then
        DisplayMessage txtPolicyNumber
        Cancel = True                          'Keep the focus
    End If
End Sub

Private Sub txtState_Validate(Cancel As Boolean)
    'Validate a changed State

    On Error Resume Next
    mPatient.State = txtState.Text

    If Err.Number <> 0 Then
        DisplayMessage txtState
        Cancel = True                          'Keep the focus
    End If
End Sub

Private Sub txtStreet_Validate(Cancel As Boolean)
    'Validate a changed Street

    On Error Resume Next
    mPatient.Street = txtStreet.Text

    If Err.Number <> 0 Then
        DisplayMessage txtStreet
        Cancel = True                          'Keep the focus
    End If
End Sub

Private Sub txtZipCode_Validate(Cancel As Boolean)
    'Validate a changed ZipCode
```

```
      On Error Resume Next
      mPatient.ZipCode = txtZipCode.Text

      If Err.Number <> 0 Then
         DisplayMessage txtZipCode
         Cancel = True                              'Keep the focus
      End If
End Sub
```

```
'****General Procedures****
```

```
Private Sub AssignData()
   'Transfer the value from the Patient object to the interface

   With mPatient
      txtPatientNumber.Text = .PatientNumber
      txtLastName.Text = .LastName
      txtFirstName.Text = .FirstName
      txtStreet.Text = .Street
      txtCity.Text = .City
      txtState.Text = .State
      txtZipCode.Text = .ZipCode
      mskPhone.Text = .Phone
      txtPolicyNumber.Text = .PolicyNumber
   End With
End Sub
```

```
Private Sub DisableControls()
   'Disable navigation buttons

   cmdNext.Enabled = False
   cmdPrevious.Enabled = False
   cmdFirst.Enabled = False
   cmdLast.Enabled = False
   cmdDelete.Enabled = False
   mnuFind.Enabled = False
   mnuSelect.Enabled = False
   mnuSort.Enabled = False
End Sub
```

```
Private Sub DisplayMessage(ctlCurrent As Control)
   'Display a message for field validation

   MsgBox Err.Description, vbExclamation, "Data Entry Error"
   With ctlCurrent
      .SelStart = 0                       'Select the current entry
      .SelLength = Len(.Text)
   End With
End Sub
```

```
Public Sub DisplayRecordCount()
   'Display the record count

   staAdvVision.Panels(1).Text = "Record " & _
      mPatient.AbsolutePosition & " of " & mPatient.RecordCount
End Sub
```

```
Private Sub EnableControls()
   'Enable navigation buttons
```

```
      cmdNext.Enabled = True
      cmdPrevious.Enabled = True
      cmdFirst.Enabled = True
      cmdLast.Enabled = True
      cmdDelete.Enabled = True
      mnuFind.Enabled = True
      mnuSelect.Enabled = True
      mnuSort.Enabled = True
End Sub
```

```
Private Sub SetUpAdd()
    'Set up controls for the Add, clear out the fields

    With txtPatientNumber
        .Locked = False
        .Text = ""
        .SetFocus
    End With
    cmdSave.Enabled = True                'Enable the Save button
    cmdAdd.Caption = "&Cancel"            'Allow a Cancel option
    txtLastName.Text = ""
    txtFirstName.Text = ""
    txtStreet.Text = ""
    txtCity.Text = ""
    txtState.Text = ""
    txtZipCode.Text = ""
    mskPhone.Text = ""
    dbcInsurance.Text = ""
    txtPolicyNumber.Text = ""
End Sub
```

CPatient

```
'Project:       Chapter 07 Advanced Vision and Beyond
'               Chapter Hands-On Example
'Module:        CPatient
'Date:          2/2000
'Programmer:    Bradley/Millspaugh
'Description:   Business Services Tier.
'               Defines properties and methods for Patient objects
'Folder:        Ch07AdvancedVision
Option Explicit

'Create an instance of the Data Services class
Private mDataService    As CDataService

'Declare a BindingCollection to bind data source and data consumer
Private mbndPatient     As BindingCollection

'Declare properties for Patient (Note alphabetic order)
Private mstrCity                   As String
Private mstrFirstName              As String
Private mstrInsuranceCompanyCode   As String
Private mstrLastName               As String
Private mintPatientNumber          As Integer
Private mstrPhone                  As String
Private mstrPolicyNumber           As String
Private mstrState                  As String
Private mstrStreet                 As String
Private mstrZipCode                As String
```

```
'Enum for error codes
Public Enum paError
    paValidationError = vbObjectError + 512 + 100
End Enum
```

```
'****Property Procedures****
```

```
Public Property Get Insurance() As DataSource
    'Expose the data source to bind to the DataCombo box

    Set Insurance = mDataService
End Property
```

```
Public Property Get City() As String
    'Retrieve current value

    City = mstrCity
End Property
```

```
Public Property Let City(ByVal strCity As String)
    'Assign property value

    mstrCity = StrConv(strCity, vbProperCase)
    PropertyChanged "City"
End Property
```

```
Public Property Get FirstName() As String
    'Retrieve current value

    FirstName = mstrFirstName
End Property
```

```
Public Property Let FirstName(ByVal strFirstName As String)
    'Assign property value

    mstrFirstName = StrConv(strFirstName, vbProperCase)
    PropertyChanged "FirstName"
End Property
```

```
Public Property Get InsuranceCompanyCode() As String
    'Retrieve current value

    InsuranceCompanyCode = mstrInsuranceCompanyCode
End Property
```

```
Public Property Let InsuranceCompanyCode(ByVal _
    strInsuranceCompanyCode As String)
    'Assign property value

    mstrInsuranceCompanyCode = strInsuranceCompanyCode
    PropertyChanged "InsuranceCompanyCode"
End Property
```

```
Public Property Get LastName() As String
    'Retrieve current value

    LastName = mstrLastName
End Property
```

```vb
Public Property Let LastName(ByVal strLastName As String)
    'Assign property value

    mstrLastName = StrConv(strLastName, vbProperCase)
    PropertyChanged "LastName"
End Property
```

```vb
Public Property Get PatientNumber() As Variant
    'Retrieve current value

    PatientNumber = mintPatientNumber
End Property
```

```vb
Public Property Let PatientNumber(ByVal varPatientNumber As Variant)
    'Assign property value

    If IsNumeric(varPatientNumber) Then
        mintPatientNumber = CInt(varPatientNumber)
        PropertyChanged "PatientNumber"
    Else
        Err.Raise paValidationError, "CPatient", "Invalid Patient Number"
    End If
End Property
```

```vb
Public Property Get Phone() As String
    'Retrieve current value

    Phone = mstrPhone
End Property
```

```vb
Public Property Let Phone(ByVal strPhone As String)
    'Assign property value

    If IsNumeric(strPhone) Or Len(strPhone) = 0 Then
        mstrPhone = strPhone
        PropertyChanged "Phone"
    Else
        Err.Raise paValidationError, "CPatient", "Invalid Phone Number"
    End If
End Property
```

```vb
Public Property Get PolicyNumber() As String
    'Retrieve current value

    PolicyNumber = mstrPolicyNumber
End Property
```

```vb
Public Property Let PolicyNumber(ByVal strPolicyNumber As String)
    'Assign property value

    mstrPolicyNumber = strPolicyNumber
    PropertyChanged "PolicyNumber"
End Property
```

```
Public Property Get State() As String
    'Retrieve current value

    State = mstrState
End Property
```

```
Public Property Let State(ByVal strState As String)
    'Assign property value

    Select Case Len(strState)
        Case 2        'Right length
            mstrState = UCase(strState)
            PropertyChanged "State"
        Case 0
            'Empty field OK
        Case Else
            Err.Raise paValidationError, "CPatient", _
                "Invalid State Code. Must be two characters only."
    End Select
End Property
```

```
Public Property Get Street() As String
    'Retrieve current value

    Street = mstrStreet
End Property
```

```
Public Property Let Street(ByVal strStreet As String)
    'Assign property value

    mstrStreet = strStreet
    PropertyChanged "Street"
End Property
```

```
Public Property Get ZipCode() As String
    'Retrieve current value

    ZipCode = mstrZipCode
End Property
```

```
Public Property Let ZipCode(ByVal strZipCode As String)
    'Assign property value

    If Len(strZipCode) >= 5 Or Len(strZipCode) = 0 Then
        mstrZipCode = strZipCode
        PropertyChanged "ZipCode"
    Else
        Err.Raise paValidationError, "CPatient", _
            "Invalid Zip Code. Must be at least five digits."
    End If
End Property
```

```
'****Event Procedures****

Private Sub Class_Initialize()
    'Instantiate the data source and binding collection
    Set mDataService = New CDataService
    Set mbndPatient = New BindingCollection
```

```
    'Set up the Binding Collection
    Set mbndPatient.DataSource = mDataService
    With mbndPatient
        .DataMember = "Patient"
        .Add Me, "PatientNumber", "Patient Number"
        .Add Me, "LastName", "Last Name"
        .Add Me, "FirstName", "First Name"
        .Add Me, "Street", "Street"
        .Add Me, "City", "City"
        .Add Me, "State", "State"
        .Add Me, "ZipCode", "Zip Code"
        .Add Me, "Phone", "Phone"
        .Add Me, "InsuranceCompanyCode", "Insurance Company Code"
        .Add Me, "PolicyNumber", "Policy #"
    End With
End Sub
```

```
Private Sub Class_Terminate()
    'Release resources

    Set mbndPatient = Nothing
    Set mDataService = Nothing
End Sub
```

```
'****General Procedures****
```

```
Public Function AbsolutePosition() As Integer
    'Call the Data Services

    AbsolutePosition = mDataService.AbsolutePosition
End Function
```

```
Public Sub Add()
    'Call the method from Data Services

    On Error Resume Next
    mDataService.Add

    If Err.Number <> 0 Then
        Err.Raise Err.Number, Err.Source, Err.Description
    End If
End Sub
```

```
Public Sub CancelUpdate()
    'Call the Data Services

    mDataService.CancelUpdate
End Sub
```

```
Public Sub Delete()
    'Call the method from Data Services

    On Error Resume Next
    mDataService.Delete
```

```
        If Err.Number <> 0 Then
            Err.Raise Err.Number, Err.Source, Err.Description
        End If
    End Sub

Public Sub Filter(strFieldName As String, strSearchValue As String, _
                ByRef blnMatchFound As Boolean)
    'Call the Data Services

    mDataService.Filter strFieldName, strSearchValue, blnMatchFound
End Sub

Public Sub Find(strFieldName As String, strSearchValue As String, _
                ByRef blnMatchFound As Boolean)
    'Call the Data Services

    mDataService.Find strFieldName, strSearchValue, blnMatchFound
End Sub

Public Sub MoveFirst()
    'Call the method from Data Services

    mDataService.MoveFirst
End Sub

Public Sub MoveLast()
    'Call the method from Data Services

    mDataService.MoveLast
End Sub

Public Sub MoveNext()
    'Call the method from Data Services

    mDataService.MoveNext
End Sub

Public Sub MovePrevious()
    'Call the method from Data Services

    mDataService.MovePrevious
End Sub

Public Function RecordCount() As Integer
    'Call the Data Services

    RecordCount = mDataService.RecordCount
End Function

Public Sub Save()
    'Call the Data Services

    On Error Resume Next
    mDataService.Save

    If Err.Number <> 0 Then      'Error occurred
        Err.Raise Err.Number, Err.Source, Err.Description
    End If
End Sub
```

```
Public Sub ShowAllRecords()
    'Call the Data Services

    mDataService.ShowAllRecords
End Sub
```

```
Public Sub Sort(strSortString As String)
    'Call the Data Services

    On Error Resume Next
    mDataService.Sort strSortString
    If Err.Number <> 0 Then          'Error occurred
        Err.Raise Err.Number, Err.Source, Err.Description
    End If
End Sub
```

CDataService

```
'Project:        Chapter 07 Advanced Vision and Beyond
'                  Chapter Hands-On Example
'Module:         CDataService
'Date:           2/2000
'Programmer:     Bradley/Millspaugh
'Description:    Data Services tier. Defines properties and methods.
'                  Contains the connection to the database.
'Folder:         Ch07AdvancedVision

Option Explicit
Private conAVB              As ADODB.Connection
Private rsPatient          As ADODB.Recordset
Private rsInsurance        As ADODB.Recordset

Public Enum dsError
    dsDuplicateAdd = vbObjectError + 512 + 1
    dsOperationFailed = vbObjectError + 512 + 2
    dsEmptyRecordset = vbObjectError + 512 + 3
End Enum
```

```
'****Event Procedures****

Private Sub Class_GetDataMember(DataMember As String, Data As Object)
    'Determine the Recordset to return

    Select Case DataMember
        Case "Patient"
            Set Data = rsPatient
        Case "Insurance"
            Set Data = rsInsurance
    End Select
End Sub
```

```
Private Sub Class_Initialize()
    'Create the Recordsets
```

```
    On Error GoTo HandleError
    Set conAVB = New ADODB.Connection
    Set rsPatient = New ADODB.Recordset
    Set rsInsurance = New ADODB.Recordset

    'Open the Connection
    conAVB.ConnectionString = "Provider=Microsoft.Jet.OLEDB.3.51;" & _
        "Persist Security Info=False;Data Source=" & App.Path & _
        "\AVB.mdb;Mode = readwrite"
    conAVB.Open

    'Open the rsPatient Recordset
    With rsPatient
        .CursorLocation = adUseClient
        .CursorType = adOpenDynamic
        .LockType = adLockOptimistic
        .Open "Select * from Patient", conAVB, , , adCmdText
    End With

    'Open the rsInsurance Recordset
    With rsInsurance
        .CursorLocation = adUseClient
        .CursorType = adOpenDynamic
        .LockType = adLockOptimistic
        .Open "Select Code, Name from InsuranceCompany", _
                conAVB, , , adCmdText
    End With

    'Add Recordsets to the DataMembers collection
    With DataMembers
        .Add "Patient"
        .Add "Insurance"
    End With

Class_Initialize_Exit:
    Exit Sub

HandleError:
    Err.Raise dsOperationFailed, "CDataService", "Recordset open failure"
End Sub
```

```
Private Sub Class_Terminate()
    'Release resources

    Set conAVB = Nothing
    Set rsPatient = Nothing
    Set rsInsurance = Nothing
End Sub
```

```
'****General Procedures****

Public Function AbsolutePosition() As Long
    'Return the Recordset absolute position

    On Error GoTo HandleError
    AbsolutePosition = rsPatient.AbsolutePosition

AbsolutePosition_Exit:
Exit Function
```

```
HandleError:
    AbsolutePosition = 0
    Resume AbsolutePosition_Exit
End Function
```

```
Public Sub Add()
    'Add a new record

    On Error GoTo HandleError
    rsPatient.AddNew   'Clear out fields for new record

Add_Exit:
    Exit Sub

HandleError:
    Err.Raise dsOperationFailed, "CDataService", "AddNew operation failed"
End Sub
```

```
Public Sub CancelUpdate()
    'Cancel the Add

    On Error GoTo HandleError
    With rsPatient
        .CancelUpdate 'Cancel the Add
        .MoveLast
    End With

CancelUpdate_Exit:
    Exit Sub

HandleError:
    Err.Raise dsOperationFailed, "CDataSource", "CancelUpdate failed"
End Sub
```

```
Public Sub Delete()
    'Delete the current record

    On Error GoTo HandleError
    With rsPatient
        .Delete                         'Delete the current record
        .MoveNext                       'Move to the following record
        If .EOF Then                    'If last record deleted
            .MovePrevious
            If .BOF Then                'If BOF and EOF true, no records remain
                On Error GoTo 0
                Err.Raise dsEmptyRecordset, "CDataSource", _
                    "The last record was deleted"
            End If
        End If
    End With

Delete_Exit:
    Exit Sub

HandleError:
    Err.Raise dsOperationFailed, "CDataService", "Delete operation failed"
End Sub
```

```vb
Public Sub Filter(strField As String, strName As String, _
                ByRef blnMatchFound As Boolean)
    'Select by selected field

    On Error GoTo HandleError
    With rsPatient
        .Filter = strField & " Like '" & strName & "*'"
        If .EOF Then
            blnMatchFound = False
            .Filter = ""
        Else
            blnMatchFound = True
        End If
    End With

Filter_Exit:
    Exit Sub

HandleError:
    blnMatchFound = False
    Resume Filter_Exit
End Sub

Public Sub Find(strFindString As String, strSearch As String, _
                ByRef blnMatchFound As Boolean)
    'Find by strFindString
    Dim vntBookmark As Variant

    On Error GoTo HandleError
    With rsPatient
        vntBookmark = .Bookmark
        .Find strFindString & " Like '" & strSearch & "*'"
        If .EOF Then
            blnMatchFound = False
            .Bookmark = vntBookmark
        Else
            blnMatchFound = True
        End If
    End With

Find_Exit:
    Exit Sub

HandleError:
    blnMatchFound = False
    Resume Find_Exit
End Sub

Public Sub MoveFirst()
    'Move to the first record

    On Error Resume Next
    rsPatient.MoveFirst
End Sub
```

```vb
Public Sub MoveLast()
    'Move to the last record

    On Error Resume Next
    rsPatient.MoveLast
End Sub
```

```vb
Public Sub MoveNext()
    'Move to the next record

    On Error Resume Next
    With rsPatient
        .MoveNext
        If .EOF Then
            .MoveLast
        End If
    End With
End Sub
```

```vb
Public Sub MovePrevious()
    'Move to the previous record

    On Error Resume Next
    With rsPatient
        .MovePrevious
        If .BOF Then
            .MoveFirst
        End If
    End With
End Sub
```

```vb
Public Function RecordCount() As Integer
    'Return the number of records in the Recordset

    On Error GoTo HandleError
    RecordCount = rsPatient.RecordCount

RecordCount_Exit:
    Exit Function

HandleError:
    RecordCount = 0
    Resume RecordCount_Exit
End Function
```

```vb
Public Sub Save()
    'Save the current record

    On Error GoTo HandleErrors
    rsPatient.Update

Save_Exit:
    Exit Sub

HandleErrors:
    Err.Raise dsDuplicateAdd, "CDataService", "Save operation failed"
End Sub
```

```
Public Sub ShowAllRecords()
    'Set Filter to nothing

    rsPatient.Filter = ""
End Sub
```

```
Public Sub Sort(strSortString As String)
    'Sort data by strSortString argument

    On Error GoTo HandleError
    rsPatient.Sort = strSortString

Sort_Exit:
    Exit Sub

HandleError:
    Err.Raise dsOperationFailed, "CDataService", "Sort operation failed"
End Sub
```

MCSD Exam Notes

Exam Objectives Covered in This Chapter

Deriving the Physical Design

- Assess the potential impact of the logical design on performance, maintainability, extensibility, and availability.

Creating User Services

- Use data binding to display and manipulate data from a data source.

- Implement error handling for the user interface in desktop applications.
  - Handle inline errors.

Questions/Tricks to Watch for

- Know the steps in each design phase.

- Know how to bind data from a data source to a data consumer.

- Set the DataSourceBehavior to vbDataSource to create a data-aware class. The GetDataMember event is added to the class.

- The BindingCollection is the link between the data source and the data consumer.

Summary

1. Design can be divided into four stages: conceptual design, logical design, physical design, and deployment. Validation compares the conceptual design with the logical design.
2. A good logical design can speed coding time and reduce the amount of maintenance a system requires.

3. Good design is important to a good system or application and can be measured through performance, maintainability, extensibility, and availability.

4. A database application can be divided into multiple tiers for future enhancement and flexibility.

5. The User Services tier, or layer, should handle only the user interface. The Business Services tier handles all business rules, calculations, and validation. Data Services handles all storage and retrieval of data. Together these three layers are called the *services model*.

6. UML is a tool for planning, designing, and documenting object-oriented systems.

7. To create UML class diagrams, you use rectangles to represent objects and draw lines and arrowheads to show the relationships, which may be association, dependency, aggregate, or generalization.

8. A data-aware class can be a data source or data provider; a form or object that uses the data is a data consumer.

9. A data-aware class can create Connections and Recordsets. Set the DataSourceBehavior property to vbDataSource to make a class data aware.

10. A form that instantiates a data-aware class object becomes a data consumer for the class module that is the data source.

11. The DataMembers class holds one DataMember for each Recordset or Command that you want to expose to other classes.

12. The controls on the form call methods of the data-aware class to perform all database functions.

13. Bind the form's controls to the data-aware class by setting each control's DataSource and DataMember properties in code after creating an instance of the data source class. Set each control's DataField property at design time.

14. In a two-tier application, place the field validation in the data-aware class. For a three-tier application, all validation, as well as data formatting and calculations, belongs in the Business Services tier.

15. The properties of a class module that is a data consumer can be bound to the fields in a data source by using a BindingCollection. The DataBindingBehavior property of a data consumer class must be set if the class contains a BindingCollection.

16. To perform inline error handling, use `On Error Resume Next` and check the error number after each operation that could cause an error.

17. In the form module use each control's Validate event to set the field property in the Business Services object. In the Property Let procedure, perform any validation or formatting required.

K e y   T e r m s

Add method
  (BindingCollection) *317*
aggregate *305*
association *302*
availability *299*

BindingCollection *316*
Business Objects *300*
Business Services *300*
conceptual design *298*
data-aware class *306*

Review Questions

1. Name and define the four stages of design.
2. What does the term *validation* mean in reference to the design stages?
3. Why are comments, naming conventions, and standards important?
4. Why take the time to do all that "design stuff"?
5. Explain the significance of the three areas within the UML symbol for an object.
6. Which relationship does a dashed line in UML represent? a solid line? a one (1) and a zero (0)?
7. Explain the concept of a multitier application. Discuss the benefits.
8. Differentiate between the DataBindingBehavior property of a class and the DataSourceBehavior property.
9. What step is needed to make a class module data aware?
10. Describe the function of the BindingCollection.
11. Explain why a DataMember would be added to a data source class.
12. What is the purpose of the Add method of the BindingCollection?

Programming Exercises

7.1 Modify exercise 5.1 to be a two-tier client-server application.
7.2 Modify exercise 5.1 to be a three-tier application.
7.3 Modify exercise 5.4 to be a three-tier application.
7.4 Create a multitier application for updating the Authors table in Biblio.mdb.

CASE STUDIES

1. Modify your Chapter 5 project 1 to be a two-tier application.

Video Bonanza

2. Modify your Chapter 5 project 1 to be a three-tier application.

1. Modify your Chapter 5 project 1 to be a two-tier application.

VB Auto

2. Modify your Chapter 5 project 1 to be a three-tier application.

8

Creating and Managing ActiveX Code Components

At the completion of this chapter, you will be able to . . .

1. Recognize the terminology associated with COM and ActiveX components.

2. Understand the concept and purpose of type libraries.

3. Differentiate between server applications and client applications.

4. Set up VB project groups.

5. Register and unregister components.

6. Use Friend to share procedures among the classes in a component.

7. Create an ActiveX Dll project.

8. Implement the rules for component shutdown.

9. Trace the life cycle of a component.

10. Create an ActiveX Exe project.

11. Understand the purpose of asynchronous notifications using event notification or callback procedures.

12. Design an abstract class to implement multiple interfaces.

13. Recognize the significance of version compatibility.

In Chapter 6 you created new classes using class modules. In this chapter you will learn to create COM components for both ActiveX Dll and ActiveX Exe projects. You will store COM objects in a type library and use the objects either in-process or out-of-process. You will also register and unregister components, define Friend procedures, and use asynchronous communications.

The Component Object Model

The idea of reusing objects sounds great. It shouldn't be necessary to rewrite code to perform the same (or nearly the same) action in multiple applications. But how do someone else's objects work with your project, and how can your software components work with others? The answer is **Component Object Model (COM),** Microsoft's standard that defines how software components interact with each other.

ActiveX technology is based on COM. A component, sometimes called a *code component,* is simply a class module that is compiled and stored for reusability.

The COM model provides for communication through standard interfaces. The term *interface,* when used with an object, refers to the Public properties and methods of the class module. These properties enable an object created from a code component to "communicate" with an application. The application that uses a software component is called a *consumer* or *client application.* When you create a software component that can be shared, your project is considered the **provider** or **server application.** Fortunately for VB programmers, the compiler does most of the interface work for you.

COM is an implementation of OOP. Well-written components provide encapsulation and a high degree of reusability. COM standardizes interface rules, which make it possible to reuse components.

COM components are language independent. In your VB projects you can use components from other applications, such as Excel or PowerPoint, or those written in another programming language, such as C, C++, Java, or Delphi. Many prewritten components are available from third-party vendors and shareware or freeware for download. The components that you write in VB can be used in applications written in many other languages. Which language a third-party developer used in creating an ActiveX component should not matter to you; it will work with your VB application because the interface is standardized. Microsoft calls this feature **interoperability.** See MSDN Component Tools Guide for more information.

ActiveX Code Components

You can create two types of code components: ActiveX Dlls and ActiveX Exes (Table 8.1). An **ActiveX Dll** code component runs in the memory space of the

ActiveX Dll	ActiveX Exe
In-process provider.	Out-of-process provider.
Runs in the same address space as the consumer (client) application.	Runs in its own address space. An independent application.

consumer application and is referred to as **in-process.** An **out-of-process** code component runs in its own memory space and is created as an **ActiveX Exe.** Make this association: a Dll is always in-process; an Exe is always out-of-process. The terms are used almost interchangeably.

If you are familiar with the extensions Dll and Exe, you'll find it easy to distinguish the component types. Dll stands for *dynamic link library.* Dll files store code components in a library that can be accessed by an application. An Exe file is an executable application on its own and therefore executes out-of-process. Out-of-process components also go by the names ***application provider, application server,*** or ***automation server application.***

An ActiveX code component may be a single class module or an entire application. Microsoft Excel is sometimes used as an object by other programs. Excel objects are considered out-of-process providers, which run in their own address space.

The concept of a *user* gets a little fuzzy when you speak of COM components. When you create a provider component, you are the component's **author.** But who is the user? the programmer who uses your component in an application? the end user of the entire application? This situation requires another term: a person (programmer) who uses a component is called the ***developer.*** Sometimes the author and developer are the same person; sometimes not. Both author and developer must conform to the rules of COM to share and reuse components.

Two other types of visual components, ActiveX controls and ActiveX documents, are covered in the next chapter.

The Instancing Property

Each class module that you create as a code component (in-process or out-of-process) has an **Instancing property.** The Instancing property specifies how an object of the class can be instantiated (Table 8.2). The default setting is MultiUse, which allows you to create multiple objects from one copy of the class. MultiUse provides the most efficient use of memory for out-of-process components. SingleUse, on the other hand, creates a new copy of the component for every object that is created. SingleUse is available only for Exes; it is not allowed for Dlls.

Instancing Value	Purpose	ActiveX Dll	ActiveX Exe
Private	Cannot be used in other applications.	√	√
PublicNotCreatable	Object must be created by component; other applications cannot use `New` keyword.	√	√
MultiUse	One instance can create multiple objects.	√	√
GlobalMultiUse	Properties and methods act as global functions. There is no need to create an instance of the class because it is automatically created. (MultiUse)	√	√
SingleUse	Each object created requires a copy of the component.		√
GlobalSingleUse	Properties and methods act as global functions. There is no need to create an instance of the class because it is automatically created. (SingleUse)		√

Both SingleUse and MultiUse have a variation that makes the properties and methods of the class act like global functions. With GlobalMultiUse and GlobalSingleUse, an instance of the class is created automatically the first time a procedure or method of the class is called. Objects created automatically are also referred to as **global objects.** An advantage of using global objects is that you don't have to explicitly instantiate an object to be able to use the properties and methods of the class. However, this feature can also be a disadvantage, since it's easy to inadvertently instantiate the object; client-side code is more ambiguous, and it's easy to confuse multiple instances of global information.

The other two choices for the Instancing property are Private and PublicNotCreatable. Private means that no other component can create an object of the class. Use PublicNotCreatable for a class that should not be instantiated by the consumer. Instead the class's objects should be created only by another class within the component. A good example of using PublicNotCreatable is for the objects in a collection, such as the DispensaryItems collection of DispensaryItem objects. Make the individual object (DispensaryItem) PublicNotCreatable and then only allow objects to be created by using the Add method of the collection (DispensaryItems). Objects with an Instancing property of PublicNotCreatable are called **dependent objects.**

Type Libraries

When you display information in the Object Browser, you are actually displaying type libraries. A **type library** for a component holds a definition of the Public objects, properties, methods, events, and constants. Type libraries enable other applications to reference the component.

Type libraries are stored in files with the extension Tlb (type library) or Olb (object library), or they may be included in the component's Exe or Dll file. When you compile an ActiveX project, VB adds the type library to the Exe (out-of-process) or Dll (in-process) file. Also, the component's type library is added to the list in the *References* dialog box. The name of your component is the project's Name property; the description that displays in the References list and at the bottom of the Object Browser is the Project Description, which you enter on the *Project Properties* page (Figure 8.1). Make sure to use a descriptive description!

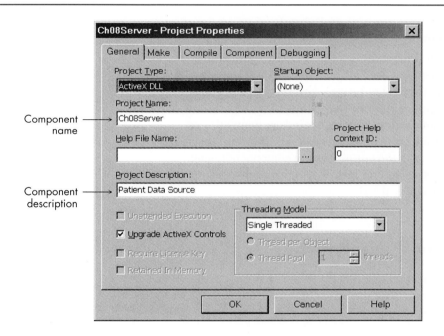

Component name

Component description

The Project Properties page for an ActiveX Dll project. The Project Name property becomes the component name; the Project Description displays in the References list and the description in the Object Browser for this component.

When you want to use a component in a client (consumer) application, you must add a reference to the component by using the *References* dialog box. You are familiar with adding references. In fact, you did so in Chapter 7 when you set a reference to the BindingCollection. Your project then became a client application using binding.

COM does not actually require type libraries, and some components do not have one. If a type library does not exist, the object cannot be added to the project from References, cannot use early binding, and cannot allow the client to respond to events.

Testing Components

As you write code components, you need some way to test them. You need one project that creates a component (the provider or server) and another project that uses the component (the consumer or client). The method that you use depends on whether you are creating an in-process Dll or an out-of-process Exe.

Testing In-Process Components

To test in-process components, you can use the **Project Group** feature. A project group allows you to have more than one project open in one instance of VB. You can have your server application (class module code component) running at the same time as the client application (a second project that instantiates an object).

Use *Step Into* debugging and watch the execution in the server and client applications. Another good learning technique is to add some Debug.Print methods into your code; the Immediate window displays the Print output as actions occur during execution.

Testing Out-of-Process Components

Out-of-process components must run separately from their client applications. Therefore, when you test an out-of-process code component, you need two instances of VB running at the same time. The ActiveX Exe server component runs in one copy while your client application runs in the other.

After the component is thoroughly tested, it is registered permanently on the system and does not need to be running in an instance of VB. But until testing is complete, you must compile and run the out-of-process component (using Ctrl + F5 or *Run/Start with Full Compile*) in one instance of VB and then run your client (consumer) in another instance of VB.

Registering and Unregistering Components

If another application is going to use a component, it must be registered on the system. Each component is assigned an ID called a *GUID* (which stands for "globally unique identifier"), a 128-bit number that is guaranteed to be unique for each component. The Windows Registry maintains a list of all identifiers for all components that are registered on the system along with the path for retrieving the component. Each Registry entry also contains a ClassID, a name given to the component that is used in late binding. With late binding the program refers to the ClassID, which in turn references the Registry to get the path.

When you compile an ActiveX component, the compiler automatically registers the component on your system. This registration is fine for your system, but if you move a project to a different computer, the component must also be registered there. You can manually register a component, but the best way to register components on another system is to use the VB Package and Deployment Wizard, which creates a Setup program that automatically registers components. (See Chapter 14 to create Setup programs.)

Registering In-Process Components

You can manually register a Dll by using the Regsvr32.Exe file located in the Windows/System directory. (If the file is not on your system, you can find it on the VB CD.) This program calls the COM Registry interface and needs only the name and path of the compiled component.

From the Windows *Start* menu, select *Run.* In the *Run* dialog box, type the following line:

```
REGSVR32 a:\MyProjectFolder\MyComponent.Dll
```

To unregister a component, use the /u parameter:

```
REGSVR32 /u a:\MyProjectFolder\MyComponent.Dll
```

Note: You must include the complete path and filename, which are case-sensitive. You can include a /i parameter to delete the entry from the VB References list.

After you have unregistered a component, make sure to empty the Recycle Bin. Sometimes when a component remains there, the system acts as if that component is still registered.

Registering Out-of-Process Components

When an Exe code component is compiled into an executable file, a Registry entry is created. After a file is registered, the Windows Registry keeps track of the component's path even if the file is moved to a new folder.

If you move an Exe component to another machine, you must register the component there. You can use the Regsvr32.Exe program described earlier or use the VB Package and Deployment Wizard to create a Setup program (see Chapter 14).

Friends

Some components have multiple class modules that may need to access each other's properties and methods. But if you declare the properties and methods as Public, the client application will also have access. The solution is to use the **Friend keyword,** which you can use in place of Public or Private. Using Friend has the advantage of sharing the information among the classes of the server project, but not to the client. Only those properties needed by a client should be made Public.

You can use the Friend keyword on the declaration of a Sub, Function, or Property procedure, but not on a variable declaration. The only place you can declare a Friend is in a class module; it is not allowed in standard code modules or form modules.

For example, this Public procedure allows the client application to change the RecordKey property:

```
Public Property Let RecordKey(ByVal strKey As String)
    'Assign value to RecordKey property

    mstrRecordKey = strKey
End Property
```

Instead, you can change the code as follows so that only another module in the same component can make a change to the property:

```
Friend Property Let RecordKey(ByVal strKey As String)
    'Assign value to RecordKey property

    mstrRecordKey = strKey
End Property
```

Now the RecordKey property is available within the component but is not added as a Public member in the type library.

Feedback 8.1

1. Specify the file type for the following extensions:
   (a) Dll
   (b) Exe
   (c) Tlb
2. What is the difference between GlobalMultiUse and MultiUse instancing?
3. How do you test an in-process component? an out-of-process component?
4. Why use COM? Give as many reasons as you can.
5. What is the name of the utility that you can use to register or unregister a COM component?
6. Give an example where Friend might be used.

Creating an ActiveX Dll

The following step-by-step tutorial demonstrates creating an ActiveX Dll server component (a provider) to enter patient information. The server maintains a PatientNumber static variable to assign the next sequential number to each new patient. The server consists of a single class module (CPatient) and a standard code module. Notice that the standard code module is loaded once, the first time a CPatient object is instantiated. Although CPatient objects can be created and destroyed, the standard code module remains loaded until the last reference to the module is set to Nothing.

You will also create a client project that uses the Dll server component.

Create an ActiveX Dll—Step-by-Step Tutorial

Follow each step to create your own in-process server.

Set up the ActiveX Dll Server Project

STEP 1: Start VB and begin a new project. For Project Type, select ActiveX Dll. You will have a project with one class module.

STEP 2: Name the class module *CPatient*.

STEP 3: Select *Project/Project1 Properties* and make these entries in the *Properties* dialog box:

- Change the *Startup Object* to *Sub Main*.

- Name the project *PatientDll*.

● Change the *Project Description* to *Patient ActiveX Dll.*

Remember, the project description is the name that will appear in the References list and the description in the Object Browser for your component.

STEP 4: Add a standard code module to your project. Call the module *PatientCodeModule.*

STEP 5: Save the project in a new folder called Ch08ActiveXDll. Call the project *Ch08ActiveXDllServer.*

Write the Code in the Standard Code Module

Although an ActiveX Dll component does not need a standard code module, in this case we will use one. Sub Main will be the startup object for your component, so we can track execution with the Debug.Print output. The standard code module is needed for this component to maintain the sequential patient numbers.

STEP 1: Enter the remarks for the standard code module.

```
'Project:        Chapter 08 ActiveX DllServer
'Module:         Patient Standard Code Module
'Date:           Today's Date
'Programmer:     Your Name
'Description:    Code for component
'Folder:         Ch08ActiveXDll
Option Explicit
```

STEP 2: Enter Sub Main. Notice that the only line of code generates debug output for tracking execution.

```
Sub Main()
    'Start component execution

    Debug.Print "In Sub Main of Server Component"
End Sub
```

STEP 3: Create the GetPatientNumber function. This function maintains the count and returns the next sequential number each time it is called.

You must declare the patient number variable and increment it in a standard code module rather than in the class. Each new instance of the class has a new set of property variables, and when an object is destroyed the property variables are also destroyed. To maintain a variable for all instances, you must place the variable in a standard code module.

```
Public Function GetPatientNumber() As Long
    'Generate consecutive patient numbers

    Static lngPatientNumber As Long         'Store the Patient Number
    lngPatientNumber = lngPatientNumber + 1 'Generate the next Number
    GetPatientNumber = lngPatientNumber     'Return the value
End Function
```

Enter the Code for the CPatient Class

STEP 1: Enter the remarks and property module-level variables for the CPatient class.

```
'Project:        Chapter 08 ActiveX Dll
'Module:         CPatient
'Date:           Today's Date
'Programmer:     Your Name
'Description:    Create an in-process component
'Folder:         Ch08ActiveXDll
Option Explicit

Private mstrName              As String
Private mlngPatientNumber     As Long
```

STEP 2: Enter the property procedures.

```
Public Property Let PatientName(ByVal strName As String)
    'Assign property value

    mstrName = strName
End Property

Public Property Get PatientName() As String
    'Return property value

    PatientName = mstrName
End Property

Public Property Get PatientNumber() As Long
    'Return the Patient Number

    PatientNumber = mlngPatientNumber
End Property
```

STEP 3: Code the Class_Initialize and Class_Terminate procedures.

```
Private Sub Class_Initialize()
    'Initialize the class
    '  Called when an object is instantiated

    'Generate next Patient Number
    mlngPatientNumber = GetPatientNumber
    'Show what's happening
    Debug.Print "Patient # " & PatientNumber & " Instantiated"
End Sub

Private Sub Class_Terminate()
    'Terminate the class
    '  Called when an object is destroyed

    Debug.Print "Patient # " & PatientNumber & " Name: " & _
    mstr   Name & " Destroyed"
End Sub
```

STEP 4: Press Ctrl + F5 (or *Run/Start with Full Compile*) and click OK on the dialog box that appears. This step compiles the component and lets you know of any syntax errors. If you get an error, fix it and press Ctrl + F5 again until you don't see any more errors. Then stop execution of the project (nothing is happening, anyway).

That's it for the server project. Now it's time to create the client project.

Create a Client Application

You are going to add a second project, creating a project group. A project group allows you to have more than one project open at the same time, which means that both projects are listed in the References and Object Browser. This feature allows you to test the client and server applications together. When we know the component works, we will make the Dll file so that it can be accessed from any project.

Add the Client Project

STEP 1: Select *File/Add a Project* and select Standard Exe. Check the Project Explorer window; you should now have two projects inside a project group.

Set the Client Project Properties

STEP 1: Right-click on Project1 in the Project Explorer window and select *Set as Startup* from the shortcut menu. Now this project will begin execution first when you select *Run.*

STEP 2: Name the form *frmPatient.*

STEP 3: Select *Project/References* and select *PatientDll*; it should be near the top of the list.

STEP 4: Click on the Save toolbar button to save the entire project group.

- Name the Form *frmPatient.*

- Name Project1 *ActiveXDllClient.*

- Name the group *ActiveXDllDemo.*

Set up the Client Form

STEP 1: Give the form a Caption: *ActiveX Dll Client Application.*

STEP 2: Add a command button to frmPatient (Figure 8.2).

Figure 8.2

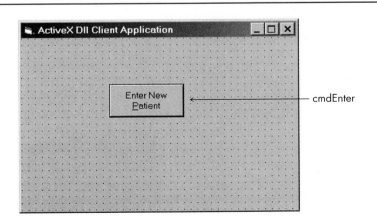

The form for the client application.

cmdEnter

STEP 3: Write the remarks and module-level variable for the form module:

```
'Project:        ActiveX Dll Client
'Module:         frmPatient
'Date:           Today's Date
'Programmer:     Your Name
'Description:     The client application; uses the server component.
'Folder:         Ch08ActiveXDll
Option Explicit
Private mPatient As CPatient
```

STEP 4: Write the code for the cmdEnter button. This code instantiates a new CPatient object, inputs the patient name from the user, and assigns the name to the PatientName property of the new object.

```
Private Sub cmdEnter_Click()
    'Instantiate a new Patient object

    Set mPatient = New CPatient
    mPatient.PatientName = InputBox("Enter Patient Name")
End Sub
```

STEP 5: Write the Form_Unload procedure, to release the object variable.

```
Private Sub Form_Unload(Cancel As Integer)
    'Release resources

    Set mPatient = Nothing
End Sub
```

Test the Project

STEP 1: Save the project group and run the project. If the Immediate window isn't visible, display (Ctrl + G) and resize it so that you can see the form and the window.

You didn't get a compile error (User-defined type not allowed), did you? If so, you must set a reference to PatientDll in the *References* dialog box.

STEP 2: Click the Enter Patient button and keep your eye on the Immediate window. Enter a patient name and watch what happens.

STEP 3: Enter two or three more patients and watch the execution.

STEP 4: Close the application; check the Immediate window to see that the server application calls Class_Terminate when the client application unloads.

STEP 5: Try pressing F8 to begin execution again. Repeatedly press the F8 key to single-step and watch the execution.

Raise an Event in the Server Component

You can raise an event in the ActiveX Dll server component to which the client application can respond. In this continuation of the step-by-step tutorial, you will maintain an array of the names entered so far. If a new name duplicates a previous entry, the CPatient class will raise an event.

You must store the array in the component's standard code module rather than in the class module, since each new instance of the class destroys the

previous instance. But a standard code module cannot raise an event, so you
will raise the event in the class module.

Add a Dynamic Array to the Server Component's Code Module

STEP 1: Switch to the server component and dimension a dynamic array at the
module level of the standard code module:

```
Dim mstrName()  'Store the names in a dynamic array
```

STEP 2: Give the array one element in Sub Main:

```
ReDim mstrName(0)   'Start the array with one element
```

STEP 3: Write a function with a Boolean return—True if the name is added and
False if it is a duplicate.

```
Public Function AddedToArray(strName As String) As Boolean
    'Add a name to the array if it doesn't already exist
    Dim intElement As Integer
    Dim varElement As Variant

    AddedToArray = True                      'Assume OK to begin
    For Each varElement In mstrName          'Look for a match
        If UCase(strName) = UCase(varElement) Then
            AddedToArray = False             'Match found
            Exit Function
        End If
    Next
    'No match found--Add to the array
    intElement = UBound(mstrName) + 1    'Find the next index
    ReDim Preserve mstrName(intElement) 'Increase the array size by 1
    mstrName(intElement) = strName       'Store the name in the next element
End Function
```

Add the Event to the Class Module

STEP 1: Switch to the CPatient class module. Declare the event in the General
Declarations section of the CPatient class module.

```
Event DuplicateName()
```

STEP 2: In the Property Let procedure for the PatientName property, call the
AddedToArray function and raise an event for a duplicate name.

```
Public Property Let PatientName(ByVal strName As String)
    'Assign property value

    mstrName = strName
    If Not AddedToArray(strName) Then

        RaiseEvent DuplicateName

    End If
End Property
```

Modify the Client Form to Check for the Event

STEP 1: In the client project, add `WithEvents` to the declaration of the object variable.

```
Private WithEvents mPatient    As CPatient
```

STEP 2: Drop down the Object list in the Code window and select mPatient. A code template for the mPatient_DuplicateName event procedure will appear. Write the code to display a message.

```
Private Sub mPatient_DuplicateName()
   'Display a message to the user

   MsgBox "Duplicate name entered"
End Sub
```

Test the Event

STEP 1: Save the project and run it. Try entering different names and some duplicates. You should see a message box for the duplicates.

STEP 2: For a very interesting exercise, try watching the processing of the array by setting a breakpoint in the `AddedToArray` function. Display the Locals window, expand the entries for PatientCodeModule and mstrName, and view the names being added to the array.

Create the Component's Dll File and Type Library

After you have thoroughly tested the component and you know it is ready to be used by client applications, it's time to compile the component, create the Dll file, and make the type library. This process also registers the component automatically so that it appears in the References list and can be used in any project.

STEP 1: In the Project Explorer window, select the server project: PatientDll.

STEP 2: From the *File* menu, select *Make Ch08ActiveXDll.dll*. Check the folder and filename and click OK. This step compiles the project, creates the Dll file with its type library, and registers the components in the Registry.

STEP 3: Now we'll test it. First save the project group again; then right-click on the PatientDll project and select *Remove Project*. Answer Yes to the *Are you sure?* message. Now you should have only the form in the project group.

STEP 4: Run the project. Does it run properly without the class module in the project? (If not, check the References list and select *Patient ActiveX Dll.*)

STEP 5: Close VB but don't save the project again. This way you can reopen the project group and continue to experiment with the component.

Create a Component That Implements Business Rules

In the preceding tutorial you learned the basics of creating an ActiveX Dll component. In this chapter's hands-on example, you will apply those concepts in a project that implements business rules.

Feedback 8.2

1. Assume that you are writing code in a module that responds to an event called FoundOne, which is fired by another class called LookForOne.
   (a) What line should you add to the General Declarations section of the module that responds to the event?
   (b) Where do you write code to respond to the event?
   (c) What line of code do you need in the General Declarations section of the LookForOne class so that it can fire the event?
   (d) What line of code do you need to actually fire the event? Name two ways to register an ActiveX Dll component.

The Life Cycle of a Component

The lifetime of a component depends on where it is created. A component created in a sub procedure (local) exists only until the procedure finishes; one declared at the module level lasts for the life of the module. Yes, it's the same rule as for variables but with a few wrinkles. As a client application developer, you usually declare a component in the General Declarations section. The component then goes out of scope when the project ends. However, it may not release all references to the objects and properties in the component, so you must always set the references to Nothing.

The component developer's job is to see that the component does not terminate early or remain when it shouldn't. A "properly behaved" ActiveX component should release memory when all connections to the client are made and no sooner. Your component should never shut down with an End statement. This practice could be a problem with out-of-process components.

Several strange situations might cause a component to shut down unexpectedly or not shut down when you think you have released all references to it. If you plan to take the MCSD certification exam, you need to be familiar with these possibilities. See the "MCSD Exam Notes" section at the end of this chapter for more information.

Feedback 8.3

1. What is the lifetime of a component declared at the module level and instantiated in a procedure?
2. What is the lifetime of a component declared and instantiated in a procedure?

ActiveX Exe Code Components

ActiveX Exe code components execute in their own address space. The result is that your client application can call a code component and then continue with its own processing while the component "does its thing." When the out-of-process component is finished with its task, that component notifies the client application with an **asynchronous notification.**

When you are testing an out-of-process component, you will need to run two copies of VB—one for the client application and one for the server application.

There are several things to consider when choosing to use an ActiveX Dll or an ActiveX Exe component. Dlls beat Exes for performance. Exes are best for background, asynchronous processing and are better for exposing an application's object model to clients.

Create an ActiveX Exe—Step-by-Step Tutorial

In this tutorial you will modify an existing project into an out-of-process code component.

Create the Project and Set the Project Properties

STEP 1: Make a copy of your Ch06 hands-on project (Ch06SBSCollection).

> *Note:* If you don't have this project, you can find a copy on your student CD.

STEP 2: Name the new folder Ch08ActiveXExe.

STEP 3: Display the project properties and change the project type from *Standard Exe* to *ActiveX Exe.*

STEP 4: Change the startup object to Sub Main.

STEP 5: For project name, enter *Ch08ActiveXExe.*

STEP 6: For project description, enter *Dispensary Collection Component.* (Remember that this name appears in the References list.)

STEP 7: For both of the classes, change the value of the Instancing property to *5 - MultiUse.*

Add the Sub Main

STEP 1: Add a standard code module to the project. Name the module StandardCode.

STEP 2: Enter the following code:

```
'Project:      Maintain Collection
'Module:       StandardCode.bas
'Programmer:   Your Name
'Date:         Today's Date
'Description:  Load the form
'Folder:       Ch08ActiveXExe

Option Explicit
```

```
Private Sub Main()
   'Load the form

   frmDispensaryItem.Show
End Sub
```

Fix the Menu

You want a component's menu command to be *Close* rather than *Exit*.

STEP 1: With the Menu Editor change the form's Exit option to &Close and the name to mnuFileClose.

STEP 2: In the form's code change mnuFileExit_Click() to mnuFileClose_Click().

Compile the Project

STEP 1: Use Ctrl + F5 or *Run/Start with Full Compile* and click OK on the dialog box. This step just compiles the project; it does not show the form. You are checking for syntax errors.

STEP 2: If there are no errors, stop execution.

STEP 3: Select *File/Make DispensaryItem Exe* to create an executable file. Note: If your project name is different from DispensaryItem, you will see that name instead. Check the folder and filename and click OK.

STEP 4: Close the project.

Use the Component from a Client Application

STEP 1: Take off your component-author hat and put on your developer hat. You are going to develop an application that uses a component that an author has written.

STEP 2: Create a new Standard Exe project called *Ch08ActiveXExeClient* and save it in a folder of the same name.

STEP 3: Name the form frmDispensary and set its Caption to *Dispensary Client*.

STEP 4: On the form add a command button named cmdDispensary with the Caption *&Dispensary*.

STEP 5: Set a reference to *Dispensary Collection Component*.

STEP 6: Display the Object Browser. Select *Ch08ActiveXExe* from the Libraries list and look at the objects, properties, methods, and error constants of the Exe component.

STEP 7: Write the code for the client application. Note that you instantiate the class to call the component. Because Sub Main is the startup object, the form will display.

```
'Project:      ActiveX Exe Client
'Module:       frmDispensary
'Programmer:   Your Name
'Date:         Today's Date
'Description:  Client application to use the Dispensary Collection Component
'Folder:       Ch08ActiveXExeClient

Option Explicit
Private mDispensaryItems As CDispensaryItems
```

```
Private Sub cmdDispensary_Click()
    'Instantiate the dispensary collection component

    Set mDispensaryItems = Nothing 'In case we've been here before
    Set mDispensaryItems = New CDispensaryItems
End Sub

Private Sub Form_Unload(Cancel As Integer)
    'Release the resources

    Set mDispensaryItems = Nothing
End Sub
```

STEP 8: Run the application.
STEP 9: Click the command button. Your dispensary form should appear.

Asynchronous Communication

One advantage of using Exe code components is that the component runs in a separate process. Your application can continue to execute in its own processing area. Asynchronous processing requires the component to alert the client when the process is finished. This step can be accomplished through event notification or callback procedures.

Event Notification

You can use an event in a code component to let the client know that asynchronous processing is complete. You already know how—the component declares and raises an event; the client declares the component WithEvents and can choose to respond to the event. This procedure can work well in some situations, but not so well in others.

If multiple clients are using a single-server component at the same time, event notification may not work out well. The server application merely raises the event with no knowledge of which clients, if any, receive the message. For multiple clients the out-of-process component has no control over the order in which the clients are notified of the event. The component must wait until all clients have handled the event before regaining control. And if the event has any ByRef arguments, the component receives only one change, from the last client that changed the argument. And finally, any errors not handled by the client cannot be sent back to the server. If any of these situations are a problem for your application, you must use a callback procedure.

Callback Procedures

Callback procedures require extra steps but can resolve potential conflicts. The extra work is divided between the author of the component and the developer who uses the component. With callbacks the client identifies itself to the server component and requests notification.

The server component must contain a class that manages the notification. It may be the same class that performs the processing. This manager class must have a Public callback method and properties to keep an ID of the client. The type library must include these methods in the interface accessible to the client.

To see an example of a callback procedure, refer to the VB sample applications in MSDN. If the samples are installed on your system, you should find

Tip

If you get an error message "Object does not support automation events," make sure your Dispensary ActiveX file is not running in another instance of VB.

them in the path *Program Files\Microsoft Visual Studio\MSDN98\98VS\1033\ samples\VB98*. The Coffee sample includes an ActiveX Exe with asynchronous notification using events, whereas the Coffee2 sample uses callback procedures.

Feedback 8.4

1. What is the difference between an in-process server and an out-of-process COM server?
2. How can you change a component defined as in-process to out-of-process?
3. Name two ways that an out-of-process component can notify the calling module that an operation is complete.

Interfaces

Recall that the interface of a class is its Public properties and methods (Figure 8.3). The class is said to "expose" the properties and methods. All variables and procedures that are declared as Private are hidden and not exposed. In VB a class may have more than one interface, exposing a different set of properties and methods in the second interface than it does in the first (Figure 8.4). And often one interface is used for more than one class (Figure 8.5), which can provide consistency and polymorphism (more on this topic later in the section "Implementing Polymorphism through Interfaces").

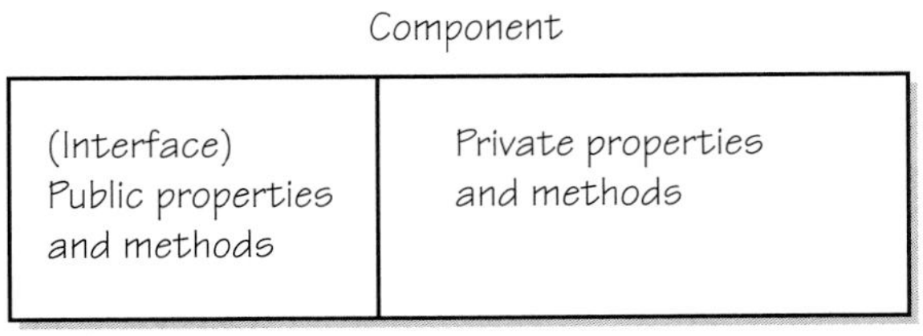

Figure 8.3

The Public properties and methods of a class are its interface. The Private properties and methods are hidden from other modules.

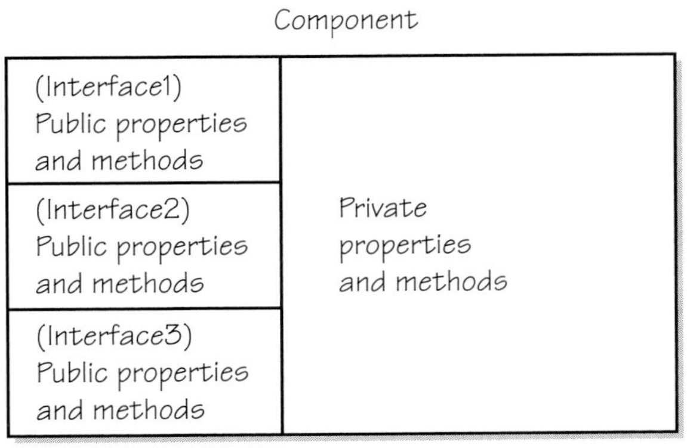

Figure 8.4

A class can expose more than one interface.

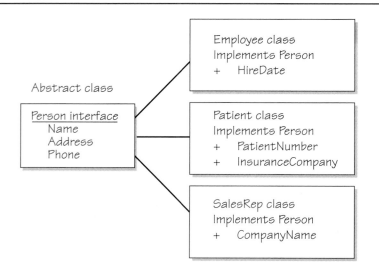

To expose more than one interface or to use a predefined interface, you must write the interface as a separate class. An interface class declares Public properties and methods but has no code to implement those properties and methods. The class that uses the interface is said to "implement" the interface. The implementing class must have code to handle (implement) every property and method of the interface.

Interface Classes

An interface class has procedures that contain no code. Classes that contain these "empty" procedures are called ***abstract classes*** and cannot be used to instantiate objects. Their purpose is to create a superclass from which sub-classes can be built.

How many applications are based on information about a person? Consider a Person class. The Person class could be an abstract class that contains prop-erties for Last Name, First Name, Phone, and so on. The Person class could be used to create a Patient in our application; it could also be used to create an Employee, a SalesRep, or a Student.

The superclass forces the other classes to contain all of the properties and methods in the abstract class. When using multiple interfaces, all Public items must be the same. However, additional properties and methods can be added to a subclass.

Creating an Abstract Class

You can create a class to use as an interface. Add a new class module to a proj-ect and give it a name. The convention is to name interface classes with a pre-fix of capital *I*. In this example we'll name the interface class IPerson. Add Public variables for each property and empty Public procedures (Subs and Functions) for the methods. Do not add any code to the procedures.

```
'Project:      Multiple Interfaces
'Module:       IPerson
'Date:         2/2000
'Programmer:   Bradley/Millspaugh
'Description:  Interface Superclass
'Folder:       Ch08MultipleInterfaces

'Declare properties for Person
Public LastName              As String
Public FirstName             As String
Public Phone                 As String

Public Sub Save()
   'Method to save the property values
End Sub
```

The Implements Keyword

When you create the subclass, you use the Implements statement. By doing so, you agree to implement all properties and methods of the superclass. In fact, you will get a compile error if you neglect to write code for any procedures of the superclass.

```
'Project:      Multiple Interfaces
'Module:       CPatient
'Date:         2/2000
'Programmer:   Bradley/Millspaugh
'Description:  Patient class that implements the IPerson interface.
'Folder:       Ch08MultipleInterfaces

Option Explicit
Implements IPerson
```

After you include the Implements statement, the Object list includes the name of the interface (Figure 8.6). Now pull down the Procedure list; all Property procedures are listed (Figure 8.7). When you add a Property Let,

F i g u r e   8 . 6

The Object list includes the name of the interface you are implementing.

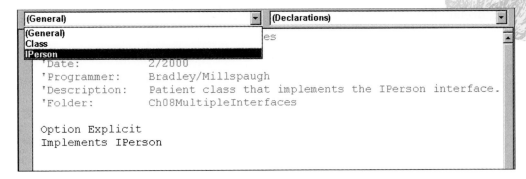

Figure 8.7

The Procedure list includes all of the properties (Property Lets and Property Gets) and methods for the implemented interface.

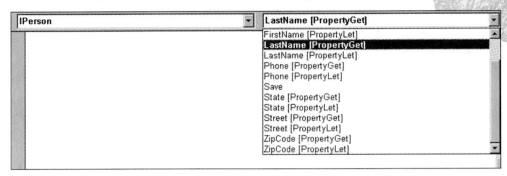

notice that the variable for the argument is set to *RHS*, which stands for "right-hand side" (the right-hand side of an assignment statement). RHS is just a placeholder for the variable name, which you can change if you wish.

```
Private Property Get IPerson_FirstName() As String
    'Retrieve current value of FirstName property
    IPerson_FirstName = mstrFirstName
End Property

Private Property Let IPerson_FirstName(ByVal RHS As String)
    'Assign value to FirstName property
    mstrFirstName = RHS
End Property
```

Notice that in the interface class, you declare properties as Public variables and methods as Public Subs and Functions. Then in the class that implements the interface, you declare the Property Lets, Property Gets, Subs, and Functions as Private. Actually, VB creates the procedure templates for you, with the keyword Private everywhere it is required.

Using the Class That Implements an Interface

When you use a class that implements an interface, such as in a form module, you declare an object variable of the interface type. Then, when you instantiate the variable, declare it as a new instance of the class that implements the interface.

```
'Project:       Multiple Interfaces
'Module:        frmPatient
'Date:          2/2000
'Programmer:    Bradley/Millspaugh
'Description:   Form to use the CPatient class
'Folder:        Ch08MultipleInterfaces

Option Explicit
Private mPerson      As IPerson
```

```
Private Sub Form_Load()
    'Instantiate the class

    Set mPerson = New CPatient
End Sub
```

When you reference the object variable in code, the properties of the interface are available (Figure 8.8).

The properties defined in the interface pop up when you refer to the class.

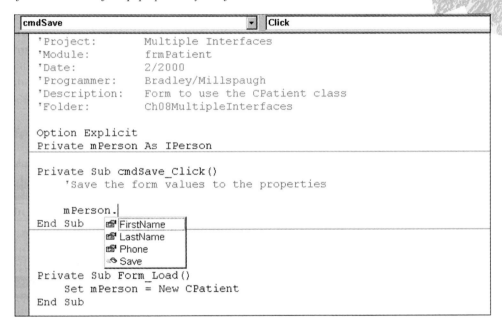

Implementing Polymorphism through Interfaces

You will recall that polymorphism is a feature of object-oriented programming that allows a class to behave in different ways, depending on how it is used. The way to implement polymorphism in VB is to define and use interfaces. For example, you can define an interface such as Person, with methods like Save and Print. The interface defines the names of the properties and methods, but does not define their behavior. Therefore, a program that implements the interface can determine that Save means to save to a collection, to a database, or to a sequential file; and Print may be to the printer, the screen, or perhaps a file formatted for printing. But every class that implements the interface will use the Save and Print methods. As mentioned earlier, using interfaces not only facilitates polymorphism but also provides for consistency in programming. This approach prevents programmers from using Save in one program, SaveRecord in another, and perhaps AddToCollection in another.

Maintaining the Integrity of Interfaces

After you create an interface and it is being used, you must be careful about making changes. If you add or delete properties or methods, any client applications that implement the interface will fail. Basically, the rule is that you cannot modify any Public portion of the interface. If you want to add properties and/or methods, you must create a new interface. An existing interface is a contract with the programs that implement it; the interface must never change.

Fortunately, it's still possible to improve applications based on interfaces. A class can implement multiple interfaces. Although implementing multiple interfaces is beyond the scope of this text, you can find additional information in MSDN in the following topics: "Polymorphism, Interfaces, Type Libraries, and GUIDs" and "Providing Polymorphism by Implementing Interfaces" in the section "General Principles of Component Design" and "Polymorphism" in the section "Programming with Objects," in the *Visual Basic Programmer's Guide.*

Version Compatibility

When you modify classes that are already in use, you must be very careful to maintain compatibility. One way to do so is to create a new interface for any changed features. You should also be aware of the **version compatibility** options located on the Component tab of the *Project Properties* dialog box (Figure 8.9). The compatibility options are *No Compatibility, Project Compatibility,* and *Binary Compatibility.*

F i g u r e   8 . 9

Select the Version Compatibility option on the Component tab of the Project Properties dialog box.

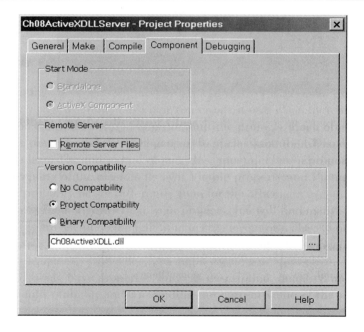

If you opt for *No Compatibility,* each time the project is compiled a new type library is generated. Applications that used the earlier version will not work with a different version. Use this option when you basically want to Save As— you want to make a new component based upon an older one but are not trying to maintain compatibility. Change the name of the component and the name of the project (for the type library) and then set the option to *No Compatibility.* This step will change the IDs for the new version without affecting other applications.

Project Compatibility is new to VB 6. It works well for new development and testing situations where you recompile multiple times as you work. If you do not use this option while developing, you may end up with a message in the *References* dialog box that your component is missing. However, be aware that if you modify any existing class that is already in use elsewhere, choosing *Project Compatibility* is the same as choosing *No Compatibility*—the existing projects will no longer work.

Binary Compatibility is true version compatibility, allowing new applications and older applications to execute with a component after modification. When programmers speak of version compatibility, they are referring to *Binary Compatibility.*

Compatibility has three levels: version identical, version compatible, and version incompatible. When using version identical or version compatible, increase the version number on the Make tab of the *Project Properties* dialog box (Figure 8.10). You can check the box to automatically increment the version number, or you can enter the number yourself. You can enter *Major, Minor,* and *Revision* numbers. For version identical, you keep the same name for your component and do not add any new properties or methods. For version compatible, the component name is unchanged, but additional items may be added to the interface.

Figure 8.10

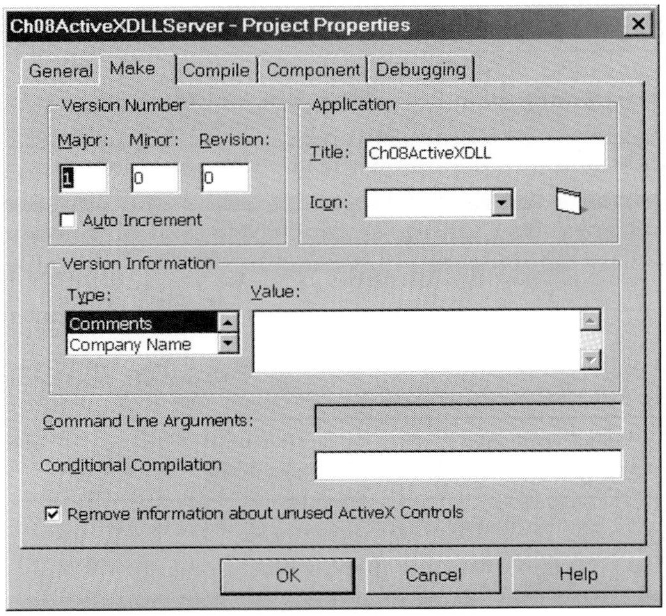

Set the version number on the Make tab of the Project Properties *dialog box.*

If changes need to be made to the interface and will affect the data type, arguments, or identifier names, your interface is version incompatible. In this case you should consider the use of multiple interfaces with the `Implements` clause.

Feedback 8.5

1. What is an interface? What is meant by the statement that a class exposes properties and methods?
2. What is an abstract class and how would you write one?
3. Give an example of a superclass and subclasses.
4. What line of code do you need to include in the General Declarations section of a class that will expose properties of an interface class?
5. Why worry about version compatibility?
6. Explain how to use multiple interfaces to maintain compatibility.

The Visual Component Manager

New to VB 6 is the **Visual Component Manager (VCM),** a tool for organizing components. VCM is designed to help you locate components and organize the components into folders in a database. The database, called a *repository,* can be a local Access database or a SQL Server database on the server.

You can use the Visual Component Manager to

- Publish components. Publishing a component makes it available for others to use.

- Find components. When you are developing an application, you can search for an already-developed component that fits your needs.

- Reuse components. After you find a component that you want to use, incorporate it into your project.

To display the Visual Component Manager, select *View/Visual Component Manager* or use its toolbar button (Figure 8.11). (If the button does not appear on your toolbar, select *Add-ins/Add-in Manager,* locate *Visual Component Manager,* and select *Loaded* and *Load on Startup.*)

Figure 8.11

The toolbar button for the Visual Component Manager.

In the Visual Component Manager window (Figure 8.12), you can open the Local Database folder to find several folders already created for you. Initially you will probably see the panes set up like the figure, but you can display or hide the Explorer pane and the Properties pane, so your display may differ.

Figure 8.12

The Visual Component Manager window.

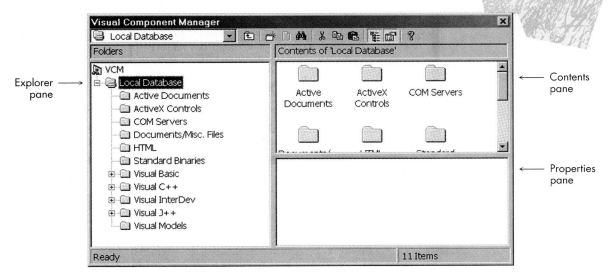

Publishing a Component

You add a component to the repository database by publishing the component. You can choose to publish only the compiled version of your component or also the source code. To publish the source code, you must first save the project (or VCM will give you a message telling you to do so). Of course, to publish the compiled version, you must first compile the component.

You use the Publish Wizard to guide you through the publishing process. You can begin the wizard by first opening a folder and then clicking on the Publish a New Component toolbar button in the VCM window (Figure 8.13).

Figure 8.13

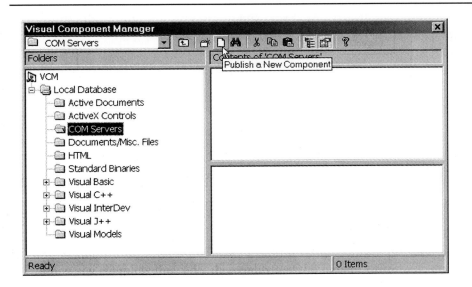

Press the Publish a New Component toolbar button to invoke the Publish Wizard.

You can also begin the wizard by right-clicking your component in the Project Explorer window in the VB IDE (Figure 8.14).

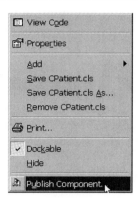

Right-click on the project or component in VB's Project Explorer and select Publish Component to begin the Publish Wizard.

The Publish Wizard

Follow the screens through the wizard to add your component to the repository database.

- Select a Repository/Folder screen: Choose the database (may be more than one) and folder within the database.
    - New Item name: You can give the item a name, which is for information only; it will not affect the project or Registry name.

- Title and Properties screen: You can use the Browse button to locate the project file or component file that you want to add.
    - Set the Type to VB Project.
    - Select Source Code.

- More Properties screen: Add a description and keywords. You and other developers will use the description and keywords to locate the component later.

- Select Additional File(s) screen: This screen lists the files that will be published. You can add or remove files if you wish.

- COM Registration screen: You can indicate which files require entries in the Registry. The wizard is pretty smart and makes a good guess about which components to register. The wizard won't allow you to register source code.

- Finish: Your project will display in the VCM.

Finding and Reusing Components with Visual Component Manager

You can use VCM's Find to locate a published component and add it to your current project. If the source code was published, you can add the source to your project. If only the compiled version was published, you can add it to your

References list. For ActiveX controls (covered in Chapter 9), you can choose to have the control added to your toolbox.

Click on the Find Item(s) toolbar button to open VCM's *Find Items* dialog box (Figure 8.15). You can search by component name, by type, by keywords, or by text in the annotations.

Open the Find Items dialog box to search for a published component.

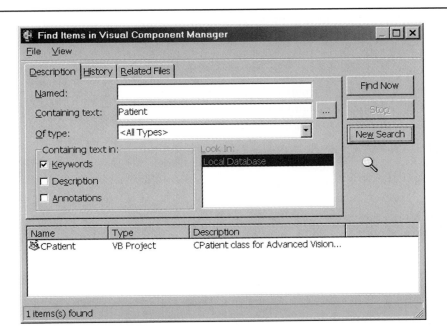

After you locate the desired component, double-click its name. When the *Select Folder* dialog box appears place the component in the same folder as your current project. If the selected component includes source code, you will see it in your Project Explorer window; COM components are added to the References list, and controls are added to the toolbox.

Feedback 8.6

1. What is the purpose of Visual Component Manager?
2. How do you access Visual Component Manager?
3. What does it mean to publish a component, and how do you do it?

Your Hands-on Programming Example

In this hands-on exercise, you will create an ActiveXDll component that implements business rules. We will start with the two-tier project from Chapter 7 (Ch07DataAwareClass) and separate it into two distinct projects in one project group. Then we will convert the data-aware class into an in-process server component that can be used by many projects. Figure 8.16 shows the component design.

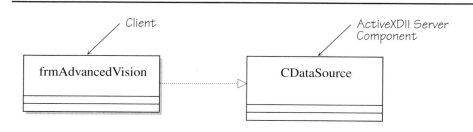

The component design for the
Hands-on Programming
Example.

Set up the Project Group

The easiest way to set up the two projects in a project group and maintain the references is to duplicate the project file and move the modules into the correct project.

STEP 1: Copy your Ch07DataAwareClass folder to a new location and name the new folder *Ch08ClientServer.*

STEP 2: Create a new folder inside the project folder, calling the new folder *Ch08Client.*

STEP 3: Copy the Vbp file from Ch08ClientServer into the Ch08Client folder. Rename the Vbp file in the Client folder to Ch08Client.Vbp; rename the Vbp file in the ClientServer folder to Ch08Server.Vbp.

Now you have two copies of the project file, and both copies have references to all modules.

STEP 4: Move the Frm and Frx files from Ch08ClientServer to Ch08Client. The form is the client application.

STEP 5: Open the project file for Ch08Client. Answer *Yes* to the question about the missing class file. In the Properties window, rename the project to *Ch08Client.*

STEP 6: Select *File/Add Project* and add Ch08Server.Vbp. Answer *Yes* to the question about the missing form file. Make sure the added project is selected in the Project Explorer window and rename the project in the Properties window to *Ch08Server.*

Set the Project Properties

STEP 1: Right-click on the Ch08Server project in the Project Explorer window and choose *Ch08Server Properties.*

STEP 2: In the *Project Properties* dialog box, General tab, make these selections; then close the dialog box and click OK on the informational message box.

- Project type: *ActiveX Dll.*

- Startup object: *(None).*

- Project description: *Patient Data Source.*

STEP 3: Click on the CDataSource class module in the Project Explorer window. In the Properties window change the Instancing property to *5 - Multiuse.*

STEP 4: In the Project Explorer window, right-click on Ch08Client and choose *Set as Start Up*. This step makes the form in the client application display when you run the project group.

STEP 5: With Ch08Client still selected, open the *References* dialog box and select Ch08Server. Now the client application has a reference to the server application.

The only reason that Ch08Server appears in the References list is because the project is open as part of the project group.

Run and Test the Project

STEP 1: Save the project group as Ch08ClientServerGroup.

STEP 2: Press Ctrl + F5 to run with a full compile. Test the various program functions.

Compile and Register the Server

STEP 1: Click on the server project in the Project Explorer and select *File/Make Ch08Server.Dll*. In the resulting dialog box, change the filename to *Ch08PatientDataServer*.

This step will make the Dll file and place an entry in the Windows Registry.

Separate the Projects

STEP 1: In the Project Explorer window, right-click on the Ch08Server project and choose to remove the project, answering *Yes* twice. Remember, you are removing the project from the group, but the files remain on your disk. You can always add the project back if you need to.

STEP 2: Save the project group again. It should hold only the client application.

STEP 3: Run the client application again.

Interesting aside: Open the *References* dialog box. VB has changed the selected reference from Ch08Server to Patient Data Source, the project description of the server project.

You now have a Dll in-process component that you can use with this client application or with any others that you or someone else writes.

Run on Another Machine?

As a further exercise, move your project to another machine and make it run there. You must copy the Dll file, register it using Regsvr32.Exe, set a reference to the Dll file in the client application, and make it (the client) run.

Most Dlls are stored in the Windows/System folder, but that location is not a requirement. You can actually register the Dll from a diskette folder.

Create a New Client

Try carrying this project a little further. Create a new VB project with a form. Write a new user interface for the patient data—it isn't necessary to display all fields. Set a reference to Patient Data Source and code a few of its methods, such as MoveNext and Sort. Again, you don't have to implement all functions of the server in every client.

Publish the Component Using Visual Component Manager

Now that you have a registered Dll component that is actually useful, publish it using the VCM.

The Project Code

The code for this project is unchanged from the Ch07DataAware project.

MCSD Exam Notes

Exam Objectives Covered in This Chapter

Deriving the Physical Design
● Design VB components to access data from a database.

● Design the properties, methods, and events of components.

Creating User Services

Instantiate and Invoke a COM Component

● Create a VB client application that uses a COM component.

● Create a VB application that handles events from a COM component.

Create Callback Procedures to Enable Asynchronous Processing between COM Components and VB Client Applications

Creating and Managing COM Components

Debugging a COM Client Written in VB

Compiling a Project with Class Modules into a COM Component
● Implement an object model within a COM component.

● Set properties to control the instancing of a class within a COM component.

Use Visual Component Manager to Manage Components

Register and Unregister a COM Component

Testing the Solution

Implementing Project Groups to Support the Development and Debugging Processes

- Debug Dlls in-process.

- Test and debug a control in-process.

Questions/Tricks to Watch for

Watch for questions that ask about the rules for component shutdown.

Component Shutdown Rules

Four factors cause component shutdown relating to references, forms, code, and startup. The effect differs for in-process and out-of-process components. Table 8.3 shows the component shutdown rules.

Table 8.3

Component Shutdown

A Component Will Shut down if	
In-Process Component	**Out-of-Process Component**
No references to Public objects.	No external references are held by client applications.
No forms are visible.	No forms are loaded.
No code executing or in the Calls list.	No code executing or in the Calls list.
Component is not in the process of starting.	Component is not in the process of starting.

References A component is shut down when there are no references to Public objects, which means the Public properties of the class. Notice the word *Public;* if all references are to Private properties, the component is released. This action can cause a problem for an in-process component. If the component shuts down and then the client attempts to refer to it, a program fault occurs. The moral: Don't pass an instance of a Private class to a client.

This situation would occur if you pass a reference (send an argument ByRef) of a Private property of the component to the client. When there are no Public properties, the component will shut down and then the reference becomes invalid. If you need to pass the information to the client, use a PublicNotCreatable instancing property for the object.

Another problem can occur when multiple components are in use and they contain references to each other (a circular reference); VB will not shut them down. VB cannot distinguish between an internal reference (inside the component) and an external reference (from the client) for in-process components. The client may release the component, but it is not released from memory because of the internal reference.

A circular reference occurs when two objects contain a reference to each other. You may wonder why you would do this. It's very common to set up a circular reference if you refer to the Parent property of an object. This property is frequently used in an object model to find which collection contains a specific object. If the property is used, the object contains a reference to its parent and the parent contains a reference to the child object. Many common controls such as a check box or an ADO data control contain a Parent property. Be wary of using the Parent property in component creation because doing so may interfere with the component shutdown.

With out-of-process components, only external references keep the component from shutting down. VB maintains a count of the external references of a component because several clients may use the component. When there are no external references, the component shuts down. If there is a circular reference or a global object in a component and a second client is using the same server component, the internal references from the first client are not released from memory. For more information refer to "Visual Basic Component ShutDown Rules" in MSDN.

Forms A component is shut down if no forms are visible for an in-process component and if no forms are loaded for an out-of-process component. The moral on this one: Make sure to unload all forms when your program terminates. This practice should become a habit.

Code Components will not shut down while code is executing. This situation can occur if you are running code from another component or from the Windows API.

Startup Startup is something you don't need to worry about when coding, but you should be aware of the concept. If there is a time lapse during startup when forms are not loaded, no external references exist, and no code is executing, the component will not shut down.

Summary

1. The Component Object Model (COM) is a standard for creating interfaces that communicate with other software components. ActiveX is based on COM.
2. An object interface is the Public properties and methods that can be accessed by a client application.
3. Client or consumer applications use the services of provider or server applications.
4. Class modules can be compiled into ActiveX Dll (in-process) or ActiveX Exe (out-of-process) code components.
5. The person who writes a component is the author; the person who uses the component in an application is the developer.
6. The Instancing property controls the times and ways in which a component can be instantiated.
7. The properties and methods of a class are stored in a type library when the class is compiled.
8. Access to a software component is made through the *References* dialog box.

9. A VB project group contains more than one project and is an ideal way to test an in-process code component in a client application.

10. Out-of-process components must be tested in a second instance of VB.

11. ActiveX components are registered when they are compiled. In-process components can be registered on a client machine by using RegSvr32 in the Windows/System directory. The same program can be used to unregister a component.

12. A GUID is a globally unique identifier used to identify a component.

13. The Friend keyword allows the classes of a component to share procedures without making them Public and available to the client.

14. A server component can raise an event; the client application can respond to that event.

15. The life cycle of a component depends on a set of shutdown rules that differ for in-process and out-of-process components.

16. ActiveX Exe components are out-of-process components that execute in their own address space.

17. An out-of-process component executes asynchronously; it can notify the client that processing is complete by using an event or a callback procedure.

18. A component may expose multiple interfaces. You can create an interface class that defines the properties and methods of the class but has no code to implement the procedures. This type of class is called an *abstract class*.

19. VB implements polymorphism by using multiple interfaces.

20. Once it is put into production, an interface should never be changed.

21. The Visual Component Manager is a tool that organizes and helps to locate software components.

Key Terms

abstract class *376*

ActiveX Dll *358*

ActiveX Exe *359*

application provider *359*

application server *359*

asynchronous notification *372*

author *359*

automation server application *359*

callback procedure *374*

client application *358*

code component *358*

Component Object Model (COM) *358*

consumer application *358*

dependent object *360*

developer *359*

Friend keyword *363*

global object *360*

in-process *359*

Instancing property *359*

interface *358*

interoperability *358*

out-of-process *359*

project group *362*

provider application *358*

server application *358*

type library *361*

version compatibility *380*

Visual Component Manager *382*

R e v i e w   Q u e s t i o n s

1. What is the COM standard and how does it relate to ActiveX?
2. What is an interface?
3. Why would an application be referred to as a client? a server?
4. Differentiate between in-process and out-of-process components.
5. Define the terms *author* and *developer* in the context of programming with components.
6. What is the purpose of the Instancing property of a class?
7. How is a type library created? What does it contain?
8. Why would you want to use a project group?
9. What steps are required to register a component on a client's machine?
10. Explain what is meant by *Friend.*
11. Explain the shutdown rules for components.
12. What is the lifetime of a component that is instantiated in a command button's click procedure?
13. Discuss the concept and purpose of asynchronous processing.
14. Differentiate between asynchronous communication using event notification versus callback procedures.
15. Why would multiple interfaces be needed?
16. What are the functions of the Visual Component Manager?

P r o g r a m m i n g   E x e r c i s e s

8.1 Create an in-process code component for simple annual interest. The code component will have properties for principal, rate, and time and a method for calculating interest.

Interest = Principal * Rate * Years

Add a client project creating a group. The client will have a form that allows a user to enter principal, rate, and years. These values will be assigned to the properties in the component. Display the result of the method that calculates interest.

8.2 Change the project type of exercise 8.1 to ActiveX Exe, compile, and test the project. Note: Because the Exe is out-of-process, you must use a separate instance of VB to test the client application.

8.3 Create an ActiveX Dll code component for Payroll. A form will input an employee name and hours worked. A check box will ask "Salaried?". If the answer is No, a dropdown list will give options for levels 10, 11, and 12. For a salaried employee display a dropdown list with salary levels A, B, and C. Use the amounts in the table to calculate and display gross pay for the week. On salaried use 1/52 of the annual pay. With an hourly employee calculate overtime at time and a half for all hours over 40.

Hourly Level	Hourly Rate	Salary Level	Annual Pay
10	7.50	A	27,000
11	10.50	B	35,000
12	14.00	C	42,000

Create a client application that calls the payroll component.

8.4 Using the specifications for exercise 8.2, create an out-of-process component and test with a client application.

8.5 Modify a two-tier application from Chapter 7 to be an in-process Dll project.

C A S E   S T U D I E S

Modify project 1 from Chapter 7. **Video Bonanza** in-process Dll component. Make the data source class into an

Modify project 1 from Chapter 7. **VB Auto** in-process Dll component. Make the data source class into an

9

ActiveX Documents and ActiveX Controls

At the completion of this chapter, you will be able to . . .

1. Create an ActiveX document.

2. Manage UserDocument and UserControl events: Initialize, InitProperties, ReadProperties, WriteProperties, and Terminate.

3. Navigate to other active documents and Web sites.

4. Define menus for a UserDocument, which are merged with the container's menus.

5. Save and restore property values using the PropertyBag.

6. Create an ActiveX control that exposes properties.

7. Understand the sequence of events as a control executes at design time and run time.

8. Raise and respond to control events.

9. Create a Property Page for a control.

10. Understand how to create an ActiveX control that is a data consumer or a data source.

In Chapter 8 you learned about two types of COM components: Dlls and Exes. In this chapter you will become familiar with two more types of ActiveX COM components: **ActiveX documents,** which run in a container, such as Internet Explorer; and **ActiveX controls**—visual components that you can add to the VB toolbox to place on forms or place on your Web pages.

ActiveX Documents

An ActiveX document is similar to the other components that you learned about in Chapter 8, but it executes in a different environment called a ***container.*** The container can be an Internet Explorer browser or Microsoft Binder. The examples in this chapter use Internet Explorer 5.0 for the container.

Note: According to Microsoft documentation, other container applications may soon be able to host ActiveX documents.

The code component for an ActiveX document can run either in-process or out-of-process. In the *New Project* dialog box (Figure 9.1), you will notice two project types for ActiveX documents: *ActiveX Document Dll* and *ActiveX Document Exe.* Recall that a Dll is an in-process provider and an Exe is an out-of-process provider.

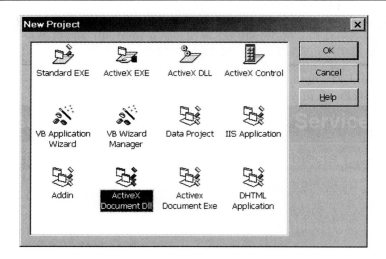

Select ActiveX Document Dll or ActiveX Document Exe to create either an in-process or out-of-process ActiveX document.

When you create a new project of either type, a new UserDocument object is added to the project (Figure 9.2). A Designer window opens for the document, which looks very similar to a form in a Designer window. In fact, a UserDocument is similar to a form in many ways. You place controls on the document and write code to respond to the control events, but the document appears as a Web page instead of an independent form.

Figure 9.2

A UserDocument project with a Document Designer window.

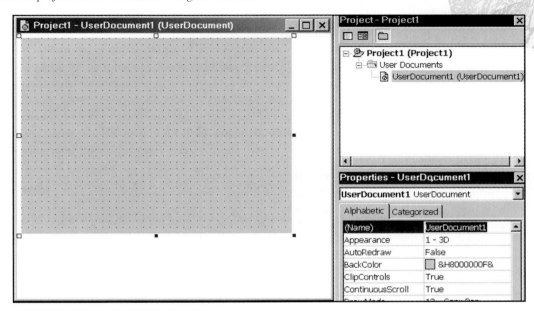

Many ActiveX document events differ from those of forms. Because a UserDocument runs inside a container, which is a separate application, many of the events of a form just wouldn't make sense. For example, UserDocuments do not have events for Activate, Deactivate, Load, QueryUnload, Unload, or any of the Link events. On the other hand, a UserDocument has some events that a form does not. They include InitProperties, ReadProperties, Scroll, Show, and WriteProperties events.

UserDocument Events

When a UserDocument is created, the first event to execute is Initialize, followed by InitProperties or ReadProperties. The **InitProperties event** occurs when a new instance of an object of ActiveX document type is created. As the name implies, the properties of the component are initialized. The **ReadProperties event** occurs when an existing object is loaded and has stored values.

You store the property value by using a WriteProperty method, which saves the properties into a **PropertyBag object.**

The Hyperlink Object

Because a UserDocument runs in a browser, you may want to include a link that "jumps" to a Web site. You can use a Hyperlink object to link to a Web

URL as well as to transfer to a different UserDocument. Use the NavigateTo
method of the HyperLink object.

```
Hyperlink.NavigateTo txtURL.Text
HyperLink.NavigateTo App.Path & "\docPatient.vbd"
Hyperlink.GoBack
```

Other methods of the Hyperlink object are GoForward and GoBack. These
work like the Forward and Back buttons in a browser.

Menus

You can create a menu for a UserDocument with the VB Menu Editor exactly
as you do for a form. However, since the document appears in a browser window, which has a menu of its own, differences occur during execution. VB
merges the menu of the document with the menu of the container. *Help* remains
on the far right on the menu bar, and by default, your document menu items
precede *Help*. You can adjust the location of your menus by using the
NegotiatePosition dropdown list in the Menu Editor. You can also merge your
Help menu with that of the browser. You will see how to set up menus in the
step-by-step tutorial that follows.

UserDocument Files

When you add an ActiveX document to a project, the object is called a
UserDocument. VB stores a UserDocument in file with an extension of .dob.
The compiled version, which runs in a container, has a .vbd extension. When
you are testing an ActiveX Document project in the VB environment, VB stores
the .vbd file in its program folder. After you compile the project to a Dll or Exe,
the Vbd file will be in the folder that you specify. When you test a project that
navigates from one document to another, you need to be aware of which path
you are using.

Creating an ActiveX Document—Step by Step

Note: To complete this tutorial, you must have Internet Explorer on your system. At this time ActiveX documents cannot run in Netscape Navigator or any
other browsers.

Begin the Project

STEP 1:   Open a new project, selecting ActiveX Document Dll for the type.
STEP 2:   In the Properties window, change the project name to
ActiveXUserDocuments.
STEP 3:   Double-click on UserDocument1 to open it in the Designer window.
Change the document's Name property to *docOne.*
STEP 4:   Add the following controls to the UserDocument (Figure 9.3).

Figure 9.3

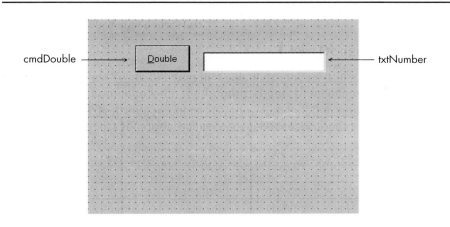

The UserDocument for the step-by-step tutorial.

Control	Property	Value
txtNumber	Text	(empty)
cmdDouble	Caption	&Double
	Default	True

STEP 5: Code cmdDouble to double the number in the text box.

```
Private Sub cmdDouble_Click()
    'Double the value in the text box

    txtNumber.Text = 2 * Val(txtNumber.Text)
End Sub
```

STEP 6: Run the project. You will see the Property Page, Debugging tab. Click OK.

Internet Explorer opens, if it isn't already open, and displays your ActiveX document.

STEP 7: Notice the Address box, which shows a Vbd file with its complete path. Make note of the path; you will need it later. VB uses this path for the temporary Vbd files for testing ActiveX documents.

STEP 8: Enter a numeric value and double it. In fact, you can double it as many times as you wish.

STEP 9: Close the browser.

STEP 10: Stop the VB application.

STEP 11: Save your project, creating a new folder called Ch09ActiveX UserDoc.

The UserDocument has a .dob extension. The file displayed in the browser has a .vbd extension. You can use the Windows Explorer to locate the Vbd file. In fact, you can double-click on the Vbd filename to open the file in Internet Explorer, assuming that your system has been set up correctly to point Vbd files to Internet Explorer.

Set up to Navigate to a URL

Note: To navigate to a URL, you must have an open connection to the Internet. You can also complete this section by linking to an HTML file on disk.

STEP 1: Add another command button and a text box to the UserDocument (Figure 9.4).

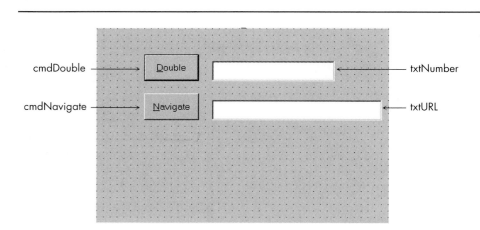

Add a command button and a text box to the document.

Control	Property	Value
txtURL	Text	(empty)
cmdNavigate	Caption	&Navigate

Although we could set the Text property of txtURL at design time, we are going to initialize it in code, which will add flexibility later as well as demonstrate initializing properties of a UserDocument.

STEP 2: In the General Declarations section, add the opening remarks and declare a string constant with the default value for the URL.

```
'Project:      Chapter 09 ActiveX Document
'Module:       docOne
'Date:         Today's Date
'Programmer:   Your Name
'Description:  A UserDocument with a calculation and a hyperlink
'Folder:       Ch09ActiveXUserDoc
Option Explicit
Private Const mstrDefaultURL = "http://msdn.microsoft.com/"
```

Feel free to substitute another URL, such as your own home page. But make sure to include the complete protocol at the beginning ("http://"). If you don't have an Internet connection, store the file Test.htm from your student CD into your project folder. Then enter the complete path for the constant. For example:

```
Private Const mstrDefaultURL = "a:\Ch09ActiveXUserDoc\Test.htm"
```

STEP 3: Select *UserDocument* from the Object list and *Initialize* from the Procedure list and write the code to initialize the value for the URL.

```
Private Sub UserDocument_Initialize()
    'Initialize properties

    txtURL.Text = mstrDefaultURL
End Sub
```

STEP 4: Write the code for cmdNavigate.

```
Private Sub cmdNavigate_Click()
    'Use the Hyperlink object's NavigateTo
    'method to go to the URL in txtURL

    On Error GoTo HandleNavigateErrors
    Hyperlink.NavigateTo txtURL.Text

cmdNavigate_Exit:
    Exit Sub

HandleNavigateErrors:
    MsgBox "Invalid URL", vbOKOnly, "Hyperlink Failure"
    Resume Next
End Sub
```

STEP 5: Save and run the project again. Test the Navigate button. Enter a new URL and test again. Test the browser's Forward and Back buttons.

STEP 6: Switch to the VB window and stop execution. Answer *Yes* to the *Are you sure?* question.

Add a UserDocument

Just like a regular project can have multiple forms, a container project can have multiple documents. You use the Hyperlink object to navigate from one document to another.

STEP 1: Select *Project/Add User Document* to add a document.

STEP 2: Name the document *docTwo*.

STEP 3: Add a command button named *cmdReturn* with a Caption of *&Return*.

STEP 4: Code the command button.

```
Private Sub cmdReturn_Click()
    'Use Hyperlink to go back

    Hyperlink.GoBack
End Sub
```

Create a Menu for a UserDocument

We will add a menu to docOne with a command to navigate to docTwo. We will also integrate the new menu with the browser's menus.

STEP 1: Switch to docOne and use the Menu Editor to create a menu command.

Caption:	&Switch Documents
Name:	mnuSwitchDocuments

Drop down the list for NegotiatePosition and choose Middle. (Later you can try the other choices, which determine the placement of your menu within the existing browser menus.)

STEP 2: Enter the menu command indented one level.

Caption: Doc &Two
Name: mnuSwitchDocTwo

STEP 3: Code mnuSwitchDocTwo. Note: The menu does not appear on the UserDocument in design view. To code the procedure, drop down the Object list and choose mnuSwitchDocTwo.

For now, we will hard-code the complete path for the Vbd file. Later we will clean it up a bit. Use the path that you made note of earlier.

```
Private Sub mnuSwitchDocTwo_Click()
    'Display another document
    ' Use the path on your system where VB stores its temporary files.

    Hyperlink.NavigateTo "C:\Program Files\Microsoft Visual Studio\VB98\docTwo.vbd"
End Sub
```

STEP 4: Save the project and run it. Pull down the menu and go to Doc Two. Test the Return button.

Note: If the document does not appear, use Windows Explorer to find the Vbd file and check the exact path and filename, including spaces.

STEP 5: Return to the VB environment and stop execution.

Display a Form from a UserDocument

You can add a form to an ActiveX Document project just as you can in a standard project. We will create an About form.

STEP 1: Use *Project/Add Form* and select the option to add an About Dialog to the project.

STEP 2: Modify the interface as indicated in Figure 9.5 and remove all extra code, leaving only the cmdOK_Click procedure.

F i g u r e   9 . 5

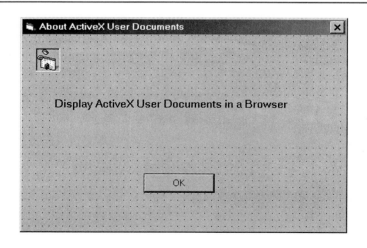

The About Dialog form.

STEP 3: Add the remarks.

```
'Project:      Chapter 09 ActiveX Document
'Module:       frmAbout
'Date:         Today's Date
'Programmer:   Your Name
'Description:  Show a form with User Documents
'Folder:       Ch09ActiveXUserDoc
Option Explicit

Private Sub cmdOK_Click()
    'Close the form

    Unload Me
End Sub
```

STEP 4: On docOne add a menu item *mnuHelp* and under it *mnuHelpAbout.* Set the NegotiatePosition for mnuHelp to *Right.*

STEP 5: Add the code for the menu command.

```
Private Sub mnuHelpAbout_Click()
    'Show the About form

    frmAbout.Show vbModal
End Sub
```

> *Note:* Some containers cannot handle modeless forms so be sure to include the vbModal.

STEP 6: Run the project and drop down the browser's *Help* menu. It has a submenu called *docOne Help.* Display your About form.

Persisting Data Using the PropertyBag Object

A PropertyBag object is a handy object that you can use to store property values. Each ActiveX document and ActiveX control has a built-in PropertyBag. You can also add a PropertyBag to any class by setting the class's Persistence property to True. Or you can create your own instance by declaring an object of type PropertyBag and instantiating it with the New keyword.

You use the built-in PropertyBag to save the values of a document's properties. For example, you may display a UserDocument, navigate to another document, and return to the first document. Each time you display a document (or redisplay one using the Back button), you create a new instance of the document. Any values that the user entered in controls on the first document are gone when it is redisplayed. But if you save the properties in a PropertyBag, you can restore the properties when the document is redisplayed.

VB saves the PropertyBag object in a document's Vbd file. If you are testing an application in the VB environment, each time you run you create a new, temporary Vbd file. Therefore, the property values persist for only the one execution of the application. But if you compile the project into a Dll or Exe, VB saves the Vbd files in the folder with the compiled project. And each time you run, the PropertyBag is saved in the Vbd file, so the property values persist from one run to the next.

PropertyBag Methods and Events

Use the PropertyBag's **WriteProperty** and **ReadProperty** methods and the
UserDocument's events to store and retrieve properties.

Method	
WriteProperty	Save the current value of a property in the PropertyBag.
ReadProperty	Retrieve the saved value of a property.
Event	
WriteProperties	Store property values into the PropertyBag using the WriteProperty method in the WriteProperties event procedure.
ReadProperties	Retrieve saved values by executing the ReadProperty method in the ReadProperties event procedure.

You use the UserDocument's PropertyChanged method to ensure that the
WriteProperties event will fire.

The WriteProperty Method—General Form

```
Object.WriteProperty PropertyName, Value[, DefaultValue]
```

The PropertyName is a name that you make up. It does not have to be the name
of a property that you have defined in the object. You can think of the property
names as declaring variable names. You declare a name and a value. Use the
optional default value if you want to give the property a default value.

The WriteProperty Method—Examples

```
PropBag.WriteProperty "UserName", mstrUserName, ""
PropBag.WriteProperty "URLEntry", txtURL.Text
PropBag.WriteProperty "NumberValue", txtNumber.Text, ""
```

In these examples, taken from the step-by-step tutorial that follows, you
can see that the value may come from a variable or a control property.

The ReadProperty Method—General Form

```
Object.ReadProperty(PropertyName[, DefaultValue])
```

The ReadProperty method returns a value, which you assign to a variable
or control property. The PropertyName must be the name that was used when
the property was saved. The optional default value is a fallback value; it is used
if no value was saved for the property.

The ReadProperty Method—Examples

```
txtUserName.Text = PropBag.ReadProperty("UserName", "")
txtURL.Text = PropBag.ReadProperty("URLEntry", mstrDefaultURL)
txtNumber.Text = PropBag.ReadProperty("NumberValue", "")
```

Persisting Properties with a PropertyBag—Step by Step

In this continuation of the chapter step-by-step tutorial, we will persist property values from one instance of a document to the next. We will also code differently for testing mode than for production mode.

Add Controls and a Property to the UserDocument

STEP 1: Add a text box, label, and check box to docOne. Set the properties to match Figure 9.6.

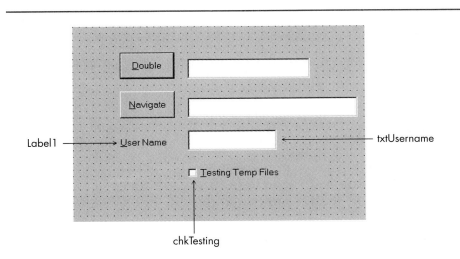

Add a text box, label, and check box to docOne.

STEP 2: Test the project. Enter a numeric value and double it, enter a user name, and enter a new URL. Navigate to a different page by using the menu option (or the URL) and return to docOne.

What happens? Because returning to a document creates a new instance, all properties are reinitialized.

STEP 3: Add a UserName property to the docOne code. We are going to make this property a read-only property, as we are planning to later retrieve it from a second document.

```
Private mstrUserName As String

Public Property Get UserName() As String
    'Retrieve the current value of the Username property

    UserName = mstrUserName
End Property
```

STEP 4: Code the txtUserName Change event to save a new UserName as it is
entered.

```
Private Sub txtUserName_Change()
    'Save a changed user name

    mstrUserName = txtUserName.Text
    PropertyChanged "UserName"
End Sub
```

STEP 5: Code the PropertyChanged method for the other controls.

```
Private Sub chkTesting_Click()
    'Save a changed entry

    PropertyChanged "Testing"
End Sub

Private Sub txtNumber_Change()
    'Save a changed entry

    PropertyChanged "NumberValue"
End Sub

Private Sub txtURL_Change()
    'Save a changed URL entry

    PropertyChanged "URLEntry"
End Sub
```

Save the Properties in the PropertyBag

STEP 1: Select *UserDocument* from the Object list, select *WriteProperties* from
the Procedure list, and write the code to save properties into the
PropertyBag. Note that only one of the properties (UserName) is actually set up as a property of the class. For the others, we just made up a
name to hold the value of a control.

```
Private Sub UserDocument_WriteProperties(PropBag As PropertyBag)
    'Save property values in the property bag

    PropBag.WriteProperty "UserName", mstrUserName
    PropBag.WriteProperty "URLEntry", txtURL.Text
    PropBag.WriteProperty "NumberValue", txtNumber.Text
    PropBag.WriteProperty "Testing", chkTesting.Value
End Sub
```

STEP 2: Add the code for the UserDocument_ReadProperties. Be sure to use
exactly the same property names that we used to save them.

```
Private Sub UserDocument_ReadProperties(PropBag As PropertyBag)
    'Retrieve the saved properties from the property bag

    txtUserName.Text = PropBag.ReadProperty("UserName", "")
    txtURL.Text = PropBag.ReadProperty("URLEntry", mstrDefaultURL)
    txtNumber.Text = PropBag.ReadProperty("NumberValue", "")
    chkTesting.Value = PropBag.ReadProperty("Testing", False)
End Sub
```

STEP 3: Test the project by entering a value in each control, navigating to docTwo, and returning to docOne. You will see a dialog box asking whether you want to save the changes (Figure 9.7); this question refers to the changed properties of the document, so choose Yes. When you return to docOne, the values should persist. Note that we have not yet coded the check box.

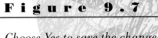

Figure 9.7

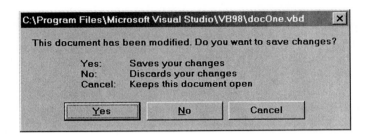

Choose Yes to save the changed properties in the PropertyBag.

STEP 4: Stop execution and restart. Your property values do not persist from one run to the next when VB's temporary Vbd files are used, since new files are created each time you run.

Compile the Project to a Dll

STEP 1: Close Internet Explorer and stop program execution.

STEP 2: Select *Make ActiveXUserDocuments.dll* from the *File* menu. Save the Dll file in your project folder. In addition to the Dll file, VB places the Vbd files for the two documents in the project folder.

Now that you have compiled versions of the document files, you can choose to run the compiled versions or the temporary versions created by the VB environment.

Implement the Testing Check Box

STEP 1: Modify the code for switching to docTwo. (Keep the complete path that you were already using.)

```
Private Sub mnuSwitchDocTwo_Click()
    'Display another document
    '  Use the path on your system where VB stores its temporary files

    If chkTesting Then
        Hyperlink.NavigateTo _
            "C:\Program Files\Microsoft Visual Studio\VB98\docTwo.vbd"
    Else
        Hyperlink.NavigateTo App.Path & "\docTwo.vbd"
    End If
End Sub
```

STEP 2: Recompile the project by selecting *File/Make ActiveXUserDocuments.dll*.

STEP 3: Test the project using the temporary Vbd files: Run from the VB environment and notice the address showing in the Internet Explorer Address box. Navigate to docTwo from the menu and notice the address. Return to docOne and check the Testing check box, navigate to docTwo, and notice the address.

STEP 4: Switch to the VB environment, stop execution if your program is in run time, and answer Yes to the *End program at this time?* message.

STEP 5: Switch to Internet Explorer. Select *File/Open* and browse to find your docOne.vbd file in your project folder. Make sure to set the *Files of type* to *All Files.* Open the file and notice the address displayed.

STEP 6: Navigate to docTwo and again notice the address. Try selecting the check box for Testing and navigate to docTwo again. No temporary document to display?

STEP 7: Enter a number and double it, enter a username, navigate to docTwo, and answer *Yes* to the *Save?* question. When you return to docOne, the values should persist.

STEP 8: Close Internet Explorer and reopen it.

STEP 9: Open your docOne.vbp file from your project folder again. This time the properties should persist, since the PropertyBag is saved in the Vbp file.

Sharing Data between Documents

If you want values from one document to be available in a second document, you must create a global object variable that refers to the first document. You must add a standard code module to the project for the global variable.

Add a Standard Code Module

STEP 1: Select *Project/Add Module* to create a standard code module.

STEP 2: Code a global declaration for an object variable.

```
'Project:        Chapter 09 ActiveX Document
'Module:         StdCode
'Date:           Today's Date
'Programmer:     Your Name
'Description:    Declare global object
'Folder:         Ch09ActiveXUserDoc
Option Explicit

Public gobjDocument As Object
```

STEP 3: Name the module *stdCode* and save it as *stdCode.bas.*

Set the Reference to the Global Variable

STEP 1: In docOne, add a line to the UserDocument_Initialize event procedure to set the reference to this document.

```
Set gobjDocument = Me
```

Modify docTwo to Retrieve the Property from docOne

STEP 1: Add two labels to docTwo to display and identify the user name.

Label1	Caption: User Name
lblUserName	Caption: (Blank)

STEP 2: Add code in docTwo's UserDocument Initialize event procedure to display the UserName property of docOne. We added the check for Nothing to illustrate the difference between using the temporary version of the Vbd file and the compiled version.

```
Private Sub UserDocument_Initialize()
    'Display global data on document

    If gobjDocument Is Nothing Then
        lblUserName.Caption = "Nothing"
    Else
        lblUserName.Caption = gobjDocument.UserName
    End If
End Sub
```

Test the Project

STEP 1: Recompile the project using *File/Make ActiveXUserDocuments.dll.*

STEP 2: Run the project from the VB environment. Enter a username and switch to docTwo. Does the username appear? Which version of docTwo are you displaying? Actually, more important, which version of the standard code module is it using? docTwo uses the global object reference in the code module that is in the same folder as the Vbd file. Check the Testing check box on docOne, enter a username, and navigate to docTwo. This step should display the username on docTwo.

STEP 3: This time test the compiled versions of both documents. In Internet Explorer choose *File/Open*, set to *All Files*, and open docOne.vbd from your project folder.

STEP 4: Enter a username and do *not* check the Testing check box. Navigate to docTwo. This step should work correctly. You must use both document files from the same location.

Using the Migration Wizard

VB's **Migration Wizard** makes it easy to convert an existing form application into a UserDocument. You can easily convert a project into one that will run in a browser.

The Migration Wizard is a VB add-in called *VB6 ActiveX Doc Migration Wizard.* We'll use it to quickly change your form from the three-tier application in Chapter 7 into an ActiveX document. The wizard modifies the form's code and comments out any code that will not work with a UserDocument.

STEP 1: Make a copy of your Ch07AdvancedVision files in a folder called Ch09ActiveXDocWizard.

STEP 2: Open the project in VB.

STEP 3: From the *Add-Ins* menu load *VB6 ActiveX Doc Migration Wizard* and then run it.

   Note: If the Migration Wizard does not appear on your Add-Ins menu, select *Add-In Manager* and load the wizard.

STEP 4: Click *Next* on the *Introduction* dialog box.

STEP 5: Check frmAdvancedVision and click Next.

STEP 6: On the Options screen, select

   ● Comment out invalid code.

- Remove original forms after conversion.
- Convert to an ActiveX EXE.

Click Next.

STEP 7: Click Finish.

STEP 8: Click OK on the message that you've created the document.

STEP 9: Read the summary report now or copy and paste into a word processor to read later.

STEP 10: Run the project. Click OK on the box about using components.

STEP 11: Notice that your menu was added to the browser menu. Also notice the second *File* menu that doesn't do anything. For a production job, you would remove the *File* menu from the document.

STEP 12: Stop execution of the project and open the UserDocument's Code window. View the changes made by the wizard.

Feedback 9.1

1. When do the following UserDocument events occur:
   (a) InitProperties
   (b) WriteProperties
   (c) ReadProperties
   (d) Initialize
   (e) Terminate
2. Code the statement to link a UserDocument to www.Microsoft.com.
3. Code the statement to link a UserDocument to a second user document, called *docInsurance.vbd,* which is stored in the same folder as the project.

ActiveX Controls

An ActiveX control is any VB control that is not one of the intrinsic controls. In Chapter 2 you learned to use many different ActiveX controls, such as the Toolbar, StatusBar, and ImageList. You can also create your own controls or modify existing controls.

When you create a new ActiveX control, you can either use existing controls to create a **composite control** or build your own from scratch. The example in this chapter uses a composite control.

An ActiveX control is similar to the other ActiveX components we have worked with, which are all based on COM standards. A control that you create appears in the *Components* dialog box, just like the other ActiveX controls you have used. When you select a control from the list, the control appears in the toolbox. Each control is stored in a file with an .ocx extension.

The Control Author versus the Developer

The distinction between a contol's author and the **developer** who uses the control is much more important with ActiveX controls than it is in any of the other module types. The **author** creates the control (and tests and compiles it), and the control appears in the toolbox. When the developer adds an instance of the control to a form (instantiates the object), the control's code begins executing;

the Initialize, InitProperties, and ReadProperties events occur while the developer is still in design time. When you author a control, you must plan for the design-time behavior of your control as well as its run-time behavior.

Controls at Design Time

To plan for design-time behavior of a new control, you should be aware of how the VB environment handles control creation and destruction. Think about what happens when you add one of VB's intrinsic controls to a form: You create a new instance of, say, a text box control. VB gives the new text box a set of properties based on default values. The Name property is based on the control's classname; the Text property is based on the Name; the Top, Left, Height, and Width are as you created them. Most of the other properties are set to a default value, which you can change at design time. If you close the Form Designer window or the VB environment and then redisplay the form, you expect that all of your property settings will still be there, right? Of course. But for your new control, the property values set by the developer will not persist unless the control author writes code to make it happen.

At design time each control is created and destroyed many times:

Developer Action	Control Action	Event Occurs
Place a new instance of a control on the form (site the control).	Control is instantiated.	Initialize InitProperties
Close the Form Designer window with the control's container.	Control is destroyed.	Terminate
Reopen the Form Designer window with the control's container.	Control is created.	Initialize ReadProperties
Run the application.	Control is destroyed (temporarily). Program is loaded into memory, and the control is created.	Terminate Initialize ReadProperties
Stop application execution.	Control is destroyed as program stops. When the VB environment redisplays and the container shows in the Form Designer window, the control is created.	Terminate Initialize ReadProperties
Close VB environment.	Control is destroyed.	Terminate
Open VB environment, open project, and open Form Designer window for control's container.	Control is created.	Initialize ReadProperties

Notice that InitProperties occurs only once—when the control is first **sited** (placed) on the form. Every other time that the control is created, the ReadProperties event occurs.

With this information you can see the best location to place code. You will give a control its initial default values in the InitProperties event procedure, which happens only once in the lifetime of the control. In the ReadProperties event procedure, you must restore the property settings as the developer last set them. Notice also that if you set default properties in the Initialize event, rather than InitProperties, the developer's property settings will be lost, since the Initialize event happens so often.

Creating a New Control

When you create a new control, you can either add a new UserControl module to a project or begin a new project, choosing ActiveX Control as the project type. The new UserControl object appears as a design surface, similar to a form, in a Designer window (Figure 9.8).

A UserControl in a Designer window.

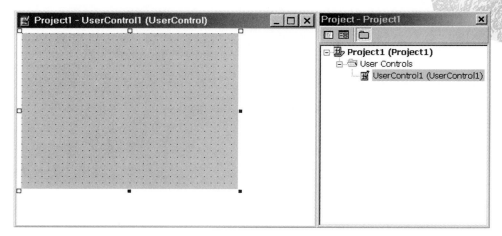

You design the visual interface for your control in the Designer window. If you are creating a composite control, you place the constituent controls on the UserControl surface. You, as the control's author, have access to all properties of the constituent controls. The developer will not be able to access those properties unless you expose the properties as Public properties of your control.

Setting Properties of a New Control

As soon as you begin a new control, give it a name and a bitmap image. The name that you choose for the UserControl object is the name that will display in the Components list and the toolbox. Make sure to not use the same name for the control and the project; VB raises an error if you try it.

The ToolboxBitmap Property

All UserControls initially display the same image in the toolbox, just as all forms have the same icon unless you change them. You will want an appropriate image in the toolbox to represent your control. To set a bitmap image for your control, set the **ToolboxBitmap property.** The image can be a bitmap with a file extension of .bmp, .dib, .pal, .gif, or .jpg; the image cannot be an icon. You can select from the VB Graphics library or use an image of your own.

When creating projects, place the file for the graphic in the same folder as your application. This practice makes your job easier during development, but keeping the graphic with the application is also important for distribution, as you will learn in Chapter 14.

Other Properties of the UserControl

The UserControl has some other properties that you may find useful. If you want to allow an application to set the Default property of your control, you must set the control's DefaultCancel property to True. Your control can become a container for other controls if you set its ControlContainer property to True. And guess what InvisibleAtRuntime does.

Exposing Properties of a Control

You can set up new properties of a control class, just as you do for all other classes. Declare a module-level Private variable to hold the property and write Property Get/Property Let procedures.

Example

```
Private mdblMilesMax          As Double  'MilesMax property

Public Property Get MilesMax() As Variant
    'Retrieve current value of MilesMax property

    MilesMax = mdblMilesMax
End Property

Public Property Let MilesMax(ByVal vNewValue As Variant)
    'Set value for MilesMax property

    mdblMilesMax = CDbl(vNewValue)
    PropertyChanged "MilesMax"
End Property
```

Notice in this example that the property values are passed as Variant data type, even though within the control's module the values are stored and used as Double. Passing values as Variant is a precaution so that a run-time error will not occur for a nonnumeric value or a container specifying the wrong data type.

Delegating a Property

Rather than set up a module-level variable to hold a property, you can store the property's value in one of the constituent controls. In this example the Miles property is stored in txtMiles.Text. This technique is called ***delegating*** the control's property. In this case it gives the developer access to the Text property of txtMiles, which would not be visible otherwise.

Example

```
Public Property Get Miles() As Variant
    'Retrieve current value for Miles property

    Miles = CDbl(txtMiles.Text)
End Property
```

```
Public Property Let Miles(ByVal vntMiles As Variant)
    'Set value for Miles property

    If IsNumeric(vntMiles) Then
        txtMiles.Text = Format$(CDbl(vntMiles), "0.00")
        PropertyChanged "Miles"
    End If
End Property
```

Persisting Properties by Using the PropertyBag

You use the PropertyBag to save and restore properties for an ActiveX control, just as you do for an ActiveX document. Use the **WriteProperties event** of the UserControl object to save the properties and retrieve the saved values in the ReadProperties event procedure.

```
Private Sub UserControl_WriteProperties(PropBag As PropertyBag)
    'Save changed properties in the property bag

    With PropBag
        .WriteProperty "Miles", txtMiles.Text, "0"
        .WriteProperty "KM", txtKM.Text, "0"
        .WriteProperty "MilesMax", mdblMilesMax
        .WriteProperty "KMMax", mdblKMMax
        .WriteProperty "BackColor", Ambient.BackColor
    End With
End Sub

Private Sub UserControl_ReadProperties(PropBag As PropertyBag)
    'Retrieve saved property values from property bag

    With PropBag
        txtMiles.Text = .ReadProperty("Miles", "0")
        txtKM.Text = .ReadProperty("KM", "0")
        mdblMilesMax = .ReadProperty("MilesMax", 200)
        mdblKMMax = .ReadProperty("KMMax", 321.8)
        BackColor = .ReadProperty("BackColor", Ambient.BackColor)
    End With
End Sub
```

Using the Ambient Object's Properties

You may have noticed the entries in the previous examples referring to Ambient.BackColor. This code retrieves the BackColor property of the control's container.

Each control has an Ambient object, which holds information about the control's container. You can use the Ambient properties in your control to set such things as the BackColor, ForeColor, or Font. The Ambient properties are read-only; you cannot change any properties of the container by changing an Ambient property.

You can respond to changes in the control's environment in the UserControl_AmbientChanged event procedure. For example, if the developer changes the form's font or color at design time, you may want to change the corresponding property of your control. The event passes one argument—PropertyName, which holds the name of the property that changed.

Example

```
Private Sub UserControl_AmbientChanged(PropertyName As String)
    'Check for changes in the container

    If UCase$(PropertyName) = "BACKCOLOR" Then
        BackColor = Ambient.BackColor
    End If
End Sub
```

The Extender Object and Properties

When you create a new control, you define the properties that you want to expose. You also get a group of properties "for free" (Figure 9.9). VB provides these properties in the Extender object. This feature means that a control's author doesn't have to declare every property. For example, you can use the Name property, perhaps to set a Caption or pass as an argument of an event, without first setting up a Name property.

Figure 9.9

When you create a new control, these properties are automatically created. They are provided by the Extender object.

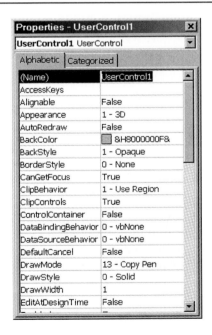

As a control author, you don't need to be concerned about the Extender properties; they are there mostly for the developer using your control.

Responding to Resize Events

While a developer is setting up a control at design time, he or she may resize
the control. You (the control author) may want to resize or reposition the elements in your control when this occurs. You may want to resize any constituent
controls and/or change the font or position of control elements. Or you may
want to restrict the size and not allow the developer to resize smaller or larger
than some set amount. You can place any such code in the UserControl_Resize
event procedure.

```
Private Sub UserControl_Resize()
    'Resize the control but not smaller than the minimum size
    Const intMinControlSize As Integer = 3824

    If Width < intMinControlSize Then
        Width = intMinControlSize 'Cannot resize below minimum
    End If
End Sub
```

Raising Events

You can declare and raise events in a control, just as you do in other classes.

```
Public Event ValueOverMax()

Private Sub cmdSetMiles_Click()
    'Set the value based on text box entry
    Dim dblMiles   As Double

    With txtMiles
        dblMiles = CDbl(.Text)              'Convert text to numeric
        If dblMiles <= mdblMilesMax Then    'Within range
            Miles = dblMiles
            sldDistance.Value = dblMiles * 100
        Else                                'Outside range
            RaiseEvent ValueOverMax
        End If
    End With
End Sub
```

Responding to Events

You, as the application developer, can write code to respond to the control's
events. You don't declare any class WithEvents, you just add the control to the
project. The control's name appears in the Code window Object list and the
event is in the Procedures list.

```
Private Sub conDistance_ValueOverMax()
    'Respond to error event

    MsgBox "The value entered is greater than the maximum", _
        vbOKOnly, "Convert Distance"
End Sub
```

Creating and Using an ActiveX Control—Step by Step

In this step-by-step tutorial, you will create a control that converts between miles and kilometers. The user can use the slider to set the value or enter a value in the text box and click *Set*. Figure 9.10 shows the completed control.

Figure 9.10

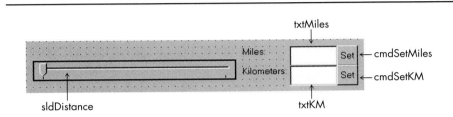

The completed ConvertDistance control for the step-by-step tutorial.

Set up the Project

STEP 1: Begin a new project, selecting ActiveX Control for the project type.

STEP 2: Rename UserControl1 to *ConvertDistance* in the Properties window.

STEP 3: Name the project *ConvertDistanceControl*. Note that you cannot give the project the same name as the control.

STEP 4: Save the control as *ConvertDistance.ctl* in a new folder called *Ch09ActiveXControl*. Save the project as *ConvertDistanceControl.vbp*.

STEP 5: Set the ToolboxBitmap property: Although you can select a bitmap file in any location, for distribution purposes, it's best to store the file in your project folder. Locate Entirnet.bmp and copy it into your project folder.

> *Note:* You can use the Explorer's Find command or look in the location for a default VB install: Program Files\Microsoft Visual Studio\ Common\Graphics\Bitmaps\Outline\Nomask\Entirnet.bmp.
> After copying the file, make sure to set the control's property.

Create the User Interface

STEP 1: Select *Project/Components* and check *Microsoft Windows Common Controls 6.0*. This step adds the Slider control to your toolbox.

STEP 2: Resize the control surface and add the slider, two labels, two text boxes, and two command buttons. Refer to Figure 9.10 for placement and the control names.

STEP 3: Set these additional properties for the controls:

Control	Property	Setting
sldDistance	BorderStyle	1 - ccFixedSingle
	ToolTipText	Select Miles or KM

continued

Control	Property	Setting
two labels	BackStyle	0 - Transparent
two text boxes	Alignment	1 - Right Justify

Set up the Properties

The plan is to create new properties for Miles, KM, MilesMax, and KMMax. You will store Miles and KM in their corresponding text boxes and store MilesMax and KMMax in module-level Private variables. You will set up constants for the default values of Miles and MilesMax.

You will store all four distance properties as Double data type to allow for large and fractional values. However, the slider requires integer values, so you must convert to integers. In this control you will round to two decimal places and multiply by 100 to produce integers for the slider values.

STEP 1: Write the remarks and code the module-level variables and constants.

```
'Project:        ActiveX Control
'Module:         ConvertDistance.ctl
'Date:           Today's Date
'Programmer:     Your Name
'Description:    ActiveX control to convert between miles and
'                kilometers.
'Folder:         Ch09ActiveXControl

Option Explicit

Private Const mdblDefMiles    As Double = 0
Private Const mdblDefMilesMax As Double = 200
Private mdblMilesMax          As Double    'MilesMax property
Private mdblKMMax             As Double    'KMMax property
```

STEP 2: Write the property procedures for the four properties. Notice that Miles and KM are stored in text boxes rather than variables. Also notice that we are passing arguments as Variant data type to avoid run-time errors.

```
'*** Property Procedures ***

Public Property Get KM() As Variant
    'Retrieve current value for KM property

    KM = CDbl(txtKM.Text)
End Property

Public Property Let KM(ByVal vntKM As Variant)
    'Set value for KM property

    If IsNumeric(vntKM) Then
        txtKM.Text = Format$(CDbl(vntKM), "0.00")
    End If
    PropertyChanged "KM"
End Property
```

```
Public Property Get KMMax() As Variant
    'Retrieve the current value of KMMax property

    KMMax = mdblKMMax
End Property

Public Property Let KMMax(ByVal vNewValue As Variant)
    'Set value for KMMax property

    If IsNumeric(vNewValue) Then
        mdblKMMax = CDbl(vNewValue)        'Set KMMax property
        MilesMax = ConvertKMToMiles(mdblKMMax) 'Set MilesMax property
    End If
End Property

Public Property Get Miles() As Variant
    'Retrieve current value for Miles property

    Miles = CDbl(txtMiles.Text)
End Property

Public Property Let Miles(ByVal vntMiles As Variant)
    'Set value for Miles property

    If IsNumeric(vntMiles) Then
        txtMiles.Text = Format$(CDbl(vntMiles), "0.00")
        PropertyChanged "Miles"
    End If
End Property

Public Property Get MilesMax() As Variant
    'Retrieve current value of MilesMax property

    MilesMax = mdblMilesMax
End Property

Public Property Let MilesMax(ByVal vNewValue As Variant)
    'Set value for MilesMax property

    mdblMilesMax = CDbl(vNewValue)
    With sldDistance    'Set the slider's Max property
        .Max = Round(mdblMilesMax * 100)
        .LargeChange = Round(.Max / 10)
        .SmallChange = Round(.LargeChange / 10)
        .TickFrequency = .Max / 10
    End With
    mdblKMMax = ConvertMilesToKm(mdblMilesMax)
    PropertyChanged "MilesMax"
    PropertyChanged "KMMax"
End Property
```

Initialize the Default Properties

STEP 1: Recall that the InitProperties event occurs only once, when the developer places the control on the container. This event procedure is where you set the default properties for the control.

As you add procedures, it is a good idea to keep them organized. Although it takes a little extra time as you write, you will save that time many times over when you are looking for procedures.

The recommended organization:

- All property procedures, arranged alphabetically disregarding the prefix.

- All event procedures, arranged alphabetically.

- All general procedures, both functions and sub procedures, arranged alphabetically.

```
Private Sub UserControl_InitProperties()
    'Initialize default properties

    Debug.Print "InitProperties" 'To demonstrate event sequence
    Miles = mdblDefMiles
    KM = ConvertMilesToKM(CDbl(txtMiles.Text))
    mdblMilesMax = mdblDefMilesMax
    mdblKMMax = ConvertMilesToKm(mdblMilesMax)
    BackColor = Ambient.BackColor
    With sldDistance
        .Max = CInt(mdblMilesMax * 100)
        .LargeChange = Round(.Max / 10)
        .SmallChange = Round(.LargeChange / 10)
        .TickFrequency = .Max / 10
    End With
End Sub
```

Notice that we are calling a function called ConvertMilesToKM. We will write that function shortly.

Persist the Properties by Using WriteProperties and ReadProperties

STEP 1: Write the code for the WriteProperties and ReadProperties procedures. Notice that we are storing the BackColor property in addition to the properties that we defined.

```
Private Sub UserControl_WriteProperties(PropBag As PropertyBag)
    'Save changed properties in the property bag

    With PropBag
        .WriteProperty "Miles", txtMiles.Text, "0"
        .WriteProperty "KM", txtKM.Text, "0"
        .WriteProperty "MilesMax", mdblMilesMax
        .WriteProperty "KMMax", mdblKMMax
        .WriteProperty "BackColor", Ambient.BackColor
    End With
End Sub

Private Sub UserControl_ReadProperties(PropBag As PropertyBag)
    'Retrieve saved property values from property bag

    With PropBag
        txtMiles.Text = .ReadProperty("Miles", "0")
        txtKM.Text = .ReadProperty("KM", "0")
        mdblMilesMax = .ReadProperty("MilesMax", 200)
        mdblKMMax = .ReadProperty("KMMax", 321.8)
        BackColor = .ReadProperty("BackColor", Ambient.BackColor)
    End With
```

```
    With sldDistance   'Set the properties for the slider
        .Max = CInt(mdblMilesMax * 100)
        .LargeChange = Round(.Max / 10)
        .SmallChange = Round(.LargeChange / 10)
        .TickFrequency = .Max / 10
    End With
End Sub
```

Respond to a Change in an Ambient Property

STEP 1: Write the code to respond to a changed BackColor property for the control's container.

```
Private Sub UserControl_AmbientChanged(PropertyName As String)
    'Check for changes in the container

    If UCase$(PropertyName) = "BACKCOLOR" Then
        BackColor = Ambient.BackColor
    End If
End Sub
```

Write the Two Conversion Functions

STEP 1: Write the functions to convert between miles and kilometers. These general procedures belong at the end of the code.

```
Private Function ConvertKMToMiles(dblKM) As Double
    'Calculate miles from KM

    ConvertKMToMiles = dblKM * 0.6214
End Function

Private Function ConvertMilesToKM(dblMiles) As Double
    'Calculate KM from miles

    ConvertMilesToKM = dblMiles * 1.609
End Function
```

Write the Slider Event Procedures

When the user moves the slider's thumb, by dragging the thumb, clicking along the slider, or using keyboard keys, the Change event occurs once—when the move is complete. As the thumb is moving, the Scroll event occurs continuously, so you must write code for both events if you want the distance values to update while the slider is in motion and when it stops.

The slider's value is kept in miles, so you must convert to kilometers and then set both the Miles and KM properties.

```
Private Sub sldDistance_Change()
    'Set properties to reflect new value

    KM = ConvertMilesToKM(sldDistance.Value) / 100
    Miles = sldDistance.Value / 100
End Sub

Private Sub sldDistance_Scroll()
    'Set values on control

    sldDistance_Change
End Sub
```

Declare an Event

STEP 1: Add an event declaration in the General Declarations section.

```
Public Event ValueOverMax()
```

We will raise this event if the user enters a value for miles or kilometers that is greater than the maximum.

Write the Command Button Event Procedures

The user can enter a new value into a text box and click on Set. The cmdSet event procedures should validate the entry and set the slider's Value property to the chosen value. Remember that the slider's value is in miles * 100.

STEP 1: Write the event procedures for the two command buttons. Afterward you will write the general procedure SelectValue.

```
Private Sub cmdSetMiles_Click()
    'Set the value based on text box entry
    Dim dblMiles   As Double

    With txtMiles
        If IsNumeric(.Text) Then            'Check for numeric
            dblMiles = CDbl(.Text)
            If dblMiles <= mdblMilesMax Then 'Not greater than the max
                Miles = dblMiles
                sldDistance.Value = dblMiles * 100
            Else
                RaiseEvent ValueOverMax
                SelectValue txtMiles
            End If
        Else
            SelectValue txtMiles
        End If
    End With
End Sub

Private Sub cmdSetKM_Click()
    'Set the value based on text box entry
    Dim dblKM       As Double

    With txtKM
        If IsNumeric(.Text) Then
            dblKM = CDbl(.Text)
            If dblKM <= mdblKMMax Then
                KM = dblKM
                sldDistance.Value = ConvertKMToMiles(dblKM) * 100
            Else
                RaiseEvent ValueOverMax
                SelectValue txtKM
            End If
        Else
            SelectValue txtKM
        End If
    End With
End Sub
```

Write More Procedures

These procedures make your control more professional. When the user enters a value in a text box, the corresponding Set command button becomes the default so that the user can press just the Enter key. Also, if the entered value doesn't pass validation, the value should appear highlighted.

STEP 1: Enter the SelectValue procedure. This procedure highlights the text in the text box that is passed as an argument.

```
Private Sub SelectValue(txtBox As TextBox)
    'Make the text appear selected

    With txtBox
        .SelStart = 0
        .SelLength = Len(.Text)
        .SetFocus
    End With
    Beep
End Sub
```

STEP 2: Switch to the Designer window and set the UserControl's DefaultCancel property to True. This step is needed before you can set any constituent control's Default or Cancel property to True.

STEP 3: Code the GotFocus events of the two text boxes.

```
Private Sub txtKM_GotFocus()
    'User typing in text box

    cmdSetKM.Default = True
End Sub

Private Sub txtMiles_GotFocus()
    'User typing in text box

    cmdSetMiles.Default = True
End Sub
```

Testing a Control

You must test a control in a container. For most of your testing, you will place the control on a form and run it. But a quick and easy way to test a control is to run it in Internet Explorer on a Web page. If you click Run in the VB environment and the control project is the Startup project, VB will open Internet Explorer and run an instance of your control on a Web page.

To test a control on a form, add a Standard Exe project, creating a project group, and set the new project as the startup project. On the form in the second project, you can add an instance of your control and run it. To make your control appear in the toolbox, you must close the control's Designer window.

Sometimes during testing you need to play around a little. For example, after you have sited a control on a form, you may decide to modify the control's code and run again. Remember that the InitProperties event never fires a second time for one instance of a control. At times you may need to delete the control and re-add it if you want to test the initialization process. Also, if you switch to your form's Designer window while the control's Designer window is open, you will see lines across the control on the form (Figure 9.11). You need to close the control's Designer window.

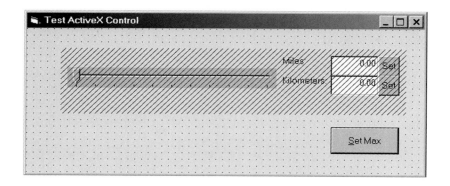

The control appears cross-hatched on the form if the control's Designer window is open.

Add a Project and Test the Control

STEP 1:   Close the control's Designer window. The icon for your control should appear in the toolbox.

STEP 2:   Choose *File/Add Project* and add a Standard Exe project.

STEP 3:   Resize the form and add an instance of your control (Figure 9.12).

Add an instance of the ConvertDistance control to the form.

STEP 4:   Change the form's Name and Caption properties and name the ConvertDistance control *conDistance.*

STEP 5:   Right-click on the new project in the Project Explorer window and choose *Set as Start Up* from the shortcut menu. This setting makes the form the startup object.

STEP 6:   Click on Run. Your control should appear on the form in run time.

STEP 7:   Test the slider and check the values for Miles and KM.

STEP 8:   Enter a value for Miles and press Enter or click Set. Does it correctly set the miles and kilometers?

STEP 9: Enter a value for KM. Does it work correctly?

STEP 10: Try a value higher than the maximum. The default maximum miles is 200.

> Note that we haven't yet written code to respond to the ValueOverMax event.

STEP 11: Close the form to stop execution.

> If you need to do any debugging, you must reopen the control's Code window. You may find it useful to add Debug.Print statements in multiple procedures so you can trace the execution of the control's code.

Respond to the Control's Event

STEP 1: Open the form's Code window, drop down the Object list, and select your control name, conDistance. Code the conDistance_ValueOverMax procedure.

```
Private Sub conDistance_ValueOverMax()
   'Respond to error event

   MsgBox "The value entered is greater than the maximum", _
      vbOKOnly, "Convert Distance"
End Sub
```

STEP 2: Test the project again. Enter both miles and kilometers greater than the maximum. Try changing the maximum miles and entering new values.

Test the BackColor Property

STEP 1: In the form's Designer window, change the form's BackColor property to something pretty. Does your control change to match? You can change the form multiple times; every time it triggers your control's UserControl_AmbientChanged procedure. Your control is running while the form is in design time.

Add the Resize Event Code

STEP 1: In the form's Designer window, resize the control. What happens? What should happen?

> We are going to add code in the control's Resize event to resize the slider and reposition all the controls. We could also resize text boxes and change font sizes, but we'll leave that for you to try on your own.

STEP 2: Switch to the control's Code window and select UserControl and Resize. Write the following code:

```
Private Sub UserControl_Resize()
   'Reposition the controls
   Const intMinControlSize As Integer = 3824
   Const intSliderLeft As Integer = 120
   Const intSpaceAfterSlider As Integer = 108
   Const intLabelWidth As Integer = 852
   Const intTextWidth As Integer = 852
   Const intButtonWidth As Integer = 372
   Const intRightBorderWidth As Integer = 120
```

```
    If Width < intMinControlSize Then
        Width = intMinControlSize 'Cannot resize below minimum
    End If

    With sldDistance
        .Left = intSliderLeft
        .Width = Width - (.Left + intSpaceAfterSlider + _
            intLabelWidth + intTextWidth + intButtonWidth + _
            intRightBorderWidth)
        lblMiles.Left = .Left + .Width + intSpaceAfterSlider
        lblKM.Left = .Left + .Width + intSpaceAfterSlider
    End With
    txtMiles.Left = lblMiles.Left + intLabelWidth
    txtKM.Left = lblKM.Left + intLabelWidth
    cmdSetMiles.Left = txtMiles.Left + intTextWidth
    cmdSetKM.Left = txtKM.Left + intTextWidth
End Sub
```

STEP 3: Close the control's Designer window and switch to the form's Designer window.

STEP 4: Resize the control on the form. Try making it a little smaller, lots smaller, and wider. The slider should resize, and the rest of the controls should reposition. You cannot resize smaller than the minimum width.

Did you try resizing vertically? We didn't code anything for that feature, but you can do so on your own if you wish.

Change the MilesMax Property at Run Time

You have seen how to change the properties of your new control at design time. You can also change them at run time. We are going to write code to change the MilesMax property at run time, which will also change the scale of the slider.

STEP 1: Add a command button to the form.

Name:	cmdSetMax
Caption:	&Set Max

STEP 2: Code the cmdSetMax_Click event procedure to input a new value for the maximum number of miles and set the control's MilesMax property.

```
Private Sub cmdSetMax_Click()
    'Set the maximum number of miles
    Dim varMax As Variant

    varMax = InputBox("Enter new maximum miles")
    If Val(varMax) > 0 Then
        conDistance.MilesMax = Val(varMax)
    End If
End Sub
```

STEP 3: Test the project again. Change the maximum number of miles to larger numbers and smaller numbers. Notice how the scale of the slider changes.

Creating a Property Page

When you, as developer, place an instance of your new control on a form, you see the control's properties in the Properties window. You have probably noticed that the properties you defined, such as Miles and KM, appear in the Properties list, where you can view and change them. You have also noticed that most custom controls have **Property Pages** that you can use to set properties. This is especially true for the more complicated properties, such as a grid control, toolbar, or image list.

You (the control author) can easily add a Property Page to your ActiveX control. The easiest way is to use the Property Page Wizard and then make any modifications that you wish. We will add a Property Page to the ConvertDistance control and then discuss any possible modifications.

Add a Property Page

STEP 1: Select your ConvertDistance control in the Project Explorer window, right-click, and choose *Add/Property Page* from the *Project* menu; select *VB Property Page Wizard.*

STEP 2: In the first wizard screen, click Next.

STEP 3: On the Select the Property Pages screen, click Add. For the new page name, enter *Miles.*

Each tab of the *Property Pages* dialog box is defined as a separate page; you are creating the Miles tab.

Note: Most often you will create a General tab, for the general properties. In this case Miles is more appropriate.

STEP 4: Your new Miles page should appear checked. Click Next.

STEP 5: On the Add Properties screen you see your public properties. Select Miles and MilesMax and send them to the list on the right side by clicking >. Click Next.

STEP 6: On the Finished screen, select the Yes option button and click Finish. The report that the wizard displays is quite informative and can help you to create more complicated Property Pages. You can save the report for later study.

STEP 7: Close the control's Designer window and open the form's Designer window. Right-click on the DistanceControl on the form and choose *Properties.* Your Property Page should appear. You should be able to view the current values for the properties and make changes.

Note: You, the author, don't want to allow you, the developer, to modify both the miles and the kilometer values. That would require a complicated validation and conversion problem for the Property Page code, which is best left to the control.

Examining and Modifying the Property Page

You can create multiple Property Pages. Each displays as a separate tab in the *Property Pages* dialog box and is saved as a separate file with a .pag extension.

Any application that uses your compiled control (Ocx) has access to the Property Page.

A Property Page is a separate module with a visual interface and code. You can display and modify both. Figure 9.13 shows the visual interface for the Miles Property Page in a Designer window, and Figure 9.14 shows the code for the Property Page.

Figure   9.13

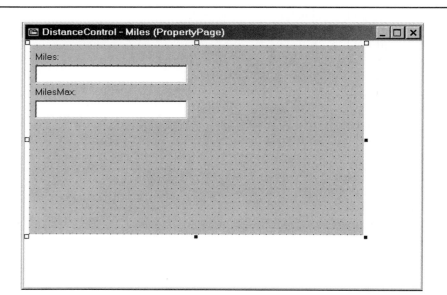

The visual interface for the Miles Property Page. You can add, remove, and edit the controls on the page.

Figure   9.14

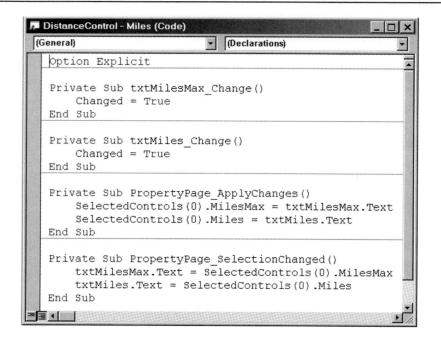

The code for the Miles Property Page, generated by the VB Property Page Wizard.

The Property Page Visual Interface

The Property Page visual interface is very much like a form. You can add and remove controls, as well as change properties for the controls. If you decide to add controls for more properties, you will have to add code to connect the controls to the properties.

You are not limited to text boxes for property values. You can add drop-down lists, option buttons, and check boxes for those controls that would benefit from such a selection. You can also enable, disable, validate, set focus, or hide any controls in the Property Page code.

The Property Page Code

The Property Page code generated by the Property Page Wizard (Figure 9.14) requires a little explanation. You have no doubt noticed that when a Property Page first displays, the Apply button is disabled, but as soon as you make any entry, the button is enabled. The `Changed = True` in the Change event for the two text boxes causes the Apply button to become enabled, which also triggers the PropertyPage_ApplyChanges event when the user (developer) selects *OK/Apply,* or switches to another tab.

The SelectedControls Collection Recall that you can select several controls, such as a group of text boxes on a form, and change many properties at once. You can change such properties as Alignment and Font, but you are not allowed to change properties that presumably would be different for each control, such as the Name and Text properties.

If you are going to create a robust Property Page, you need to provide for the possibility that a developer will place multiple instances of your control on a form. The developer may select multiple instances and expect to change the properties for all controls at the same time. If you are going to code for this situation, you must determine which properties you will allow to be changed as a group and disable or ignore the others. You will find a good example of this technique in the VB sample CtlPlus that comes with MSDN.

The Property Page's SelectedControls collection holds a reference to all controls that are selected. The collection is zero based, so the first (and only) selected control is SelectedControl(0). The PropertyPage_ApplyChanges procedure assigns the values in the text boxes to the correct property of the selected control. The PropertyPage_SelectionChanged procedure assigns the current properties of the selected control to the text boxes. This event occurs when the Property Page is first displayed and when the developer changes the selected controls. Since the *Property Pages* dialog box is modeless, the developer can select and deselect controls while the box displays.

Connecting a Property Page to a Control

You can connect a Property Page to a control without using the wizard. Select the control's module so that its properties display in the Properties window. Then select the PropertyPages property build button. You will see a list that includes any pages that you created plus some standard pages, which you can use to set such properties as font, color, picture, and data format (Figure 9.15).

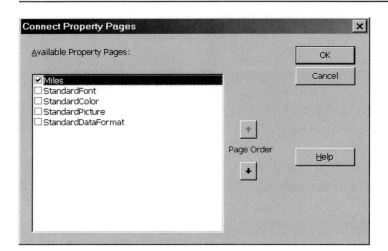

Data-Aware Controls

You can create ActiveX controls that are data aware. A control can be a data source, very much like the ADO data control, or a data consumer, such as a text box or label. The UserControl's DataSourceBehavior and DataBindingBehavior are the keys to creating data-aware controls.

To create a control that is a data source, you must set the DataSourceBehavior to vbDataSource. The default is vbNone. When a control is set up as a data source, you can bind other controls, such as text boxes and labels, to the control. For a complete step-by-step example, see the MSDN topic *Creating Data Sources*.

Data Consumer Controls

You are used to using data-aware controls such as text boxes, labels, and grids, which can be bound to a data source. These data-bound controls are considered *data consumers*. You can set an ActiveX control to be **bindable,** which makes it a data-aware control. Set the control's DataBindingBehavior to vbSimpleBound; this setting gives your control new properties for DataSource, DataMember, DataFormat, and DataField.

Binding a Single Field

If your data-aware ActiveX control has only one field to bind to the data (Figure 9.16), setting up the field is relatively simple. Create a property for the data field and write the Property Get and Property Let procedures. The property can be a delegated property, which stores its value in a control. (We'll get to the CanPropertyChange method soon.)

Example

```
Public Property Get Patient() As String
    'Return current value of Patient property

    Patient = txtPatient.Text
End Property
```

Figure 9.16

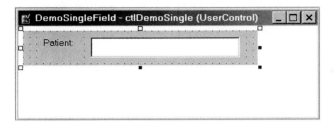

An ActiveX control with a single bindable field is easy to make data aware.

```
Public Property Let Patient(ByVal strPatient As String)
    'Assign a new value to Patient property

    If CanPropertyChange("Patient") Then
        txtPatient.Text = strPatient
        PropertyChanged "Patient"
    End If
End Property
```

One more small step, and the field will be properly bound. Open the *Procedure Attributes* dialog box from the *Tools* menu and click on Advanced (Figure 9.17). In the Data Binding frame, select *Property is data bound*. Also select *This property binds to DataField* and *Property will call CanPropertyChange before changing*. If you have multiple properties to bind, only one of them can be set to *This property binds to DataField*, but all can be set to *Property is data bound*.

Figure 9.17

Set the property to be data bound in the Procedure Attributes dialog box.

Procedure Attributes

Name: Patient

Description:

Project Help File: Help Context ID:
                       0

Use this Page in
Procedure ID: Property Browser: Property Category:
(None)   (None)   (None)

Attributes
☐ Hide this member   ☐ User Interface Default
  ☐ Don't show in Property Browser

Data Binding
Select for → ☑ Property is data bound
data bound   ☑ This property binds to DataField
                ☐ Show in DataBindings collection at design time
                ☑ Property will call CanPropertyChange before changing
                ☑ Update immediate

OK   Cancel   Apply   Advanced >>

At this point you can add a project, create a form, add an instance of the new control, and add an ADO data control or a Data Environment. After setting up the connection for the data control, you can set the properties of the ActiveX control. Your control will have properties for DataSource, DataMember, DataField, and DataFormat. Ignore the DataMember property and set the DataSource and DataField properties. Your application should display data in the bound field.

Binding Multiple Fields

It's more likely that you will want to bind multiple fields, rather than a single field. The sample project *Ch09DataAware* creates an address label for a patient (Figure 9.18).

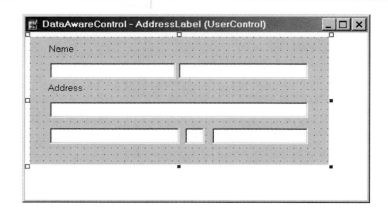

The user interface for the AddressLabel data-aware ActiveX control.

Create a delegated property for each constituent control, similar to the one described above for Patient. Then set the Property Attributes (refer again to Figure 9.17) for each property. Set each property to *Property is data bound, This property binds to DataField,* and *Property will call CanPropertyChange before changing.* In addition, select *Show in DataBindings collection at design time.* Although only one of your properties can be set to *This property binds to DataField,* the other properties can be bound through the Bindings collection.

The developer using the control implements the DataBindings collection. The author of the control just sets the properties to *Show in DataBindings collection at design time.*

If you plan to allow updates to the bound data, you need to include the PropertyChanged method in the Property Let. You should also include a PropertyChanged method in the control's Change event, since the user can change the data in the control.

```
Public Property Get LastName() As String
    'Retrieve the current value of LastName property

    LastName = txtLastName.Text
End Property
```

```
Public Property Let LastName(ByVal strLastName As String)
    'Assign a new value to the LastName property

    If CanPropertyChange("LastName") Then
        txtLastName.Text = strLastName
        PropertyChanged "LastName"
    End If
End Property

Private Sub txtLastName_Change()
    'Check if user changes value

    PropertyChanged "LastName"
End Sub
```

The CanPropertyChange Method

You have noticed the calls to the CanPropertyChange method, as well as the reference on the *Procedure Attributes* dialog box. Microsoft recommends that you call this method before updating and update only if the return is True. Actually, in the current implementation of VB the method always returns True, even if the database is read-only. But be warned, be prepared, write your programs this way, and answer the question on the MCSD exam this way.

The DataBindings Collection

In the ActiveX control, you include all properties that you want to bind in the DataBindings collection. The application that uses the control must reference the properties in the collection. After you add an instance of your data-aware control to a form, click in the property for DataBindings to open the *DataBindings* dialog box (Figure 9.19). You can set each property of the control to bind it to a data field.

F i g u r e   9 . 1 9

Set the properties to bind each control in the Data Bindings dialog box.

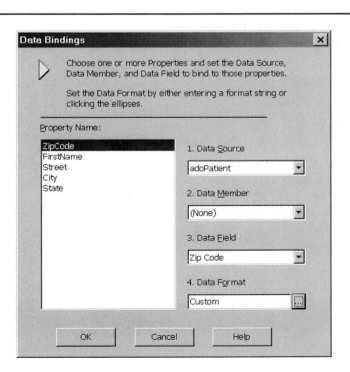

Using the Control in an Application

You may want to open the Ch09DataAware project on your CD. You will find the AddressLabel control and a form with an instance of the ActiveX control. Make sure that you close the control's Designer window before looking at the form. For simplicity this example uses an ADO data control; you could also use a Data Environment or Object Model for the data source.

Check the properties for the instance of the AddressLabel control on the form, making sure to open the *DataBindings* dialog box. Only the first property (LastName) is bound using the DataField property; the rest are bound by using the DataBindings.

If you want to run the project, make sure to press Ctrl + F5 (Run with full compile) so that the control is registered.

Compiling and Distributing a Control

You can compile an ActiveX control to an Ocx file. Select *File/Make ControlName.ocx* to create the file. Once you compile the control, it is registered on your system. The control then appears in the Components list so that you can add the control to any project. You can also move the Ocx file to another machine and register it there using the Regsvr32.exe utility, as discussed in Chapter 8 for ActiveXDll components.

When you want to distribute a control for use in other projects, you have two choices. You can distribute the source code (the Ctl file), which the developer includes in another project, or you can distribute the compiled version. Each method has its advantages.

Distributing the source version is easy, and you don't have to be concerned about versioning or licensing issues. The developer can view and modify the code for the control if necessary. The control just becomes a module in the new project. However, if modifications to the control are necessary, it may be difficult to update all copies in all projects. And of course, if a developer modifies a copy of the control, you have the likelihood of many versions of the control in existence.

If you distribute an Ocx file and need to make modifications later, you can easily distribute a new version. Of course, the modifications should not cause problems in the other applications. You can add properties and methods to a control, but you should never remove any. And don't change any significant properties of your control that might make applications fail, such as changing the DataField property of a data-aware control or the DefaultCancel property.

In Chapter 14 you will learn to use the Package and Deployment Wizard to create setup files for your applications containing controls or for just the controls. The setup file created by the wizard automatically registers the components on the destination computer.

Feedback 9.2

1. Explain the behavior of an ActiveX control during an application's design time. What events occur if the developer closes the form's Designer window and then reopens it?

2. Why must you avoid setting a control's default values in the Initialize event procedure?
3. What is property delegation, and what is its purpose?
4. What is the Extender object, and what is its purpose?
5. What is the Ambient object, and what is its purpose?
6. Explain how to create a Property Page using the wizard.

MCSD Exam Notes

Exam Objectives Covered in This Chapter

Creating and Managing COM components

Create a COM component that implements business rules or logic. Components include Dlls, ActiveX controls, and active documents

Create ActiveX controls

- Create an ActiveX control that exposes properties.
- Use control events to save and load persistent properties.
- Test and debug an ActiveX control.
- Create and enable Property Pages for an ActiveX control.
- Enable the data binding capabilities of an ActiveX control.
- Create an ActiveX control that is a data source.

Create an active document

- Use code within an active document to interact with a container application.
- Navigate to other documents.

Questions/Tricks to Watch for

- Make sure you know the difference between a component's Initialize, InitProperties, and ReadProperties events. Set default values for properties in the InitProperties event procedure. If you set default values in the Initialize event procedure, you will wipe out any settings made by the developer.

S u m m a r y

1. An ActiveX document executes in a container such as Internet Explorer or Microsoft Binder.
2. ActiveX documents can be either in-process or out-of-process components.

3. A UserDocument does not have many of the events of a form, such as Load, Unload, QueryUnload, Activate, and Deactivate.

4. UserDocuments and UserControls have Initialize, InitProperties, ReadProperties, and WriteProperties events.

5. The Hyperlink object can be used to navigate to another document, a Web site, or forward or backward through documents.

6. Menus for documents are merged with the container's menus.

7. You can display a form from an ActiveX document.

8. A PropertyBag is an object that stores property values. Use the WriteProperty method to save properties in the WriteProperties event procedure. The properties are retrieved from the PropertyBag with the ReadProperty method in the ReadProperties event procedure.

9. To share data between documents, declare a global object variable in a standard code module, set a reference to the document that holds the data, and refer to those data in the second document as a property of the global object.

10. The Migration Wizard converts existing applications and components into documents that can be used in a browser.

11. In addition to the intrinsic VB controls and the ActiveX controls on the Components list, you can build your own ActiveX controls.

12. A composite control contains other controls.

13. An ActiveX control must be programmed to execute during application design time as well as run time.

14. The control's InitProperties event occurs only once, when the control is first sited on a form (or other container). Use the InitProperties event procedure to set up default values for properties.

15. During the lifetime of a control, it is destroyed and re-created many times. Each time, the Initialize, ReadProperties, and Terminate events occur.

16. Use a control's Ambient object properties for information about the control's container. The control's AmbientChanged event occurs when any of the Ambient properties change.

17. The VB Extender supplies a group of default properties for every control.

18. You can create a Property Page and attach it to a control. This practice makes it easier for the developer to set properties.

19. You can create an ActiveX control that is data aware. It can be either a data source or a data consumer.

Key Terms

ActiveX control   *396*

ActiveX document   *396*

author   *410*

bindable   *430*

composite control   *410*

container   *396*

delegating   *413*

developer   *410*

InitProperties event   *397*

Migration Wizard   *409*

PropertyBag object   *397*

Property Page   *427*

ReadProperties event   *397*

ReadProperty method   *404*

R e v i e w   Q u e s t i o n s

1. Differentiate between the events of a form and those of a UserDocument module.
2. Explain when each event occurs and the actions that should be performed in their event procedures: Initialize, Terminate, ReadProperties, WriteProperties, and InitProperties.
3. How do you navigate from one ActiveX document to another? from a document to a Web site?
4. When you define menus for a UserDocument, where do the menus appear during run time? How can you change the location of the menus?
5. What is the PropertyBag object, and what is its purpose?
6. What is the Ambient object, and what is its purpose?
7. What is the Extender object, and what is its purpose?
8. Explain the execution of an ActiveX control during design time for an application. What occurs when the developer closes the form Designer window and reopens it?
9. What is property delegation? When would it be useful?
10. Explain how to create a Property Page and attach it to an ActiveX control.
11. What is the difference between a control that is a data source and one that is a data consumer? What properties must be set to make a control either a data source or a data consumer?

P r o g r a m m i n g   E x e r c i s e s

9.1   Write an ActiveX Dll document project that calculates the shipping charge for a package if the shipping rate is $0.12 per ounce.

UserDocument: Use labeled text boxes for the package-identification code (a six-digit code) and the weight of the package—one box for pounds and another one for ounces. Use a label to display the shipping charge. Include command buttons for Calculate and Clear.

Code: Include event procedures for each of the command buttons. Use a constant for the shipping rate, calculate the shipping charge, and display it formatted in a label.

Calculation hint: There are 16 ounces in a pound.

9.2   Create an ActiveX Exe document project that calculates rental charges for the local car rental agency. The agency charges $15 per day plus $0.12 per mile.

UserDocument: Use text boxes for the customer name, address, city, state, ZIP code, beginning odometer reading, ending odometer reading, and the number of days the car was used. Use labels to display the miles driven and the total charge. Format the output appropriately. Include a command button and text box to allow the user to navigate to another Web site or document.

Form: Add an About form to be displayed from the *Help* menu. Include menu commands for Calculate and Clear.

Code: For the calculation, subtract the beginning odometer reading from the ending odometer reading to get the number of miles traveled. Use a constant for the $15 per day charge and the $0.12 mileage rate.

9.3   Modify exercises 9.1 and 9.2. The first document will display a command button for Shipping Charges and one for Rental Charges. Each command will take the user to a new document to display and calculate the appropriate data. The secondary documents should have command buttons to go back to the first document. Use a PropertyBag to persist the data.

9.4   Create a control that holds a label and a text box. Make the text in the text box appear selected when your control receives the focus. Delegate the Text property of the text box and the Caption of the label. Expose the text box Change event to the client application. (Hint: You must raise an event when the contents change.)

Write an application that has at least two instances of the control.

9.5   Create a control that contains a label captioned *Departments* and a drop-down list box that contains the following department names: Accounting, Human Resources, Information Technology, Purchasing, and Sales. Make the control size just large enough to hold the two elements. Test the control in a browser. Can you add new values to the list at run time?

Modify the control so that it reflects the background color of the container.

....

C A S E   S T U D I E S

Video Bonanza

1. Design and code an ActiveX document project to calculate the amount due for rentals. Movies may be in VCR (videotape) format or DVD format. Videotapes rent for $1.80 each, and DVDs rent for $2.50. New releases are $3 for DVD and $2 for videotape.

On the UserDocument include a text box to input the movie title and option buttons to indicate whether the movie is DVD or videotape format. Use one check box to indicate whether the person is a member; members receive a 10 percent discount. Another check box indicates a new release.

Use command buttons for Calculate, Clear for Next Item, Order Complete, and Summary. The Calculate but-

ton should display the item amount and add to the subtotal. The Clear for Next Item clears the check box for new releases, the movie title, and the option buttons; the member check box cannot be changed until the next customer is processed. Include validation to check for missing data.

The Order Complete button clears the controls on the form for a new customer.

The Summary button displays the number of customers and the sum of the rental amounts in labels. Make sure to add to the customer count and rental sum for each customer order.

2. Create a data consumer control that displays the movie title, category, and length. Test the control

in a browser. Compile and test the control in a group project.

Be sure to set the Ambient object property for the background and foreground color for each label.

VB Auto

Create a data consumer control that displays the automobile manufacturer, model, year, and sales price. Test the control in a browser. Compile and test the control in a group project.

Be sure to set the Ambient object property for the background and foreground color for each label.

C H A P T E R

10

Programming for the Internet

At the completion of this chapter, you will be able to . . .

1. Use VB Internet WebBrowser control.

2. Develop DHTML applications.

3. Import an existing HTML page.

4. Explain the Dynamic HTML object model.

5. Manipulate the style and content of HTML pages.

6. Understand IIS application terminology.

7. Recognize the methods and events unique to a WebClass.

8. Describe the relationship of Active Server Pages, WebClasses, and WebItems.

9. Store and Retrieve state information.

10. Understand sequencing in WebClasses.

11. Create a Web-based database application.

This chapter introduces controls and applications related to the Internet. Your application can contain controls as simple as a WebBrowser to display Web sites or the Internet Transfer control to use the HTTP (Hypertext Transfer Protocol) and FTP (File Transfer Protocol) protocols. The need to create Web-based applications is increasing, and VB provides the ability to create dynamic Web-based applications using DHTML (Dynamic HTML) or IIS (Internet Information Server). IIS applications are server-side Internet applications, while DHTML applications can respond to HTML pages without transferring control to the server. In this chapter you will learn the features of DHTML applications and of the DHTML Page Designer. The section on IIS explains the relationships among Active Server Pages, WebClasses, and WebItems. An application on Web-based database is also covered. The chapter assumes that you are familiar with the Internet, its basic terminology, and HTML.

Internet Controls

You can use VB controls to access and use the Internet. As the name implies, the **WebBrowser control** can be used to browse the Web by navigating to any URL. The **Internet Transfer control** gives your VB application access to the Internet HTTP protocol (Hypertext Transfer Protocol) and FTP protocols (File Transfer Protocol). The **WinSock control** enables you to connect to a remote computer by using TCP (Transmission Control Protocol).

Browsing the Web from a Visual Basic Project

One option available on the *Components* dialog box is *Microsoft Internet Controls.* (This control appears only if Internet Explorer is installed on the system.) Select this option to place the WebBrowser control in your toolbox. Placing a WebBrowser control on your form creates a window on the form and allows you to link your VB application to the Internet. The control's default name is WebBrowser1; when naming your control use the prefix *web*.

One method of the WebBrowser control is Navigate, which allows you to specify a specific Web site URL. Place the link as a string following the call to the method. This code brings up the Microsoft home page if you have a current connection to the Internet:

```
webBrowser.Navigate "www.microsoft.com"
```

The WebBrowser control works with a browser, which may be Netscape Navigator as well as Internet Explorer. If no browser is open, the project attempts to open Internet Explorer. If you want to use Netscape, open the browser before executing your VB project. Note: You must have an active Internet connection for either browser to work.

You can allow your user to specify the Web site. Use a text box and add a command button to your application. Check for a blank text box. If the URL does not exist, Internet Explorer cancels the navigation.

```
'Project:        Web Browser
'Programmer:     Bradley/Millspaugh
'Date:           2/2000
'Description     Navigate the Web with the
'                WebBrowser control
'Folder:         Ch10WebBrowser
Option Explicit

Private Sub cmdGo_Click()
    'Navigate to the desired Web site
    On Error GoTo HandleError

    If txtURL.Text <> "" Then
        webBrowser.Navigate txtURL.Text
    Else
        MsgBox "Type the URL in the text box", vbOKOnly, "NO URL Specified"
    End If

cmdGo_Exit:
    Exit Sub

HandleError:
    Resume Next
End Sub
```

The WebBrowser control has many properties and methods, which you can view by using the Object Browser. You can also find Help in MSDN under WebBrowser Object; the Help screens look different than VB Help, because the WebBrowser is documented as part of Internet Explorer.

Dynamic HTML

You are probably already familiar with HTML (Hypertext Markup Language) which is used to create Web pages. **Dynamic HTML (DHTML),** new with VB 6, is a superset of HTML that provides for dynamically altering the elements on the page in response to user actions. DHTML enables you to respond to events, insert and delete elements on the page, and dynamically alter the design style of elements on a page.

DHTML applications run on the client machine; in contrast, IIS applications run on the server. Using DHTML can cut down on network traffic and server activity, and applications can run considerably faster.

Another advantage of DHTML over HTML is that the page can store the **state** (information from/about a page). This feature allows the page to "remember" how it displayed last time, redisplay data entered by the user, and share data between pages. In addition, you can access a DHTML page offline, since it is stored on the client machine. DHTML is also more secure than HTML. DHTML pages are compiled and cannot be accessed and altered as can standard HTML.

The disadvantage of DHTML? It runs only in Internet Explorer 4.01 or higher. It does not run on other browsers, such as Netscape. This restriction makes DHTML useful for applications that will run on an intranet but not for

Internet applications that will be run in other browsers. An **intranet** is a Web site designed for the exclusive use of systems within a company or network. An intranet can be used to allow employees easy access to company information without exposing that information to the rest of the Internet.

Viewing a Dynamic Web Page

You can quickly see what a dynamic page looks like and how it can change content and style. Open and run the clever sample project DHShowMe, which comes with VB. Depending on the installation, the sample projects may be in Program Files\Microsoft Visual Studio\Msdn98\98vs\1033\Samples\Vb98. You can also find individual sample projects on the MSDN CD1. It isn't necessary to install all projects—just copy the one you want.

Figure 10.1 shows the first page of the DHShowMe project. You will learn a lot by executing the project and examining the code.

Tip

If you have problems with DHTML, make sure that you have applied the VB service packs and are using the latest version of Internet Explorer.

F i g u r e   1 0 . 1

Open and run the VB sample project DHShowMe to see Dynamic HTML in action.

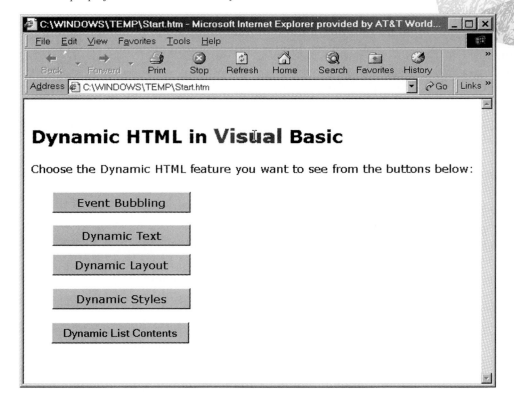

Creating DHTML Applications

A DHTML application combines VB code with HTML, creating an interactive browser application. A project consists of several files: a project file (.vbp), one or more DHTML Designer files (.dsr), and possibly standard code module(s)

(.bas). Each Web page has a separate Designer file, which is quite similar to a form file—it holds a definition of the visual interface and code for the event procedures and general procedures. Designers may also generate a .drx file that holds binary information (similar to the .frx file for a form). When the project is complete, you compile the project to a .dll, which is the run-time component.

When you begin a new project, one of the choices is *DHTML Application.* The VB environment looks somewhat different when you work on a DHTML application, and the toolbox has tools that are specific to the elements on a DHTML page. The Project Explorer window contains two elements: a DHTML Page Designer (DHTMLPage1) and a code module (modDHTML).

Web Page Elements

The terminology for DHTML applications is slightly different from the terminology for form-based programs. In DHTML the visual user interface is a document (Web page) rather than a form. Controls are called *elements,* which are similar to their form-based counterparts. But the elements have different names, slightly different properties (called *attributes*), and different events. The elements resemble many familiar controls including text boxes, command buttons, option buttons, dropdown combo boxes, and check boxes. Table 10.1 shows some DHTML elements and the similar VB controls. Notice the TextField and TextArea elements; a TextField is for a single-line entry, and a TextArea is for multiple line input/display. The SubmitButton is normally used to send information to the server, and the ResetButton clears information from the screen.

T a b l e   1 0 . 1

DHTML Elements and Similar VB Controls

Web Page Element	Similar VB Control
Button, SubmitButton, ResetButton	command button
TextField	text box
TextArea	multiline text box
Option	option button
Checkbox	check box
Select	dropdown combo
Image	image
Hyperlink	(none)
HiddenField	(none)

The attributes (properties) for the elements also differ a little from those you are used to. Instead of the Name property, the Id attribute identifies each control that you want to refer to in code.

DHTML Element Events

The events for DHTML elements are mostly similar to control events, with the addition of the prefix *on.* For example, instead of a Click event, the Button element has an onclick event, and the events for a document are similar to those for a form. Table 10.2 shows some of the events for documents and forms.

Web Page Element Event	VB Form Event
onload	Load
onunload	Unload
onreadystatechange	Initialize
onclick	Click
onfocus	GotFocus
onblur	LostFocus
onmouseup	MouseUp

The DHTML Page Designer

You create new Web pages or modify existing ones by using the DHTML Page Designer. Each page in the application has its own Designer. Working with the Designer requires some familiarity with HTML.

You can create pages with the DHTML Page Designer or import existing Web pages.

Figure 10.2 shows the Designer. The right pane is called the Detail pane, and the left pane holds a TreeView that displays elements added to the page. Notice the dropdown lists for Styles above the TreeView (the default style is Normal). Other styles include Headings, Address, Bulleted List, and Definition Term, Definition, and Paragraph (standard HTML styles).

Creating a DHTML Page—Step by Step

In this tutorial you will create a DHTML page that inputs a value and performs a calculation. It also has a hyperlink to display a second page. Figure 10.2 shows the (nearly) complete page.

Begin the Project

STEP 1: Open a new project, selecting *DHTML Application.*

STEP 2: In the Project Explorer window, open the Designers folder. Double-click on DHTMLPage1 to open the Designer and maximize its window.

STEP 3: With DHTMLPage1 selected in the Properties window, set the BuildFile property to AVBPatient.htm. This step identifies the file that VB will create when you compile and run the project.

Enter the Text

STEP 1: Click in the Detail pane and type *Advanced Vision and Beyond.* A Paragraph entry (P) appears in the TreeView under the Body entry. (Click the plus sign to expand the entry.)

Figure 10.2

The DHTML Page Designer. Each Web page has its own Designer.

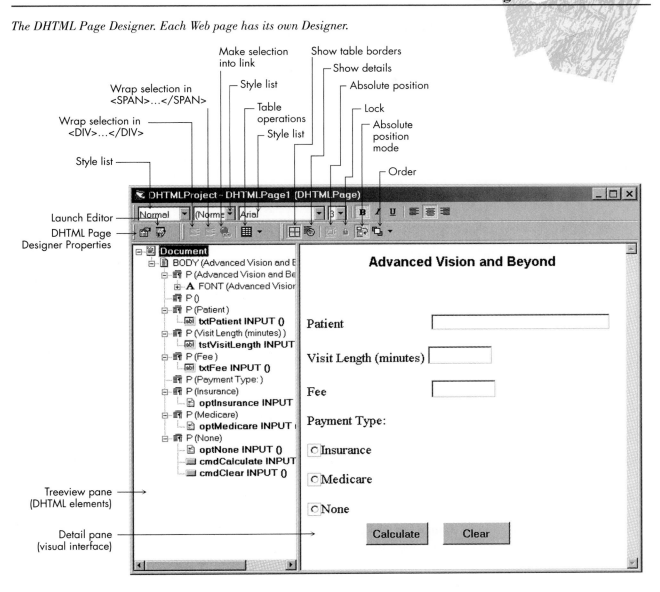

> *Note:* You can turn on and off the display of tags in the Detail pane by using the Show Details toolbar button.

STEP 2: Select the text and change the font to Arial, size 3, bold, and centered. This setting centers the entry on the Web page, regardless of the size of the browser window.

STEP 3: Click after the text and press Enter twice. Change to Times New Roman font, click the Align Left button, and type *Patient*. Press the spacebar a few times and press Enter.

STEP 4: Type *Visit Length (minutes)*, space a few times, and press Enter.

STEP 5: Type *Fee*, space a few times, and press Enter.

STEP 6: Type *Payment Type:*, space, and press Enter.

STEP 7: Type *Insurance* and press Enter; type *Medicare* and press Enter; type *None* and press Enter.

Add Elements

STEP 1:   Add a TextField (not a TextArea) from the toolbox. Notice that the pointer does not become a crossbar; just draw the control using the I-beam pointer.

By default, the control is placed in an **absolute position** (which has a fixed position on the page). This mode gives you control of where you want elements placed but can cause real problems when the application runs. Since the user can resize the browser window, you need to make sure that the TextField always appears next to the word *Patient.* To do that, you need to use a **relative position,** which places elements relative to the text.

STEP 2:   Right-click on the TextField and deselect the *Absolute Position* option. The element jumps down to the bottom of the page; drag it back up and to the right of *Patient.*

Using relative positioning, you must insert spaces to move the elements into the position you want.

Note: the proportional spacing of fonts hampers your ability to place elements where you want them when you are using this method. A better method to align elements is to use a table, but that approach is more involved than this example warrants.

STEP 3:   In the Properties window set the Id property to *txtPatient* and the Value property to blank.

STEP 4:   Add another TextField, change it to relative positioning, and drag it next to *Visit Length (minutes).*

STEP 5:   Set the Id property to *txtVisitLength* and the Value to blank.

STEP 6:   Add a TextField, with an Id of *txtFee* and Value of blank. Use relative positioning and place the field after *Fee.*

STEP 7:   Double-click on the Option tool in the toolbox to create a default-size option button. Change the button to relative positioning and drag it to the left of *Insurance.* Change the button's Id to *optInsurance* and its Name to *optPaymentType.*

To make option buttons function as a group, where only one of the group can be selected, all must have the same Name property. The Id property must still be unique for each button.

STEP 8:   Create another option button with relative positioning to the left of *Medicare.* Change the Id to *optMedicare* and the Name to *optPaymentType.*

STEP 9:   Create a third option button with relative positioning to the left of *None.* Change the Id to *optNone* and the Name to *optPaymentType.* Set the button's Checked property to True, which makes this button appear selected when the page first displays.

STEP 10:   Create a Button element at the location on the page that you want it to appear. For the buttons, we will use absolute positioning. Change the Id to *cmdCalculate* and the Value to *Calculate.* (As you can see, the Value attribute is the same as the Caption of a command button.) Set the AccessKey to *C.* (You cannot show the access key on the button, however.)

STEP 11:   Add a ResetButton with an Id of *cmdClear* and a Value of *Clear.* Set the AccessKey to *L.*

Write Code

STEP 1: Switch to the Code window, select *cmdCalculate*. Drop down the list of events, take a look at them, and select the onclick event. Enter the code for calculation.

```
Private Function cmdCalculate_onclick() As Boolean
    'Calculate the fee
    Const Rate As Currency = 1.5

    txtFee.Value = Format$(Val(txtVisitLength.Value) * Rate, "Currency")
End Function
```

STEP 2: Write the code for the onclick event of cmdClear.

```
Private Function cmdClear_onclick() As Boolean
    'Clear the fields

    txtVisitLength.Value = ""
    txtFee.Value = ""
    optNone.Checked = True
    With txtPatient
        .Value = ""
        .focus
    End With
End Function
```

STEP 3: Add code for BaseWindow_onload to set the focus to the first text box.

```
Private Sub BaseWindow_onload()
    'Set the initial focus

    txtPatient.focus
End Sub
```

STEP 4: Add the remarks to the top of the code.

```
'Project:     DHTML Demo
'Module:      DHTMLPage1
'Programmer:  Your Name
'Date:        Today's Date
'Description: Uses the DHTML Page Designer to create an interactive Web page.
'Folder:      Ch10DHTML
```

Test the Application

STEP 1: Save the application in a folder called *Ch10DHTML*.

STEP 2: Run the application. The first time you run, the Property Page appears. Click OK.

STEP 3: Test the application. Enter a patient name and type *15* for *Visit Length*. Test the option buttons; only one should be selected at any one time. Click Calculate. The display for the fee should be $22.50.

STEP 4: Press Clear.

STEP 5: Experiment with resizing the browser window.

STEP 6: Look at the URL displayed in the Address box. Make a note of the path that VB is using for development; you will need it later. (The normal path on a desktop system is C:\Windows\Temp.)

STEP 7: Switch to the VB environment and stop the application.

STEP 8: At this point you may want to modify the spacing on the page. Insert spaces to reposition any relative elements; drag any absolute elements to their new location.

Import a Page

You can create pages in other applications and import them into the DHTML project, where you can add elements and VB code.

STEP 1: Use Windows Explorer to locate the Web page and graphic file to add to the project. Find AboutAVB.htm and Eye.gif in the *Ch10ImportHTML* folder (on the text CD) and copy them into the current project folder (Ch10DHTML). Although you can add a page from a different location, for this demo it's easier to use files in the same folder.

STEP 2: Choose *Add DHTML page* from the *Project* menu.

STEP 3: Select the option button for Save HTML in an external file.

STEP 4: Click on Open and browse to select AboutAVB.htm. Click Open and OK.

The imported page appears but without the graphic.

STEP 5: Right-click on the image and select *Properties*. Click on the Build button for Image Source and browse to find Eye.gif. Now the graphic appears in the image element but is hard-coded for the path on your system, which is not a good thing.

STEP 6: Display the properties for DHTMLPage2 and notice the two entries for SourceFile and BuildFile. We need to change them both.

You can store an HTML file either external to the project or within the project. The SourceFile entry determines whether the file is external or internal; a blank entry means that it's internal. The BuildFile entry determines the name of the HTML file that the VB compiler creates. By default, the two entries are the same, but you can change them.

STEP 7: Delete the entry for the DHTMLPage2 SourceFile property. You will have to respond to a dialog box to confirm this choice. Say Yes.

STEP 8: Change the BuildFile property to *AboutAVB.htm*.

STEP 9: Switch to the Code window and add the comments.

```
'Project:       DHTML Demo
'Module:        DHTMLPage2
'Programmer:    Your Name
'Date:          Today's Date
'Description:   Displays Advanced Vision about with a cookie
'Folder:        Ch10DHTML
```

STEP 10: Save the project.

Development versus Deployment

When you finish development of your project, compile it, and deploy it, VB resolves the path references to all point to the same location. But during design and development, the paths of Web pages and graphics can be an annoying problem, especially if you need to move the project from one computer to another. VB uses a temporary directory for development, usually Windows\Temp, depending on your system configuration. The project needs to find all of its HTML and graphic files in the Temp directory or else have them hard-coded to an absolute path for development. Neither choice is ideal for development when you may move the project from one computer to another or run projects on your computer from the text CD.

The solution we are adopting for this book is to work from Windows\Temp and not hard-code any paths. Therefore, you must copy the graphic files that you want to display to the Windows\Temp folder. Remember, you won't face this problem with deployed applications, which use relative paths for all elements.

Set up the Temp Directory

STEP 1: Copy Eye.gif to Windows\Temp (or the path that you noted earlier as the temporary working path).

STEP 2: Remove the path from the Src (source) property of the image on AboutAVB.htm. Make it say only *Eye.gif* and press Enter. VB will change the entry to *about:blankEye.gif.*

STEP 3: Check the BuildFile property of both pages. It should be set to the HTML file with no path.

STEP 4: Check the SourceFile property of both pages. They should both be blank.

Connecting to a Second Page

You can create a hyperlink to link to a second page in two ways: (1) Type the display text, select it, and click on the Make selection into link toolbar button or (2) use the Hyperlink tool from the toolbox. Set the Hyperlink object's Id property to *lnkSomething*.

You can set up the link either by setting the Href property of the Hyperlink object or by using the BaseWindow's Navigate method. The simplest approach is to set a reference for the Hyperlink using the Href property in code.

```
lnkAboutAVB.href = "AboutAVB.htm"
```

You can also specify a path name in the reference, but for development omitting the path name is preferable.

```
lnkAboutAVB.href = App.Path & "\AboutAVB.htm"
```

When the user clicks on a hyperlink, control passes to the next page immediately. If you want to do some other processing first, such as validating or saving information from the page, you can write code in the Hyperlink object's onclick event procedure. However, if you code the procedure, you won't get the automatic link. Instead you should use the Navigate method.

```
Private Function lnkAboutAVB_onclick() As Boolean
    'Use the Navigate method when the link is clicked

    BaseWindow.Navigate "AboutAVB.htm"
End Function
```

Sometimes you may want the user to move to a second page when he or she takes another action, such as clicking a specific button or moving the mouse over an object. In that case you can use the Navigate method in the appropriate procedure.

Add a Hyperlink

STEP 1: Return to the first page and click at the bottom. Press Enter twice, if necessary, to place the insertion point below the buttons.

STEP 2: Type *About Advanced Vision* and click on the Center Alignment button. Select the text and choose the next smaller font size.

STEP 3: With the text selected, click on the Make selection into link button on the toolbar.

STEP 4: Change the Id property of the Hyperlink object to *lnkAboutAVB*.

STEP 5: Switch to the Code window and set the Href property in the BaseWindow_onload event procedure.

```
Private Sub BaseWindow_onload()
    'Set the initial focus

    lnkAboutAVB.href = "AboutAVB.htm"
    txtPatient.focus
End Sub
```

STEP 6: Save the project and run it.

STEP 7: Test the link to the second page.

> *Note:* If the graphic did not appear, first check the Address box on the browser. It should be the Temp directory. Then make sure that the graphic is also in that directory.

STEP 8: Click the browser's Back button to return to the first page.

STEP 9: Switch back to the VB environment and stop execution.

Dynamic Styles and Content

You can change the style of the page or any of the elements on the page. You already know how to change the properties of elements at design time, but you can also change style properties while the page is executing. If you ran the VB sample, you saw many examples of dynamic style changes.

Each element has a Style collection that has properties such as color and font (Table 10.3). You can assign a value to the Style properties in code. To change a property for the document itself, place the code in the DHTMLPage_Load event procedure. Note that the document contains a bgcolor property and no Style object.

```
Private Sub DHTMLPage_Load()
    'Set background color of the page

    Document.bgColor = "azure"
End Sub
```

Style	Purpose
bgcolor	Background color of the Document object (page).
fgcolor	Foreground color of the Document object (page).
backgroundcolor	Background color of control elements.
color	Foreground color of control elements.
border	Border around an element.
font	Font setting includes fontsize, fontstyle, etc.

You can make changes to the Style properties of elements in any appropriate event procedure. If you want to set initial properties of elements, use the BaseWindow_onload event procedure.

```
Private Sub BaseWindow_onload()
    'Set the initial focus

    txtFee.Style.backgroundColor = "lightgrey"
    lnkAboutAVB.href = "AboutAVB.htm"
    txtPatient.focus
End Sub
```

Assign a value by giving the name of the element, followed by the word *Style,* and then the property—for example,

```
txtFee.Style.backgroundColor = "lightgrey"
```

The color names are not the same as those used in VB and offer many more choices. The colors are defined by Internet Explorer and include blue, blueviolet, slateblue, and cadetblue. For a great list, look at the Color Table topic in MSDN. Set your MSDN Active subset to *Platform SDK, Internet/Intranet/ Extranet Services* and do a search for *Color Table.* After you find the page, you might want to add it to your Help favorites.

The Style object has many properties, such as backgroundColor, border, borderColor, font, fontSize, fontWeight, margin, textAlign, and textDecorationUnderline. You can see the complete list in the Object Browser under IHTMLStyle.

Modify the Style of Elements

Continuing with the step-by-step DHTML tutorial, you will change the background color of the text boxes during execution.

STEP 1: In the first page, add this line to the BaseWindow_onload event procedure:

```
txtFee.Style.backgroundColor = "lightgrey"
```

STEP 2: Set the color of the page in the DHTMLPage_Load event procedure.

```
Private Sub DHTMLPage_Load()
    'Set the background color of the document

    Document.bgColor = "lightgrey"
End Sub
```

STEP 3: Modify the cmdClear_onclick event procedure to set the background
color of the two text boxes when the user clicks Clear. (The changes are
highlighted.)

```
Private Function cmdClear_onclick() As Boolean
    'Clear the fields

    With txtVisitLength
        .Value = ""
        .Style.backgroundColor = "white"
    End With
    txtFee.Value = ""
    optNone.Checked = True
    With txtPatient
        .Style.backgroundColor = "white"
        .Value = ""
        .focus
    End With
End Function
```

STEP 4: Set the color to grey when the focus is lost. The onblur event is similar
to the LostFocus event for a VB control.

```
Private Sub txtPatient_onblur()
    'Change color of text element when focus is lost

    txtPatient.Style.backgroundColor = "lightgrey"
End Sub

Private Sub txtVisitLength_onblur()
    'Change color of text element when focus is lost

    txtVisitLength.Style.backgroundColor = "lightgrey"
End Sub
```

STEP 5: Save and test the project again. Stop execution when finished.

You can also use DHTML to change the content of a page, such as adding
and deleting elements through code. Refer to the VB sample DHShowMe.

The DHTML Object Model

The object model for DHTML (Figure 10.3) is based on a **BaseWindow
object,** the instance of the browser that the application runs in. Each page displayed in the BaseWindow is called a **Document object.** The Document
object handles the events from the user and contains the **DHTMLPage
object,** which acts more like a form in a VB project. The Page object has

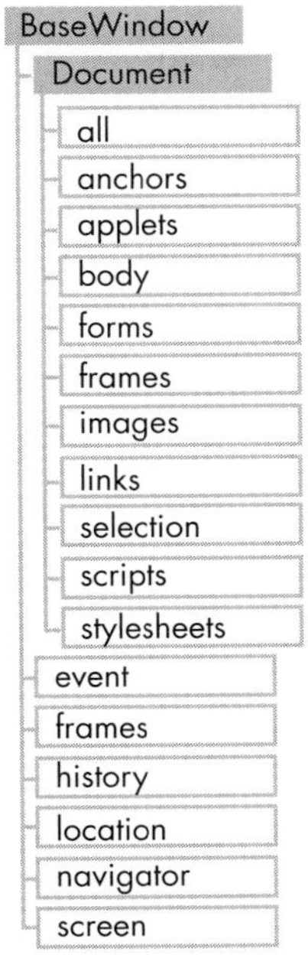

Figure 10.3

```
BaseWindow
  Document
      all
      anchors
      applets
      body
      forms
      frames
      images
      links
      selection
      scripts
      stylesheets
   event
   frames
   history
   location
   navigator
   screen
```

The DHTML object model. The two primary objects used in VB are the BaseWindow and Document objects.

Initialize, Load, Unload, and Terminate events. Asynchronous loading fires the Load event when the first object is loaded, but synchronous loading does not fire the Load event until all elements on the page have been created. (You can choose the mode by setting the AsyncLoad property of the DHTMLPage object.)

You can use the object model to access any element or event at run time. One important difference between DHTML events and VB events occurs when no event procedure (event handler) is written for a specific event. In VB, if you don't write an event procedure for a particular event, such as the MouseDown event of a control, that's the end of that. But in DHTML, if no event procedure exists for the event, the event is passed up to its container. And if the container doesn't handle the event, it is passed up to the container's container, until the event reaches the document level. This process is called **event bubbling.**

Managing State

One useful technique is to allow the user to make entries or choices on a page and then to restore those entries the next time the page displays or to transfer values from one page to another. The conditions you want to save are called the **state**. Saving and restoring the values is called *managing* the state. Applications that cannot manage the state, such as normal HTML, are called *stateless* applications.

Using DHTML, you use the PutProperty and GetProperty procedures to save and retrieve values in a manner very similar to a Property Bag. The property names and values are concatenated together and saved in a packet called a **cookie.**

When you begin a new DHTML project, it includes a standard code module. Inside the module are two procedures: the PutProperty sub procedure and the GetProperty function procedure. Use these procedures to store information in a cookie (Put) or to retrieve information from a cookie (Get).

The arguments for the PutProperty are the HTML Document object, the name of the property, a value for the property, and, optionally, an expiration date. The Cookie property of the HTML Document object stores the information.

Automatically Generated Code Module

```
'PutProperty: Store information in a cookie by calling this
'             function.
'             The required inputs are the named Property
'             and the value of the property you would like to store.
'
'             Optional inputs are:
'                expires : specifies a date that defines the valid lifetime
'                          of the property. Once the expiration date has been
'                          reached, the property will no longer be stored or
'                          given out.
'

Public Sub PutProperty(objDocument As HTMLDocument, strName As String, _
    vntValue As Variant, Optional Expires As Date)

        objDocument.cookie = strName & "=" & CStr(vntValue) & _
            IIf(CLng(Expires) = 0, "", "; expires=" & Format(CStr(Expires), _
                "ddd, dd-mmm-yy hh:mm:ss") & " GMT") ' & _
End Sub
```

The GetProperty function retrieves the concatenated string of all of the stored properties. Notice that the arguments are the HTML document object and a string name of the property you want. The function splits the cookie into an array (zero based) of substrings. (The Join function joins strings into an array.)

```
'GetProperty: Retrieve the value of a property by calling this
'             function. The required input is the named Property,
'             and the return value of the function is the current value
'             of the property. If the property cannot be found or has expired,
'             then the return value will be an empty string.
'

Public Function GetProperty(objDocument As HTMLDocument, strName As String) _
                As Variant
    Dim aryCookies() As String
    Dim strCookie As Variant
    On Local Error GoTo NextCookie

    'Split the document cookie object into an array of cookies.
    aryCookies = Split(objDocument.cookie, ";")
    For Each strCookie In aryCookies
        If Trim(VBA.Left(strCookie, InStr(strCookie, "=") - 1)) _
            = Trim(strName) Then
            GetProperty = Trim(Mid(strCookie, InStr(strCookie, "=") + 1))
            Exit Function
        End If
```

```
NextCookie:
        Err = 0
    Next strCookie
End Function
```

Important note: Internet Explorer 5 causes these procedures to fail with a Type Mismatch error. You must change the argument type of objDocument to Variant. The two lines highlighted in the preceding code must be changed to

```
Public Sub PutProperty(objDocument As Variant, strName As String, _
                vntValue As Variant, Optional Expires As Date)
Public Function GetProperty(objDocument As Variant, strName As String) _
                As Variant
```

Saving and Retrieving Cookies

If you want to save state information in a cookie, place the PutProperty in code somewhere after the value has been set but before the user leaves the page. You can use either the BaseWindow's onunload event or the DHTMLPage's Unload event—both events occur each time the user leaves a page.

```
Private Sub BaseWindow_onunload()
    'Store the name and visit as cookies

    If txtPatient.Value <> "" Then
        PutProperty BaseWindow.Document, "Name", txtPatient.Value
    End If
    If txtVisitLength.Value <> "" Then
        PutProperty BaseWindow.Document, "Visit", txtVisitLength.Value
    End If
End Sub
```

"Empty" cookies cannot be stored. Test for a blank field before using the PutProperty. It's also a good idea to use an OnError in the procedure that retrieves the data in case the cookie has not yet been saved.

The location for the GetProperty is a little bit trickier. You cannot reference page elements in the Load event for the DHTMLPage. Use the BaseWindow's onload event instead.

```
Private Sub BaseWindow_onload()
    'Load values from the last page

    On Error Resume Next
    txtName.Value = GetProperty(BaseWindow.Document, "Name")
End Sub
```

Get and Put Properties

In this continuation of the DHTML step-by-step tutorial, you will save the patient name and visit length as the user leaves the page. Then display the patient name on the About form. For the cookies to pass correctly, you must be using the same directory for both Web pages. Refer to the section "Development versus Deployment" earlier in this chapter and make sure that the

BuildFile property of both DHTMLPage objects holds the page name with no path.

STEP 1: Open the standard code module for the project and change the argument type for *both* the `GetProperty` function and PutProperty sub procedure. The argument must read `objDocument As Variant` in both procedures.

> *Note:* This step is necessary only if you are using Internet Explorer 5.

STEP 2: Switch to the code window for the first page and save the cookies in the onunload event of the BaseWindow.

```
Private Sub BaseWindow_onunload()
    'Store the name and visit as cookies

    If txtPatient.Value <> "" Then
        PutProperty BaseWindow.Document, "Name", txtPatient.Value
    End If
    If txtVisitLength.Value <> "" Then
        PutProperty BaseWindow.Document, "Visit", txtVisitLength.Value
    End If
End Sub
```

STEP 3: Switch to the second DHTML Designer and add a TextField element to AboutAVB.htm. We are going to use this element to display the patient name from the main page.

STEP 4: Set the Id property of the TextField element to *txtName*.

STEP 5: Retrieve the cookies in the BaseWindow_onload event procedure of AboutAVB.htm.

```
Private Sub BaseWindow_onload()
    'Load values from the last page

    On Error Resume Next
    txtName.Value = GetProperty(BaseWindow.Document, "Name")
End Sub
```

STEP 6: Save and test the project. Enter a name and amount on the first page and switch to the second page. The patient name should appear in the text box.

Feedback 10.1

1. Name the controls that VB provides for working with the Internet. When would each control be used?
2. Give three possible reasons to dynamically change a page during execution.
3. Name the three objects in the DHTML object model.
4. Write the code to dynamically change the background color of a TextField called txtProductNumber when the field receives the focus.

Internet Information Server

Note: To complete the exercises in this section, you must have installed IIS or Personal Web Server. IIS runs only on NT; Personal Web Server can run on Windows 95/98 and NT Workstation. See "Creating an IIS Application—Step by Step" for information on locating and installing Personal Web Server.

IIS (Internet Information Server) applications are dynamic applications that run in a browser, similar to DHTML. The two big differences between IIS and DHTML are that IIS applications run on the server rather than on the client machine and that IIS applications produce standard HTML that can display in any browser. That's a big one. It means that you can write IIS applications to run on the Internet and work with any platform and most browsers.

In an **IIS application** you use VB programming to respond to user events on the Web page and dynamically modify the page. The user takes some action, such as entering information or clicking a button, and that action is communicated to the IIS application. The application generates new HTML in response to the action and sends the standard HTML page to the browser.

You can write robust VB programs, such as programs that display information from a database, as Web-based applications.

The Structure of an IIS Application

The primary object in an IIS application is a WebClass. You can create one or more WebClasses, which each represents a Web page. When a WebClass is compiled, it produces an **Active Server Page (ASP),** which has an object model that controls program execution. Compiling an IIS application produces a Dll, which also needs the run-time component, MSWCRUN.dll, to run.

The browser interacts through the Web server (IIS or Personal Web Server). Figure 10.4 (p. 460) illustrates the relationships among the elements of an IIS application.

An IIS application produces HTML pages in two ways. Most of the pages will be already-created Web pages with some elements that need modification under program control. These .htm files are added to a WebClass as templates. You can also output the actual HTML tags from VB code in the WebClass and produce an entire Web page.

WebClasses

A **WebClass** is a component that resides in a Web server and responds to input from a browser. The URL for the WebClass is the path to the Active Server Page. When a user links to or types in the URL, the WebClass displays an HTML page and enters into the application.

As an example, let's say that Advanced Vision has a Web site at AV.com. The IIS application is stored in the Patient directory on the company's server. If the WebClass is called *PatientInfo* (NameInURL property) and the Project is *AdvVision*, the URL for the page is

```
http://www.AV.com/Patient/AdvVision_PatientInfo.asp
```

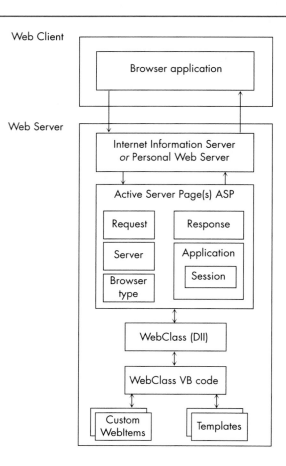

The organization of an IIS application.

When you begin a new IIS application, VB adds one WebClass Designer, which you use to create the WebClass. If you want to add another WebClass, you must add another Designer (one WebClass per Designer). Developers often prefer to create a project using multiple WebClasses so that other applications can reuse the individual classes.

WebItems and Templates

You can add **WebItems** and **templates** to a WebClass. A template is a file that contains an HTML page. The page contains items that can be modified by the WebClass before sending it to the browser.

Custom WebItems do not contain their own HTML page. Basically they contain only code to handle events on Web pages. A custom WebItem is similar to a standard code module for an IIS application; both hold code but no user interface.

Both custom WebItems and template WebItems can expose events. You then write the associated event procedures in VB code.

Active Server Pages

The IIS application can use several of the objects from the Active Server Page's object model to access and process information. The WebClass has access to the Request, Response, Session, Application, Server, and BrowserType objects. For example, in an application you can check the BrowserType object to determine the capabilities of the browser running the program and generate different HTML and/or applets depending on the features supported.

ASP Request Object

The **Request object** holds information about the current user, data entered by the user, and arguments to an HTTP request. The information about the user is stored in cookies that can pass information in both directions between the browser and the server.

We will use the Request when we want to retrieve data from a form on the Web page. An input box (text field) on the Web page has a name, which is used with the Request.

```
strName = Request.Form("LastName")
```

This line of code retrieves the contents of the input box named *LastName* and stores it in a string variable.

ASP Response Object

The **Response object** sends information from the server to the browser. The Write method of the Response object can send HTML directly to the browser. The following code is generated inside each new WebClass that you create. As you can see, the code writes out HTML tags and text, which a browser can interpret and display.

```
With Response
    .Write "<html>"
    .Write "<body>"
    .Write "<h1><font face=""Arial"">IIS Demo Startup Page</font></h1>"
    .Write "<p>This response was created in the Start event of wbclDemo.</p>"
    .Write "</body>"
    .Write "</html>"
End With
```

Another method of the Response object is Redirect, which sends the user to a URL other than the one requested. You can use the Response object's Cookies collection to save and retrieve user information.

Session and Application Objects

The Session and Application objects are used to store state information in IIS. The **Session object** can store information about the current user such as what pages have been accessed within the IIS application. If you want to track information about multiple users such as a hit count, use the **Application object.**

Hyperlinks

Your project can connect to other WebItems in your application. It is unlikely that while coding the application you will know exactly where the application will ultimately reside. The **URLFor method** allows you to specify the item you want and the correct URL will be substituted. You include the name of the WebItem in a Response.Write.

```
.Write "<A HREF = """ & URLFor(PatientInfo) & """ & Advanced Vision Home Page</A>"
```

The link on the page will appear as <u>Advanced Vision Home Page</u>. The run-time Dll sends the processing to the correct location.

It is important to design your application without coding the drive and directory for the URL. The path of the production project is likely to differ from that of the development system or may change over time. You can save yourself considerable trouble if you place all files for the project, including the images, in the project folder.

WebClass Events

A WebClass is a class module, very similar to other class modules you have created and used. When the application begins, the Initialize event of the WebClass executes and creates the WebClass object. A WebClass does not have a Load or Unload event. These form events are replaced with the BeginRequest and EndRequest events. Use these events to get and release any resources or data from the server, set values for variables, read and write state, and do any necessary cleanup.

The Start event of the WebClass executes after the BeginRequest unless the application specifies a different event. The following step-by-step example uses the Start event procedure.

Creating an IIS Application—Step by Step

Before you begin this tutorial, you must have a Web server available. If you are running Windows NT, you can install IIS on the network server. For desktop applications on Windows 95/98 or NT Workstation, you can simulate the environment by using Personal Web Server (also called Peer Web Server).

IIS and Personal Web Server are available on the Windows NT Option Pack. Personal Web Server is available on the VB/VS CD, as well as the Windows 98 CD.

Installing Personal Web Server

To install Personal Web Server from the VB or Visual Studio CD, run the Setup program and select *Add/Remove Options.* Then select *Server Applications and Tools (Add Only).* Under *Server Components,* select *NT Option Pack (for Windows 9x)* and click *Install.* Step through the wizard screens, selecting *Typical* installation. When the wizard finishes server installation, it will set up a virtual directory to host applications.

If you want to install from the Windows 98 CD, use Windows Explorer to find the file. It should be in add-ons/pws/setup.exe. This file also runs the Installation Wizard.

Set up the Folders

STEP 1: Create two new folders and name them *Ch10IISTemplate* and *Ch10IIS.*

STEP 2: Locate the Ch10Templates folder on the text CD. Copy WebItemDemo.htm into the Ch10IISTemplate folder and copy Image2.gif into Ch10IIS (the project folder).

Begin the Application

STEP 1: Open VB and begin a new project, selecting the IIS Application icon.

STEP 2: Double-click on the WebClass Designer in the Project Explorer window. The Designer opens, showing the TreeView and Detail panes (Figure 10.5).

Figure 10.5

The WebClass Designer.

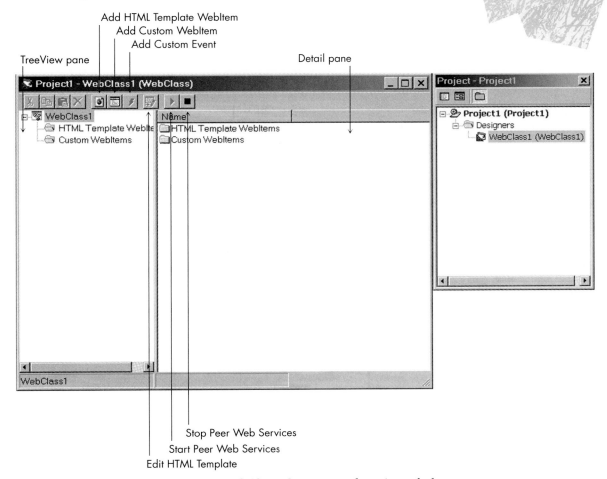

STEP 3: View the WebClass code. The WebClass_Start procedure is coded using the Response object. The Reponse `Write` method writes a Web page with HTML tags.

```
Private Sub WebClass_Start()

    'Write a reply to the user
    With Response
        .Write "<html>"
        .Write "<body>"
        .Write "<h1><font face=""Arial"">WebClass1's Starting Page</font></h1>"
        .Write "<p>This response was created in the Start event of WebClass1.</p>"
        .Write "</body>"
        .Write "</html>"
    End With
End Sub
```

STEP 4: In the Properties window, change both the WebClass Name and NameInURL properties to wbclDemo.

STEP 5: Save the project by clicking on the VB Save Project toolbar button. Save into the Ch10IIS folder; you will be prompted to save the designer file (.dsr) and the project file (.vbp).

Add a WebItem

STEP 1: In the TreeView pane of the Designer, right-click on wbclDemo and choose *Add HTML Template* from the shortcut menu (or you can use the toolbar button). Browse to select *WebItemDemo.htm* from your Ch10IISTemplate folder. The template appears with its name highlighted, waiting for you to rename it. Change its name to *TemplateDemo*.

A copy of the template file is added to your project. If you decide to modify the template, you will edit the copy in your project.

STEP 2: Switch to the Code window, add comments, and modify the HTML to include a hyperlink. (The added lines are highlighted.)

```
'Project:      Internet Information Server
'Programmer:   Bradley/Millspaugh
'Date:         2/2000
'Description: A demonstration using a WebClass to create an Active Server Page
'             file. Requires Personal Web Server or IIS to compile.
'Folder:       Ch10IIS
Option Explicit
Option Compare Text

Private Sub WebClass_Start()
    'This is the first event that will execute; it displays a simple page.

    With Response
        .Write "<html>"
        .Write "<body>"
        .Write "<h1><font face=""Arial"">IIS Demo Startup Page</font></h1>"
        .Write "<p>This response was created in the Start event of wbclDemo.</p>"
        .Write "<p>"
        .Write "<A HREF = """ & URLFor(TemplateDemo) & _
                """ & >Click here to go to a WebItem</A></p>"
        .Write "</body>"
        .Write "</html>"
    End With
End Sub
```

Code the Respond Event

Adding a template WebItem to the WebClass makes the WebItem's name appear in the Objects list in the Code window. When the user clicks on the link for the TemplateDemo page, the page object's Respond event occurs.

STEP 1: Select TemplateDemo from the list of objects, select Respond from the list of procedures, and enter the code.

```
Private Sub TemplateDemo_Respond()
    'Display the page

    TemplateDemo.WriteTemplate
End Sub
```

Test the Project

STEP 1: Run the program. The first time you run, you have to respond to the Project Properties Debugging options. Click OK and accept the Virtual Root suggested. The Web server begins, the default browser loads, and your page displays. (The first time you run, it takes a little while to begin.)

STEP 2: Click on the link.

You can use the browser's Back button to return to the first page. It would be better to have a link on the second page to return to the main page or other location appropriate for the application. We'll do that in the hands-on example at the end of the chapter.

STEP 3: Close the browser, return to VB, and stop program execution.

The URLFor Method

In the WebClass Start event procedure that we just coded, you used the URLFor method to link to the next item. The URLFor method triggers an event, by default the Respond event. However you can specify a different (custom) event instead. The section on "UserEvents" shows how to respond to a custom user event.

The URLFor Method—General Form

```
Object.URLFor(WebItemObject As WebItem,[EventName])
```

The URLFor Method—Examples

```
URLFor(TemplateDemo)
URLFor(PatientInfo, "UserEventInTemplate1")
```

Substitution Tags

You can use substitution tags in an HTML template to dynamically modify the page. For example, you might want to change the font, style, page color, or text color, or insert information on the page such as the user name or ID or the date. To use substitution tags, you must

• Place substitution tags in pairs in the HTML template file.

• Write code in the WebClass to respond to the template object's ProcessTag event. In the event procedure you determine which tag to process and substitute the correct HTML.

- Make sure to include the WriteTemplate method of the template object as we did in the preceding step-by-step tutorial. This method triggers any events for the template object.

You can think of substitution tags as variables in the HTML. When the template is sent to the browser, the variable names are replaced with their value.

You specify substitution tags as a pair of tags, similar to the format of most other HTML tags.

```
<WC@TAGNAME>TagValue</WC@TAGNAME>
```

The name of the tag begins with a prefix. By default the tag prefix is *WC@*, but you can choose something else by setting the TagPrefix property of the template object.

For example, here is some standard HTML code that sets the background color of the page and the foreground color of the text. We are using the hex color numbers found on the *Color Table* page in MSDN.

```
<BODY bgColor= #F0F8FF>
<FONT FACE="Arial" SIZE=6 Color=#6495ED>
```

To use substitution tags so that you can specify the color when the page displays, replace the color numbers with substitution tags.

```
<BODY bgColor=<WC@BACKCOLOR>BackColor</WC@BACKCOLOR>>

<FONT FACE="Arial" SIZE=6 Color=<WC@FORECOLOR>ForeColor</WC@FORECOLOR>>
```

These tags appear in the template file. When the template is sent to the browser for display, the code in the template object's ProcessTag event procedure substitutes the desired value in place of the tags.

The ProcessTag Event

Use the ProcessTag event of the template object to replace the tag value. The name of the tag and its current contents are passed to the procedure, which should set the TagContents to the desired value.

```
Private Sub WebItemDemo_ProcessTag(ByVal TagName As String, _
        TagContents As String, SendTags As Boolean)
    'Fill in substitution tags

    Select Case UCase$(TagName)
        Case "WC@FORECOLOR"
            TagContents = "#6495ED"
        Case "WC@BACKCOLOR"
            TagContents = "#F0F8FF"
    End Select
    SendTags = False
End Sub
```

After this procedure executes once for each tag, the HTML template file will look like this:

```
<BODY bgColor= #F0F8FF>
<FONT FACE="Arial" SIZE=6 Color=#6495ED>
```

Add Substitution Tags to the Step-by-Step Example

To add substitution tags, you first edit the template and then write the code.

STEP 1: Right-click on the TemplateDemo and choose *Edit HTML Template* from the shortcut menu (or use the toolbar button). The default HTML editor for your system (Notepad, unless you have changed it) opens with the template file.

> *Note:* If the file doesn't open in an editor, the default HTML editor has not been set up on your system.

STEP 2: Edit the two lines.

```
<BODY bgColor=<WC@BACKCOLOR>BackColor</WC@BACKCOLOR>>

<FONT FACE="Arial" SIZE=6 Color=<WC@FORECOLOR>ForeColor</WC@FORECOLOR>>
```

STEP 3: Save the HTML file and close the editor. The VB project will ask whether you want to refresh the template. Say Yes.

STEP 4: Open the Code window for the WebClass. Select TemplateDemo and ProcessTag and then write the code.

```
Private Sub TemplateDemo_ProcessTag(ByVal TagName As String, _
                TagContents As String, SendTags As Boolean)
   'Fill in substitution tags

   Select Case UCase$(TagName)
      Case "WC@FORECOLOR"
         TagContents = "#6495ED"        'Cornflower
      Case "WC@BACKCOLOR"
         TagContents = "#F0F8FF"        'Aliceblue
   End Select
   SendTags = False
End Sub
```

STEP 5: Test the project again. The background and foreground colors on the template (second page) should be two beautiful shades of blue.

STEP 6: Close the browser and stop the application.

Use Substitution Tags to Customize a Page

You can use substitution tags to customize the elements on a page.

```
<P>Please call <WC@Patient>LastName</WC@Patient> to remind of appointment on
<WC@Appt>ApptDate</WC@Appt></P>
```

The ProcessTag procedure can then substitute with variable data or database fields.

```
Sub Notify_ProcessTag(ByVal TagName As String, TagContents As String, _
      SendTags As Boolean)
'Determine which tag is being replaced
```

```
    Select Case (TagName)
        Case "WC@Patient"
            TagContents = rsPatient![First Name] & " " & rsPatient![Last Name]
        Case "WC@Appt"
            TagContents = mstrApptDate
    End Select
    SendTags = False
End Sub
```

UserEvents

You can declare and use custom UserEvents. Your WebClass code can then execute a procedure based on the event that occurs.

You could place this line in an HTML template file called *Appointment* to trigger the Followup event:

```
<URLFor(Appointment, "Followup")>
```

In the UserEvent of the template object, you can determine which event fired and take appropriate action. Create a procedure for each event that you need and then use an If or a Select Case to determine which procedures to execute.

```
Private Sub Appointment_UserEvent(ByVal EventName As String)
    'Select the correct event

    Select Case EventName
        Case "Followup"
            Followup
        Case "Annual"
            Annual
    End Select
End Sub
```

Controlling Sequence by Using the NextItem Property

You can use the NextItem property of the WebClass to transfer control to another WebItem template. You may decide while processing one page that you need to display a different page, without giving the user a choice in the matter. You can also set the NextItem property in the WebClass_Start event procedure to display the initial page. The NextItem property holds a reference to an object; therefore, you must use the Set keyword to assign a value to the property.

```
Private Sub WebClass_Start()
    'Transfer control to the PatientInfo template,
    '    which triggers the PatientInfo Respond event

    Set NextItem = PatientInfo
End Sub
```

State Management

You can manage state in an IIS application in a variety of ways. The WebClass object or another VB object can store information on the server side, information can be stored in a database, or information can be passed between the server and the browser using cookies, the URLDataProperty, or hidden HTML fields.

Using Objects

If a WebClass remains instantiated between requests, you can store information in variables in the WebClass. Or you may decide to create a VB object that remains instantiated by setting the StateManagement property of the WebClass to wcRetainInstance. A third alternative is to save values or VB objects in the Application and Session objects of the Active Server Page.

The life of a WebClass normally ends when a response is sent to the browser. The **wcRetainInstance property** provides the opportunity to keep the WebClass instantiated until the application is terminated. The disadvantage of keeping the WebClass alive is that all requests must be made to the same Web server and the Active Server Page must be sure that the proper thread is used in processing the request. If you need to retain a WebClass for only part of an application, you can call the ReleaseInstance method when appropriate.

The Session and Application objects of the Active Server Page are treated as properties of the WebClass. You can use these objects without setting the wcRetainInstance property of the WebClass and, therefore, eliminate the problem of requiring the same Web server. Specify the property name in quotes.

```
Session("Visit") = 15
intPageCount = Application("PageCount")
```

Cookies

The number and size of cookies are limited. Cookies are best suited for small items of information such as an ID or a key that will be used to access a database. However, some browsers do not support cookies, and some allow the user to turn off the use of cookies. A cookie stores information for a specific server. If you need to store information for a specific page in your application, it is better to use the URLData property.

The **URLData property** allows you to set or return a parameter that is appended to a URL. This method eliminates the need to store information on either the server or browser side. You can set the URLData property to a value, such as the username or ID. When the user returns to the page, the data can be restored.

Requesting Input from the User

You may want the user to enter a value that you can retrieve into the program, such as text boxes on a form. To do this, set up the Web page template with a form. You will need to give each input field a name, which you can then use in the WebClass code.

You can create a form on a Web page by using an HTML editor. Microsoft Word has tools to create a form and place controls on the form. Figure 10.6 shows the Web page for the hands-on example being created in Word 97.

Using Word 97 to create a Web page. A form is needed to allow data entry.

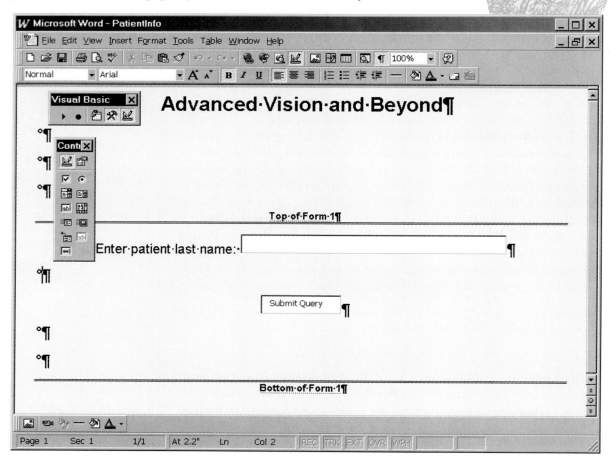

- Use the *File/New* command and create a new blank Web page.

- Type the title of the page, centered, with the desired font and size. Press Enter a few times to space down the page.

- Display the Visual Basic toolbar (*View/Toolbars/Visual Basic*).

- Click on the Toolbox button to open the VB HTML control toolbox.

- Click on the TextBox control, and Word will create a new form that contains a text box of default size. If line centering is still in effect, the text box will appear centered.

- Drag the handles of the text box to resize it. You can only select and resize controls when in design mode. Notice that both the VB toolbar and toolbox have a Design Mode button.

- Click to the right of the text box to get an insertion point. Then press Enter a few times to enlarge the form area.

- Click to the left of the text box and type the prompt you want for the text box, such as *Enter patient name:*

- Add a Submit button and drag it into the form below the text box.

- With the Submit button selected, display the properties (using the Toolbox button). Change the HTMLName property to *cmdSubmit* and the Caption to *Submit Query*.

- Select the text box and display its properties. Change the HTMLName to LastName.

- Save as HTML.

- You can view the page by using the Web Page Preview button or *File/Web Page Preview*.

- You can view the HTML source by using *View/HTML Source*. When you are viewing the HTML source, a new button appears at the left of the toolbar to *Exit HTML Source*.

- In the HTML source, notice the input tags that begin with <INPUT.

- The value is the equivalent of a Caption, the name is used in a request method, and the Id is the programmable reference to the element.

- Insert *Id = txtLastName* between the tags for the text box.

- When you add the HTML file to a WebClass, you will receive a dialog box similar to Figure 10.7. Accept all suggestions.

Figure 10.7

Respond OK to this dialog box.

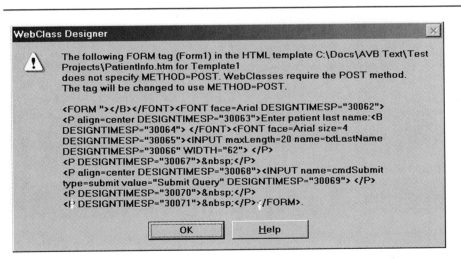

- When you execute, you may need to change the method of the button to Post.

● If you use Word to create your HTML document, you may find that if you edit your page later, the command button is opened as a text box. View the document as a Web page, and the button displays properly.

Feedback 10.2

1. If VB will not allow you to open an IIS application project, what software must be installed on the system?
2. Where does an IIS application reside?
3. Why can an IIS application, with embedded VB code, run on all different browsers and computer systems?
4. How is an Active Server Page created?
5. Write the URLFor method to link to the Order event of a WebItem called Sales. The link should display as <u>Order New Item.</u>

Your Hands-on Programming Example

Advanced Vision needs a Web page for accessing patient names and phone numbers within the office; the page needs to run on most browsers. It was decided that an IIS application would best meet the needs. The home page will display the company name, an input box for the patient last name to be entered, and a submit button.

A search for names keyed on the letters typed (an A/a should retrieve all last names starting with A/a) will display a table of names and phone numbers for all matches. If no match is found or the name input box is left blank, an appropriate message should display on the Web page. The second page must contain a link back to the first page.

The first page is an HTML file that you can create with an HTML editor (or you may include the .htm file from the student files).

Add this Web page as an HTML template file. Add a custom event named FindName to the WebItem.

Plan the Project

Sketch the Web page (Figure 10.8), which your user signs off.

Plan the WebClass, WebItems, and Properties

Object	Property	Value
WebClass	Name	wbclPatient
	NameInURL	AdvancedVision
PatientInfo (Template file)	Name	PatientInfo
FindName (custom event of PatientInfo)	Name	FindName

Figure 10.8

The Web page for the hands-on example.

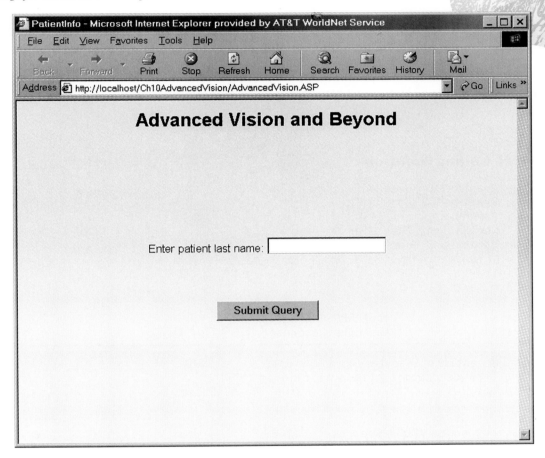

Plan the Procedures

Plan the event procedures.

Object	Procedure	Pseudocode
WebClass	Start	Set the NextItem to PatientInfo.
PatientInfo	Respond	Write the template file.
PatientInfo	FindName	Retrieve name from Web page. If name not blank Open the Recordset. If not end of recordset Do Until end of Recordset Write name and phone in table. Loop Else msg for no records Else msg for blank input Print link to return to first page.

Write the Project

● Create a Web page according to the specifications or load the one from the CD.

● In the WebDesigner, add a template file for the Web page.

● Working from the pseudocode, write the procedures.

● When you complete the code, thoroughly test the project.

The Project Coding Solution

```
'Project:      Chapter 10 Advanced Vision
'Programmer:   Bradley/Millspaugh
'Date:         2/2000
'Module:       wbclPatient (Web Class)
'Description:Database access with IIS
'Folder:       Ch10AdvancedVision
Option Explicit
Option Compare Text

Private conAVB              As ADODB.Connection
Private rsPatient          As ADODB.Recordset
```

```
Private Sub PatientInfo_FindName()
    'Event occurs when submit button is clicked
    'Create a page with a table of names from the database
    Dim strName As String
    Dim strSQL As String
    Set rsPatient = New ADODB.Recordset
    Set conAVB = New ADODB.Connection

    'Get name from the form
    strName = Request.Form("LastName")

    'Check for blank name
    If strName <> "" Then
        'Open the Connection
        With conAVB
            .ConnectionString = "Provider=Microsoft.Jet.OLEDB.3.51;" & _
            "Persist Security Info=False;Data Source=" & App.Path & _
            "\AVB.mdb;Mode = readwrite"
            .Open
        End With

        'Open the Recordset
        strSQL = "Select [Last Name], [First Name], Phone from Patient " _
                 & "Where [Last Name] Like '" & strName & "%'"
        With rsPatient
            .CursorLocation = adUseClient
            .CursorType = adOpenDynamic
            .LockType = adLockOptimistic
            .Open strSQL, conAVB, , , adCmdText
        End With
```

```
        'Create a table with the Recordset
        If Not rsPatient.EOF Then
            With Response
                .Write "<TABLE BORDER CELLSPACING = 1 CELLPADDING = 7>"
                Do While rsPatient.EOF = False
                    'New row and cell
                    .Write "<TR><TD>"

                    'Display fields from the Recordset
                    .Write rsPatient![Last Name] & ", " & rsPatient![First Name]
                    .Write "</TD><TD>"
                    .Write Format(rsPatient!Phone, "(###) ###-####")
                    .Write "</TD><TR>"

                    rsPatient.MoveNext
                Loop
                'End of table
                .Write "</TABLE>"
            End With
        Else
                Response.Write "No Records matched"
        End If
    Else
        Response.Write "You must enter a name"
    End If
    Response.Write "<p><p><a href = """ & URLFor(PatientInfo) _
        & """ >Advanced Vision Home Page<a>"
End Sub
```

```
Private Sub PatientInfo_Respond()
    'Write out the PatientInfo template

    PatientInfo.WriteTemplate
End Sub
```

```
Private Sub WebClass_Start()
    'Transfer control to the PatientInfo template,
    '    which triggers the PatientInfo Respond event

    Set NextItem = PatientInfo
End Sub
```

MCSD Exam Notes

Exam Objectives Covered in This Chapter

Creating User Services

Create a Web page by using the DHTML Page Designer to dynamically change attributes of elements, change content, change styles, and position elements

Questions/Tricks to Watch for

● Be familiar with creating Web pages with the DHTML Page Designer and with importing pages using DHTML Page Designer Property Page.

● Understand the differences among Active Server Pages, WebClasses, and WebItems.

S u m m a r y

1. A WebBrowser control allows your application to browse the Web or to place a specific site on your form. The Navigate method, used to specify the URL, may be coded to one location, or you can use a text box to allow the user to specify an address.

2. The Internet Transfer control allows applications to use FTP and HTTP protocols.

3. The WinSock control can make TCP connections.

4. Dynamic HTML is an enhanced version of HTML that allows Web pages to change dynamically at run time. The processing is primarily on the client machine, which reduces Internet traffic. DHTML is best suited for an intranet because it requires Microsoft products to run.

5. Each DHTML page of an application requires a Page Designer in the VB project. The Designer allows the developer to create Web pages or add VB programming to existing pages.

6. The elements for creating a Web page appear in the toolbox and resemble controls that are used on forms.

7. You can use either relative or absolute positioning to place elements on a Web page.

8. The DHTML object model consists of a BaseWindow object, Document objects, and the DHTMLPage objects.

9. Event bubbling allows an event that is not handled at one level to move up the hierarchy of objects until it is handled.

10. Storing information about an Internet session is referred to as *state management*.

11. IIS makes Web pages interactive using HTML that can run under multiple browsers. With IIS, VB code can be used to handle events.

12. An IIS application resides on the server side. The application consists of WebClasses that contain one or more WebItems and templates. Each WebClass is associated with an Active Server Page (ASP) that is generated when the IIS application is compiled.

13. The Request, Response, Session, Application, Server, and BrowserType objects of ASP are used by IIS.

14. The UrlFor method substitutes the actual URL for a page before sending the HTML page to the browser.

15. Substitution tags allow variable data to appear on a Web page. The ProcessTag event occurs once for each tag in the page.

16. Cookies are packets of information about the user. Using DHTML, cookies are stored on the client machine. Using IIS, cookies may be stored on either the server or client machine.

17. You can handle state management for IIS applications in several ways. The wcRetainInstance property can keep a session alive through multiple requests. Data can be stored in the Session and Application objects, and data can be appended to the URL by using the URLData property.

Key Terms

Review Questions

1. What method is used to link to a URL with the WebBrowser control?
2. Differentiate between DHTML applications and IIS applications in terms of browsers, object model, and location of processing.
3. List and explain the components of the DHTML object model.
4. The DHTML Page Designer has two panels. Describe the purpose of each.
5. Give an example of dynamically changing the contents of a DHTML page.
6. What is an intranet?
7. Describe the relationships among an Active Server Page, a WebClass, and a WebItem.
8. List and define the purpose of the objects of the ASP object model that are used by IIS.
9. Define three methods of state management available with IIS.

Programming Exercises

10.1 Use the WebBrowser control in an application to link to a site for an optometrist/optician. Use your favorite search engine to locate an appropriate URL.

10.2 Create a DHTML application that allows employees to Clock In/Out. The Web page must have a text field for the employee to enter an ID number; the page must also have an option button to select clocking in or clocking out. Store the ID number and the system time as a cookie.

Change the background color of the text boxes to indicate whether the user is clocking in or out.

10.3   Create a personal Web page using any editor, or use your existing Web page if you already have one. Create a DHTML application and import your Web page.

   After importing the page to a DHTML Page Designer, add elements and programming.

   Hint: Use Microsoft Word. You can select any background color or texture. Use an image if you wish. When you have your page arranged, use *Save As HTML*.

10.4   Write an IIS database application. Convert one of your database applications to IIS.

C A S E   S T U D I E S

Video Bonanza

Create a DHTML application to calculate the amount due and provide a summary of rentals. All movies rent for $1.80, and all customers receive a 10 percent discount.

The page should contain input for the member number and the number of movies rented. Inside labels, display the rental amount, the 10 percent discount, and the amount due. Calculate the results as the movie number is entered.

Include a command button for Clear.

VB Auto

Create a Web page that displays an advertisement for the location and services of VB Auto. Have a link for sales that allows the user to input a make of car. Search the VBAuto database and display a Web page that lists the year, model, and price for any cars that match the criteria.

11

Extending VB Using the Windows API

At the completion of this chapter, you will be able to . . .

1. Write applications that call procedures from the Windows API to extend the power of VB.

2. Understand the purpose and placement of `Declare` statements for API procedures.

3. Use the API Viewer add-in.

4. Differentiate and understand argument data types, including those from C++.

5. Use SendMessage to communicate with controls.

Windows has thousands of functions, procedures, and constants, and many of them are not directly available in VB. The dynamic link libraries (**DLLs**) that Windows applications use for such tasks as moving and resizing windows are referred to as the Windows **application programming interface (API).**

One extremely useful feature of VB is that a project can call and use library procedures used by the Windows system. Consequently, functions available in Windows but not available in VB can still be used. VB uses many API DLLs to create the VB environment. In this chapter you learn to call the library routines of the Windows API to expand the capabilities of an application.

Dynamic Link Libraries

Windows uses (DLLs) to store collections of procedures. Your project links to the DLL file at run time. A VB project can call a function from the library and pass arguments if needed. The function is maintained separately from the program that calls it. As you learned in Chapter 8, changes can be made to the internal workings of a function in a dynamic link library without having to recode all the projects that call the function.

Two steps are required for using a DLL. Any time you call a procedure that is in a library, you must include a **Declare statement.** Declare statements tell VB the name of the procedure and the library where it can be found, along with the arguments the procedure needs. Once you have included the Declare, you can call the procedure as you would one of your own. You can call both sub procedures and functions from DLLs; the Declare statement specifies the type of procedure. (Recall that a function returns a value.)

The Declare Statement

Declare statements appear at the module level. You can include them in the General Declarations section of a form module or in a standard code module. Calls to the library procedures may appear in any module in the scope of the Declare. If the Declare appears in a form module, it must be Private; usually in a standard code module, you want the Declare to be Public, so it can be used globally.

The Declare Statement—General Form

```
[Public|Private] Declare Sub Name Lib LibName [Alias AliasName] ([ArgumentList])
[Public|Private] Declare Function Name Lib LibName [Alias AliasName] _
    ([ArgumentList]) [As Datatype]
```

The Name parameter refers to the name of the procedure. If the name of the procedure is the same as a reserved word in VB or one of your existing procedures, you will need to use an alias to give the procedure a new name within your project. The word *Lib* precedes the name of the DLL file. The argument list specifies the arguments expected by the procedure.

In the first of the following examples, the function procedure is called *sndPlaySound* from the Winmm system library file.

The Declare Statement—Examples

```
Private Declare Function sndPlaySound Lib "winmm" Alias "sndPlaySoundA" _
    (ByVal lpszSoundName As String, ByVal uFlags As Long) As Long
Declare Function GetWindowsDirectory Lib "kernel32" Alias "GetWindowsDirectoryA" _
    (ByVal lpBuffer As String, ByVal nSize As Long) As Long
```

The arguments may have a data type specified and can be passed ByVal or ByRef.

Passing Arguments ByVal and ByRef

Remember that arguments may be passed to a called procedure by value or by reference. When passed ByVal, only a copy of the original value is passed; the called procedure cannot alter the original value. When items are passed ByRef, the memory address of the original value is passed to the procedure, allowing the procedure to change the original value. You will pass ByVal or ByRef based upon the requirements of the specific DLL. If no specification is made, the default is ByRef.

When you are calling Windows API procedures, always declare a string argument ByVal. Most API functions are written in C, and VB and C do not store strings in the same way. A VB string holds the length of the string at the beginning; strings in C are variable in length and terminated by a NULL character. C does not actually have a string data type, but treats strings as an array of characters.

The treatment for string arguments and array arguments is different from that for other (nonarray) arguments. You should declare string and array arguments as passing ByVal, but what is actually passed is the address of the first element of the array.

Calling a DLL Procedure

You can call a DLL procedure from within any procedure in the scope of the `Declare` statement. The call will look the same as calls to procedures that you have written. The passed arguments may be either variables or constants.

The following procedure uses the `sndPlaySound` function to play a sound wave file (.wav extension). This shareware wave file sounds like the Laurel and Hardy "Look at the fine mess you've gotten us into now" routine. Although this example plays the sound when a command button is clicked, you might consider playing it in a game program or in a validation routine when the user makes a mistake.

```
Private Sub cmdPlay_Click()
    'Play the sound
    Dim lngTalk As Long
    Dim strWaveFile As String
    Const lngSync = 1

    strWaveFile = App.Path & "\l&h.wav"
    lngTalk = sndPlaySound(ByVal CStr(strWaveFile), lngSync)
End Sub
```

The first parameter converts the path and filename string to a "C string" by using the CStr function. The second argument being passed is a long constant. Compare these arguments with the Declare used for this DLL procedure. (Note: The path indicated must be valid for your system. This shareware file is included on your CD.)

```
Declare Function sndPlaySound Lib "winmm" Alias "sndPlaySoundA" _
(ByVal lpszSoundName As String, ByVal uFlags As Long) As Long
```

The sndPlaySound function is very useful for including sounds in a multimedia program. You might consider scanning in your own pictures, recording a voice description, and playing back the sound file when the appropriate selection is made from a menu or command button.

Finding the Reference Information for DLLs

You are not expected to learn the names and arguments for DLL procedures. You will find small code samples in magazines, in articles that present tips, or in question-and-answer features. If you ask a *How do I do . . . ?* question online, the answer you receive may include a few lines of code that include a Declare and a call to the procedure.

The API Viewer

Obviously there is no need to reinvent the wheel or to rewrite code that already exists. It is much more efficient to incorporate existing functions into your application. How will you know what features already exist in the Windows API? VB comes with a reference database for the procedures in the Windows API. You can use the API Viewer add-in to look up the names of library files, procedures, constants, and the format of the Declare for each call.

Running the Viewer

Load and run the VB 6 API Viewer from the *Add-Ins* menu. When the Viewer starts, there's nothing to view (Figure 11.1). You must first load the text file that holds the reference information. Select *File/Load TextFile* (Figure 11.2) and load Win32API.txt. This file should be in a folder called WinAPI, most likely beneath Microsoft Visual Studio\Common\Tools, depending on how VB was installed on your system. Notice the second option on the *File* menu, to load a database file. If you use the API Viewer frequently, you can save time in future searches by loading the text file and converting it to an .mdb (Jet) database file.

Tip

To use this add-in, it must be selected when you install VB on your system.

Figure 11.1

The API Viewer as it first appears.

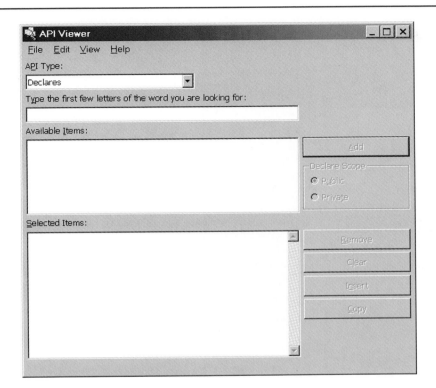

Figure 11.2

Select File/Load TextFile to load the information file.

Drop down the API Viewer's *API Type* list, and you can select *Constants, Declares,* or *Types* (Figure 11.3). Examine the available Constants and Types; then look at the Declares. You can choose the procedure you want, such as PlaySound, select the option button for Public or Private, and click Add. The correct `Declare` statement appears in the Selected Items list. From there you can copy to the Clipboard and paste the statement(s) into your code.

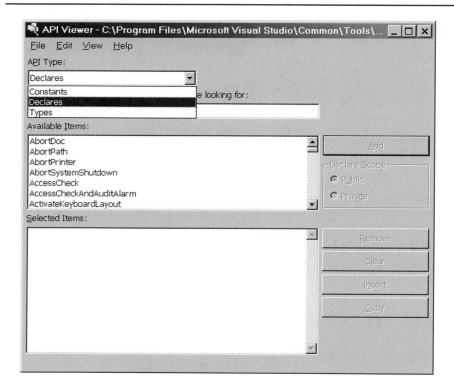

Library Files

The Windows API code is written in C or C++ and stored in library files. Look at the list of library selections in the VB *References* dialog box from the *Project* menu. The line near the bottom of the dialog box shows the path including the .DLL extension. Use Windows Explorer to look in the Windows and Windows\System folders; you will see many library files with the .DLL extension. Since most of the Windows DLL code is written in C or C++, calling procedures requires some use of C syntax. Don't worry if you don't know C. You don't have to write any C statements; you only have to pass arguments to the library procedures. The `Declare` statements displayed in the viewer are used to connect your VB application to the API.

Calling DLL Procedures

Here are some examples of calling API procedures. You can find many more examples in online tips and the excellent book *Dan Appleman's Visual Basic Programmer's Guide to the Win32 API.*[1]

Accessing System Information with a DLL

Your project may need to know the specific hardware or software on the computer system running the program. Windows maintains this information, and

---

[1]Sams, Feb. 1999, by Dan Appleman and Galen Grimes.

you can access it with a DLL. The following program determines the current
version of Windows and the video configuration.

Figure 11.4 shows the form for this program example.

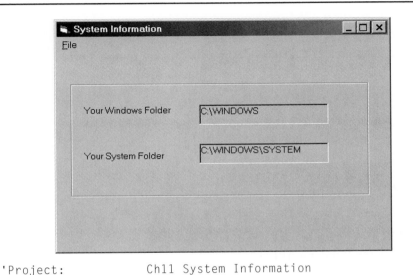

*The form for the system
information program that uses a
Windows API DLL.*

```
'Project:              Ch11 System Information
'Programmer:           Bradley/Millspaugh
'Date:                 2/2000
'Module:               DeclareDLLs.bas
'Description:          Declares DLL procedures to find the Windows
'                      and System folders.
'Folder:               Ch11SysInfo

    'Declare the DLL procedures
    Declare Function GetWindowsDirectory _
        Lib "kernel32" Alias "GetWindowsDirectoryA" _
        (ByVal lpBuffer As String, ByVal nSize As Long) _
        As Long
    Declare Function GetSystemDirectory Lib _
        "kernel32" Alias "GetSystemDirectoryA" _
        (ByVal lpBuffer As String, ByVal nSize As Long) _
        As Long
```

```
'Project:              Ch11 System Information
'Programmer:           Bradley/Millspaugh
'Date:                 2/2000
'Module:               frmSysInfo
'Description:          Uses DLL procedures to find the Windows
'                      and System folders.
'Folder:               Ch11SysInfo

Option Explicit

Private Sub Form_Load()
    'Call the DLL procedures and assign return
    '    values to labels
    Dim strWinPath As String
    Dim vntTemp

    'Create a string of 145 null characters
    strWinPath = String(145, Chr(0))
```

```
    'Fill the string with the path name
    vntTemp = GetWindowsDirectory(strWinPath, 145)
    'Take the left characters up to the null
    lblWindowsDir.Caption = Left(strWinPath, InStr(strWinPath, Chr(0)) - 1)
    strWinPath = String(145, Chr(0))
    vntTemp = GetSystemDirectory(strWinPath, 145)
    lblSystemDir.Caption = Left(strWinPath, InStr(strWinPath, Chr(0)) - 1)
End Sub
```

```
Private Sub mnuFileExit_Click()
    'Terminate the project

    Unload Me
End Sub
```

Using SendMessage to Communicate with Windows and Controls

VB implements only a subset of the capabilities of windows and controls. You can perform many additional operations using the Windows API SendMessage function, which communicates with windows and controls. (Most controls are actually considered windows by the Windows operating system.) Here are just a few of the things you can do with SendMessage:

- Close a window.
- Set margins inside text boxes and combo boxes.
- Determine which line of a multiline entry is selected.
- Set the height of each entry in a list box or combo box.
- Set the width of the dropdown portion of a dropdown list.
- Display the dropdown portion of the list.
- Set tab stops in a list box or combo box.

The SendMessage Declare Statement

Using the API Viewer, copy the SendMessage Declare statement.

```
Private Declare Function SendMessage Lib "user32" _
    Alias "SendMessageA" (ByVal hwnd As Long, _
    ByVal wMsg As Long, ByVal wParam As Long, _
    lParam As Any) As Long
```

The SendMessage Parameters

hwnd	"Handle" to the window. This is the name of the window or control. VB example: cboName.hwnd
wMsg	The message to send. You should use one of the predefined constants that you can find in the API Viewer. All combo box constants begin with CB, list box with LB, window with WM, text box with EM.
wParam	A long parameter; use depends on the message.
lParam	A long parameter; use depends on the message.

Using SendMessage to Automatically Drop Down a List

Have you ever wanted to make the dropdown portion of a list automatically drop down when the control receives the focus? VB doesn't have a built-in method to do this, but the SendMessage API function will do it for you.

Select the SendMessage Declare from the API Viewer and also locate and select the CB_SHOWDROPDOWN constant. Select *Private* from the option button (Figure 11.5); then copy the statements to the Clipboard and paste them into your project.

F i g u r e   1 1 . 5

Select the SendMessage Declare *and the CB_SHOWDROPDOWN constant in the API Viewer and copy them into a project.*

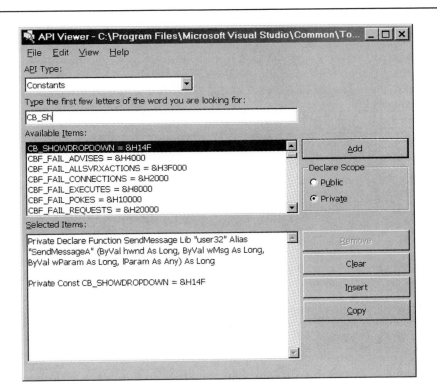

For the CB_SHOWDROPDOWN message, the two long parameters are

wParam	(Long) Any nonzero value to drop down; zero to close the list.
lParam	Unused for this message. Set to zero.

The function's return value (a long) has no value and should be ignored.

The Program Listing

```
'Project:        API SendMessage
'Date:           2/2000
'Programmer:     Bradley/Millspaugh
'Description:    Drop down a list using an API function call.
'Folder:         Ch11SendMessage

Option Explicit

'Copy the Declare and Const statements from the API viewer
Private Declare Function SendMessage Lib "user32" _
    Alias "SendMessageA" (ByVal hwnd As Long, _
    ByVal wMsg As Long, ByVal wParam As Long, _
    lParam As Any) As Long
Private Const CB_SHOWDROPDOWN = &H14F
```

```
Private Sub cboText_GotFocus()
    'Drop down the list
    Dim lngReturn As Long
    Const lngShow As Long = -1  'Any non-zero value will do the job


    lngReturn = SendMessage(cboText.hwnd, CB_SHOWDROPDOWN, lngShow, 0)
End Sub
```

Exiting Windows

Some applications automatically shut down or reboot Windows. You can place
API code in the standard code module of an application to perform the
shutdown.

```
'Project:        Ch11 System ShutDown
'Programmer:     Bradley/Millspaugh
'Date:           2/2000
'Module:         frmMain
'Description:    Uses DLL procedures to shut down the system
'Folder:         Ch11ShutDown
Option Explicit

Private Declare Function ExitWindowsEx& Lib "user32" _
    (ByVal uFlags&, ByVal wReserved&)

'Constants needed for exiting Windows
Const EWX_FORCE = 4
Const EWX_LOGOFF = 0
Const EWX_REBOOT = 2
Const EWX_SHUTDOWN = 1
```

```
Private Sub cmdShutDown_Click()
    'Call the API code to exit Windows
    Dim lngExitWindows As Long

    lngExitWindows = ExitWindowsEx(EWX_SHUTDOWN, 0&) 'Shut down the computer
End Sub
```

By changing the first argument to EWX_LOGOFF, you can log off or use EWX_REBOOT to restart.

S u m m a r y

1. Dynamic link libraries (DLLs) are procedures in library files, outside of VB, that can be linked and called when a project is running.
2. DLLs used by Windows are referred to as the Windows application programming interface (API).
3. DLL procedures may pass arguments by value (pass a copy of the value) or by reference (pass the address of the value).
4. You can find API `Declares`, constants, and `Types` by using the API Viewer, and you can copy and paste the statements into a project.

K e y   T e r m s

application programming interface   `Declare` statement *480*
  (API) *480*   DLL *480*

R e v i e w   Q u e s t i o n s

1. What are the purposes of a `Declare` statement?
2. Explain the difference between ByVal and ByRef. When is each used?
3. What information is available from the API Viewer?
4. What function gets the path of the Windows directory? the System directory?
5. What is the purpose of the `SendMessage` function?
6. What arguments are available for the `ExitWindowsEx` function?

P r o g r a m m i n g   E x e r c i s e s

11.1   If you have access to a multimedia system with a microphone, record a short message to a .wav file. Write a project that plays back the sound file—a description of an item being displayed, for example.

11.2   Rewrite either of the chapter examples on page 488 to place the `Declare` statement in a standard code module.

11.3   Examine the .wav files in your Windows directories. Write a project that prompts the user to guess a number. Have the project generate a random number from 1 to 100. Allow the user to enter a number. Display a message that indicates whether the response is too high or too low. If the user gives the correct answer, use the Tada.wav file to generate a sound.

11.4 Add the SendMessage call to one of your previous projects with a drop-down list. Place the Declare and Const statements in a standard code module (making them Public). When the user tabs into the combo box, the list should automatically drop down.

12

Optimizing Applications

At the completion of this chapter, you will be able to . . .

1. Understand the purpose and advantages of native code compilation.

2. Optimize for speed or size.

3. Perform conditional compilation.

4. Set constants for conditional compilation.

5. Persist values by using the Windows Registry.

6. Use the Resource Editor to create resource files.

7. Use resource functions to load information from a resource file at run time.

This chapter explains the various compiler options that are available to you, along with the effect of each advanced setting. You will learn about conditional compilation, which allows you to determine which program lines to include when compiling a program. You will find out how to use VB statements and functions to store information in the Windows Registry and learn about resource files and the VB 6 Resource Editor.

Setting Compiler Options

You can make several choices as to how a project is compiled. These choices determine the format and size of the compiled module, as well as the execution speed of the completed program.

The compile choices you make should depend on several factors. Programs that depend heavily on mathematical calculations can run considerably faster if optimized for speed. However, programs that spend most of their time sending and receiving database information, displaying forms, and calling DLL routines may benefit little or not at all from optimization. If your program will be run on computers with limited memory, you would certainly not want to load all the forms at startup and slow down the system; in fact, even the size of your executable file may be significant. However, when the system capacity is sufficient, the processing speed may be the more important factor.

You can choose the compile options by selecting *File/Make FileName.exe* and clicking on *Options* (Figure 12.1) when you are ready to compile. Or you can choose *Project/ProjectName Properties* to display the same information (Figure 12.2). Both dialog boxes have a Make tab (Figure 12.3) and a Compile tab (Figure 12.4, p. 494). The following discussion focuses on the options on the Compile tab.

F i g u r e   1 2 . 1

The Make Project dialog box. Select Options to display the Compile options.

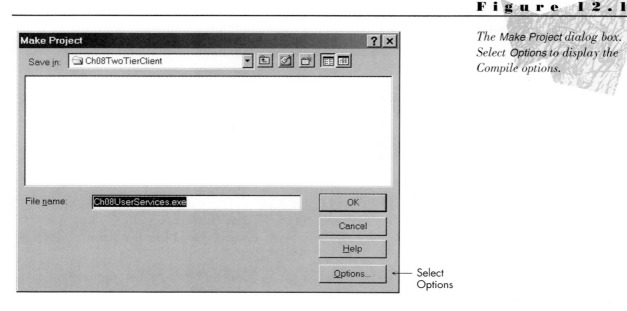

Select Options

Figure   12.2

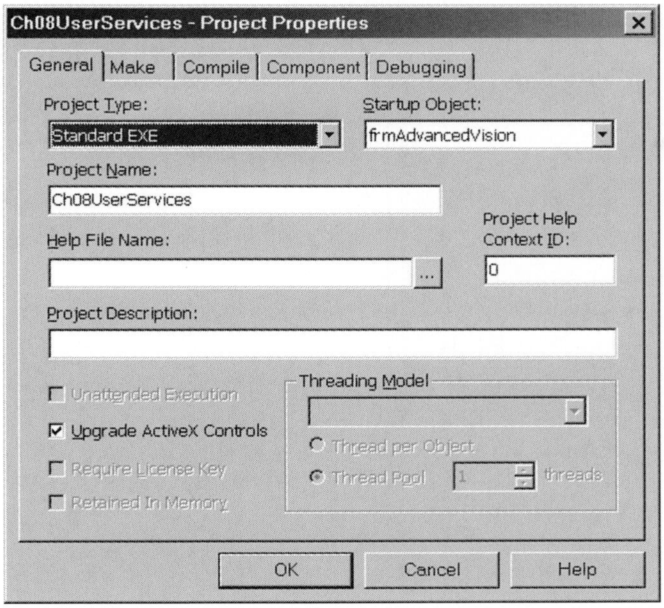

The Project Properties dialog box.

Ch08UserServices - Project Properties

General | Make | Compile | Component | Debugging

Project Type:
Standard EXE

Startup Object:
frmAdvancedVision

Project Name:
Ch08UserServices

Help File Name:

Project Help Context ID:
0

Project Description:

☐ Unattended Execution
☑ Upgrade ActiveX Controls
☐ Require License Key
☐ Retained In Memory

Threading Model

○ Thread per Object
○ Thread Pool   1   threads

OK   Cancel   Help

Figure   12.3

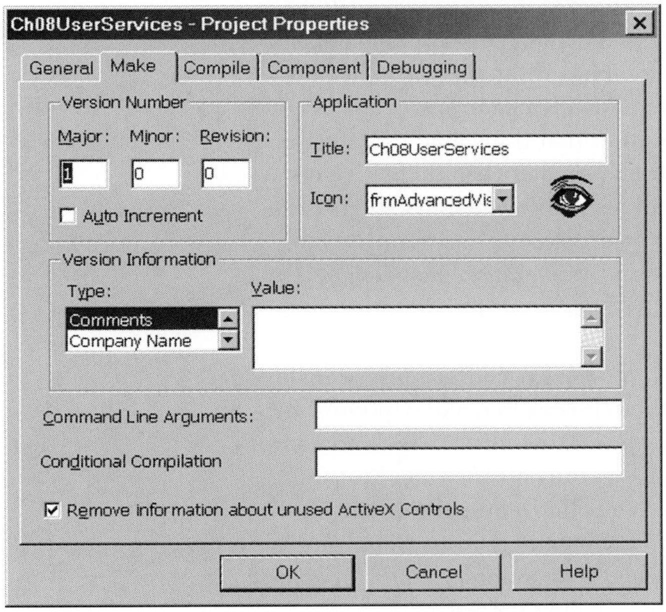

The Make tab of the Project Properties dialog box and the Make Project dialog box.

Ch08UserServices - Project Properties

General | Make | Compile | Component | Debugging

Version Number

Major: Minor: Revision:
1   0   0

☐ Auto Increment

Application

Title: Ch08UserServices

Icon: frmAdvancedVis

Version Information

Type: Value:
Comments
Company Name

Command Line Arguments:

Conditional Compilation:

☑ Remove information about unused ActiveX Controls

OK   Cancel   Help

P-Code versus Native Code

VB programmers have the option of creating the executable file in p-code (short for pseudocode) or in native code. When an executable file is created, the source code is translated into some form of machine language that the system

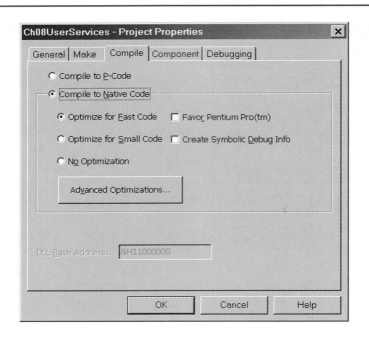

The Compile tab of the Project Properties dialog box and the Make Project dialog box.

can run. The earliest versions of Basic used an interpreter rather than a compiler. Each time the program was run, one line of code was translated to machine code, then executed, and on to the next line. This approach was a memory advantage for the earliest microcomputers with their limited memory because the executable file was never permanently created.

Later advances allowed VB to use a compiler that translated the program into an executable file called **p-code.** The file is smaller than the native code used by other languages such as C++ but still requires some translation at run time. With VB 5 and later, the programmer has the option of using **native code** to reduce the processing time during execution. As memory has become less expensive, the idea of faster processing has become more important than the size of the executable file.

The dialog box contains option buttons to select p-code or native code. When native code is selected, there are further choices to make. Optimize for speed or for size (small code) is one such choice. The others are check boxes to determine whether optimization should be made to run on a Pentium Pro and/or to create Symbolic Debug info. If you opt for Symbolic Debug, the debug information is placed in a .pdb file and your application can then be debugged in Visual C++ or any editor that has a Debug view. This option is handy for components that are used with applications written in other languages.

Advanced Optimizations

Click on the Advanced Optimizations button to see the options (Figure 12.5) but beware of these choices. Some of these options can speed up processing but can also be fatal to your application or, worse, produce erroneous results. So why would they be offered? Well, if you are absolutely sure that your

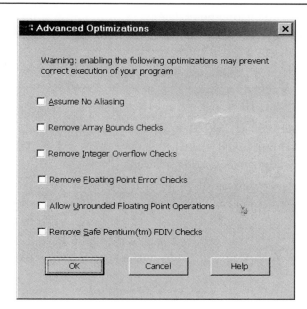

*The Advanced Optimization
options can improve execution
speed by removing VB's
error-checking routines.*

application can run without errors, you can omit VB's error checking and produce a smaller and faster compiled module. But this approach also means that you need a thorough understanding of the implications of each choice. Note: If the program was working fine and then develops errors after optimization, make sure to change the optimization before debugging the code.

Assume No Aliasing

When you pass values ByRef, the value can be referred to by two different names, a situation that is referred to as an **alias.** If your program does not need to track aliasing, this option can be selected.

Remove Array Bounds Checks

Normally an error occurs if an index is outside of the dimensioned range of an array. If this situation cannot occur in an application, you may wish to remove array bounds checks. This option might be appropriate when the index is always selected from a list and the user cannot enter an invalid number.

Remove Integer Overflow Checks

This option can speed up integer calculations that use Byte, Integer, Long, and Currency data types. Normally every time any Integer data type is used in a calculation, a check is made to be sure that the number falls into the range allowable for the specific data type. If you always carefully validate all numeric values, you could select this option and speed up your program. But beware, you won't receive a run-time error for bad data—you'll just get the wrong answer.

Remove Floating-Point Error Checks

This option checks for division by zero and performs range checks for floating-point data types (Single or Double). Again, if your program attempts to calculate with invalid numbers, the result of the calculation may be incorrect.

Allow Unrounded Floating-Point Operations

Do not select this option if your program compares two floating-point data types to determine whether they are equal. Normally the compiler rounds the numbers to the same precision before comparing two numbers. This option eliminates the rounding, which can speed up processing but maintains the numbers at a larger precision than necessary and may result in incorrect comparison results.

Remove Safe Pentium FDIV Checks

If all systems that will run the application are Pentium based, this option can speed up execution. Important note: Performance suffers if the application runs on other systems.

Feedback 12.1

1. Name the compiler optimization feature on the *Advanced* menu that checks for the following conditions:
   (a) Subscript out of range.
   (b) Division by zero.
   (c) Valid range for integer numbers.
   (d) Valid range for floating-point numbers.
2. If you want to optimize for speed, would you use p-code or native code?

Conditional Compilation

You may need to compile different lines of code depending on the situation. An example of **conditional compilation** may occur when software is created to run on multiple platforms. For example, a developer can use VB 4 to create a version for Win 3.1 or Win 95 (VB 6 does not support Win 3.1, though). Another example of multiple-version software could be an application for international distribution. The application itself can have arguments that specify which language version is to be compiled, maybe French, Italian, Spanish, or English. Conditional compilation is also frequently used in debugging.

When the compiler reads program lines, it converts those lines to machine code. Compiler directives are statements to the compiler, telling it to skip certain program lines if a condition is true.

The #If Directive

The **#If directive** has a format similar to the VB If statement but determines whether lines of code will be compiled or not.

The #If Directive—General Form

```
#If condition Then
    VB statement(s)
[#Else|#ElseIf condition Then
    VB statement(s)]
#End If
```

The condition is tested for True or False but is actually stored in an Integer. Any nonzero value tests as True; zero is False.

The #If Directive—Examples

```
#If English Then
    'Code for English version
#ElseIf Italian Then
    'Code for Italian version
#End If

#If Debugging Then
    Debug.Print "Counter value: "; intCounter
#End If
```

Specifying Arguments for the Application

Now you may be wondering where the value for the condition is coming from, such as the *English, Italian,* or *Debugging* in the previous examples. You can set the values of the variables in three different ways: in the Make tab under *Project/Properties,* in a directive line in the VB code, or on the command line when you start VB. If you set a variable's value in code, the scope of the variable is Private for the module in which it is set; the other two methods create a Public value for the entire project.

Make Tab

The Make tab on the *Project Properties* dialog box has a text box for Conditional Compilation arguments (Figure 12.6). You can type assignment statements for the project here. A colon must separate multiple statements.

```
English = 1:Italian = 0
```

Figure 12.6

Set the initial value for conditional compilation arguments on the Make tab of the Project Properties dialog box.

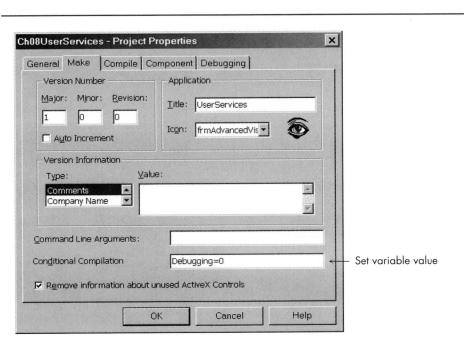

Command-Line Arguments

You use command-line arguments when you start VB. You can type a command line from the Windows *Start/Run* menu option. You can invoke VB and compile a project directly from the command line. The /d parameter indicates that a conditional compilation argument follows. The following example starts VB, loads the AdvVision.vbp project, begins the compile, and passes a compiler directive variable:

```
vb6.exe /make AdvVision.vbp /d English = 1
```

#Const Directive

You can set the value of a conditional compilation argument in code by using the **#Const directive**.

```
#Const Debugging = 1    'Turn on debugging mode
```

Feedback 12.2

1. Conditional compilation arguments have a module-level scope for which of the following:
   (a) Set in code using #Const directive.
   (b) Command-line argument.
   (c) Conditional Compilation argument on the Make tab of the *Project Properties* dialog box.
2. Write the compound condition that will Debug.Print the value of intCustomerCount when Testing is set to True.
3. Write the Conditional Compilation argument to make the Debug.Print statement in question 2 print.

Storing Data in the Windows Registry

Suppose you want to store a small amount of information from one execution of an application until the next. Perhaps you have user preferences, a date of last run, a count, or a property setting that you need next time the program runs. Although you could create a database, that's a bit of overkill. One solution is to store the information in the Windows **Registry,** a database that stores user, application, and system information. The Registry in Windows 95 and higher replaces the .ini files from Windows 3.1.

VB provides a standard Registry location where you can store information from your applications. You can save, retrieve, and delete Registry settings. If you save items to the Registry, you should always clean up after yourself and delete the settings when you are finished. You probably won't be allowed to make Registry entries on shared computers in a classroom or lab.

Saving a Setting

You save a value by using the **SaveSetting statement. The Registry key** is a name that you make up to identify the value in the Registry. Use something meaningful for your keys; prefixes are not usually included. You must also specify the name of the application and a Registry section.

The SaveSetting Statement—General Form

```
SaveSetting ApplicationName, Section, RegistryKey, Value
```

The SaveSetting Statement—Example

```
SaveSetting App.Path & "\RegistrySettings", "Startup", "ButtonCount", _
    mintButtonClickedCount
```

In this example the name of the application is RegistrySettings, and the information will be stored as ButtonCount in the Startup section of the application's Registry. You would likely place this line of code in the Form_Unload event procedure.

Retrieving a Setting

You can retrieve a single setting or retrieve all the settings at once. Place the code to get the setting(s) in the Form_Load event procedure so the information is available to the application. The **GetSetting function** returns a single key.

The GetSetting Function—General Form

```
GetSetting(ApplicationName, Section, RegistryKey[, DefaultValue])
```

The GetSetting Function—Example

```
mintButtonClickedCount = Val(GetSetting(App.Path & _
    "\RegistrySettings", "Startup", "ButtonCount", "0"))
```

If you don't include the default value, VB uses an empty string (" "). Supplying a default value is a more efficient approach.

You can use the **GetAllSettings function** when you want to retrieve several key values. The information is retrieved as a two-dimensional array as Variant type.

The GetAllSettings Function—General Form

```
GetAllSettings(ApplicationName, Section)
```

The GetAllSettings Function—Example

```
strSettings = GetAllSettings(App.Path & "\RegistrySettings", "Startup")
```

Deleting a Setting

If you no longer need Registry items, it's a good idea to clean them out. Use the **DeleteSetting statement** to remove entries.

The DeleteSetting Statement—General Form

```
DeleteSetting ApplicationName, Section[, Key]
```

The DeleteSetting Statement—Example

```
DeleteSetting App.Path & "\RegistrySettings", "Startup"
```

```
'Project:        Window Registry Settings
'Module:         frmRegistrySettings
'Date:           2/2000
'Programmer:     Bradley/Millspaugh
'Description:    Store and Retrieve a value from the registry.
'Folder:         Ch12WindowsRegistry

Option Explicit
Dim mintButtonClickedCount As Integer

Private Sub cmdPress_Click()
    'Add one to the button clicked count

    mintButtonClickedCount = mintButtonClickedCount + 1
    lblCount.Caption = mintButtonClickedCount
End Sub

Private Sub Form_Load()
    'Get the current setting

    mintButtonClickedCount = Val(GetSetting(App.Path & _
            "\RegistrySettings", "Startup", "ButtonCount", "0"))
    lblCount.Caption = mintButtonClickedCount
End Sub

Private Sub Form_Unload(Cancel As Integer)
    'Save setting in registry

    SaveSetting App.Path & "\RegistrySettings", "Startup", _
            "ButtonCount", mintButtonClickedCount
End Sub

Private Sub mnuFileExit_Click()
    'Terminate the project

    Unload Me
End Sub
```

Feedback 12.3

1. In which event procedure should a `SaveSetting` statement be placed?
2. Write the statement to retrieve the setting of a key called *RunDate* from the Startup section of the Registry for Payroll.vbp (store the value in mdtmRunDate).

Resource Files

A **resource file** contains strings, icons, sound files, cursors, and bitmaps for an application. This file's primary use in VB is to handle multiple versions of an application in an efficient way. Each item in the resource file has a unique identifer. Each project can have only one resource file.

One advantage of using resource files is that items are loaded as the resource is needed rather than when the form loads. This approach can speed up the initial load time for an application. The resource file has an extension .res. After compilation the file is a standard Window resource file that can be loaded with any Windows-based Resource Editor.

Resource files are also used for international distribution of applications. The string text and icons for the user interface can be stored in several languages to **localize** the application. The sample applications in MSDN include a program called the Automated Teller Machine (Atm.vbp) that allows bank transactions in English, German, French, Italian, and Spanish. In that example the first screen displays buttons for various languages, and then the following forms display text in the appropriate language. The hands-on example in this chapter demonstrates the concept by changing a form's Caption.

Resource Editor

The VB 6 Resource Editor is an add-in that you load with the Add-in Manager on the *Add-Ins* menu. This add-in creates two new menu options: *Add New Resource File* is placed on the *Project* menu, and *Resource File* is added to the *Tools* menu.

Adding a Resource File

The *Add New Resource File* option displays an *Open* dialog box. To create a new file, type in the filename and you will see the following message: *xxxxxx.RES file does not exist, Do you want to create it?* Of course, you want to click Yes. The new resource file is added into the list of files in the Project Explorer window.

You can also add a resource file by selecting *Resource File* from the *Tools* menu and selecting the icon for *Open*.

Editing the Resource File

The *Tools* menu *Resource File* option displays the Resource Editor window with its own toolbar (Figure 12.7). The tools to the right are

- Edit String Tables

- Add Cursor . . .

- Add Icon . . .

- Add Bitmap . . .

- Add Custom Resource . . .

The Resource Editor window.

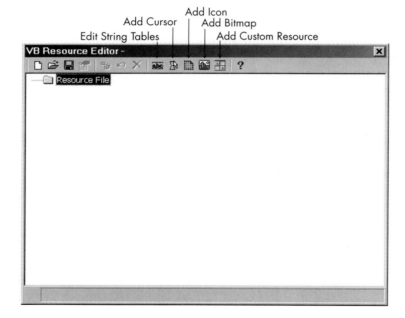

These options allow you to add existing files of the specified type to your new resource file with the exception of the String Table. The **String Table** contains strings that can be used for screen text. Each string in the table has its own identifier.

When you add a resource to the file, the Resource Editor assigns a numeric ID to that resource. You can display the properties for the resource and change the ID to something more meaningful (Figure 12.8).

Figure 12.8

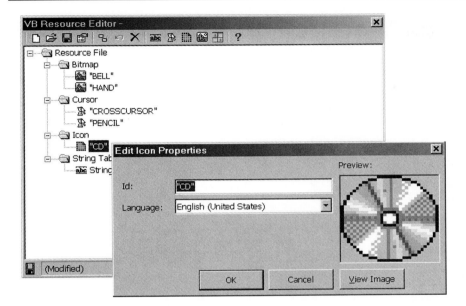

Display the properties for a resource and change the ID to a meaningful string.

Loading a Resource File at Run Time

VB has three functions for retrieving resources from the resource file: LoadResString, LoadResPicture, and LoadResData. Use the functions to assign values at run time.

```
lblName.Caption = LoadResString(101)
picDisplay.Picture = LoadResPicture("Hand")
```

Feedback 12.4

1. What are the advantages of using resource files?
2. How can resource files be used for "localizing" applications?

Your Hands-on Programming Example

Create a project that uses a resource file to store the form Caption in English and in Italian. The main form contains two buttons, one for each language. The Caption will be blank when the application begins.

Plan the Project

Sketch the form (Figure 12.9), which your user signs off.

Figure 12.9

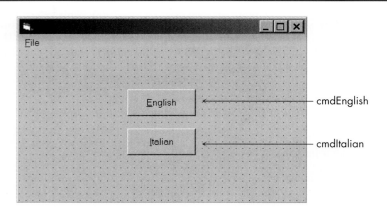

cmdEnglish

cmdItalian

The form for the hands-on example that uses the Resource Editor.

Plan the Properties

Object	Property	Value
frmMain	Caption	(blank)
cmdEnglish	Caption	&English
cmdItalian	Caption	&Italian
mnuFile	Caption	&File
mnuFileExit	Caption	E&xit

Plan the Procedures

Plan the event procedures.

Object	Procedure	Pseudocode
cmdEnglish	Click	Display the English caption.
cmdItalian	Click	Display the Italian caption.
mnuFileExit	Click	Display message box in appropriate language. Unload the form.

Plan the Resource File

Add two strings to the string table.

101	Introduction to Visual Basic
102	Introduzione a Visual Basic

Write the Project

● Create a form to meet the specifications.

● Add a resource file to the project.

- Enter the strings into the String Table.

- Working from the pseudocode, write the procedures.

- When you complete the code, thoroughly test the project.

The Project Coding Solution

```
'Project:        Resource Editor
'Module:         frmMain
'Date:           2/2000
'Programmer:     Bradley/Millspaugh
'Description:    Display different captions from the
'                resource file string table.
'Folder:         Ch12Resources
Option Explicit
Dim mstrLanguage As String
```

```
Private Sub cmdEnglish_Click()
    'Display caption in English

    frmMain.Caption = LoadResString(101)
    mstrLanguage = "English"
End Sub
```

```
Private Sub cmdItalian_Click()
    'Display caption in Italian

    frmMain.Caption = LoadResString(102)
    mstrLanguage = "Italian"
End Sub
```

```
Private Sub mnuFileExit_Click()
    'Display message box in selected language
    Dim strMessage As String

    If mstrLanguage = "English" Then
        strMessage = "Good Bye"
    Else
        strMessage = "Ciao"
    End If
    MsgBox strMessage, vbOKOnly, mstrLanguage
    Unload Me
End Sub
```

MCSD Exam Notes

Exam Objectives Covered in This Chapter

Testing the Solution

- Given a scenario, select the appropriate compiler options.

- Control an application by using conditional compilation.

Questions/Tricks to Watch for

● Know the optimization options under the Advanced Optimizations on the Compile tab of the *Project Properties* dialog box.

● Know appropriate data types for specific situations.

S u m m a r y

1. VB executable files can be compiled into native code or p-code. Native code runs faster because it does not require the additional translation step needed with p-code.

2. Native code executable files can be optimized for speed, for size, or for execution on a Pentium machine.

3. Several compiler options can speed up processing but can result in errors if not added in the proper situations. Checking for aliasing, array boundary checks, integer overflow, and division by zero can be eliminated, as well as the rounding of floating points used in comparisons.

4. Conditional compilations can be used for debugging or for distributing a single version of software for use under various conditions such as multiple operating systems or screen-text languages.

5. The #If directive allows the application to check for a condition and determine specific lines to be compiled.

6. Values can be assigned to a conditional compilation variable in the *Project Properties* dialog box, the command line, or code using the #Const directive.

7. You can persist data by saving it in the Windows Registry and then retrieving the data during the next program run.

8. A resource file can include bitmaps, icons, sound files, and string text. When using a resource file, the appropriate file is not loaded until it is needed.

9. Resource files may contain resources for different versions of the software.

K e y   T e r m s

Review Questions

1. Differentiate between native code and p-code.
2. When would it be inappropriate to use each of the following options:
   (a) Assume No Aliasing
   (b) Remove Array Bounds Checks
   (c) Remove Integer Overflow Checks
   (d) Remove Floating-Point Error Checks
   (e) Allow Unrounded Floating-Point Operations
   (f) Remove Safe Pentium FDIV Checks
3. Give an example of where it may be necessary or helpful to use conditional compilation.
4. How is conditional compilation implemented in VB code?
5. Specify three methods for supplying values for conditional compilation.
6. What steps are necessary to store and retrieve information from the Windows Registry?
7. How can existing settings be removed from the Registry?
8. What is a resource file?
9. Why would you want to create a resource file?
10. What features are available in the VB 6 Resource Editor?

Programming Exercises

12.1 Test the optimization settings for size. Select one of your VB applications and make executable files from your code using different settings. Compare the size of the executable files using various compiler options.
   • Set the compiler options to p-code.
   • Set the compiler to native code and optimize for speed.
   • Set the compiler to native code and optimize for size.

12.2 Create a project that allows the user to type in his or her name. Store the name in the Windows Registry so that the text box will display the name as the program starts.

12.3 Modify the hands-on project to load strings for the message box in the Exit procedure. Also include an image or icon representing the country selected. (You may use the icon in the toolbar or display it on the form.)

12.4 Run the Automated Teller Machine sample application in MSDN VB Samples.
   • Print out the code and study the Form_Load procedure.
   • Check the String Table.
   • How many resources relate to each language?

13

Creating Help Files

At the completion of this chapter, you will be able to . . .

1. Differentiate between WinHelp and HTML Help files.

2. Create the necessary files to set up HTML Help.

3. Use the HTML Help Workshop to create a Help file with a table of contents, index, and display pages.

4. Connect the Help file to a VB project.

5. Set up and display F1 context-sensitive Help.

6. Set up and display WhatsThisHelp.

Windows applications support the use of two types of Help files: **WinHelp** and **HTML Help.** Traditionally, all Windows programs have used WinHelp files, but Microsoft has switched to HTML Help for all new applications and development tools. The newer applications and MSDN display HTML Help files with a browser look and feel.

This chapter covers HTLM Help; WinHelp is covered in Appendix A.

Using either WinHelp or HTML Help, you can display Help to your user in several formats, including a Help facility with topics, an index, and a table of contents; context-sensitive Help; and WhatsThisHelp.

HTML Help Workshop

HTML Help Workshop is a separate application from VB. You use the program to organize and assemble your pages and then compile the various files into one compiled Help file with an extension of .chm.

HTML Help Workshop also includes the **Microsoft HTML Help Image Editor** for creating screen shots and working with images, an HTML editor, an **HTML Help ActiveX control** that you can use to add navigation to an HTML page, and **HTML Help Java Applet** if you plan to run using a browser that does not support ActiveX. The **Help Viewer** provides a three-paned window for displaying online Help topics, many Help screens, and an extensive reference to HTML tags, attributes, character sets, and style sheets.

HTML Help Workshop comes on the Visual Studio or VB CD, but is not automatically installed with the software. You can find the HTMLHelp.exe file in the HTMLHelp folder. The Exe file is a compressed file that will uncompress itself when you run it. You have to run Setup on the uncompressed file to install the application on your computer.

You may prefer to download the latest version from Microsoft's Web site, however. As of this writing, version 1.22 is current, and it still has a few bugs that we hope will be corrected in a newer release soon. You can download the file from msdn.microsoft.com/Workshop/author/htmlhelp/default.asp.

One advantage of using HTML Help rather than WinHelp is that the size of the files is not limited. The Workshop condenses the files as it compiles, reducing storage requirements. It also includes a feature that can convert WinHelp files to HTML Help.

Setting up Help

The first step in setting up a Help system is to plan its organization. Decide on the main subject headers and the topics beneath each header. Each page that you display is a separate HTML file, which you organize and connect together by using HTML Help Workshop.

A Help Facility

Figure 13.1 shows a Help screen for HTML Help Workshop, which illustrates how your Help pages will appear. The left pane holds tabs for Contents and

Figure 13.1

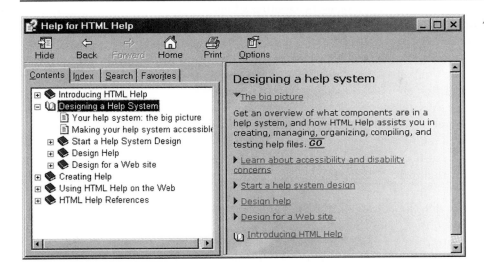

A window displaying HTML Help.

Index (also Search and Favorites tabs, which this chapter doesn't cover). Each book icon represents a heading, and each page icon represents an HTML page.

To get a better idea of the look and feel of Help, take a closer look at the Contents tab of MSDN (Figure 13.2), which is just a very large application of

Figure 13.2

An MSDN screen, which is HTML Help.

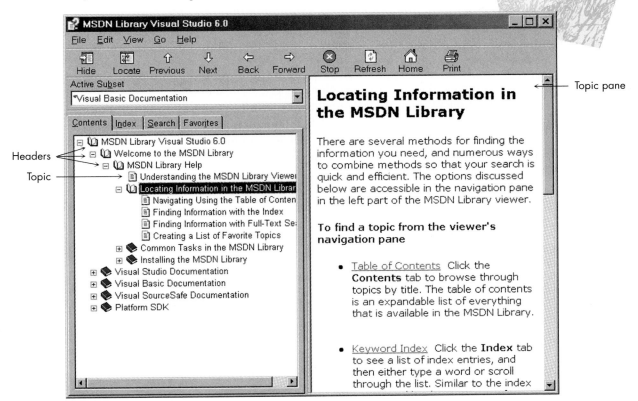

HTML Help. Each header (book icon) can display open or closed. Beneath each header are topics (page icons) and/or additional headers, creating a hierarchy of headers and topics. Notice too that if you select a header and display it in the right pane (the Contents pane), a screen appears that usually has some introductory information and links to the topics beneath the header.

Every screen that displays in the Contents pane is a called a **Help topic** and is a separate HTML file. So your first step is to design the header pages, topic pages, and any extra pages that you want to display from links. You may also think of Help topics that you want to display only from context-sensitive Help. Plan the links that you want to include on each page before you begin creating the pages. Although you can add links later, you'll save yourself considerable time by entering the links when you create the pages. You must create all the pages as HTML documents (file extension .htm). You can use Word, FrontPage, or any HTML editor to create the pages. (The HTML files for this chapter were created in Microsoft Word 97.)

Save yourself some trouble and first create a folder for the Htm files. Place any graphics, sounds, and multimedia files that you want to use in the folder. When you create links to any files or other documents, link to the file in the folder, but do not include a path as part of the link. For example, if a PageA.htm requires a link to PageB.htm, do not allow the editor to specify "a:\MyProjectFolder\HTMLHelpFiles\PageB.htm". Instead make the link say simply "PageB.htm" (no backslashes). Later you will be able to move or rename the folder without changing the links. And if no path is provided, the current folder is searched first.

This text is not intended to be a tutorial on creating HTML pages. The chapter illustrations assume that you have already created the HTML files.

Context-Sensitive Help

If you have gotten this far in developing applications, you have probably used context-sensitive Help. You place the cursor on an element, press F1, and a Help topic (presumably about the element you selected) pops up.

You can implement context-sensitive Help in your VB applications by giving each element (forms and controls) a HelpContextID, which is a unique integer. In HTML Help Workshop you use a **Map file** and an **alias** to relate each integer HelpContextID to a specific HTML file.

WhatsThisHelp

The Windows WhatsThisHelp feature also pops up Help while the user is working, but in a little different manner. When the user selects WhatsThis from a button or a menu option, the pointer changes into the question mark (Figure 13.3). Then the user can click on an element, and a Help topic pops up (Figure 13.4).

You can create WhatsThisHelp and display it in VB by using the WhatsThisHelp property of each control for which you want to supply pop-up help. (As you will see later in this chapter, this is one of the weak points of HTML Help Workshop; we're hoping for improvement in the next release.)

Figure 13.3

⌕?

*The WhatsThisHelp pointer. The
user can click on an object and
pop up Help text.*

Figure 13.4

Font Color ⌕

Formats the selected text with the color you
click.

File Types

An HTML Help project consists of several files. Some you create yourself,
using a text editor; others are created as you work in HTML Help Workshop.

File Type	File Extension	Purpose
Project Header file	.hhp	Holds references to the rest of the files in the project. Similar to the project file in a VB project. The Workshop creates this file when you begin a new project.
Topic files	.htm	Holds the screens to display in the Help Contents pane, one file for each screen. These files are in HTML (Web page) format. You create Topic files by using an HTML editor or text editor.
Graphic and multimedia files	.jpeg, .gif, .png, .wav, .midi, .avi, and others	Images, sounds, and videos for which you supply links on HTML pages. You supply these files.
Map file	.h	Defines the **Topic ID** numbers that VB will use to connect to topics, along with a unique identifier for each topic, which is used in the Workshop. You create this file by using a text editor.
Table of Contents file	.hhc	Stores the headings and organization for the Contents tab. Created by the Workshop when you define the table of contents.
Index file	.hhk	Holds the entries for the searchable index. Created by the Workshop when you define the index.
WhatsThisHelp Topic file	.txt	Holds a unique identifier for each topic that you want to display and the text to display. You create this file by using a text editor.
Compiled Help file	.chm	Holds the compiled Help project. The Workshop creates this file when you compile the project.

Creating the Files

Before you begin using HTML Help Workshop, you should plan your Help system and create the files that must be created with an editor. Create all the topic files and the Map file. If you plan to implement WhatsThisHelp, you also need to create its topic file. WhatsThisHelp is covered later, after the tutorial for the Help facility and context-sensitive Help.

Creating a Help Facility and Context-Sensitive Help— Step by Step

For this tutorial you can design and create your own HTML pages, or you can use the pages supplied on your text CD in the folder *Ch13SBS/HTML*. Figure 13.5 shows the completed Help facility, and Figure 13.6 shows the Dispensary topic page with two additional links.

F i g u r e   1 3 . 5

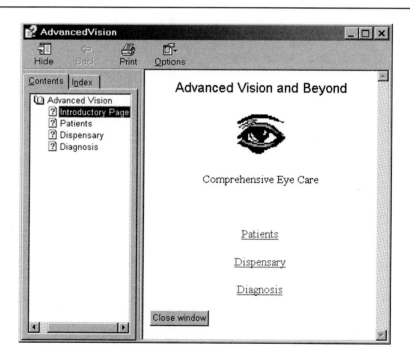

The completed Help facility for the step-by-step tutorial.

Before you begin the tutorial, make sure that you have HTML Help Workshop on your system. If not, refer to "HTML Help Workshop" earlier in this chapter.

Begin the Project

STEP 1: Locate the Ch13SBS folder on your text CD and copy it to a diskette or the hard drive. Examine the files. You should have VB project and form files and an Html folder holding six .htm files.

Figure 13.6

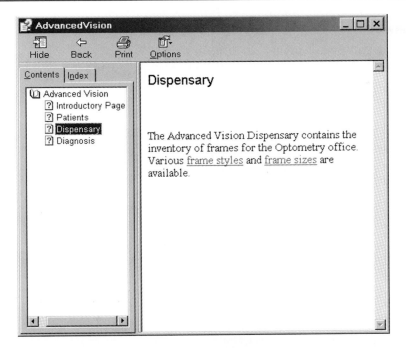

The Dispensary topic has links to two additional pages. These linked pages are included in the Help project but do not appear in the Contents.

Create the Map File

STEP 1: Use Notepad, Word, or a text editor of your choice to create this Map file. The Map file defines a unique identifier for each topic that you want to connect to a VB object and gives a numeric Topic ID to each.

```
#define IDH_DEFAULT 10
#define IDH_PATIENT 20
#define IDH_DISPENSARY 30
#define IDH_DIAGNOSIS 40
```

Note that the prefix, *IDH_*, is a Windows standard. The prefix isn't required, but if you use it, the HTML Help Workshop checks to make sure that there are no missing associations.

STEP 2: Take care when you save this file. Its name should be Context.h, and its file type must be text. If you are using Notepad, for *Files of type* select *All files (*.*)*; otherwise, Notepad will add .txt to the filename. If you are using Word, for *Save as type* select *Text Only*. Save the file in the Html folder.

Begin a Project in the Workshop

STEP 1: Open HTML Help Workshop.

STEP 2: Select *New* from the *File* menu. Notice that several components are listed; choose *Project*. Click OK.

STEP 3: On the first wizard screen, click Next.

STEP 4: On the New Project Destination screen, use the Browse button to locate the Html folder beneath your project folder; name the file AdvancedVision. (The wizard will add the extension .hhp). Click Next.

STEP 5: On the Existing Files screen, select *HTML files (.htm).* Click Next.

> *Note:* You can choose to add the files now, with the wizard, or wait and add them later.

STEP 6: On the HTML Files screen, click Add. You can add all .htm files at once: Click on the first filename, shift-click on the last one (to select them all), and click Open. Back on the HTML Files screen, you should see all six files. Click Next.

STEP 7: On the final wizard screen, click Finish. You will see a listing of the beginnings of your project file.

STEP 8: Take a look at the menus and buttons (Figure 13.7). The buttons down the left edge of the window change, depending on which tab is displayed. You will see this feature later as we create Contents and Index tabs.

Figure 13.7

The HTML Help Workshop window, showing the entries in the project file.

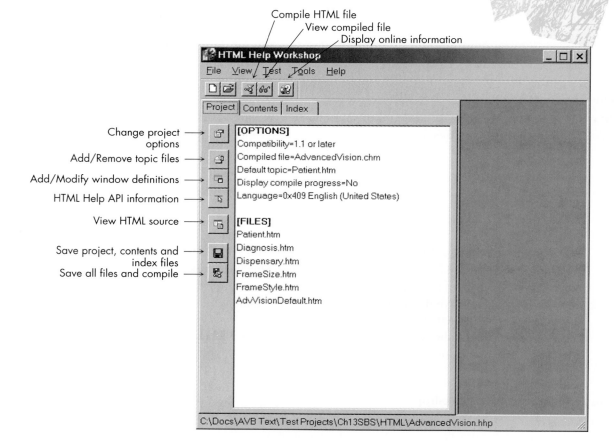

Set up the Topic IDs and Aliases

In this section you associate the topic identifiers and Topic IDs with the actual HTML pages. Recall that in the Map file you set up unique identifiers and

517

Topic IDs. Now you will set up an alias for each topic. In HTML Help, a topic is known by its identifier. In the VB program you refer to the Topic ID, which points to the identifier, which points to the actual HTML topic file.

Map File		Alias	
Identifier	**Topic ID**	**Identifier**	**HTML File**
IDH_DEFAULT	10	IDH_DEFAULT	AdvVisionDefault.htm
IDH_PATIENT	20	IDH_PATIENT	Patient.htm
IDH_DISPENSARY	30	IDH_DISPENSARY	Dispensary.htm
IDH_DIAGNOSIS	40	IDH_DIAGNOSIS	Diagnosis.htm

STEP 1: Click on the HtmlHelp API Information button. The dialog box has tabs for Map, Alias, and Text Pop-ups.

STEP 2: On the Map tab, click on the Header file button and add *Context.h*, the Map file that you created earlier.

Note that you could include multiple Map files.

STEP 3: Switch to the Alias tab and click the Add button. Type in the first identifier, *IDH_DEFAULT*, and drop down the list for the HTML file. Choose *AdvVisionDefault.htm*.

STEP 4: Refer to the alias list before step 1 and enter the aliases for IDH_PATIENT, IDH_DISPENSARY, and IDH_DIAGNOSIS (Figure 13.8). Click OK to close the dialog box.

Notice the new [Alias] and [Map] sections in your project header (Figure 13.9).

F i g u r e   1 3 . 8

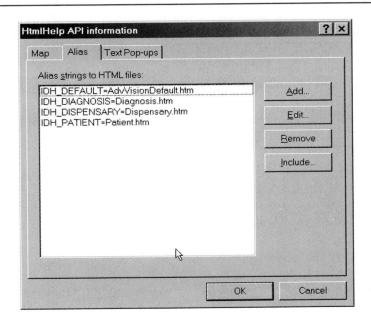

Add an alias for each topic.

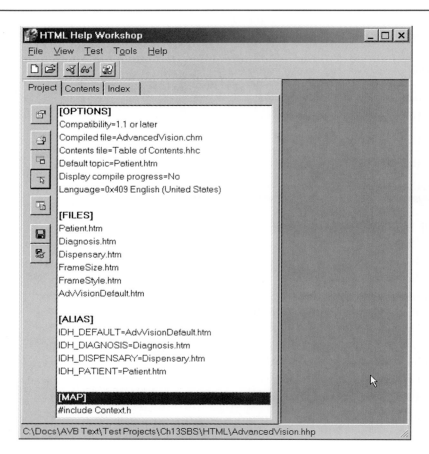

Create the Table of Contents

STEP 1: Switch to the Contents tab. On the next dialog box, select the option to create a new Contents file and then accept the default name: *Table of Contents.hhc.* Click Save.

STEP 2: Notice that a different set of buttons displays (Figure 13.10). Click on Contents properties and view the General tab.

STEP 3: Deselect the option to *Use folders instead of books* (if it is selected). Notice also that you can supply your own images—one for the closed state and one for the open state. Click OK.

STEP 4: Click on *Insert a heading* and enter the title that you want to display for the first heading icon: *Advanced Vision.* Click on Add and select the topic AdvVisionDefault. Click OK, and OK again to return to the Contents tab.

STEP 5: Click on *Insert a page* and answer No to the query asking whether you want the new entry to go at the beginning. The new entry will then go after your heading entry. Enter *Introductory Page* and add the AdvVisionDefault topic.

STEP 6: Add an entry for *Patients,* selecting the Patient topic.

STEP 7: Add an entry for *Dispensary,* selecting the Dispensary topic.

STEP 8: Add an entry for *Diagnosis,* selecting the Diagnosis topic.
        The table of contents should be complete.

Figure 13.10

Create the Table of Contents on the Contents tab.

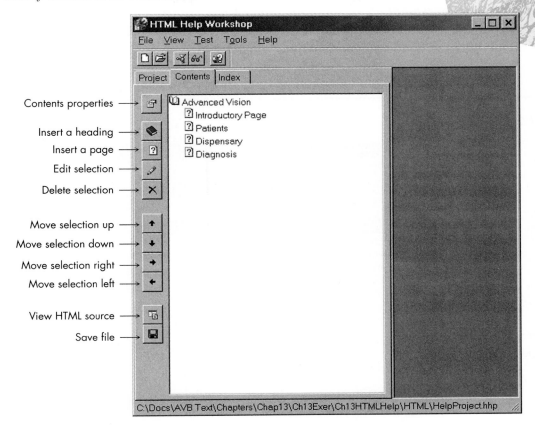

Create the Index

The index takes some planning. You should select words that a person would be apt to search for; it sometimes takes a little creativity to think of topics that people might enter. However, you don't want to clutter the index by including every word in the Help file. One page may have multiple entries in the index.

STEP 1: Click on the Index tab and select the option to create a new index file. Accept the default name *Index.hhk*. Notice that the buttons have changed for the Index tab.

STEP 2: Click on *Insert a keyword* and enter the word *patient*, which will display in the index. Click on the Add button and select the Patient topic file.

If more pages refer to the patient keyword, you can add them now. (In this case, none do.) Click OK and OK again to return to the Index tab.

STEP 3: The Patient topic could use some more keywords in the index: Add *insurance company; name* (or "name, two-word") and *policy number* keywords, each referring to Patient.

Note that the order of entry is not important. The Workshop knows how to sort.

STEP 4: Add the keyword *diagnosis* that refers to the Diagnosis topic.

STEP 5: Add the keyword *dispensary* that refers to the Dispensary topic.

STEP 6: Add the keyword *frames* that refers to the FrameStyle topic. Then add a second topic to the same keyword. Select the FrameSize topic.

STEP 7: Examine the buttons and notice that you can edit or delete an entry, as well as move an entry up, down, left, or right (Figure 13.11), to create hierarchical relationships.

Figure 13.11

The index keywords in the Index tab.

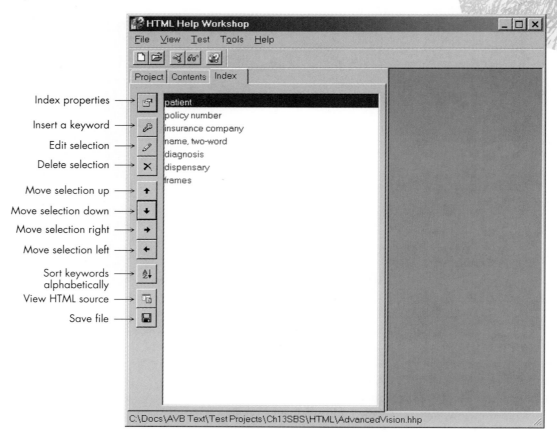

STEP 8: Click the Sort button to sort in alphabetic order.

The index should be finished now. You can always add more entries later.

Compile the Help Facility

STEP 1: Switch back to the Project tab and click the *Save all files and compile* button from the left. The Workshop compiles the file and displays statistics in the right pane (Figure 13.12). You may want to widen the pane a little to view the results. If the compiler detects any problems with missing or misspelled files or links, it displays error diagnostics in the right pane. No error diagnostics means a clean compile, and we are ready to connect this file to the VB project.

Figure 13.12

The compiler displays any error diagnostic messages and statistics.

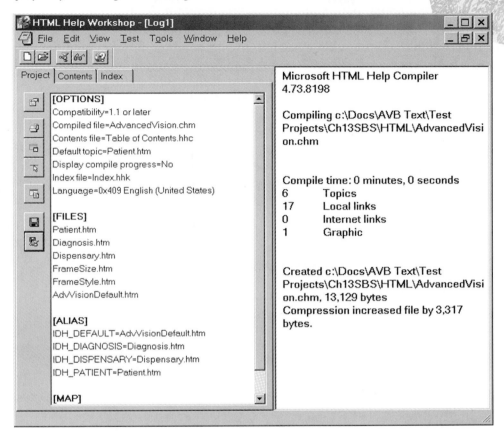

If you have any error diagnostic messages, you must locate them, fix them, and recompile. When you do, you will be prompted to save the Log file. Accept the defaults.

View and Test the Help Facility

STEP 1: Click on the View compiled file toolbar button (the glasses) or select *View/Compiled Help File.* Your Help file should open in a new window.

STEP 2: Test the entries in the Contents tab and the Index tab. Test each link on the pages to make sure that they work.

If a link doesn't work, you may have to return to the HTML editor and correct a page. Any time you change a page or any entry, *you must recompile the Help project.*

When you are finished, close the viewer window and return to the main window with the Project tab displayed.

Add Navigation Using the ActiveX Control

The HTML Help Workshop comes with a control, called the *HTML Help ActiveX control,* which you can add to Web pages.

STEP 1: In the [Files] section of the main window, double-click on AdvVisionDefault.htm, which opens the page in the HTML editor.

STEP 2: Look at the tags and text and scroll down to the bottom of the file.

STEP 3: Click just before the closing </HTML> tag and verify that you have an insertion point rather than selected text.

STEP 4: Double-click on the HTML Help ActiveX Control button on the toolbar, which starts a wizard. Drop down the list for commands and notice the many choices. Select *Close window* and click Next.

STEP 5: Select *As a button* and click Next.

STEP 6: On the Button Options screen, choose to display text on the button and enter *Close window* for the text. Click Next and then Finish.

STEP 7: Notice in the HTML editor window that code has been added for an object. Save and compile again. (Any time you change *anything*, you must recompile.)

STEP 8: View your compiled Help file again. After you are sure that everything else works, test the new button on the introductory page.

STEP 9: Close the HTML Help Workshop.

Connecting the HTML Help File to an Application

To activate F1 Help for your VB project, all you have to do is set the **HelpFile property** of the App object to the Help's Chm file. You can do this step in one of two places—either on the *Project Properties* dialog box or in code. It's easier to set the property at design time in the *Project Properties* dialog box, but setting the property in code gives you the flexibility to set the path and to select different files in different situations.

Open the VB Project File

STEP 1: Open the HTMLHelp VB project in the Ch13SBS folder. Note that all Help files should be in the Html folder, and only the VB files should be in the Ch13SBS folder.

Connect the Help File for F1 Help

STEP 1: Open the *Project Properties* dialog box and notice the entry for Help File Name. Click the Build button, drop down the Files of type list, and select *HtmlHelp Files (*.chm)*. Then browse for your Chm file and close the *Help File* dialog box. Notice that the entire path is included for filename. Delete the path, all except the Html folder and filename. The entry should read *HTML\AdvancedVision.chm* (no leading backslash).

For the alternative method, you can add this line of code to the Form_Load event procedure:

```
App.HelpFile = App.Path & "HTML\AdvancedVision.chm"
```

Note that if you assign the HelpFile property in code, that action overrides any setting made at design time.

STEP 2: Run the program and press F1. Your Help screen should pop up.

Tip

If you have a problem displaying the compiled Help file from your VB application, try this: With Windows Explorer, double-click on the AdvancedVision.chm file. The file should open and will likely work in VB after this step.

Display Help from a Menu Command

To display HTML Help from a menu command, you will add a control to the project.

STEP 1: Open the *Components* dialog box and choose *hhOpen OLE Control Module.* The control will appear in the toolbox.

> *Note:* This control should be installed and registered with HTML Help Workshop. If you don't have it, you can find it on the text CD. You can also display HTML Help using a Windows API function instead of the HhOpen control. See the project Ch13HTMLHelpAPI on the text CD.

STEP 2: Add an instance of the HhOpen control to the form. This control will be invisible at run time.

STEP 3: Write the code to display Help from the menu.

```
Private Sub mnuHelpContents_Click()
    'Display the default page in the Help system
    Dim strHelpFile As String

    strHelpFile = App.Path & "\Html\AdvancedVision.chm"
    Hhopen1.OpenHelp strHelpFile, "AdvVisionDefault.htm"
End Sub
```

STEP 4: Run the project and select *Contents and Index* from the *Help* menu. Your Help system should display.

Connecting Context-Sensitive Help

Recall that you gave each Help topic a Topic ID. You can associate each Topic ID with a form or control in your project. Then when the user selects the object and presses F1, Help displays the correct topic.

> *Note:* If the Topic ID is invalid, no Help displays.

Set the HelpContextIDs for Context-Sensitive Help

STEP 1: In design time set the **HelpContextID property** of the following objects. This step associates each object with a particular topic in the Help file.

Object	HelpContextID Property
form	10
cmdPatient	20
cmdDispensary	30
cmdDiagnosis	40

STEP 2: Run the project. To test context-sensitive Help, you must point to a control or the form, press the mouse button (and keep it down), and press F1. Then you can move the mouse pointer off the object if you wish. Help should always open to the correct topic.

Tip

Close the Help project in HTML Help Workshop when you are working on a VB project and close the VB project when you are working in the Workshop. One application cannot work on the file if the other is using it.

Modifying Help Files

You can modify the Help Web pages, add pages to Help, and change the organization of the Help project. You must always remember to recompile after any change. The compiled Help Chm file holds the HTML pages in compressed form. When Help displays, only those compressed pages display, not the individual HTML pages. When you distribute an application, only the Chm file is needed, not the many files that make up the Help project.

WhatsThisHelp

You cannot implement both context-sensitive Help and WhatsThisHelp at the same time. Turning on WhatsThisHelp turns off context-sensitive Help.

The Help files produced by the current version of HTML Help Workshop do not handle WhatsThisHelp correctly. It almost works, but not quite. We hope that by the time you read this chapter, a new version will correct the problem. (As of this writing, version 1.22 is current.) You need to know a little about implementing WhatsThisHelp for the MCSD exam.

Create a Topic File

The first step in creating WhatsThisHelp is to create a Topic file by using a text editor. You create one entry in the Topic file for each object that should have pop-up WhatsThisHelp. Give each topic a unique Topic ID, which is different from the Topic IDs you used for the Help topics. Then write one line of text to pop up.

The format for the WhatsThisHelp Topic file looks like this:

```
.Topic 100
Advanced Vision and Beyond Helpful Application
.Topic 200
Enter patient information.
.Topic 300
Select the frame size and frame style.
.Topic 400
View the standard codes for diagnoses.
```

Save the file with a .txt extension in the same folder as your Help files.

You must add the WhatsThisHelp Topic file to the Help project in HTML Help Workshop. Add the filename to the [Files] list. (Even though the dialog box seems to accept only .htm files, enter the entire filename and .txt extension and it will be accepted.) Save and recompile the Help file and close the Workshop.

To connect the WhatsThisHelp to the VB project, you must do these things:

● Set the App.HelpFile property in code, adding the second filename:

```
Private Sub Form_Load()
    'Set up the file for WhatsThisHelp

    App.HelpFile = App.Path & "\Html\AdvancedVision.chm::WhatsThis.txt"
End Sub
```

● Set the form's WhatsThisHelp property to True (this option turns off context-sensitive Help and enables WhatsThisHelp).

● Set the WhatsThisHelpID property of each control for which you want to pop up a Help topic. Use the IDs that you created in the Topic file.

Object	Value for WhatsThisHelpID
cmdPatient	200
cmdDispensary	300
cmdDiagnosis	400

● Write code to turn on WhatsThisHelp.

```
Private Sub mnuHelpWhatsThis_Click()
    'Turn on WhatsThisMode

    Me.WhatsThisMode
End Sub
```

Try It

You can try this and see it work (sort of, in the current version). Run the VB project, select the *Help/Whats This* menu command, and use the question-mark pointer to point to a control and click. If you are lucky, the message will pop up on top of the form. Or it may pop up behind the form (that's the bug). If you see an hourglass pointer instead of the pop-up text, look at the Windows taskbar—you should have an extra button. Right-click on the extra taskbar button to bring the pop-up message to the front.

Note: If you receive a message that the Help file can't be opened, make sure that HTML Help Workshop is closed and check the code line in Form_Load very carefully.

Adding a WhatsThisHelp Button

You can add the WhatsThisHelp button to the window's title bar (Figure 13.13). The user can invoke Help from the button without any code in the program. To display the button, set the form's WhatsThisButton property to True. For the button to display, you must also set the form's ControlBox property to True and set one of these conditions:

BorderStyle property = Fixed Dialog.

or

MinButton and MaxButton = False and BorderStyle = Fixed Single or Sizeable.

Other Forms of User Assistance

Good programs provide assistance to the user. In this chapter you learned about providing Help, context-sensitive Help, and WhatsThisHelp. You can also provide helpful information using ToolTips and status bars. You might consider

Figure 13.13

WhatsThisHelp button

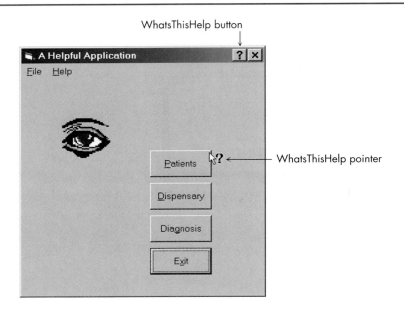

WhatsThisHelp pointer

Display the WhatsThisHelp button on the title bar. When the user clicks the button, the pointer changes to the WhatsThisHelp pointer.

showing the formula for a calculation in a ToolTip, as well as instructions for data entry. Instructions in status bars can be very useful and unobtrusive. It's a good idea to use the MouseOver event of controls to change the message in a status bar; then use the MouseOver event of the form to reset the status bar text.

Feedback 13.1

1. Give the file type and purpose of each of the following file extensions.
   (a) .hhk
   (b) .hhc
   (c) .chm
   (d) .jpeg
   (e) .avi
   (f) .htm
   (g) .chm
2. List five types of user assistance that can be added to an application.

MCSD Exam Notes

Exam Objectives Covered in This Chapter

Implement Online User Assistance in a Desktop Application
- Set appropriate properties to enable user assistance. Help properties include HelpFile, HelpContextID, and WhatsThisHelp.

- Create HTML Help for an application.

Questions/Tricks to Watch for

● If an invalid value is given for HelpContextId, no Help will be displayed.

S u m m a r y

1. Windows supports Help files in the WinHelp format and HTML Help.
2. The HelpFile can be assigned to the VB project at design time or run time.
3. HTMLHelp combines topic files (HTML pages), graphics and multimedia files, contents files, and index files into a Help project. The compiled file has the extension .chm.
4. ToolTips and status bars can also be considered parts of an application's Help system.

K e y   T e r m s

alias *512*	HTML Help Image Editor *510*
Help Topic *512*	HTML Help Java Applet *510*
Help Viewer *510*	HTML Help Workshop *510*
HelpFile property *522*	Map file *512*
HelpContextID property *523*	Topic ID *513*
HTML Help *570*	WinHelp *510*
HTML Help ActiveX control *510*	

R e v i e w   Q u e s t i o n s

1. How is each Help topic defined in HTML Help?
2. Explain how the Map file and aliases are used together and what they accomplish.
3. How is the Help file connected to a VB project for F1 Help?
4. How do you connect individual forms and controls to specific Help topics?
5. What Help file(s) must be distributed with a VB application?
6. What is WhatsThisHelp?

P r o g r a m m i n g   E x e r c i s e s

13.1 Use Word or any HTML editor to create Web pages about your favorite hobbies or sports. Include at least one image.

Assemble and compile the file by using HTML Help Workshop.

Add the Help file to a small VB project.

13.2   Add an HTML Help to any of your previous projects. Include appropriate help topic files and a Map file for the Topic IDs. Include a Table of Contents and an Index. Display the Help from a menu option under a Help menu in your application.

C A S E   S T U D I E S

Video Bonanza

Create an HTML Help file to explain how to locate a video. Add the Help facility to the Help Menu in one of the projects you have created for Video Bonanza. Add other topics as you wish, creating a topic file and a Topic ID in the Map file for each entry. Create a Table of Contents and an Index.

VB Auto

Create an HTML Help file to explain how to look up an automobile. Add the Help facility to the Help menu in one of the projects you have created for VB Auto. Add other topics as you wish, creating a topic file and a Topic ID in the Map file for each entry. Create a Table of Contents and an Index.

14

Distributing Your Applications and Components

At the completion of this chapter, you will be able to . . .

1. Create .cab distribution files.

2. Select the Internet, networks, CDs, or diskettes as media for distribution.

3. Understand which files can be legally distributed.

4. Differentiate between packaging and deployment.

5. Use a wizard to package and deploy applications.

6. Test a setup process.

7. Manually create a setup file (.lst).

8. Create uninstall procedures.

9. Deploy localized ActiveX controls.

10. License an ActiveX control.

You might think that you can compile your VB project to an Exe file, copy it to another computer, and run it there. And maybe you can if the destination computer has all the VB support files and components that your project needs. A VB Exe cannot run without these support files. The Package and Deployment Wizard can determine which files are needed and create a package that you can use to install your project on other computers.

In this chapter you will learn how to distribute applications and components. As the developer, you can choose to distribute applications on floppy disks or CDs, to a network, or by making them downloadable from a Web site. You can use the Package and Deployment Wizard or set up the distribution manually with the Setup Toolkit. For most applications the wizard works fine; the toolkit is more flexible than the wizard and provides additional options.

The Package and Deployment Wizard

After you create and compile an application, you can distribute copies for installation on other systems running Microsoft Windows. You have several choices for media—you can distribute an application on floppy disks, a CD, a network, or the Web.

To distribute the application, you must **package** it and then deploy it. Packaging is the process of assembling all the files needed to run the application and creating a compressed file, called a cabinet or **.cab** file. The .cab file holds all necessary files and a Setup program. Copying the package to the media or location from which you want to distribute the application is called *deployment.* The VB Package and Deployment Wizard can walk you through the entire process.

One way to run the Package and Deployment Wizard is to load it from the Add-in Manager in the VB environment. You can also run from the desktop by using the Windows *Start/Programs* menu. Under either the *Visual Basic 6.0* menu or *Microsoft Visual Studio 6.0/Microsoft Visual Studio 6.0 Tools,* you will find an option for *Package and Deployment Wizard.* One other alternative is to run an existing script from the DOS prompt; this *silent mode* is used when you want to rerun a script without having to respond to the wizard's prompts.

If you run the wizard from the *Add-Ins* menu in the VB environment, the wizard assumes that you want to package the current project and does not give you the option of choosing a different project. If you are working on a multi-project group, make sure to select the project you want before beginning the wizard.

The wizard offers three initial choices: *Package, Deploy,* and *Manage Scripts* (Figure 14.1). The *Package* option asks questions to determine which files are needed in the distribution package. *Deploy* walks you through the transfer of the package to the desired media. Each time you use the wizard, it creates a script that records the choices you made. The *Manage Scripts* option allows you to modify or reuse existing scripts.

Packaging an Application

You can create a **standard package,** which can be used for all types of deployment except through the Web, or an **Internet package,** which can be

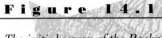

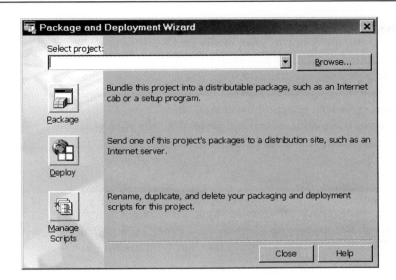

The initial screen of the Package and Deployment Wizard. The Browse button does not appear if you open the wizard from the Add-Ins menu of the VB environment.

distributed over the Internet. You can also create a **dependency file,** which contains dependency information needed by components, such as ActiveX Dlls, Exes, and controls. If you want to package both a component that you have written and an application using the component, you should first create a dependency file for the component and then package the application. If you attempt to first package the application, the wizard will not be able to find the dependency information that it needs for the component, and you'll have to back up and restart.

Files That Can Be Distributed

You can legally distribute all executable files (.exe), controls (.ocx), and components (.dll) that you have created. Microsoft also allows you to include any icons that were distributed with your edition of VB. With the Professional and Enterprise editions, you are also allowed to include any Microsoft graphics files (from \Visual Studio\Common\Graphics) or the ODBC files (in \Program Files\Common Files\ODBC subdirectory).

If your application needs any other controls or components, you must have permission from the author. Check the license agreement for any third-party items that you have purchased.

VB requires several files for an application to run, including Msvbvm60.dll, Stdole2.tlb, Oleaut32.dll, Olepro32.dll, Comcat.dll, Asyncfilt.dll, and Ctl3d32.dll. The Package and Deployment Wizard includes these for you if they are needed.

Creating a Package

STEP 1: Create an executable file (Exe) for the application you want to distribute. Or you can wait—the wizard will prompt you to create one.

STEP 2: Start the wizard, preferably from the Windows *Start/Programs* menu. Depending on how the programs were installed on your system, you'll find the Package and Deployment Wizard under either *Microsoft Visual Basic 6.0 Tools* or *Microsoft Visual Studio 6.0 Tools.*

STEP 3: Select the project to distribute, using the Browse button to find the file (refer again to Figure 14.1). (If you are using the Add-in Manager, the project is already listed and there is no Browse button. If the correct project isn't listed, you'll have to exit, select the correct project, and restart.)

STEP 4: Click on the big Package button in the left section of the dialog box. If you haven't compiled to an Exe, or compiled more recently than the changes to your source files, the wizard prompts you to compile (Figure 14.2).

The Package and Deployment Wizard prompts you to compile your project or browse to find the Exe file.

STEP 5: Depending on whether the wizard has run on this computer before, you may see a Packaging Script list; choose *NONE* and click on Next.

STEP 6: On the *Package Type* dialog box, select *Standard Setup Package* (Figure 14.3) and click Next. If you were packaging a component, rather than a stand-alone program, you would choose *Dependency File* instead.

Select Standard Setup Package from the Package Type dialog box.

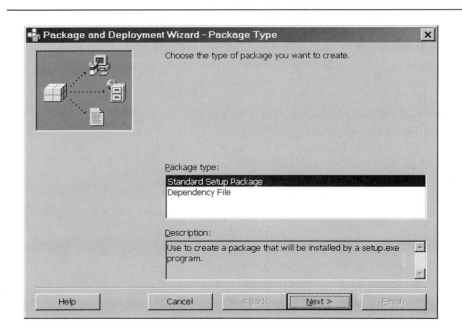

STEP 7: On the *Package Folder* dialog box, select *New Folder* and create one called *Package*. (This process uses a lot of memory, and you may want to delete your package easily.) Click Next.

STEP 8: The wizard attempts to determine the files necessary for distribution and displays the list in the *Included Files* dialog box (Figure 14.4). The list includes all dependent files, your Exe, and the files that VB needs. You can also add files at this point. For example, the wizard cannot determine that you need to include a database file, but you can add it yourself. Take a look at the list and click Next.

Figure 14.4

The wizard displays all the files needed to package your application. You can add and remove files if needed.

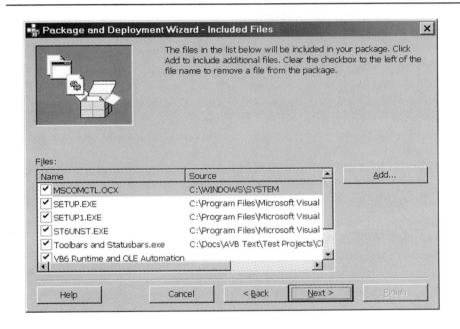

STEP 9: On the *Cab Options* dialog box, you can choose how to create the .cab file(s). If you want to distribute on floppy disks, you must have multiple .cab files, each one fitting in 1.44 MB, so click the *Multiple cab* option. If you plan to distribute on CDs or a network, choose *Single cab*. Click Next.

STEP 10: On the *Installation Title* dialog box, enter the title that should appear when users run your setup program. Click Next.

STEP 11: The *Start Menu Items* dialog box allows you to decide where the application will appear on your user's *Start* menu (Figure 14.5). Accept the defaults and click Next.

STEP 12: In the *Install Locations* dialog box, you can control the location of each installation file. The ones listed are the standard locations for Microsoft systems. Click Next.

STEP 13: You now specify whether your files will be considered shared files. If the user uninstalls your application, shared files may not be deleted. Click Next.

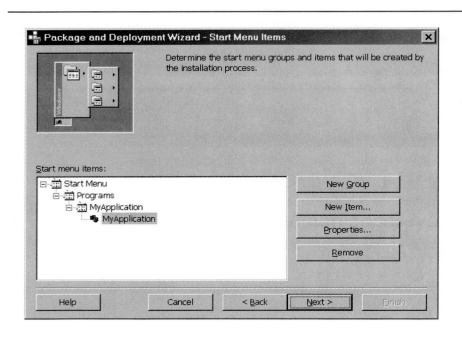

*Select the location on the Start
menu that you want your
application to appear.*

STEP 14: The final screen in the wizard enables you to name the script. The choices you just made can be saved and used again. Click Finish, and the wizard creates the .cab file(s).

After you create your distribution package, take a look at the contents of your Package folder. You will see a setup application (Setup.exe), Setup.lst, and the Cab file(s). There is also a folder called *Support* to hold the dependency files.

Deployment

Once you have created the distribution package, you can copy the files for distribution or you may opt to have the wizard do it for you.

Deploying Your Application

STEP 1: Select the large Deploy button from the Package and Deployment Wizard.

STEP 2: On the *Package to Deploy* dialog box, a list of scripts appears; select the one for your application and click Next.

STEP 3: Decide on your deployment method: floppy disks, folder (for a network install), or Web publishing (Figure 14.6).

- Floppy disk: The next dialog box asks for the drive name to which the files will be copied.

- Folder: The next dialog box checks for a folder for installation. Use this option also for CDs and then write to the CD from the folder.

- Web: The next two dialog boxes ask which files you want to deploy and then request a URL.

STEP 4: The final screen allows you to give a name to your deployment script.

After the deployment the wizard displays a report of the copied files, which you can optionally save. Note that you don't have to use the wizard for deployment; you could copy the files yourself to the floppy disk, CD, or network folder.

Packaging an Application with ActiveX Components

If the project you want to package has an ActiveX class module, such as a Dll, Exe, or a control, you must go through the wizard twice. Otherwise it will tell you that it doesn't have dependency information for the component. First select the class module and choose Dependency File. After you complete the wizard steps for the component, package the main application as you did above. The wizard will find the dependency information and the entire application, including the component, will be packaged together.

You can also package and distribute just the component. When the user runs Setup, the component is copied to the selected location and automatically registered on the system.

Managing Scripts

The option on the wizard for managing scripts has tabs for Packaging Scripts and Deployment Scripts. Command buttons allow you to Rename, Duplicate, Delete, or Close.

Testing Setup

After you complete the packaging and deployment of your application, you need to test the Setup program. You should perform the test on a system that *does not* have VB installed to be certain that all critical files are present.

Make sure to test running the Setup program and then actually running the application.

Uninstalling an Application

The VB Setup program places a file called *St6unst.log* in the folder where the application is installed. The log file keeps track of information for uninstalling the application from the Windows *Add/Remove Programs* option.

The log file tracks directories created for installation, files installed, which files are shared, Registry entries, links, startup menus, and any self-registered files. Windows maintains a count for each shared file. As programs are removed, the count is reduced by one. Theoretically, Windows will prompt you to remove the file when the count reaches zero.

If the installation fails, the application's uninstall runs automatically.

Feedback 14.1

1. Explain the difference between packaging and deployment.
2. Which of the following files can be legally included for distribution?
   (a) .exe
   (b) .ocx
   (c) .dll
   (d) Eye.ico
   (e) Msvbvm60.dll

Manually Creating a Setup File

The Package and Deployment Wizard uses a program called the Setup Toolkit. The toolkit generates the Setup.exe for preinstall steps, which then executes the Setup1.exe files. You can modify the Setup1.exe or the Setup.lst file.

Setup1.Exe

You can use the Setup Toolkit to modify the screens the user sees when running the Setup program. This feature is useful if you have files that are optional for installation. For example, when you install VB, you can choose whether or not to add the graphics features; they are not automatically included in the install files.

Setup.lst

The Setup.lst file contains a list of all files needed to install an application along with information about where the file should be installed and how it is to be registered. A listing of the file will display five sections: Bootstrap, Bootstrap Files, IconGroups, Setup, and Setup1 Files. Additional comment lines are included at the end for customization.

Setup.lst Example

```
[Bootstrap]
SetupTitle=Install
SetupText=Copying Files, please stand by.
CabFile=Grid1.CAB
Spawn=Setup1.exe
Uninstal=st6unst.exe
TmpDir=msftqws.pdw
Cabs=7

[Bootstrap Files]
File1=@VB6STKIT.DLL,$(WinSysPathSysFile),,,6/18/98 12:00:00 AM,102912,6.0.81.69
File2=@COMCAT.DLL,$(WinSysPathSysFile),$(DLLSelfRegister),,5/31/98 12:00:00
AM,22288,4.71.1460.1
File3=@STDOLE2.TLB,$(WinSysPathSysFile),$(TLBRegister),,6/2/98 3:46:22
PM,17920,2.30.4261.1
File4=@ASYCFILT.DLL,$(WinSysPathSysFile),,,6/2/98 6:24:06 PM,147728,2.30.4261.1
File5=@OLEPRO32.DLL,$(WinSysPathSysFile),$(DLLSelfRegister),,6/2/98 6:24:08
PM,164112,5.0.4261.1
File6=@OLEAUT32.DLL,$(WinSysPathSysFile),$(DLLSelfRegister),,6/2/98 6:24:04
PM,598288,2.30.4261.1
File7=@MSVBVM60.DLL,$(WinSysPathSysFile),$(DLLSelfRegister),,6/25/98 12:00:00
AM,1409024,6.0.81.76

[IconGroups]
Group0=Grid
PrivateGroup0=True
Parent0=$(Programs)

[Grid]
Icon1="Grid.EXE"
Title1=Grid
StartIn1=$(AppPath)

[Setup]
Title=Grid
DefaultDir=$(ProgramFiles)\Project1
AppExe=Grid.EXE
AppToUninstall=Grid.EXE

[Setup1 Files]
File1=@MDAC_TYP.EXE,$(AppPath),,,6/26/98 12:00:00 AM,8124720,4.71.1015.0
File2=@MSSTDFMT.DLL,$(WinSysPath),$(DLLSelfRegister),$(Shared),6/18/98 12:00:00
AM,118784,6.0.81.69
File3=@MSBIND.DLL,$(WinSysPath),$(DLLSelfRegister),$(Shared),6/18/98 12:00:00
AM,77824,6.0.81.69
```

continued

```
File4=@MSDATGRD.OCX,$(WinSysPath),$(DLLSelfRegister),$(Shared),6/24/98 12:00:00
AM,260920,6.0.81.69
File5=@MSADODC.OCX,$(WinSysPath),$(DLLSelfRegister),$(Shared),6/24/98 12:00:00
AM,118064,6.0.81.71
File6=@Grid.exe,$(AppPath),,,5/3/99 9:30:06 AM,20480,1.0.0.0

; The following lines may be deleted in order to obtain extra
; space for customizing this file on a full installation diskette.
;
; XXXXXXXXXXXXXXXXXXXXXXXXXXXXXXXXXXXXXXXXXXXXXXXXXXXXXXXXXX
; XXXXXXXXXXXXXXXXXXXXXXXXXXXXXXXXXXXXXXXXXXXXXXXXXXXXXXXXXX
```

The name of the main Setup program, the name of a temporary directory used during installation, uninstall directions, and the text for installation instructions are listed in the Bootstrap section. Files needed for installation are in the Bootstrap Files section. All other files that are needed to run the application are in the Setup1 Files section. Any information that may be required by the programs in the Setup1 Files section is stored in the Setup section.

Manual Distribution

You can create the distribution media without using the wizard. For a CD, just copy the packaged files. For a network, the files must be copied to the proper locations. If the package is for the Internet, the files need to be copied to the appropriate Web site. Microsoft has a WebPublishing Wizard in the ActiveX Software Developer's Kit.

Distribution on floppy disks requires a bit more consideration because the sequence of files is important. The first disk must contain the Setup.exe and the Setup.lst files. Next come all files in the Bootstrap Files section, followed by other .cab files. You will probably need several disks.

Feedback 14.2

What is contained in each of the following sections of setup?

1. Bootstrap
2. Bootstrap Files
3. Setup
4. Setup1 Files

Deploying and Licensing Controls

ActiveX controls can be packaged as source code (.ctl file) or compiled (.ocx file). If the control is Public (the Public property is set to True), it can be compiled as part of an ActiveX project file. The .ocx that is generated can then be distributed individually or as part of an application package. The best way to include all required files is to use the Package and Deployment Wizard, which also automatically registers the control.

Another alternative is to include the UserControl code module in a project. When that project is compiled, the control becomes part of the application without the need for an .ocx file. However, the control cannot be updated within the project in the same way as replacing an .ocx with modifications. By including the code module in the project, anyone with access to the project has the ability to modify the source code.

If you distribute a control as an .ocx file, other developers can use the control in applications. This practice raises concerns about licensing and versioning controls. You can require a license key, which keeps the control from being used in a project. In the *Project Properties* dialog box, use the check box for *Require License Key.* This setting causes the license key of the control to be added to the Registry of the user's system at setup. Any time an instance of the control is created, it checks for the key. If someone has a copy of the .ocx file but has not run setup, there will be no Registry key and the component cannot instantiate itself.

When licensed controls are used on the Internet, the browser creates a runtime instance and passes the license key. If the license is not available, the control cannot be created.

A control can be "translated" for use in many languages and is then referred to as a **localized control.** The distribution procedure is the same but also includes a **satellite DLL** containing the translated strings. When making modifications, you must keep the version of the control and the version of the satellite DLL in sync; otherwise, the strings may be incorrect.

The Visual Studio Installer

As of this writing, Microsoft has just announced a new tool for distributing applications, the Microsoft Visual Studio Installer. According to Microsoft the new Installer handles "centralized distribution for maintenance and updates, application self-repair, and powerful installation rollback facilities" and will "reduce the overall cost of distribution." This new application will run on Windows NT, Windows 95, Windows 98, and Windows 2000. The application creates setup programs that work on any 32-bit Windows desktop platform.

MCSD Exam Notes

Exam Objectives Covered in This Chapter

Deploying an Application

- Use the Package and Deployment Wizard to create a Setup program that installs a desktop application, registers the COM components, and allows for uninstall.

- Plan and implement floppy disk–based deployment or CD-based deployment for a desktop application.

- Plan and implement Web-based deployment for a desktop application.

S u m m a r y

1. An application that is going to be distributed is packaged into compressed .cab files and then copied to the distribution media (deployed).
2. The deployment media can be floppy disks, CDs, networks, and the Web.
3. The Package and Deployment Wizard can be loaded with the Add-in Manager or from the Windows *Start/Programs* menu and then used to walk through the process of packaging and deployment.
4. During the packaging phase, the wizard adds all files that are needed to run the program. These include forms, projects, executable files, controls, graphics, databases, and the VB library modules. You can also add and remove files from the list.
5. Scripts are generated for both the packaging and the deployment portions of distribution. These scripts can be reused on later applications or used from the DOS prompt.
6. Always test the Setup program on a machine other than the development computer—one that does not have VB installed.
7. An Uninstall application is created when the Setup program executes.
8. Additional features can be added to the setup process by manually editing the Setup1.exe and the Setup.lst files.
9. The deployment of the files can be done manually. The sequence of files is critical for floppy disks.
10. Controls require consideration about licensing, versioning, and distribution.

K e y   T e r m s

.cab file   *530*
dependency file   *531*
deployment   *530*
Internet package   *530*

localized control   *539*
package   *530*
satellite DLL   *539*
standard package   *530*

R e v i e w   Q u e s t i o n s

1. Define the following terms:
   (a) Deployment
   (b) Packaging
2. What is a .cab file?
3. What does a package consist of?
4. What files can be legally distributed?
5. List and describe the steps in packaging.
6. List and describe the steps in deployment.
7. What media can you use to distribute applications?
8. Describe a wizard script.

9. What does a Setup Toolkit project contain?
10. List and describe the sections in a Setup.lst file.

Programming Exercises

14.1   Select your project from Chapter 13 containing the Help files. Package
       and deploy the application to floppy disks. How would you modify this
       process to distribute your application on a CD? Test your distribution
       disks by installing them on another computer.
14.2   Copy your Dll project from Chapter 8. Rename the folder and run the
       Package and Deployment Wizard. Make sure to create a dependency
       file for the Dll before packaging the application.

CASE STUDIES

Video Bonanza

Create an Exe file for your application from a previous chapter. Package and deploy the application to floppy disks.

VB Auto

Create an Exe file for your application from a previous chapter. Package and deploy the application to a folder on the hard drive.

Creating WinHelp Files

At the completion of this appendix, you will be able to . . .

1. Add Help to a project using the WinHelp format.

2. Create a Topic file using a word processor.

3. Use the Help Workshop to compile Windows Help files.

4. Understand the use of the HelpFile and HelpContextID properties.

5. Set up What's This Help.

To create Help files using the WinHelp format, you create text files with codes and compile the files with a compiler such as **Help Workshop.** Help Workshop is included as a part of Visual Studio and is installed along with Visual C++. If you have only VB installed from Visual Studio on your system, you will not have access to the application. You can also download the file Hcwsetup.exe from Microsoft's Web site.

Creating the Contents of the Help File

You can use a word processor to create the contents of your Help topic file and then save the file in rich text format. Your word processor must be able to insert custom footnotes, allow hidden text, and have single and double underlining capabilities. Individual items in the file are referred to as Help topics and contain text and/or graphics. The topic holds explanatory information in the form of words and/or pictures. Each topic can contain hotspots to link to other topics.

You mark the text by using footnotes and hidden text. Use footnotes to indicate the words or ID to use for the Help topic ID, the topic title, and any keywords for the index. Use hidden text to create links to other topics. The text to be used as a link is underlined (single or double underlines) prior to the hidden text. Single underlines cause a pop-up, frequently used for definitions. Double underlines create a link that jumps to the new topic.

Topics files are stored in rich text format (.rtf), one topic to a page. A topic file can have an unlimited number of topics. You can include multiple topic files when compiling a Help file.

Creating a Topic File

Create a topic in the file for each subject in your Help file.

STEP 1: Open a new file in Word or another word processor that can save in rich text format (.rtf).

STEP 2: Type the following:
Dispensary
The Advanced Vision Dispensary contains the inventory of frames for the Optometry office. A variety of frame styles are available.
Diagnosis
The diagnoses are based on industry numbers. Some are indicated in the table below.
Frame Styles
Frames are available in both Plastic and Metal.

STEP 3: Copy and paste the Diagnosis table from AVB.mdb below the Diagnosis topic.

Code	Description
367.00	Hypermetropia
367.10	Myopia
367.20	Astigmatism
367.40	Presbyopia

Note that you can copy and paste bitmap graphics to your topic file.

STEP 4: Insert a hard page break between the topics (before *Diagnosis* and before *Frame Styles*).

STEP 5: Place the insertion point before *Dispensary* and insert a footnote. Select the option for *Custom mark,* click on the Symbol command button, change the Font to *(normal text)* in the dropdown list, and then select the # sign. Click OK on the *Symbol* dialog box. Click OK on the *Footnote* dialog box.

STEP 6: For the footnote, type the ID that will link to this topic. We'll use *Dispensary.*

STEP 7: Repeat the process for a footnote in front of *Diagnosis* and *Frame Styles.*

STEP 8: Save the Help topic file, setting type to Rich Text Format and naming the document *AVB.*

Tip

Users can jump to a specific location in a topic if you insert a topic ID at that point.

Creating a HotSpot in the Topic File

STEP 1: Position the insertion point immediately after the underlined frame style. Type in the topic ID of the link; do not leave a space.

STEP 2: Select just the characters in the ID and single underline. Hint: Because there is no space, you may find it easier to position your insertion point after the last letter and hold the Shift key while you backspace.

STEP 3: Hide the underlined text. Make sure the text is highlighted; then use *Format/Font* and mark the check box for hidden.

Creating the Contents List

STEP 1: Insert a page break before your first topic. On the first page you can create a list of topics.

STEP 2: Place the word or phrase for your list; for this example, create a link for *Dispensary* and one for *Diagnosis.* Use double underlines on the phrase for the link and then follow it (no space again) with the related topic ID in hidden text. (To set double underlines, select your text, use the *Format/Font* menu option, and use the dropdown list of underline styles.)

Dispensary

Diagnosis

Help File Footnotes

Footnote Symbol	Purpose	Item Displays In
#	Help topic ID	Link, locate topic
$	Topic title	Search results
K	Keyword	Index tab

Compiling the Help Project

You must compile the topic files into a Help file (.hlp). Use Help Workshop to accomplish this.

Help Workshop

From *Start /Programs* select *Microsoft Visual Studio 6.0* and *Microsoft Visual Studio 6.0 Tools.* There you will find *Help Workshop.* Note: If you don't find it on the menu, you may not have installed it with Visual Studio. Help Workshop is installed along with Visual C++.

Because Help Workshop is a separate application, it has its own Help files. See *Help* under *Workshop* for more information on creating .rtf files or compiling your Help files.

Using Help Workshop

STEP 1: Open the Help Workshop program.

STEP 2: From *File/New* select *Project* and click OK.

STEP 3: Give the name *Dispensary* for your .hlp file, placing it in the directory with the application.

STEP 4: Click on the Files command button on the next screen. Click on *Add* and select your .rtf file. Click on OK to close. Note that you can add as many topic files as you want to be compiled into a single Help file.

STEP 5: At the bottom of the window, click on the *Save and Compile* command button.

STEP 6: Any warnings or error messages will appear. Most are quite easy to understand (if you read carefully) and require you to modify the .rtf file and then recompile. This example produces a note stating that table cell borders are not supported. This condition doesn't cause any problem, and we can ignore the warning.

Coding the Visual Basic Program

First you want to create a place in your application for the user to access Help files. The standard location is under a *Help* menu.

To display Help from a VB program, you add a Common Dialog control to the form and use the ShowHelp method. The Common Dialog control has two properties that control how Help is accessed. Set the HelpFile property to the name of the .hlp file and the HelpCommand Property to *cdlHelpContents*. In your menu command's event procedure, assign values to the HelpFile and HelpCommand properties of the Common Dialog control and use the ShowHelp method.

Adding Help to a Project

STEP 1: Open the Advanced Vision project from the hands-on example in Chapter 2.

STEP 2: Add a menu item under *Help* called *Index . . .* preceding the *About* command.

STEP 3: Add a Common Dialog control named *dlgCommon* to the form. You will have to add a reference to the *Microsoft Common Dialog Control 6.0* on the *Components* dialog box.

STEP 4: Type in code for the menu option.

```
Private Sub mnuHelpIndex _Click()
        'Set property values for the Common Dialog and display Help

        dlgCommon.HelpFile = App.Path & "\Dispensary.hlp"
        dlgCommon.HelpCommand = cdlHelpContents
        dlgCommon.ShowHelp 'Display Visual Basic Help contents topic
End Sub
```

STEP 5: Test the Program. Under the *Dispensary* topic try the hotspot for *Frame Styles.*

Help Properties

The code for the ShowHelp method also sets values for the HelpFile and the HelpCommand properties. The HelpFile property is rather obvious in its use. The name of the Help file can be assigned at design time through *Project/Properties*. The Property Page has a dropdown list that allows the developer to specify the file type as WinHelp (.hlp) or HTMLHelp (.chm).

The HelpCommand property specifies the type of display that will appear for the Help window. In this example the value is set to cdlHelpContents to select the Contents tab. Other values are cdlHelpContext for a specific topic and cdlHelpIndex for the Index tab.

Context-Sensitive Help

Have you ever used the F1 key to search for Help on a particular keyword? This feature is called *context-sensitive Help*. The topic that is displayed depends on where the cursor is located at the time the F1 key is pressed. To set the topic ID, use the HelpContextID property. This property exists for your controls as well as the menu items. To invoke context-sensitive Help, you only need to connect a control to a topic ID. If no ID is specified, general Help is displayed. However, an invalid topic ID results in no display for Help.

What's This Help

Another type of Help is *WhatsThisHelp*. Each form has a property for WhatsThisHelp set to False. If you set the property to True and HelpContextIDs have been set, the user will see a pop-up window with the related Help topic.

Feedback

1. What is the difference between a Help topic file and a Help file?
2. Write statements to assign the Property values for HelpFile and HelpCommand for MyHelp.hlp (the Common Dialog is named dlgCommon).
3. How many topic files can be included in a Help file?

Questions/Tricks to Watch for

If an invalid value is given for ContextHelpID, no Help will be displayed.

S u m m a r y

1. Help Workshop is an application for creating Help content files and for compiling the Help files.
2. WinHelp uses a rich text format with footnotes to designate topic IDs, topic titles, and keywords. Hidden text is used for a jump (link) or pop-up.
3. Double underlines create a link to the hidden topic ID, while a single underline generates a pop-up for definitions.
4. A Help project file can contain as many Help topic files as you want, but an application can have only one compiled Help file.
5. The HelpContextID specifies the Help topic for context-sensitive Help.
6. The type of display in WinHelp is determined by the value of the HelpCommand property.
7. The HelpFile can be assigned at design time or run time.

K e y   T e r m s

Help Workshop   *544*

R e v i e w   Q u e s t i o n s

1. How is the Help file connected to a VB project?
2. What is the purpose of Help Workshop?
3. Identify the following file types:
   (a) .rtf
   (b) .hlp
   (c) .cnt
   (d) .htm
   (e) .chm
4. What is *What's This Help*?
5. How is a WinHelp file connected to an application?

Programming Exercises

A.1   Use a word processor to create a rich text file containing contents and topics about your favorite hobbies or sports. Format the text in any color and font that you wish. Include at least one image and one pop-up.

Compile the file with Help Workshop.

Add the code to an application by using the Common Dialog control.

A.2   Add Help to a project that you have already completed.

B

Sequential and Random Data Files

At the completion of this appendix, you will be able to . . .

1. Create data files.

2. Read and write records to disk.

3. Differentiate between sequential and random files.

4. Incorporate fixed-length strings into user-defined data types.

5. Read and write random files.

6. Perform add, delete, and edit operations on random files.

7. Allow the user to input data using the InputBox function.

Data Files

Many computer applications require data to be saved from one run to the next. Some examples are personal tasks, such as budgeting, mailing lists, and sports-team records, and business applications, such as inventory records, customer files, and master files. You are probably already familiar with using a database; this section deals with methods to store and access **data files** on disk.

Data Files and Project Files

In computer terminology anything that you store on a disk or hard disk is given its own unique name and called a **file.** Each of your VB projects requires multiple files—for the forms, standard code modules, and project information. However, the files you will create now are different; they contain actual data, such as names and addresses, inventory amounts, and account balances.

Data File Terminology

The entire collection of data is called a file. The file is made up of **records**—one record for each entity in the file. Each record can be broken down further into **fields** (also called *data elements*). For example, in an employee file, the data for one employee are one record. In a name and address file, the data for one person are a record.

In the name and address file, each person has a last name field, a first name field, address fields, and a phone number field. Each field in a record pertains to the same person. Figure B.1 illustrates a name and address file.

The rows in this data file represent records; the columns represent fields.

Last Name	First Name	Street	City	State	Zip	Phone	Email
Maxwell	Harry	795 W. J Street	Ontario	CA	91764	909-555-1234	
Helm	Jennifer	201 Cortez Way	Pomona	CA	91766	818-555-2222	JHelm@ms.org
Colton	Craig	1632 Granada Place	Pomona	CA	91766	909-555-3333	

A record

A field

The data stored in files are nearly always entered in an organized manner. Records may be stored in account number order, alphabetically by name, by date, or by the sequence in which they are received. One field in the record is the organizing factor for the file (such as account number, name, or date). This field, which is used to determine the order of the file, is called the *record key,* or *key field.*

A key field may be either a string or numeric field. In an employee file, if the records are in order by an employee number, then the employee number is the key field. If the order is based on employee name, then the name is the key field, although key fields are normally unique data items.

File Organizations

The manner in which data are organized, stored, and retrieved is called the *file organization*. Two common file organizations are *sequential* and *random*. In this chapter you will learn to read and write both sequential and random files.

Opening and Closing Data Files

Three steps are necessary to process data files:

1. *Open* the file. Before any data may be placed on the disk or read from the disk, the file must be opened. Generally you will open the file in the Form_Load procedure.
2. *Read* or *write* the data records. You will read or write in a save procedure associated with the data entry form.
3. *Close* the file. You must always close a file when you are finished with it.

The Open Statement—General Form

```
Open "FileName" For {Input|Output|Append|Random} As #FileNumber [Len = RecLength]
```

The **Open statement** elements shown in the braces are the **file mode,** indicating the way in which a file will be accessed. The braces indicate that a choice may be made but that the entry is required. The first three choices are used for sequential files. The FileNumber may be from 1 to 511. The record length can be up to 32,767 characters.

File Mode	Description
Output	Data are output from the project and written on the disk. New data are written at the beginning of the file, overwriting any existing data.
Input	Data are input into the project from the disk. This mode reads data previously stored on the disk.
Append	Data are output from the project and written on the disk. New data are added to the end of the file.
Random	Data can be input or output and records may be accessed in any order.

The Open Statement—Examples

```
Open "A:\DataFile.Dat" For Output As #1
Open "C:\VB6\CHO701\Names" For Input As #2
```

The first example opens a file called *DataFile.Dat* as an output file, calling it file #1. The second example opens a file in the C: drive called *Names* as an input file, calling it file #2.

Remember that a data file must always be opened prior to being used. When a data file is opened, the following actions are taken:

1. The directory is checked for the named file. If the file does not exist, a directory entry is created for this file, with the exception of Input mode, which will cause an error message if the file does not exist.
2. For sequential files a **buffer** is established in memory. A buffer is simply an area of main storage. As the program instructs VB to write data on the disk, the data are actually placed in the buffer. When the buffer is filled, the data are physically written to the disk. The size of the buffer for a random file is the number specified in the Len = clause of the Open statement.
3. A **file pointer** is created and set to the beginning of the file for all modes except Append, in which the pointer is set to the end of the file. The pointer is always updated to indicate the current location in the file.
4. The file is given a **file number** for future reference. Each file used in a project must be assigned a unique number; however, the numbers need not begin with one. After a file is closed, the number may be reused for a different file.

The Close Statement—General Form

```
Close [#filenumber...]
```

The Close Statement—Examples

```
Close #1
Close #1, #2
Close
```

The Close statement terminates processing of a disk file. When used without a file number, all open files are closed. The Close statement performs many housekeeping tasks:

1. Physically writes the last partially filled buffer on the disk (sequential files only). The Write statement places data in the buffer, and the data are written to the disk when the buffer is filled. Generally, the buffer will contain data when the project terminates. Those data must be written to the disk.
2. Writes an end-of-file mark (**EOF**) at the end of the file.
3. Releases the buffer.
4. Releases the file number.

Note: Executing an End statement will automatically close all open files, but you should not rely on this technique. A good rule is to always explicitly Close every file that has been opened in the project.

The FreeFile Function

You must assign a file number to each file you open. For a small project with one or two data files, most programmers assign #1 and #2. But in a larger project, selecting a file number can be a problem. If your code will be part of a larger project with code from other programmers and other libraries, you must make sure to avoid any conflicting file numbers. To solve this problem, you can allow the system to assign the next available file number. Use the FreeFile function to assign the next available file number to your file, and you will never have conflicts.

```
Dim intFileNumber As Integer
intFileNumber = FreeFile 'Get next available file number
Open "FILE.DAT" For Output As #intFileNumber
```

Viewing the Data in a File

You can use the Windows Notepad or WordPad application (or any other text editor) to look at the data in your file. Sequential files appear as text with commas separating the fields. Random data files, however, may contain some strange characters; these represent numeric fields. Numeric data types such as integer, single, and currency are stored in two or four bytes that can be read by a project but look cryptic when displayed by a text editor. When you finish viewing your data file, make sure to exit without saving; your text editor may insert special control characters that will corrupt your file.

Trapping Errors for Data Files

Several errors might occur while you are saving or reading a data file. Use an On Error statement to turn on error trapping and a Select Case or If when testing for possible error conditions.

Sequential File Organization

Sequential files contain data elements that are stored one after another in sequence. When you read the data from the disk, it must be read in the same sequence in which it was written. To read any particular element of data, all preceding elements must first be read.

As data elements are written on disk, string fields are enclosed in quotation marks and the fields are separated by commas. Records are generally terminated by a carriage return character.

A sequential name and address file on the disk might look like this:

"Maxwell", "Harry", "795 W. J. Street", "Ontario", "CA", "91764"<CR>
"Helm", "Jennifer", "201 Cortez Way", "Pomona", "CA", "91766"<CR>
"Colton", "Craig", "1632 Granada Place", "Pomona", "CA", "91766"<EOF>

Writing Data to a Sequential Disk File

Use the **Write # statement** to place data into a sequential data file. Before the Write # statement can be executed, the file must be opened in either Output mode or Append mode. Remember that for Append mode the file pointer is placed at the end of the file. If there are no records, the beginning of the file *is* the end of the file. In Output mode the pointer is placed at the beginning of the file. Use Output mode when you want to create a new file or write over old data.

The list of fields to write may be string expressions, numeric expressions, or both and may be separated by commas or semicolons.

The Write Statement—General Form

```
Write #FileNumber, ListOfFields
```

The Write Statement—Examples

```
Write #1, txtAccount.Text, txtDescription.Text, txtPrice.Text
Write #2, strAccount
Write #intFileNum, mintCount; mintQuantity; mcurTotal
```

The `Write #` statement outputs data fields to the disk. As the elements are written on disk, commas are written between elements, string data are enclosed in quotation marks, and a carriage return and a line feed are inserted after the last element.

Creating a Sequential Data File

Sequential files are most commonly used to store small quantities of data that will rarely change. A common use of a sequential file is to store the information from a list box from one run to the next. The following save procedure writes the contents of a list box to a sequential file:

```
Private Sub mnuFileSave_Click()
    'Save the list box contents to a sequential file
    Dim intIndex   As Integer
    Dim intMaximum As Integer

    Open "Coffee.Dat" For Output As #1
    intMaximum = cboCoffee.ListCount - 1
    For intIndex = 0 To intMaximum
        Write #1, cboCoffee.List(intIndex)
    Next intIndex
    Close #1
End Sub
```

After execution of this procedure, the Coffee.Dat file on disk will hold the elements from the list box. VB automatically writes a carriage return at the end of each `Write #` statement and an EOF mark at the end of the file.

Disk File Contents
"Chocolate Almond"<CR>"Espresso Roast"<CR>
"Jamaica Blue Mtn."<CR>"Kona Blend"<CR>"Vanilla Nut"<EOF>

Reading the Data in a Sequential File

When you want to read a sequential file from the disk, you must open it for input. A successful `Open` sets the file pointer to the beginning of the file. After you have opened the file in Input mode, you can read the records by using the **Input # statement.** One word of warning: Recall that if you open a file for input and it does not exist, a run-time error occurs and the program terminates. Later in this appendix you will learn to check for errors and avoid the error message.

The Input # Statement—General Form

```
Input #FileNumber, ListOfFields
```

The Input # Statement—Examples

```
Input #1, lblName.Caption, lblStreet.Caption, lblCity.Caption, lblZipCode.Caption
Input #2, strAccount
Input #intFileNum, intSavedCount, intSavedQuantity, curSavedTotal
```

The FileNumber named on the Input # statement must be the number of a previously opened data file. The field names should be separated by commas. It doesn't matter what variable names were used when the data were written to the disk. When the data elements are read from the disk, they may be called by the same variable names or by completely different ones.

If you plan to load a list box from the data stored in a sequential file, the Open in the Form_Load must be followed by a loop that adds the data to the list. The loop will terminate when the EOF mark is read.

Finding the End of a Data File

When reading data from the disk, you must know when to stop. Recall that closing the file created an EOF mark. You can read until the EOF mark has been reached. (Attempting to read past the EOF mark causes a run-time error.)

The EOF(n) Function—General Form

```
EOF(FileNumber)
```

The EOF(n) function returns True when the EOF mark is read on the last good record. You can test for EOF with an If statement, but a better solution is to use a loop that continues until the condition is True. This example uses a Do/Loop:

```
Do Until EOF(1)    'Continue processing until EOF condition is True
    Input #1, strCoffeeFlavor         'Read a record from the data file
    cboCoffee.AddItem strCoffeeFlavor   'Assign the variable to the list box
Loop
```

Feedback

1. Write the Visual Basic statements to
   (a) Open a sequential file called Vendor.dat for output.
   (b) Write the items in the lstVendor list box to the Vendor.dat file.
   (c) Close the Vendor.dat file.
   (d) Open the Vendor.dat file so it can be used to read the records.
   (e) Read the records from the disk file into a list box.
2. What function is used to find the end of the file?

Sequential File Programming Example

This programming example contains a dropdown combo box with flavors of coffee. The user can add new flavors to the list, remove items from the list, or clear the list. A data file saves the list contents from one program run to the next. For each program run the list will be loaded from the data file during the Form_Load procedure of the startup form. If the flavors file does not yet exist, the program skips over loading the combo box to allow the user to add coffee flavors and create the file.

The user can choose to save the coffee list into a disk file by selecting a menu choice. Also, when the *Exit* menu choice is selected, if any changes have been made to the list, the project prompts the user to save the file. A Boolean variable is used to determine whether any changes have been made since the file was last saved.

```
'Module:        frmFlavors
'Programmer:    Bradley/Millspaugh
'Date:          2/2000
'Description:   Save Coffee flavors from a dropdown list in a sequential file
'Folder:        AppBSeqFile

Option Explicit
Dim mblnIsDirty As Boolean
```

```
Private Sub cmdAddCoffee_Click()
    'Add a new coffee flavor to the coffee list

    If cboCoffee.Text <> "" Then
        With cboCoffee
            .AddItem cboCoffee.Text
            .Text = ""
        End With
        mblnIsDirty = True
    Else
        MsgBox "Enter a coffee name to add.", vbExclamation, "Missing data"
    End If
    cboCoffee.SetFocus
End Sub
```

```
Private Sub Form_Load()
    'Load the Coffee list
    Dim strCoffee As String
    Dim strFilePath

    On Error GoTo HandleErrors
    strFilePath = App.Path & "\Coffee.Dat"
    Open strFilePath For Input As #1
    Do Until EOF(1)
        Input #1, strCoffee
        cboCoffee.AddItem strCoffee
    Loop
    Close #1

Form_Load_Exit:
    Exit Sub

HandleErrors:
    Dim intResponse As Integer

    Select Case Err.Number
        Case 53, 76                     'File or path not found
            intResponse = MsgBox("Create a new file?", _
                vbYesNo + vbQuestion, "File not Found")
            If intResponse = vbYes Then
                Resume Form_Load_Exit   'Exit the procedure
            Else
                mnuFileExit_Click       'Exit the project
            End If
        Case 71                         'Disk not ready
            intResponse = MsgBox("Disk not ready. Retry?", _
                vbRetryCancel + vbQuestion, "Disk Error")
            If intResponse = vbRetry Then
                Resume                  'Try again
            Else
                mnuFileExit_Click       'Exit project
            End If
        Case Else               'All other errors should cancel execution
            Err.Raise Err
        End Select
End Sub
```

```
Private Sub Form_QueryUnload(Cancel As Integer, UnloadMode As Integer)
    'Ask user to save the file
    Dim intResponse As Integer

    If mblnIsDirty = True Then
        intResponse = MsgBox("Coffee list has changed. Save the list?", _
            vbYesNo + vbQuestion, "Coffee List Changed")
        If intResponse = vbYes Then
            mnuFileSave_Click
        End If
    End If
End Sub
```

```
Private Sub mnuEditAdd_Click()
    'Add a new coffee to list

    cmdAddCoffee_Click
End Sub
```

```
Private Sub mnuEditClear_Click()
    'Clear the coffee list
    Dim intResponse   As Integer

    intResponse = MsgBox("Clear the coffee flavor list?", _
        vbYesNo + vbQuestion, "Clear Coffee List")
    If intResponse = vbYes Then
        cboCoffee.Clear
        mblnIsDirty = True
    End If
End Sub
```

```
Private Sub mnuEditRemove_Click()
    'Remove the selected coffee from list
    Dim strMsg       As String

    If cboCoffee.ListIndex <> -1 Then
        cboCoffee.RemoveItem cboCoffee.ListIndex
        mblnIsDirty = True
    Else
        strMsg = "First select the coffee to remove."
        MsgBox strMsg, vbInformation, "No Coffee Selection Made"
    End If
End Sub
```

```
Private Sub mnuFileSave_Click()
    'Save the list box contents to a sequential file
    Dim intIndex     As Integer
    Dim intMaximum   As Integer
    Dim strFilePath As String

    strFilePath = App.Path & "\Coffee.Dat"
    Open strFilePath For Output As #1
    intMaximum = cboCoffee.ListCount - 1
    For intIndex = 0 To intMaximum
        Write #1, cboCoffee.List(intIndex)
    Next intIndex
    Close #1
    mblnIsDirty = False
End Sub
```

```
Private Sub mnuFileExit_Click()
    'Terminate the project

    Unload Me
End Sub
```

Notice that the error handling in the Form_Load procedure traps for any error on the Open. If there is no error, the combo box is loaded with a Do/Loop.

If error number 53 or 76 occurs (File not found or Path not found), a message box asks the user whether or not to create the file. An answer of No terminates the program, but a Yes continues execution without attempting the read.

The user can enter new flavors during program execution, remove flavors, or clear the list. If any changes are made to the list, the Boolean variable mblnIsDirty is set to True. When the project exits, if mblnIsDirty is True, the user is prompted to save the list.

Random Data Files

The primary difference between sequential files and random files is that you may read and write the data in any order in a **random file.** With sequential files you must always start at the beginning of the file and proceed in order through the file. Random files offer greater speed as well as the capability for random access.

You can visualize random files as a table in which each entry may be referenced by its relative position. Each entry in a file is one record, which is referred to by its record number. Any record in the file may be read or written without accessing the preceding records.

All records in a random file are exactly the same size. The fields within the record are fixed in length and position. That is, if the name takes the first 30 bytes (characters) in one record, every record will allocate the first 30 bytes for the name. This scheme is a departure from sequential files with their variable-length fields and records. Before reading or writing a random file, the record structure or layout must be defined. The Type/End Type statements set up record structures. The only modification you will need is to use fixed-length strings.

Fixed-Length Strings

String variables may be variable length or fixed length. Until this point, all strings have been variable length. But for random files you will need to specify fixed-length strings. You can define a specific number of characters for elements of user-defined data types, and you can dimension fixed-length single variables and arrays.

If the value you store in a field is less than its specified length, the extra positions are filled with spaces. If you assign a value that is longer than the fixed length, the extra characters are truncated (chopped off) when the value is stored in the fixed-length string.

To specify the string length, add an asterisk (*) followed by the size to the string declaration.

```
Dim strName        As String * 30

Type FullName
    strLastName    As String * 20
    strFirstName   As String * 20
End Type
```

Defining a Record for a Random File

To define a record for a random file, first set up its structure with a Type statement. Then dimension a record variable of the data type.

Note: You can code Type statements in a standard code module or the General Declarations section of a form module. In a form module you must specify Private.

```
Private Type MemberStructure
    strLastName        As String * 20
    strFirstName       As String * 20
    strPhone           As String * 12
End Type

Dim mudtMemberRecord As MemberStructure
```

Opening a Random File

The Open statement for a random file is the same as for sequential files, using a file mode of Random. This mode allows you to input and output to the same file without closing and reopening it.

```
Open "B:\Data\Names.txt" For Random As #1 Len = 52
Open "A:Members.Dat" For Random As #2 Len = Len(mudtMemberRecord)
```

For a random file the Len (length) entry refers to the length of a single record. In the second example the second Len is actually the Length function that returns the size in bytes of the item enclosed in parentheses. The item in parentheses is the name used for the record variable you declared.

Reading and Writing a Random File

The input/output statements that you will be using for a random file differ from those used for sequential files. When accessing a random file, the data are handled a record at a time. The statements used are Get and Put, which include the record position in the file and the name of the variable defined as the record.

You can Get and Put records in a random file in any order you choose. That is, you may first write record #5, then #1, then #20, or any other order. When record #5 is written in the file, VB skips enough space for four records and writes in the fifth physical location. Record positions 1 to 4 are skipped until such time as records are written in those locations.

The record numbers start at record 1. This rule will probably feel strange to you, since you are used to arrays and lists beginning with an index of zero. If you attempt to Get or Put a record number of zero, you receive a *Bad Record Number* error.

The Get Statement—General Form

```
Get [#]FileNumber, [RecordNumber], RecordName
```

The Get Statement—Examples

```
Get #2, intRecNumber, mudtMemberRecord
Get #1, intRecordNumber, mudtInventoryRecord(intRecordNumber)
Get #2, intCustomerNumber, gudtCustomerRecord(intIndex)
Get #3, 4, udtAccountRecord
Get #1, , mudtMemberRecord
```

The **Get statement** reads data from a random disk file and places the data into the record-name variable. This variable should be declared with a user-defined data type. If the variable is an array, the appropriate subscript number must be included.

When you omit the record number, the *next* record (after the last Get or Put that was processed) is read from the file. Either a variable or a constant may be used for the record number. Generally you will want to use a variable to allow selection of any record in the file.

The Put Statement—General Form

```
Put [#]FileNumber, [RecordNumber], RecordName
```

The Put Statement—Examples

```
Put #2, intRecNumber, mudtMemberRecord
Put #1, intRecordNumber, mudtInventoryRecord(intRecordNumber)
Put #2, intCustomerNumber, gudtCustomerRecord(intIndex)
Put #3, 4, udtAccountRecord
Put #1, , mudtMemberRecord
```

The **Put statement** takes the contents of the specified record and writes it on the disk. The record number determines the relative location within the file for the record. If the record number is omitted, the record will be placed in the *next* location from the last Get or Put. Note that the next location is likely not the end of the file. Be careful not to write over other data by accident. If you wish to add a record to the end of the file, add 1 to the current number of records and Put the record at that position.

Accessing Fields in a Random Record

The Get and Put statements always read or write an entire record. To access the individual fields within the record, the elements must be referenced by the record name, a period, and the element name that is defined with the Type statement.

```
Get #1, intRecordNumber, mudtMemberRecord
lstName.AddItem mudtMemberRecord.strLastName
```

Finding the End of a Random File

To find the end of a random file, use the **LOF function** (length of file) rather than the EOF function. The LOF function returns the size of the file in bytes. Although EOF can sometimes be used, problems can occur if records are written randomly and any gaps exist in the file.

The FileNumber entry is the file number from a currently open file.

To determine the highest record number in the file, divide the return value of the LOF function by the size of one record (the name dimensioned using the user-defined data type).

The LOF Function—General Form

```
LOF(FileNumber)
```

The LOF Function—Example

```
intNumberRecords = LOF(1) / Len(mudtMemberRecord)
```

You can use the LOF function to find out how many records are in the file prior to using a For/Next loop that might load the data into a table or list.

```
'Read a random file and store member names into a list box
Dim intNumberRecords As Integer
Dim intIndex As Integer 'Index for the loop

intNumberRecords = LOF(1) / Len(mudtMemberRecord)
For intIndex = 1 To intNumberRecords
Get #1, intIndex, mudtMemberRecord
    lstNames.AddItem mudtMemberRecord.strLastName
Next intIndex
```

When you are adding to the end of the file, you can use a calculation to find the next record number.

```
intRecordNumber = LOF(1) / Len(mudtMemberRecord) + 1
Put #1, intRecordNumber, mudtMemberRecord
```

The Seek Function

At times you may need to determine the position of the file pointer within the file. The **Seek function** returns the current location of the pointer. For a sequential file the current byte number is returned. For a random file Seek returns the position (record number) of the *next* record in the file.

The Seek Function—General Form

```
Seek(FileNumber)
```

FileNumber is the file number of a currently open file.

The Seek Function—Example

```
intNextRecord = Seek(1)
```

Using a List Box to Store a Key Field

When you Get or Put a record in a random file, you need to know the record number. However, keeping track of record numbers is inconvenient. Who wants to remember record numbers?

A slick visual solution to the record number problem is to display the name or identifying information in a list box. The list box can have its Sorted property set to True, which makes it easy for the user to find the desired record. Each name's corresponding ItemData property can hold the record number. When the user selects a record from the list, you can use the number stored in ItemData to retrieve the correct record. In Figure B.2 a list box is used for record selection.

Figure B.2

The list box holds employee names in the List property and corresponding keys (record numbers) in the ItemData property.

	List Box List Property	ItemData Property	
User selects this name from list.	Brooks, Barbara	5	
	Chen, Diana	3	
	Dunning, Daniel	1	
	Khan, Brad	6	Program displays record 6 from the file.
	Lester, Les	2	
	Nguyen, Ahn	4	
	Potter, Pete	8	
	Stevens, Roger	7	

The following code segment concatenates a first and last name, adds to the list box, and then assigns the record number to the ItemData property.

```
Public Sub AddtoList(iIndex As Integer)
    'Add to the list box and the ItemData
    Dim strName As String

    strName = Trim(gudtEmployee.strLastName) & ", " & gudtEmployee.strFirstName
    lstEmployee.AddItem strName
    lstEmployee.ItemData(lstEmployee.NewIndex) = intIndex
End Sub
```

When concatenating fixed-length strings, the entire string length, including the spaces, is used. You can use a trim function to avoid printing the extra spaces.

Trimming Extra Blanks from Strings

The **Trim, LTrim,** and **RTrim functions** remove extra blank characters in a string. When you have fixed-length strings, such as the fields in a random file, the strings are usually padded with extra spaces. The LTrim function removes extra spaces at the left end of the string; RTrim removes extra spaces on the right, and Trim removes extra spaces from both the left and right ends of the string.

The Trim, LTrim, and RTrim Functions—General Form

```
Trim(StringExpression)
LTrim(StringExpression)
RTrim(StringExpression)
```

The Trim, LTrim, and RTrim functions return a string with the extra spaces removed.

The Trim, LTrim, and RTrim Functions—Examples

```
Trim(" Harry Rabbit ")  'Returns "Harry Rabbit"
LTrim(" Harry Rabbit ")  'Returns "Harry Rabbit "
RTrim(" Harry Rabbit ")  'Returns " Harry Rabbit"
```

Navigating through a Random File

When displaying information from a file, you should allow your user to move through the records within the file. Common options for navigation are First, Last, Previous, and Next. The First button or command displays the first record from the file, and Last displays the last record. Previous and Next move one record in the desired direction.

Because we are using a sorted list box to control the sequence of the records, the option for Next takes you to the data for the next item in the list box. This task is easy to accomplish by using the properties of the list box. ListIndex indicates the currently selected record. You can move to the next or previous record by adding or subtracting 1 to/from the ListIndex property. Make sure that the result of the calculation will be a valid record number, not less than one and not exceeding the record count.

Coding the Navigation Buttons

```
Private Sub cmdPrevious_Click()
    'Display the previous record from sorted list

    With frmMain.lstEmployee
        If .ListIndex < 1 Then
            cmdLast_Click
        Else
            .ListIndex = .ListIndex - 1
            ReadRecord
        End If
    End With
End Sub
```

```
Private Sub cmdNext_Click()
    'Display the next record from sorted list

    With frmMain.lstEmployee
        If .ListIndex < .ListCount - 1 Then
            .ListIndex = .ListIndex + 1
            ReadRecord
        Else
            cmdFirst_Click
        End If
    End With
End Sub
```

You can find the first and last records using list box properties. Remember that the ListIndex of the first record is 0. The ListIndex of the last record is one less than the ListCount.

```
Private Sub cmdFirst_Click()
    'Display the first record from sorted list

    frmMain.lstEmployee.ListIndex = 0
    ReadRecord
End Sub
```

```
Private Sub cmdLast_Click()
    'Display the last record from sorted list

    With frmMain.lstEmployee
        .ListIndex = .ListCount - 1
    End With
    ReadRecord
End Sub
```

Navigation during an Add or Delete

If the user is allowed to click on the navigation button when an Add or Delete operation is in progress, a problem can arise. You can avoid this problem by disabling the navigation buttons during an Add or Delete. You will need to enable the buttons during an Update or Browse operation.

```
Private Sub DisableNavigation()
    'Disable the navigation commands

    cmdLast.Enabled = False
    cmdFirst.Enabled = False
    cmdPrevious.Enabled = False
    cmdNext.Enabled = False
End Sub
```

```
Private Sub EnableNavigation()
   'Enable the navigation commands

   cmdLast.Enabled = True
   cmdFirst.Enabled = True
   cmdPrevious.Enabled = True
   cmdNext.Enabled = True
End Sub
```

Locking the Contents of Controls

Another technique for keeping the user out of trouble is to lock text boxes when you don't want to allow any changes. Although you can set the Enabled property of a text box to False, the contents will display as grayed. A better approach is often to set the Locked property to True. If you lock text boxes, make sure to unlock them again when you *do* want to allow changes.

```
txtLastName.Locked = True
txtFirstName.Locked = True
txtStreet.Locked = True
```

Updating a Random File

A file update generally consists of routines to add records, update records, delete records, and browse through records. The procedures for these options might be selected from a command button or a menu command.

Each routine must display the fields from the file, so we will use one form and refer to it as the *data form*. This form will contain text boxes for each field of a record along with the appropriate labels.

Adding and Editing Records

When the user wants to add a record, all of the text boxes must be cleared. After the data are entered, the record will be written to the disk file. The record will be written at the end of the file. The list box must be updated and the record number stored in the ItemData property for the list. It is a good idea to set the current ListIndex to the new record.

```
mintIndex = LOF(1) / Len(gudtEmployee) + 1  'Find next available record number
gudtEmployee.strDeleted = "N"
SaveData                             'Send text box fields to record variables
WriteRecord                          'Write record variable in file
With frmMain
    .AddtoList (mintIndex)           'Add entry to list box on main form
    .lstEmployee.ListIndex = .lstEmployee.NewIndex  'Set ListIndex
End With
```

An alternative approach is to search through the records in the file to find the location of a deleted record. You can then add a new record in the location of the deleted record. For this example we will add all new records at the end of the file.

Deleting a Record

You can delete a record from a random file in several ways. A common method is to mark a record in some way to indicate that the record is deleted, rather than to actually remove it. If you actually remove a record, you also have to move forward all the remaining records. That process takes time and also changes the record numbers. (Often the record number is used as a form of identification.)

One technique is to write some special character in a field of the record to indicate that the record has been deleted. A drawback of this method is that the data in the record cannot be recovered later if you want to add undelete routines.

A more popular way to delete a record is to add a special field to the record description. The field, commonly called a *delete flag* or *delete code,* holds one of two values, such as *Y* and *N, A* for *active* and *D* for *deleted,* or True/False values. We will use this approach.

In the following data type, the field stDeleted indicates whether a record is deleted. A *Y* in stDeleted means that the record is deleted. When a record is added, *N* is placed in the field.

```
Type udtEmployee
    strLastName      As String * 15
    strFirstName     As String * 10
    strStreet        As String * 20
    strCity          As String * 15
    strState         As String * 2
    strZipCode       As String * 11
    strPhone         As String * 11
    strEmail         As String * 20
    strEmployeeCode  As String * 4
    strDeleteCode    As String * 1
End Type
Public gudtEmployee      As udtEmployee
```

To mark a record as deleted, store a *Y* in the stDeleted field.

```
gudtEmployee.strDeleted = "Y"
```

When records are loaded into the list box, only those without the *Y* will be loaded.

```
If gudtEmployee.strDeleted <> "Y" Then
    AddtoList (intIndex)
End If
```

Keep the List Box Up-to-Date

Whenever a record is deleted from the file, the list box must also be updated. Use a RemoveItem method to delete the reference to the deleted record from the list. The next code segment puts together the steps for deletion.

```
'Set the record number to match the list box ItemData property
With frmMain.lstEmployee
    mintIndex =.ItemData(.ListIndex)
    gudtEmployee.strDeleted = "Y" 'Set the delete field to indicate deleted record
    WriteRecord                    'Write the record back into the file
    'Remove the current list element from the list box
    .RemoveItem.ListIndex
End With
```

Confirm the Deletion

You may want to verify that the record is really to be deleted. If you do so, make sure to offer a Cancel button.

The Read and Write Procedures

Good programming technique uses a single procedure for reading a file and one for writing to the data file. Write a procedure to write a record and call it from any location that needs a write. Then code a single procedure to read a record and call it as needed. The following code segment writes a record in the file:

```
Private Sub WriteRecord()
    'Write to disk

    Put #1, mintIndex, gudtEmployee
End Sub
```

For this procedure to work correctly, mintIndex must be set to the record number, and gudtEmployee must have the fields for the record.

The Read procedure is very much the same, but it must find which record to read by checking the selection in the list box. Notice that the ItemData property is used to get the record number, mintIndex. After the record is read, the data are displayed.

```
Private Sub ReadRecord()
    'Use ItemData to directly access record in the file

    'Set the record number to the current ItemData
    With frmMain.lstEmployee
        mintIndex = .ItemData(.ListIndex)
        Get #1, mintIndex, gudtEmployee 'Read the record
        DisplayData                     'Move fields into text boxes to display
    End With
End Sub
```

Feedback

1. Write the Type statement called *Inventory*, which contains 30 characters for a description, 5 characters for a part number, a price (currency), and a quantity (integer).
2. Declare a variable called *mudtInventoryRecord* that will use the Inventory data type.
3. Write the statement to open a random file using the disk file Inventory.Dat on the C: drive.
4. Write the statement(s) to find the number of records in the Inventory.Dat file.

5. Write the statement to write one record to the Inventory.Dat file using a record number called *intRecordNumber*.
6. What value does the Seek function return if the current record is record # 5?
7. Write the statement to read one record from the Inventory.Dat file.

Random File Programming Example

An employee file will be maintained by using a random file with two forms: a main form and a data form. The main form will have a list box of employee names and command buttons for Add, Delete, Update, and Browse. When the user clicks on a command button, the data form will display, set for the correct action.

The data form for the file will display the fields in text boxes and provide OK and Cancel buttons for changes to the file. The data form will also include navigation buttons (First, Last, Next, and Previous), which are enabled for the Update and Browse options but disabled for the Add and Delete options. The project will use the list box on the main form for navigation. The user selects a record by the employee name, and the correct record is read from the file. The list box ItemData property holds the record number for the random reads.

Add option	Display the data form with the fields empty. When the user clicks the OK button, save the record in the next available record position.
Delete option	Display the data form with the selected record displayed. The user can then choose OK to delete the record or to cancel the operation.
Update option	Display the data form with the selected record displayed. The user can then choose OK to save any change or to cancel the operation.
Browse option	Display the data form with the text boxes locked. The user can use the navigation buttons to move through the file, but cannot make any changes.

The Project Coding Solution

Standard Code Module

```
'Module          Filetype.Bas
'Programmer:      Bradley/Millspaugh
'Date:            2/2000
'Description:     Define the record
'Folder:          AppBRandomFile

Type Employee
     strLastName  As String * 15
     strFirstName As String * 10
     strStreet    As String * 20
     strCity      As String * 15
     strState     As String * 2
     strZip       As String * 5
     strPhone     As String * 15
     strEmail     As String * 25
     strDeleted   As String * 1
End Type
```

```
Public gudtEmployee   As Employee
Public gstrFileAction As String
```

Main Form: frmMain

```
'Form          frmMain
'Programmer:   Bradley/Millspaugh
'Date:         2/2000
'Description:  This project uses a random file to store employee
'              information. It stores employee names in a list box
'              and allows file updating and browsing.
'Folder:       AppBRandomFile

Private Sub cmdAdd_Click()
    'Display a blank form for an add

    gstrFileAction = "A"
    frmFile.Show vbModal
End Sub
```

```
Private Sub cmdBrowse_Click()
    'Look at the file

    gstrFileAction = "B"
    frmFile.Show vbModal
End Sub
```

```
Private Sub cmdDelete_Click()
    'Display and delete the selected item from list

    If lstEmployee.ListIndex <> -1 Then
        gstrFileAction = "D"
        frmFile.Show vbModal
    Else
        MsgBox "Select record to Delete", vbOKOnly + vbInformation, "Delete"
    End If
End Sub
```

```
Private Sub cmdUpdate_Click()
    'Display the selected item from list

    If lstEmployee.ListIndex <> -1 Then
        gstrFileAction = "U"
        frmFile.Show vbModal
    Else
        MsgBox "Select record to update", _
            vbOKOnly + vbInformation, "Update"
    End If
End Sub
```

```
Private Sub Form_Load()
    'Read the file and store in the sorted list box.
    'Store the random record number into ItemData.
```

```
    Dim intIndex        As Integer
    Dim strName         As String
    Dim intResponse     As Integer

    On Error GoTo HandleErrors
    Open App.Path & "\Employee.Dat" For Random As #1 Len = Len(gudtEmployee)
    If LOF(1) / Len(gudtEmployee) > 0 Then   'If file not empty
        For intIndex = 1 To LOF(1) / Len(gudtEmployee)
            Get #1, intIndex, gudtEmployee
            If gudtEmployee.strDeleted <> "Y" Then
                AddtoList (intIndex)
            End If
        Next intIndex
    Else
        iResponse = MsgBox("File is empty. Create new file?", _
            vbYesNo + vbQuestion, "No File")
        If intResponse = vbNo Then
            mnuFileExit_Click         'Exit project
        End If
    End If

Form_Load_Exit:
    Exit Sub

HandleErrors:
    If Err.Number = 71 Then
        intResponse = MsgBox("No disk. Retry?", _
            vbRetryCancel + vbQuestion, "No Disk in Drive")
        If intResponse = vbRetry Then
            Resume                    'Try again
        Else
            mnuFileExit_Click         'Exit project
        End If
    Else
        On Error GoTo 0               'Turn off error handling
    End If
End Sub
```

```
Private Sub mnuFileExit_Click()
    'Terminate the project
    Unload frmFile
    Unload Me
End Sub
```

```
Private Sub mnuViewEmployee_Click()
    'Display the Employee file form

    gstrFileAction = "B"             'Browse
    frmFile.Show vbModal
End Sub
```

```
Public Sub AddtoList(intIndex As Integer)
    'Add to the list box and the ItemData

    With gudtEmployee
        strName = Trim(.strLastName) & ", " & .strFirstName
    End With
```

```
    With lstEmployee
        .AddItem strName
        .ItemData(.NewIndex) = intIndex
    End With
End Sub
```

Data Entry Form: frmFile

```
'Form:          frmFile
'Programmer:    Bradley/Millspaugh
'Date:          2/2000
'Description:   Obtain and display data for the employee file
'Folder:        AppBRandomFile
Option Explicit
Dim mintIndex As Integer

Private Sub cmdCancel_Click()
    'Return to main form with no action

    frmFile.Hide
End Sub
```

```
Private Sub DisplayData()
    'Transfer from record to text fields

    With gudtEmployee
        txtLastName.Text = .strLastName
        txtFirstName.Text = .strFirstName
        txtStreet.Text = .strStreet
        txtCity.Text = .strCity
        txtState.Text = .strState
        txtZip.Text = .strZip
        txtPhone.Text = .strPhone
        txtEmail.Text = .strEmail
    End With
End Sub
```

```
Private Sub SaveData()
    'Transfer from text fields to data record

    With gudtEmployee
        .strLastName = txtLastName.Text
        .strFirstName = txtFirstName.Text
        .strStreet = txtStreet.Text
        .strCity = txtCity.Text
        .strState = txtState.Text
        .strZip = txtZip.Text
        .strPhone = txtPhone.Text
        .strEmail = txtEmail.Text
    End With
End Sub
```

```
Private Sub cmdFirst_Click()
    'Display the first record from sorted list

    frmMain.lstEmployee.ListIndex = 0
    ReadRecord
End Sub
```

```
Private Sub cmdLast_Click()
    'Display the last record from sorted list

    With frmMain.lstEmployee
        .ListIndex = .ListCount — 1
    End With
    ReadRecord
End Sub
```

```
Private Sub cmdNext_Click()
    'Display the next record from sorted list

    With frmMain.lstEmployee
        If .ListIndex < .ListCount — 1 Then
            .ListIndex = .ListIndex + 1
            ReadRecord
        Else
            cmdFirst_Click
        End If
    End With
End Sub
```

```
Private Sub cmdOK_Click()
    'Choose action depending upon the command
    Dim strName As String

    Select Case gstrFileAction
    Case "A"
        mintIndex = LOF(1) / Len(gudtEmployee) + 1
        gudtEmployee.strDeleted = "N"
        SaveData
        WriteRecord
        With frmMain
            .AddtoList (mintIndex)
            .lstEmployee.ListIndex = .lstEmployee.NewIndex
        End With
    Case "D"
        With frmMain.lstEmployee
            mintIndex = .ItemData(.ListIndex)
            gudtEmployee.strDeleted = "Y"
            WriteRecord
            .RemoveItem .ListIndex
        End With
    Case "U"
        SaveData
        With frmMain.lstEmployee
            mintIndex = .ItemData(.ListIndex)
            WriteRecord
            'Change name in list box if needed
            .RemoveItem .ListIndex
            frmMain.AddtoList (mintIndex)
        End With
    End Select

    'Return to main form
    Me.Hide
End Sub
```

```
Private Sub cmdPrevious_Click()
    'Display the previous record from sorted list

    With frmMain.lstEmployee
        If .ListIndex < 1 Then
            cmdLast_Click
        Else
            .ListIndex = .ListIndex - 1
            ReadRecord
        End If
    End With
End Sub
```

```
Private Sub DisableNavigation()
    'Disable the navigation commands

    cmdLast.Enabled = False
    cmdFirst.Enabled = False
    cmdPrevious.Enabled = False
    cmdNext.Enabled = False
End Sub
```

```
Private Sub ReadRecord()
    'Use ItemData to directly access record in the file

    With frmMain.lstEmployee
        mintIndex = .ItemData(.ListIndex)
    End With
    Get #1, mintIndex, gudtEmployee
    DisplayData
End Sub
```

```
Private Sub WriteRecord()
    'Write to disk

    Put #1, mintIndex, gudtEmployee
End Sub
```

```
Private Sub ClearTextBoxes()
    'Clear all of the text boxes

    txtLastName.Text = ""
    txtFirstName.Text = ""
    txtStreet.Text = ""
    txtCity.Text = ""
    txtState.Text = ""
    txtZip.Text = ""
    txtPhone.Text = ""
    txtEmail.Text = ""
End Sub
```

```
Private Sub Form_Activate()
    'Set the focus to the name field

    Select Case gstrFileAction
        Case "A"
            lblCommand.Caption = "Add a Record"
```

```
            ClearTextBoxes
            DisableNavigation
            UnlockTheControls
            txtLastName.SetFocus
        Case "D"
            ReadRecord
            lblCommand.Caption = "Delete this record?"
            DisableNavigation
            LockTheControls
        Case "U"
            ReadRecord
            lblCommand.Caption = "Update"
            EnableNavigation
            UnlockTheControls
        Case "B"
            lblCommand.Caption = "Browse"
            LockTheControls
            EnableNavigation
            cmdFirst_Click
    End Select
End Sub
```

```
Private Sub LockTheControls()
    'Lock the text boxes so no edits can be made

    txtLastName.Locked = True
    txtFirstName.Locked = True
    txtStreet.Locked = True
    txtCity.Locked = True
    txtState.Locked = True
    txtZip.Locked = True
    txtPhone.Locked = True
    txtEmail.Locked = True
End Sub
```

```
Private Sub UnlockTheControls()
    'Unlock the text boxes

    txtLastName.Locked = False
    txtFirstName.Locked = False
    txtStreet.Locked = False
    txtCity.Locked = False
    txtState.Locked = False
    txtZip.Locked = False
    txtPhone.Locked = False
    txtEmail.Locked = False
End Sub
```

```
Private Sub EnableNavigation()
    'Enable the navigation commands

    cmdLast.Enabled = True
    cmdFirst.Enabled = True
    cmdPrevious.Enabled = True
    cmdNext.Enabled = True
End Sub
```

The InputBox Function

When you need to request input from the user, you can always use a text box, either on the current form or on a new form. VB also provides a quick and easy way to pop up a new form that holds a text box, using the InputBox function.

The InputBox function is similar to MsgBox. In the input box you can display a message, called the *prompt,* and allow the user to type input into the text box.

The InputBox Function—General Form

```
VariableName = InputBox("Prompt" [, "Title"] [, Default] [, XPos] [, YPos])
```

The prompt must be enclosed in quotation marks and may include NewLine characters (vbCrLf) if you want the prompt to appear on multiple lines. The Title displays in the title bar of the dialog box; if the Title is missing, the project name appears in the title bar. Any value you place in *Default* appears in the text box when it is displayed; otherwise, the text box is empty. (If *Default* is a string, it must be enclosed in quotation marks.) *XPos* and *YPos,* if present, define the measurement in twips for the left edge and top edge of the box.

The InputBox Function—Examples

```
strName = InputBox("Enter your name.")
intQuantity = InputBox("How many do you want?", "Order Quantity")
```

Using the InputBox to Randomly Retrieve a Record

You will find the input box to be a great tool when you need to retrieve a record from a random file. Many applications use the record number as a method of identification, such as customer number or product number. If you request this number, you can read the correct record in the random file directly.

```
Dim intRecordNumber As Integer
intRecordNumber = Val(InputBox("Enter Customer Number"))
If intRecordNumber >= 0 And intRecordNumber <= LOF(1) / Len(udtCustomer) Then
    Get #1, intRecordNumber, udtCustomer
Else
    MsgBox "Invalid Customer Number"
End If
```

S u m m a r y

1. A data file is made up of records, which can be further broken down into fields or data elements. The field used for organizing the file is the key field.

2. An Open statement is needed to access data files. The Open allows modes for Input, Output, Append, and Random. A FileNumber is associated with a file at the time the file is opened.

3. A Close statement should be used prior to the termination of a program that uses data files.

4. The FreeFile function can be used to find the next available file number.

5. Sequential files use the Write # and Input # statements for writing and reading records. Each field to be written or read is listed in the statement.

6. The records in a sequential file must be accessed in order, and the file is either input or output, not both. With a random file the records may be accessed in any order and may be read or written without closing the file.

7. Random file access uses fixed-length records and requires the string fields to be a specified length. Use the Type statement to define the record structure for a random file.

8. The Get and Put statements read and write records in a random file.

9. A file update program allows the user to make changes to the data file, such as adding a record, changing the contents of a record, and deleting a record.

10. The LOF function returns the length of a random file in bytes. You can use the result to calculate the number of records in the file and the record number of the next available record.

11. You can use a list box to allow the user to select a record from a random file. The ItemData property of the list box is set to the record number so that random reads can retrieve the correct record.

12. The Trim, LTrim, and RTrim functions remove extra spaces from fixed-length strings.

13. The input box is similar to a message box; it allows the user to enter information that can be returned to the project.

K e y   T e r m s

buffer *554*
data element *552*
data file *552*
EOF *554*
field *552*
file *552*
file mode *553*
file number *554*
file pointer *554*
Freefile function *554*
Get statement *563*
Input # statement *557*
key field *552*

LOF function *564*
LTrim function *566*
Open statement *553*
Put statement *563*
random file *561*
record *552*
record key *552*
RTrim function *566*
Seek function *564*
sequential files *555*
Trim function *566*
Write # statement *555*

R e v i e w   Q u e s t i o n s

1. What is the difference between a VB project file and a data file?
2. Explain what occurs when an `Open` statement is executed.
3. List and explain the file modes for data files.
4. What is the significance of a file number?
5. Differentiate between the Output and Append modes.
6. What is the format for the statements to read and write sequential files?
7. When would an `On Error` statement be used?
8. Explain the function and use of the Err object.
9. Differentiate between a random file and a sequential file.
10. What does *updating a data file* mean?
11. Give examples for using the `InputBox` function.
12. What function can be used to determine an available file number?

P r o g r a m m i n g   E x e r c i s e s

B.1   Create a *sequential file* for employee information and call it *Employee.dat.* Each record will contain fields for first name, last name, Social Security number, and hourly pay rate.

Write a project to process payroll. The application will load the employee data into an array of user-defined types from the sequential file with an extra field for the pay. The form will contain labels for the information from the array and display one record at a time.

A command button called *FindPay* will use a `For Next` loop to process the array. First you will display an input box for the number of hours worked, calculate the pay, and add to the totals. Then you will display the labels for the next employee. (Place the pay into the extra field in the array.)

The Exit button will print a report on the printer and terminate the project. (Print the array.)

Processing: Hours over 40 will receive time-and-a-half pay. Accumulate the total number of hours worked, the total number of hours of overtime, and the total amount of pay.

Sample Report

Ace Industries

Employee Name	Hours Worked	Hours Overtime	Pay Rate	Amount Earned
Janice Jones	40	0	5.25	210.00
Chris O'Connel	35	0	5.35	187.25
Karen Fisk	45	5	6.00	285.00
Tom Winn	42	2	5.75	247.25
Totals	162	7		929.50

B.2   (Random file) Create a project that stores and updates personal informa-
      tion for a little electronic black book. The fields in the file should include
      last name, first name, street, city, state, ZIP code, birthday, phone num-
      ber—home, phone number—work, phone number—pager, and e-mail
      address.

B.3   Create a random file project that stores and updates student information.
      Use a list box to display the student names, and store record numbers in
      the ItemData property, similar to the programming example.

      The fields include
      Name
      Major—use a dropdown combo box to list available majors.
      Class level—use option buttons for Freshman, Sophomore, Junior, and
      Senior.
      Dean's list—use a check box.

· ·

C A S E   S T U D Y

VB Auto Center

Create a project that maintains a
random file for vehicle inventory.
The fields contained in each record should be an
inventory ID number, manufacturer, model name,
year, vehicle ID number, and cost value.

Hint: Refer to the programming example in this appendix for
ideas for the data entry screen, menus, and command
buttons.

C

Review of Introductory Visual Basic Topics

This appendix is intended as a review of VB topics generally covered in an introductory course.

You should always treat the MSDN Help files as your primary reference and look there when you need more explanation about any of these topics.

Visual Basic Projects

A VB project consists of several files. Always create a project folder first and keep all project files in the folder.

Project File

The VB project file is a text file that stores the names of all files needed for the project and references to library routines needed by the project. You can examine and modify the project file with a text editor. The file extension is .vbp.

Form Modules

Each form in a project is a separate module and is stored in a separate file. A form is saved with an extension of .frm. Binary information about the form, including any graphics that you have assigned to the Picture property of the form or Image or Picture controls, is stored in an .frx file.

You can add an existing form to a project by using *Project/Add Form/Existing.*

Standard Code Modules

Standard code modules contain only code with no visible user interface. Usually you use a standard code module to define elements to be shared with all modules in a project. You can declare global variables and constants, user-defined Types, and `Declares` for API procedure calls. You can also write sub procedures and functions in the standard code module.

Data Types, Variables, and Constants

The data values you use in a VB project may be variables or constants. They may be stored and manipulated as one of the intrinsic data types, a user-defined Type, or one of the many object types.

Data Types

Visual Basic data types:

Data Type	Type of Information Stored	Range of Values	Amount of Storage Used
String	Text	Zero to approximately 2 billion characters	10 bytes plus 1 byte for each character for variable-length strings; 1 byte for each character for fixed-length strings
Integer	Whole numbers	−32,768 to 32,767	2 bytes
Long	Whole numbers	−2,147,483,648 to 2,147,483,647	4 bytes
Byte	Whole numbers	0 to 255	1 byte
Single	Fractional (floating-point) values	−3.402823E38 to −1.401298E−45 and 1.401298E−45 to 3.402823E38	4 bytes
Double	Fractional (floating-point) values	−1.79769313486232E308 to −4.94065645841247E−324 and 4.94065645841247E−324 to 1.79769313486232E308	8 bytes
Currency	Decimal fractions	−922,337,203,685,477.5808 to 922,337,203,685,477.5807	8 bytes
Decimal (subtype of Variant; cannot be declared with Dim)	Extremely large decimal fractions or whole numbers	Whole numbers: +/−79,228,162,514,264,337,593,543,950,335 Fractional values: +/−7.9228162514264337593543950335	14 bytes
Boolean	True or False values	True or False True stored as −1 and False stored as 0	2 bytes
Date	Date and time, stored as a floating point, where fractional part represents the time and the whole number part represents the date	1/1/100 to 12/31/9999	8 bytes
Variant	Any type of data	Depends on the type of data stored	The amount of memory to hold the type of data stored plus 22 bytes
Object	Reference to an object	Any object reference	4 bytes

Selecting the Data Type

Always choose String for text characters and for numbers that are used for identification, such as part numbers, Social Security numbers, and ID numbers. As a general rule, do not use numeric data types for numbers unless you plan to calculate with the numbers.

When dealing with whole numbers, use Integer for any values that you don't expect to surpass the 32K limit. For example, all counters and ages should be Integer. Use Long for whole numbers that may be larger than the limit. Use Byte only for compatibility with routines that require it, such as reading byte data from a file or for calling Dlls written in C; a C Char data type requires a VB Byte data type.

For fractional values you can choose Single, Double, or Currency. Single and Double are stored as floating-point numbers, which can have some rounding errors when working with decimal fractions, such as dollars and cents. Use Currency for dollar amounts as well as other values stored in tenths and hundredths, such as interest rates or temperatures.

Decimal data type is actually a subtype of Variant and cannot be declared with a `Dim` statement. To convert a numeric value to Decimal, use the `CDec` function.

```
decBigAnswer = CDec(dblOneNumber * dblAnotherNumber)
```

Variant data type, the default type, is the least efficient. Use Variant only when you cannot know ahead of time what type of data will be stored. You must use a Variant when accessing the elements of an array with `For Each... Next`. A Variant can store any type of data and is therefore easy to use, but has a negative impact on memory usage and performance. VB must perform internal conversions every time a Variant is accessed.

Variables

You declare variables by using the `Dim` statement (for dimension). A variable name (identifier) can be 1 to 255 characters in length; may consist of letters, digits, and underscores; cannot contain any spaces or periods; cannot be a VB keyword; and must begin with a letter.

```
{Dim|Public|Private|Static} VariableName As DataType
```

Examples

```
Dim strName       As String
Public gcurTotal  As Currency
Private mobjItem   As Object
Dim objMyForm     As Form
Static EventCount As Integer
```

If you omit the data type, the variable will be Variant. One important note: You can declare multiple variables on one line, but the data type declaration applies to one variable only. For example, the statement

```
Dim intCount, intSum, intIndex As Integer
```

declares one Integer variable and two Variant variables.

Naming Conventions

Good programming practice dictates that variable names should always be meaningful. The prefixes you see are not required by VB but are recommended to indicate the data type and scope. You will find different conventions in different books and programming shops, but the important thing is to choose one standard and stick to it. The prefixes recommended by Microsoft in MSDN for data type are shown below. Use the lowercase prefix and capitalize each word of the name. Always use mixed case, never all uppercase.

Examples

blnAllDone
curSalesAmount
strFirstName

Data Type	Prefix
Boolean	bln
Currency	cur
Double	dbl
Date/Time	dtm
Integer	int
Long	lng
Single	sng
String	str
Variant	vnt

Note: To see the complete Microsoft list of coding conventions, see the MSDN topic:

Visual Basic Documentation
    Using Visual Basic
        Programmer's Guide
            Visual Basic Coding Conventions
                Constant and Variable Naming Conventions
                Object Naming Conventions

Constants

Declare a constant for a value that will not change during program execution. Naming rules and conventions are the same for constants as for variables. Note: Earlier versions of VB recommended using all uppercase to identify a constant, so you may see some examples of this style.

```
Const strCompanyName  As String = "Advanced Vision and Beyond"
Const intTypeOne      As Integer = 1
```

Scope

You can declare a variable or constant to be local, module level, or global in scope. The scope is the area of the project in which the variable or constant can be seen and referenced. For example, a local variable is available only in the procedure where it is declared. Coding conventions dictate that you add one additional prefix character at the beginning of the identifier to indicate the scope.

You determine the scope by the placement and form of the `Dim` statement. A variable or constant declared inside a procedure is local to that procedure. Its value cannot be seen or used in any other procedure. Local variable names do not have an additional prefix for the scope.

Any `Dim` or `Const` statements that appear in the General Declarations section of a module are considered module level. The variables or constants are available in all procedures of that module. Use *m* for the scope prefix.

Global variables and constants are declared with the Public keyword and are available in all procedures of all modules of the project. You can declare global variables and constants in the standard code module or in the General Declarations section of a form module. (Good programming practices say that you should limit the use of globals as much as possible. It's much better to declare properties of a form than to use global variables to pass data from one form to another. Global variables violate encapsulation rules.) The scope prefix for global variables is *g*.

Lifetime

The lifetime of a variable is the length of time that the variable exists. For example, a local variable exists only as long as the procedure executes. Each time the procedure begins execution, the variable is created and when the procedure terminates the variable is destroyed. For this reason a local variable cannot be used to accumulate a count or a total unless the variable is declared as Static.

A module-level variable exists as long as the module is loaded. For example, if you declare a module-level variable called mintCounter in a form module, you can reference the variable in any procedure of the form, and the counter can continue to accumulate as long as the form is loaded. Hiding the form does not destroy the variable, but unloading the form does.

A global variable declared with the `Public` keyword in a standard code module exists as long as the project is active. If a global variable is declared in a form module, the variable is destroyed when the form is unloaded.

Public, Private, and Static Variables

The form for a `Dim` statement is

```
{Dim|Public|Private|Static} VariableName As DataType
```

The default is Public, so if you use either the `Dim` or `Public` keyword, the variable is Public. It's best to declare a variable as Private unless you intend to make it Public for a reason. (Public variables are global in scope and violate encapsulation rules.)

Static variables are local variables with a lifetime that matches the module rather than the procedure. If you declare a variable as Static, it is not destroyed each time the procedure exits. Instead, the variable is created once the first time the procedure executes and retains its value for the life of the module. You can use a static variable to maintain a running count or total, as well as keep track of whether a procedure has executed previously.

```
Static blnDoneOnce As Boolean    'Boolean variables are initialized as False
If blnDoneOnce Then
    Exit Sub        'Already been here before
Else
    'Coding that you want to do one time only
    blnDoneOnce = True
End If
```

Conversion between Data Types

VB automatically converts numbers between data types when you assign one data type to another, rounding if necessary. You can use the conversion functions to explicitly convert when you want to make sure that the correct type is used.

Function	Purpose	Example
CCur	Convert to Currency	curAmount = CCur(sngAmount)
CDbl	Convert to Double	dblAmount = CDbl(txtBigAmount.Text)
CInt	Convert to Integer	intNumber = CInt(curDollars)
CLng	Convert to Long	lngNumber = CLng(dblBigNumber)
CSng	Convert to Single	sngAmount = CSng(txtInputNumber.Text)
Val	Convert to the appropriate numeric data type	intMyNumber = Val(txtMyNumber.Text)

Calculations

Make sure to convert any input value to numeric before calculating. Although VB can make assumptions and convert correctly most of the time, any non-numeric value, including a blank text box, causes a run-time error. You can use the Val function or one of the type conversion functions to convert the Text property of a text box to numeric.

```
mcurTotal = mcurTotal + Val(txtAmount.Text)
```

Calcluations are performed according to the hierarchy of operations:

1. All operations within parentheses. Multiple operations within the parentheses are performed according to the rules of precedence.
2. All exponentiation, using the ^ operator. Multiple exponentiation operations are performed from left to right.
3. All multiplication and division (* /). Multiple operations are performed from left to right.
4. All addition and subtraction (+ −) are performed from left to right.

There are no implied operations in VB. For example, the algebra expression 2Y must be written as 2 * Y in VB.

Arrays

You can define two types of arrays in VB: static arrays and dynamic arrays. For static arrays you declare the number of elements, which does not change during the run of the program. Dynamic arrays can be resized during program execution.

All elements of an array must be the same data type. You can get around that restriction, however, by declaring an array of Variants. Variant variables may hold any type of data.

Static Arrays

Use the Dim statement to declare a static array. You can declare the upper and lower bounds of the array or declare only the upper bound. If you don't specify the lower bound of the array, zero is assumed unless you include an Option Base 1 statement.

```
Dim curTotal(1 To 25) As Currency
Dim sngTemp(-10 To 10) As Single
Dim strPerson(10) As String    'Elements 0 to 10
Option Base 1
Dim strPerson(10) As String    'Elements 1 to 10
Private mintQuestion(1 To 5, 1 To 100)   'Two-dimensional array
Static strAnswer(100, 25, 5) As String   'Three-dimensional array
```

To reference one element of the array, use an integer variable or constant for the index (also called a *subscript*).

```
curTotal(1) = curTotal(1) + curNewValue
strPerson(intPersonNumber) = txtPerson.Text
strAnswer(intPersonNumber, intQuestionNumber, txtAnswer.Text)
```

Dynamic Arrays

With a dynamic array, you can resize an array at run time, clear an array, and free the space used by an array. Declare the array using Dim, Private, or Static (but not Public) with empty parentheses. Then use the ReDim statement to set the size of the array in code. Note: The ReDim statement clears the array. If you want to preserve the values already in the array, use the Preserve keyword.

```
Private mcurSale() As Currency   'Usually declared at the module level
Private mintSaleNumber As Integer
-----
Private Sub SaveSale()
   'Add a new sale to the array

   mintSaleNumber = mintSaleNumber + 1
   ReDim Preserve mcurSale(1 To mintSaleNumber)
   mcurSale(mintSaleNumber) = Val(txtSale.Text)
```

Collections

A collection is similar to an array but much more powerful. You can declare a collection and add elements by using the Add method. You can remove elements by using the Remove method, and you can access the Count property.

The Item method returns one element of the collection. You can specify the element by using an index, as in an array. And you can reference an element of the array by a key, which is a unique string.

VB has many built-in collections, such as a form's Controls collection and a project's Forms collection. The preferred method of traversing all elements of a collection is to use the For Each loop. See the "For Each...Next" section later in this appendix for further information.

```
Dim colPurchases As New Collection   'Declare at module level
-----
    'Add an item and its key to the collection
    colPurchases.Add txtItemName.Text, txtItemID.Text   'Item and key
    ----
    'Retrieve one item by its key
    Dim strItemKey As String
    strItemKey = InputBox("Enter item key")
    Debug.Print strItemKey, colPurchases(strItemKey)   'Display key and corresponding item
    ---
    'Display all elements of collection
    Dim vntPurchase As Variant
    For Each vntPurchase In colPurchases
        Debug.Print vntPurchase
    Next
```

User Defined Types

You can combine related variables into a new data type by using the Type and End Type statements. Once you have declared a new data type, you can dimension variables of that type.

Type and End Type statements belong in the General Declarations section of a form module or a standard code module. In a standard code module, the new Type is Public by default. In a form module, you must specify Private.

```
Private Type Employee
    strLastName       As String
    strFirstName      As String
    strEmployeeID     As String
End Type

Dim mudtEmployee      As Employee
```

The location of the Dim statement determines the scope of the variable, just as with any variables. The recommended prefix for a variable is *udt*.

To refer to individual elements of a user-defined type, specify the variable name, a dot (period), and the element name.

```
mudtEmployee.strLastName = txtLastName.Text
mudtEmployee.strFirstName = txtFirstName.Text
mudtEmployee.strEmployeeID = txtID.Text
```

You can also declare an array of a user-defined type.

```
Dim mudtMyEmployees(1 To 100) As Employee
------
   mudtEmployee(intIndex).strLastName = txtLastName.Text
   mudtEmployee(intIndex).strFirstName = txtFirstName.Text
   mudtEmployee(intIndex).strEmployeeID = txtID.Text
```

Control Structures

You use control structures to modify the sequence of the logic flow in a program. Each control structure tests conditions to determine the path to take.

Conditions

You test a condition for True or False. A condition may be based on the value of a Boolean variable or on the relationship of two or more values. You can form a condition by using the six relational operators and the logical operators.

Relational Operators		Logical Operators
>	(greater than)	And
<	(less than)	Or
=	(equal to)	Not
>=	(greater than or equal to)	
<=	(less than or equal to)	
<>	(not equal to)	

Comparisons must be on like types and may compare strings and/or numeric values.

If...Then...Else

Although you will see examples of the single-line If statement, the block If statement is the recommended form.

The Single-Line If Statement

```
If Condition Then ActionToTakeWhenTrue Else ActionToTakeWhenFalse
```

Example

```
If intCount > 0 Then DisplayTheCount
```

The Block If Statement

```
If Condition Then
   Action(s)ToTakeWhenTrue
[ElseIf Condition Then
   Action(s)ToTake]
[Else
   Action(s)ToTake]
End If
```

```
If blnFirstTime Then
    InitializeVariables
    blnFirstTime = False
End If

If txtName.Text <> "Smith" Then
    'Take some action
Else
    MsgBox "Hello Ms. Smith"
End If
```

Select Case

The Select Case structure can test for several values and is easier to read and debug than a deeply nested If statement. The Select Case is often used for error handling.

```
Select Case Expression
    Case ConstantList
        Statement(s)ToExecute
    [Case ConstantList
        Statement(s)ToExecute]
    ...
    [Case Else]
        [Statement(s)ToExecute]
End Select

Select Case Err.Number
    Case 53, 76                  'File or path not found
        'Action to take for this error
    Case 71                      'Disk not ready
        'Action to take for this error
    Case Else                    'All other errors
        Err.Raise Err            'Re-raise the error for the system to handle
End Select
```

Loops

A loop repeats program statements and checks a condition to determine when to exit the loop. VB has several constructs for forming loops, including the For...Next, Do...Loop, and For Each...Next.

    Each time execution passes through a loop is called one *iteration*.

For...Next

A For...Next is the preferred looping construct when you know ahead of time how many iterations you need. You must declare a variable to use as the loop index, which can be any of the numeric data types. The initial value, test value, and step may be constants, variables, numeric property values, or expressions.

```
For LoopIndex = InitialValue To TestValue [Step Increment]
    'Statement(s) to execute inside the loop
Next [LoopIndex]
```

When Step is omitted, the increment defaults to one.

```
For intIndex = 1 To 10
    Debug.Print intIndex
Next intIndex
```

The loop index is compared to the test value. If the loop index is *greater than* the test value, control passes to the statement following the Next statement. Otherwise, the statement(s) inside the loop are executed. At the Next statement, the loop index is incremented and tested again.

You can use a negative increment. In this case, the test is made for *less than* the test value.

```
For intIndex = 10 To 1 Step - 1
    Debug.Print intIndex
Next intIndex
```

Do Loops

Do Loops begin with the Do keyword and end with the Loop keyword. You can test a condition at the top of the loop, which might prevent the statements within the loop from executing even once, or at the bottom of the loop. You can form the condition for ending the loop with either the While or Until keywords. The While continues execution of the loop as long as a condition is True; the Until continues execution until the condition becomes True.

```
Do {While | Until} Condition
    'Statement(s) to execute inside the loop
Loop
```

or

```
Do
    'Statement(s) to execute inside the loop
Loop {While | Until} Condition

Do Until EOF(1)
    'Read the next record from file #1
Loop

Do
    'Statements inside the loop
    intCount = intCount - 1
Loop While intCount < 10
```

For Each...Next

The For Each...Next loop is the preferred construct for stepping through all elements of an array or a collection. You declare a Variant variable to hold each element of the array. For a collection of objects, you can declare a Variant variable or a variable of the specific object type.

Inside the loop the variable holds the current object or array element.

One great advantage of using the `For Each...Next` is that you don't have to manipulate indexes or test for the number of elements.

```
For Each VariableName In {ArrayName | CollectionName}
    'Statements to execute inside the loop
Next

Dim vntItem As Variant
For Each vntItem In MyArray
    Debug.Print vntItem
Next

Dim objForm As Form
For Each objForm In Forms
    Debug.Print objForm.Name, objForm.Caption
Next
```

Early Exit

For each loop construct you can exit early, before the test condition is True. Although many structured-programming purists advise against this practice, it is widely used in programming.

Use the `Exit For` or `Exit Do`, depending on the type of loop you are using.

```
Do Until EOF(1)
    Input #1, strName, strAddress, strZIP
    If strZIP = "93035" Then
        Exit Do
    End If
Loop

For intIndex = 1 To 10
    Debug.Print intIndex
    If intIndex = intMatchValue Then
        Exit For
    End If
Next intIndex
```

Sub and Function Procedures

Modern programs are made up of a series of procedures, which are the building blocks of programming. In VB you *must* write event procedures to respond to the events caused by the user. You can also create *general* procedures, which are not associated with any event but are called from other procedures.

Good programmers tend to break a program into many procedures, each to accomplish a specific task. Certainly any task that must be performed many times or from different locations should be written in a procedure that can be called.

In addition to event procedures, you can write sub procedures, function procedures, and property procedures. A sub procedure is a block of code that does not return a value. A function procedure (or just *function*) is a block of code that always returns a value. Property procedures are used to get or set the values of properties in class modules and form modules.

Calling Procedures

You can call a sub procedure in two ways. Assuming that you have written a sub procedure named PrintHeadings that requires an ending date as an argument, you can call it in either of these two ways:

```
PrintHeadings dtmEndingDate
```

or

```
Call PrintHeadings(dtmEndingDate)
```

Notice that you use parentheses only in the second format, with the keyword Call.

You call a function procedure by using it in an expression, just like calling one of VB's built-in functions. Assuming that you have written a function called *AverageCost* that requires three Currency arguments and returns a Currency result, you can call the function like this:

```
curAverage = AverageCost(curCostOne, curCostTwo, curCostThree)
```

Passing Arguments

The values that you pass to procedures are called *arguments*. You absolutely *must* supply the arguments in the correct order and in the correct data type. The names of the variables are not passed to the called procedure, only the address of the data value or a copy of the data. You can specify whether to pass the address or a copy of the data by specifying ByRef or ByVal in the procedures. See the "ByRef and ByVal" section later in this appendix.

When you write sub procedures and functions, you must specify the values to be passed. Inside the procedures those values are referred to as *parameters*. (Remember, the calling code passes *arguments*; the called procedure receives those values and calls them *parameters*.)

Writing Sub Procedures

When you write a new procedure, you can use one of two methods—either use the menu option or type the procedure header directly. The menu choice *Tools/Add Procedure* gives you a dialog box where you can specify the name of the procedure, whether it is a sub, function, or property procedure, and whether it is Public or Private. The alternative, preferred by most programmers, is to place the insertion point on a blank line between procedures and type the procedure header (without the parentheses). For example, you can type Private Sub PrintHeading and press Enter. VB adds the parentheses and the End Sub or End Function statement.

```
Private Sub PrintHeadings()

End Sub
```

Of course, you can also type the parameter list and the parentheses if you wish.

```
Private Sub PrintHeadings(dtmEndingDate As Date)
```

The parameter passed to the PrintHeadings sub procedure is a local variable to the procedure. Note that the name of the parameter does not have to be the same as the variable name passed as an argument from the calling procedure. You can call the PrintHeadings sub procedure in any of these ways:

```
PrintHeadings Date       'Pass today's date
PrintHeadings dtmMyFavoriteDate
PrintHeadings "2/2/2000"
```

The PrintHeadings sub procedure uses the dtmEndingDate parameter inside the procedure to reference the value passed for the parameter.

```
Private Sub PrintHeadings(dtmEndingDate As Date)
    'Print the report headings

    Printer.Print Tab(10); "Advanced Vision and Beyond"
    Printer.Print Tab(14); "As Of "; FormatDateTime(dtmEndingDate, vbShortDate)
End Sub
```

Writing Function Procedures

Functions return a value, so a function procedure must have a data type for the return value. The procedure header for a function looks like this:

```
[{Public | Private}] Function FunctionName(ParameterList) As DataType
```

If you omit the Public | Private, the function defaults to Public.

When you declare a function, VB creates a local variable with the same name as the function. Somewhere inside the function, before exiting, you must assign a value to that variable. That value is returned to the calling statement.

```
Private Function AverageCost(curCost1 As Currency, _
    curCost2 As Currency, curCost3 As Currency) As Currency
    'Calculate the average of three numbers

    AverageCost = (curCost1 + curCost2 + curCost3) / 3
End Function
```

ByRef and ByVal

By default, arguments are passed ByRef (by reference), which means that the address of your program variable is passed to the procedure. Therefore, if the called procedure makes any changes to the argument's value, the change will be made to the variable. To protect your variables and provide better separation of program tasks, you can specify that an argument be passed ByVal (by value), which forces VB to make a copy of the data and pass the copy. If the called procedure makes any changes to the argument, it has no effect on the original variable that you passed.

The primary way of specifying how data values pass is by declaring ByVal on the procedure header:

```
Private Sub PrintHeadings(ByVal dtmEndingDate As Date)
```

A date passed to this procedure will be passed by value. You can specify passing an argument by value on the Call by enclosing the argument in parentheses:

```
PrintHeadings (dtmMyEndingDate)
```

Notice that this format resembles the format using the `Call` statement. If you want to specify `ByVal` and use the `Call`, two sets of parentheses are required:

```
Call PrintHeadings((dtmMyEndingDate))
```

Public and Private

You can declare sub procedures and functions as Public or Private. Private procedures can be executed only from within the same module. A Public procedure can be executed by any module in the project. The only time that you should code Public procedures is to expose methods of a class module. If you omit the `Private` keyword when writing a procedure, the default is Public.

VB Functions

VB provides many intrinsic functions for financial calculations, numeric operations, string manipulation, and date/time processing.

The VB editor helps you type the arguments of functions. When you type the parentheses, the arguments pop up, showing the correct order. The argument to enter is shown in bold. The order of the arguments is important because the function uses the values based on their position in the argument list. If the arguments are supplied in the incorrect order, the result is wrong. And if the data types are incorrect, a run-time error occurs.

Financial Functions

VB provides functions for many standard financial operations. Each function returns a value that you can assign to a variable or to a property of a control.

Category	Function	Purpose
Depreciation	DDB	Double-declining balance
	SLN	Straight line
	SYD	Sum-of-the-years digits
Payments	Pmt	Payment
	IPmt	Interest payment
	PPmt	Principal payment

Category	Function	Purpose
Return	IIR	Internal rate of return
	MIRR	Rate of return when payments and receipts are at different rates
Rate	Rate	Interest rate
Future value	FV	Future value of an annuity
Present value	PV	Present value
	NPV	Present value when values are not constant
Number of periods	NPer	Number of payments

Example—The Pmt Function

You can use the Pmt function to find the amount of each payment on a loan if the interest rate, the number of periods, and the amount borrowed are known.

```
Pmt(InterestRatePerPeriod, NumberOfPeriods, AmountOfLoan)
```

The interest rate must be specified as a decimal and adjusted to the period. For example, if the loan has an annual rate of 10 percent and you want to find monthly payments, you must convert the yearly interest rate to monthly (.10/12).

The number of periods is the number of payments. If you want to know the monthly payment for a five-year loan, convert the number of years to the number of months (5*12).

The monthly payment for a five-year loan at 10 percent for $10,000 can be calculated like this:

```
curPayment = Pmt(.1/12, 5*12, 10000)
```

Numeric Functions

Function	Returns
Abs(x)	The absolute value of x. $\|x\| = x$ if $x \geq 0$ $\|x\| = -x$ if $x \leq 0$
Atn(x)	The angle in radians whose tangent is x.
Cint(x)	The even integer closest to x (rounded).
Cos(x)	The cosine of x where x is in radians.
Exp(x)	The value of e raised to the power of x.
Fix(x)	The integer portion of x (truncated).
Int(x)	The largest integer $\leq x$.
Log(x)	The natural logarithm of x where $x \geq 0$.

continued

Function	Returns
Rnd	A random number in the range 0–1.
Round(*x*[, *DecimalPlaces*])	The rounded value of *x*, rounded to the specified number of decimal positions. Note: Values round to the nearest even number.
Sgn(*x*)	The sign of *x*. −1 if $x < 0$ 0 if $x = 0$ 1 if $x > 0$
Sin(*x*)	The sine of *x* where *x* is in radians.
Sqr(*x*)	The square root of *x* where *x* must be ≥ 0.
Tan(*x*)	The tangent of *x* where *x* is in radians.

String Manipulation Functions

You can perform many operations on strings by using VB's string functions.

Function	Returns
Asc(*StringExpression*)	The number corresponding to the ASCII code for the first character of String.
Chr(*NumericCode*)	A string character that corresponds to the ASCII code in the range 0–255. Reverse of the Asc function.
Filter(*InputStrings*, *FilterValue*[, *Include*[, *CompareSetting*]])	An array that contains a subset of the input string array based on a specified filter criteria.
Format(*Expression* [, *Format* [, *FirstDayOfWeek* [, *FirstWeekOfYear*]]])	A string formatted as described in the format.
FormatCurrency(*Expression* [, *NumDigitsAfterDecimal* [, *IncludeLeadingDigit* [, *UseParensForNegativeNumbers* [, *GroupDigits*]]]])	A string formatted as currency according to the computer's *Regional Settings Currency* setting unless specified differently in the optional arguments.
FormatDateTime(*Date* [, *NamedFormat*])	A string formatted as a date and/or time, depending on the named format. Choices are vbGeneralDate, vbLongDate, vbShortDate, vbLongTime, vbShortTime; defaults to vbGeneralDate.
FormatNumber(*Expression* [, *NumDigitsAfterDecimal* [, *IncludeLeadingDigit* [, *UseParensForNegativeNumbers* [, *GroupDigits*]]]])	A string formatted as a number. Any omitted arguments default to the computer's *Regional Settings Number* setting.
FormatPercent(*Expression* [, *NumDigitsAfterDecimal* [, *IncludeLeadingDigit* [, *UseParensForNegativeNumbers* [, *GroupDigits*]]]])	A string formatted as a percentage ($\times$ 100) with a trailing % sign. Any omitted arguments default to the computer's *Regional Settings Number* setting.
Instr(([*StartingPosition*,] *StringExpression*, *SubString*	A numeric value that is the position within the string where the substring begins; returns zero if the substring is not found.

Function	Returns
InstrRev(*StringExpression, SubString*[, *StartingPosition*[, *CompareSetting*]])	A numeric value that is the position within the string where the substring begins, starting from the end of the string; returns zero if the substring is not found.
Join(*ArrayOfSubstrings* [, *DelimiterToInsert*])	A string formed by concatenating all strings from the array. Omitting the delimiter makes one long string of the text. Reverse of Split function.
LCase(*StringExpression*)	The string converted to lowercase.
Left(*StringExpression, NumberOfCharacters*)	The left-most characters of the string for the indicated number of characters.
Len(*StringExpression*)	A numeric count of the number of characters in the string.
Mid(*StringExpression, StartingPosition* [, *NumberOfCharacters*])	A substring taken from the string, beginning at StartingPosition for the specified length.
MonthName(*MonthNumber* [, *Abbreviate*])	A string that holds the month name for the specified number (1–12). Not abbreviated if the Boolean Abbreviate argument is omitted.
Replace(*StringExpression, FindString, ReplacementString,* [, *StartingPosition*[, *Count* [, *CompareSetting*]]])	A string that has the FindString replaced with the ReplacementString the specified number of times.
Right(*StringExpression, NumberOfCharacters*)	The right-most characters of the string for the indicated number of characters.
Space(*NumberOfCharacters*)	A string of blank spaces for the specified number of characters.
Split(*StringExpression*[, *Delimiter*[, *Count*[, *CompareSetting*]]])	An array of strings formed by separating a single string into array elements. Delimiter character used to split strings. Reverse of Join function.
Str(*NumericExpression*)	The string value of the numeric expression; used to convert numeric values to strings. Reverse of the Val function.
String(*NumberOfCharacters, StringExpression*)	A string of the named character(s) for a length of the specified number of characters.
StrReverse(*StringExpression*)	A string with the characters reversed.
UCase(*StringExpression*)	The string converted to uppercase.
Val(*StringExpression*)	The numeric value of the string expression used to convert strings to numeric values. Reverse of the Str function.
WeekdayName(*DayNumber* [, *Abbreviate* [, *FirstDayOfWeek*]])	A string holding the day of the week, based on the DayNumber (1–7). FirstDayOfWeek defaults to Sunday.

Example—The Format Function

The VB Format function has been largely replaced by the (new to VB 6) FormatNumber, FormatCurrency, FormatDateTime, and FormatPercent functions. However, you may have occasions to use the older Format function.

For the `Format` function you can use named formats or create a custom format by using formatting mask characters. The named formats are "General Number", "Currency", "Fixed", "Standard", "Percent", "Scientific", "Yes/No", "True/False", "On/Off".

Examples

```
lblAnswer.Caption = Format(curAnswer, "Currency")
lblOutput.Caption = Format(sngNumber, "###,###.00")
```

Formatting characters for custom format masks:

Format Character	Purpose	Example
0	Placeholder for a digit. Display a zero if no digit exists for that position.	0.00
#	Placeholder for a digit. Display a blank if no digit exists for that position.	###.##
.	Decimal point	###.00
%	Percent placeholder. Value is multiplied by 100.	##.00%
,	Thousands separator.	###,###
:	Time separator	hh:mm
+ − $ ( )	Display literal character	+###
\	Display the following character as a literal.	*###

Example—UCase and LCase

The `UCase` and `LCase` functions convert to uppercase or lowercase. This feature can be useful when testing for a particular value and the user may input in either case.

```
If UCase(strAnswer) = "YES" Then
    'Take action based on 'yes' answer
End If
```

Date/Time Functions

The VB date functions can retrieve the system date, break down a date/time into component parts, test whether the contents of a field are compatible with the Date data type, and convert other types to a date.

Function	Return
CDate(VariableOrProperty)	Converts to a Date data type. The value to convert must be a valid date or time. (Use the `IsDate` function to find out.)
Date	The system date.

Function	Return
`DateDiff("Interval", Date1, Date2)`	The difference between Date1 and Date2. The interval determines how the comparison is made: "yyyy" = years, "q" = quarters, "m" = months, "d" = days, "w" = weekdays, "ww" = weeks, "h" = hours, "n" = minutes, "s" = seconds.
`DatePart("PartType", Date)`	The specified element of the date, using the codes shown for interval in the `DateDiff` function.
`IsDate(Expression)`	True or False, depending on whether the expression is a valid date or time value.
`MonthName(MonthNumber [, Abbreviate])`	A string that holds the month name for the specified number (1–12). Not abbreviated if the Boolean Abbreviate argument is omitted.
`Now`	The system date and time.
`WeekdayName(DayNumber [, Abbreviate [, FirstDayOfWeek]])`	A string holding the day of the week, based on the DayNumber (1–7). FirstDayOfWeek defaults to Sunday.

Example—Converting to a Date

```
If IsDate(txtEndingDate.Text) Then
    dtmEndingDate = CDate(txtEndingDate.Text)
End If
```

Functions for Determining the Data Type

At times you may need to determine the data type of a value, as in the preceding example for checking a date.

Function	Return / Purpose
`IsArray(VariableName)`	True or False, depending on whether the variable is an array.
`IsDate(Expression)`	True or False, depending on whether the expression is a valid date or time value.
`IsNumeric(Expression)`	True or False, depending on whether the expression evaluates to a numeric value.
`IsObject(VariableName)`	True or False, depending on whether the variable represents an object.
`Is Nothing`	True or False, depending on whether an object variable is set to Nothing. Example: `If objMyObject Is Nothing Then`

`TypeOf`	Checks the type of an object variable. This special syntax can be used only in a logical expression:
	`If TypeOf ObjectVariable Is ObjectType Then`
	Example:
	`If TypeOf MyControl Is TextBox Then`

`TypeName(VariableName)`	Returns the data type of a nonobject variable. Example: `Debug.Print TypeName(varMyValue)`

Forms

A project may have one or more forms. Each form is a separate module that has a visible user interface plus code. A form is actually a class and you can add properties to a form by declaring a module-level variable and Property Get/Let procedures.

The Startup Object

When a project begins execution, the startup object is loaded into memory. The startup object can be a form or a procedure called Sub Main in a standard code module. Set the startup object in *Project/Properties*.

Loading and Unloading Forms

The Load statement loads a form into memory but does not show it. If you have many forms in a project, it's a good idea to load them ahead of time and just show them on demand.

```
Load FormName
```

Unloading a form removes it from the computer's memory. To terminate a project, always unload all forms.

```
Unload FormName
Unload Me          'Unload the form that is executing code
```

Hiding and Showing Forms

You can show a form modally or modelessly using the Show method. A modal form requires action from the user and must be responded to and closed before execution can continue. Forms such as message boxes and dialog boxes should always be displayed modally. Modeless forms are similar to the VB environment, where several windows are open and the user can switch from one to another while working.

```
FormName.Show [{vbModal|vbModeless}]
```

If you omit the modal entry, the default is modeless.

```
frmAbout.Show vbModal
```

If you use the Show method for a form that isn't loaded, the reference to the form causes it to first load and then show.

Form Properties

The main properties of a form that you always set are the Name and Caption. You can also choose whether to display minimize and maximize buttons, a close button, and a control box (the system menu that pops up at the left end of the title bar). If you want to display a form with no title bar, you must set ControlBox to False and the Caption to an empty string.

Size and Location Properties

When a form is first displayed, it uses several properties to determine the location and size. Set the StartUpPosition to set its position on the screen. WindowState determines whether the form displays in the original size you created or maximized or minimized.

The Top and Left properties determine the form's placement in its container, such as an MDI form. The Height and Width properties determine the size.

Set the MDIChild property to True for a child form that will display inside a parent (MDI) form.

Form Events

These events occur in this order when a form loads into memory:

Initialize	Occurs once, the first time a form is loaded in an application. If the form is unloaded and reloaded, the event does not occur again, unless the form's instance is set to Nothing. You can program this event to set customized form properties.
Load	Occurs each time the form is loaded. The controls on a form are not available during the Load event; therefore, you cannot set the focus in this event procedure. Most programmers use this procedure as the location for initialization tasks.
Activate	Occurs when a form becomes the active window. During a project with multiple forms, the Activate event occurs each time the user switches from one form to another. The Deactivate event occurs for the form losing active status.

These events occur as a form's life ends. The exact order depends on the situation.

DeActivate	Occurs when the form loses focus to another form in the project. It does not occur if the user switches to another application, the application closes, or the form unloads.
QueryUnload	Occurs just before the Unload event, giving the programmer a chance to determine the cause of the unload and cancel the unload process if necessary.
Unload	Occurs right after the QueryUnload event. Most programmers place cleanup code in this event procedure. The Unload can also be canceled in this event procedure, but the cause of the unload is not available here as it is in the QueryUnload.
Terminate	Occurs only after a form is unloaded, all form variables have been set to Nothing, and the form has been set to Nothing.

The GotFocus and LostFocus events may or may not occur for a form.

GotFocus	Occurs after the Activate event when a form becomes active *only if the form has no visible enabled controls.* This event is not a good place to place code; use the Activate event instead.
LostFocus	Occurs only if the GotFocus event previously fired, which is not often.

Using Multiple Forms

A project can hide and show multiple forms. Each form is a class and can have Public and Private members. You can access the Public members (variables and procedures) of one form from another. However, this practice is considered poor form, as it violates rules of encapsulation.

You can share data between forms by using global variables (again, poor form) or by setting properties of the form. If you need to pass data between forms, create a property of the form, write Property Get/Let procedures, and set the properties as needed.

Controls

The VB intrinsic (built-in) controls appear in the toolbox, and you can add more controls to the toolbox by setting a reference on the *Components* dialog box (*Project/Components*). Controls appear in the Components list when they are registered on your system.

Create an instance of a control class on a form by clicking on the control's icon and drawing the control on the form or by double-clicking the control's icon, which creates a control of default size in the center of the form. You can create multiple controls of one class by Ctrl-clicking on the icon—the pointer remains a crossbar, and you can create as many controls of that type as you wish. Press the Esc key or click on the toolbox arrow when you are finished drawing that control type.

You can select multiple controls by using Ctrl-click or Shift-click. The selected controls are treated as a group, and you can move them, delete them, or change their properties.

Common VB Controls

Most VB programming uses just a few controls: Label, TextBox, CheckBox, OptionButton, ListBox, ComboBox, and CommandButton.

The Label Control

Use a Label control for the words and instructions on the form as well as program output that you don't want the user to be able to modify. Set the Caption property for the words that you want to appear. You can also set the font and size. You can make a label look similar to a TextBox by settting the label's BorderStyle and BackColor properties. A label cannot receive the focus.

The TextBox Control

Use a TextBox for user input. The Text property holds the contents of the TextBox. You can enable/disable a TextBox.

The CheckBox Control

Use a CheckBox for options the user can select or deselect. Each CheckBox operates independently, so any number of check boxes may be selected.

The Value property of a CheckBox holds its current state and may be Unchecked, Checked, or Grayed. You can test and set the Value property in code.

```
If chkMyCheckOption.Value = Checked Then
    'Take some action
    chkMyCheckOption.Value = Unchecked
End If
```

The OptionButton Control

Option buttons, also called *radio buttons*, appear in groups. Only one option button in a group can be selected at one time. A group is defined as all the buttons that belong to one container. A container can be a form, a Frame, or a PictureBox control.

When you create Option buttons, do not double-click on the toolbox tool unless you want the button's container to be the form. Dragging an Option button into a Frame does not make it belong to the Frame. You must click on the toolbox icon and draw the Option button inside the container. You can also change the container of an Option button by cutting it to the Clipboard and pasting it into a container.

The Value property of an Option button holds its state and can be True or False. The Caption determines the words next to the button. You can test or change the Value in code.

```
If optMyOptionButton.Value Then
    'Take action for the selected button
    optMyOptionButton.Value = False
End If
```

ListBoxes and ComboBoxes

ListBoxes and ComboBoxes are very similar. A ListBox appears on the form in the size that you create it; a ComboBox can be made to appear small and drop down when the user clicks on the down arrow. You can set the Style property of a ComboBox control to Dropdown Combo, Simple Combo, and Dropdown List. Both a Dropdown Combo and a Simple Combo have a text box, which allows the user to make an entry as well as select from the list.

List controls have a List property that holds the items that appear in the list. You can set the List property at design time or add elements at run time by using the AddItem method.

```
cboNames.AddItem "John"
```

You can remove items from the list by using the RemoveItem method and clear the list by using the Clear method.

Each item in the list can be referenced by an index (zero based). The ListIndex property holds the index of the currently selected list element and is -1 if nothing is selected. The ListCount holds a count of the number of elements in the list. Setting the Sorted property to True causes VB to keep the list sorted in alphabetic order.

Each list control has a second unseen list, called the ItemData, which can hold a value of Long data type for each list element. The ItemData property is usually used to hold a key for each list element.

```
'Add an item to the list and the key to ItemData
With cboPerson
    .AddItem txtPerson.Text    'Add to the list
       'For a sorted list, NewIndex holds the index of the new item
    .ItemData(NewIndex) = CLng(txtKey.Text)   'Save the key in the corresponding ItemData
End With
```

The CommandButton Control

Command buttons typically carry out the actions of a program. Set the button's Name property before writing any code for its Click event and set its Caption for the words you want to appear on the button.

Command buttons should be accessible from the keyboard, so set their Captions with a keyboard access key. Place an ampersand in front of the letter that you want to be the access key. For example, set the Caption to *&Print* in order to display *Print*.

Default and Cancel Properties

One of the buttons on a form should be the Default button, and one should be the Cancel button. When a user types information on a form, generally he or she wants to press the Enter key when finished, rather than pick up the mouse and click a button. The button with its Default property set to True receives a Click event when the user presses Enter. The button with its Cancel property set to True receives a Click event when the user presses the Escape key. Good programmers make sure to set a Default button on every form and a Cancel button when appropriate.

Setting the Tab Order

When the user presses the Tab key, the focus should move from one control to the next, in sequence. Each control on the form has a TabIndex property, and most have a TabStop property. The TabIndexes (zero based) determine the order that the focus moves when using the Tab key. You can set the TabIndex of a control to a new value, and all indexes after that point are increased by one, effectively inserting the control into the tab sequence.

Labels do not have a TabStop property, since they cannot receive the focus. But labels *do* have a TabIndex property. This feature allows you to use a label to set up keyboard access keys for the text boxes that accompany the labels. For example, set a label's Caption to &Name and its TabIndex property to zero. Then set the corresponding text box's TabIndex to one (one higher than the TabIndex for its label). When the user enters the access key (Alt + N in this case) the focus attempts to go to the label and instead goes to the next higher TabIndex for a control that can receive the focus.

Using the Validate Event and Causes Validation Property

The Validate event and Causes Validation property were added to controls in VB 6. Using this event and property greatly simplifies field-level validation on a form. You can check the validity of each field in its Validate event procedure.

Each control on the form has a Causes Validation property that is set to True by default. When the user finishes an entry and presses Tab or clicks on another control, the Validate event occurs for the control just left. That is, the event occurs if the Causes Validation property of the *new* control is set to True. You can leave the Causes Validation property of most controls set to True so that validation occurs. Set Causes Validation to False on a control such as Cancel or Exit to give users a way to bypass the validation if they don't want to complete the transaction.

Control Arrays

A control array is a series of controls of a single class that have the same name. The control array receives only one Click event, where you can determine which control of the group caused the action. When you have a control array, you reference each individual control with an index. For example, create a series of OptionButtons as a control array and name each button optChoice. If you check the Properties window for each button, you will find that each has an Index property (zero based). Refer to the first button as optChoice(0).

Because the Option button array has only one Click event, you can check in its event procedure to see which button is selected and set a module-level variable to its Index value.

```
Dim mintOptionIndex  As Integer  'Module-level variable
Private Sub optChoice_Click(Index As Integer)
    'Save the index of the selected button
    mintOptionIndex = Index
End Sub
```

Later in the program where you want to know which button was selected, you can reference the module-level variable.

```
Private Sub cmdOK_Click()
    'Take some action
    Select Case mintOptionIndex
        Case 0
            'Action for first button
        Case 1
            'Action for second button
        'Additional Cases for each button
    End Select
End Sub
```

Menus

It's easy to create menus with VB's Menu Editor. With a form displaying, click the Menu Editor toolbar button or select *Tools/Menu Editor*. In the *Menu Editor* dialog box, you can define menus, menu commands, and submenus.

The Caption of each item is the word(s) that you want to appear; the Name is the identifier that you use in code. Create keyboard access keys by using an ampersand before the letter you want to use. You can also define keyboard shortcuts, such as Ctrl + P for Print, which execute without opening the menu.

You use indentation in the dialog box to define menus, menu commands, and submenus. The following example shows the Captions and Names of each item, following the recommended naming guidelines.

Caption	Name	Description
&File	mnuFile	*File* menu
&Print	mnuFilePrint	*Print* menu command
-	mnuFileSeparator	Separator bar
E&xit	mnuFileExit	*Exit* menu command
&Edit	mnuEdit	*Edit* menu
&Sort	mnuEditSort	*Sort* menu command
By &Name	mnuEditSortName	Pop-up submenu item below *Sort*
By &City	mnuEditSortCity	Pop-up submenu item below *Sort*
&Help	mnuHelp	*Help* menu
&About	mnuHelpAbout	*About* menu command

Notice the separator bar entry under the *File* menu. To create a separator, the Caption should be a single hyphen and have a unique name.

Printing

VB is designed to create programs with a graphical user interface, but not to create nicely formatted reports. The Data Report, added in VB 6, is a nice feature if you want to print a report from a database, but doesn't help at all for program output. Many third-party vendors sell products that can create reports from a VB program.

That said, you *can* print from VB, but printing is inflexible and not easy to format well.

PrintForm

The easiest way to print from VB is to set up a form the way you want it and execute the PrintForm method. The entire form prints as a graphic.

The Print Method

You can use VB's Print method to print on a form, on the Printer object, or in the Debug window. It's a good idea to set up your Prints initially for the Debug window, test the program, and change all lines later to the Printer object.

```
Debug.Print Tab(10);"Report Title"; Tab(25); "Page "; intPageNumber
```

After the program is tested and you like the spacing of the report in the Debug window, use *Edit/Replace* to replace all occurrences of `Debug.Print` to `Printer.Print`.

The Printer Object

VB sets up a Printer object in memory. Every time you issue a Printer.Print method, another line is added to the object in memory. When the page fills, or you execute a NewPage method or an EndDoc method, the page is actually sent to the printer.

The format of a print line uses punctuation from earlier versions of Basic—the comma and semicolon, as well as the `Tab` and `Spc` functions. When you print multiple items on a line, the items are separated by commas or semicolons. The items to print can be expressions made up of literals, variables, and properties of controls.

You need to consider the font used for printing. Most fonts have proportional spacing, which means that columns won't align properly. You can use a fixed-pitch font, such as Courier, if you want every character to take the same amount of space.

Spacing with Commas

The output page has preset tab settings with five columns per line. Each column is referred to as a *print zone*. A comma advances printing to the next print zone. The statement

```
Printer.Print , "Advanced Vision"
```

prints "Advanced Vision" in the second print zone. Use two consecutive commas to advance two print zones:

```
Printer.Print "Name", , "Phone"
```

The string literal "Name" prints in the first print zone, and "Phone" prints in the third print zone.

The width of a print zone is 14 characters, based on the average size of a character for the current font. If you print many narrow characters, such as *i* and *t*, more than 14 characters fit, but if you print many wide characters, such as *w* and *m*, fewer than 14 characters print in a print zone. The only way to change the size of a print zone is to change the font.

Spacing with Semicolons

To print one item after another without advancing to the next print zone, separate the items with a semicolon. For example, if txtName.Text is "Mary", the line of code

```
Printer.Print "Name: "; txtName.Text
```

will output as

```
Name: Mary
```

Notice that the literal "Name: " includes a space, which is necessary to separate the items in the output.

Trailing Commas and Semicolons

If the last character on a print line is a comma or semicolon, the next Print method continues on the same line without advancing the line.

```
Printer.Print "First this ",
Printer.Print "Then this"
```

will output as

```
First this    Then this
```

The second item prints in the second print zone.

Printing Blank Lines

If you want blank lines for spacing on the report, you must "print" blank lines.

```
Printer.Print            'Print a blank line
```

The Tab Function

The Tab function spaces along the line, similar to pressing the Tab key when typing in a word processor. You can use Tabs to align columns. Specify the tab position as a number, which may be an arithmetic expression, a constant, or a variable. Fractional values are rounded up. Tab positions are relative to the start of the line.

```
Printer.Print Tab(20); "Advanced Vision and Beyond"
Printer.Print Tab(10); "Name"; Tab(30); "Pay"
Printer.Print Tab(intColumn1); txtName.Text; Tab(intColumn2); curPay
```

If you try to tab to a column that precedes the previous output on the line, the Tab advances to the specified position on the next line. Do not use a comma following a Tab function; doing so causes a jump to the next print zone.

The Spc Function

The Spc function inserts spaces into the line, relative to the last item printed.

```
Printer.Print Tab(20); "Name"'; Spc(5); "Phone"; Spc(5); "Address"
```

Notice that you can combine Tab and Spc on one line.

Printing Strings and Numeric Data

When you print a string item, such as a literal, variable, or Text property, the item prints with no additional spacing. But when you print a numeric item, such as a numeric variable, you must be aware of the spacing. VB inserts a space in front of the number for the sign (which it fills with a minus sign for a negative number); another space is inserted after the number.

Selecting the Font

You can change the Font property of the Printer object in code. However, you must know the exact name of a font on the target printer. If you aren't sure of the target computer or the supported fonts, stick with the TrueType fonts that come with Windows, such as Arial, Times New Roman, and Courier New.

```
Printer.Font.Name = "Times New Roman"
Printer.Font.Size = 12
```

You need to change the font name and size only once, before the first item to print.

Terminating the Page or the Job

The NewPage method sends the current page to the printer and clears the Printer object in memory so you can begin a new page. The EndDoc method sends the current page to the printer and terminates the printer job. Note: When a program terminates, VB automatically sends an EndDoc.

```
Printer.NewPage          'Send page and begin a new page
Printer.EndDoc           'Send page and terminate the print job
```

D

Solutions to Chapter Feedback Questions

Chapter 1

Feedback 1.1

1. No. VB 6 requires a minimum of a 486/DX 66 MHz processor.
2. Yes. VB 6 will run under Windows 95, Windows 98, Windows 2000, or NT. For NT, the processor should be a Pentium.
3. VB 6 requires a CD-ROM drive for installation.
4. The Professional edition includes

   - Additional ActiveX controls.

   - Internet Information Server (IIS) Application Designer.

   - Integrated data tools and the Data Environment.

   - ActiveX data objects (ADO).

   - Dynamic HTML (DHTML) Page Designer.

   - A native code compiler.

5. The Enterprise edition also includes

   - SQL Server.

   - Microsoft Transaction Server.

   - Internet Information Server.

   - Visual SourceSafe.

   - Visual Database tools (Query Designer and Database Designer).

   - SNA Server.

   - Application Performance Explorer.

   - Visual Modeler.

   - Stored Procedure Editor.

   - Visual Component Manager.

   - Remote Data Control.

   - Other BackOffice tools.

Feedback 1.2

1. Place an `Option Explicit` statement in the General Declarations section or make sure that *Require Variable Declaration* is checked on the Editor tab.
2. Select the *Save Changes* option on the Environment tab found under *Tools/Options.*
3. *Auto Syntax Check.*
4. *Tools/Options* is grayed out when no project is open.
5. General Declarations section.
6. *Full Module View.*

7. *Compile on Demand* means that the run can begin before the entire project is compiled.

Feedback 1.3

1. You can use a Watch expression to display in the Watch window; set a breakpoint at the line containing the expression and look at the Data Tips; use a `Debug.Print` for the expression to display in the Immediate window, or View the Locals window.
2. At break time, point to an expression to display the Data Tips. Set a breakpoint on a line of code to force the break.

    In the Immediate window you can enter a line of code to display the contents of an expression or modify program variables.

    Set a Watch expression or a QuickWatch. The Watch window displays values for expressions that have a watch set.

    The Locals window automatically displays all variables in the current module; the only step is to view the window.
3. Run the project with one of the single-stepping options: *Step Into, Step Over,* or *Step Out.* These options can be accessed from the *Run* menu or by using a shortcut key. For example, you can press F8 to begin execution and single-step program lines.
4. An array can be displayed in the Watch window by dragging the name of the array into the window. The Locals window can also be used to display values for an array.
5. The properties of the active form are available in the Locals window at break time.

Chapter 2

Feedback 2.1

1. Many people are color blind or have difficulty reading bright colors. Overall, people have an easier time reading from the muted color.
2. Initialize, Load, Activate, QueryUnload, Unload, and Terminate.

    Program initialization tasks are usually placed in the Form_Load event; verifying an exit is placed in the QueryUnload.
3. `cmdPrint.Enabled = False`
4. The `End` statement terminates a project immediately; the QueryUnload, Unload, and Terminate events never occur.

    The following code is used to unload all forms using the Forms collection.

```
Private Sub Form_Unload (Cancel As Integer)
    'Loop through the forms collection and unload each form.
    Dim OneForm as Form

    For Each OneForm In Forms
        Unload OneForm
    Next
End Sub
```

Chapter 3

Feedback 3.1

1.
- **(a)** txtTeacher.DataSource = adoClasses
- **(b)** txtTeacher.DataField = Name
- **(c)** It doesn't matter how the Text property is set; the field contents will display there.

2. ConnectionString and RecordSource
3. A CommandType specifies the type of record source: table, SQL command, or stored procedure.

Feedback 3.2

Control	Property	Setting
lblInvoiceNumber	DataSource	adoSales
	DataField	InvoiceNumber
lblDate	DataSource	adoSales
	DataField	Date
dbcCustomer	DataSource	adoSales
	DataField	CustomerNumber
	RowSource	adoCustomers
	ListField	Name
	BoundColumn	CustomerNumber

Feedback 3.3

1. The BOFAction property is set at design time in the Properties window of a data control. BOFAction determines the action to be taken when the beginning of the file is reached. This property should be used when a project contains navigation buttons for moving through the database records.
2. Set the EOFAction property to adStayEOF.

```
Private Sub cmdNext_Click()
    'Move to the next record

    With adoPatients.Recordset
        .MoveNext
        If .EOF Then
            .MoveLast
        End If
    End With
End Sub
```

Feedback 3.4

1. `frmAdvVision.staAdvVision.Panels(1).Text = "Record " & _`
   `        .AbsolutePosition & " of " & .RecordCount`
2. ADO MoveComplete event.

Feedback 3.5

1. Add a Connection object, setting its ConnectionString to the database.
2. Add a Command object and set the database object to *Table*.
3. Select the appropriate table.
4. With the right mouse button, drag the Command object to the form.
5. Select *Bound Controls* from the menu.

Feedback 3.6

1. Report Header   Appears once at the top of the report.
   Page Header   Appears at the top of each page.
   Group Header   Appears at the top of each group.
   Detail   One for each record.
   Group Footer   At the end of each group (for subtotals).
   Page Footer   At the end of each page.
   Report Footer   At the end of the report.
2. The record count should be placed in the report footer by using *Insert Control* to place a function on the line. Set the function type to *rptFuncRCnt*.
3. The page number can appear in the page header or the page footer. Use *Insert Control* and *Current Page Number*.
4. Grouping places records together according to a field that matches. To use grouping the records must be sorted in order by the grouping field. It is very handy when subtotals are needed, such as a subtotal of sales by department.
5. The functions for *Insert Control* contain a Sum (the default), use the function in the group footer for a subtotal, and use the function in the report footer for a report total. Specify the field to be totaled.
6. Use the Show method to display a report in Print Preview mode.

Chapter 4

Feedback 4.1

1.
   (a) Forward only.
   (b) Static.
2.
   (a) Read only.
   (b) Optimistic.

Feedback 4.2

1. `deAcmePayroll.rsEmployee`
2. `deAcmePayroll.rsEmployee.AddNew`
   `(deAcmePayroll.rsEmployee.Update)`
3. `deAcmePayroll.rsEmployee.Delete`
   `(deAcmePayroll.rsEmployee.MoveNext)`

Feedback 4.3

1. The Validate event executes when the user leaves a control and the control he or she moves to has its CausesValidation property set to True.
2. If all controls are set to CausesValidation = True, the user would not be able to cancel a transaction or take any other action without entering "good" data. The focus will remain in the text box.
3.
      (a) File not found: VB
      (b) Duplicate key field: ADO provider
      (c) Empty key field: ADO provider
4. The Errors collection is contained in the Connection object. The collection contains one member for each error that occurs.

```
For Each errDBError In deAdvancedVision.conAVB.Errors
    strMessage = strMessage & errDBError.Description & vbCrLf
Next
```

Feedback 4.4

1. `deAdvancedVision.rsVisit.Find "[Visit Date] = #1/5/00#"`
2. `deAdvancedVision.rsVisit.Find "[Visit Date] = #" & txtDate.Text & "#"`
3. Check for the end of the Recordset:

```
If .EOF Then
    MsgBox "Record Not Found", vbExclamation, "Search"
End If
```

4. A bookmark stores the location of a record within the Recordset so that you can return to that record later.

Feedback 4.5

1. `deAdvancedVision.rsDispensary.Find "Quantity < 20"`
2.
      (a) `deAcmePayroll.Employee.Sort = "Rate"`
      (b) `deAcmePayroll.Employee.Sort = "[Employee Name]"`
3. `deAcmePayroll.Employee.Filter "YTD > 45000"`

Feedback 4.6

1. SELECT \`Last Name\`, \`First Name\`, \`Patient Number\`, Phone FROM Patient
2. SELECT Patient.\`Last Name\`, Patient.\`First Name\`,
    Patient.\`Patient Number\`, Patient.Phone,
    InsuranceCompany.Name
   FROM Patient, InsuranceCompany

Chapter 5

Feedback 5.1

1. Connection object.
2. Last Name, First Name, Phone, Street, City, etc.
3. Needs `WithEvents` on the `Dim` statement.
4. `rsInsurance.Open "InsuranceCompany", conAVB, , , adCmdTable    'Open the Recordset`
5. "Patient"   Table name (source)
   conAVB   Connection
   adOpenDynamic   CursorType
   adLockOptimistic   LockType
   adCmdTable   Record source type

Feedback 5.2

1. Select [Last Name], [First Name], [Patient Number], Phone From Patient
2. Select [Last Name], [First Name], [Patient Number], Phone, Name
    From Patient, InsuranceCompany
    Where Patient.[Insurance Company Code] = InsuranceCompany.Code
3. Select [Last Name], [First Name], [Patient Number], Phone, [Insurance Company Code], Name
    From Patient
    LEFT JOIN InsuranceCompany
    ON Patient.[Insurance Company Code] = InsuranceCompany.Code

Chapter 6

Feedback 6.1

1.
```
Private mstrLastName        As String
Private mstrFirstName        As String
Private mstrStudentNumber    As String
Private mcurGPA              As Currency
```

In the General Declarations section.

```
2. Public Property Let LastName(strLastName As String)
      'Assign value to the property

      LastName = strLastName
   End Property
3. Public Property Get GPA() As Currency
      'Retrieve property value

      GPA = mcurGPA
   End Property
```

Feedback 6.2

1. The class is code that defines the properties and methods. An object is an actual instance of the class that reserves memory to store the values for the properties, similar to the relationship between a data type and a variable.
2. mDispensaryItem an object; CDispensaryItem a class.
3. The value of the text box is assigned as the value for the Quantity property of mDispensaryItem. The Property Let procedure of the class module will execute.

Feedback 6.3

```
1. Private mPerson As CPerson 'General Declarations
   Set mPerson = New CPerson
   'In the procedure that uses the object, probably Form_Load.
2. Set mPerson = Nothing
```

Feedback 6.4

1. Declare the event in the General Declarations section of the class module.

```
Public Event WillSoundAlarm
```

   Raise the event in code. When a condition occurs that should generate the event, use the RaiseEvent statement.

```
If mblnTimeElapsed Then
    RaiseEvent WillSoundAlarm
End If
```

2. Declare the object using the WithEvents keyword.

```
Private WithEvents mMyTask As CMyTask
```

   Next write the code for the event procedure. You will find your object, mMyTask, in the Code window's Object list and all events that you have defined in the Procedure list.

```
Sub mMyTask_WillSoundAlarm()
```

Feedback 6.5

1. `CPersons.Item(strKey)`
   `CPersons.Item(intIndex)`
2. An index is the relative position of an element within the collection and may change as items are deleted. A key is unique to the element and is not affected by updates to the collection.
3. Item.
4. `cPersons.Remove strKey`

Feedback 6.6

1.
```
Enum myErrorConstants
    InvalidFrameSize = 1
    InvalidFrameStyle = 2
    InvalidQuantity = 3
End Enum
```

2.
```
Public Property Let FrameSize (intFrameSize As Integer)
    'Assign value to the property

    If intFrameSize >= 1 And intFrameSize <= 4 Then
        FrameSize = intFrameSize
    Else
        Err.Raise InvalidFrameSize
    End If
End Property
```

3.
```
On Error GoTo HandleError
    '(Program statements here)
    Exit Sub

HandleError:
    If Err.Number = InvalidFrameSize Then
        MsgBox "Frame size must be between 1 and 4", vbInformation, _
            "Error in Frame Size"
    Else
        MsgBox "Unexpected Error", vbInformation, "Error"
    End If
```

Chapter 7

Feedback 7.1

1. **(a)** Distributing on a network: deployment.
   (b) Coding: physical design.

    (c) Interviewing users: conceptual design.
    (d) Designing an interface: logical design.
    (e) Determining objects and relationships: logical design.

2. Documentation and planning. It creates a visual representation of the design of a system and the relationship among the objects.

- An **association**—the most general type of relationship. You can initially define all relationships to be associations and add more precision later.

- A **dependency**—a relationship that indicates that the client class uses services from the supplier class. The provided services may be constants, variables, or methods of the supplier class.

- An **aggregate**—a whole and part relationship. The whole end of the relationship (also called the aggregate class or the container) is the client.

- A **generalization**—an inheritance relationship, which shows an "is a" relationship between classes.

Feedback 7.2

1. Set the DataSourceBehavior property to vbDataSource. Add "Visit" to the DataMembers collection.
2. `DataMembers.Add "Visit"`
3. `Set mDataSource = New CDataSource`
4.
```
'Bind the controls to the data -- DataField set at design time
With txtDate
    .DataMember = "Visit Date"
    Set .DataSource = mDataSource
End With
```

Feedback 7.3

1. In which tier do the following belong? For the objects and Recordset, tell where they are first defined and where they will be referenced.
    (a) Patient object: used in User Services, defined in Business Services, values from Data Services.
    (b) Visit Update form: User Services.
    (c) Visit object: used in User Services, defined in Business Services, values from Data Services.
    (d) Patient Recordset: defined in Data Services, accessed from the Business Services, displayed on the form in User Services.
2. Define a binding collection in the Business Services. Bind the properties of the business object to the fields in a Recordset by using the Add method of the binding collection.

```
Private mbndPatient    As BindingCollection
With mbndPatient
    .DataMember = "Patient"
    .Add Me, "PatientNumber", "Patient Number"
    .Add Me, "LastName", "Last Name"
    .Add Me, "FirstName", "First Name"
    .Add Me, "Street", "Street"
    .Add Me, "City", "City"
    .Add Me, "State", "State"
    .Add Me, "ZipCode", "Zip Code"
    .Add Me, "Phone", "Phone"
    .Add Me, "InsuranceCompanyCode", "Insurance Company Code"
    .Add Me, "PolicyNumber", "Policy #"
End With
```

3. Each time a new record is current, you must assign the properties from the CPatient class to the form's controls.

```
Private Sub AssignData()
    'Transfer the value from the Patient object to the interface

    With mPatient
        txtPatientNumber.Text = .PatientNumber
        txtLastName.Text = .LastName
        txtFirstName.Text = .FirstName
        txtStreet.Text = .Street
        txtCity.Text = .City
        txtState.Text = .State
        txtZipCode.Text = .ZipCode
        mskPhone.Text = .Phone
        txtPolicyNumber.Text = .PolicyNumber
    End With
End Sub
```

4. Assign the text box value to a member of the business object.

```
mPatient.City = txtCity.Text
```

Chapter 8

Feedback 8.1

1.
   (a) Dll   Dynamic-link library
   (b) Exe   Executable file
   (c) Tlb   Type library

2. With a Global instancing property, an instance of the class is created automatically the first time a procedure or method of the class is called.

3. In-process components are tested in the same VB environment by creating a project group. Out-of-process components require two copies of the VB environment to be running at once (one for the client application and one for the server application).

4. COM is a standard that allows components written in different languages to work together (interoperability). Components can be reused in multiple

applications reducing development time, increasing productivity, and creating a more consistent system.
5. Regsvr32.exe
6. In a component that has more than one class module and needs to share data among the modules but not make them Public.

Feedback 8.2

1. Assume that you are writing code in a module that responds to an event called FoundOne, which is fired by another class called LookForOne.
   (a) `Dim WithEvents`
   (b) `Private Sub LookForOne_FoundOne()`
   (c) `Event FoundOne()`
   (d) `RaiseEvent FoundOne`
2. Dll components can be registered by doing a full compile or by using the RegSvr32 application.

Feedback 8.3

1. Lifetime of the module.
2. Lifetime of the procedure.

Feedback 8.4

1. An in-process server runs in the same process as the client and cannot run standalone; it is stored as a .dll. An out-of-process component is an .exe file that can be set to run standalone. It runs in its own processing area.
2. Project Properties has a dropdown list to determine the type of component.
3. Event notification or callback procedure.

Feedback 8.5

1. An interface refers to the properties and methods of a class that are public. Only Public members are "exposed" because Private members can be used only within the class itself. An object of a class has access to only the Public properties and methods.
2. An abstract class is used to create a superclass from which other classes are created. It may contain empty methods to force the method name to become a part of the interface. Any class created from the abstract class must define the code for the member.
3. Option buttons and check boxes share many properties and methods. A superclass could define the functionality for both and then the specifics would be defined in the appropriate subclass.
4. `Implements`
5. Version compatibility allows users with an earlier version of the component to still function.
6. A newer version could implement the older interface and then update the code within methods as needed. New members can be added to the newer class.

Feedback 8.6

1. Tool for organizing components.
2. Visual Component Manager is accessed from the *View* menu. If it is not there, add it by using the Add-in Manager.
3. With the Visual Component Manager, publishing a component refers to adding it to the repository database. Compile and save the project before using the Publishing Wizard in Visual Component Manager.

Chapter 9

Feedback 9.1

1.
(a)	InitProperties	After Initialize, first time the document is accessed.
(b)	WriteProperties	Before document is terminated.
(c)	ReadProperties	Every time the document is accessed.
(d)	Initialize	First event to execute when a document is created.
(e)	Terminate	Last event to execute when document is destroyed.

2. `HyperLink.NavigateTo "www.Microsoft.com"`
3. `HyperLink.NavigateTo App.Path & "\docInsurance.vbd"`

Feedback 9.2

1. Placing the control on the form causes the Initialize, InitProperties, and ReadProperties events to occur. Closing the form calls the WriteProperties. Reopening the form causes the ReadProperties event.
2. The Initialize event occurs only when the control is first placed on a form; the InitProperties and ReadProperties follow and can override values.
3. Store the property's value in one of the constituent controls, rather than a module level variable, to give the developer access to the value.
4. A group of properties provided "for free" by VB so that the control author does not need to create them.
5. It holds information about the control's container so the developer or user can change corresponding properties.
6. Choose *Add/Property Page* from the *Project* menu; select *VB Property Page Wizard.* Follow the steps to name the properties that are to appear on the tab.

Chapter 10

Feedback 10.1

1. VB contains a WebBrowser control that creates a window on a form for browsing to a Web site. The Internet Transfer Control provides the FTP and HTTP protocols to VB, and the WinSock control uses TCP/IP for email or chat capabilities.
2. You may want the user to control the style of the page. You may want to add or delete text. The properties of elements can be changed.

3. The three objects in the DHTML object model are the Base Window, the Document, and the DHTML Page.

4.
```
Private Sub txtProductNumber_onfocus()
    'Change color of text element when focus is received

    txtProductNumber.Style.backgroundColor = "lightgrey"
End Sub
```

Feedback 10.2

1. Install IIS (on NT only) or Personal or Peer Web Server.
2. An IIS application resides on the server.
3. IIS produces standard HTML.
4. An Active Server Page is created when a WebClass is compiled.
5.
```
Response.Write "<A HREF = """ & URLFor(Sales, "Order") & _
            """ & >Order New Item</A></p>"
```

Chapter 12

Feedback 12.1

1. **(a)** Subscript out of range: Remove Array Bounds Checks.
   (b) Division by zero: Remove Floating-Point Error Checks.
   (c) Valid range for integer
           numbers: Remove Integer Overflow Checks.
   (d) Valid range for floating-point
           numbers: Remove Floating-Point Error Checks.

2. Native code.

Feedback 12.2

1. Command-line argument and Conditional Compilation argument on the Make tab of *Project/Properties*.
2.
```
#If Testing Then
    Debug.Print intCustomerCount
#End If
```
3. `#Const Testing = True`

Feedback 12.3

1. Form_Unload event procedure.
2.
```
mdtmRunDate = Val(GetSetting(App.Path & _
"\Payroll", "Startup", "RunDate"))
```

Feedback 12.4

1. Resource files can hold the images, multimedia, and string text for an application in a single place.

2. The resource file can contain multiple string text and/or images needed for various versions.

Chapter 13

Feedback 13.1

1. **(a)**	.hhk	Index file	Entries for a search
(b)	.hhc	Table of contents	Contents tab information
(c)	.chm	Compiled help file	Used in the application
(d)	.jpeg	images	Used on Web page
(e)	.avi	sound	Used on Web page
(f)	.htm	Topic file	Text for Help pages
(g)	.hhp	Project file	Contains references for all files in .chm

2. Help file
Context-sensitive Help
What's This Help
ToolTips
Status bar text

Chapter 14

Feedback 14.1

1. Packaging creates the files for distribution; deployment is the process of distributing the files to the desired media.

2. **(a)**	.exe	Yes, it's your file.
(b)	.ocx	Yes, if you have rights to the file.
(c)	.dll	Yes, if you have rights to the file.
(d)	Eye.ico	Yes, Microsoft allows the graphics in the common folder to be distributed.
(e)	Msvbvm60.dll	Yes.

Feedback 14.2

What is contained in each of the following sections of setup?

1. The name of the main Setup program, the name of a temporary directory used during installation, uninstall directions, and the text for installation instructions.
2. Files needed for installation.
3. Other files that are needed to run the application.
4. Information that may be required by the programs in the Setup1 Files.

Appendix A

1. The Help file is a compiled file that contains all the topics, contents, and index files. The topic file contains the text of the *Help* menu.
2. `dlgCommon.HelpFile = App.Path & "\MyHelp.hlp"`
   `dlgCommon.HelpCommand = cdlHelpContents`
3. As many as you need.

Appendix B

Feedback

1. **(a)** `Open "Vendor.Dat" For Output As #1`
   (b) `For intIndex = 0 To lstVendor.ListCount − 1`
   `        Write #1, lstVendor.List(intIndex)`
   `   Next intIndex`
   (c) `Close #1`
   (d) `Open "Vendor.Dat" For Input As #1`
   (e) `Do Until EOF(1)`
   `        Input #1, strVendor`
   `        lstVendor.AddItem strVendor`
   `   Loop`
2. `EOF`

Feedback

1. ```
   Type Inventory
        strDescription    As String * 30
        strPartNumber     As String * 5
        curPrice          As Currency
        intQuantity       As Integer
   End Type
   ```
2. `Dim mudtInventoryRecord As Inventory`
3. `Open "C:\Inventory.Dat" For Random As #1 Len = Len(mudtInventoryRecord)`
4. `intNumberRecords = LOF(1) / Len(mudtInventoryRecord)`
5. `Put #1, intRecordNumber, mudtInventoryRecord`
6. 6; the position of the next record.
7. `Get #1 , , mudtInventoryRecord`
   ```

Glossary

#Const directive   Assigns a value to an argument used in conditional compilation.

#If directive   A condition that the compiler uses to determine which lines of code to include in the compile. Used for debugging or selecting code for different versions.

absolute position   Placing an element on a Web page at a specific location. Not recommended because of problems with resizing and varying screen resolutions and dimensions.

AbsolutePosition property   Recordset property that holds the actual record number.

abstract class   Class module that cannot be used to instantiate objects. Contains empty procedures.

Active Server Pages (ASP)   A Microsoft technology that allows a server, such as IIS, to dynamically generate the HTML that it sends to Web browsers. Each WebClass is associated with an ASP file that is generated when the WebClass is compiled.

ActiveX data objects (ADO)   A database access technology compliant with Universal Data Access (UDA). Provides a data access model that can be referenced directly through code as well as by a data control or a data environment.

ActiveX Dll   A code component that conforms to the COM standard and runs in-process.

ActiveX Exe   A code component that conforms to the COM standard and runs out-of-process.

Add method   Member of a collection interface that adds an element to the collection. You must create a "wrapper" method when creating collection classes.

AddNew method   An update method for beginning a new record in a Recordset. Clears the bound data fields for new data. Used with the Update method for saving the data.

ADODB   Library for ADO. A reference to ADODB must be included in an ADO project.

ADOR   Subset of full ADO library; used with browser applications to minimize size.

aggregate   Calculate a single value from a group. Includes Sum, Average, Min, Max, and Count.

alias   An alternative name, often shorter, for use in a query.

API   Application programming interface. The set of functions available from Windows.

Application object   ASP object to track information about multiple users, such as a hit count.

Application programming interface   See API.

application provider   A project that supplies a class module for use in a client/consumer application.

application server   A project that supplies a class module for use in a client/consumer application.

association   General type of relationship in Unified Modeling Language (UML).

asynchronous notification   An indication that a process is complete when using an asynchronous operation.

asynchronous operation   Processing occurs independently, such as for an out-of-process component. The client application continues execution while another process is being performed.

attribute   Term for a property; used in Dynamic HTML.

author   Individual who creates an ActiveX control or code component.

automation server application   Another name for a provider or server application.

availability   A program can recover and continue after encountering errors.

BaseWindow object   The browser object in a DHTML application.

BeginTrans method   Connection object method to start a

<section>
633
</section>

transaction. The update(s) that occur as part of the transaction are treated as a group and are either all applied or all rolled back.

BindingCollection Used with a class acting as a data consumer. Items added to the binding collection connect properties to a field from the data source.

BOF A Boolean condition that indicates beginning of file.

BOFAction property Specifies the action to take when a Recordset is at BOF.

BookMark property Holds the position of a record in a Recordset. Can be used to store a record's position in order to return there after an unsuccessful search.

BoundColumn property A member of the interface for a DataCombo or DataList control. Specifies the field in the data source that is used to retrieve data or save changes.

Break mode Halt in execution of an application; used in testing and debugging projects.

break time Refers to a project in Break mode; as opposed to a program in run time.

breakpoint Allows programmer to mark a line of code at which program execution should move to Break mode; used for debugging.

buffer Temporary storage used to hold records that are being transferred to or from a database or file.

business objects A class module designed to handle business rules, including calculations and

validation. Middle tier of a three-tier application.

Business Services Business tier of a multitier application; contains business objects.

.cab file A "cabinet" file used to store the necessary files for distributing an application.

Call Stack A list of the procedure calls leading up to the current location in the program. Can be displayed in a window as a debugging aid.

callback procedure A procedure executed by a server application to notify the client that an operation is complete. Used in asynchronous operations.

CancelUpdate method A method that cancels the current update or add operation in a database application.

child form A dependent form in a multiple-document interface (MDI) application. The child form closes automatically when the parent form is unloaded.

child node The lower or dependent node in a ListView.

class A prototype or blueprint for an object indicating the properties and methods.

class module Code module for creating a class. Can contain properties, methods, and events for use in instantiating objects.

Class_Initialize event Event that occurs when a class is instantiated.

Class_Terminate event Event that occurs when an object is set to Nothing or goes out of scope.

client application Application containing/implementing an

ActiveX code component. Also called a consumer application.

code component Class module stored as a Dll or Exe; provides reusability in consumer applications.

collection class A class that can contain a group of member objects. A collection has Add, Delete and Item methods and a, Count property.

column A single field of data in a table.

Command object A member of ADO used to connect to a table, stored procedure, or SQL statement.

CommitTrans method Saves all updates in the group and ends the transaction.

Component Object Model (COM) A standard for creating interfaces for code components.

conceptual design Initial information gathering to determine the system or application requirements.

conditional compilation Tells the compiler whether to compile certain lines of code into the application. Uses a #If directive to determine whether specific lines of code are to be compiled.

Connection object A member of ADO used to connect to a database.

ConnectionString Property of a Connection object. Used to specify the source of the data.

consumer application Application containing/ implementing an ActiveX code component. Also called a client application.

context menus   Shortcut menus that pop up when you right-click an item.

Controls collection   A VB collection that holds all of the controls in a container such as a form.

cookie   Packet of information stored between displays of Web pages. Usually stored on the client machine but may be stored on the server using IIS.

cursor   The resources for managing a set of records that returns a specific row of the Recordset. Using ADO, the cursor may be implemented either as client-side or server-side.

CursorLocation property   Determines whether the ADO data cursor is implemented on the client or server system.

CursorType property   Determines the access type of an ADO data cursor. May be set to read-only, to locked, or to run in batch mode.

data-aware class   A data-consumer class that is connected to a data source.

data-bound control   A control that is connected to a field in a Recordset.

data consumer   An application that uses the data provided by a data source.

Data Environment Designer   A VB feature that sets up the definitions for a data source, which can be accessed from any form in an application.

data file   Disk file that holds values for a sequential or random file.

Data Report Designer   VB feature used to create reports from database records.

Data Services   Database tier of a multitier application. Contains all references and events pertaining to the database connection, maintenance, and update commands.

data shaping   Language used to perform hierarchical database access.

data source   An object or application that provides the data to a data consumer.

Data Tip   Debugging tool to display the current value of an expression at break time. Similar to ToolTips.

Data View window   Part of the Data Environment Designer. Displays the relationships among data.

DataBindingBehavior property   Class module property allowing objects to use a Binding collection.

DataCombo control   An ADO control that is bound to a field in a Recordset. The control receives its input from one data field and can display data from a related field.

DataEnvironment object   An object created with the Data Environment Designer, which can be bound to multiple data sources and accessed from all forms in an application.

DataField property   The property of a data-bound control that specifies the field from the data source.

DataForm Wizard   VB tool to generate forms containing data-bound controls.

DataList control   Similar to a DataCombo control. An ADO control that can be bound to one data field but display related data from another field.

DataSource property   Used to connect a control to a data source.

DataSourceBehavior property   A Boolean property that when True makes a class a data provider.

DDL   Data definition language. Used to create and modify the structure of a database.

Declare statement   Statement that defines a procedure external to VB so that the procedure may be called from VB code. Required for accessing API functions. Gives a prototype of the function or sub procedure with arguments and data types.

DECommand   A Command object in the data environment.

DEConnection   A Connection object in the data environment.

Delete method   Included in the interface for collection classes and database manipulation for deleting a member of the collection or Recordset.

DeleteSetting statement   Deletes a Registry setting from the Windows Registry.

dependency   UML relationship that indicates that the client class uses services from the supplier class.

dependency file   Required file for a program to be properly packaged and deployed.

dependent object   Objects with an Instancing property of PublicNotCreatable.

deployment   Process of distributing applications.

developer   Individual creating an application that uses an ActiveX control or code component.

DHTML page object   DHTML object model element that is similar to a form in a VB project. The page object has Initialize, Load, Unload, and Terminate events.

DLL   Dynamic-link library. A file containing a code component, function, or procedure that can be accessed by applications.

Document object   DHTML object model element that handles the events from the user and contains the DHTML page object.

drill-down interface   A style of displaying hierarchical data that allows expansion and hiding. The user can move down through levels.

Dynamic HTML (DHTML)   An enhancement of HTML that allows styles and content of a Web page to change at run time. Runs only with Microsoft browser.

early binding   Declaring the object type so that the compiler is aware of the type and can verify the properties, methods, and events. See also *late binding*.

element   Web page component that resembles a control: text field, text area, and submit button are a few.

encapsulation   The combination of an object's properties, methods, and events. The internal workings of the object are hidden from other classes.

Enterprise edition   The version of VB that contains a full set of features.

Enum statement   Used to declare Public numeric constants in a class module.

EOF   End of file. A Boolean condition that is True at the end of a Recordset or data file.

EOF function   Function to test for end of a sequential file.

EOFAction   A property to specify which action should be taken when the EOF condition is True.

Error object   Member of the ADO object model. Stores information about processing errors.

error trapping   Coding to control the action when an error occurs.

Errors collection   A collection of Error objects.

event bubbling   In IIS applications an event that is not handled by an object moves up to its container until the event is handled or the top level is reached.

event consumer   An object that responds to an event.

event provider   An object that generates or raises an event.

event sink   An object that responds to an event.

event source   An object that generates or raises an event.

Event statement   Declares an event in the General Declaration section of a class module. Must appear if a class raises an event.

Execute method (ADO)   Used to open a Connection or Command object; less flexible than the Open method for creating Recordsets.

extensibility   The ability to add features to an application at a later date.

field   Individual element in a record. Corresponds to a column in a table of rows.

Field object   ADO object for an individual field within a record.

Fields collection   An element of the ADO object model; collection class that holds all fields.

file (database)   A collection of tables, such as an Access .mdb file.

file mode   Specification for the manner that data can be accessed from a disk file, including Input, Output, Append, Random, and Binary.

file number   Number used to logically reference a random or sequential file.

file pointer   Position within a random or sequential data file. Used to determine the position to read or write.

Filter property   Recordset method for selecting all records that meet criteria.

Find method   Recordset method for selecting the first record that meets criteria.

Forms collection   A collection that holds a reference to all loaded forms.

Friend keyword   Provides access to Private members of a class. Used in place of Public or Private to allow access to other classes in the application but not to code outside the component.

generalization   Unified Modeling Language (UML) inheritance relationship; displays "is a" relationship between classes.

Get statement Retrieve a record from a random data file.

GetAllSettings function Returns all settings for an application from the Windows Registry.

GetSetting function Returns one setting for an application from the Windows Registry.

global object Implicit instantiation of an object. An object declared as Public.

grid Control for displaying database records.

Help Workshop Application to compile WinHelp files; found on the Visual Studio installation CD.

Hide method Hides a form without unloading it.

HTML Hypertext Markup Language. The standard language used to create Web pages. Recognized by all browsers, such as Netscape or Internet Explorer.

HTML Help Microsoft's current technique for displaying Help in an application. Uses HTML pages and replaces WinHelp.

IIS Internet Information Server. Microsoft's Web server that runs on NT. Can be simulated on Windows 9x and NT Workstation by Personal Web Server.

IIS application A type of VB application that can enhance HTML templates with ASP code before submitting them to Internet Information Server. The HTML produced by the server is standard HTML and can display in any browser.

ImageList control Control used to contain images for other controls such as a toolbar or TreeView.

Immediate window Debugging window displays data from a `Debug.Print` and can be used to execute single VB statements.

Index property Numeric position within a list.

inheritance The ability to derive a new object class based on an existing class.

inline error handling Error-handling technique using the `On Error Resume Next` statement and checking for an error after any statement likely to cause an error.

inner join A join of two database tables where a record is included only when there are matching values in both tables.

in-process Code component that executes in the same process (memory space) as the client application. Dlls are in-process components.

Input # statement Read data from a sequential data file.

instance Single object created from a class module.

Instancing property Determines whether and how a class can be instantiated.

instantiate Create an object of a type defined by a class module.

Integrated development environment (IDE) VB environment provides ability to edit, compile, and execute applications during development.

interface The Public properties and methods exposed by a code component.

Internet package Method of deployment. Packaging allows for distribution on networks, Internet sites, and disks.

Internet Transfer Control A VB Internet control used for FTP and HTTP transfers.

interoperability COM feature that allows ActiveX components written in different languages to work together through a standardized interface.

intranet An "internet" that runs only within a company or network.

join Combine two or more database tables by a common field using SQL.

key field Uniquely identifies each record; field used to perform a search.

late binding Declaring objects `As Object`, which prevents the compiler from knowing the object class until run time. Does not allow for syntax checking during the compile; slower and less efficient than early binding.

Learning edition Version of VB designed for education.

left join A join of two database tables that includes all records from the first table and only those from the second table that have matching values in the common field.

line label Line of code followed by a colon; used for branching code in error trapping.

ListField property DataCombo and DataList control property to specify the field to display in the list.

ListView control Windows common control used to display

objects as large icons, small icons, list, or report (detail).

localize Develop for distribution in different locales; having different versions for different countries or languages.

localized control Control designed for use in a particular locale or country. Text may be in different languages.

Locals window A window used for debugging; displays all local variables and the properties of objects.

LockType property Data Environment property for controlling the access of data by multiple users.

LOF function Length of file function; returns the number of bytes in the file. Can be used to determine the number of records in a random data file.

logical design The phase of solution development in which the business objects are identified.

LTrim function Trims spaces from the left of a string.

maintainability A goal of system design that makes a program easily modifiable without crashing the system and with a minimum amount of effort by the software developers. Coding standards and documentation can improve maintainability.

MaskedEdit control Similar to a text box control with formatted input and output.

MDI Multiple-document interface. An application containing a parent (MDI) form and child forms.

Me Keyword that refers to the current form or class.

Microsoft Developers Network (MSDN) A library of Help files, including articles, periodicals, tutorials, and programming samples.

Mode property ADO DataEnvironment property that determines the access rights of the user.

MoveComplete event ADO Recordset event that occurs after a move from one record to another.

MSHFlexGrid Grid control designed for displaying data for a hierarchical Recordset.

multitier database application Application functionality is divided into components based on User Services, Business Services, and/or Data Services.

native code Machine language instructions produced by a compiler, which are translated for the processor and operating system on which the application will run. VB can compile to native code or pseudocode (p-code), which is portable to other computer systems but is less efficient.

New keyword Creates a new instance of an object; reserves memory for the object.

node One entry on a TreeView control.

Nodes collection Holds all root and child nodes for a TreeView control.

object An instance of a type defined by a class.

Object Browser Tool to display the interface (Public properties, methods, and events) of objects, arguments of functions and procedures, and constants.

object model A plan of the relationships among the objects in a system.

OLE DB Standardized interface that allows the developer to refer to data from any source using the same set of programming tools, whether the data is stored in a database, a text file, or a spreadsheet.

Open method ADO method for Command and Recordset objects; can accept table names or SQL queries.

Optimize property ADO property that dynamically creates an index for a field in a Recordset.

out-of-process A code component that executes in a different process (memory space) than the client application.

package Files prepared for distribution of an application or component.

panel A section on a status bar.

parameter Supplies needed information for a function or sub procedure.

Parameter object Supplies needed information to an ADO Command object.

Parameters collection ADO collection object for storing Parameter objects.

parent form MDI form controlling the life of the application; may contain child forms.

p-code Pseudocode. Code produced by the compiler; creates smaller executable files than native code but runs slower and requires additional translation and library files at run time.

performance Applications optimized for user needs as well as speed and least use of resources.

Personal Web Server Microsoft's Web server that runs on Windows 95/98 and NT Workstation. Can emulate IIS for a desktop system.

physical design The phase in software development that converts the logical design to physical requirements, such as specific hardware and software components.

polymorphism Allows different classes of objects to have similar methods that behave differently for that particular object.

pop-up menu Shortcut menus that pop up when you right-click an item.

Professional edition The "middle" version of VB; has more functionality than the Learning edition but less than the Enterprise edition.

ProgID (programmatic ID) String representing the class name of a control in the type library.

programming object model Relationship of objects in an application.

project group Multiple projects executing in a single VB environment.

Properties collection ADO object. Connection, Command, Recordset, and Field objects each has a Properties collection.

Property Get Retrieves a property value from an object.

Property Let Assigns a property value for an object.

Property object Represents the characteristics, descriptions, or behavior for each object in the ADO object model.

provider application Server application supplying a code component or control.

Put statement Writes records to a random data file.

Quick Watch Debugging tool for displaying values of a variable or expression as an application executes.

RaiseEvent statement Fire an event, or cause it to occur.

random file Low-level data file; records can be accessed in any sequence.

record Represents the data for one item, person, or transaction in a database Recordset. Corresponds to a row in a table.

RecordCount property Holds the number of records in a Recordset.

Recordset object A temporary set of data that represents a table, the output of an SQL query, or a stored procedure; kept in local storage.

RecordSource property Specifies the table, command, or stored procedure to create a Recordset.

Registry Windows file for storing configuration and persistent data for applications.

Registry key Reference name for a field with a value stored in the Registry.

relation hierarchy ADO parent Command object and a child Command object relating data from two tables.

relative position Position elements on Web page in relationship to the text. Preferred method for positioning; allows element to move when the page is resized.

Remove method Method for deleting an object from a Collection.

Request object ASP object that holds information about the current user, data entered by the user, and arguments to an HTTP request.

resource file Contains images and text for an application; items are loaded as needed. Often used to provide text strings in different languages to localize an application.

Response object ASP object that sends information from the server to the browser.

Resume statement Continues execution after an error has occurred.

reusability Obtain the functionality from one class of object when you have another similar situation.

right join A join of two database tables that includes all records from the second table and only those from the first table that have matching values in the common field.

right-mouse menu Shortcut menus that pop up when you right-click an item.

RollbackTrans method Connection object method to cancel all updates made during a transaction.

root node Top-level node in a TreeView, which cannot be collapsed.

row Represents the data for one item, person, or transaction; a record.

RowSource property Property of DataList and DataCombo control; specifies the data control or Data Environment to use to retrieve the data for the list.

RTrim function Trims spaces from the right end of a string.

satellite Dll Contains translated strings for a localized control.

SaveSetting statement Stores a value and its associated Registry key in the Windows Registry.

SDI Single-document interface; contains no forms with parent/child relationship.

Seek function Statement used to search for a specific record in a random file and position the file pointer.

sequential files Low-level data storage; data must be written and read in sequence.

server application A project that supplies a class module for use in a client/consumer application.

Session object ASP object that stores information about the current user such as which pages have been accessed within an IIS application.

Set statement An assignment statement for object variables.

Shape command Efficient alternative to the SQL join; creates a hierarchical Recordset when joining tables, rather than return multiple rows of matching fields.

Shape data manipulation language ADO 2.0 language designed for working with the parent/child relationship.

siting Process of connecting an ActiveX document to its container.

Sort property ADO property to temporarily reorder records in a Recordset by any field.

SQL Structured Query Language; a standard database language for query, navigation, and maintenance of database tables.

standard package Distribution package used for all types of deployment except through the Web.

state Information stored between pages of an Internet application. Applies to ActiveX documents, DHTML applications, and IIS applications.

StatusBar control Control used to create a status bar for an application. Properties allow including text, date, time, settings (such as Cap Lock).

Step Into Debugging tool that executes one line at a time, including the lines in called sub procedures and functions.

Step Out Debugging tool used only when single-stepping in a called procedure to quickly finish execution of the current procedure; execution breaks again after the call in the calling procedure.

Step Over Debugging tool; shows the line-by-line execution of the current procedure but does not show the code in any called procedures.

String table Resource file element used to store text.

Tabbed Dialog control Control for displaying information on multiple tabs or pages; optimizes use of screen.

table A database set of data containing rows and columns.

template A file that contains an HTML page. A Web page that can be added as a WebItem to a WebClass.

toolbar A bar that usually appears across the top of a window; contains buttons for shortcuts to menu items.

Toolbar control Windows common control for creating toolbars.

transaction One or more database update statements that execute or fail as a group. Starts with BeginTrans method and ends with CommitTrans; can also be abandoned with RollbackTrans.

TreeView control Windows common control displaying information with a root and nodes; easily expandable/collapsible.

Trim function Removes spaces from left and right ends of a string.

type library Definition of the Public objects, properties, methods, events, and constants of a code component.

Unified Modeling Language (UML) Diagramming design tool for object-oriented systems.

Universal Data Access (UDA) Microsoft's strategy for accessing data from multiple providers.

Unload statement Removes a form from memory.

update   Adds, deletes, and modifications performed on a database.

Update method   ADO method used to submit edits for a record in a Recordset.

URLData property   Used to pass state in IIS applications; concatenates the state information to the URL.

URLFor method   Allows a WebItem name to be specified and the correct URL will be substituted by the Web server.

User Services   User interface tier of a multitier application; the forms.

validation   Verification of data values entered by the user.

version compatibility   Defines relationship among modified versions of code. Options are No Compatibility, Project Compatibility, and Binary Compatibility.

Visual Component Manager (VCM)   A tool for organizing components.

Visual SourceSafe (VSS)   A VB tool for identifying and man-

aging versions of source code. Keeps a database of users (developers) and source code versions.

Watch expression   Variable or expression value displayed during debugging.

Watch window   Debugging window that displays Watch expressions.

wcRetainInstance property   Provides the opportunity to keep the WebClass instantiated until the application is terminated.

Web   World Wide Web; an application that runs on the Internet.

WebBrowser control   A VB Internet control that displays a window on a form for browsing the Web.

WebClass   The primary object in an IIS application. Each WebClass may contain multiple WebItems; a component that resides in a Web server and responds to input from a browser.

WebItem   Web pages or code (custom WebItems) that are added to a WebClass.

WillChangeRecord event

ADO Recordset event that occurs prior to a change to the database.

Windows Registry   Windows file for storing configuration and persistent data for an application.

WinSock control   Internet control that can be used for email or setting up a "chat."

`WithEvents` **keyword**   Added to a declaration (`Dim`|`Public`|`Private`) of an object variable. Provides access to the events of an object.

working model   Limited version of VB designed for educational purposes.

wrapper method   A Public method written in a class module to provide access to an existing Private method.

Write # statement   Output data to a sequential file.

Index